America
in the
Twentieth
Century

A HISTORY

America in the Twentieth Century

A HISTORY

JAMES T. PATTERSON

Brown University

HARCOURT BRACE JOVANOVICH, INC.

New York   Chicago   San Francisco   Atlanta

COPYRIGHTS AND ACKNOWLEDGMENTS

For permission to use the selections reprinted in this book, the author is grateful to the following publishers and copyright holders:

IRVING BERLIN MUSIC CORPORATION for excerpts from lyrics of "This Time" by Irving Berlin on page 316. © Copyright 1942 Irving Berlin. © Copyright renewed 1969. Reprinted by permission of Irving Berlin Music Corporation.

DOUBLEDAY & COMPANY, INC. for "The Reckoning," copyright 1941 by Theodore Roethke, from the book *The Collected Poems of Theodore Roethke*. Reprinted by permission of Doubleday & Company, Inc.

FARRAR, STRAUS & GIROUX, INC. for "When I get to the other side" from *Anyplace But Here* by Arna Bontemps and Jack Conroy. Reprinted with the permission of Farrar, Straus & Giroux, Inc., from *Anyplace But Here* by Arna Bontemps and Jack Conroy, Copyright © 1945, 1966 by Arna Bontemps and Jack Conroy.

MARCUS GARVEY, JR. for "Black queen of beauty, thou hast given color to the world" by Marcus Garvey, Sr. Reprinted by permission of Marcus Garvey, Jr., literary executor of the estate of Amy Jacques Garvey.

HARPER & ROW for "Superman" from *The Carpentered Hen and Other Tame Creatures* by John Updike. Copyright © 1955 by John Updike. Reprinted by permission of Harper & Row, Publishers, Inc.

HOUGHTON MIFFLIN COMPANY for "When the organizers needed dough" from *Coming of the New Deal* by Arthur M. Schlesinger, Jr. Reprinted by permission of the publisher.

EILEEN LAMB for "Where are You, God?" from *So Far, So Good! An Autobiography* by Elsie Janis. Reprinted by permission of Eileen Lamb.

MACMILLAN PUBLISHING CO., INC. for "The Leaden-Eyed" by Vachel Lindsay. Copyright © 1914 by Macmillan Publishing Co., Inc., renewed 1942 by Elizabeth C. Lindsay.

SANGA MUSIC for "I don't want your millions mister" by Jim Garland. © Copyright 1947 by Stormking Music Inc. All rights reserved. Used by permission.

CHARLES SCRIBNER'S SONS for "Richard Cory" by Edwin Arlington Robinson. Reprinted by permission of Charles Scribner's Sons from *The Children of the Night* by Edwin Arlington Robinson.

TWAYNE PUBLISHERS, INC. for "If We Must Die" from *Selected Poems of Claude McKay;* copyright 1953 by Twayne Publishers, Inc., and reprinted by permission of Twayne Publishers, a Division of G. K. Hall & Co., Boston.

To Nancy, Steve, and Marnie

Preface

America in the Twentieth Century brings together my thoughts concerning United States history from about 1900 to the present, a field in which I have taught for some twelve years. Although the book pays due attention to the traditional areas of political and diplomatic history, it also focuses on areas of increasing interest to students and scholars: black history, women's history, urbanization, the role of ethnic groups, the rise of presidential power and of the federal bureaucracy, the power of corporations and the conflict of economic groups, changing sexual mores, and trends in regional and national values.

I have tried to give pace to the narrative by including anecdotes and quotations, by describing key personalities, and by setting aside selections from primary sources that illuminate passages in the text. I hope, however, that readers will not conclude that my purpose is to entertain or to avoid serious issues. On the contrary, I have tried to offer up-to-date interpretations and to state my conclusions on major questions. Without sacrificing my own viewpoint, I have also tried to present various sides of controversial issues. My aim is to stimulate the thinking of college-level students in survey courses and in courses dealing with twentieth-century American history.

Many people helped me during the writing and production of this book. These include Thomas A. Williamson and William J. Wisneski, my editors at Harcourt Brace Jovanovich, and Carla Hirst Wiltenburg, who did an excellent job of finding pictures and cartoons. I am also indebted to Alexandra Roosevelt for her careful attention to the details of the manuscript. Sidney Zimmerman of HBJ was an especially intelligent, well informed, and thought-provoking manuscript editor. Professor John Thomas of Brown University helped greatly by reading early drafts of two chapters, as did Daniel Fischel, a Brown graduate student. Professor John Morton Blum of Yale University criticized the entire manuscript with great care and discrimination, and Professor Lawrence Veysey of the University of California, Santa Cruz, also read the whole manuscript and offered extensive and extremely valuable criticism of it. Both scholars immeasurably improved the book.

James T. Patterson

Contents

13

The 1960s: from altruism to disenchantment

411

14

Turmoil, 1965–1968

449

15

The unsettled 1970s

485

The Constitution of the United States of America

521

Presidential elections, 1900–1972

534

Index

537

Tables

Maps and Graphs

America in the Twentieth Century

A HISTORY

1

A
frayed society:
America
at the turn
of the century

The historian Frederick Jackson Turner had every reason to rejoice as the nineteenth century ended. In 1893, when he was only thirty-one years old, he had delivered his widely acclaimed paper describing the influence of the frontier on American history, and by 1899 he was a well-established professor at the University of Wisconsin. Although his salary was only $3000 per year and he usually had to teach summer school six days a week to pay his bills, Turner still lived comfortably. Food, fuel, and light for him, his wife, and three small children cost less than $1000 a year, taxes and interest on his house around $500, clothes $200, and medical bills $100. Like other Americans, he paid no income tax, and he did without such later "necessities" as a car, freezer, or refrigerator. He owned his lake front home, employed two servants, and had ample time for the bicycling, fishing, and walking that kept him close to the beauty of his native state.

Turner felt secure and content like many contemporaries born and raised on farms and in small towns at the turn of the century. Burton Wheeler, later a senator from Montana, grew up in Hudson, Massachusetts, a small industrial town twenty-five miles from Boston. His father was a cobbler, and the family owned an eight-room frame house on the outskirts of town. They kept a horse and cow, and raised pigs and chickens. Wheeler recalled easy-going days when he picked blueberries for pocket money and wandered through Hudson, a "classic Victorian setting." Hugo Black, who was later to achieve fame as a Supreme Court justice, also had a youth in which he enjoyed lazy days of horseshoe pitching, baseball, croquet, and fishing in east-central Alabama. Paul Douglas, later a senator from Illinois, cherished the Maine woods in which he lived as a small boy and where his mother and uncle cleared land for cabins and a summer hotel. Bruce Catton, the Civil War historian, recalled fondly the measured pace and opportunity of the lumber country in upstate Michigan during the 1890s. Born in 1901, Margaret Mead was perhaps most rhapsodic of all in remembering her early years in Hammonton, New Jersey, not far from Philadelphia. Like the others, she was struck by the simplicity of life and the immediacy of the outdoors, where she could roam at will. Among her joys were playing with her mother's possessions and, living in an extended family, listening to her grandmother's imaginative stories.

These young people enjoyed life styles enormously more comfortable than those endured by the large number of people who crowded the cities or scratched at the land. Class distinctions existed, but opportunity also beckoned, and right conduct (or "character," as it was popularly called) was believed to count for almost as much as social standing. As the historian William Leuchtenburg described it, the life of middle-class youth featured "the clang of the trolley, the cry of the carnival pitchman, the oompah of the military band on a summer evening, the clatter of Victorian sulkies, the shouts of children playing blindman's buff and run-sheep-run." For nostalgic Americans in later decades this description offered an image of a world that seemed to have been overwhelmed by the complexity, breathlessness, and divisiveness of twentieth-century life.

Movement and tension

Only an elite, however, could hope to enjoy such an idyllic existence. America had 76 million people in 1900, of whom 35 million were generally underprivileged Negroes, Indians, or immigrants. Of the remaining 41 million, few enjoyed the advantages of people like the Turners. For every socially secure girl like Margaret Mead there were scores, like Theodore Dreiser's Sister Carrie, who fled farm or small town, only to be buffeted about in the cities. For every upward-mobile young man like Wheeler or Douglas there were many more who moved constantly without ever advancing up the social ladder. Continuous geographical mobility and social insecurity, not the static gentility of Currier and Ives prints, describe the lives of all but the favored few at the time.

Moreover, memories suffused with nostalgia have a way of distorting historical reality. Even for people like Turner and his well-placed contemporaries, that reality could be frightening indeed. For Turner the blows were personal, and they came with the suddenness that made life so uncertain for people of that generation. In 1899 he lost both a daughter and a son, his wife had an emotional breakdown and was confined for a period in a sanitarium, and he, stricken by the events, went briefly into seclusion. Personal tragedies also disrupted the early lives of Mead and Douglas. When Mead was a young girl her father became cold and withdrawn from the family following the death of her baby sister. When Douglas was four his mother died, his father took to drink, made life intolerable for his second wife and two sons, and virtually forced them to flee to the Maine woods. Black and Catton were spared similar family crises, but lived amid social and economic dislocations: Black in an agrarian depression and Catton in a once thriving lumber region cut barren by the loggers. By 1900 conservationists began to lament this reckless commercial exploitation of natural resources.

Sensitive Americans worried about this social instability. Some young people reacted by finding opportunity in the city, and some by moving West— young Burt Wheeler did both. Others, like Douglas, who watched lumberjacks killed or maimed every year, came to demand action from the government, which in the 1890s was still more a symbol of unity than an agency directly affecting lives. Many others, however, turned to saloons, prostitution, and, perhaps most fearfully for the rest of their contemporaries, to socialism, radicalism, and the formation of interest groups. The apprehension about potential class warfare, intensified by the feeling that the frontier was a thing of the past, obsessed many respectable Americans in the depression-ridden 1890s. As the historian Henry Adams complained, "the individual crawled as best he could, through the wreck, and found many values of life upset."

Ethnic and racial tensions, already acute in the large American cities, disturbed even the lives of small-town Americans. Black's area of Alabama had comparatively few Negroes, but they were supposed to know their place. When a local white boy shot and killed a Negro, he was acquitted because his father was respectable. Black's father, a well-to-do storekeeper, lamented the court's decision—not because it revealed racial injustice but because in mocking the law the acquittal would leave no one safe. Wheeler had no such experience with Negroes, but when he tried to date local Catholic girls, he was driven from their neighborhood by people throwing rocks. And Douglas recalled that the Irish in Maine were stoned as they tried to walk to parochial schools. These racial and ethno-cultural tensions, so sharp and open in late-nineteenth-century America, profoundly shaped the residential, educational, and political contours of the era.

Epidemics, high mortality rates, drunkenness, immorality, agricultural disaster, unemployment, radicalism, ethnic and racial divisions—all these (whether real or imagined) frightened well-placed Americans in the 1890s. A supposed harmony of interests seemed in danger of destruction. In retrospect it is clear that the established ways showed striking longevity, that the wellborn were to maintain their social and economic hegemony under a capitalistic economy and a republican form of government—in short, that in twentieth-century America much from the nineteenth century would be preserved. Yet such continuity was by no means so clear at the time, for three overwhelming forces seemed destined to transform the nation. These were urbanization, mass immigration, and industrialization.

FEAR OF THE CITY

The extent of urbanization in America by 1900 is sometimes exaggerated. According to the Census Bureau, which defined urban areas as places with populations of 2500 or more, only a little more than 40 percent of Americans lived in urban areas in 1900; and because this definition included many small towns, it is probable that three out of four Americans were not city dwellers. Many cities that later became metropolises were still moderate in size: the population of Dallas in 1900 was 42,000, of Houston, 44,000. In all but a few large cities it was still possible to climb aboard a trolley and ride quickly into the country. The slums, tenements, and ghettos described by Jacob Riis and other urban reformers proliferated in only a few older, predominantly eastern urban areas. Only one city, Boston, had a subway, and very few had skyscrapers. New York , whose tallest building in 1900 had only twenty-nine stories, was not the vertical wonder it was to become in the next thirty years, but a sprawling conglomeration of low, grey tenements, brownstones, and iron-decked commercial buildings.

Yet contemporaries were correct in pointing to the sweep of urban growth, for it had been and would continue to be astonishing. In 1860 Pittsburg had a population of 67,000 people; by 1900 it had 450,000. During the same period the population of Minneapolis grew from 2500 to 200,000, that of Los Angeles from 5000 to 100,000. In 1900, Chicago, which had only 30,000 inhabitants in 1850, had 1.7 million, and Kansas City, only a small town in 1850, had 200,000. By 1900 not only Chicago but also Philadelphia, with 1.3 million, and New York–Brooklyn, with 3 million, had over a million residents. By 1920 the inevitable occurred: America, by census definition, was more than 50 percent urban.

At the root of this growth were sweeping developments in technology. Electrification made possible trolleys, which allowed urban areas to spread beyond the old cities of antebellum days. It led also to the installation of elevators, without which the vertical metropolis could not have developed. Steam and electricity also accelerated the urban concentration of industry, which had previously scattered to sources of water power. The mechanization of farming, the growth of railroads, and the increasing use of the refrigerator car facilitated the rapid shipment of foodstuffs and other raw materials in the quantities necessary to support huge agglomerations of people. The growth of

The growth of cities: the ten largest cities from 1860 to 1900 and in 1970
(in thousands)

1860		1880		1900		1970	
New York[a]	1,072	New York[a]	1,773	New York[a]	3,437	New York	11,571
Philadelphia	585	Philadelphia	847	Chicago	1,699	Los Angeles[b]	7,032
Baltimore	212	Chicago	503	Philadelphia	1,294	Chicago	6,978
Boston	178	Boston	363	St. Louis	575	Philadelphia	4,817
New Orleans	169	St. Louis	351	Boston	561	Detroit	4,199
Cincinnati	161	Baltimore	332	Baltimore	509	San Francisco[c]	3,109
St. Louis	161	Cincinnati	255	Pittsburgh	452	Washington	2,861
Chicago	109	Pittsburgh	235	Cleveland	382	Boston	2,753
Buffalo	81	San Francisco	234	Buffalo	352	Pittsburgh	2,401
Newark	72	New Orleans	216	San Francisco	343	St. Louis	2,363

SOURCE: Donald B. Cole, *Handbook of American History* (New York, 1968), p. 166; and George E. Delury, *World Almanac and Book of Facts 1975* (New York, 1974) p. 148
[a]Manhattan and Brooklyn [b]Includes Long Beach [c]Includes Oakland

cities, like much else in modern American history, stemmed in large part from the technological imperative.

Technological change also caused lasting disruptions in rural and small-town life. The mechanization of agriculture contributed to regular overproduction of cash crops and to plummeting prices (especially before 1897) on domestic and world markets. Small farmers, tenants, and rural laborers found themselves squeezed off the land or burdened with ever greater debts. Faced with ruin, thousands of people, especially in the Plains and the South, joined the Populists in the early 1890s and cursed their enemies. "The great common people of this country are slaves," said Mary Ellen Lease, a prominent Populist orator, "and monopoly is the master. The West and South are prostrate before the manufacturing East." The folk singer Woody Guthrie, son of poor rural folk from the Plains, remembered his mother rocking him to sleep:

> Rock-a-bye baby, on the tree top;
> When you grow up, you'll work in a shop.
> When you are married, your wife will work, too
> So that the rich will have nothing to do.

> Hush-a-bye baby, on the tree top;
> When you grow old, your wages will stop.
> When you have spent the little you've made
> First to the poorhouse, then to the grave.

The reforms sought by the agrarian rebels—the eight-hour day, popular election of senators, governmental control of railroads and utilities—later became part of American life. In the 1890s, however, the Populists succeeded

Changing population distribution, 1860–1920
(in thousands)

	1860	1870	1880	1890	1900	1910	1920
Urban[a]	6,216	9,902	14,129	22,106	30,159	41,998	54,157
Rural	25,226	28,656	36,026	40,841	45,834	49,973	51,552
Total	31,442	38,558	50,155	62,947	75,993	91,971	105,709

SOURCE: Adapted from U. S. Bureau of the Census, *Historical Statistics of the United States, Colonial Times to 1957* (Washington, D. C., 1960), p. 14
[a] Persons living in places of 2500 or more inhabitants

chiefly in frightening "respectable" people, who perceived them as harbingers of class warfare. More important, the embattled farmers were fighting a losing battle against inexorable technological forces, and thousands gave up the struggle every year by fleeing to the cities. Though America's rural population continued to rise, from 36 million in 1880 to 50 million in 1910, the urban population jumped much more rapidly, from 14 to 42 million in the same period. About 10 million of these 28 million "new" urbanites were immigrants from abroad. The remaining 18 million, however, came from the American countryside. This vast rural-urban migration was vivid testimony to the unsettled economic and social conditions of the age.

Many motives impelled the millions who left the farms and small towns. For some, like Sister Carrie, the city was a magnet—a place where bright lights, noise, and color might bring excitement to life. For others, urban life was the new frontier—a place that promised to enhance social status or economic opportunity, a "safety valve" for economic discontent, cultural isolation, and social stagnation. To such migrants rural life was not so much joyful as monotonous, lonely, and exhausting. "I'm sick of farm life," one of Hamlin Garland's characters complained bitterly. "It's nothing but fret, fret, fret, and work the whole time, never seeing anybody but a lot of neighbors just as big fools as you are. I spend my time fighting flies and washing dishes and churning. I'm sick of it all."

Many Americans responded to the massive shift from country to city by reaffirming the mythical virtues of rural life. In spite of Garland's realistic portrayals of rural hardship, rhapsodies about life in small towns survived as staples of fiction until writers like Sherwood Anderson and Sinclair Lewis delivered powerful (though still not fatal) blows to them in the teens and 1920s. Booth Tarkington's *Gentleman from Indiana,* published in 1900, was typical of small-town fantasies. The inhabitants of fictional Plattville, a Tarkington character observed, were "one big happy family." Plattville was "the one place for a man to live who likes to live where people are kind to each other, and where they have the old-fashioned way of saying 'Home.'" Even Theodore Dreiser, product of a harsh, lower-class background in small-town Indiana, was moved by a trip through his native state in 1916. "Every one of

> *When Aunt Em came there to live she was a young pretty wife. The sun and wind had changed her, too. They had taken the sparkle from her eyes and left them a sober gray; they had taken the red from her cheeks and lips, and they were gray also. She was thin and gaunt, and never smiled now. When Dorothy, who was an orphan, first came to her, Aunt Em had been so startled by the child's laughter that she would scream and press her hand upon her heart whenever Dorothy's merry voice reached her ears; and she still looked at the little girl with wonder that she could find anything to laugh at.*
>
> *Henry never laughed. He worked hard from morning till night and did not know what joy was. He was gray also, from his long beard to his rough boots, and he looked stern and solemn, and rarely spoke.*
>
> The reality of life on the Plains, as described by Lyman Frank Baum in his *The Wonderful Wizard of Oz* (1900). Aunt Em and Uncle Henry were the guardians of Dorothy, the heroine, who is swept away from her humdrum life.

those simple towns through which we had been passing," he conceded, "has its red light district." But "the center of Indiana is a region of calm and simplicity, untroubled to a large extent . . . by the stormy emotions and distresses which so often affect other parts of America and the world."

The celebration of the small town was but one sign of the tension under which many Americans, swept up in social change, were living. Other indications were the nostalgia implicit in Turner's thesis that democracy and individualism were products of the frontier, the joyful release many Americans felt at William McKinley's triumph over the "radical" William Jennings Bryan in 1896, and the passion with which people embraced the "splendid little war" against Spain in 1898, a conflict that William James thought might "hammer us into decency." Buffeted about by social change, many Americans persistently emphasized the virtues of their agrarian past. Accordingly, their portrayal of cities was hardly flattering, and even historians have echoed their emphasis on the dingy, the violent, and the pathological side of urbanization. Such a portrayal, distorted and overgeneralized, deserves a careful look.

THE QUALITY OF URBAN LIFE

James Bryce, the sophisticated English observer whose *American Commonwealth* (1888) remains one of the most discerning descriptions of late-nineteenth-century American life, put forward one theme that underlay the verbal assault on American cities. This was aesthetic revulsion. American cities, he observed, "differ from one another only herein, that some are built more with brick than with wood, and others more with wood than with brick." A year later, his countryman Matthew Arnold agreed. "American cities," he wrote, "have hardly anything to please a trained or a natural sense for beauty . . . a great void exists in the civilization over there [in America]; a want of what is elevating and beautiful, of what is interesting."

Bryce and Arnold reflected a widespread view that American cities, among the fastest growing in human history, were unplanned and therefore ugly. The architect Louis Sullivan described Chicago as "this flat smear, this endless drawl of streets and shanties, large and small, this ocean of smoke. . . . New York may be revolting to you, but this Chicago thing is infinitely repulsive to me. . . . Seventy years ago it was a mudhole—today it is a human swamp." Rudyard Kipling concluded simply of Chicago, "I urgently desire never to see it again," while the novelist Henry James, who moved to London to escape the crassness of his native land, called the American city a "huge continuous 50-floored conspiracy against the very idea of the ancient graces."

To contemporary observers ugliness was merely the most obvious manifestation of urban pathology. Another was city government, which by 1900 was too often in the hands of immigrant political "machines" to suit old-stock residents and "goo-goos," or "good government" reformers. In fact, these urban machines served important functions, sometimes offering to city government the same organization and regimentation that graded urban schools were contributing to education. At their most humane they also furnished welfare services to people in need. As Martin Lomasney, the boss of Boston, put it, "there's got to be in every ward somebody that any bloke can come to—no matter what he's done—and get help. *Help, you understand; none of your law and justice, but help.*" Men like Lomasney or New York's Charles Murphy, boss of Tammany Hall, provided on the local level the beginnings of welfare functions that state and federal government were later to assume.

Some of these bosses proved wasteful or corrupt. More often, they treated politics as an occupation, not as a forum for disinterested public service. "There's an honest graft," Tammany's George Washington Plunkitt observed, "and I'm an example of how it works. I might sum up the whole thing by sayin': I seen my opportunities and I took 'em." Jimmy Walker, the colorful mayor of New York in the 1920s, added, "there comes a time in politics when a man must rise above principle." The immigrant machines reflected not only the trend toward centralization and the service state but also the social mobility of newer ethnic groups via classic forms of adaptation. It was not surprising that such organizations tended to overturn the older elites.

Many people recoiled from such machines, especially because immigrants ran them. Bryce contemptuously referred to the "ignorant multitude, largely composed of recent immigrants, untrained in self-government." Novelists of the period commonly agreed. The progressive David Graham Phillips in his political novel *The Plum Tree* (1905) described the boss, Dominick, as a "huge tall man, enormously muscular, with a high head like a block, straight in front, behind and on either side; keen, shifty eyes, pompous cheeks, a raw, wide mouth; slovenly dress, with a big diamond on his puffy little finger." Tarkington in "The Aliens," a short story, portrayed a precinct chairman as a "pockmarked, damp-looking, soiled little fungus of a man." Even the social

Cities grew rapidly; they were unplanned and often became congested: Chicago, 1910.

worker Jane Addams believed that immigrants were "densely ignorant of civic duties."

Observers of the city around 1900 were also distressed by crowding. Actually, urban densities were generally manageable in American cities, most of which sprawled outward rather than upward. But in a few older areas like New York City, the situation seemed ominous. The urban reformer Jacob Riis estimated in 1890 that 330,000 people lived in one square mile of the lower east side, and that the death rate for children under five in some of these blocks was almost 140 per thousand, compared to 88 per thousand for the city at large. The density of population in Manhattan in 1894 was 143.2 people per acre. One section had 986.4 people per acre, a density surpassing even that of Bombay.

The cause of such crowding, then and later, was the increasingly high value attached to urban land, which led builders and landlords to make optimal use of space. The result in New York was the "dumbbell" tenement, the dominant form of residential construction in that city between 1879 and 1900. These tenements were five- or six-story buildings, each floor of which had two hallway water closets and fourteen rooms divided into four apartments. The buildings occupied small lots of 25 x 100 feet, and the largest rooms were 10½ x 11 feet. The tenements left no space for landscaping and were attached to each other in front and back. The name "dumbbell" was applied because of narrow (28-inch) air shafts that separated the buildings in the middle and provided the only lighting for the interior rooms. One New York block in 1900 contained thirty-nine such tenements with a total of almost 2800 inhabitants. In that block only forty apartments had running water, and thirty-two cases of tuberculosis had been recorded in the previous five years.

Tenement dwellers: fire escapes were the chief place to get relief from summer heat in the slums.

Writers of the time were almost unanimous in deploring the results of this crowding. Frequently the water closets jammed, leaving overpowering odors that mingled with those of horse manure on the streets and garbage tossed down the air shafts. These odors, a report on sanitation in Philadelphia concluded, created "such a pernicious influence upon the atmosphere that one feels an indescribable sense of relief in going to the park or moving out of town, where the air is not laden and polluted with the fetid vapors and foul odors everywhere prevailing." The air pollution of the 1970s, however noxious, has been considerably less pungent than in the days of outdoor plumbing and the horse.

Middle-class reformers, forgetting the stench of the farmyards and the primitive amenities of small towns, were often appalled. And, though they worried about disease, they tended in that Victorian age to dwell on the presumed connection between slum life and sexual immorality. Charles Loring Brace, organizer of the Children's Aid Society, stressed that theme as early as 1880 in his book *The Dangerous Classes of New York*. "If a female child be born and brought up in a room of one of those tenement houses," he wrote, "she loses very early the modesty which is the great shield of purity. Personal delicacy becomes almost unknown to her. . . . it is well nigh impossible for her to retain any feminine reserve, and she passes almost unconsciously the line of purity at a very early age."

Complaints such as these ignored the fact that privacy—new to the Victorian era—had hardly characterized rural life in America. Still, others followed Brace's lead. Crowding, said the Tenement House Commission of New York in 1894, led to a "condition of nervous tension; interfering with the separateness and sacredness of home life; leading to the promiscuous mixing of all ages and sexes in a single room—thus breaking down the barriers of modesty and conducing to the corruption of the young, and occasionally to revolting crimes." Josiah Strong, a widely read Protestant minister and reformer, called slum life a "commingled mass of venomous filth and seething sin, of lust, of drunkenness, of pauperism and crime of every sort." And a popular song concluded:

> She wanted to roam so she left the old home
> The old people's hearts were sore,
> She longed for the sights and the bright city lights
> Where hundreds had gone before.
> She went to the heart of the city
> And mingled with strangers there,
> But nobody said, "You are being misled,"
> For what did the stranger care?
>
> In the heart of the city that has no heart
> That's where they meet, and that's where they part,
> The current of vice had proved too strong
> So the poor little girlie just drifted along,
> Nobody cared if she lived or died,
> Nobody cared if she laughed or cried,
> She's just a lost sister and nobody's missed her,
> She's there in the city
> Where there's no pity,
> In the city that has no heart.

Street scene, Staten Island. The horse lies dead, overwhelmed by the heat.

Rear tenement bedroom, New York City, *c.* 1910

Songs like these conveniently overlooked a vast folklore about farmers' daughters: there seems no end of ways to "ruin" demure damsels from the countryside. What was true, however, was that thousands of immigrant and lower-class women lived lives of squalor and desperation. Margaret Sanger, one of eleven children whose mother died young of tuberculosis, became a nurse on the lower east side of New York at the turn of the century. What she saw made her a pioneer for birth control. The way women live, she wrote later, "is almost beyond belief. They hate and fear any prying into their homes or into their lives. They resent being talked to. The women slink in and out of their homes on their way to market like rats from their holes. The men beat their wives sometimes black and blue, but no one interferes. . . . Women whose weary bodies refuse to accommodate themselves to their husbands' desires find husbands looking with lustful eyes upon other women, sometimes upon their own little daughters, six and seven years of age."

Not all lower-class enclaves were as disorganized and miserable as those that Sanger saw in New York. Workers in Paterson, New Jersey, for instance, maintained such a coherent sense of community in the late nineteenth century that they were able to enlist the backing of police and municipal leaders against factory owners. Similarly, Italian-American families in Buffalo retained the tradition of the old country that males earned the family's daily bread while the wives worked, if at all, in the home; for these families urban life caused no harm. Cities, for all their problems, still offered displaced or discontented people a standard of living they could not have found any place else, and thousands of Americans flocked to them through most of the twentieth century.

Nevertheless, the vision of the city as ugly, corrupt, crowded, disease-ridden, and above all immoral caught hold with many Americans who were small-town born and bred and who were adults by the turn of the century. The slum, and by extension the city, appeared a frightening symbol of the decline of civilization and the disruption of the natural order of things.

THE FOREIGNERS

In 1908 Israel Zangwill scored a hit on Broadway with his play, *The Melting Pot.* "The real American," one of his characters explained, "has not yet arrived. He is only in the Crucible, I tell you—he will be the fusion of all the races, the coming superman." Four years later a young Russian-Jewish immigrant, Mary Antin, wrote a book, *The Promised Land,* that sold more than 85,000 copies in the next four decades. Like Zangwill, she advanced the idea that America could melt all newcomers into a superior common national-ity. "I have been made over," she exulted. "I am absolutely other than the person whose story I have to tell."

It is doubtful, however, that the many Americans who saw the play or read the book really believed in the optimistic message of assimilation. On the contrary, hostility to free immigration mounted steadily after the 1870s. As early as 1882 Congress excluded Chinese immigration, and in 1897 it approved a law that required incoming migrants to pass a literacy test. President Cleveland vetoed it, as did President Wilson in 1913 and 1915. But in 1917, only five years after Antin's cry of affirmation, Congress overruled Wilson's veto, and in the 1920s it went further by applying quotas that discriminated against "undesirable" southern and eastern Europeans. The nativism revealed by these laws was not new to the late nineteenth century, for Americans had periodically erupted in waves of ethnocentrism, religious intolerance, and alien persecutions. But the depth of turn-of-the-century nativism—which ultimately overrode the pressure of otherwise powerful industrialists seeking cheap labor—exposed a lack of confidence in the nation's ability to absorb the "wretched refuse" (as even the Statue of Liberty labelled immigrants) of foreign lands. The "immigrant problem," along with the rise of cities, profoundly unsettled many turn-of-the-century Americans.

The anti-immigrationists worried first about the sheer size of the "inva-sions," which dwarfed all previous mass movements in Western history. Besides migrants from Asia and from Mexico, approximately 25 million Europeans entered the United States in the five decades before 1900. The census of that year showed that 26 million of America's 76 million people were foreign born or children of immigrants. In the next fourteen years, the peak of immigration, another 14.5 million arrived—a rate of more than a million per year. Alarmed, the head of the Daughters of the American Revolution con-cluded in 1910 that "we must not so eagerly invite all the sons of Shem, Ham, and Japhet, wherever they may have first seen the light, and under whatever traditions and influences and ideals foreign and antagonistic to ours they may have been reared, to trample the mud of millions of alien feet into our spring."

The restrictionists also worried about the nature of this latest wave of immigration. Prior to the 1890s close to 90 percent of immigrants had come from northern or western Europe. Many, like the Irish, spoke English; others, like the Germans or Scandinavians, physically resembled Americans of Anglo-Saxon stock. Most of these migrants had eventually brought their families and had settled on farm land rather than congregating in cities. Increasingly, however, the new migrants fled from southern or eastern Europe, which provided 70 percent of the wave that came in between 1900 and 1914. To Anglo-Saxons they seemed poorly educated and politically ignorant (or subversive). They were also much more likely than the earlier immigrants to be Catholic or Jewish. Arriving in a country with little good land left for farming, they concentrated in eastern and middle western cities. By 1910 one-third of the population of America's eight largest cities was foreign-born.

Preoccupation with such a picture led contemporaries into several over-simplifications. One was that the new migrants, as Woodrow Wilson said in 1902, were "men out of the ranks where there was neither skill nor energy nor any initiative of quick intelligence." In fact, the bottom elements of European society lacked the money to migrate. More commonly, the newcomers were

Relation of total immigration to total population, 1870–1930

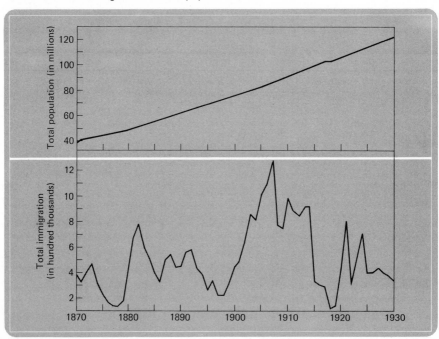

SOURCE: Adapted from *Historical Statistics of the United States*, pp. 7, 56, 57

Immigration from Europe and Asia, 1870–1930

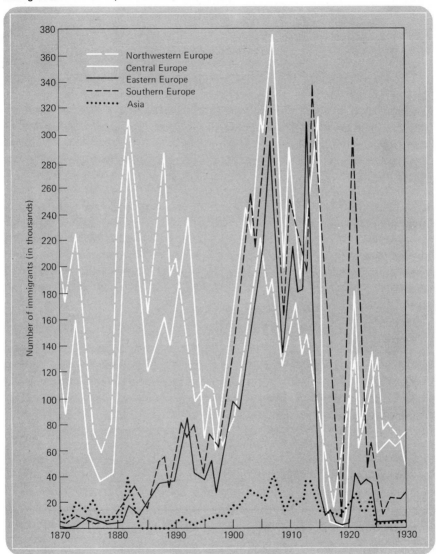

SOURCE: Adapted from *Historical Statistics of the United States*, pp. 56–59. *Northwestern Europe:* comprises Great Britain, Ireland, Scandinavia, Netherlands, Belgium, Luxembourg, Switzerland, France; *Central Europe:* comprises Germany, Poland (which was included in figures for Germany, Austro-Hungary, and Russia between 1899–1919), Austria, Czechoslovakia, Yugoslavia, Hungary; *Eastern Europe:* comprises Russia (USSR after 1917) in Europe, Latvia, Estonia, Lithuania, Finland, Rumania, Bulgaria, Turkey in Europe; *Southern Europe:* comprises Italy, Spain, Portugal, Greece, Albania; *Asia:* comprises Turkey in Asia, China, Japan, Philippine Islands.

restless sons and daughters of peasant families that could subdivide their meager acreage no further. Or they were people who had already been uprooted to European cities and had moved again to America. Or, if Jewish, they had fled from persecution in Russia and eastern Europe. Far from being lazy or unenterprising, these new migrants were willing to work long hours at heavy physical labor—perhaps to give their children the advantages they had lacked, perhaps to save the money necessary to buy a house in the city or land in the old country.

Contemporaries also assumed wrongly that foreign-born Americans were growing rapidly as a percentage of the population. That was not the case. Thousands of the new migrants left their families behind, and those who brought them did not reproduce faster than native Americans. Most of these immigrants were single men who came to America in search of jobs. If they were lucky, they found them, worked hard, and amassed savings far beyond what they could have accomplished in their native lands. If they were unlucky—and millions were after the panics of 1893 and 1907—they suffered. Either way, many yearned to escape the grinding physical labor of America, and thousands availed themselves of the cheap (as low as $10) steamship voyage home to the old country—for good. Between 1870 and 1900 it is estimated that 24 percent of the immigrants—"birds of passage," they were called—left America; between 1900 and 1914 the percentage approached 40. For these reasons the foreign-born in America in 1914 comprised only 14.5 percent of the population, barely higher than the 13.2 percent discovered by the census of 1860.

The extent of this out-migration suggests that images of ethnic concentration also need revision. Even between 1900 and 1914 in America the ethnic ghetto did not exist in the eastern European sense of the term, which usually was a rigidly bounded area to which Jews were confined. Large concentrations of ethnic groups developed, primarily in those few older cities or mill and factory towns where abundant aged (and therefore cheap) housing existed. Moreover, these enclaves were not "spider webs" trapping all who blundered in or "spawning grounds" for crime and immorality, to use the words of one contemporary observer. On the contrary, they were usually highly fluid neighborhoods that featured huge in- and out-migrations. And statistics on crime and immorality in these enclaves or among foreign groups are so notoriously imprecise as to be useless. Even the Mafia, often considered a characteristically criminal outgrowth of "ghetto" life, was in fact part of the cultural baggage of some of those who emigrated from Palermo.

Historians have qualified the notion that there was one representative immigrant experience or that different ethnic groups perceived each other as going through the same process. While the bulk of southern and eastern Europeans fled peasant or village backgrounds, thousands, especially from Italy, came from cities. Also, the foreign arrivals from any given country possessed such a bewildering variety of mores and dialects that it is hazardous at best to speak of a common experience by nationality. Southern and northern Italians, for instance, might as well have come from different countries. Such differences prevented the unified class consciousness that labor organizers eagerly but vainly attempted to develop.

But just as rural Americans exaggerated the seamy side of the city, so old-stock residents, the majority, failed to appreciate the complexity and variety of the foreign migrations. The result was a nativism as varied as the immigrants themselves. As early as the 1870s nativists included some people like the New Jersey professor who was aesthetically disgusted by the "beer-drinking" and "brute-like" people who "eat, drink, breed, work, and die" and who require the "rich and more intelligent classes" to "guard them with police and standing armies, and to cover the land with prisons, cages, and all kinds of receptacles for the perpetrators of crime." Others joined the antialien American Protective Association and campaigned for such abiding institutions as Flag Day and the pledge of allegiance to the flag. Anglo-Saxons also established increasingly exclusive orders to separate themselves from the immigrant masses (and from native whites scrambling up the social ladder). Between 1883 and 1897 these people founded such organizations as the Sons of Revolution, Groton School, the Social Register, the Colonial Dames, the DAR, the Society of Mayflower Descendants, the Aryan Order of St. George, and the Baronial Order of Runnymede. By 1897 the DAR, founded in 1890, had 397 chapters in thirty-eight states.

Not all those who worried about the rising tide of immigration were political and social conservatives. In 1885 a group of progressive economists founded the American Economic Association to promote social reform. At the same time they offered a prize of $150 for the best essay on the "Evil Effects of Unrestricted Immigration." Free immigration, they recognized, was welcomed by employers seeking cheap labor. It promoted poverty. The sheer size of the migrations—of people who had had no experience with democratic institutions—threatened to overwhelm America's political system.

The depression of the mid-1890s temporarily decreased the rate of immigration, but it also sharpened the social tensions under which nativism could spread. Accordingly, the use of nasty stereotypes increased. *The New York Times* referred to "hatchet-faced, pimply, sallow-cheeked, rat-eyed young men of the Russian-Jew colony," while Francis Walker, an eminent economist and restrictionist, talked of "beaten men from beaten races, representing the worst failures in the struggle for existence." The appearance of heightened nativism at the very moment that immigration was decreasing suggests that restrictionism stemmed from a significant loss of confidence among Americans in the 1890s as well as from alarm about the numbers of foreign-born people who were arriving.

Walker's use of the phrase "struggle for existence" revealed a growing use of Darwinian language in the battle against free immigration. This kind of argument received its most scholarly support in the writings of William Z. Ripley, who published his *Races of Man* in 1899. Ripley used cephalic indexes to describe three "races," the Teutonic, the Alpine, and the Mediterranean.

Though Ripley avoided ranking these "races," restrictionists were not so careful, and his book became a Bible for proponents of a Darwinian view that justified Anglo-Saxon imperialism as well as discrimination against certain ethnic groups. The focus of the restrictionist case shifted accordingly—from a concern about the impact of immigration on working conditions to arguments that some groups were by nature better "fit" to assimilate. And because assimilation to the dominant—the white Anglo-Saxon Protestant descendants of the earlier immigrants—was the perceived ideal, those immigrants who failed to assimilate were not only less "fit" but by definition inferior.

Thus it was that scientific ethnocentrism became common during the first decade of the twentieth century, and articles advocating eugenics proliferated in the magazines and newspapers. Between 1907 and 1917, sixteen states passed laws permitting sterilization of various types of presumably hereditary defectives (none of the laws was regularly enforced). The Dillingham Commission of congressmen and other experts, which set out to discover "whether there may not be certain races which are inferior to other races," not surprisingly concluded (in a forty-two-volume study published in 1911) that restriction of the newer groups was justified by "economic, moral, and social considerations." And Madison Grant, an anthropologist with the American Museum of Natural History, brought the racist argument to its ultimate conclusion in 1916 with publication of his *Passing of the Great Race*. Grant's book exalted the "specialized traits of Nordic man; his stature, his light colored eyes, his fair skin and light colored hair, his straight nose and his splendid fighting and moral qualities." Grant lamented the emancipation of the slaves and ridiculed the notion of human brotherhood. *Science* magazine, impressed, called it a "work of solid merit."

This science infected some reformers as well. In California, progressives talked of the "Yellow Peril" and forced anti-Japanese laws through the legislature. At the time California had approximately 50,000 Japanese residents in a total population of 2,250,000. Members of the Immigration Restriction League included Robert A. Woods, Boston's leading social worker, John R. Commons and Edward A. Ross, eminent reformers and economists at the University of Wisconsin, and President David Starr Jordan of Stanford University. Florence Kelley, a socialist and a militant social reformer, worried after the Lawrence textile strike of 1912 that anarchy had "become hereditary from generation to generation among immigrants and their children."

In 1916 the progressive *New Republic* revealed how far America had departed from the model proposed by Zangwill and Antin. "Only recently," it observed, "we had absolute confidence in our power of assimilation. Serb, Armenian, Lithuanian, we assured ourselves, would put off their national characters and become good Americans . . . as Irish, Germans, and Scandinavians had become merged with the original English stock. . . . This optimism is hard to remember." The older ways of small-town, Anglo-Saxon America appeared to be vanishing as rapidly as the frontier, and with them went some of the characteristic American confidence in the future.

RAMPAGING INDUSTRIALIZATION

"Every American who lived into the year 2000," Henry Adams wrote in 1904, "would know how to control unlimited power. He would think in complexities unimaginable to an earlier mind. . . . To him the nineteenth century would stand on the same plane with the fourth—equally childlike—and he would only wonder how both of them, knowing so little, and so weak in force, should have done so much."

Adams was merely expressing the awe that many people felt about the rampages of industrialization. As early as the 1880s the value of manufactured goods exceeded for the first time that of farm products, and the number of nonagricultural workers rose above the number working on the farms. In 1860 American industries had ranked fourth in the world with products totaling $1.9 billion. By 1890 they were worth $10 billion, and by 1900 the United States ranked first in the world with goods valued at $13 billion.

Other statistics suggest the magnitude of this growth, which even in the depression-ridden 1890s averaged 4.6 percent per year. Between the mid-1860s and 1900 railroad truckage increased from 35,000 to 193,000 miles, steel rose from 20,000 long tons produced per year to 10 million, and bituminous coal jumped from 13 million short tons extracted per annum to 212 million. Oil production rose from zero in 1860 to 1 billion gallons of kerosene, 300 million gallons of fuel oils, and 170 million gallons of lubricating oils in 1900, while horsepower from all sources (steam, electricity, wind, water, and work animals) increased from 2,535,000 in 1860 to 46,215,000 forty years later. It was no wonder that Adams added, "power leaped from every atom. . . . Man could no longer hold it off. Forces grasped his wrists and flung him about as though he had hold of a live wire."

Inventions accompanying this growth seemed equally astonishing to contemporary observers. Before 1860 Americans had taken out 30,000 patents;

The clock in the workshop,—it rests not a moment,
It points on, and ticks on: eternity—time;
Once someone told me the clock had a meaning,
In pointing and ticking had reason and rhyme. . . .
At times, when I listen, I hear the clock plainly;
The reason of old—the old meaning—is gone!
The maddening pendulum urges me forward
To labor and still labor on.
The tick of the clock is the boss in his anger.
The face of the clock has the eyes of the foe.
The clock—I shudder—Dost hear how it draws me?
It calls me "Machine" and it cries [to] me "Sew"!

A poem by Morris Rosenfeld described working conditions at the turn of the century.

The explosion of industrial growth, 1860–1920

	1860	1880	1900	1910	1920
Population (millions)	32	50	76	92	106
Urban population (percent of total)[a]	20	28	40	44	51
Railroad miles in operation	30,626	93,262	193,346	240,293	252,845
Exports of merchandise (millions of current dollars)	316	824	1,371	1,710	8,030
Nonagricultural exports (millions of current dollars, followed by percent of total)	49(16)	122(15)	485(35)	767(45)	4,163(52)
Iron ore production (thousands of tons)	2,873	7,120	27,300	57,015	67,604
Steel ingots and castings produced (thousands of tons)	20[b]	1,247	10,188	26,094	42,132
Crude petroleum production (thousands of barrels)	500	26,286	63,621	209,557	442,929
Bituminous coal production (thousands of tons)	9,057	50,757	212,316	417,111	568,667
Workers in nonfarm occupations (thousands, followed by percent of all workers)	4,325(41)	8,807(51)	18,161(63)	25,779(69)	30,985(73)
General imports (millions of current dollars)	354	668	850	1,557	5,278
GNP (billions of dollars, 1929 prices)	9.1[c]	16.1[c]	37.1[c]	55.0[c]	71.9[c]

SOURCE: Adapted from *Historical Statistics of the United States*, pp. 7, 14, 72, 139, 356, 357, 360, 361, 365, 366, 416, 417, 427, 429, 544, 545, 552, 553
[a] Persons in places of 2500 or more inhabitants [b] 1867 [c] Annual averages, 1869–73, 1877–81, 1897–1901, 1907–11, and 1917–21

during the next thirty years they took out 440,000. These led to such developments as the transatlantic cable, the telephone, refrigerator cars, typewriters, the linotype, and the Pullman car. After 1900 the parade of technological advances and innovations continued: the first transmittal of speech by wireless (1900), the Wright brothers' airplane (1903), the first connected film story, *The Great Train Robbery* (1903), the Diesel engine (1904), the nickolodeon (1905), and Ford's Model T (1908).

Despite these innovations, America remained an awkward giant in many ways. Roads were so poor as late as 1901 that Roy Chapin, publicizing the new "Merry Oldsmobile" by driving it from Detroit to New York, followed the Erie Canal towpath for 150 miles rather than trusting the highways. The trip took seven and a half days. Cars were so frightening that President Theodore Roosevelt was commended for his "characteristic courage" in riding in one. Urban housewives used canned vegetables and some processed foods, but they lacked modern conveniences like refrigerators. City dwellers as a rule relied on gas jets or candlepower for lighting and more often than not did without indoor plumbing or central heating. Cuspidors were more common than bathtubs in the American home. Even the telephone, developed in the 1870s, was a rarity in private houses—only 1.3 million existed for 16 million American households in 1900. It was not until the 1920s that the middle classes enjoyed the domestic conveniences that the elite possessed at the turn of the century.

Yet technological changes were leading to a host of less-publicized but profoundly influential industrial innovations. In the glass industry, machines were developed after 1880 that made bulbs, bottles, tumblers, glass tubing, and continuous sheets of window glass. Innovations also transformed the media. In 1840 editions of large urban newspapers consisted of between four and six pages; they had circulations of up to 4000, and their cost was between five and ten cents. By 1890 there were not only machines that set type but also that printed both sides of a continuous sheet of paper, then automatically folded and cut the pages. By the turn of the century the *New York World,* a giant among papers, was reaching perhaps a million readers daily with editions of sixteen or more pages, which sold for two cents. Sunday editions, including colored supplements, were sometimes as large as sixty-four pages.

Perhaps the most astonishing improvements occurred in the production and handling of grains, lumber, and metals. Corn production increased from 800 million bushels in 1860 to 3 billion in 1915, while wheat output in bushels rose during the same period from 173 million to 1 billion. Developments in mining iron ore after 1880 included not only exploitation of the rich Mesabi Range in Minnesota but also new loading procedures. In 1890 it took a week to discharge 2000 tons of ore from a lake ship onto railroad gondolas, but by 1910 it was possible to load a 10,000-ton cargo in less than two hours. Trains filled with ore clattered down the Duluth, Missabe, and Iron Range Railroad every forty-five minutes.

Many nontechnological developments assisted these improvements. Among them were the techniques of "scientific management" popularized by Frederick Winslow Taylor. Taylor did not welcome vast technological change or mass production. His aim was primarily to increase output by organizing work more efficiently. Higher productivity, he argued, would allow for better wages, more harmonious labor-management relations, and, ideally, lower prices on manufactured goods. These lower prices, in turn, would decrease the cost of living for consumers, including factory workers. These ideas anticipated Henry Ford's dramatic announcement in 1914 of a $5-a-day minimum wage and led to the slow realization by employers of the relationship between decent wages and the profits to be made through mass consumption.

But Taylor's methods usually meant that workers toiled at the ever faster, machine-ruled pace so memorably caught in Charlie Chaplin's film, *Modern Times*. "If a man won't do what is right," he said, "*make* him." "Remember," he told students, "that the kind of engineering that is most wanted is that which saves money; that your employer is first of all in business to make money and not to do great and brilliant things." By 1901 Taylor was secure enough to become an independent consultant, and by 1915 his theories on scientific management were widely applied throughout the western world.

The increasing capital derived from profits also contributed to growth, especially among large concerns. Between 1860 and 1890 the average rate of savings by American business was 5 percent yearly, and so funds were available for reinvestment and expansion. Successful manufacturers were able to set up their own warehouses, eliminate jobbers, develop their own advertising, patent brand names, and sell directly to wholesalers. Retailers, assisted by Rural Free Delivery, starting in 1896, and parcel post, starting in 1913, were able to branch into a mass national market. The circulation of the Sears general catalogue increased from 318,000 in 1897 to 3 million for the fall of 1907. Well before the mid-1920s, when some 75 million Sears catalogues circulated annually, they were known as the "Farmer's Bible." With other developments, such as the interurban railway and the mass circulation newspapers, the Sears catalogues did much to bridge the gap between urban and rural life-styles and to chip away at the insularity of the countryside.

A final important source of industrial development was urban growth. In many consumer goods industries the enticement of this vast urban market led entrepreneurs to develop new business strategies and structures that were as innovative as technological changes. In meat packing and tobacco men like Gustavus Swift and James B. Duke created vertical combinations permitting them to control operations from production through sales to consumers. Other entrepreneurs worked out horizontal mergers, especially during the depression of the 1890s, which ruined weaker competitors. Either way, these giant combinations boomed as cities grew. And by the 1890s the urban market also brought huge growth to producer goods industries. In 1887, for instance, the Carnegie Steel Company shifted its production at the Homestead Works from steel rails to building materials for the booming urban construction industry. The continued urban and suburban growth of the three decades after 1900 remained a prime source of the dramatic increases in American industrial power.

The pains of growth

As Americans quickly discovered, such unprecedented growth did not come without serious pressures and pains. Among these was the concentration of financial power in the hands of a few well-situated bankers and life insurance executives, particularly in New York City. Their command of vast pools of capital for investment, especially in the 1890s, when many businessmen were scrambling for cash, gave them considerably more leverage over the economy than that possessed by the national government, which in the 1890s had to turn to J. P. Morgan's syndicate for a high-interest loan. Because the money market was in the hands of private entrepreneurs, the economy was subject to periodic overspeculation, mismanagement of stockholders' funds, and occasional panics. One of these panics, in 1901, left half the brokerage firms in New York bankrupt.

Another, in 1907, was more serious, forcing banks to close their doors to frightened depositors who wanted to withdraw their money. Further damage was averted only when Morgan himself gathered the top financiers in his imposing library, locked the door, and took the key to make certain that none of them resumed the selling that had been slashing market values. The congressional investigating committee formed in the aftermath of this panic later published findings showing that Morgan and Rockefeller interests controlled 341 directorships in 112 corporations with aggregate resources of $22,245,000,000. This sum was more than the assessed property in all states west of the Mississippi.

The power of the investment bankers (which later declined as rich corporations developed their own funds for expansion) was but one sign of an alarming concentration of resources in the hands of a few industrial giants. Though some of these, like Rockefeller's Standard Oil Company, existed before the 1890s, the main wave of mergers occurred after the depression of the 1890s, which suggested that size could be a hedge against hard times. During the 1890s, 95 percent of railroad trackage fell into the hands of six large combines dominated by men like Morgan. By 1900 there were 73 industrial combinations with capitalizations exceeding $10 million, 53 of which had been chartered in 1898 or 1899. By 1904 the 305 largest firms in America, with an aggregate capital of some $7 billion, controlled almost two-fifths of manufacturing capital in the country.

The most frightening monopoly of all developed in 1901, when Charles Schwab, Carnegie Steel's chief executive, concluded a deal with Morgan. The result was the United States Steel Company, America's first billion-dollar corporation. In many ways the deal made sense, for it prevented the excess in capacity that was already hurting the railroads. The new corporation was able to pay higher wages than other steel companies and to maintain satisfactory dividends. For Morgan, who argued that concentration maximized profits and rationalized growth, the deal was amply justified.

But the new corporation terrified many of Morgan's contemporaries. U. S. Steel swallowed 213 manufacturing plants and transportation companies; 41 mines; 1000 miles of railroad; 112 ore boats; 78 blast furnaces; and vast coal, coke, and ore holdings, including those in the Mesabi. It controlled more than 60 percent of America's steel capacity and exercised enormous leverage over the production of finished goods. It directly employed some 170,000 workers. Its capitalization, at $1.4 billion, was three times the amount spent annually by the federal government. It was falsely capitalized at twice the value of the stocks and bonds of the companies it had absorbed, enabling the House of Morgan to make an initial profit of $12.5 million on the new watered stock. The huge, unprecedented size of the combination caused President Hadley of Yale, a conservative, to warn that if the trusts were not "regulated by public sentiment," there could be an "emperor in Washington within twenty-five years."

The profits amassed by people like Morgan also gave Americans concern. In 1900 Carnegie himself earned $23 million and paid no income taxes (which were then regarded as unconstitutional by the Supreme Court). The Vanderbilt family had seven houses worth a total of $12 million within seven blocks on New York's Fifth Avenue. In 1900, 1 percent of the population owned more national wealth than did the remaining 99 percent, and by 1910 it was estimated that seventy Americans owned $35 million or more each, or one-sixteenth of the nation's total wealth. Far from hiding these fabulous riches, many of the new millionaires flaunted them in displays of conspicuous consumption.

At the other end of the income ladder millions of Americans lived in conditions best described by Robert Hunter, who published his widely read book *Poverty* in 1904. Hunter discovered that during the prosperous years between 1897 and 1903 approximately half of America's families owned no property, and that 10 million Americans, one-eighth of the population, were "underfed, underclothed, and poorly housed." Such people, Hunter warned, "live miserably, they know not why. They work sore, yet gain nothing. They know the meaning of hunger and the dread of want. They love their wives and children. They try to retain their self-respect. They have some ambition. They give to neighbors in need, yet they are themselves the actual children of poverty." The poet Vachel Lindsay simply called them the "Leaden-Eyed."

> Not that they starve, but that they starve so dreamlessly,
> Not that they sow, but that they seldom reap,
> Not that they serve, but have no gods to serve,
> Not that they die, but that they die like sheep.

These 10 million people were but a fraction of the total who were poor by twentieth-century American standards. In all, approximately half the population lacked the wealth to make ends meet. Such widespread deprivation helps explain some staggering statistics about turn-of-the-century America. In 1900 only 95,000 Americans graduated from high school. This was only 7 percent of young people aged seventeen. The average educational level was between grades five and six. Sixty years later 65 percent of seventeen-year-olds graduated from high school, and the average level attained was grade twelve. More staggering still are health statistics. The infant mortality rate in 1900 was 1 per 100 live births; sixty years later it was 1 per 400. Life expectancy at birth for whites was forty-eight years, for nonwhites only thirty-three; sixty years later the figures had jumped to seventy-one and sixty-four years respectively.

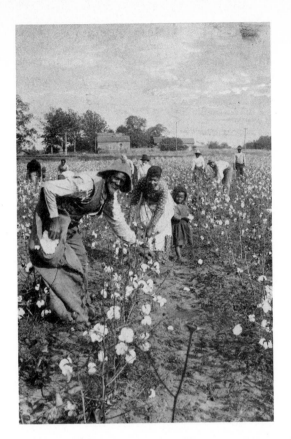

The different life styles of rich and poor
c. 1900: the cotton pickers in the South;
an immigrant family making cigars at
home; Cornelius Vanderbilt mansion in
New York City.

While comparative statistics leave something to be desired, it is probable that these health figures ranked America in 1900 at the bottom of the industrialized western world.

Books like Hunter's, or John Spargo's *The Bitter Cry of the Children* (1906) and John A. Ryan's *A Living Wage* (1906), also offered insights into the impact of industrialization on American labor. By 1900 18 million of America's work force of 29 million people were engaged in nonagricultural jobs. (In 1880 there had been only 8 million such workers or one-half the total work force of 16 million.) Those in essentially blue-collar positions (perhaps 11 to 13 million people) earned an average annual wage of around $500, often too low to match the cost of living for an urban family of four. The work force also included 1.75 million children under fifteen and more than five million women, many of whom worked in southern mills at wages as low as ten cents for a ten-hour day. Most industrial workers labored sixty or more hours per week, and many, including those at U. S. Steel, toiled more than seventy hours, which included one twenty-four-hour shift per week. Close to a million industrial workers were hurt per year in uncompensated work-related accidents. A total of 146 women died in a fire in 1911 at the Triangle Shirt Waist Company in New York City. These women had been working a seventy-four-hour week for between $14 and $15, or approximately twenty cents an hour.

Well before 1900 such conditions had prompted militant reactions from labor spokesmen. Such confrontations as the Haymarket Affair (1886), the Homestead Strike (1892), and the Pullman Strike (1894) had already terrorized

O masters, lords and rulers in all lands,
Is this the handiwork you give to God,
This monstrous thing distorted and soul-quencht?
How will you ever straighten up this shape;
Touch it again with immortality;
Give back the upward looking and the light;
Rebuild in it the music and the dream;
Make right the immemorial infamies,
Perfidious wrongs, immedicable woes?

O masters, lords and rulers in all lands,
How will the future reckon with this Man?
How answer his brute question in that hour
When whirlwinds of rebellion shake all shores?
How will it be with kingdoms and with kings—
With those who shaped him to the thing he is—
When this dumb Terror shall rise to judge the world,
After the silence of the centuries?

Edwin Markham's "The Man With the Hoe," first printed in the *San Francisco Examiner* in 1899, "flew eastward across the continent like a contagion." The frightened reaction to it suggested the concern Americans felt about potential class conflict.

Why workers struck: company-owned houses in a coal mining town.

the upper classes. After the turn of the century the agitation continued, including a general strike in San Francisco in 1900, a national hatters' strike in 1901, a walkout of anthracite miners (1902), which forced presidential involvement, and a bitter strike in the Colorado coal fields (1904), which led to the imposition of martial law. Between January 1902 and June 1904 such outbreaks caused the death of 180 men, injuries to 1651, and arrests of 5000 more. Total union membership, only 440,000 in 1897, increased to more than 2 million by 1904.

But the American labor movement, which even in 1904 attracted only 12 percent of the nonagricultural work force, stalled during the next decade, and by 1915, unions represented only 8 percent of the nonfarm labor. Many formidable obstacles caused this poor showing by unions, which were considerably less successful than in industrial areas of western Europe at the time.

One of these was the ethic of work that equated success with individual effort. "You cannot wetnurse people from the time they are born until the time they die," proclaimed Henry Havemeyer, the sugar baron. "They have got to wade in and get stuck." The popular preacher Henry Ward Beecher added, "no man in this land suffers from poverty unless it be more than his fault—unless it be his *sin*." Underlying such statements was the sweeping power of social Darwinism, which applied evolutionary theory to the marketplace. Champions of this view like William Graham Sumner, an influential Yale professor, asserted that successful human beings were those most fit to survive. Failures—the poor—were by definition unfit. Institutions such as labor unions artificially assisted people who were destined not to survive; they interfered with evolution by natural selection. "Leave things as they now are," Carnegie counseled in promoting his "Gospel of Wealth." "If asked what important law I should change, I must perforce say none; the laws are perfect."

Another obstacle to unionization was the fear, especially in the turbulent 1890s, that labor agitation would erupt in class warfare. During the Pullman strike William Howard Taft, later a mild progressive, complained that the police "have only killed six . . . as yet. This is hardly enough to make an impression . . . it will be necessary for the military to kill more." Theodore Roosevelt added, "the sentiment now animating a large proportion of our people can only be suppressed as the Commune in Paris was suppressed, by taking ten or a dozen of their leaders out, standing . . . them against a wall, and shooting them dead. I believe it will come to that. These leaders are plotting a social revolution and the subversion of the American Republic."

Though reactionary groups such as the National Association of Manufacturers continued to resort to such language in the 1900s, leaders of big business like J. P. Morgan used more sophisticated arguments aimed at co-opting labor agitators. By promising company pension plans, employee representation, and profit sharing, they popularized "welfare capitalism." To advance this cause, Morgan and others collaborated with labor leaders like Samuel Gompers, head of the American Federation of Labor, to form the National Civic Federation. Business and labor, federationists believed, had a natural identity of interests that would prevent conflict. As if to practice what he preached, Morgan also induced recalcitrant coal mine executives (over whom he had financial control) to accede, during a nationwide strike in 1902, to arbitration.

This welfare capitalism was hardly popular with smaller businessmen, most of whom could ill afford to be generous amid the fierce competition and insecurity of the age. Businessmen, indeed, were in no sense a united interest group. Moreover, the welfare capitalists were scarcely prolabor. Those few corporations that inaugurated pension plans ordinarily required workers to stay on the payroll for fifteen (or even thirty) years before qualifying for benefits. Meanwhile employees who agitated for unions ran the risk of being fired. Employee representation plans were euphemisms for company-run unions. Profit-sharing, really wages withheld for distribution later, reached only a handful of workers. Still, welfare capitalism sounded more enlightened than the crass social Darwinism of the Robber Barons. The flexibility of magnates like Morgan, then and later, did much to maintain the peculiarly unchallenged power of corporations in modern America.

The ethnic composition of the work force also posed difficulties for labor unions. Most recent migrants knew little of labor organizations, and they did not like to pay union dues. Contrary to the prevailing stereotype of the time, they tended to be politically apathetic: few were radicals. They were too anxious about job security and their savings to risk becoming blacklisted. Many immigrant steel workers, for instance, readily endured twelve-hour shifts, stumbled home to boarding house dormitories, and fell into the beds just vacated by laborers taking the next shift; long hours meant more pay. If they could survive the backbreaking toil and avoid accidents, they could acquire enough money to return home, find a wife (or rejoin one), buy land, and achieve a standard of living undreamed-of before their voyage to the New World.

The American economy conspired against unions. Working hours and conditions were probably worse in America than in the industrialized parts of Europe. But the simple fact was that American real wages, however inadequate, were between two and four times higher than they were in England or France, and incomparably better than those in eastern Europe. For thirty years after the Civil War native as well as immigrant workers also benefited from a long deflationary spiral that had the effect of increasing real wages even when dollar wages stayed the same.

These facts suggest that the processes of industrialization and technological change were not the destructive forces that some modern writers have described. Witness the occupational structure in 1900. Though still heavily weighted toward industrial labor (11 to 13 million workers) and farming (11 million), it also included 1.2 million professional and technical workers, 1.7 million managers and officials (not counting farm owners), 900,000 clerical workers, 1.3 million sales workers, and 1 million service workers, or more than 6 million in all. These white-collar workers, who had numbered less than 1 million in 1870, were engaged in the fastest growing areas of the economy. Moreover, of the 11 to 13 million industrial workers in 1900, 3 million were defined by the census as "craftsmen, foremen and kindred workers." Despite the pace of change, these people had managed to retain their skills or to develop new ones. Many achieved positions of status in their neighborhoods or moved to better locations. Many others were able to acquire property, or money that enabled their children to stay in school or go to college. But this upward social and geographical mobility—which may have benefited 30 percent of the sons of manual workers—was less common than the novels of Horatio Alger suggested. Moreover, business leaders were recruited from among the children of the educated middle classes—the rags to riches saga was essentially a myth. People did move gradually up the social ladder, however, and many more thought they could, which was more important than the reality. Union organizers constantly confronted this refusal of industrial workers to consider themselves part of a permanent laboring class.

For all these reasons the dominant union, the American Federation of Labor, tended to recruit only among skilled workers and to eschew the task of organizing industry-wide unions. Gompers, the longtime head of the AFL, typified this mentality. The son of a Dutch-Jewish cigar maker, Gompers was apprenticed at the age of ten to a shoemaker and then to his father. At age thirteen, in 1863, he migrated to America and assumed his trade in New York. Young Gompers became a union member at fourteen and knew well the writings of Marx and Engels, but he never joined the Socialist party. He branded theoreticians as "so-called intellectuals or butters-in." Socialism, he added, "is a proposition to place the working people of this country in a physical material strait-jacket.'' Gompers insisted instead on skilled craftsmen working within capitalism for better conditions. ''Unions, pure and simple,'' he said, ''are the natural organization of wage workers to secure their present material and practical improvement and to achieve their final emancipation. . . . The way out of the wage system is through higher wages.'' Gompers distrusted the state, which he argued (with considerable truth at the time) was as likely to oppress as to assist working people, and he was open in his contempt for blacks and Orientals, who were competing with other workers for jobs. ''Caucasians,'' he announced, ''are not going to let their standard of living be destroyed by Negroes, Japs, or any others.''

Not surprisingly, Gompers' brand of craft unionism held little appeal for unskilled workers. He also offended socialists and militants. Eugene Debs, head of the Socialist party, said that to work with Gompers was as ''wasteful of time as to spray a cesspool with attar of roses.'' But the socialists, like other militants, found that generating class consciousness among geographically mobile, ethnically divided workers, especially amid an extremely hostile judicial and governmental climate, was a very difficult struggle. For all his limitations, for all his racism, Gompers and men like him came close to anticipating one model of the future: a nation of increasingly self-conscious, tightly knit interest groups, each with an existing stake in the system, and with a set of practical economic goals.

But a nation of interest groups was of course precisely what so many influential Americans were fearful of at the turn of the century. ''Welfare capitalists,'' for instance, denounced such a development precisely because they, as a dominant group, had the most to gain by arguing that society was harmonious as it was. And Richard T. Ely, the progressive economist, felt obliged to defend himself against charges of having uttered heretical ideas by denying that he had ever counseled workers to strike or that he favored the principle of the closed shop. To hold such beliefs, Ely said, would ''unquestionably unfit me to occupy a responsible position as an instructor of youth in a great University.'' In making such a statement Ely, product of a small-town, middle-class background, joined his colleague Frederick Jackson Turner—and many others at the time—in asserting the hope that the turbulent social forces of turn-of-the-century America could be directed into peaceful channels. This effort to maintain order amid the forces of urbanization, immigration, and industrialization—in short, to halt the dangerous fraying of society—was to be a central theme of the ''progressive era'' that followed.

Suggestions for reading

Among the many books offering interpretations of American life at the turn of the century are Robert Wiebe, *The Search for Order, 1877–1920** (1968); Samuel Hays, *The Response to Industrialism** (1957); and Rowland Berthoff, *An Unsettled People* (1971), and Robert Wiebe, *Segmented Society* (1975), both of which offer a broader view of American history. Small-town existence is covered in Lewis Atherton,

Main Street on the Middle Border (1954); Robert Walker, *Life in the Age of Enterprise* (1967); and Mark Sullivan's six-volume *Our Times* (1926–34). For descriptions of life on the farms, and for accounts of Populism, see Ray Allen Billington, *Westward Expansion: A History of the American Frontier** (1967); Fred Shannon, *The Farmer's Last Frontier* (1945); John Hicks, *The Populist Revolt** (1931); Norman Pollack, *The Populist Response to Industrial America** (1962); Walter T. K. Nugent, *The Tolerant Populists: Kansas Populism and Nativism* (1962); Theodore Saloutos, *Farmer Movements in the South, 1865–1933* (1960); C. Vann Woodward, *Tom Watson* (1938), and *Origins of the New South, 1877–1913** (1951).

For urban history consult Howard Chudacoff, *Evolution of American Urban Society** (1975); Constance M. Green, *The Rise of Urban America** (1965); Charles Glaab and A. T. Brown, *A History of Urban America** (1967); and Zane Miller *Urbanization of America** (1973). All are useful surveys. Studies of mobility include Stephan Thernstrom, *Poverty and Progress** (1964), which deals with Newburyport, Massachusetts, and *The Other Bostonians**, which covers 1880–1970; and Howard Chudacoff, *Mobile Americans: Residential and Social Mobility in Omaha, 1880–1920* (1972). Sam Bass Warner's *Streetcar Suburbs: The Process of Growth in Boston 1870–1900* (1971) is excellent. Morton and Lucia White, *The Intellectual Vs. the City** (1962) surveys antiurban attitudes of selected American thinkers. Books on immigration and nativism include Oscar Handlin, *The Uprooted** (1951); Maldwyn Jones, *American Immigration** (1960); John Higham, *Strangers in the Land: Patterns of American Nativism** (1955); Moses Rischin, *The Promised City: New York's Jews, 1870–1914* (1970); Humbert Nelli, *The Italians in Chicago, 1880–1930** (1973); Barbara Solomon, *Ancestors and Immigrants* (1956); and Milton Gordon, *Assimilation in American Life** (1964).

For developments in business and technology students might start with Daniel Boorstin, *The Americans,** vol. 3 (1870–1960) (1974). See also Adolf Berle, Jr., *The Twentieth-Century Capitalist Revolution** (1954); Frederick Lewis Allen, *The Big Change** (1969); Edward Kirkland, *Industry Comes of Age, 1860–1897* (1961); and Thomas Cochran and William Miller, *The Age of Enterprise** (1942). William Miller, ed., *Men in Business* (1952), contains stimulating essays, as does Thomas Cochran's *Inner Revolution** (1964). Books on business leaders include Joseph Wall, *Andrew Carnegie** (1970); Keith Sward, *The Legend of Henry Ford** (1948); and Matthew Josephson, *Edison* (1959). Useful works on turn-of-the-century social and economic thought are Sidney Fine, *Laissez Faire and the General Welfare State** (1956); Samuel Haber, *Efficiency and Uplift: Scientific Management in the Progressive Era, 1890–1920** (1964); Harold U. Faulkner, *The Decline of Laissez Faire, 1897–1917** (1951); Richard Hofstadter, *Social Darwinism in American Thought** (rev. ed. 1959); Robert McCloskey, *Conservatism in The Age of Enterprise, 1865–1910** (1951); and James Weinstein, *The Corporate Ideal in the Liberal State, 1900–1918** (1969).

Accounts of the poor and of labor include Robert Bremner's excellent *From the Depths: The Discovery of Poverty in America* (1956); David Brody, *Steelworkers in America: The Nonunion Era** (1970); Henry Pelling, *American Labor** (1960), a survey; and Bernard Mandel, *Samuel Gompers, a Biography* (1963).

Important primary sources are Jacob Riis, *How the Other Half Lives** (1890); Jane Addams, *Twenty Years at Hull House** (1910); Lincoln Steffens, *Shame of the Cities** (1904); Robert Hunter, *Poverty* (1904); John Spargo, *The Bitter Cry of the Children* (1906); and Mary Antin, *The Promised Land* (1969 ed.), a glowing account by an immigrant.

The ambiguities of progressive solutions 1900-1917

In 1906 William James complained of the "moral flabbiness born of the exclusive worship of the bitch-goddess SUCCESS. That—with the squalid cash interpretation put on the word success—is our national disease." Andrew Carnegie made the complaint more personal by observing that "the amassing of wealth is one of the worst species of idolatry. . . . To continue much longer overwhelmed by business cares and with most of my thoughts wholly upon the way to make more money in the shortest time, must degrade me beyond hope of permanent recovery."

It was no great feat, however, to identify the pervasive materialism and commercialization of the age. It was much harder for social critics to transcend social Darwinism or village values. The effort to do so began in the late nineteenth century, but many who joined the search for change remained prisoners of their backgrounds.

Among those who found it difficult to escape nineteenth-century notions were reformers who worried about poverty. Until 1900 they usually called themselves "charity workers," and they considered poverty—revealingly referred to as "pauperism"—the result of individual failings, not of environmental conditions. Leaders in the field, while well-intentioned, believed that generous assistance bred dependency, and they usually doled out as little aid as possible. One critic of this cost-conscious approach wondered later if the Charity Organization Society was really just a "business enterprise, designed to keep poverty out of sight and make life more comfortable for the rich." A poet concluded:

> The organized charity scrimped and iced
> In the name of a cautious, statistical Christ.

Even Jacob Riis, the reporter whose *How the Other Half Lives* (1890) did so much to alert people to poverty, could not blot out happy memories of village life in Denmark, whence he had emigrated at the age of twenty-one. Though he supported reforms ranging from model tenement legislation to settlement houses, he hated the city, and he relied heavily on such palliative solutions as playgrounds, home economics teaching, kindergartens, and boys' clubs. Like other nineteenth-century reformers, Riis opposed public housing legislation, and he despised "bums," tramps, and people who relied on charity. "Nothing is more certain," he said, " . . . than this, that what a man wills himself, that he will be." He added, "Luck is lassoed by the masterful man, by the man who knows and who can."

Reformist ministers promoting the so-called social gospel revealed much of the same nostalgia. Younger social gospellers like Monsignor John A. Ryan, the leading Catholic reformer, and Walter Rauschenbusch, a Baptist theologian, called after 1900 for collectivist programs. More typical of late-nineteenth-century social gospellers, however, was Washington Gladden, a Congregational minister of small-town background who refused to welcome an urbanized, bureaucratized, society. Gladden supported compulsory education, abolition of the saloon, and child labor legislation, but he also quoted social Darwinists on the evils of "over-legislation." Frightened by growing class divisions, he yearned for the harmony he had experienced as a boy.

The social gospellers also had to contend with more reactionary forces within their own churches. The most widely known figures in American Protestantism in the 1890s were not men like Gladden but roving evangelists like Dwight Moody, who brought the techniques of salesmanship to his campaign against irreligion. Moody was contemptuous of the social gospellers. "I have heard of reform," he said, "until I am tired and sick of the whole thing. It is regeneration by the power of the Holy Ghost that we need." Though vague concerning dogma, Moody's message encouraged the fundamentalist thinking that culminated in the Scopes trial of 1925. It also led some young people to reject the Church. The novelist Frank Norris called God a "prodigious mechanism of cogs and wheels," and Edward Bellamy forbade his family to go near a church.

Our scientific political economy has long been an oracle of the false god. It has taught us to approach economic questions from the point of view of goods and not of man. It tells us how wealth is produced and divided and consumed by man, and not how man's life and development can best be fostered by material wealth. It is significant that the discussion of "Consumption" of wealth has been most neglected in political economy; yet that is humanly the most important of all. Theology must become christocentric; political economy must become anthropocentric. Man is Christianized when he puts God before self; political economy will be Christianized when it puts man before wealth. Socialistic political economy does that. It is materialistic in its theory of human life and history, but it is humane in its aims, and to that extent is closer to Christianity than the orthodox science has been.

Walter Rauschenbusch's *Christianity and the Social Crisis* (1907) expresses a militant critique of materialism and of capitalism. Men like Washington Gladden, however, expressed a more characteristically moderate view.

The social gospellers suffered above all from their ambivalence about the major forces of the age: urbanization, immigration, and industrialization. Caught in an increasingly secularized world, their response as churchmen was to demand the Christianization of society. This message appeared to be well received. But it was an appeal that aimed more at awakening the conscience of individuals than at developing collectivist approaches to social problems. It failed also to give serious enough attention to whether Christianity, under assault from secular values, retained the power to move individual men toward reform. Such a probing assessment of religion itself had to await the writings of men like Reinhold Niebuhr in the 1930s.

Nothing reveals better the ambivalence inherent in late-nineteenth-century reformism than the ideas of the two towering social thinkers of the age, Henry George and Edward Bellamy. George, Philadelphia-born, sailed as a young man to California, where he published his immensely influential book *Progress and Poverty* in 1879. The book offered contemporary readers a sharp indictment of the wastefulness and rapaciousness of American capitalism. It influenced a galaxy of later activists and intellectuals, including the municipal reformers Tom Johnson and Newton Baker of Cleveland, Samuel ("Golden Rule") Jones and Brand Whitlock of Toledo, the writer and muckracker Lincoln Steffens, and the "people's lawyer," Clarence Darrow. Bellamy, a newspaper reporter and novelist, published the even more lasting utopian novel *Looking Backward* in 1888. By 1890 American readers of Bellamy's book had already founded 127 so-called Nationalist clubs to promote his doctrines.

George's solution for the problem of capitalistic excesses was the so-called single tax on unused or unimproved land. The threat of such a tax, he argued, would force landowners to develop their property for the good of society. Revenue from the tax would enable government to abolish other levies. George did not want to create a centralized, positive government that would develop a welfare state. Instead he wanted to rely on the single tax as the simple panacea for the ills of society. Populists in the 1890s rejected George's antistatist perspective, and a later reformer dubbed his ideas "a single draft of Socialism with unstinted individualism thereafter." These critics were harsh, for George's writings did much to challenge the rusty "iron laws" of economics. But they were correct in noting that George tended to look backward to a Jacksonian society of freeholders and entrepreneurs, not forward to a nation of cities and interest groups.

Bellamy's vision was more modern. Few social thinkers, in fact, were keener about the potential of rational planning and centralization. His utopia accepted urbanization, and it glorified technological progress. It was run by a highly bureaucratic state in the hands of benevolently inclined former workers. But this utopia, aptly named the "Republic of the Golden Rule," was above all free of class division and unrest, the specter of which in the 1880s had prompted his creative outburst. His world of the future was antiseptic, harmonious, free of factious interest groups—an urbanized version of small-town values. Bellamy, and many other Americans in the late nineteenth century, yearned for community, stability, for virtues supposedly associated with the small towns in which they had grown up.

THE GENTEEL TRADITION

Another manifestation of turn-of-the-century thought was what the philosopher George Santayana in 1911 called the Genteel Tradition. Narrowly defined, the Genteel Tradition meant discreet and decorous optimism in the arts. Painters and sculptors were supposed to depict what one critic called "beautiful things seen beautifully." The business of art, another proclaimed, "is to afford joyance . . . what a shame it is the great gifts of expression should be wasted on heinous and joyless subjects." When Thomas Eakins, one of America's most gifted artists, painted a picture of doctors operating on a human body, an outraged critic denounced it as a "degradation of art . . . the scene is so real that [people with nerves] might as well go to a dressing room and have done with it." In 1886 Eakins was dismissed from his teaching post at the Philadelphia Academy because he posed nude males with females.

Similar conventions governed literature at the turn of the century. Critics praised the optimistic mysticism of Emerson while fearing (or ignoring) the more tragic visions of Poe or Melville. The editor of *Century,* an elite magazine, deleted as offensive a passage that read "the bullet had left a blue mark over his brown nipple." Theodore Roosevelt seriously dismissed *Anna Karenina* as "altogether needlessly filthy." Among the best sellers in 1901 were historical romances and novels celebrating traditional values. Included were such titles as *Quo Vadis, When Knighthood Was in Flower,* and *Alice of Old Vincennes.* Even a "realist" like the novelist William Dean Howells, who honestly portrayed the tensions of middle-class life, appeared to Sinclair Lewis in 1930 to be a "pious old maid whose greatest delight is to have tea at the vicarage." Lewis (as usual) was unfair, but his remark revealed the contempt that later writers held for the literary traditions of 1900.

Much popular fiction of the time featured masculine individuals overcoming seemingly overwhelming odds. One of these was the hero Frank Merriwell, a Yale man who always scored the winning touchdown and who refused to drink or smoke. Similar heroes stood out in the widely read tales of William T. Adams, who wrote under the pen name Oliver Optic and whose motto was "First God, then Country, then Friends." Western stories, like Owen Wister's *The Virginian* (1902), also sold well. These portrayed strong, silent cowboy heroes who reminded nostalgic Americans of frontier individualism. Such books also transformed killers like Jesse James and Billy the Kid into Robin Hoods taking money from the rich. The appeal of such characters at the turn of the century probably reflected a prevailing concern that individuals were being swallowed up in an urban, collectivized world and were being victimized by plutocrats and corporations. One hundred twenty-one novels about Jesse James were published between 1901 and 1903. They sold 6 million copies.

The Genteel Tradition in culture reflected a broad affirmation of pious beliefs, which the historian Henry May called the "reality, certainty, and eternity of moral values." These included truth, justice, patriotism, and decency, all of which the educated classes had a duty to inculcate in other people. Thus Roosevelt insisted that "the greatest historian should also be a great moralist. It is no proof of impartiality to treat wickedness and goodness as on the same level." A manual for high school teachers in 1914 asserted: "My teacher of history should increase my capacity for real happiness, and sharpen my appreciation for all things beautiful and for all persons noble and honorable. He should help me to see that righteousness exalts a nation, and that sin not only is a reproach to my people, but has also been the downfall of great empires."

Decorous relations between the sexes was an integral part of the Genteel Tradition. Proper women in America and abroad imprisoned themselves in corsets, wore layers of skirts covering their ankles, and never let young men know how they felt. Well-bred suitors had to pursue their quarry with punctilious respect. "Even when I was thirty years old," a New York gentleman recalled, "if I had asked a girl to dine with me alone, I would have been kicked down the front steps. If I had offered her a cocktail, I would have been tossed out of society for my boorish effrontery." Such precise behavior was not typical of informal courtship in the country or the still more casual encounters of lower-class urban life. But it represented an ideal that well-bred young people followed. Even G. Stanley Hall, a prominent psychologist and expert on adolescent behavior, felt obliged to be positively saccharine about the subject of sex. "In the most unitary of all acts," he wrote of sexual intercourse, "which is the epitome and pleroma of life, we have the most intense of all affirmations of the will to live and realize that the only true God is love, and the center of life is worship. Every part of mind and body participates in a true pangenesis. This sacrament is the annunciation hour, with hosannas which the whole world reflects. Communion is fusion and beatitude. It is the supreme hedonic narcosis, a holy intoxication."

By 1910 the "conspiracy of silence" against the mere discussion of sexual questions was under assault. But many of the warriors against it were not incipient Freudians demanding sexual expression, but doctors and other guardians of traditional values who led the social hygiene and "purity" movements. Alarmed at statistics indicating the spread of gonorrhea and syphilis, some of these reformers went so far as to call for frank sex education in the schools. But the main thrust of these movements was not liberation, but preservation of marriage and the family. Indeed, "purity" reformers also campaigned against prizefighting, ballet, and intercollegiate football. Meanwhile, traditionalists stood firm against perceived breeches of the code. In 1910, 30,000 readers of the *Ladies Home Journal* cancelled their subscriptions in protest against an article that suggested that ignorance about sex could cause illegitimate conceptions.

As the career of Theodore Roosevelt was to reveal, there was no necessary contradiction between adhering to traditional moral values and adopting a "progressive" position on political issues. Progressivism for such people was frequently counterrevolutionary in its intent—a way of rejecting trusts, class conflict, and commercialization and returning to the older ways. So long as the Genteel Tradition remained intact it would be difficult for more "modern" thinkers to receive a hearing.

THE ASSAULT ON GENTEEL VALUES

One of the guardians of traditional values, *Nation* magazine, complained in 1913 of "the tango, eugenics, the slit skirt, sex hygiene, . . . the double standard of morality . . . a conglomerate of things important and unimportant, of age-old problems and momentary fads, which nevertheless have this one thing in common, that they do involve an abandonment of the old proprieties and the old reticences." In the same year, another magazine, *Current Opinion,* phrased it more simply by saying that in America it had now struck "Sex O'Clock."

Many manifestations of this cultural change were indeed merely "momentary" or faddish. These included such dances as the turkey trot, the chicken scratch, the kangaroo dip, the bunny hug, and the grizzly bear. Traditionalists also worried about more serious matters such as the rise of the "flapper," the popularity of jazz and abstract art, and the spread of cigarette smoking, which by 1914 led ten predominantly rural states to pass laws banning the sale of

> *It was understood that no girl was interested in a man or showed any liking for him until he had made all the advances. You knew a man very well before you wrote or received a letter from him, and those letters make me smile when I see some of the correspondence today. There were few men who would have dared to use my first name, and to have signed oneself in any other way than "very sincerely yours" would have been not only a breach of good manners but an admission of feeling which was entirely inadmissible.*
>
> *You never allowed a man to give you a present except flowers or candy or possibly a book. To receive a piece of jewelry from a man to whom you were not engaged was a sign of being a fast woman, and the idea that you would permit any man to kiss you before you were engaged to him never even crossed my mind.*
>
> Eleanor Roosevelt's recollections of girlhood at the turn of the century.

cigarettes. Americans especially feared more alarming manifestations of cultural change like divorce, which ended approximately one marriage in twelve by the eve of World War I. It seemed that the formerly solid props maintaining the genteel way of life had been cut away.

An increasingly self-aware group of literary leaders, many of whom were congregating in places like Greenwich Village, welcomed these changes in behavior. As early as 1900 some of them founded *Smart Set,* a magazine aimed at promoting new cultural forms, and by 1908, when bright young critics like George Jean Nathan and H. L. Mencken worked for it, *Smart Set* enjoyed a circulation approaching 200,000. Four years later, in 1912, radical young intellectuals like Max Eastman, John Reed, and Floyd Dell founded the *Masses.* Though known especially for its left-wing political views, the *Masses* also ridiculed genteel values. Its masthead proclaimed it a "Revolutionary and not a Reform Magazine: A Magazine with a Sense of Humor and No Respect for the Respectable: Frank, Arrogant, Impertinent, Searching for the True Causes . . . A Magazine Whose Final Policy Is To Do As It Pleases and Conciliate Nobody, Not Even Its Readers."

By 1917 these cultural radicals—aptly named the "lyrical left" by one historian—had found two especially articulate spokesmen for their cause. One of them, the sharp-tongued Randolph Bourne, celebrated America's first youth movement. "How well we know the type of man of the older generation who has been doing good all his life," Bourne wrote bitterly. "How his personality has thriven on it! How he has ceaselessly been storing any moral fat in every cranny of his soul! How goodness has been meat to him." The other, Van Wyck Brooks, broke decisively with genteel ("highbrow") writers, who "produced a glassy inflexible priggishness on the upper levels that paralyses life," and with "lowbrow" writers, who appealed to "self-interested practicality." He concluded by demanding a "middle plane. . . . On the economic plane this implies socialism; on every other plane it implies something which a majority of Americans in our day certainly do not possess—an object in living.''

Many of these cultural critics were visionaries: socialism, sexual liberation, and youthful values would sweep away bourgeois conventions. Other young writers, however, were affected by a deep pessimism about contemporary conditions. Three such pessimistic books were Stephen Crane's *Maggie—A Girl of the Streets* (1896), Frank Norris's *McTeague* (1899), and Theodore Dreiser's *Sister Carrie* (1900). All embraced a literary naturalism that asserted the inexorable power of the environment over humankind. As Crane's title suggested, Maggie fell victim to urban living and became a prostitute. The book, Crane told a friend, showed that "environment is a tremendous thing in this world, and often shapes lives regardlessly." *McTeague,* which one genteel critic termed "about the most unpleasant American story that anybody has ever ventured to write," sketched the moral and social decline of a San Francisco dentist. Dreiser's novels were relentless in describing the adverse effects of urban life. "The rich were rich and the poor poor," he said, "but all were in the grip of imperial forces whose ruthless purposes or lack of them made all men ridiculous, pathetic, or magnificent as you choose."

This pessimistic naturalism was as crude and unscientific as the more optimistic versions of social Darwinism that it attacked. It encouraged cynicism about reform (Dreiser said he "didn't care a damn for the masses"), gross stereotyping of small-town life as in Edgar Lee Masters' grim *Spoon River Anthology* (1915), and the sophomoric despair of men like Mencken or Sherwood Anderson. As Anderson put it in 1916, "the idea is very simple; so simple that if you are not careful you will forget it. It is this—that everyone in the world is Christ and they are all crucified." Yet for all their oversimplification the naturalists ripped away the façade of propriety that the genteel writers had erected.

SOCIAL DARWINISM UNDER SIEGE

Paralleling the assault on the Genteel Tradition was a gradual, ultimately successful war against social Darwinism. By 1917 this war was still being fought, but the major battles had been won. Among the many writers engaged in these battles were young journalists who wrote scathing indictments of American conditions for the new mass circulation magazines. These included Upton Sinclair, a phenomenally productive socialist whose book *The Jungle* (1906) exposed conditions in the meat-packing industry; David Graham Phillips, whose *Treason of the Senate* (1906) attacked congressional irresponsibility and corruption; and Lincoln Steffens, a bright young reporter whose *Shame of the Cities* (1904) exposed the links between urban malfeasance and corporate power.

These men were reporters, not philosophers engaged in intellectual combat with formal social Darwinian thought. They were stronger on providing facts than in offering theoretical solutions. They tended to exaggerate, so much so that Roosevelt denounced them as "muckrakers." However labeled, they were reformers who rejected the older faith in the unimpeded blessings of evolution. They also enjoyed an unprecedented readership. If they did not cause a reorientation in popular thinking, they surely reflected and reinforced it.

Other critics of social Darwinism used universities or scholarly organizations to voice their views. These included such figures as John R. Commons, a Wisconsin economist; Lester Ward, a sociologist and paleontologist who became the first president of the American Sociological Society in 1905; and Franz Boas, a cultural anthropologist at Columbia who attacked the theories underlying racial and ethnic discrimination. Though these academicians differed widely in their views, they shared the basic belief that men and women could redirect evolutionary forces toward more progressive ends. Academicians such as these exercised growing influence within their disciplines and on the early generations of American graduate students in the social sciences.

There is filth on the floor, and it must be scraped up with the muck-rake; and there are times and places where this service is the most needed of all the services that can be performed. But the man who never does anything else, who never thinks or speaks or writes, save of his feats with the muck-rake, speedily becomes, not a help to society, not an incitement to good, but one of the most potent forces of evil.

Theodore Roosevelt's view of muckrakers, 1906.

Perhaps the most influential of these turn-of-the-century thinkers was the iconoclastic Thorstein Veblen. Conventional in some ways—he defended the profit motive—he was very unconventional in others. Veblen had little use for entrepreneurs like Carnegie or financiers like Morgan. Such men, he argued, were motivated not by an "instinct for workmanship" but by "pecuniary emulation." His heroes were engineers, who, if given power, could deliberately reshape the economy along more efficient, rational lines. This emphasis on planning was the clearest sign of Veblen's break with established economic thinking and an inspiration to younger, reform-oriented economists of the 1920s and 1930s.

New developments in legal thought assisted this revolt against social Darwinism. As early as the 1880s Oliver Wendell Holmes, Jr., began questioning the prevailing nineteenth-century view that abstract judicial principles, or precedent, must form the essence of decisions. "The life of the law has not been logic; it has been experience," Holmes argued in *The Common Law* (1881). "The felt necessities of the time, the prevalent moral and political theories . . . even the prejudices which judges share with their fellow men, have had a good deal more to do than the syllogism in determining the rules by which men should be governed." Named to the Supreme Court by Theodore Roosevelt, Holmes quickly disappointed the President by refusing to vote in 1904 for the dissolution of the Northern Securities Company, a railroad combine. But Holmes's view that experience must be the basis for the law also led him to insist that judicial decisions reflect changing social conditions. Thus Holmes dissented when a majority of the court in *Lochner* v. *New York* (1905) overturned a state law setting a ten-hour day for bakers. The court justified its decision by arguing that laws regulating work violated the freedom of contract guaranteed by the Constitution. Holmes, however, insisted that the Constitution was "not intended to embody a particular economic theory." He argued also for judicial restraint: courts should avoid striking down democratically enacted legislation. This practical view, dubbed "sociological jurisprudence" by Harvard law professor Roscoe Pound, rarely convinced a majority of the Supreme Court before 1937. But well before World War I it had attracted such able lawyers as Louis D. Brandeis, who used social statistics to defend labor legislation. In law, as in economics, new ways of thinking were sweeping away the abstractions of the past.

Educational theorists joined this revolt against nineteenth-century dogmas. One such theorist was G. Stanley Hall, a psychologist, philosopher, and educator who led the so-called child study movement at the turn of the century. To Hall, as to other "progressive" educators, the graded, formalistic schools of late-nineteenth-century America placed so much emphasis on rote learning that the needs of individual children were ignored. The title of his best-known book, *Adolescence: Its Psychology and Its Relation to Physiology, Anthropology, Sociology, Sex, Crime, Religion, and Education* (1904), suggested the range of his interests and the depth of his belief that educators should be prepared to adapt to particular needs of individual children.

Let me quote from Dr. Ely Van der Warker (1875): Woman is badly constructed for the purposes of standing eight or ten hours upon her feet. I do not intend to bring into evidence the peculiar position and nature of the organs contained in the pelvis, but to call attention to the peculiar construction of the knee and the shallowness of the pelvis, and the delicate nature of the foot as part of a sustaining column. The knee joint of woman is a sexual characteristic. Viewed in front and extended, the joint in but a slight degree interrupts the gradual taper of the thigh into the leg. Viewed in a semi-flexed position, the joint forms a smooth ovate spheroid. The reason of this lies in the smallness of the patella in front, and the narrowness of the articular surfaces of the tibia and femur, and which in man form the lateral prominences, and thus is much more perfect as a sustaining column than that of a woman. The muscles which keep the body fixed upon the thighs in the erect position labor under the disadvantage of shortness of purchase, owing to the short distance, compared to that of man, between the crest of the ilium and the great trochanter of the femur, thus giving to man a much larger purchase in the leverage existing between the trunk and the extremities. Comparatively the foot is less able to sustain weight than that of man, owing to its shortness and the more delicate formation of the tarsus and metatarsus.

The Brandeis brief in the case of *Muller* v. *Oregon* (1908). The court's important decision sustained Brandeis's defense of a state law setting maximum hours for women. Thus was "sexism" enlisted in the cause of reform.

Among the younger men influenced by Hall was John Dewey, whose almost unending stream of books and articles (including his brief, readable *School and Society* [1899]), lambasted contemporary educational methods. Schools, Dewey argued, should be "embryonic communities" that could "shape the experiences of the young so that instead of reproducing current habits, better habits shall be formed, and thus the future adult society be an improvement on their own." Dewey hoped schools would sponsor a cooperative community spirit such as he had known as a boy in rural Vermont. But Dewey was not nostalgic, for he wished such cooperativeness to promote collective social action. Education, he said, was the "fundamental method of social progress and reform."

Like many educational theorists, Dewey placed entirely too much faith in the potential of schools to alter society—generally they remained highly structured and bureaucratic reflections of society at large. Dewey's ideas also left an ambiguous legacy on progressive educational theory. Some of his followers used him to promote industrial education (which he often favored), and others, to defend unstructured "play schools" (which he opposed). Many self-styled progressive educators forgot that Dewey, far from opposing intellectual training, wanted to develop in students what he called a "creative intelligence," which could be put to "pragmatic" or "instrumental" use in improving society. Like Veblen, Dewey ultimately hoped that institutions, if led by purposeful, intelligent people, could become flexible, adaptable agents of change.

But if it was not always clear what Dewey's "instrumentalism" stood for, it was easy to tell what he was against: dogma, rigidity, formalism. Like the philosopher William James, who advocated what he termed "pragmatism," Dewey insisted that human intelligence (what James called "will") could alter the course of history. "The knower is the actor," James said. "There belongs to mind from its birth upward, a spontaneity, a vote." In this sense Dewey and James ranged well beyond their chosen disciplines of philosophy, psychology, and educational theory, and offered the opponents of social Darwinism a powerful set of arguments.

Men like Dewey, Veblen, and Holmes also provided reformers with a rationale for replacing older abstract "principles" with empirical study. "The man of the future," Holmes said, "is the man of statistics and the master of economics." W. E. B. DuBois, the militant black leader, added, "there is only one sure basis of social reform, and that is Truth—a careful, detailed knowledge of the essential facts of each social problem." A host of contemporary developments—muckraking, the collection of labor statistics, "scientific" studies of social conditions, the Brandeis brief—suggest that reformers questioned one older method of effecting change: creating moral outrage leading to conversion. Instead, experts must collect the facts, and planners use them in rational ways.

This faith in expertise, in administration, in planning properly struck some critics as undemocratic. How "progressive" was it to rely on an intellectual elite? Others predicted that "experts" could never be wholly impartial and that it was naive to suppose that administrators could free themselves from moral or political pressures. The assertion that truth was relative, that it depended in part on the facts one could amass, also alarmed observers who argued that pragmatism ultimately disavowed moral principles. "The younger cosmopolitan America," Santayana complained later, "has favored the impartial confrontation of all sorts of ideas. . . . Never was the human mind master of so many facts and sure of so few principles." As Santayana and others correctly perceived, the faith in facts could easily cause political and economic leaders to substitute what was practical for what was just and honorable.

Still, pragmatism developed a growing appeal after the turn of the century. To younger, forward-looking members of the professional classes it substituted empiricism for metaphysics. The stress on planning promised to give direction to modernization as well as to take control of society away from corrupt bosses and plutocrats and place it in the hands of "experts." Finally, pragmatism gave little offense even to conservatives. For all their ridicule of social Darwinism, instrumentalists like Dewey, who celebrated community cooperativeness, planners like Veblen, who glorified the ethic of meaningful work, and philosophers like James, who insisted that human beings could impose their wills on the course of events, still believed deeply in the potential of individuals to survive the collectivization of life. The pragmatic revolt, in short, promised to preserve as well as to plan. Like the "progressivism" that embraced it in the name of reform, it was counterrevolutionary as well as reformist.

Progressivism

Broadly speaking, the attacks on the Genteel Tradition and social Darwinism were part of intellectual currents throughout the industrialized western world. In the United States they accompanied the so-called progressive era between roughly 1900 and 1917. But intellectual ferment is ordinarily as much a reflection as a cause of broader forces. Such was the case during the years before 1917, a complex era when the major social forces—industrialization, bureaucratization, urbanization—grew so threatening that people felt they had to adopt new methods to control them. In a society as geographically diverse and complex as the United States, these methods necessarily varied widely. Some people organized to battle high tariffs, others to eliminate the slum or restrict immigration. Still others promoted conservation, urban reform, trust-busting, or improvement in the status of blacks, labor, or women. Most of these people called themselves "reformers" or "progressives." But they also worried, naturally enough, about their own well-being. Confronted with collectivization, they concluded that they had to develop pressure groups of their own. From this perspective the progressive era was not simply a morality play starring "reformers" against "special interests." Rather, it featured a galaxy of specialized and increasingly bureaucratized "reform" groups, many of which developed their own self-propelling subcultures without coalescing with each other.

The proliferation of pressure groups at the time supports this functionalist description of progressive reform movements. The pressure groups included reform-conscious organizations like the Anti-Saloon League, the General Federation of Women's Clubs, the Farmers' Union, the Immigration Restriction League, and the National Association for the Advancement of Colored People. More specialized business groups included the National Civic Federation, the Chamber of Commerce, the National Business League, and the National Rivers and Harbors Congress, all of which sought to change, or "reform," the existing order. The growing number of professional organizations included the American Medical Association, the American Sociological Society, and the American Association of University Professors. These groups, and many more like them, were either first organized or expanded rapidly during this period. All became increasingly self-interested (and, with some exceptions, more powerful) as professionalization and specialization advanced later in the century. The universalist reform impulse of Edward Bellamy no longer seemed as applicable in the modern age.

Why these organized groups gathered strength when they did remains difficult to explain. Simple economic interpretations confront the fact that America enjoyed unprecedented prosperity in the twenty years following the depression of 1893–97: large-scale commercial farmers, the vanguard of protest in the 1890s, benefited as never before—or since—from rising prices for their produce. The view that "the people revolted" against exploitation fails to identify the "people" or to answer why they did not do so earlier. The explanation of "social lag"—that people only belatedly articulate their problems and turn to reform—tells more about what happened than why.

An equally unsatisfactory answer holds that progressive leaders were middle-class Americans concerned primarily about enhancing their social status. Such a view correctly identifies the rapid growth of the middle class in the late nineteenth century. It also argues persuasively that many professional people—lawyers, doctors, teachers, ministers—felt threatened by immigrants beneath them and plutocrats above them. But this theory of "status revolt" is based on the questionable psychology that threatened people become reformers, when in fact they might have become revolutionaries or drones. The theory also tends to forget that most political movements in modern societies are led by people in the middle or upper middle classes. It fails to explain why such people, who had been threatened long before 1900, waited until then to lash out. And it is empirically wrong, for studies of reform on the state level have shown no significant difference in the social origins of progressives and standpatters. The theory of status revolt, while helpful in directing attention to the social tensions of the age, cannot explain why some middle-class Americans became reformers after 1900 and others did not.

Still, socioeconomic forces did contribute to pressures for change. The years after 1897, while free of serious depression, featured periodic panics and much financial uncertainty. They were also the first years of sustained inflation since the 1860s. The cost of living increased some 30 percent between 1897 and 1917, while wages and salaries remained approximately the same. It is not certain that middle-class people caught in this economic squeeze comprised the backbone of support for progressive causes, or that blue-collar workers provided a mass following. Indeed, later inflationary periods such as the mid-1940s or early 1970s caused people to demand budgetary retrenchment, not reform. But it is clear that Americans at the time complained often against the cost of living, and that for them retrenchment—and honest government—was the essence of reform.

The depression of the mid-1890s, which angered not only farmers but also thousands of urban dwellers, also moved people to call for change. It temporarily drove closer together various disaffected groups that previously had been divided along ethnic, class, or regional lines. These disaffected groups began by demanding an end to waste and then went on to demand that politicians eradicate special privilege, support progressive taxation, and finally be held accountable themselves (through initiative, referenda, recall, and direct election of senators) to the people. As economic conditions improved, these groups insisted that their politicians offer not only efficient but positive government. In this way the depression of the 1890s, like the hard times of the 1930s, helped develop new ideas of what government could and should do.

Any satisfactory explanation of the sources of progressivism must finally keep in mind the regional differences of turn-of-the-century America. Massachusetts seemed quite "conservative" simply because it had already accomplished many of the social reforms being demanded after 1900 in less industrially advanced regions of the nation. In Virginia, "progressivism" was promoted by anti-industrial reactionaries anxious to restore the state's Jeffersonian heritage. In many areas of the South and the Plains, progressives complained most bitterly about absentee corporate ownership of their economic resources: such people were not embattled former Populists but merchants, entrepreneurs, and professional people angry at freight rates. In California, progressivism began as a movement of antirailroad ranchers and landowners and developed later into a coalition of urbanites, labor unions, and ethnic groups. And in highly urbanized states like New York, workers and city machines provided steady support for a host of social and political reforms. In this general way each local coalition tended naturally to call for changes befitting its peculiar situation.

Viewing progressivism as a mixed collection of self-interested pressure groups helps explain why it was difficult to identify its base. For though it enjoyed diverse support (an advantage the Populists had lacked), it depended always on the cooperativeness of its potentially conflicting groups. Thus, many small businessmen gladly supported efforts to regulate railroad rates, but opposed the NAACP, the AFL, or women's suffrage. Social reformers included those who promoted immigration restriction, those who favored labor legislation, and those who worked for both. Feminists divided, often explosively, into those who proclaimed the virtues of suffrage, those who demanded sexual liberation, and those who sought to protect women workers from economic exploitation.

These divisions among reformers accounted for the limitations of progressive visions, for each group concentrated on its own objectives. Few reformers sought such fundamental changes as would be brought about by socialism or even a welfare state. Many, in fact, promoted "reform" in order to stem the tide of socialism, and few supported civil rights or civil liberties. Some reforms, like prohibition and immigration restriction, were animated in part by nativism or fear of the masses. The staunch backing for compulsory education, which spread widely in the period, reflected the hope that schools, like prohibition or immigration restriction, could "Americanize" the population and restore order to society. Organize, these activists argued, and excise the blemishes; but don't destroy capitalism. They were counterorganizers seeking to divert social change into safe directions.

James Addams—"Saint Jane"
to followers—in the early days
of Hull House.

BROAD VISIONS

Social Justice The most satisfactory way to understand progressivism is not to talk generally about motives and ideas but to see what the reform groups did. Among such groups were the advocates of better working conditions. These reformers, who ranged from settlement house workers to Marxists, fell far short of achieving their objectives. But many of them offered a vision of social justice that transcended the interest group model of progressivism. Of all the reformers before 1917 the crusaders for social justice seemed most willing to accept the more urban, collectivist reforms of the New Deal.

Many of these reformers were young well-educated, middle-class women. Among them was Florence Kelley, daughter of a Pennsylvania congressman. She graduated from Cornell University in 1882. But because she was a woman, the University of Pennsylvania refused to admit her to law school. Kelley traveled to Europe, attended the University of Zurich, and even translated into English Friedrich Engels's *The Condition of the Working Class in England*. In 1886 she returned to America, lived briefly at Jane Addams's Hull House in Chicago, and became chief factory inspector in Illinois. In 1899 she became general secretary of the National Consumers' League, which battled for laws protecting women and children workers. She also joined the Socialist party, helped organize the NAACP, and in 1919 became a founding member of the Women's International League for Peace and Freedom.

The most revered social worker of the time was Jane Addams. Like Kelley, she came from a solid middle-class background. But after dropping

Fostering a different life in the city: the Henry St. Settlement, New York.

out of medical school she became restless, traveled twice to Europe, and returned home determined to found a settlement house for the poor. Hull House, started in 1889, offered services including a day nursery, a dispensary, a boarding house, a music school, and an art gallery. In its broadest sense it was an alternative to life in a nuclear family, for it offered communal living of a sort to people of differing generations. Addams also branched out to crusade for child labor laws, juvenile courts, women's suffrage, and international peace. In 1912 she seconded the nomination of Theodore Roosevelt for the presidency on the Progressive party ticket.

Addams did not pretend to be wholly altruistic. Social work, she argued, gave middle-class women something useful to do; it was a "subjective necessity." She also rejected socialism, supporting Roosevelt in 1912 in part because she distrusted the power of labor unions within the Democratic party.

Though sensitive to the cultural distinctiveness of immigrants, she said that they could learn much from America, which "represented a distinctly superior standard of life and thought." Part of Addams's great appeal to Americans was the image of almost maternal moderation she seemed to present.

The settlement house movement, vigorous before 1917, declined rapidly after the 1930s. One reason was the cutting off after 1917 of mass immigration; another was competition from governmental services, especially under the New Deal, which revealed that settlement workers seldom reached poor people beyond their neighborhoods. Indeed, they seldom tried, for most social workers during the progressive era were cool to the idea of a welfare state. Unlike more radical reformers, they wished to humanize the social community, not to restructure it.

Still, the social justice movement left an impact on its times. By 1914 there were some 400 settlement houses in America. By 1916, thirty-two states had passed laws providing workmen's compensation, thirty-nine were regulating working hours for women and children, and all had approved some controls over child labor. Eleven states were even experimenting with minimum wage legislation—for women only. Though these state laws affected relatively few people, and though the Supreme Court struck down the minimum wage laws after 1917, many social workers emerged as forceful advocates of New Deal measures in the 1930s. In the process they did much to expose social conditions, to develop model legislation, to popularize the fact-oriented investigative method of understanding social problems, and to extend the idea that environmental, not personal, problems lead to social disorder.

More radical members of the social justice movement began looking beyond the neighborhood to class action. Among these were young labor organizers who sought industry-wide unions as alternatives to the conservative craft unionism of the AFL. In 1909 the New York Women's Trade Union League and a local of the International Ladies Garment Workers Union succeeded in gaining support for a massive strike—the so-called Uprising of the Twenty Thousand—against sweatshops like the Triangle Shirt Waist Company in New York City. For three months thousands of women workers, mostly young Jewish immigrants, endured winter cold and abuse from police and thugs trying to break their picket lines. The strike resulted in the unionization of only a few shops, but even this limited success encouraged organizers. In Chicago a strike in 1910 of 40,000 men clothing workers, though again only partially successful, led to the growth under Sidney Hillman of the Amalgamated Clothing Workers Union of America. By World War I these industrial unions remained weak. But they were established as industrial unions and later became bulwarks of the CIO.

A more radical effort for social justice was the Western Federation of Miners, an industrial union whose greatest strength lay in the metal mining areas of the Far West. Led by flamboyant figures such as William ("Big Bill") Haywood, a powerful activist who had lost one eye in an accident at the age of nine, these miners engaged employers in a series of bloody strikes at places

Troops and workers during a textile strike, Lawrence, Mass., 1912.

like Coeur d'Alene, Idaho, (1899) and Cripple Creek, Colorado, (1903). In 1905 Haywood helped to gather these miners and other migratory workers such as lumberjacks into the Industrial Workers of the World. By 1910 the IWW, or Wobblies, as they were called, comprised the radical, direct action wing of American socialism, and in the next two years they branched into organizing textile workers in the East. In 1912 the IWW won a protracted struggle for unionization in the mills at Lawrence, Massachusetts. By 1915, despite an unsuccessful strike of textile mills in Paterson, New Jersey, it had attracted 60,000 to 100,000 members.

The militancy of the IWW terrified conservatives, and even the Socialist party felt obligated to expel Haywood in 1913 because he advocated violence and sabotage. The man of the future, said the IWW, was not the theorist but "the obscure Bill Jones on the firing line, with stink in his clothes, rebellion in his brain, hope in his heart, determination in his eye, and direct action in his gnarled fist." By 1919 the ideology of the IWW was overtly revolutionary.

"The worst thief is he who steals the playtime of children."
W.D.HAYWOOD.
JOIN THE I. W. W. AND HELP PUT THE THIEVES TO WORK

"The working class and the employing class," Haywood said, "have nothing in common. . . . Between these two classes a struggle must go on until the workers of the world unite as a class, take possession of the earth and the machinery of production, and abolish the wage system."

In fact, the IWW talked more militantly than it behaved, and its leaders avoided violence or sabotage. Most of the members were nonideological miners and migratory workers who supported the IWW not because it talked of socialism but because it promised them—unrealistically—a personal freedom such as they had enjoyed prior to the advent of large-scale corporate mining and lumbering. Their heroes were Lincoln, Jefferson, and John Brown, not Karl Marx. Haywood himself wanted workers, not the state, to own private property, and his goals were more bourgeois than socialist. Echoing Bellamy, he said utopia would contain a "wonderful dining room where you will enjoy the best food that can be purchased; your digestion will be aided by sweet music which will be wafted to your ears by an unexcelled orchestra. There will be a gymnasium and a great swimming pool and private bathrooms of marble."

Haywood's major mistake was adhering to direct action once America had entered World War I. After he supported a few strikes, the government retaliated in a series of unconstitutional raids on IWW offices in September, 1917. By 1918 almost all the IWW leaders were in jail on charges brought under the wartime Espionage and Sedition acts. Haywood jumped bail in 1921

One of the many children at work in South Carolina cotton mills, 1909.

to flee to Russia, where he died ignored and embittered in 1928. Meanwhile better wages during the prosperous war years removed the chief motivation for activism among the rank and file. The IWW proved an exciting, romantic model of industrial unionism that continued to attract syndicalists, cultural radicals, and even anarchists long after its demise. From the beginning, however, it attempted the almost impossible task of organizing migratory workers against corporate power, and it played a negligible role after 1918.

The Socialist party, the most tenacious wing of the social justice movement, grew dramatically during the years between 1900 and 1912. Its leader, Eugene Debs, had turned to socialism in 1897 after being jailed for his part in the Pullman Strike. Though hardly an intellectual or even an effective party organizer, Debs was charismatic, openhearted, and eloquent. Under his leadership, the party managed before 1912 to elect 160 councilmen, 145 aldermen, 1 congressman, and 56 mayors, including leaders in cities like Milwaukee, Berkeley, and Schenectady. During this same period the party published more than 300 newspapers, one of which, the Kansas-based *Appeal to Reason*, had 700,000 weekly subscribers. In 1912 the party boasted a membership of 125,000, and Debs as presidential candidate received 900,000 votes, or 6 percent of the total presidential vote. Of third-party candidates in the twentieth century, only Theodore Roosevelt the same year, Robert La Follette in 1924, and George Wallace in 1968 received higher percentages of the vote.

Eugene V. Debs speaking to a crowd in Canton, Ohio.

Debs spoke for a broad following ranging from immigrants in the cities to former Populists on the Plains to writers like Jack London and Upton Sinclair. He probably appealed above all to blue-collar workers ignored by the AFL. Though a convert to Marxism, he talked more eloquently about poverty and injustice than about the class struggle or the dictatorship of the proletariat. After the election of 1912 his following began to split apart. Some members placed their hopes in Woodrow Wilson. Others, including the IWW, were expelled. By 1917 party membership had slipped to 80,000, almost 33,000 of whom belonged to federations of clannish ethnic groups. In 1920, Debs received almost 920,000 votes in his campaign for the presidency, the most ever earned by a Socialist candidate. But observers agreed that the vote, which was only 2 percent of the total, represented disillusion with the war and admiration for Debs, who ran his campaign from a prison cell. By the mid-1920s the party was a deeply divided, insignificant political force that failed to revive substantially even in the depression-plagued 1930s.

The decline of the American Socialist party was not the fault of Debs, an inspiring leader. It stemmed rather from many sources, including savage repression by the public and government in World War I, and from internal factionalism intensified after 1920 by Communists and Trotskyites. The party also faced political obstacles such as laws making it difficult and expensive to get on the ballot. It had to appeal to mobile workers who yearned for membership in the middle class, not in the revolutionary proletariat, and who

> *The members of a trades-union should be taught the true import, the whole object of the labor movement and understand its entire program.*
>
> *They should know that the labor movement means more, infinitely more, than a paltry increase in wages and the strike necessary to secure it; that while it engages to do all that possibly can be done to better the working conditions of its members, its higher object is to overthrow the capitalist system of private ownership of the tools of labor, abolish wage-slavery and achieve the freedom of the whole working class and, in fact, of all mankind. . . .*
>
> An occasionally militant Eugene Debs on the evils of the AFL, 1904.

were divided along ethnic and racial lines. After 1917 Socialism had to survive amid widespread prosperity and the absence of new immigration. With so many obstacles it is not surprising that Debs tended to stress social justice as much as socialism, or that his party, like the IWW, failed in the long run to expand.

Women's Rights To activists like Addams and Kelley women's rights were only part of the broader crusade for social justice. For other women reformers of the era, however, they became the central issue. Though these feminists differed sharply among themselves, some of them raised arguments later revived by advocates of women's liberation.

Far on the fringe in that decorous era were a few militant champions of sexual liberation. One of the most visible was Emma Goldman, a Russian-Jewish immigrant who fled to America in 1885. After a brief and unsatisfactory marriage, she moved to New York City and embraced anarchism, birth control, and free love. Women, she said, "must no longer keep their mouths shut and their wombs open." Frequently jailed for her radical activities, she was ultimately deported to Russia in 1919. Goldman appealed more to a small group of intellectuals and anarchists than she did to most feminists or to the masses, whom she once termed "inert and indolent, crude, lame, pernicious in their demands and influence." Even before her deportation she had little influence on her times, except to serve as a symbol for all that was "dangerous" in the radical tradition.

Closer to the mainstream of feminism were the birth control advocates led by Margaret Sanger. These middle-class women rarely proposed free love or abolition of the conventional nuclear family. Many of them were conservatives motivated by fears that Anglo-Saxon Protestants were committing "race suicide": birth control, they believed, would limit or reduce the growth of the immigrant masses. The birth control advocates received steady harassment for their troubles, and in 1914 the government indicted Sanger on nine counts of obscenity that if upheld could have imprisoned her for forty-five years. But Sanger persevered, the charges were later dropped, and in 1918 the courts permitted doctors to distribute birth control information. Though state laws continued to prohibit the sale of contraceptives, the advocates of birth control had begun to show some middle-class women a way out of the tyranny of unwanted pregnancies.

A more economically oriented feminism appeared in the writings of Charlotte Perkins Gilman, whose *Women and Economics* (1898) put forth much of what the National Organization for Women was to say seventy years later. Though married in 1884 to an affectionate husband, Gilman grew so unhappy with the burdens of housework and motherhood (she had one daughter) that she had a nervous breakdown and obtained a divorce in 1894. *Women and Economics* reflected her own unhappy experience by challenging what Betty Friedan was later to call the "feminine mystique" of the joys of domesticity. "Only as we live, think, feel, and work outside the home," she wrote, "do we become humanly developed, civilized, and socialized." Gilman disagreed that sexual freedom would transform or liberate women. Rather, she argued, women were like men in finding freedom and satisfaction through meaningful work and creative effort. Gilman did not oppose marriage but crusaded for a form of communalism featuring large housing units, day nurseries, central kitchens, and maid service to relieve women of domestic chores. Because the number of working women increased at the time—from 5 million in 1900 to more than 7 million in 1910—it appeared as if she was foreseeing the future.

The National American Women's Suffrage Association seeks working-class support.

Most of these women, however, were not working because of a desire for personal satisfaction but because of economic necessity. Her vision directly challenged the traditional view that women belonged in the home, and during her time it had little influence.

The limited appeal of sexual freedom and economically oriented feminism left the field clear for women's suffrage reformers, who spearheaded the movement for women's rights by 1910. Membership in the National American Women's Suffrage Association, the central agency of the reform, increased from 17,000 in 1905 to 75,000 in 1910. In that year Washington became the first state since 1896 and only the fifth (all western) to approve women's suffrage. Four other states, including California, followed in the next two years. In 1912 Roosevelt's Progressive party endorsed the measure, and when his party started to dissolve in 1913, politicians began promoting the cause in hopes of gathering former Progressives to their side for the elections of 1914. After 1915, when the highly organized Carrie Chapman Catt assumed control of NAWSA, the movement rapidly gathered momentum. Though unenthusiastic about America's entrance into World War I, Catt shrewdly reminded politicians that women were selling war bonds, working in factories, and enlisting in the Red Cross. At the same time she maintained a prudent distance from more radical suffragists whose headline-grabbing tactics of picketing and other means of direct action probably alienated potential supporters. By the end of 1917 NAWSA claimed two million members, and in 1919 the Senate sent the proposed Nineteenth Amendment to the states. In mid-1920 the amendment was finally ratified by the necessary three-fourths of the states. The moderate, pragmatic tactics of NAWSA provided a classic illustration of a well-organized pressure group operating within the political process for well-defined ends.

Passage of the amendment led some reformers to perceive a golden age ahead. "There is little doubt," a woman wrote in 1922, "that within twenty years the corrupt city machine as we now know it, with its party bosses, its inner cliques and grafting gangs, will be a thing of the past, as extinct as the dodo." It soon became clear, however, that these were wildly euphoric expectations. Women tended to go to the polls in smaller numbers than men and to vote very much as men did. They also failed to gain admission to positions of political or economic influence. The Nineteenth Amendment, the social worker Grace Abbott admitted realistically in 1925, "provided a ticket of admission to the political fairgrounds. It does not admit us to the races nor to the side shows, nor does it insure us a place on the committees which award the prizes."

The expectation that women would abolish the "corrupt city machines" veiled a less attractive side of suffragism as it developed after 1900. In the nineteenth century crusaders like Elizabeth Cady Stanton and Susan Anthony had appealed directly from the Declaration of Independence. Women, they argued simply, deserved full equality with men. But suffragists after 1900 tended to be middle-class Protestants with sufficient education to be aware of the glaring gap between the economic status of women and their lack of political rights. Like many people in the North, they feared the immigrant and laboring masses. Like most southerners, they opposed voting by blacks. So it was that the egalitarian justification for suffrage existed alongside of the claim that women were different—purer, more sensitive. This argument enabled many suffragists to favor the imposition of a literacy test to "abolish the ignorant vote." Such a test would obviously discriminate against blacks, ethnics, and lower-class working men and women. "Those [suffragists] who thought 'Patrick' was bad enough," one historian explained, "did not want to add 'Bridget' to their problems." Other advocates of women's suffrage recognized that middle-class Protestant women, who outnumbered their ethnic sisters, would gain the most with the approval of suffrage. And still others promoted women's suffrage as a way of achieving moralistic reforms aimed in part at immigrants: all seven states that adopted prohibition between 1914 and 1917 were states in which women had recently been granted the vote. The crusade for women's suffrage, like many progressive reforms, included racism and nativism, which stained its vision.

The claim that women were purer than men showed how far feminism had to progress before it could develop as a powerful ideology. For that argument was the mirror image of statements used for years by men (and many women) to discredit the suffragists. Women, these antisuffragists said, were different from men—too protected to understand the issues, too pure to sully themselves on the hustings. The suffragists went beyond this perspective by insisting that women were not only pure but intelligent. Their basic argument, however, asserted that women deserved equal rights not because they were similar but because they were different. It was four decades before the women's movement recovered from this assertion of difference.

Still, it is hard to quarrel too severely with pragmatists like Catt who resorted to this type of appeal. Even social workers like Addams and Kelley demanded social legislation protecting women only—demands that also relied on the argument that women required special treatment. And the overwhelming majority of Americans persisted in viewing women as mothers and home-

Women of the Equal Suffrage League of St. Louis, Missouri,
visit one of the state's small country towns.

bodies. The Camp Fire Girls, founded in 1912, dressed in "authentic squaw dresses" and were ranked as "wood gatherers," "fire makers," and "torch bearers." They progressed by learning to make ten standard soups, recognizing three types of wails from babies, and beautifying yards. L. Frank Baum, widely read creater of the Wizard of Oz, reflected the contemptuous attitude toward feminists by creating a female character in 1904 called General Jinjur, leader of an "army of revolt." General Jinjur ran a female-dominated society in which "men were sweeping and dusting and washing dishes, while the women sat around in groups, gossiping and laughing." Her army, equipped with knitting needles, jabbed at guards protecting the Scarecrow (a straw man) and plotted to use the jewels of Emerald City for rings, bracelets, and necklaces, and the city's wealth to "buy every girl in the Army a dozen new gowns." These and countless other manifestations of popular attitudes explain why people like Charlotte Perkins Gilman received such a perfunctory hearing. Under the circumstances the suffragists accomplished a good deal.

Racial Justice Unlike women, America's blacks remained a relatively concentrated group in the years prior to World War I. In 1910 four-fifths of American blacks (who then numbered 10 million in all, or 11 percent of the American population), still lived in the South, where they worked at menial tasks. Harlem was described in 1893 as a white district "distinctly devoted to the mansions of the wealthy, the homes of the well-to-do, and the places of business of the tradespeople who minister to their wants." The ghettoization of blacks in northern cities had barely begun as the nineteenth century came to a close.

Yet these were years of mounting racial discrimination. In the 1890s southern whites, fearful of a developing interracial alliance under Populism, began the systematic disfranchisement of blacks (and often of poor whites). They also perfected an unsurpassed demagoguery based on Darwinian concepts of black "retrogression" or "reversion to savagery" after emancipation. Benjamin Tillman, a senator from South Carolina, announced that the Negro was "a fiend, a wild beast, seeking whom he may devour." A character in Thomas Dixon's novel *The Clansman* (1905) added that the Negro was "half child, half animal, the sport of impulse, whim, and conceit . . . a being who, left to his will, roams at night and sleeps in the day, whose speech knows no word of love, whose passions, once aroused, are as the fury of a tiger."

Disfranchisement was but the newest form of racial discrimination suffered by blacks. Segregated in schools that in 1910 spent approximately $2.20 per pupil (the amount spent for southern whites was $4.90, for the nation at large, $21.15), they were lucky if they learned to write; the illiteracy of blacks in some states approached 50 percent, four to five times that of southern whites. Three-fourths of blacks were tenants or share croppers, with an annual wage of approximately $100, and thousands were held to the land by contract labor systems that amounted literally to peonage. If blacks complained there was always the ultimate sanction of lynching. During the 1890s lynchings averaged 188 per year in the South, and blacks (who previously shared the distinction with some whites) became the almost exclusive target.

That was the end of that! Mob justice administered! And there the Negro hung until daylight the next morning—an unspeakably grisly, dangling horror, advertising the shame of the town. His head was shockingly crooked to one side, his ragged clothing, cut for souvenirs, exposed in places his bare body: he dripped blood. And, with the crowds of men both here and at the morgue where the body was publicly exhibited, came young boys in knickerbockers, and little girls and women by scores, horrified but curious. They came even with baby carriages! Men made jokes: "A dead nigger is a good nigger." And the purblind, dollars-and-cents man, most despicable of all, was congratulating the public:

> *"It'll save the country a lot of money!"*
> *Significant lessons, these, for the young!*

But the mob wasn't through with its work. Easy people imagine that, having hanged a Negro, the mob goes quietly about its business; but that is never the way of the mob. Once released, the spirit of anarchy spreads and spreads, not subsiding until it has accomplished its full measure of evil.

From Ray Stannard Baker, *Following the Color Line* (1908). This particular lynching occurred in Springfield, Ohio.

The first decade of the twentieth century saw the beginnings of a long-run decline in lynchings: 93 occurred per year between 1900 and 1910, and 62 per year in the next decade. But peonage remained so common that one Florida citizen concluded in 1907, "slavery is just as much an 'institution' now as it was before the war." And tensions occasionally erupted into race riots, one of which took place in 1908 in Abraham Lincoln's home town of Springfield, Illinois, and prompted the founding of the National Association for the Advancement of Colored People a year later. By then northerners as well as southerners regularly demanded racial discrimination, viewing blacks as "children" in need of protection or as biologically inferior brutes. The novelist Jack London spoke of "the dark-pigmented things, the half-castes, the mongrel bloods, the dregs of long-conquered races," and the progressive editor William Allen White conceded that "we [whites] are separated by two oceans from the inferior races." Henry L. Mencken added in 1910:

> The educated Negro of today is a failure, not because he meets insuperable difficulties in life, but because he is a Negro. His brain is not fitted for the higher forms of mental effort; his ideals, no matter how laboriously he is trained and sheltered, remain those of a clown. He is, in brief, a low caste man, to the manner born, and he will remain inert and inefficient until fifty generations of him have lived in civilization. And even then, the superior white man will be fifty generations ahead of him.

In the face of such attitudes it is not surprising that the accommodationist advice of Booker T. Washington, head of Tuskegee Institute, remained popular among American blacks until early in the twentieth century. "The agitation of questions of social equality," he insisted, "is the extremest folly, and progress in the enjoyment of all the privileges that will come to us must be the result of severe constant struggle rather than of artificial forcing." Yet even in Washington's time blacks were far from passive. In 1890 the black editor T. Thomas Fortune helped found the National Afro-American League as an alternative to the two major parties. In that same year an estimated one million blacks belonged to the Colored Farmers Alliance, which eventually joined white Populists in the fight for agrarian reform. Throughout the period Washington himself—in public so accommodating—privately funded the legal struggle against peonage.

After 1900 men like William E. B. Du Bois began rebelling against Washington's leadership. A product of the middle class, Du Bois was raised in Massachusetts and educated at Fisk and Harvard, where he received his PhD degree in 1895 and where he grew highly sensitive to racial slurs. In his *Souls of Black Folk* (1903) he declared that "the problem of the twentieth century is the problem of the color line." Two years later he joined other militants to demand equality. Blacks, he said in criticizing Washington, could not sit in "courteous and dumb self-forgetting silence" until time rescued them. Four years later, in 1909, he co-founded the NAACP. By the time of Washington's

> *If somewhere in this whirl and chaos of things, there dwells Eternal Good, pitiful yet masterful, then anon in His good time America shall rend the Veil and the prisoned shall go free. Free, free as the sunshine trickling down the morning into these high windows of mine, free as yonder fresh young voices welling up to me from the caverns of brick and mortar below—swelling with song, instinct with life, tremulous treble and darkening bass. My children, my little children, are singing to the sunshine, and thus they sing:*
>
> > *"Let us cheer the weary traveler,*
> > *Cheer the weary traveler,*
> > *Let us cheer the weary traveler*
> > *Along the heavenly way."*
>
> *And the traveler girds himself, and sets his face toward the Morning, and goes his way.*
>
> W. E. B. Du Bois, *Souls of Black Folk* (1903).

death in 1915 Du Bois was already recognized as the leader of militant blacks. "We must lay at the soul of this man," Du Bois wrote of his departed rival, "a heavy responsibility for the consummation of Negro disfranchisement, the decline of the Negro college and public school, and the firmer establishment of color caste in this land."

Whether Du Bois offered a wholly realistic argument is another question. Surely he was uncharitable toward Washington, whose accommodationism flowed from awareness of harsh southern racial patterns and whose stress on blacks helping themselves inspired later black nationalists. Du Bois was also reluctant to admit that racial segregation in the North, while primarily the result of white racism, was also promoted by black retailers, funeral directors, evangelists, and real estate operators who depended on black patronage. Finally, Du Bois was an elitist who at that time relied rather too heavily on what he called the "talented tenth" for black leadership and on primarily legalistic answers to discrimination. This faith in a black elite failed to recognize that there were few blacks as militant and well educated as he, few white liberals who could be counted upon, and few judges who were willing to challenge white attitudes. As the "civil rights revolution" of the 1960s demonstrated, the black masses—the very group to whom Washington had pitched his more accommodationist appeal—would have to be organized before meaningful racial progress could occur.

Yet Du Bois's growing bitterness, which led him to pan-Africanism, socialism, and (as a very old man) communism, was easy to understand, for "progressivism" had little time for people of color. Southern states, led by progressive governors like James K. Vardaman of Mississippi and Jeff Davis of Arkansas, proceeded with the efficient disfranchisement of blacks, while urban ghettos began to spread in northern cities such as Chicago and New

W. E. B. Du Bois.

York. As early as 1905 white school children in Chicago rioted when officials attempted to transfer them to a predominantly black school, and in the next decade blacks in Chicago were banned from amusement parks, dance halls, and even the YMCA. And stereotypes hardened. New York plays about blacks carried such titles as "Gentlemen Coons' Parade," "The Coon at the Door," "Dat Watermillyon," and "The Coon and the Chink." Negro songs at the time, the black writer James Weldon Johnson recalled, were known as "'coon songs,' and were concerned with jamborees of various sorts and the play of razors, with the gastronomical delights of chicken, pork chops and watermelon, and with the experiences of red-hot 'mammas' and their never too faithful people." In 1915 D. W. Griffith drew all the worst stereotypes together by making Dixon's *The Clansman* into a cinematographically brilliant movie, *Birth of a Nation*. It portrayed the Ku Klux Klan preserving southern womanhood from bestial black men roaming the post-bellum South.

Confronted with such universal prejudice, militants like DuBois understandably failed to accomplish much before the 1930s. But their failure was primarily one of timing. When the broadened perspectives of white liberalism,

Harlem, *c*. 1900.

the centralization of political power, and the large migration of southern blacks into northern cities meshed in the 1950s, DuBois's dream of militant interracial cooperation leading to full equality finally began to take place.

NARROW VISIONS

Prohibition   The campaigns for social justice, women's rights, and racial equality, for all their compromises and imperfections, possessed a core of altruism that sustained them in later years. Other reforms sponsored by progressives exposed a more nativist, self-interested side of progressivism.

Among these was prohibition, which critics like H. L. Mencken ridiculed as the creation of fundamentalist preachers and rural Puritans. This image is correct to a point, for the "dry" crusade was strongest in the predominantly rural, Protestant sections of the South and West and was championed by their most revered spokesman, William Jennings Bryan. But as Bryan's involvement revealed, prohibition was also a plank in the platform of many progressive leaders. Frances Willard, the head of the Women's Christian Temperance Union, fought for social justice as well as for prohibition, and the muckraking novelist Upton Sinclair wrote an antiliquor book, *The Wet Parade,* as late as 1932. These progressives ultimately favored prohibition because they believed that nothing less drastic could curb the plague of alcoholism and the disorderly behavior of "drunks" on the streets and around saloons. This middle-class Christian impulse, rooted in the social gospel, gave the crusade against alcohol an appeal far broader than men like Mencken were prepared to acknowledge.

Yet later "wets" were correct in pointing to the darker side of the crusade. The most effective workers for the cause were the highly organized lobbyists of the Anti-Saloon League, which converted from support of local option laws to prohibition after 1907. The League was a one-issue pressure group whose lobbyists admitted that they did not care whether people drank or not, so long as they voted dry. The league reminded legislators (as if they needed much reminding) that the liquor interests corrupted politics and that saloons assisted immigrant political machines. It also appealed to employers who wanted a more reliable, efficient labor force. In Sinclair Lewis's novel *Babbitt,* Vergil Gunch, the coal dealer, sips a cocktail and says to his companion, " . . . don't . . . forget prohibition is a mighty good thing for the working classes. Keeps 'em from wasting their money and losing their productiveness."

For all these reasons the Anti-Saloon League scored success in twenty-six states representing half the population by April, 1917; prohibition was not the product of wartime emotions but an ongoing part of prewar progressivism. And when America entered the war, the League's pressure became irresistible. The grain used for making liquor, it appeared, was so necessary to feed soldiers that Congress in 1917 approved legislation banning the use of grain for distilling or brewing. This provision in effect made America dry. Germans, it seemed, controlled most of the breweries. And it did seem unpatriotic to talk about the freedom to drink when the nation was fighting to save the world. In December 1917 the proposed Eighteenth Amendment passed Congress, and in January 1919 it received the necessary ratification of three-fourths of the states. The Volstead Act, approved nine months later, banned the manufacture or sale of liquor (defined as one-half of one percent alcohol by volume) after the amendment took effect in January 1920. The crusade against alcohol was thus transformed into the coercive and divisive "Great Experiment" of the 1920s.

Reform of City Government Like the drive for prohibition, the demand for urban reform involved a wide variety of people. Two of these were Tom Johnson, who served as mayor of Cleveland from 1901 to 1909, and Hazen Pingree, mayor of Detroit from 1890 to 1897. Johnson, product of a poor southern family, rose in classic fashion from newsboy to hard-driving owner and operator of street railways in Cleveland. An advocate of free trade, he became a disciple of Henry George. By the time he became mayor, however, he had moved beyond the single tax to support municipal ownership of public utilities, women's suffrage, urban home rule, and progressive taxation. At his death in 1911 he was perhaps America's best-known urban reformer. Pingree, like Johnson, was a self-made man (in shoe manufacturing) who brought a solid business background to public life. He too began as a moderate reformer concerned with providing honest, efficient service, but was moved by the depression of the 1890s to call for progressive taxation, municipal ownership of utilities, the direct election of senators, and the abolition of child labor. To relieve unemployment he provided workers with "potato patches," an early version of direct governmental relief.

A still more advanced social reformer was Samuel "Golden Rule" Jones, mayor of Toledo from 1897 to 1904. He too was a capitalist who began as an oil roustabout and ultimately made a fortune manufacturing oil-well machinery. As an enlightened employer he established an eight-hour day, paid vacations, profit-sharing, and a minimum wage. As mayor he called for a "Cooperative Commonwealth, the Kingdom of Heaven on Earth," and he practiced what he preached. He recognized labor unions, inaugurated a minimum wage for city employees, started kindergartens, constructed a municipal golf course, took clubs away from police, planned playgrounds, and maintained a free lodging-house for tramps. Essentially a pragmatic Christian socialist, he argued that "private ownership is a high crime against democracy." Jones's heretical views earned him the emotional support of workers and ethnic groups. Elected four times, he died in office and was succeeded by Brand Whitlock, a disciple who carried on his work.

The careers of such capitalists turned reformers reveal the impact of the depression in shaping the impulse for social justice in America. They suggest also that some progressives embraced reform not because they feared for their social status but because their experiences in the ruthless world of business shattered their faith in nineteenth-century solutions.

But such advanced reformers were relatively rare in city halls during the early years of the century. More common were men and women aptly described by the historian Melvin Holli as "structural reformers." Some of these propagandized for the so-called Galveston Plan of 1901, which attempted to take government "out of politics" and entrust it to a commission of businessmen. Others favored hiring an expert city manager, as Staunton, Virginia, did in 1908. These reformers demanded a nonpartisan ballot, the overthrow of corrupt political machines, and the application of scientific management to government. "Ignorance should be excluded from control," wrote Abram Hewitt, the reform mayor of New York in 1901. "The city business should be carried on by trained experts selected upon some other principle than popular suffrage."

Hewitt's distrust of popular suffrage made it quite clear that these structural reformers yearned to destroy the power of the immigrants—specifically the Irish—in city politics. Good government, they said, meant rule by the wellborn. "A man's occupation," the reformist Voters League of Pittsburg argued in 1911, "ought to give a strong indication of his qualifications for membership on a school board . . . small shopkeepers, clerks, workmen at many trades . . . could not, no matter how honest, be expected to administer properly the affairs of an educational system." These reformers began calling for literacy tests as qualifications for voting, for stringent voter registration laws (which tended to exclude the mobile working classes), and for city-wide districting, which broke down the ward-based structure of the immigrant machine.

Such structural reformers were not hypocrites, for urban corruption did exist. But they were self-interested. Former businessmen like Johnson and Jones—and writers like Steffens—knew better that the ultimate source of corruption was not the immigrant bosses but entrepreneurs seeking favors and franchises. The structural reformers also assumed wrongly that it was possible to take politics (by which they often meant immigrant machines) out of government. This view was not only nativist, but naive, because politics in the broad sense meant the balancing of interest groups, and there was little reason to believe that efficiency-conscious commissioners or appointed city managers could do that any better than could elected, and therefore responsive, politicians. It was not surprising that men like Hewitt seldom lasted in power for long, that commission-style government rarely proved popular in the larger, ethnically diverse cities, or that the political power of ethnic groups persisted long after the crusade for municipal reform at the turn of the century.

Reform in the States   By 1900 many political figures concluded that the city offered too small a field for meaningful change, and they turned to reform on the state level. "The state, and the state alone," Richard Ely explained in 1898, "stands for all of us." The most prominent among these politicians were Robert La Follette of Wisconsin and Hiram Johnson of California. Both were fiery, outspoken opponents of trusts and special interests who developed formidable vote-getting appeal in their states. La Follette served as governor from 1900 to 1906 and then as senator until his death in 1925. Johnson was chosen for three terms as governor between 1910 and 1916, and then for five terms in the Senate. To many of their generation they were the very symbols of enlightened, progressive government.

Their exalted reputations rested on undeniable accomplishments. La Follette pressed for more stringent control of railroads and public utilities. He got the legislature to approve the nation's first meaningful direct primary, and he established stiffer tax rates on corporations. By using the resources of the University of Wisconsin he established a model for informed, precise preparation of legislation. Johnson, who rode to power on the slogan, "Kick the Southern Pacific [Railroad] out of politics," achieved laws regulating utilities, curbing child labor, and establishing an eight-hour day for working women, workmen's compensation, and political reforms such as the initiative and referendum.

Both men were considerably less altruistic or enlightened than they appeared to their admirers. Like many progressive politicians, La Follette had been a regular Republican in the 1880s and 1890s, whereupon he gradually emerged as a leader of an "out" faction within the party. His ideas were less advanced than those of many others in Wisconsin, and he did much less for social justice than did his less-publicized gubernatorial successors. Once elected he used state employees to construct a potent political machine that helped his family to dominate the state for forty years. "Give us this law," he reputedly said in demanding the direct primary, "and we can hold this state forever." Johnson, a narrow, abusive man who seldom forgave an enemy, was as vain and personally ambitious as La Follette. He was also the champion, especially in his early years, of moderates who proclaimed themselves as leading a "movement in behalf of the businessman, the tax-payer, and decent government." As late as his campaign for governor in 1910 he did not even know what such reforms as the initiative and referendum were. In 1913 he encouraged racists to pass a bill prohibiting aliens from owning property, and he led sharp crackdowns on strikers. Such was the ambiguous reality behind the façade of progressive achievement.

Men like La Follette prided themselves especially on their laws setting up commissions to regulate railroads and public utilities. But though these commissions helped curb intrastate discrimination in rate-making, they varied so considerably that carriers came to demand uniform federal regulation. Most commissioners also realized quickly that economic nationalism made state regulation rather meaningless. And few commissioners possessed even the authority to examine company records in order to compute fair rates. Accordingly they accomplished much less than progressive rhetoric claimed.

A case in point was the model Wisconsin railroad commission law of 1905. Like most state laws that followed, it permitted railroads to set initial rates and granted broad review powers to the conservative courts. As the price for passage, moderates let it be known that they would refuse to confirm nominations of La Follette men to the commission, and the body as finally established became dominated by a member who conceded in 1907 that "no railway commission has ever lived which can prescribe carefully adjusted rates for a state with considerable railway mileage." By 1910 the commission had dropped all pretense of battling the railroad interests and was seeking instead ways of establishing fair, "scientific" rates. A final irony was that La Follette insisted on making the commission appointive, while his enemies, resenting this "undemocratic" plan, called (unsuccessfully) for the popular election of commissioners. The controversy showed that it is dangerous to swallow progressive rhetoric about the virtues of popular rule.

The demand for these state regulatory commissions rarely came from the "common" people, most of whom were too poor even to ride as passengers. Rather, it stemmed chiefly from large-scale commercial farmers and businessmen seeking reduced shipping rates. To the extent that railroads discriminated against certain regions, these businessmen-reformers had a case. But their argument rarely acknowledged that the overall level of railroad rates had remained stable since the 1890s, despite increased railway labor and material costs. They also refused to concede that many American railroads, already struggling to stay alive economically, could not afford rate reductions. It is too much to argue—as some have—that regulation (which was seldom punitive) killed the railroads. Conversely, it is cynical to say that men like La Follette were pawns of shipping interests. But it is true that the drive for regulatory commissions was led by well-organized shipper groups with economic motives. This contest between shippers and carriers indicated that business interests often opposed one another—there was no united "industrial complex." It suggested also that it is better to see the politics of regulation as a conflict among interest groups than as a dualistic contest between railroadmen and reformers.

Perceiving the regulatory issue as a battle among interests helps to explain why the commissions frequently left progressives unhappy. Even those few commissions with access to company records found that there was no such thing as "scientific" rate-making. They also discovered that it was impossible to define the "public interest" or to take the rate question "out of politics." For setting rates meant assigning economic priorities, and someone—shipper, carrier, consumer—inevitably got hurt. Efficiency-conscious progressives refused to abandon this ideal of regulation by "experts," and when state commissions proved unable to oversee interstate commerce, they clamored for federal agencies. These, it turned out, were useful in providing a forum for reconciling diverse interests—which legislatures could not have done so well. But to the extent that experts assumed the authority to assign priorities, they took control of basic economic policy from democratically elected officials. In this way the commission idea was more "political" and more elitist than progressives like La Follette ever cared to admit.

ELECTORAL REFORM

If regulation of the "interests" was plank number one for many state progressives, "direct democracy" was second. "The voice of the people," said the progressive Kansas editor William Allen White, "is indeed the will of God." "The people," La Follette also observed, "have never failed in any great crisis in history." To prove they meant what they said, many progressives demanded the direct election of senators, the direct primary, and the initiative, referendum, and recall. All were supposed to take government away from politicians and special interests and return it to the "people."

The rhetoric behind such reforms—that the cure for the ills of democracy is more democracy—had a powerful appeal. It sustained arguments for broadening the suffrage, and it was later to lead Americans into thinking that democratic institutions could be exported to authoritarian countries abroad. But the reformers tended to set up a false dualism between the "interests" and the "people" and to ignore the pluralism of American life. They also forgot that these innovations stood little chance of success in the absence of a relatively egalitarian society and an engaged, almost Athenian, electorate.

For these reasons "direct democracy" fell far short of expectations. The popular election of senators, established by constitutional amendment in 1913, caused no discernible improvement in the operations of the Senate. And the procedures of initiative, referendum, and recall ordinarily required large numbers of signatures, a cumbersome process that served well-financed interest groups better than it did poor people. Partly for this reason such measures had little impact on state legislation. Many states ignored or repealed them in the years to follow.

Direct primaries also had mixed effects. In some states they occasionally assisted reformist politicians who appealed to the voters and overturned entrenched oligarchies. In these cases the primaries helped "return government to the people," or at least to different people. More commonly, however, the primary tended to have one of four unsatisfying consequences: to make intraparty competition (already severe in most states) so expensive that politicians demanded repeal; to assist machines, which possessed the resources to bring out their regulars on primary day; to be used cynically by well-organized "out" groups with no program save that of gaining power themselves; or to play into the hands of demagogic orators previously screened out at conventions. By 1920 it was already clear that the direct primary was working no magical transformation of politics.

The attention given such supposedly democratic innovations as the direct primary obscured three other developments which reveal the limitations of using "progressivism" as the model for describing state politics. One of these was the continued prominence of ethnic and religious issues like prohibition, Sunday baseball, blue laws, and aid to parochial schools. Voting patterns as well as legislative roll calls during the period suggest that these ethnic and cultural divisions had more to do with forming political allegiances than did remoter issues like the tariff, trust busting, or political democratization. The progressive-conservative dichotomy, while a force in states such as Wisconsin, often was a poor description of political reality in the other states, and even in Wisconsin a Scandinavian newspaper suggested the depth of cultural feelings by proclaiming in 1914 that "the history and record of the Catholic power is black, blood-stained, and rotten, and cannot bear the light of day." Such ethno-cultural cleavages prevented social reformers from getting dependable mass support for economic programs.

The second development was a drop after 1890 in the percentage of eligible voters who went to the polls. Why this decline, which persisted until the 1930s, occurred is not wholly clear. One cause was the tighter registration laws and voter "purges" directed at immigrants. Another was the secret ballot, aimed at discouraging the practice of buying the votes of indigent people. A third cause was closer supervision of the polls, a reform that prevented people from voting several times. But while these changes discouraged voting in ethnic areas, they do not account for declines in turnout almost everywhere in the country. Another explanation for the decline was the realignment of political parties following the depression of the 1890s, the demise of Populism, and Bryan's presidential candidacy in 1896. These events shattered the Democratic party in many eastern and midwestern urban states.

Indeed, state politics at the time were less competitive than at any time in American history. Voters, left with little choice, may have become apathetic, perhaps even alienated, except concerning cultural and religious issues. But whatever the cause of this decline in turnout, it is clear that the progressive era, far from attracting Americans into an increasingly broad-based democratic system, witnessed the growing nonparticipation of millions. No other aspect of state politics revealed more clearly that "progressive" reforms failed to engage the masses.

The third sign that progressive reform had only a limited impact on state politics was what the political scientist Walter Dean Burnham has called the "withering away of the parties." Measures such as the secret ballot and registration laws discouraged massive efforts at recruitment, while the direct primary occasionally promoted the politics of personality or of "friends and neighbors" at the expense of organizational unity. To many progressives, who praised the "people" and denounced the machines, these were steps for the good. In fact, however, they contributed to the factionalization of American parties, to unpredictable shifts in party control, to short-lived coalitions of interest groups, to the deliberate blurring of economic and social programs, and perhaps to the decline in partisan loyalty and participation. In so doing they helped sustain the decentralization of parties at a time of rampant economic centralization and interest group consciousness, and to leave public power at a disadvantage against private power. Because America was a huge, sectionally divided, and ethnically diverse country, it is questionable whether the parties, which had to appeal to broad constituencies, could have developed otherwise. It is also not at all certain that the nation would have benefited from a splintering of parties along class, ethnic, or ideological lines. But it is clear that American parties were unable to implement the kind of coherent social programs occasionally being promoted at that time in western Europe.

The successes and failures of progressivism

Progressive reformism was remarkable because it lasted as long as it did—from approximately 1900 to 1920—and because it broadened as time passed. Progressive ideas captured sizeable segments of both parties by 1912 and culminated in "success" in many ways: settlement houses, social legislation, women's suffrage, the NAACP, prohibition, municipal reform, the popular election of senators, the direct primary, and regulatory commissions. Without these reforms, progressives thought, the imbalances of American capitalism could have led to serious class conflict, to socialism, to authoritarian government, or to other fundamental changes in American institutions.

In the process of fighting for these reforms many advanced progressives recognized that modern developments like the metropolis and the corporation had come to stay. They also realized that evangelical crusades or appeals to conscience could not reverse the imperatives of technology, industrialization, and urbanization. So these people counterorganized. They established professional associations and legislative lobbies, and they struggled for their own increasingly well defined objectives. Such self-interested "reform" helped prevent the activists from mounting a broadly humane progressive "movement." But their resorting to counterorganization and pressure groups represented practical ways of contending with forces that would otherwise have been beyond their control. And their emphasis on ideals of efficiency and rational administration, however elitist, presaged the future.

Their very successes reveal that these progressives worked within existing institutions. They let pragmatic tactics divert them from broader visions; they did not strive for fundamental social change—which usually involves social conflict—but for more modest alterations in the status quo. Many reformers therefore preferred moralizing or tinkering to planning for a more equitable system. Others displayed a fear, sometimes bordering on paranoia, of immigrants, blacks, and workers. It would take the depression to expose what they could hardly have been expected to recognize: that their modest reforms were considerably less significant in preventing social upheaval than was the steady, solid growth of the American economy.

Suggestions for reading

General interpretations of the progressive era include Arthur Ekrich, *Progressivism in America** (1974); William O'Neill, *The Progressive Years** (1975); John D. Buenker, *Urban Liberalism and Progressive Reform* (1973); and the books by Wiebe and Hays cited in the bibliography for chapter one. Gabriel Kolko, *The Triumph of Conservatism** (1963), focuses on the regulation of business during the period, while Albro Martin, *Enterprise Denied: Origins of the Decline of American Railroads, 1897–1917* (1971), offers a contrasting point of view. Richard Hofstadter's *Age of Reform** (1955) contains original comments on reform thought during the progressive era and afterwards. State studies that offer wide-ranging interpretations include David Thelen, *The New Citizenship, 1885–1900* (1972), which deals with Wisconsin; Richard Abrams, *Conservatism in a Progressive Era: Massachusetts Politics, 1900–1912* (1964); and Sheldon Hackney, *Populism to Progressivism in Alabama* (1969).

Among the books that cover trends in thought are Morton White's valuable *Social Thought in America: The Revolt Against Formalism** (1957); Eric Goldman's *Rendezvous with Destiny** (1952), Daniel Levine's brief *Varieties of Reform Thought** (1964); David Chalmers, *Social Ideas of the Muckrakers** (1964); Nathan G. Hales's *Freud and the Americans: The Beginnings of Psychoanalysis in America, 1876–1917* (1971); and Lawrence Cremin's pioneering *Transformation of the School: Progressivism in American Education, 1876–1956** (1961). On education see too Laurence Veysey, *The Emergence of the American University* (1970). Also important are Henry May, *The End of American Innocence, 1912–1917** (1959), which details the attack on the genteel tradition; William O'Neill, *Divorce in the Progressive Era* (1967); Donald K. Pickens, *Eugenics and the Progressives* (1968); Jack Holl, *Juvenile Reform in the Progressive Era* (1971); Charles Forcey, *Crossroads of Liberalism** (1961), on Walter Lippmann, Herbert Croly, and Walter Weyl; R. Jackson Wilson, *In Quest of Community: Social*

Philosophy in the United States, 1860–1920* (1970); and George Frederickson, *The Black Image in the White Mind, 1817–1914** (1971). Gilman Ostrander's *American Civilization in the First Machine Age, 1890–1940* (1970) interprets social and cultural developments.

Other important books dealing with aspects of the period are Roy Lubove, *The Progressives and the Slums: Tenement House Reform in New York City, 1890–1917* (1962), and *The Professional Altruist: The Emergence of Social Work as a Career, 1880–1930* (1965); Allen Davis, *Spearheads of Reform: The Social Settlements and the Progressive Movement, 1890–1914** (1967), and *American Heroine: Life and Legacy of Jane Addams** (1973). See also David F. Musto, *The American Disease* (1973), a study of efforts to control the use of narcotics, 1905–40; C. Roland Marchand, *The American Peace Movement and Social Reform, 1898–1918* (1973); Samuel Hays, *Conservation and the Gospel of Efficiency, 1890–1920** (1959); and James Timberlake, *Prohibition and the Progressive Movement, 1900–1920** (1963). Books dealing with urban reform and bossism include Melvin Holli, *Reform in Detroit** (1973); and Zane L. Miller, *Boss Cox's Cincinnati** (1968).

Trends in religious thought are covered in Henry May, *Protestant Churches and Industrial America* (1963); C. H. Hopkins, *The Rise of the Social Gospel in American Protestantism, 1865–1915* (1940); John T. Ellis, *American Catholicism** (2nd ed., 1969), a survey; and Nathan Glazer, *American Judaism** (rev. ed., 1972), also a survey. See especially William McLoughlin, *Modern Revivalism** (1959). Books dealing with militant labor include Howard Quint, *The Forging of American Socialism* (1964); Ray Ginger, *The Bending Cross** (1949), a biography of Eugene Debs; Melvyn Dubofsky, *We Shall Be All: A History of the Industrial Workers of the World** (1969); John Laslett, *Labor and the Left* (1970); Graham Adams, Jr., *Age of Industrial Violence, 1910–1915* (1971); David Shannon, *Socialist Party in America** (1967 ed.); Daniel Bell, *Marxian Socialism in the United States** (1952); and James Weinstein, *The Decline of Socialism in America, 1912–1925** (1967). John P. Diggins, *The American Left in the Twentieth Century** (1973), is excellent.

Books concerning the status of women and of feminism include William O'Neill, *Everyone Was Brave: The Rise and Fall of Feminism in America** (1969); Aileen Kraditor, *The Ideas of the Women's Suffrage Movement, 1890–1920* (1965); David Kennedy, *Birth Control in America: The Career of Margaret Sanger** (1970); and Lois Banner, *Women in Modern America** (1974), a readable survey of twentieth-century developments. See also John Sirjamki, *The American Family in the Twentieth Century* (1953). On black life and protest see Elliott Rudwick, *W. E. B. DuBois** (1969); B. Joyce Ross, *J. E. Spingarn and the Rise of the NAACP* (1972); Nancy Weiss, *The National Urban League, 1910–1940* (1974); Louis Harlan, *Booker T. Washington,* vol. 1 (1972), and August Meier, *Negro Thought in America, 1880–1915** (1963). Thorough studies of black life in the city are Gilbert Osofsky, *Harlem: Making of a Ghetto, 1890–1930** (1966); and Allan Spear, *Black Chicago: The Making of a Negro Ghetto, 1890–1920** (1967). The spread of discrimination by law in the South is described in C. Vann Woodward, *The Strange Career of Jim Crow** (rev. ed., 1974).

Important primary sources for the period are Upton Sinclair, *The Jungle** (1906); W. E. B. Du Bois, *Souls of Black Folk** (1903); Edgar Lee Masters, *Spoon River Anthology** (1915); John Dewey, *Child and the Curriculum* and *School and Society** (1899); Charlotte P. Gilman, *Women and Economics** (1898); William James, *Pragmatism and Other Essays** (1905); Edward Bellamy, *Looking Backward** (1888); and Henry George, *Progress and Poverty** (1879).

3

National politics

1900-1917

"It's easy enough to be President," naval hero George Dewey said in 1900. "All you have to do, I see, is take orders from Congress, and I have been taking orders all my life."

Dewey's image of a weak presidency mirrored Grover Cleveland's a few years earlier. "I shall keep right on doing executive work," Cleveland had said. "I did not come here to legislate." In 1900 President William McKinley handled official business by relying on only ten staff members, four of whom were doorkeepers or messengers. Cabinet departments such as Commerce, Labor, Transportation, HEW, and HUD were not yet established; nor were such agencies as the Federal Trade Commission, the Federal Communications Commission, the Federal Reserve, the Securities and Exchange Commission, and the Social Security Administration.

The small scale of the executive branch did not mean that the federal government was wholly powerless or that it pursued a philosophy of laissez faire. On the contrary, land grants and high tariffs had assisted entrepreneurs throughout the nineteenth century. Federal spending at the turn of the century—for internal improvements, defense, the post office, and other purposes—approximated $500 million annually. This was 3 percent of the Gross National Product, roughly the same percentage as in the mid-1920s.

These statistics do not alter the central fact that the federal government remained weak at the turn of the century. To the extent that Americans looked at all for public services, they turned to states and municipalities, which spent twice as much as Congress. Even during the Spanish-American War, soldiers identified themselves with their local units, not with the Regular Army, and newspapers concentrated on the actions of these local units to the virtual exclusion of political events in Washington. Few newspapers, indeed, bothered sending a correspondent to Washington before 1900, for they recognized that federal activity rarely affected ordinary citizens. As Cleveland had put it, "while the people should patriotically and cheerfully support their government, its functions do not include the support of the people."

Prior to the 1890s, few people had complained about this state of affairs. By 1900, however, many writers and politicians were arguing that the growth of private power threatened to overwhelm public authority. As the political scientist M. I. Ostrogorski said in 1902, "from one end of the scale to the other, the constitutional authorities are unequal to their duty; they prove incapable of ensuring the protection of the general interest. . . . The spring of government is weakened or warped everywhere."

Congress and the court

Those seeking to strengthen this "weakened spring" after 1900 had some advantages over earlier advocates of reform. One such advantage lay in the growth of federal employment. In 1861 there were 36,000 civilian federal employees, in 1900 almost 240,000, and in 1910, 389,000. Though most of these 389,000 were post office workers (210,000), or employees of navy yards and arsenals (59,000), the growth showed that government, like other large institutions, was already developing a bureaucracy that could consider national approaches to problems. A second advantage was the gradual spread of the merit system, which covered 222,000 of these employees by 1910. This merit system was a mixed blessing, for it protected bureaucrats who were impervious to popular pressures. It also tended to discriminate against lower-class applicants, who were at a competitive disadvantage in taking the civil service examinations. But elitist reformers welcomed these developments, for government could now rely on "experts" or at least on "nonpolitical" men and women presumed to be honest. In the absence of the merit system, it is doubtful that many Americans would have supported subsequent efforts of national reformers to expand federal activity.

Formidable obstacles to governmental effectiveness outweighed these advantages. These obstacles included the same barriers that had impeded progressive action on the state level: factionalized political parties, conflicting interest groups, and ethno-cultural divisions precluding the development of a mass base for social reform. National reformers had to confront two additional

Has Aldrich intellect? Perhaps. But he does not show it. He has never in his twenty-five years of service in the Senate introduced or advocated a measure that shows any conception of life above what might be expected in a Hungry Joe. No, intellect is not the characteristic of Aldrich—or of any of these traitors, or of the men they serve. A scurvy lot they are, are they not, with their smirking and cringing and voluble palaver about God and patriotism and their eager offerings of endowments for hospitals and colleges whenever the American people so much as looks hard in their direction!

A progressive view of Nelson Aldrich. By David Graham Phillips, "Aldrich, the Head of It All." *Cosmopolitan,* April, 1906.

institutions, Congress and the courts, which consistently resisted efforts for change.

One problem with Congress was leadership, which in 1900 meant "Uncle Joe" Cannon of Illinois in the House and Nelson Aldrich of Rhode Island in the Senate. Cannon had first entered Congress in 1873. By 1901, when he became speaker, he was a curt sixty-five-year-old whose villainous black cigars smeared his lips with tobacco shreds. Known as "foul-mouthed Joe," he made no pretense of sharing his power over committee assignments with proponents of change. "I am god-damned tired," he said, "of listening to all this babble for reform." Aldrich, more cultivated and sophisticated, owed his dominance in the Senate to considerable intellect and personal force. But to reformers, he was a plutocrat whose ties to big business were symbolized by his daughter's marriage in 1901 to John D. Rockefeller, Jr. As progressives realized, Aldrich was a Hamiltonian who championed firm ties between big business and government and an elitist who justified his dominance over the Senate by commenting, "Most people don't know what they want."

As the tide of progressivism advanced, new faces appeared to challenge the almost absolute power that men like Cannon and Aldrich enjoyed in the early 1900s. In the Senate these included men like La Follette of Wisconsin and Albert Beveridge of Indiana. In the House they were led by George Norris of Nebraska, who staged a revolt in 1910, stripping Cannon of his power over committee assignments. By 1913 these "insurgents" were strong enough to give President Woodrow Wilson important backing. Many of them (like Norris, who served as a senator from 1913 to 1943) remained forceful and widely admired progressives for decades thereafter.

The growing strength of these congressional progressives attracted considerable attention from reporters and historians, who reflected the American tendency to personalize politics. Get heroic reformers in office, they implied, and change will occur. But voters and state legislatures never sent more than a small minority of insurgents to Congress. Moreover, the insurgents rarely formed a cohesive bloc. This failure to coalesce stemmed in part from the highly individualistic personalities of men like La Follette, and in part from

> *From the time in earliest records, when Eve took loving possession of even the forbidden apple, the idea of property and the sacredness of the right of its possession has never departed from the race. Whatever dreams may exist of an ideal human nature . . . actual human experience, from the dawn of history to the present hour, declares that the love of acquirement, mingled with the joy of possession, is the real stimulus to human activity. When, among the affirmatives of the Declaration of Independence, it is asserted that the pursuit of happiness is one of the unalienable rights, it is meant that the acquisition, possession and enjoyment of property are matters which human government cannot forbid. . . .*
>
> Justice Brewer, address entitled "Protection to Private Property from Public Attack," 1891.

local pressures: Congressmen who hope to stay in office must listen to constituents. Given America's diversity of interests and regions, it is not surprising that progressives broke apart on key sectional issues like the tariff. From this perspective Congress was not the reactionary villain that reformist writers described, but simply the political institution most vulnerable before pressure groups.

In this way Congress could claim to be responsive—at least to those who were well organized. The judges of the Supreme Court, however, could not, for they were lifetime appointees free to rule as they wished. To the despair of reformers they chose to echo conservative theorists like Thomas M. Cooley and Supreme Court justices like Stephen Field and David Brewer. Cooley, the dominant legal scholar of the late nineteenth century, argued that the Constitution was intended to protect private property, that it must be interpreted literally, and that reform had to come from amendments, not from legislatures or courts. "What a court is to do," he wrote, "is to declare the law as written, leaving it to the people themselves to make such changes as circumstances may require." Field, the high priest of rugged individualism, opposed almost all governmental efforts to improve the social welfare. "Protection to property and to persons cannot be separated," he said in 1890. " . . . Protection to the one goes with the other; and there can be neither prosperity nor progress where either is uncertain."

Apologists such as these usually invoked hallowed documents like the Declaration of Independence or dogmas like laissez faire. In fact, however, men like Field were working consciously for business interests. Between 1890 and 1896 the high court struck down much state regulatory legislation (*Chicago Milwaukee and St. Paul Railway Co.* v. *Minnesota*, 1890), it temporarily undermined the Sherman Anti-Trust Act (*E. C. Knight* case, 1895), it sanctioned the separate but equal doctrine of race relations (*Plessy* v. *Ferguson*, 1896), and it overturned a progressive federal income tax (*Pollack* v. *Farm-*

ers' Loan and Trust Co., 1895). Field cast the deciding vote against the income tax by intoning that "the present assault upon capital is but the beginning. It will be but the stepping stone to others, larger and more sweeping, until our political contests will become a war of the poor against the rich; a war constantly growing in intensity and bitterness."

After 1900 the court generally avoided such blatant statements of personal preference. In 1904 (*Northern Securities* case) it began to resurrect the antitrust law and in 1908 (*Muller* v. *Oregon*), sustained a state law setting maximum working hours for women. But it still overturned state minimum wage laws and national child labor acts, and it persisted in regarding labor unions as illegal combinations in restraint of trade. In this way the court, like Congress, forced reformers to move slowly. It also led them to turn to the presidency as the only hope for change—and to lavish affection on the one man who personified the future. That man was Theodore Roosevelt, who assumed the presidency on the assassination of William McKinley in September, 1901.

Enter Theodore Roosevelt

In retrospect it is not altogether easy to understand why so many progressive Americans made Theodore Roosevelt their hero. Born to a patrician family from New York in 1858, he had been educated at Harvard, served as a regular Republican assemblyman in the 1880s, and advanced in the 1890s to become a civil service commissioner, the police commissioner of New York City, assistant secretary of the navy, hero of the Rough Riders in Cuba, governor of New York, and finally, vice-president. His career to that point, while distinguished, hardly revealed him as a forceful social reformer, and during the turbulent 90s he had echoed the militance of men of his class. He said, "I like to see a mob handled by the regulars, or by good State-Guards, not overscrupulous about bloodshed."

This lust for combat was rather frightening. "Every man who has in him any real power of joy in battle," he said, "knows that he feels it when the wolf begins to rise in his heart; he does not then shrink from blood or sweat, or deem that they mar the fight; he revels in them, in the toil, the pain, and the danger, as but setting off the triumph." During the Spanish-American War, when he galloped through a hail of bullets to capture San Juan Hill, he proudly wrote his friend Henry Cabot Lodge, "I killed a Spaniard with my own hand." Four years later he explained that he was "not in the least bit sensitive about killing any number of men if there is an adequate reason." For him as well as for many Americans the war was a test of character, and killing a patriotic necessity.

Roosevelt was an equally fierce moralist. What mattered in life, he said in urging the wellborn to have large families, were the "strong and tender virtues of a family life based on the love of one man for one woman and on their joyous and fearless acceptance of their common obligation toward their children.'' While president he overrode existing law to deny readmittance to the United States of a citizen who had traveled to Canada with a woman not his wife. He told the Boy Scouts, "Don't flinch, don't foul, hit the line hard.'' And he preached repeatedly the necessity of fair play, especially in college football, then a savage sport (it killed eighteen young men in 1905). "Brutality and foul play," he thundered, "should receive the same summary treatment given to a man who cheats at cards.'' The presidency, he believed, was a "bully pulpit," and he made the most of it.

This impulsive activism in the cause of righteousness provoked negative reactions among many contemporaries. Mark Hanna, the Republican party's dominant political boss, referred to him as "that damned cowboy." When the GOP nominated TR vice-president in 1900, Hanna wrote his friend McKinley that "your *duty* to the Country is to live for four years from next March." Even Roosevelt's admirers had to laugh at their hero's activities. "You must remember that the President is about six," one of them wrote. Elihu Root, soon to be Roosevelt's secretary of state, told him on his forty-sixth birthday in 1904, "you have made a very good start in life, and your friends have great hopes for you when you grow up."

Yet no one denied that Roosevelt cut a colorful figure. While police commissioner he occasionally sallied late at night—dressed in pink shirt and silk sash—into the worst sections of the city to check on his subordinates. At San Juan Hill he wore a sombrero with a blue polka-dot kerchief fluttering in the breeze. As a crusader against vice in New York and as an authentic war hero he was a man whom party chieftains like Hanna could hardly ignore.

His crusades for family, home, and country were as reassuring as they were entertaining. These were traditional, conserving virtues, not assaults on the established order. If part of Roosevelt's appeal lay in his color, much of it stemmed from his ability to appear as crusader and moral conservator at the same time. To the progressive William Allen White, Roosevelt was "reform in a derby, the gayest, cockiest, most fashionable derby you ever saw," and for young Walter Lippmann, he was "the image of the great leader and the prototype of Presidents." White and Lippmann spoke for thousands of contemporaries for whom TR ever remained a figure of heroic proportions.

ROOSEVELT AS PROGRESSIVE

One image of Roosevelt's seven and a half years in office can never be blotted out. It shows a toothy, swashbuckling TR, America's youngest president, slashing away at the corporations, conserving natural resources, and prodding Congress toward reform.

Like many stereotypes, that one was accurate in part. Though he moved slowly at first, he alarmed big businessmen in 1902 by instituting antitrust proceedings against the Northern Securities Company, J. P. Morgan's railroad

ROOSEVELT:— YOU'LL HAVE TO BE CAREFUL UNCLE. IT'S GETTING MIGHTY THIN ON TOP.

Conservation Tonic.

combine. Three months later he infuriated reactionaries during a bitter anthracite coal strike by threatening to dispatch troops and dispossess the owners if they refused to agree to arbitration. His threat worked and the union eventually won a modest victory. That year he also helped secure passage of the Newlands Act, an important conservation measure that set aside federal funds from the sale of public lands for reclamation purposes in the West. In 1903 he persuaded Congress to establish a Bureau of Corporations to gather information about business, and to approve the Elkins law prohibiting railroad rebates.

Reelected easily in 1904, over Democratic candidate Alton B. Parker, Roosevelt strayed still further from the path of his predecessor. In his second term he instituted antitrust suits against Standard Oil and the American Tobacco Company; he secured passage of the Hepburn Act providing for limited regulation of railroads; and he signed into law the Pure Food and Drug, and Meat Inspection acts. By executive order he appointed an Inland Waterways Commission, which drew up plans for multipurpose river development, and he named the conservationist Gifford Pinchot head of a new Forest Service. He also increased the total acreage of timber and forest reserves from 45 to 195 million acres. At the end of his second term he publicly favored stiff inheritance and income taxes on the wealthy, the regulation of railroad securities, strict limits on antilabor injunctions, and extension of the eight-hour day and workmen's compensation.

Roosevelt's economic philosophy reflected this movement from moderation toward progressive causes. In 1902, when he called in the coal operators, he had had no idea of promoting unionism; rather he felt he had to stop the strike before it paralyzed the country. And in 1904, when he proclaimed a Square Deal for all people, he spoke as a conservative animated by fears of potential class war. "It would be a dreadful thing," he wrote, "if we saw this country divided into two parties, one containing the bulk of the property owners and conservative people, the other the bulk of the wageworkers and the less prosperous people generally. . . . The friends of property, of order, of law . . . must realize that the surest way to provoke an explosion of wrong and injustice is to be shortsighted, narrow-minded, greedy, and arrogant."

By 1908 Roosevelt had moved to the left. He spoke of "certain malefactors of great wealth," referred to himself as a "radical," and lambasted the "speculative folly and flagrant dishonesty of a few men of great wealth." In 1910 he added, "I stand for the square deal, but when I say that I am for the square deal, I mean not merely that I stand for fair play under the present rules of the game, but that I stand for having those rules changed so as to work for a more substantial equality of opportunity and of reward for equally good service." The means to this end he called the New Nationalism, which would "put the national need before sectional or personal advantage" and would make the "executive power the steward of the public welfare." In pursuing this course Roosevelt supported social welfare programs, including minimum wages for women, that he would have scorned a few years earlier. His move to the left, which parallelled that of the voters, did not make him an advocate of a welfare state, but it left him a proponent of an activist federal government, of a modern presidency, and of social reform.

He also developed a thoughtful position on the dominant issue of the day: control of the trusts. Unlike some other progressive politicians, who struck out against monopolies, Roosevelt regarded centralization as a fact of modern economic life. "This is an age of combination," he said in 1905, "and any effort to prevent all combination will not only be useless, but in the end vicious, because of the contempt for law which the failure to enforce law inevitably produces." Not entirely consistent, Roosevelt used the Sherman act forty-four times against corporations. But he placed more faith in regulatory measures such as the Hepburn Act, and he tried to "bust" only those few monopolies that struck him as immoral and unreasonable in their restraint of trade. This distinction between "good" and "bad" trusts (adopted by the Supreme Court in 1911) was characteristic of his moralistic approach to problems. It tended also to leave corporations (and their critics) at the mercy of the "dead hand" of judges and officials, who later changed standards of right and wrong. Still, Roosevelt's awareness that the federal government had to become a countervailing power marked him as a more flexible thinker than many nostalgic opponents of bigness in any form.

THE LEGACY OF TR

If Roosevelt was such a spirited and realistic progressive, why did many reformers find him unsatisfactory? La Follette, for instance, complained that Roosevelt tried to appeal to all, satisfying none. TR's "cannonading," La Follette said, " . . . filled the air with noise and smoke, which confused and obscured the line of action, but, when the battle cloud drifted by and the quiet was restored, it was always a matter of surprise that so little had really been accomplished." Ray Stannard Baker, a perceptive journalist, concluded later that Roosevelt had "wholesome enthusiasms," but that he "ran full-speed on all the tracks at once. Too often he rode down opposition without understanding what it meant, or talked it down with a torrent of phrases."

La Follette and Baker spoke as political enemies of Theodore Roosevelt. Yet they were correct in saying that Roosevelt was less of a reformer than he sounded. Aware of congressional hostility, he did not move to lower the tariff and did nothing, despite the financial panic of 1907, to regulate banking. He stood by while Colorado authorities crushed the Western Federation of Miners in 1904. In 1905, angered by unsubstantiated reports that Negro soldiers had killed a man in Brownsville, Texas, he ordered the blanket discharge from the service of 160 blacks, 6 of whom had won the medal of honor. This command did not mean that he was a "racist," for he was more sensitive to the plight of minorities than many people at that time. But it did reveal his moralistic determination to punish wrongdoing as he saw it.

Critics like La Follette also noted accurately that Roosevelt remained on excellent terms with the "standpat" leaders of his party and with corporate leaders. In his 1904 campaign he received nearly $2 million from big businessmen, including $150,000 from Morgan and $100,000 from two top officials of Standard Oil. To get Morgan's help during the panic of 1907 he personally approved a deal whereby U. S. Steel secured control of the Tennessee Coal and Iron Company, one of its potentially most damaging competitors. In 1912, while he was campaigning for the presidency as a Progressive, Wall Street "welfare capitalists" served him as top advisors.

TR's detractors also pointed to the questionable "progressivism" of his legislative accomplishments. The Elkins Act regulating rebates was intended to cut costs of railroads, not to assist the public. In practice the law was easily evaded. Partly because of congressional resistance, the Pure Food and Drug Act failed to regulate patent medicines, the sale of adulterated food, or false advertising. It, too, was ignored or abused. The Meat Inspection Act stemmed in part from the demands of the major packers, who recognized that such a law could restrain their smaller competitors. "It is a wise law," Swift and Company said in large ads. "Its enforcement must be universal and uniform." The Newlands Act, ostensibly a "progressive" conservation measure, did most for western land interests, whose overrepresentation in the Senate could not be ignored. The Hepburn Act, Roosevelt's most impressive legislative achievement, permitted the ICC to set rates on complaint of shippers—an important step—but it failed to authorize the physical evaluation of railroads, and it left ICC rates subject to review by the courts. The act reflected the pressure on Congress of shippers, who benefited from ICC decisions.

Roosevelt's expansion of presidential power was also a mixed blessing. His executive action setting aside forest reserves, for instance, rested on ample statutory authority, but it also directly challenged the majority will of Congress. Should American presidents command such power? More generally, Roosevelt's activism encouraged Americans to depend on charismatic presidential leadership. Would reform have been served better by changes in the constituent basis of representation, by efforts to diminish the obstructive potential of the states, or by amendments to curb the jurisdiction of the courts? These are largely unanswerable questions. Moreover, such changes did not have much chance of adoption at the time. But it is true that Roosevelt did more than any other person to institutionalize the modern presidency, and that reformers ever since have tended to place exaggerated reliance on the magic of 1600 Pennsylvania Avenue.

But these criticisms of Roosevelt tend to exaggerate his freedom to act. He never enjoyed a progressive majority in Congress, and he had to deal with a largely conservative Republican party. Had he tried to promote tariff revision or banking reform, he would have succeeded only in alienating people. If he had insisted on a stronger Hepburn or Pure Food and Drug act, he would have emerged with no bills at all. Had he promoted welfare legislation, he would have been out of touch with his times. If he had not elevated the presidency, he would have had to acquiesce in the whims of a nonprogressive Congress and Court. Roosevelt, neither radical nor idealist, worked within the system rather than tilting against it.

Moreover, Roosevelt stood for more than preserving the status quo. He sought not only to maintain capitalism but to humanize it. He worked to increase executive power in part because he wished to harness it to change. He offered reformers flexible yet purposeful leadership, and he showed that the federal government would try to deal with industrialization. In so doing he helped to preserve the faith of influential Americans in democratic government and in capitalism. These were no mean achievements.

William Howard Taft

Roosevelt's successor, William Howard Taft, was one of the best-trained presidents in American political history. Number two in his class at Yale, he had received a law degree in his native Cincinnati and then progressed rapidly: solicitor general under President Benjamin Harrison, federal judge, high commissioner in the Philippines, and Roosevelt's secretary of war. Though immensely fat (sometimes more than 300 pounds), he was neither lazy nor slow. He had a quick, well-honed, and deeply conventional mind. La Follette, not given to excessive praise of his contemporaries, agreed in 1909 that Taft was "able, balanced, tactful, forceful . . . an honest and honorable man who regards a promise as sacred and a pledge as a bond."

Roosevelt, who handpicked Taft as his successor, emphatically concurred. "Things will be all right," he assured people when he took vacations from

Jovial William Howard Taft.

Pennsylvania Avenue. "I have left Taft sitting on the lid." He told Taft, "I do not believe that you will ever quite understand what strength and comfort and help you are to me." Taft reciprocated these warm feelings. He told reporters in 1907 that TR's views "were mine before I ever knew Mr. Roosevelt at all." A few weeks after being inaugurated in 1909 Taft wrote his predecessor as "Mr. President." "When I am addressed as Mr. President," he explained, "I turn to see whether you are not at my elbow. . . . I do nothing in the Executive Office without considering what you would do under the circumstances."

Less than two years later these two best of friends had broken apart. Roosevelt complained in 1910 that Taft was a "well-meaning, good-natured man, an excellent judge . . . but not a leader." During the acrimonious campaign of 1912 he was more blunt, calling Taft a "puzzle-wit," a "fathead," a man guilty of "naked fraud, of naked theft from the people." Taft, though less combative, accepted the challenge. "I do not want to fight," he said, "but when I do fight, I want to hit hard. Even a rat in a corner will fight." The struggle between the two men racked the Republican party and elected Woodrow Wilson president.

In part the breech was caused by differing ideas about how one should govern. Where Roosevelt was an activist, Taft was reflective and judicious, a strict constructionist concerning the separation of powers. "I have no disposition to exert any other influence than that which it is my function under the Constitution to exercise," he assured Aldrich. Taft added that he did not care for politics. "I don't like the limelight," he complained. He remarked as president-elect that he felt "just a bit like a fish out of water." He also assumed that he could function successfully as an administrator. "My sin," he confessed, "is . . . a disposition to procrastinate." By late 1910 this restrictive concept of the presidency was antagonizing progressives.

Roosevelt, still only fifty years old early in 1909, grew restive on the sidelines. He was ambitious for himself, for his loyal supporters, and for his ideas. As he turned to the left after 1909 he applauded some of Taft's moderately progressive policies, which included legislation regulating safety in mines and railroads, support of the amendment (ratified in 1913) legalizing income taxes, establishment of a Children's Bureau, passage of a law providing for employer liability in work done under government contracts, and the Mann-Elkins Act of 1910 increasing the ICC's power over railroads. But Roosevelt also recognized that Taft was unwilling to go further. "The chief function of the next administration," Taft said in 1909, "is to complete and perfect the machinery." It was Taft's misfortune to be president during a time when many reformers, accustomed to dynamic leadership, pressed for more substantial legislation, when they increased their numbers in Congress, and when their youthful hero yearned to return to the helm.

The first of many controversies that widened the break was the tariff. Roosevelt had understood that pressure from constituent interests always forced congressmen to raise rather than lower duties, and he wisely avoided the issue. But Taft, plunging earnestly ahead, called a special session in 1909 to revise the existing high rates. The result was predictable: the so-called Payne-Aldrich Tariff, which increased duties to new highs. As Taft recognized, the tariff fight of 1909 hardly exposed a clear-cut split between progressives and conservatives, for men like La Follette voted for higher duties on foreign goods competing with home-state products. Still, the insurgents complained accurately that the tariff would increase the already ascending cost of living, and that Taft had not exerted much influence on moderates in order to secure a better bill. When Taft defensively praised the act as the "best tariff bill that the Republican party has ever passed," they were incensed.

The tariff fight convinced progressives that Taft was joining forces with the standpat wing of the party. They were right. Though he initially distrusted Aldrich, he grew close to him during the long special session, and by 1910 called him a "good friend." Though he encouraged insurgents to think he would struggle against Cannon, whom he found "dirty and vulgar," he backed off when he felt he needed the votes of Cannon and his friends for tariff revision. After 1910, when Norris's insurgents stripped Cannon of his power to make committee assignments, they were bitter at the President, whom they owed nothing. Taft, meanwhile, grumbled that the insurgents were "yelping and snarling," "rather forward," and "pretty stupid."

Taft's views on control of trusts added to his growing estrangement from Roosevelt. "We must get back to competition," Taft said. The Sherman Act was a "good law that ought to be enforced, and I propose to enforce it." This social Darwinian faith in competition led him to institute more antitrust suits in four years than Roosevelt had in seven and a half. But his approach repudiated Roosevelt's faith in regulatory action and brought him directly into conflict with TR's New Nationalism, which Taft termed full of "wild ideas." His suit in 1911 against U. S. Steel particularly infuriated TR, who perceived the action as a politically motivated effort to publicize U. S. Steel's acquisition in 1907 of the Tennessee Coal and Iron Company. "To attempt to meet the whole problem by a succession of lawsuits," Roosevelt insisted, "is hopeless. . . . It is practically impossible to break up all combinations merely because they are large and successful and to put the business of the country back into the middle of the nineteenth century."

THE BALLINGER-PINCHOT CONTROVERSY

The most rancorous cause of Taft's break with progressives was the Ballinger-Pinchot controversy, which plagued his administration throughout late 1909 and 1910. This stemmed from charges by chief forester Gifford Pinchot, America's leading conservationist, that Richard Ballinger, Taft's secretary of the interior, had previously conspired to turn over Alaskan coal fields to a syndicate including Morgan interests. On carefully reviewing these charges Taft sided with Ballinger. But Pinchot (whom Taft regarded as a "radical and a crank") continued his attack by publicly accusing the administration of opposing conservation. Taft then had no choice but to fire Pinchot for insubordination. In the protracted hearings that followed, Taft loyalists in Congress exonerated Ballinger of fraud. But insurgents—and perhaps the majority of the country—sided with Pinchot, Roosevelt's good friend and the symbol of conservation.

The issue was not nearly so clear-cut as the insurgents believed. No enemy of conservation, Taft appointed a friend of Pinchot to replace Ballinger, and he used his executive power to remove more public land from private use than Roosevelt had done in a comparable period of time. Moreover, the line between Ballinger and Pinchot was thinner than many people realized. Ballinger, like many westerners, sided with settlers and entrepreneurs who wished to develop, not preserve, the land. But Pinchot, too, opposed simple preservation. Like Ballinger, he wanted valuable acreage developed, and as chief forester he permitted grazing and lumbering on government property (which he appropriately named "national forests" instead of "forest reserves"). Indeed, ardent preservationists like John Muir, founder of the Sierra Club, vainly fought the attempt of Pinchot and others to transform the beautiful Hetch Hetchy Valley in California into a reservoir for San Francisco. Muir and his friends, Pinchot snapped, were "nature lovers."

Yet Pinchot was correct in arguing that men like Ballinger favored a more "conservative" approach. For Pinchot wanted the federal government to manage national resources, while Ballinger preferred free-wheeling private development or state supervision. In this way Pinchot appealed to the anti-corporate emotions of many progressives and to the growing passion among the urban middle classes for outdoor recreation and the "strenuous life." His thinking also reflected the desire of many eastern progressives for efficient, "scientific," direction of national policy. The thrust of this argument showed that national progressives were moving far toward calling for the modern administrative state.

We have become great because of the lavish use of our resources and we have just reason to be proud of our growth. But the time has come to inquire seriously what will happen when our forests are gone, when the coal, the iron, the oil, and the gas are exhausted, when the soils shall have been still further impoverished and washed into the streams, polluting the rivers, denuding the fields, and obstructing navigation. These questions do not relate only to the next century or to the next generation. It is time for us now as a nation to exercise the same reasonable foresight in dealing with our great natural resources that would be shown by any prudent man in conserving and wisely using the property which contains the assurance of well-being for himself and his children.

Conservation as a means to promote national growth and greatness. Roosevelt, 1908.

The Ballinger-Pinchot controversy symbolized the formidable pressures besetting Taft's presidency. Judicious and legalistic, he had supported a subordinate whom Pinchot had determined to destroy. But in doing so he assisted opponents who used the appeal of conservation to brand him as a reactionary. More broadly, he encountered progressivism as it was rushing to full tide. Trite as it sounds, he was caught in a revolution of rising expectations, and was therefore the wrong man for his times.

Woodrow Wilson

By mid-1912 Taft admitted mournfully that he would be overwhelmed in his bid for reelection. "I think I might as well give up so far as being a candidate is concerned," he wrote his wife in July. "There are so many people in the country who don't like me." Though he stayed in the race, he anticipated that either Roosevelt, who stormed out of the GOP convention to head the new Progressive party, or the Democratic candidate, Woodrow Wilson, would win.

Roosevelt's campaign stirred his supporters to evangelical enthusiasm. One newspaper described a convention of Progressives as an "assemblage of religious enthusiasts. It was such a convention as Peter the Hermit had. It was a Methodist camp meeting done over into political terms." Wherever Roosevelt appeared, his backers sang hymns of praise.

> Follow, follow, we will follow Roosevelt
> Anywhere, everywhere, we will follow him.

Or:

> Thou will not cower in the dust,
> Roosevelt, O Roosevelt!
> They gleaming sword shall never rust
> Roosevelt, O Roosevelt!

TR, proclaiming himself fit as a "bull moose," did not disappoint his admirers. When shot in the chest during a speech in October, he brushed aside attempts to provide medical help and proclaimed, "I will make this speech or die. It is one thing or the other." The wound proved superficial, and he later resumed campaigning. His speeches also offered progressives the most advanced ideas of the day. Roosevelt supported women's suffrage, the direct election of senators, the initiative, referendum, and recall, a corrupt practices act, minimum wages for women, the prohibition of child labor. the eight-hour day, the abolition of the convict labor system, and the "national regulation of interstate corporations" by a "strong Federal administrative commission." He also favored the recall of judicial decisions in cases where state courts declared laws unconstitutional. His platform attracted most progressive social workers, including Jane Addams, to his side, and it terrified conservatives. *The New York Times* (which backed Wilson) said that TR preached "Socialism and Revolution, contempt for law, and doctrines that lead to destruction." The Louisville *Courier-Journal* commented, "more than ever [we] are sure of his insanity. If he be not of disordered mind, the record would show him a monster of depravity and turpitude."

In contrast to Roosevelt's "radicalism," Wilson's credentials as a reformer seemed fairly good by 1912. The son of a southern Presbyterian minister, he had graduated from Princeton and attended law school before turning to academic life. He then moved rapidly ahead, as a scholar in the field of political science, as a dynamic president of Princeton, and as the reformist governor of New Jersey in 1911 and 1912. He owed his presidential nomination to the enthusiastic support of most progressive Democrats, including Bryan.

Actually, however, Wilson's progressivism had been mild until 1909. In the 1890s he had supported the conservative Grover Cleveland, and in 1907 he had denounced "radicals" like Bryan, whom he wished to knock "into a cocked hat." In 1908 he explained that change is slow, that "living political constitutions must be Darwinian in structure and in practice." His voluminous

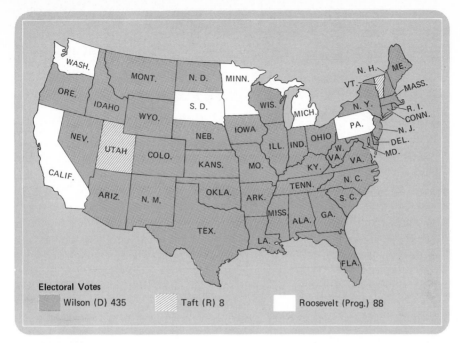

Electoral Votes
Wilson (D) 435   Taft (R) 8   Roosevelt (Prog.) 88

Election, 1912

writings on American history heaped scorn on recent immigrants (whom he called "the more sordid and hapless elements of the population"), and opposed the growth of Federal activity. "We must be careful," he said in 1906, "not to depend too much upon the federal government or turn too often from the remedy which is at hand in the power of the states."

By 1912 he appeared to have moved appreciably beyond such Jeffersonian beliefs about government. "The service rendered the people by the national government," he said, "must be of a more extended sort and of a kind not only to protect it against monopoly, but also to facilitate its life." But he remained less of a social reformer than Roosevelt, and his speeches on control of trusts, a central issue of the campaign, resembled Taft's. The way to prevent monopoly, he said, was to improve the antitrust laws, not to depend on regulatory commissions. Wilson did not oppose bigness per se, but like Taft he believed that fair competition preserved the entrepreneurial spirit that made America great. "What this country needs above everything else," he said, "is a body of laws which will look after the men who are on the make rather than the men who are already made."

This New Freedom, as Wilson called it, did not mean that TR was more "radical." Under the influence of Louis Brandeis, a key adviser in the last months of the campaign, Wilson became an extremely harsh critic of corporate leaders, many of whom supported TR. Still, his stand on trusts showed that he placed rather exaggerated faith in the ability of antitrust laws and the willingness of judges to reduce corporate concentration. Wilson's view, TR explained, was "outworn academic doctrine which was kept in the schoolroom and the professorial study for a generation after it had been abandoned by all who had experience of actual life."

Roosevelt's criticisms availed him nothing. Wilson proved an energetic campaigner and powerful orator. He also benefited from the rising cost of living, which Democrats blamed on the GOP tariff, and from a trend toward Democratic majorities that had appeared in urban areas since 1906 (probably as a reaction of many working people and immigrants against Republican support of prohibition). He capitalized especially on the division within the Republican party. In November he won easily, getting 6,296,547 votes to Roosevelt's 4,118,571, carrying the electoral college by a margin of 435 to 88, and creating Democratic margins over Republicans in Congress of 291 to 127, and 51 to 44. Taft, forgotten man of the campaign, received but 3,486,720 votes and 8 electoral votes, while Eugene Debs got 900,672 votes. The election ultimately destroyed the Progressives, who moved either to the Democrats or back to the GOP by 1916. It also showed that support for progressive candidates was overwhelming. More than TR or Taft, Woodrow Wilson came to office with a mandate for action.

Taft and Wilson on the way to Wilson's inauguration, 1913.

WILSON'S DOMESTIC PROGRAM

Eight years later when a sick and discredited Wilson left the presidency, it became almost fashionable to deride him as a priggish, self-righteous rhetorician. Abraham Flexner, an educational and medical reformer, complained that Wilson fell in love with phrase-making: "The man cannot pass an ink bottle without sitting down to pen a note." John Maynard Keynes, the English economist, called him a "blind and deaf Don Quixote." And H. L. Mencken, master of hyperbole, dismissed Wilson as a "self-bamboozled Presbyterian, the right-thinker, the great moral statesman, the perfect model of the Christian cad."

These criticisms captured one side of the new president, who had already proved so stubborn during his last years at Princeton that the university's trustees were happy to see him leave. But such criticisms overlooked his flexible direction of domestic policy between 1913 and 1916. Like Roosevelt, he had an expansive conception of the presidency. He distributed patronage effectively, compromised when he had to, and appealed eloquently to the people in support of his programs. During these four years Congress turned out more significant legislation than it had in the almost twelve years of Roosevelt and Taft.

Three major laws headed this list of legislative achievements. The first, the Underwood-Simmons Tariff of 1913, decreased *ad valorem* duties from 40 percent to between 24 percent and 26 percent and placed on or near the free list such key products as agricultural machinery, wool, sugar, shoes, iron, steel, and steel products. Taking advantage of the Sixteenth Amendment (1913), which made lawful an income tax, it also imposed a surtax on incomes ranging up to 6 percent. The second, a banking bill signed in December 1913, established twelve Federal Reserve banks regulated by a central board in Washington. This reform, Wilson's most impressive monument, was aimed at bringing some central direction to monetary policy, hitherto reserved to private bankers. The third major reform, the Federal Trace Commission, approved in 1914, attempted to give the government the same regulatory control over corporations that the ICC had over railroads.

In achieving these laws Wilson showed that he had an open, highly flexible mind. On the banking question he at first endorsed a decentralized plan that would have given the government little control over currency. When progressives complained, he reversed himself to call for a tougher bill, though one that still left bankers in control of important decisions about monetary policy. He also acceded to demands by agrarian radicals for an amendment authorizing the discounting by reserve banks of short-term agricultural paper—a measure that provided farmers with much-needed credit. Though eastern banking interests rebelled, Wilson stood firm, gathered support from businessmen, and secured a much stronger measure than he had dreamed of at the start of the battle. The final act needed substantial toughening in the 1930s, but it at least made a start toward depriving men like J. P. Morgan of their vast control over the American economy.

His turnabout on the trust issue was more startling. At first he supported the so-called Clayton bill, a measure prohibiting interlocking directorates and specifying unfair trade practices. Its central purpose, to toughen the Sherman law, closely followed his New Freedom philosophy. But he was persuaded by Brandeis in 1914 to make regulatory commissions the major line of offense against the trusts. To the dismay of the antimonopolistic progressives he dropped interest in the Clayton bill (which ultimately passed in weakened form) and supported a measure providing for a Federal Trade Commission. When Wilson signed the commission bill in late 1914, he formalized his acceptance of the New Nationalist philosophy he had denounced less than two years earlier.

Wilson's ability to shift ground manifested itself again in 1916, when, with a difficult campaign ahead against GOP candidate Charles Evans Hughes, previously a reform governor of New York, he moved to attract Progressives to the Democratic party. First, he named Louis Brandeis to the Supreme Court. He then advocated several measures he had resisted during the first two years in the White House. These included a bill banning the shipment in interstate commerce of goods made or mined by child labor; a rural credits act providing government capital to federal farm loan banks; and a workmen's compensation bill for federal employees. Faced with a railroad strike, he signed the Adamson Act establishing an eight-hour day for railway workers. Such direct governmental control over labor conditions provided a precedent for New Deal legislation two decades later. Congress also passed a Federal Highway Act authorizing matching money to states for road building, and a Revenue Act (aimed primarily at raising money for defense), which raised maximum surtaxes on incomes to 15 percent. This burst of progressive legislation in 1916 showed that Wilson had moved appreciably toward accepting federal control of American economic life. By November 1916, he stood as the almost unchallenged leader of an ethnic-worker-farmer coalition that was developing within the Democratic party.

AN EVALUATION OF WILSON

Wilson's legislative accomplishments, while impressive, did not satisfy many advanced progressives. The banking act left the reserve banks in private hands and failed to give the central board power to set discount rates. Distressed, La Follette and many other congressmen opposed it. The FTC was potent enough on paper, but it became the virtual captive of large corporate interests, in part because the Supreme Court clipped its effectiveness, in part because Wilson himself named conservative appointees to the commission. After 1914 Wilson proved more accommodating to consolidation and to financial interests than Taft or Roosevelt had been.

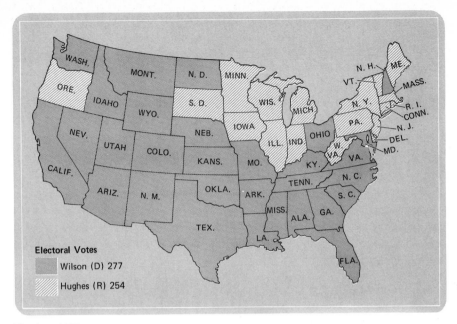

Electoral Votes

Wilson (D) 277

Hughes (R) 254

Election, 1916

Insurgents also perceived accurately that Wilson's flexibility stemmed from lack of profound conviction and from political calculation. Unlike many progressive congressmen, Wilson in 1914 considered his program completed. But sharp setbacks in the off-year elections and the prospect of defeat in 1916 gradually persuaded him that he had to move to the left or face defections from the labor and social justice wings of his party. His experience indicates that the pressures of party and of Congress were as important to the success of legislation as was dynamic presidential leadership—that the executive branch had no monopoly on "reform." It reveals that Wilson, unlike Taft or Roosevelt, was lucky in having responsive Congresses that were ordinarily to his left.

The nature of the legislation passed in these years shows also that Wilson was as much a sectional as a national leader. The income tax pleased agrarians who hoped it would lighten the burden of taxes on land. The Underwood-Simmons Tariff assisted the South and the West by placing agricultural machinery and various finished goods on the free list. The enactment of rural credits, the highway law, and the Smith-Lever Act of 1914 (which authorized federal grants to states for agricultural extension work) were aimed at gratifying the southern and western wings of the Democratic party. All these measures were "progressive" in the sense that they expanded the role of the federal government. But they also illustrated clearly the growing power of organized pressure groups in Congress.

Wilson showed many blind spots. Having assured the activists in 1912 that he favored women's suffrage, he refused to support it during his first term. The party as a whole, he argued disingenuously, opposed it. Though he vetoed nativist bills establishing literacy tests for immigrants, he did so to keep ethnics in the Democratic camp, not because he had overcome his distaste for southern and eastern Europeans. And he openly sanctioned the spread of discrimination against blacks in the government bureaucracy. "I would say," he explained in 1913, "that I do approve of the segregation that is being attempted in several of the departments."

For all these reasons Wilson does not deserve to be celebrated as an economic thinker, social reformer, or legislative magician. But he also has to be evaluated in the context of his times. Coming to office at the high tide of progressive sentiment, and blessed with receptive Congresses, he proved pragmatic and politically shrewd. He was an eloquent speaker and a dynamic congressional leader. If he had blind spots, so did many progressives at the time. His able leadership revived the Democratic party and temporarily anchored its base among urbanites and ethnics. It helped southern and western interests to feel that they too could participate in the federal management of the economy.

Above all, Wilson's first term extended years of growing federal responsiveness to pressures for change. This responsiveness was often more rhetorical than substantive, and the legislation more symbolic than effective: blacks, most of organized labor, and the urban poor continued to be excluded from federal assistance. But the very appearance of responsiveness was important, for it encouraged many Americans to believe that the presidency could deal with corporate power. This faith, however misplaced, sustained the national progressives, and preserved a measure of political stability in a time of dramatic economic change.

Suggestions for reading

Five important books on political patterns are William N. Chambers and Walter Dean Burnham, eds., *American Party Systems** (1967), a series of essays on party development; Burnham, *Critical Elections and the Mainstream of American Politics* (1972), which focuses on the twentieth century; Paul Kleppner, *Cross of Culture: A Social Analysis of Midwestern Politics, 1850–1900* (1970); Richard Jensen, *The Winning of the Midwest: Social and Political Conflict, 1888–1896* (1971); and Arthur Schlesinger, Jr., *The Imperial Presidency* (1973).

For the period prior to 1900 see L. D. White, *The Republican Era, 1869–1901* (1958), an administrative history; H. Wayne Morgan, *From Hayes to McKinley: National Party Politics, 1877–1896* (1969); David J. Rothman, *Politics and Power: The United States Senate, 1869–1901** (1966); and H. Wayne Morgan, *William McKinley and His America* (1963). The key books for national politics, 1900–17, are George Mowry, *The Era of Theodore Roosevelt** (1958); and Arthur Link, *Woodrow Wilson and the Progressive Era** (1954). Important studies are John M. Blum, *The Republican Roosevelt** (1954); and *Woodrow Wilson and the Politics of Morality**

(1956). Both are brilliantly written. Major biographies include P. C. Jessup, *Elihu Root* (2 vols., 1938); Henry Pringle, *Theodore Roosevelt** (1931), which is critical; William Harbaugh, *Power and Responsibility** (1961), a balanced biography of TR; Pringle, *Life and Times of William Howard Taft* (2 vols., 1939); Donald E. Anderson, *William Howard Taft* (1973); John J. Broesamle, *William Gibbs McAdoo: A Passion for Change, 1863–1917* (1974); and John Braeman, *Albert J. Beveridge* (1971). See also Walter Johnson, *William Allen White's America* (1947); Richard Leopold, *Elihu Root and the Conservative Tradition** (1954); Alpheus T. Mason, *Brandeis** (1946); Ray S. Baker, *Woodrow Wilson* (6 vols., 1927–37); and Alexander and Juliette George, *Woodrow Wilson and Colonel House** (1956), a provocative study using insights drawn from psychology.

Regulatory policies are covered in Gabriel Kolko, *Triumph of Conservatism** (1963), and *Railroads and Regulation, 1877–1916* (1964); and Hans Thorelli, *Federal Anti-Trust Policy* (1955). See also Morton Keller, *The Life Insurance Enterprise, 1885–1910* (1963); Robert Wiebe, *Businessmen and Reform** (1962); K. Austin Kerr, *American Railroad Politics, 1914–1920* (1968); and Melvin Urofsky, *Big Steel and the Wilson Administration* (1969).

For the Supreme Court, see Robert McCloskey, *The Modern Supreme Court** (1972), a brief survey; Loren P. Beth, *The Development of the American Constitution, 1877–1917** (1971); James W. Hurst, *Law and the Conditions of Freedom in the Nineteenth-Century United States* (1956); and Samuel L. Knoefsky. *The Legacy of Holmes and Brandeis: A Study in the Influence of Ideas* (1974 ed.).

Relevant primary sources include Herbert Croly, *The Promise of American Life** (1909), an influential call for nationalism by a leading American intellectual; Walter Lippmann, *Drift and Mastery** (1914); and Walter Weyl, *The New Democracy** (1912).

4

From expansion to war

1900 - 1917

In opposing the war against Spain in 1898, former Secretary of State Richard Olney labeled America a "nation of sympathizers and sermonizers and swaggerers." The country, he said, was too immature to pursue a policy of self-interest based on power. Instead, it oscillated between moralizing and a romantic adventurousness that was more dangerous than calculating.

Had he wished to follow this perceptive argument, Olney could have pointed to all kinds of foolish American rhetoric about foreign relations in the 1890s. Some of it came from populist opponents of expertise. Democratic Congressman Champ Clark of Missouri, Woodrow Wilson's chief opponent for the 1912 presidential nomination, urged in 1897 the abolition of America's diplomatic corps. The New York *Sun* concurred. "The diplomatic service," it editorialized in 1899, "is a nurse of snobs. . . . Instead of making ambassa-dors, Congress should wipe out the whole service." Equally extreme state-ments came from racists and jingoists who asserted that America could do no wrong. The expansionist Senator William E. Chandler of New Hampshire contended that victory over Spain would require between fifteen minutes and ninety days.

Chandler's nearly accurate but wholly uninformed prophecy reflected the nineteenth-century belief that wars need not involve total destruction. Even Alfred Thayer Mahan, a thoughtful advocate of preparedness, wrote that "war now not only occurs more rarely, but has rather the character of an occasional excess, from which recovery is easy." From this perspective the jingoism of the late 1890s, however deplorable to people who lived through twentieth-century wars, was not only understandable, but also a way of restoring a sense of purpose and unity to a divided nation.

Still, Chandler's confidence reflected the very "swaggering" that Olney described, for America's military establishment was pathetically inadequate for sustained foreign adventures. Ships commissioned in the 1880s, reveal-ingly called "seagoing coastline battleships," represented President Chester Arthur's view that "it is no part of our policy to create and maintain a navy able to cope with that of the other great powers of the world." In the early 1890s Congress authorized eight new battleships, four of which proved useful in the war against Spain in 1898. But the Regular Army remained pitifully weak. On the eve of the war, fought ostensibly to liberate Cuba from Spanish oppression, the army consisted of 28,183 officers and men (compared to 180,000 Spanish regulars in Cuba). Promotions had been so slow that Roose-velt observed white-bearded first lieutenants leading troops into battle. National guardsmen, who soon comprised the bulk of American forces, were still equipped with Civil War vintage rifles. America won that "splendid little war" primarily because Spanish admirals foolishly exposed their ships in the harbors of Cavite and Santiago, not because "heroes" like TR killed thou-sands of Spaniards. American soldiers, ill equipped, poorly trained, and seriously weakened by tropical diseases, (perhaps 2000 died of illness, four times the number killed in battle), were spared what could have been the disaster of fighting sustained battles on land in Cuba or the Philippines.

American understanding of the consequences of a war against Spain was even more primitive than its military readiness. For a while President Mc-Kinley had to use schoolbook maps to follow naval movements in the Pacific. "It is evident," he confessed, "that I must learn a great deal of geography in this war." When Admiral Dewey took Manila, McKinley did not know what to do. After much agonizing he decided that America must take over the Philippines (and Guam), for returning them to Spain would be "cowardly and dishonorable," and giving them to a European power would be "bad business and discreditable." The Philippines, he concluded, were "unfit for self-government," and "there was nothing left for us to do but to take them all, and to educate the Filipinos, and uplift and civilize and Christianize them."

McKinley's reasoning, neither impetuous nor hypocritical, rested in part on his unwillingness to let the Philippines fall under the control of Germany or some other colonial power. Similar strategic impulses explain the acquisition of Puerto Rico, which guarded sea lanes to Central America, where American expansionists wished to construct a canal. McKinley's program meant the acquisition of far-flung properties, and, in 1903, the establishment (through the so-called Platt amendment to a military appropriation bill) of an exploitative American protectorate over Cuba that lasted until 1933. Though America's administration in Cuba proved relatively enlightened for the time, military occupation of the Philippines provoked a bloody revolt—which in turn prompted brutal American countermeasures. Perhaps 200,000 Filipinos died between 1900 and 1903. One American commander, as if anticipating actions in Vietnam, ordered his men to "kill and burn and make a howling wilderness of Samar."

In the long run the Spanish-American war had ominous consequences for American policy, for the virtually indefensible Philippines, 5000 miles away, formed what Roosevelt called "our heel of Achilles." Recognizing their vulnerability—and the economic interests that had to be protected—Secretary of State John Hay sent the major powers two notes in 1899 and 1900. The first called on them to maintain equal commercial opportunities for all. The second requested that the great powers preserve the territorial integrity of China. The "Open Door" notes did not signify a change in American policy, which had regularly sought secure Asian markets. They received little backing from the other powers, which correctly regarded them as efforts to protect American influence. But in acting as if he had established the United States as the altruistic guarantor of China, Hay encouraged Americans to cherish exaggerated notions of American influence in East Asia. This gap between perception and reality had dangerous implications for policy.

Pressures of imperialism

America's sudden acquisition of a colonial empire did not go unchallenged by domestic critics. The independent Carl Schurz cried that annexation of the Philippines marked a "brutal appeal to sordid greed . . . utterly hostile to the vital principles of our free institutions." William Graham Sumner prophetically remarked that "the most important thing which we shall inherit from the Spaniards will be the task of suppressing rebellions." The pacifist Ernest Howard Crosby assailed the Christian sermonizing of men like McKinley:

> Onward Christian Soldiers
> 'Gainst the heathen crew!
> In the name of Jesus
> Let us run them through.

American enterprise abroad, 1900–1920

	FOREIGN TRADE (In millions of current dollars)					INTERNATIONAL INVESTMENTS (In billions of current dollars)		
	EXPORT		IMPORT		BALANCE (+ OR −)	U.S. INVESTMENTS ABROAD	FOREIGN INVESTMENTS IN U.S.	NET INVESTMENT POSITION (+ OR −)
	AMOUNT	% OF GNP	AMOUNT	% OF GNP				
1900	1,499	7.4[a]	930	4.3[a]	+ 570	0.7[c]	3.4[c]	−2.7
1905	1,660	5.3[b]	1,199	4.4[b]	+ 461	n.d.	n.d.	. . .
1910	1,919	4.9	1,646	4.2	+ 273	2.5[d]	6.4[d]	−3.9
1915	2,966	6.6	1,875	4.0	+1,091	3.5[e]	7.2[e]	−3.7
1920	8,664	9.3	5,784	5.9	+2,880	7.0[f]	3.3[f]	+3.7

SOURCE: Adapted from *Historical Statistics of the United States*, pp. 537, 542, 564
[a]Average of GNP percentages for 1897–1901 [b]Average of GNP percentages for 1902–06 [c]Data for 1897 [d]Data for 1908 [e]Data for 1914 (to June 30) [f]Data for 1919

These anti-imperialists were so eloquent that later critics of American expansion could add little to their case. But the opponents of colonialism could not reverse what had been done between 1898 and 1900. The popularity of the war against Spain, the initial complacency with which Americans acquired such distant territory, and the subsequent appeal of Roosevelt's expansionist foreign policy suggested that imperialist impulses flowed from powerful currents of opinion and from interest groups that knew where they were going.

One of these impulses was economic—pressures from commercial farmers and industrialists to establish and expand markets abroad. Great strides in productivity gradually enabled American manufacturers to undersell foreign competitors and to develop favorable trade balances, which ranged between $200 and $700 million every year between 1896 and 1914. The value of American exports rose from approximately $1 billion annually in the early 1890s to $2.5 billion in 1914. More important, American overseas investment increased from $700 million in 1897 to $3.5 billion in 1914.

It is easy to exaggerate the impact of this growth on the Gross National Product, 93 percent of which still depended on domestic markets. It is equally easy to overstress the political influence and commercial success of people engaged in this overseas commerce: the United States never managed to develop substantial trade with China. Still, growing numbers of American bankers and businessmen articulated an expansionist point of view by 1900, and important politicians listened. "We now hold three of the winning cards in the game for commercial greatness," the head of the American Bankers Association declared in 1898, "to wit—iron, steel, and coal. We have long been the granary of the world, we now aspire to be its workshop, then we want to be its clearing house." President Grover Cleveland argued that America must "find markets in every part of the habitable globe." McKinley stated that "it should be our settled purpose to open trade wherever we can." Secretary Hay's open-door policy merely reflected this conscious demand for commercial expansion.

This drive for markets was part of a broader feeling that grew with the supposed disappearance of the domestic frontier and with the devastating depression of the mid-1890s. These events created widespread alarm. Was the depression the result, as it seemed to be, of the end of the frontier? Could the economy be reinvigorated by expansion beyond the continent? With production escalating, would the domestic market suffice? Mahan spoke for many: "Whether they will or no, Americans must begin to look outward. The growing productivity of the country demands it."

Other expansionists argued that it was America's destiny to expand, not only to promote prosperity at home, but to bring blessings to the rest of the world. Senator Beveridge of Indiana explained in 1900 that the question of annexing the Philippines was "elemental. It is racial. God has not been preparing the English-speaking and Teutonic peoples for a thousand years for nothing but vain and idle self-contemplation and admiration. No! He has made us the master organizers of the world to establish system where chaos reigns. . . . He has marked the American people as his chosen nation to lead in the regeneration of the world." Like many other imperialists, Beveridge was an evangelical reformer who equated progress with American expansion and was not at all self-conscious about proclaiming the racial supremacy of the Anglo-Saxon peoples.

These economic and racial impulses toward expansion provided the context in which the strategic arguments of Mahan received a sympathetic hearing. Mahan, a prolific writer who headed the Naval War College, insisted in books like *The Influence of Sea Power upon History* (1890) that control over international communications was the key to success in modern war. America, he argued, should build a mighty navy that could strike at an enemy's fleet and vital points. It should construct a canal across the central American isthmus, guard access to it, and acquire bases and coaling stations for its fleet throughout the world. Mahan's arguments assisted congressional navalists like Senator Henry Cabot Lodge of Massachusetts. They also impressed Theodore Roosevelt, who tried to implement them a few years later.

Mahan especially promised Americans a national awakening. "The best hopes of the world," he wrote, did not rest in "universal harmony nor in fond hopes of universal peace." Rather, they depended on "that reviving sense of nationality . . . in the jealous determination of each people to provide first for its own. . . . In these jarring sounds . . . are to be heard the assurance that decay has not touched yet the majestic fabric erected by so many centuries of courageous battling." This argument gave Americans a rationale for engaging in the competitive struggle with other colonial powers. It offered a new frontier, a sense of purpose, a way out of the drift and divisiveness of the 1890s.

ROOSEVELT'S ROMANTIC *REALPOLITIK*

"I utterly disbelieve in the policy of bluff," Roosevelt told Taft in 1910, " . . . or in violation of the old frontier maxim, 'Never draw unless you mean to shoot.' I do not believe in our taking any position anywhere unless you mean to shoot."

Like many of TR's statements, this one was colorful and blunt. But it was not impetuous, for Roosevelt—perhaps more than any other president in this century—had pondered the role of America in foreign affairs. His basic conclusions, while clouded by moralisms, were consistent. America, he thought, had to play the large strategic and economic role that Mahan had envisioned. This policy satisfied Roosevelt's activist temperament. It rested on his characteristically American faith in the blessings of Anglo-Saxon civilization. And it appealed to what he called his "ultra-American spirit of patriotism," without which no people could achieve their destiny. But it was more than ethnocentrist moralism; it was also an approach to *Realpolitik*. Nations, he recognized, ordinarily act in their own selfish interests. They do not readily respond to "bluff" or to sermonizing. American policy, he argued, must recognize this fact by striving to preserve a stable balance of power.

Roosevelt's Asian policy attempted to put these ideas into practice. The Open Door policy, he explained later, was "an excellent thing"—on paper. But it "completely disappears as soon as a powerful nation determines to disregard it, and is willing to run the risk of war." Rather than rely on such a "bluff," TR sought ways to restrain the Russians, who appeared to be acquiring a dominant position in Manchuria. When Japan attacked Russia in 1904, Roosevelt wrote happily that Japan was "playing our game." The war would enhance American interests by destroying the potential for "either a yellow peril or a Slav peril."

At this point, however, Japan scored a series of resounding military successes that threatened to drive Russia from the scene. American magazines, easily alerted to the "yellow peril," began printing stories with headings like "Japan's Closing the Open Door," and "The Menace of Japan's Success." Roosevelt agreed that Japanese victory would signify a "real shifting of equilibrium as far as the white races are concerned." He then inaugurated a series of secret maneuvers that culminated in both Japan and Russia agreeing to attend a peace conference in Portsmouth, New Hampshire in the summer of 1905. By that time both nations were exhausted by the conflict, and Roosevelt's diplomacy encouraged them to settle. The agreement gave Japan Port Arthur and railroads in Manchuria and recognized Japan's "predominant" interests in Korea. But by preserving Manchuria as a part of China, the treaty left it officially open to the trade of all nations. Roosevelt's skillful diplomatic intervention had temporarily sustained America's economic presence in East Asia.

Roosevelt then proceeded to seek an accommodation with Japan, now the growing power in Asia. At first this seemed impossible, for migrations of Japanese laborers to the West Coast brought about ugly confrontations by 1906. In that year the California legislature debated a bill to exclude Orientals, and the San Francisco school board segregated Chinese, Japanese, and Koreans. In 1907 anti-Oriental riots exploded all along the West Coast. Roosevelt, though furious at the "idiots of the California legislature," recognized the power of the Hearst press to inflame tensions to the point of war. Accordingly, he negotiated the so-called Gentlemen's Agreement of 1907. By this informal understanding both sides agreed to put an end to all unwanted immigration. The agreement could not erase the affront to Japanese pride, but it did permit tensions to subside. And in 1908 Roosevelt further gratified the Japanese by approving the so-called Root-Takahira Agreement. This affirmed the status quo, including Japanese hegemony in Korea. Each side pledged to respect the other's interests, to observe the Open Door in China, and to protect Chinese territorial integrity.

When Roosevelt left office a few months later, he had in no sense assured stability in Asia. American businessmen continued to complain about efforts by Japan, aided by Russia and England, to exclude outside interests. Roosevelt had also refused to jettison the Open-Door policy. The instability in Asia, however, did not stem from flaws in TR's policies, but from the inviting weakness of China, which America lacked the power to change. Recognizing these limits on American influence, Roosevelt had done what little he could to develop United States interests in the area.

Considerations of power also dominated Roosevelt's more bellicose actions in the Caribbean, which he saw as an American lake. Following Mahan, he was dedicated to building an isthmian canal—in part so that the navy could move freely to defend the new possessions in the Pacific. Because the Caribbean, unlike the Orient, was well within the range of American naval forces, he was quick to react when threatened with opposition.

His actions regarding the Panama Canal revealed his willingness to resort to force. In December 1901 the Senate ratified a treaty with England that cleared the way for American construction of a canal. Secretary Hay then negotiated a draft treaty with Colombia, which controlled Panama. It granted the United States the right to build and fortify a canal, in return for which Colombia would get $10 million, plus $250,000 annual rental. The Colombian government, however, then demanded $20 million and specific guarantees of sovereignty in the canal zone. Roosevelt could have accepted the increased price, which was a fraction of the eventual cost, or he could have negotiated (as Hay suggested) with Nicaragua, where an alternative canal route beckoned. Instead, he referred to "those contemptible little creatures in Bogatá" as "foolish and homicidal corruptionists," and he determined to take control of the isthmus "without any further parley with Colombia."

The Man Behind the Egg.

At this point he was assisted by a successful revolution against Colombia. Roosevelt immediately recognized the new state of Panama, which signed an agreement granting the United States canal rights for the original price of $10 million. Eleven years later the canal opened under American control.

Roosevelt at first insisted he had behaved properly. In fact, however, he had not only encouraged talk of revolution but had led Philippe Bunau-Varilla, a Frenchman who headed the Panamanian junta, to expect American assistance. (Bunau-Varilla, Roosevelt said later, would have been "a very dull man" to have expected otherwise.) When Colombia attempted to reinforce its troops, an American warship, which had conveniently arrived at the isthmus the night before the revolution, barred the entry. Later TR admitted, indeed bragged about, his covert role in these maneuvers: "I took the isthmus, and started the canal, and I let Congress debate me instead of the canal." He added, "so far from acting unconstitutionally about the Panama Canal, I acted the way every President worth his salt ought to act."

The revolution offers a neat case study of the role of economic interests in American imperialism. Bunau-Varilla was not only leader of the junta but agent for the French canal company that had demanded $40 million for surrender of its prior right to build a canal in Panama. After the revolution he became Panama's representative in Washington, where he negotiated the treaty making possible the payment of the $40 million to his company. His co-leader was William Cromwell, a New York lawyer with excellent political connections and easy access to the State Department. As attorney for the French company Cromwell used this influence first to lobby against the route through Nicaragua, then to develop support for the revolution. The grateful French later paid him $600,000, some of which, it was later rumored, found its way into the hands of American politicians who had been stockholders in the company. Though Panama was probably the better route and though Roosevelt was not personally implicated in these financial dealings, his actions contemptuously ignored the rights of the sovereign state of Colombia. The Springfield *Republican* accurately labeled the affair "one of the most discreditable performances in our history."

Securing the canal was but part of Roosevelt's broader desire to exclude other powers from the Caribbean. As early as December 1902, when Germany (with help from England and Italy) bombarded Venezuelan ports to secure payment of debts, he had worried about possible European intervention in the area. When a revolution in Santo Domingo in late 1903 threatened to bring on similar actions, Roosevelt's suspicions mounted. Because 1904 was an election year, he acted at first with restraint, telling a friend that he had as little desire to annex the West Indian island as a "boa constrictor might have to swallow a porcupine wrong-end-to." At the same time, however, he said privately (concerning Venezuela) that "these Dagos . . . will have to behave decently," and in December, after the elections, he proclaimed a new policy to Congress. The Roosevelt Corollary, as it became known, asserted that "chronic wrong-doing" or "impotence" by a western hemispheric nation could "force the United States, however reluctantly, in flagrant cases of such

Roosevelt running a steam shovel at the Panama Canal.

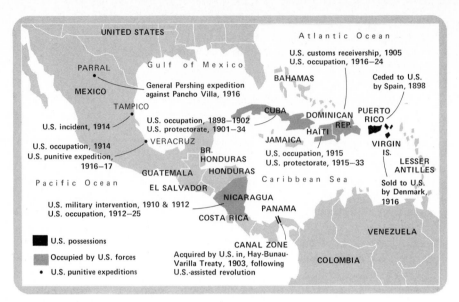

U.S. Involvement in Caribbean in Early Twentieth Century

wrong-doing or impotence, to the exercise of an international police power.''
The corollary broadened the Monroe Doctrine to assert the United States'
unilateral right to intervene whenever it deemed it necessary.

Like the Open-Door policy, the corollary was an assertion of intent by the
executive branch, not a law approved by Congress or an international agreement binding on any other power. American foreign relations, it seemed, were
falling entirely into the hands of the president. But unlike the Open Door, the
Roosevelt Corollary was well within American power to implement, and TR
acted quickly to do so by placing the finances of Santo Domingo under
American control. Meanwhile he practiced what became known as "dollar
diplomacy" by letting American bondholders know he would protect their
interests throughout the Caribbean. When the Senate refused to ratify his
agreement concerning Santo Domingo, he simply maintained it without consent, until the Senate gave way in 1907.

TR's Caribbean policies were "realistic" in using power in a region where
it was effective. They were therefore successful in the narrow sense. America
acquired a canal of strategic importance, excluded foreign rivals from the
Caribbean, and intervened with impunity to protect economic and political
interests. His policies—for all their bluster on occasion—also avoided dragging the country into war. But his actions were constitutionally high-handed.
They brought him no friends in Latin America. They encouraged Americans
to believe that might makes right, that the end justifies the means. Though
perceptive concerning the role of power in international affairs, Roosevelt
remained one of Olney's "swaggerers," something of a militarist who thrilled
to the excitement of victory.

AMERICA AND THE THIRD WORLD, 1909–1916

Both Taft and Wilson appeared to reverse the romantic *Realpolitik* of Roosevelt. Taft was legalistic, fair-minded, a leading supporter of the international peace movement, and a devoted though frustrated advocate of reciprocity with Canada and of arbitration treaties with other nations. Rejecting shows of force, he acted with restraint when unrest in Mexico threatened American interests. Wilson supported Secretary of State William Jennings Bryan's successful efforts to negotiate conciliation treaties, withdrew support for American bankers in Manchuria, and even tried (in vain) to get Congress to offer an apology and indemnity to Colombia. When revolution erupted in Mexico, he refused to let himself be swayed by American investors. "I am President of the United States," he said, "and not of a small group of American investors with vested interests in Mexico."

Both presidents, however, extended and broadened the interventionist pattern that had developed after 1898. In 1910 Taft explained that he would engage in "active intervention to secure for our merchandise and our capitalists opportunity for profitable investment." His policy of "substituting dollars for bullets," he added in 1912, was "an effort frankly directed to the increase of American trade. . . ." Under the direction of Secretary of State Philander Knox, Taft sent marines to Nicaragua to assist a conservative regime with close ties to American interests. He also prodded American bankers into investing in railroad consortiums in Manchuria. The bankers, however, struggled vainly against strong coalitions of foreign powers, which the Taft administration lacked the political and military strength to oppose. In pushing for dollar diplomacy in Asia, Taft and Knox truly hoped that American money would lessen tensions. But they succeeded only in advertising American weakness. They had misunderstood TR's essential teaching: "never draw unless you mean to shoot."

Wilson's Asian diplomacy was only slightly more productive. Though he at first encouraged nativists in California, who passed a bill early in 1913 prohibiting Japanese from owning land, he soon recognized that he would have to reduce tensions, and he sent Secretary of State Bryan to California on a mission of personal diplomacy. Bryan did not succeed in reversing Californian opinion—that was impossible—and the Japanese government remained bitter about the land law. But until Wilson's intercession it appeared that jingoists on both sides would fan the issue into a pretext for war. His belated attempts to restrain the Californians showed that he understood the desirability of avoiding a break with Japan.

Other actions in Asia indicated that he, too, had difficulty in preserving the Open Door for American interests there. On the surface he seemed motivated by a desire to act honorably. Thus he withdrew support for the American bankers in Manchuria. He was quick to recognize a nationalist regime that toppled the corrupt Manchu dynasty. He protested strongly when Japan issued the so-called twenty-one demands on China in 1915. Apparently backing down before Wilson's determined stand, the Japanese dropped their demands. But they did so only because Britain and China also resisted. And their retreat was only temporary—in 1917 Wilson himself accepted the so-called Lansing-Ishii agreement, which recognized Japan's "special" interests in China. In all, Wilson's Asian policy was neither so altruistic nor so effective as he led contemporaries to believe.

His activities in Central American affairs were still less successful. To prevent anarchy in Nicaragua, Wilson extended Taft's policy of direct intervention by imposing military rule, which assisted American financial interests. He ordered marines into politically unstable Santo Domingo, and by 1916 America ruled the country. He also initiated a military occupation of Haiti, which lasted until 1934. The Haitians, proudly independent, resisted Yankee beneficence. Before marines completed the task of pacification, some 2000 Haitians had been killed.

The irony of these interventions, which dwarfed those of his predecessors, was that Wilson thought he was acting altruistically. Unlike Roosevelt, he did not fear European pressure, for no such threats existed in Haiti or Santo Domingo. Unlike Taft, he did not cater to American investors (though they did influence the State Department). Rather, as his attempt to indemnify Colombia revealed, he hoped to promote inter-American understanding. His miscalculation, like that of many Americans before and since, was to assume that Anglo-Saxon values—stability, democracy, liberal capitalism—could be exported to countries with different cultural traditions and nationalistic aspirations.

Wilson's Intervention in Mexico   Nothing exposed this cultural blindness better than his policies in Mexico, site of one of the twentieth century's major socioeconomic revolutions. Three weeks before Wilson took office in 1913, the forces of General Victoriano Huerta betrayed and murdered Francisco Madero, the idealistic reformer who had overthrown the old autocracy in 1911. The European countries extended de facto recognition to the new regime, and American interests, seeing in Huerta the only stabilizing force in Mexico, urged Wilson to follow suit. To deny recognition to an established regime, in fact, involved a break with ordinary diplomatic practice. But Wilson took a moralistic view. "I will not recognize a government of butchers," he said. In so doing he created precedent for a doctrine of nonrecognition later used against Japan's conquest of Manchuria in 1932, and against "Red" China in 1949.

When a new Mexican leader, Venustiano Carranza, then pledged a revolution against Huerta, Wilson saw a chance to achieve his aims. Accordingly, he supported the Constitutionalists, as Carranza's forces called themselves. Carranza, however, was a nationalist who rejected Wilson's efforts to guide the revolution. In need of an excuse to intervene, Wilson found it when Huerta's forces arrested American sailors who had strayed behind Mexican lines. The local Huertista commander apologized, but the American admiral

Punch, August 27, 1913.

Woodrow on Toast.
WILSON: *If you don't take care, I shall have to treat you the same way as Europe treats the Turk.*
MEXICO: *And how's that?*
WILSON: *Well, I shall have to—to go on wagging my finger at you.*

on the scene, acting without clearance from Washington, demanded a twenty-one-gun salute to the United States flag, and Wilson supported him. The demand was ironic, for it was made to a foe whom Wilson had not deigned to recognize. It was also insulting, and Huerta declined to salute unless the Americans responded volley for volley. Because such a response would have meant recognition of Huerta's government, Wilson refused. Two days later he used the incident as a pretext to ask for congressional authority to use armed force if necessary.

Wilson then received word that a German steamer was about to land in Vera Cruz with a shipment of arms for Huerta. Without waiting for congressional action, Wilson ordered the navy to take the city. The next day, April 22, 1914, it did so, but at the cost of 126 Mexican and 19 American lives. The incident provoked anti-American demonstrations throughout Latin America, and it disturbed informed writers throughout the world. "If war is to be made on points of punctilio raised by admirals and generals," The *Economist* of London observed, "and if the government of the United States is to set the example for this return to medieval conditions, it will be a bad day for civilization."

At this stage war was averted when Wilson accepted an offer from Argentina, Brazil, and Chile to mediate the dispute. And during the summer of 1914 the Constitutionalists finally drove Huerta from power. But Wilson still resented Carranza's refusal to take American advice; so when Francisco

Pancho Villa and his army on the march.

("Pancho") Villa, a dashing but ignorant general, broke with Carranza, Wilson threw him his support. This was a serious miscalculation, for Carranza's forces were too strong for Villa. With no option remaining, Wilson was persuaded in late 1915 to offer Carranza de facto recognition. Villa then turned on his former supporter, first by hauling sixteen Americans off a train in Mexico and shooting them on the spot, and then, in March 1916, by crossing the border to burn Columbus, New Mexico, and to kill nineteen more. Wilson had backed the weaker and the more volatile man.

Villa's defiance prompted Wilson to dispatch a punitive expedition into Mexico under the command of General John J. Pershing. Vainly trying to capture the elusive Villa, Pershing expanded his army to 11,600 men and moved them more than 300 miles into central Mexico. Carranza, who had never envisioned such a formidable force, grew agitated, especially after two incidents, one at Parral in April, which resulted in the deaths of two Americans and forty Mexicans, and the second in June near Carrizal, which killed thirty Mexicans and twelve Americans and left twenty-four Americans captives of Carranza's forces.

The killing at Carrizal appeared to make war with Mexico inevitable. At this point, however, American soldiers admitted they had started the incident. Pacifists deluged Wilson with appeals for restraint. Carranza released the prisoners. Negotiations between the two countries then deadlocked over the sensitive issue of Pershing's troops, which Carranza demanded be withdrawn, and which Wilson, facing reelection, did not dare to remove. But with the election safely behind him, and the prospect of having to fight in Europe, Wilson knew he had to retreat. In January 1917 he ordered the withdrawal to begin, and in March, almost three years after Carranza had taken power, Wilson finally offered him de jure recognition.

From one perspective Wilson's handling of Mexican affairs was praiseworthy. Despite clashes such as the one at Carrizal, he had resisted the temptation to engage in full-fledged war. Despite the pressure of economic interests, he—alone among western leaders—had refused to recognize the autocratic Huerta. In so doing he had indirectly assisted the revolutionaries in their battle against autocracy and economic oppression.

From another perspective, however, his Mexican policies represented the "sympathizing and sermonizing" that Secretary of State Olney had deplored. They directly caused several armed clashes, otherwise avoidable, which led to loss of life. They aroused strong anti-American sentiment throughout Latin America. And they revealed two illusions that would plague American policy-makers in the years to come. The first assumed that foreign nationalists would welcome attempts to spread the American way of life. The second, stemming from the first, was that America, the most powerful nation on earth, could use its technology and its military force to guide revolutionary movements into channels that would safeguard American interests. These illusions continued as hallmarks of American diplomacy into the 1970s. As subsequent events—in Russia, China, Cuba, and Vietnam—were to demonstrate, Wilson's Mexican policy did not serve as an object lesson in the limitations of missionary foreign policy.

War in Europe

The movement for international peace peaked in the years before the outbreak of World War I in 1914. Andrew Carnegie established his Peace Fund in 1910 with an initial gift of $10 million. Taft worked diligently for arbitration treaties. Norman Angell's popular *The Great Illusion* (1910) argued persuasively that war was useless and obsolete. By 1912 a prominent peace leader concluded, "It looks as though this were going to be the age of treaties rather than the age of wars, the century of reason rather than the century of force."

The Great War shattered these hopes. But it did not lead Americans to plunge immediately into the action. As Wilson put it, the United States "must be neutral in fact as well as in name during these days that are to try men's souls. We must be impartial in thought as well as in action." A year later he heard rumors that the army was preparing contingency plans for battle against Germany. Furious, he summoned the acting secretary of war. If the rumors were true, he commanded, the secretary should "relieve every officer in the general staff and order him out of Washington." In hindsight his order appears

MEN WANTED
ARMY

Robert Minor, an antiwar cartoonist, expresses opposition to war in 1915. The caption, uttered by an army medical examiner, reads, "At last, a perfect soldier."

both touching and quaint, but it testified to his sincere desire to stay out of war.

In adhering to this course for almost three years Wilson found he could draw on substantial popular support. Some, including many Irish-Americans, opposed engaging in a war that would assist England. Some, including thousands of German-Americans, did not want to fight former countrymen. Others, like Theodore Dreiser, were Anglophobes. "It would be an excellent thing for Europe and the world," he wrote, "if the despicable British aristocracy . . . were smashed and a German viceroy sat in London." Untold thousands of Americans simply felt that Europe's quarrels were its own business, that America must be spared the curse of militarism. "Don't Take My Darling Boy Away," was the title of one popular song of 1915. Another went:

> There'd be no war today
> If mothers all would say,
> I didn't raise my boy to be a soldier.

But from the start of the war Wilson had to contend with many Americans who yearned to discipline the Germans. When Germany marched through neutral Belgium, Harvard President Charles Eliot urged Wilson to conclude offensive and defensive treaties with the Allies. *Life* added (a few days after the war began) that "the unanimity of sentiment in this country against Germany is surprising . . . the English, French, and Russians are fighting in

Sport.

Germany's alleged atrocities against civilians were widely publicized by advocates of pre-paredness and intervention, 1914–17. This cartoon, published in 1915, was one such effort.

behalf of the liberties of the world.'' Popular magazines published exaggerated accounts, spread via British propaganda, of German atrocities. *Harpers* (December 1914) titled a story "The Attack on New York." Another popular article, by Richard Harding Davis in *Metropolitan Magazine,* imagined spike-helmeted, bayonet-wielding Germans entrenched in headquarters at a Long Island country club.

Wilson also had to bow to economic pressures. At first he offered token support to Secretary of State Bryan, a near pacifist who refused to permit American bankers to float loans to the Allies. "Money," Bryan said force-fully, "is the worst of contrabands—it commands all other things." But influential bankers openly favored England. "Our firm had never for one moment been neutral," a Morgan partner recalled, "From the very start we did everything we could to contribute to the cause of the Allies." Wilson understood that the denial of loans to belligerent nations broke with the usual practice, that it was therefore unneutral, and that it would hurt England and France, which needed the help, much more than it would harm the Central Powers. He also realized that loans would facilitate trade and perhaps end the recession that had descended on the American economy in 1913. So in October 1914 he permitted the extension of commercial credits, in March 1915 he approved a $50 million loan from the Morgan interests to France, and in September, 1915—after Bryan's resignation from the State Department—he authorized a loan of $500 million more to the Allies. By 1917 America had loaned $2.25 billion to the Allies, and but $27 million to Germany. Trade with the Allies increased from $824 million in 1914 to $3.2 billion in 1916. (With Germany and Austria-Hungry it declined during the same period from $169 million to $1.15 million.) Long before American intervention in April 1917, the United States pursued an economic policy that was "neutral" in that it followed the ordinary practice of nonbelligerent nations in time of war, but that directly assisted both the American economy and the Allies.

By far the largest obstacle to a neutrality "impartial in thought as well as in action" was the struggle for command of the seas. England, whose ships controlled the surface, gradually imposed a far-reaching definition of contraband to be confiscated from ships bound for the Central Powers. By early 1915 its list of contraband included not only armaments but such vital raw materials as copper, iron, aluminum, rubber, gasoline, oil, and even foodstuffs. This lengthy list infuriated the Central Powers, who insisted that the Allies abide by the more restrictive definition elaborated in the Declaration of London in 1909, and it angered neutrals like the United States, whose shipments were frequently confiscated. But the English replied that it had not signed the Declaration of London, which carried no standing in international law. Desperate to prevent supplies from reaching their enemies, they tightened their economic warfare in 1916 by "blacklisting" some eighty-seven American firms from trading with British subjects in any way.

This blacklist, combined with the British suppression of the Irish, infuriated Wilson. Privately he called the English "poor boobs." He wrote Colonel Edward House, his closest adviser, that he was "seriously considering asking Congress to authorize me to prohibit loans and restrict importations to the Allies. . . . Can we any longer endure their intolerable course?" As late as November 1916 he told House to warn the English Foreign Secretary, Sir Edward Grey, that American feeling was "as hot against Great Britain as it was at first against Germany and likely to grow hotter still against an indefinite continuation of the war."

Various forces kept these tensions from escalating to the point of open conflict. Among these were the ties of sympathy and of economic interest that bound Americans to the English. Individuals also promoted understanding. One of these was America's ambassador to England, Walter Hines Page. An avid Anglophile, he behaved in a flagrantly unprofessional way by making clear to British officials that he did not share Wilson's irritation. On receiving one American protest, he took it to Grey and said, "I do not agree with it. Now let us sit down and see how we can answer it." Another was Colonel House, a shrewd Texan who served as Wilson's personal emissary on frequent missions to Europe. And still another was Robert Lansing, who succeeded Bryan as Secretary of State in 1915. Lansing felt that American security demanded the defeat of Germany. "If our people only realized the insatiable greed of those German autocrats at Berlin," he wrote early in 1917,

" . . . we would be at war today. . . . The Allies must *not* be beaten. . . . War cannot come too soon to suit me."

British sensitivity to American opinion also prevented a rupture. When southern congressmen agitated in 1915 against a British plan to place cotton on the list of absolute contraband, Lord Grey and others negotiated a secret agreement by which the British bought enough cotton to stabilize the price. Grey also instructed his ambassador in Washington to avoid unnecessary misunderstandings. "Do nothing," he advised, "which will be a cause of complaint or dispute as regards the United States government; such a dispute would indeed be a crowning calamity."

The major force driving England and America together was the German submarine, a frightening new weapon that ultimately destroyed Wilson's hopes for peaceful resolution of neutral rights at sea. From the beginning the Germans determined to use their advantage to prevent valuable materials from reaching their enemies. They made it clear that their submarines might have to sink targets on sight—surfacing to search armed ships for contraband was suicidal. Early in 1915 they imposed a "war zone" around the British Isles in which they threatened to sink all enemy vessels. Neutral ships, they warned, would be in danger because of British misuse of neutral flags.

Germany's action was a bluff, for it lacked the subs to carry out such a sweeping blockade, and it had no intention at that time of sinking neutral ships. Moreover, Wilson's response, while holding Germany to "strict accountability" for illegal destruction of American ships or lives, did not even mention the difficult issue of the rights of American citizens to travel on belligerent ships. By May 1915 German-American relations, though troubled, were far from endangered.

At this point a German submarine sank without warning the *Lusitania,* a British passenger liner. Among the 1,198 people who died were 128 Americans. The sinking shocked people not yet inured to the ravages of total war.

> *Where are You, God? . . .*
> *I can't believe that you have seen*
> *The Things that they have done . . .*
> *And yet upon this earth of Yours*
> *There still exists the Hun. . . .*
>
> *Where are You, God?*
> *In whom I put my trust?*
> *You must be there,*
> *And You are great and just.*
> *Your mighty sea they've turned into a grave,*
> *A little baby slumbers on each wave. . . .*

A poem by Elsie Janis, musical actress, 1915, expressing American feelings about the sinking of the *Lusitania.*

"All the world," Ambassador Page commented privately, "should fall to and hunt this wild beast down." The sinking narrowed Wilson's options, for many Americans demanded that he uphold the nation's honor. Distressed, he sent stiff notes demanding that Germany desist from attacking unarmed merchant ships. His sternness cost him the resignation of Bryan, who felt that Wilson should warn Americans against traveling on belligerent vessels, that he should protest the British definition of contraband, and that ships like the *Lusitania* were secretly carrying arms. Bryan observed that "a person would have to be very much biased in favor of the Allies to insist that ammunition intended for one of the belligerents should be safe-guarded in transit by the lives of American citizens."

But Wilson too was not ready to go to war, and he was cheered when he declared that "there is such a thing as being too proud to fight." Instead, he resolved to affirm "strict accountability," including the right of Americans to travel on belligerent ships. Germany refused to accede to his demands and in August 1915 sank the *Arabic,* a British liner, causing the loss of two more American lives. But Wilson persevered, and Germany backed off far enough to promise it would no longer attack unarmed passenger liners without warning, unless they tried to escape. Though the *Arabic* pledge left unresolved the status of merchant ships and of armed passenger vessels, it suggested that Germany was bending. Wilson's patience appeared to be paying off.

Wilson then labored hard to end the war, and in February 1916 Colonel House reached with Lord Grey an agreement that appeared to be a significant step in that direction. The House-Grey memorandum stated that the President "on hearing from France and England that the moment was opportune," would call a conference to end the war. "Should the Allies accept this proposal, and should Germany refuse it, the United States would probably enter the war against Germany." The memorandum marked the high point of Wilson's wartime effort to mediate for peace.

In fact, however, no such conference was held. The Germans had never shown much interest in one, and the British, who were supposed to initiate the demand for mediation, never did so. Instead, they fought grimly on. Even if a conference had been called, Wilson might have been embarrassed, for he had no authority to commit the United States to war.

Meanwhile, Secretary Lansing, operating with Wilson's approval, suggested that the Allies disarm their merchant ships, in return for which German submarines would agree to give warnings. The delighted Germans announced they would begin attacking armed merchant ships on February 29. But Grey complained that Lansing's modus vivendi made the "sinking of merchant vessels the rule and not the exception." Wilson, belatedly recognizing that the modus vivendi was disrupting House's careful diplomacy, then disavowed the plan. The lack of communication between House and Lansing revealed the uncertainty of American diplomacy. And the failure of both their approaches

The Ventriloquist.

in 1916 suggested that nothing short of total victory would satisfy the exhausted belligerents.

Wilson's rejection of the modus vivendi infuriated antiwar congressmen. What would happen, they demanded to know, if the Germans made good their threat to sink armed merchant ships, on which Americans might well be traveling? Wilson replied that he would hold the Germans accountable. Alarmed, many leading Democrats supported the Gore-McLemore resolutions warning Americans against traveling on armed belligerent ships. Wilson fought back with an open letter to Senator William J. Stone, chairman of the foreign relations committee. "Once accept a single abatement of right," he declared, "and many other humiliations would certainly follow, and the whole fine fabric of international law might crumble piece by piece." Wilson's insistence on preserving national honor (and economic interests) carried the day, and early in March the resolutions failed in the House, 276 to 142.

Having reaffirmed his policy of strict accountability, Wilson now awaited the German response. It came quickly, for on March 24, 1916 a submarine torpedoed the *Sussex,* an unarmed French channel steamer. There were eighty casualties, including several badly wounded Americans. Pressed hard by both Lansing and House, Wilson sent a stiff note to Berlin. It demanded that Germany stop attacking without warning merchant and passenger vessels, armed or unarmed, belligerent or neutral. The Germans at first reacted angrily, but on May 4 they promised that submarines would visit and search before sinking merchant vessels, both in and out of the war zone. Though the note was truculent in tone, it met Wilson's demands. The policy of strict accountability, it appeared, had prevailed.

By then, however, advocates of preparedness were strident in America. The Germans, one critic said, were "standing by their torpedoes, the British

Having Their Fling.
The cartoonist Art Young was indicted during the war for cartoons like this one.

by their guns, and Wilson by strict accountability." Tin Pan Alley turned out songs with such titles as: "I Did Not Raise My Boy to Be a Coward," and "I'd Be Proud to Be the Mother of a Soldier." Theodore Roosevelt, more militaristic than ever, charged that the president, a "peace prattler," had "done more to emasculate American manhood and weaken its fiber than anyone else I can think of." The preparedness advocates forced through a bill more than doubling the Regular Army to 11,327 officers and 208,388 men, increasing the National Guard to an authorized strength in five years of 17,000 officers and 400,000 men, and integrating the Guard into the federal defense structure. They also secured passage of a bill authorizing huge expansion of the navy within three years. House Majority Leader Claude Kitchin, a leader of the antipreparedness forces, complained that "the United States today becomes the most militaristic naval nation on earth."

Wilson dismayed men like Kitchin by signing the army bill and by applying pressure for the naval act. But as the election of 1916 approached it was clear that the president, not Charles Evans Hughes, the Republican nominee, remained the bright hope for American peace workers. Indeed, he let it be said that he had "kept America out of war." "You Are Working—Not Fighting!" read one widely circulated Democratic handbill. "Alive and Happy—Not Cannon Fodder! Wilson and Peace with Honor? or Hughes with Roosevelt and War?" The misleading refrain, "he kept us out of war," was the central one of the campaign, and except for a few Socialists (who fared poorly at the polls), Wilson attracted all the advocates of restraint. He won the election by a very narrow margin.

But even during the campaign Wilson recognized a potential danger to his policy of strict accountability: it depended on German restraint. "I can't keep the country out of war," he observed privately. "Any little German lieutenant can put us into war at any time by some calculated outrage." Early in 1917 what he feared (but hadn't explained to the voters) finally happened: Germany announced a new, drastic policy of submarine warfare. After February 1, it announced, submarines would sink without warning all ships, belligerent or neutral, discovered in a zone around Great Britain, France, and Italy, and in the eastern Mediterranean. If Germany had contented itself with practicing such warfare against belligerent ships, Wilson might have tried to compromise. But the German threat against neutral ships was clearly aimed at nations such as the United States. On February 2 the President broke off diplomatic relations with Germany.

Wilson still hoped for peace. "We do not desire any hostile conflict with the Imperial German Government," he told Congress on February 3. Though American ships clung to port, causing cargo to pile up on the docks, he resisted congressional demands that he authorize the arming of merchant vessels. But on February 25 he received an intercepted message sent by the German Foreign Secretary, Arthur Zimmermann, to the German minister in Mexico. If America and Germany went to war, the message said, the minister should suggest that Mexico fight against the United States and receive in return the "lost territory in Texas, New Mexico, and Arizona." Wilson temporarily kept the note to himself, but it stiffened his resolve to adhere to strict accountability. The next day he went to Congress and asked for authority not only to arm merchantmen but also to "employ any other instrumentalities or methods that may be necessary and adequate to protect our ships and our people in their legitimate and peaceful pursuits on the seas."

Most congressmen were prepared to arm merchant ships, even though the result would certainly be shooting on the high seas, the loss of American life, and the outbreak of war. But a minority refused to grant Wilson blanket authority to "employ any other instrumentalities or methods that may be necessary." Such power, they contended, belonged to Congress. When Wilson publicized the Zimmermann note on March 1, the stunned House of Representatives gave him the authority to arm ships, but still denied him the broader powers he wished. And in the Senate eleven or twelve pacifists and noninterventionists, including Norris and La Follette, threatened to talk the bill to death. The American presidency, while much expanded since the days of Roosevelt, could not silence congressional dissent.

Most of the antiwar senators were from the Plains or Middle West, areas with weaker commercial and sentimental ties to the Allies and (in some cases) with relatively large proportions of German-Americans. They also represented the antimonopolistic wing of the progressive movement. Remembering a simpler era, they refused to accept either bigness in business or arbitrary use of presidential power. As humantarian progressives they were horrified by the thought of sending Americans to die in far-off Europe. And as opponents of large corporations they suspected economic motives for war. "Who are the patriots of the country?" La Follette asked rhetorically. "They are the Morgans, the Rockefellers, the Schwabs, the Garys, the DuPonts and those who are back of the thirty-eight corporations most benefitted by war orders. Shades of Lincoln! What a band of patriots!" Norris added later, "we are going to war upon the command of gold. We are about to put the dollar sign on the American flag."

> *There is no necessity for war with Germany—there is no necessity for war with any of the belligerent powers. Three thousand miles of water make it impossible for us to be drawn into that vortex of blood and passion and woe if we are true to the American people. If this administration shall put a higher estimate upon human life than commerical conquest; if we shall put the immortal soul above the dollar, and regard justice of more importance than financial success, there will be no war. It is not for the vindication of the principles of human justice that imperil our peace, but rather the avaricious reaching out for pelf that threatens to involve this Nation in this world war. I submit it would be more profitable to the people of the United States— better for the peoples of the world, rather than involve the United States in that war, to suspend commerce between Europe and America so far as American shipping interests are concerned. Not that I believe that Germany or England, or any other power, has a right to prevent our ships from going where they have a right to go on the high seas. I might have a right to go in the streets where a duel was being fought by participants in a drunken mob, but it would be better for me if I exercised the prudence of a brave, sane man, and remained away from the danger zone until order should be restored.*
>
> Sen. James Vardaman of Mississippi, one of the group of "willful men," speaks out against war, March 1917.

In working for nonintervention the filibusterers probably represented a majority opinion until April. But they encountered fierce abuse from superpatriots. Newspapers called them "descendents of Benedict Arnold," while Wilson coldly branded them "a little group of willful men, representing no opinion but their own." When they prevented passage of the bill, Wilson proceeded on his own to order the ships armed and to instruct them to shoot at subs that came within striking range. This action of dubious constitutionality made a naval war inevitable, and on March 18, submarines sank three American ships, with heavy loss of life. Wilson still hesitated, but by March 20, when he called Congress into special session for April 2, he had decided that America must fight.

His call for war on April 2 was magnificently idealistic. The United States, he said, "had no quarrel with the German people." On the contrary, it would fight for "the ultimate peace of the world and for the liberation of its peoples, and the German peoples included." Wilson added that "the world must be made safe for democracy. Its peace must be planted on the tested foundations

New York's Sixty-ninth Infantry kisses the girls goodbye.

of political liberty. We have no selfish ends to serve. . . . We are but one of the champions of the rights of mankind." His eloquent speech impressed even such partisan critics as Roosevelt and Henry Cabot Lodge. And though men like Norris, Kitchin, and La Follette fought him to the end, the die was cast. The Senate adopted the resolution for war by a vote of 82 to 6, and at three in the morning of April 6 the House concurred, 373 to 50. Wilson signed the country into war the next afternoon.

AMERICAN POLICY RECONSIDERED

Two major questions arise concerning American policy toward Europe in the years between 1914 and 1917. Why did the United States go to war? Could war have been avoided?

The first question has called forth various answers. Some people, like House and Lansing at the time, thought war necessary to protect American security. Others, following Wilson's war message, assumed that American motives were primarily idealistic: to make the world safe for democracy. Critics like La Follette blamed the corporations and the bankers. Still others have qualified this economic interpretation by pointing to a broader national demand for a world in which American capitalism must be permitted to expand.

None of these answers is wholly satisfactory. The view that America fought to preserve its security simply ignores the fact that neither Wilson nor most Americans thought in such Rooseveltian terms. The argument that Wilson sought to make the world safe for democracy confuses his rhetoric of April 1917 with more prosaic—and much more important—causes relating to Germany's submarine warfare. The focus on narrow economic interests ignores the fact that bankers and corporations, though profiting immensely from war, had little impact on Wilson or Congress. The stress on broader economic considerations—or preserving an "open door" for democratic capitalism—captures part of the truth, for Wilson, like many Americans, assumed that America's future depended on its ability to protect and to expand its overseas interests. But such a view is one-sided if it underplays Wilson's peculiar rectitude. However quaint it may seem to sophisticates of the 1970s, his primary aim was to uphold his country's neutral rights—for their own sake as well as for the commercial advantages such rights might maintain. To Wilson as to many other Americans "national honor" was very much worth fighting for.

This policy worked tolerably well until 1917. It forced the Germans to back down after the sinking of the *Lusitania* in 1915 and the *Sussex* in 1916. It was politically successful, for it satisfied most noninterventionists and pacifists, as well as those who insisted that he protect neutral rights, and it left extremists like Roosevelt isolated on the fringe. Wilson's neutrality policy until early 1917 achieved its basic goal: to preserve American nonbelligerency with honor.

The problem with this policy was that it depended for its success on the restraint of Germany. More generally, it revealed how difficult it was for a nation as powerful as the United States to remain either "isolated" or "neutral" amidst total war in Europe. Having insisted on the right of American ships to sail the seas, Wilson inevitably had to protect them from attack. It was the German decision to wage unrestricted submarine warfare—a decision based on domestic perceptions of military needs—that destroyed these goals and provoked America's declaration of war.

Could American participation in the conflict have been avoided? Two schools of thought answer yes. One argues that Wilson should have worked harder for preparedness, that Germany would never have dared to embark on unrestricted submarine warfare if the United States had shown it was ready to fight. The other insists that Wilson was a "sermonizer," that he should have accepted limits on American neutral rights, that such "rights" made no sense in the age of the submarine.

The proponents of better preparedness tend to underestimate the difficulties as well as the limitations of such a policy. No such course stood much of a chance in Congress before 1916, and even after America's entrance into the war, conscription encountered stubborn congressional opposition. If Wilson had desired to arm America to the teeth, he could have done so, if at all, only by manufacturing the very crises that he properly wished to avoid. Most important, it is doubtful that the specter of a well-prepared America would have altered the German decision for unrestricted warfare. On the contrary, that ultimately fatal decision stemmed from the desperation of a government brutalized by the bloodiest war in world history, and it would probably have come regardless of the state of American preparedness.

The argument that Wilson was too righteous at first appears convincing. Seen from the perspective of the 1970s, when experience with total wars makes talk about "national honor" seem dangerous, Wilson's policy seems ill-advised. In defending the privilege—for that is what it was—of Americans to travel on belligerent ships, Wilson also affirmed a provocative definition of neutral rights. Suppose he had backed off on that point: Americans might have thought twice before traveling on such ships; many of the 175 citizens who were killed on such vessels before February 1917 might have been saved; and a major source of tension would have been dispelled. German-American relations would unquestionably have been more amicable between 1914 and early 1917 if Wilson from the start had warned Americans to stay off belligerent ships.

But his strong stand on that issue was not the major cause of war. Indeed, the United States remained at peace with Germany for almost two years after the sinking of the *Lusitania*. The basic cause—again—was Germany's decision to sink neutral as well as belligerent vessels. This decision left Wilson with three equally unpalatable courses of action. The first, to keep American ships out of the war zones, would have meant the politically perilous surrender of traditional neutral rights and of "national honor." Given America's economic and cultural ties with England, no president could have pursued such a policy without playing into the hands of militarists like TR. The second course, to affirm the right of ships to enter the zones but to leave them unarmed, in practice meant the same surrender of neutral rights, for such ships refused to sail. The remaining course was to arm the ships, to let them sail, and to hope the Germans would leave them alone. When Germany did not, Wilson was cornered. If he had still refused to ask for war, the pressure of Congress and public opinion would soon have given him no other choice.

The most compelling criticism of Wilson's inflexible policy is that it deprived the United States of the initiative. When Germany decided to embark on unrestricted submarine warfare, America was trapped. But if Wilson had shown any signs of weakening, the German decision might well have been made in 1916. However much Americans may like to think that they can always direct world events, other nations sometimes pursue policies that they know will lead to war. Such a policy was adopted by Germany in 1917, by which time the passions of warfare drove all the belligerents to acts of desperation. Given America's crucial economic and strategic role in the world by that time, it is hard to see how Wilson could have kept the United States isolated from such passions or how he or any other democratic leader could have preserved a monopoly of initiative in the cause of peace.

Suggestions for reading

General interpretations of American Foreign policy—all of which cover a much broader period than the years dealt with in this chapter—are William A. Williams, *The Tragedy of American Foreign Policy** (1962), a revisionist account emphasizing economic forces; George Kennan, *American Diplomacy, 1900–1950** (1950), a "realist's" account; and Robert Osgood, *Ideals and Self-Interest in American Foreign Policy* (1953), a well-written "realist" interpretation. Other general books are Norman Graebner, ed., *An Uncertain Tradition: American Secretaries of State in the Twentieth Century** (1961); John A. S. Grenville and George Berkeley Young, *Politics, Strategy, and American Diplomacy: Studies in Foreign Policy, 1873–1917* (1966); and Richard D. Challener, *Admirals, Generals, and American Foreign Policy, 1898–1914* (1973).

The growth of American involvement abroad is treated in Ernest May, *Imperial Years: The Emergence of America as a Great Power* (1961); H. Wayne Morgan, *America's Road to Empire: The War with Spain and Overseas Expansion** (1965); Walter LaFeber, *The New Empire: An Interpretation of American Expansion, 1860–1898* (1963); and Julius Pratt, *The Expansionists of 1898* (1936). Other relevant books are Ernest May, *American Imperialism, A Speculative Essay** (1968); Robert L. Beisner, *Twelve Against Empire: The Anti-Imperialists, 1898–1900** (1968); and E. Berkeley Tompkins, *Anti-Imperialism in the United States: The Great Debate, 1890–1920* (1970).

The Roosevelt years receive thorough treatment in Howard Beale, *Theodore Roosevelt and the Rise of America to World Power* (1956). See also Raymond Esthus, *Theodore Roosevelt and the International Rivalries* (1970), and the books on TR by Pringle and Harbaugh mentioned in the bibliography for chapter 3. For the Taft years Pringle's *Life and Times of William Howard Taft,* 2 vols. (1939), also mentioned in chapter 3, is thorough. More recent is Walter and Marie Scholes, *The Foreign Policies of the Taft Administration* (1970). Easily the most careful account of Wilson is the multivolume biography by Arthur Link listed in the bibliography for chapter 3. *Wilson: The Diplomatist** (1957), by Link, is a collection of lectures that provide important insights.

Coverage of Caribbean affairs can be found in Dexter Perkins, *The Monroe Doctrine, 1867–1907** (1937); Robert Freeman Smith, *The U. S. and Revolutionary Nationalism in Mexico, 1916–1932* (1972); Dana G. Munro, *Intervention and Dollar Diplomacy in the Caribbean, 1900–1921* (1964); Robert E. Quirk, *An Affair of Honor: Woodrow Wilson and the Occupation of Vera Cruz** (1962); and P. Edward Haley, *Revolution and Intervention: The Diplomacy of Taft and Wilson with Mexico, 1910– 1917* (1970). For Asian affairs, see Charles E. Neu, *An Uncertain Friendship: Theodore Roosevelt and Japan, 1906–1909* (1967); Akira Iriye, *Across the Pacific: An Inner History of American–East Asian Relations* (1969); Paul A. Varg, *The Making of a Myth: The United States and China, 1879–1912* (1968); and Roy W. Curry, *Woodrow Wilson and Far Eastern Policy, 1913–1921* (1968).

For American involvement in World War 1 see vols. 3–5 by Link on Wilson. Also Ernest May, *The World War and American Isolation, 1914–1917* (1959); Ross Gregory, *The Origins of American Intervention in the First World War** (1971); Daniel M. Smith. *The Great Departure: The United States in World War I, 1914–1920** (1965); and John M. Cooper, Jr., *The Vanity of Power: American Isolationism and the First World War, 1914–1917* (1969), an account of domestic opinion.

The divisiveness of war

"If this war had not come," wrote Ray Stannard Baker, "we should all have been rotten."

Baker, an ardent Wilsonian, meant that the war would put an end to all wars. Like many contemporaries, he also hoped that it would heal divisions at home. The war would bring justice to the world and unity and progress to the United States.

Much that happened in 1917 and 1918 appeared to confirm Baker's expectations. American military strength, for instance, was indispensable to the Allied cause. Early in 1917, German U-boats were sinking nearly 900,000 tons of shipping per month. By November 1917 American warships helped cut losses to less than 300,000 tons per month, and after April 1918 the Allies never lost more than 200,000 tons per month. Had the pre-1917 rate been maintained, Britain would have run out of grain within two months. On land the United States supplied a million troops by July 1918 and 2 million by November. The Americans cracked the southern front at St. Mihiel between the Argonne Forest and The Vosges Mountains and helped the Allies break the long stalemate in the trenches. The war cost 116,000 American lives (53,000 in battle) and 204,000 wounded—stiff losses for so short a time. But the deaths numbered only a third of those killed in the Civil War, and they were trifling compared to those sustained by England (900,000), France (1.35 million), and Russia (1.7 million). The apparent ease of victory encouraged Americans to maintain their faith in small peacetime armies, to reaffirm General Grant's belief in slugging it out, and to pay relatively little attention in the 1920s and 1930s to the development of tank warfare or fighter planes.

The benefits of war appeared equally salutary at home. Reformers cheered the institution of prohibition, women's suffrage, and progressive taxation, all of which were promoted by the exigencies of war. They applauded the liberal policies of the War Labor Board, which helped union membership grow from approximately 2.5 million in 1915 to more than 5 million in 1920. War orders also brought prosperity as early as 1915. Wages for all workers jumped from an average of $633 per year in 1915 to $1,407 in 1920, while stock prices, which had wallowed in 1913, broke upward in 1915 and remained high until 1920. The war made America a creditor nation for the first time, with investments abroad increasing from $3.5 billion in June 1914 to $7 billion in 1919. (Foreign investments in the United States decreased during the same period from $7.2 billion to $3.3 billion.) And war caused the GNP to leap from an average of $40 billion between 1912 and 1916 to more than $80 billion between 1917 and 1921. This was a per capita increase from $408 to $835, a rate of progress never approached thereafter.

An unprecedented Federal partnership with business interests accompanied and promoted this economic boom. The government took over the railroads, and it established new agencies such as the Food Administration, Fuel Administration, Shipping Board, and Emergency Fleet Administration to supervise and assist the private sector. The Webb-Pomerene Act of 1918 permitted corporations engaged in the export trade to combine without fear of antitrust action. The needs of war accelerated the growth of trucking, and in 1919 the administration sold 27,000 surplus trucks and bulldozers to states that used them to promote highway building, a major force for prosperity in the 1920s. And under the canny leadership of Bernard Baruch, a financier who headed the important War Industries Board, Wilson encouraged the "new competition" in business. This was a euphemism for an entente between government and big business that featured informal price fixing and collusive bidding. "The great difficulty about the distribution of work among smaller manufacturers," Baruch said frankly, "is the difficulty of getting the work done. . . . We have been trying to meet this situation by endeavoring to get a number of firms to consolidate." Baruch's partiality toward mergers assisted the long-range movement toward economic concentration.

Wilson's favoritism toward big business showed that he had moved far from the New Freedom of 1912 and that the election of Warren G. Harding in 1920, instead of signifying a return to "normalcy," meant a continuation of Federal policy already well entrenched. But the fact of business profits did not mean that large corporations overwhelmed their smaller competitors. On the contrary, big business sometimes lost ground—as was the case in steel and automobiles—to newer, more efficient companies that profited from access to the vast wartime markets. The partnership between government and business also stopped short of becoming a "military-industrial complex" or of developing into highly centralized or compulsory public planning. Both Bernard Baruch and Herbert Hoover, the efficient engineer who headed the Food Administration during the war, prided themselves on employing voluntaristic methods to secure cooperation. Still, the effectiveness of agencies like the Food Administration and the War Industries Board seemed to confirm the progressive faith in governmental planning. As early as 1917 this faith led Americans to accept such "advancements" as psychological placement and standardized testing of soldiers. In 1933 it led New Dealers to believe that the experience of government-business cooperation in World War I offered an answer to ending the depression.

The burdens of war

Almost from the beginning, however, it was clear that the war could not eradicate the prewar divisions of American society. Prosperity and economic growth, though enlarging the size of the pie, stimulated the expectations of pressure groups, who scrambled for their shares. Reflecting these pressures, Congress resisted price control and allocation of food until August 1917, four months after the American declaration of war. Controversy erupted constantly over such sensitive questions as profiteering, the location of army bases, the staffing of wartime agencies, outbreaks of pneumonia and meningitis in training camps, and shortages of coal that caused misery among the urban poor in the winter of 1917–18. Contrary to a common impression, Wilson's problems with Congress did not begin during the struggle for the League of Nations in 1919: they were commonplace during the war.

Easily the most divisive issue was inflation. Food prices more than doubled between 1915 and 1920, as did the cost of living in general. The potent southern bloc in Congress successfully resisted attempts to impose price

Because Wilson kept us out of war
He kept us out of peace
He kept us out of clothing
He kept us out of booze
He kept us out of sugar
He kept us out of beer
And made America safe
For rent hogs and profiteers.

Hiram Johnson's view of Wilson's wartime domestic policy, 1919.

Children on the east side of New York City raid a cinder pile for fuel. Scenes such as this were common in the cold winter of 1917–18, when coal shortages were serious.

controls on cotton, and clothing tripled in cost during those years. Spokesmen for the wheat farmers resented this favoritism and turned on the Democratic party in the election of 1918. Other citizens complained bitterly about the increased income taxes imposed to support the war: "progressivism" in this guise lost its appeal when people had to pay for it. For all these reasons Wilson faced a Republican Congress when he looked for help with the Versailles Treaty in 1919.

The war years also intensified racial tensions. Even before 1917, the economic boom combined with the ravages of the boll weevil in the South to spur mass migrations of blacks to northern cities. Thousands more were lured north as strike-breakers. Southern whites were so troubled by this exodus of cheap labor that they resorted to intimidation and violence. One mob in Mississippi even derailed a train to keep the blacks at home. (In the 1950s and 1960s, when agriculture was more mechanized, southern whites were happy to see the blacks go.) Northerners, alarmed by the "invasion" of 1915–19, retaliated by spreading the pattern of segregation and discrimination and then by employing violence. Racial tensions erupted in riots in twenty-six cities in 1917, including frightening confrontations in St. Louis, Omaha, and Houston.

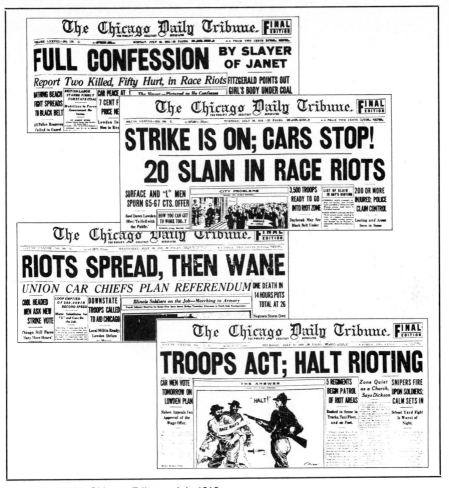

Headlines in the *Chicago Tribune,* July 1919.

We return from the slavery of uniform which the world's madness demanded of us to don to the freedom of civil garb. We stand again to look America squarely in the face and call a spade a spade. We sing: This country of ours, despite all its better souls have done and dreamed, is yet a shameful land.

It LYNCHES ... it DISFRANCHISES ITS OWN CITIZENS ... it encourages IGNORANCE ... it steals from us ... it insults us.

We return. We return from fighting. We return fighting.

Make way for Democracy. We saved it in France and by the Great Jehovah, we will save it in the USA, or know the reason why.

Black militancy, 1919.

The end of the war merely intensified these racial confrontations. Black soldiers, some 400,000 in all, deeply resented the segregation and discrimination they had encountered in the service. Those who had been abroad returned with memories of more benevolent racial patterns. The result was rising black militancy, especially in northern cities. Whites lashed back, and disturbances broke out in 1919. The worst, in Chicago, exploded in four days of fighting that killed twenty-three blacks and fifteen whites before troops stepped in. These race riots ended all hope for racial harmony and proved that the war failed to promote democracy at home.

THE WAR AND CIVIL LIBERTIES

The most frightening domestic result of the war was the encouragement it gave to superpatriotic conformity. Deluded into thinking they could stay neutral, Americans suddenly found themselves engaged in total war. To keep the doubters quiet Wilson explained that the war would end all wars, that it was a cause of righteousness against evil. Those who dissented, by definition, enlisted on the side of hell.

Such idealistic rhetoric was intended to appeal to people's nobler instincts. But other Americans used the passions of war to unleash campaigns of hatred against the enemy and against "slackers" at home. "Oh Lord," declared the popular evangelist Billy Sunday, "smite the hungry, wolfish Hun whose fangs drip with blood, and we will forever raise our voice in praise." Others saw in the passions of war the chance to exclude aliens and to preserve older ways of life. The *Saturday Evening Post* demanded the removal of "the scum of the melting pot" from American life, and a popular wartime song warned:

> If you don't like your Uncle Sammy,
> Then go back to your home o'er the sea,
> To the land from where you came,
> Whatever be its name;
> But don't be ungrateful to me!
> If you don't like the stars in Old Glory,
> If you don't like the Red, White, and Blue,
> Then don't act like the cur in the story,
> Don't bite the hand that's feeding you.

Wilson and his aides encouraged this indigenous strain of intolerance. "This is a People's war," he proclaimed. "Woe be to the man or group of men that seeks to stand in our way in this high day of resolution when every principle we hold dearest is to be vindicated and made secure for the salvation of nations." Wilson established the government's first full-blown propaganda agency, the Committee on Public Information. Headed by the dynamic

George Creel, the agency employed able writers, reformers, and intellectuals to sell bonds, popularize war aims, and encourage voluntary censorship by newspapermen. CPI volunteers distributed some 5 million "Red White and Blue" pamphlets, and gave one million patriotic "Four Minute Speeches" during the war. They also encouraged thought control and witch hunts. Free speech in wartime was simply out of the question, Creel quoted Wilson as saying. "There could be no such thing . . . it was insanity."

The CPI was an ominous sign of what a purposeful central government could do. But its function was to exhort, not to punish, so in June 1917 Congress approved the Espionage Act, which permitted the government to ban newspapers and magazines from the mails and which subjected people convicted of obstructing the draft to fines of $10,000 and twenty years in prison. Postmaster Albert S. Burleson immediately interpreted the law to mean that he could censor any printed matter that "interfered with the success of any Federal loan . . . or caused insubordination, disloyalty, mutiny, or refusal of duty in the military or naval service, or obstructed the recruiting, draft, or enlistment services . . . or otherwise embarrassed or hampered the government." Within a month he denied mailing privileges to fifteen major publications, including the *Milwaukee Leader* and the *Masses.* Because he used the classic bureaucratic method of refusing to clarify his standards, editors never knew when the government might swoop down on them. In 1918 Burleson received even greater authority through the Sedition Act, which authorized the prosecution of people who attempted to obstruct the draft or who used "disloyal, profane, scurrilous, or abusive language" concerning the government, the Constitution, the armed forces, or the flag. More than 2100 people were prosecuted under these statutes.

Conscientious objectors were one target of this campaign for "right thinking." Secretary of War Newton Baker tried to be fair by offering them the possibility of alternative noncombatant service. In fact, America's treatment of c.o.'s—some 65,000 of 24 million registrants for selective service—was

The war effort took place on many levels. Douglas Fairbanks urges people to buy bonds at a Liberty Loan rally. A woman welder works in a munitions factory. Army trainees use wooden guns in place of real weapons. The propaganda machine grinds out patriotic posters.

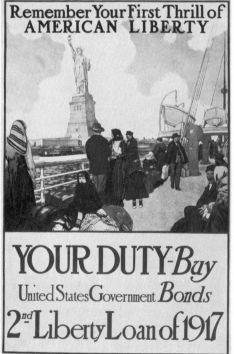

Remember Your First Thrill of
AMERICAN LIBERTY

YOUR DUTY-Buy
United States Government Bonds
2nd Liberty Loan of 1917

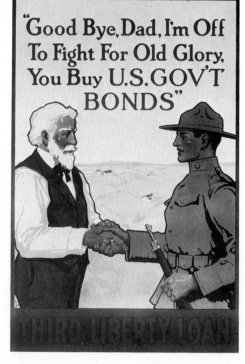

"Good Bye, Dad, I'm Off To Fight For Old Glory, You Buy U.S.GOV'T BONDS"

THIRD LIBERTY LOAN

> *I have been accused of having obstructed the war. I admit it. Gentlemen, I abhor war. I would oppose the war if I stood alone. . . . I wish to admit everything that has been said respecting me from this witness chair. I wish to admit everything that has been charged against me except what is embraced in the indictment. . . . I cannot take back a word. I can't repudiate a sentence. I stand before you guilty of having made this speech . . . prepared to take the consequences of what there is embraced.*
>
> Debs' "defense" against sedition in World War I.

more enlightened than that in other belligerent nations during the war. But only members of pacifistic religious groups, perhaps 5000 of the 21,000 c.o.'s inducted, qualified for alternative service; others took up arms or faced prison sentences ranging up to twenty-five years. An estimated 400 c.o.'s went to jail, including Roger Baldwin, head of the National Civil Liberties Bureau, which was the precursor of the American Civil Liberties Union. According to Attorney General Thomas Gregory, Baldwin was "one of a very dangerous class of persons . . . an active pacifist . . . not leading a moral life."

C.o.'s, however, were hardly numerous or threatening. Radicals and antiwar socialists, who struck many Americans as subversive, were a much more inviting target. Among socialist leaders jailed under the Espionage Act were Victor Berger of Milwaukee, who was twice denied his seat in Congress as a result of his conviction; Debs, who urged socialists to "resist militarism, wherever found" (and who spent thirty-two months in prison); and Rose Pastor Stokes, whose mistake was to assert that "no government which is *for* the profiteers can also be *for* the people, and I am for the people." The government also pounced on the IWW, confiscating its office materials (including typewriters and petty cash) and arresting 165 of its most militant members. When Baldwin interceded, Secretary of War Baker urged Wilson to drop the cases. But the President replied that the IWW was "certainly . . . worthy of being suppressed." Most of the leaders were sentenced to terms ranging up to twenty-five years.

In applying such laws men like Gregory occasionally had to confront organizations such as the American Union Against Militarism, a group of pacifists who included Norman Thomas and Jane Addams. (Its symbol for militarism was a dinosaur named "Jingo" and labeled "All Armor Plate— No Brains.") But Gregory safely challenged them, for he could rely on the greatest of all pressures for conformity: an aroused public. Patriots organized groups with names like the American Defense Society, the Sedition Slammers, the Terrible Threateners, the American Vigilante Patrol, and the Boy Spies of America. Vigilantes in Bisbee, Arizona, rounded up 1200 striking copper miners in July 1917 and dumped them in the New Mexico desert. An Indiana jury took two minutes to acquit a man who shot and killed a man who had yelled, "To hell with the United States." A motion picture producer was sentenced to ten years in jail for his movie, *The Spirit of '76,* because it allegedly aroused hostility to Britain, America's wartime ally. And almost all things German, from sauerkraut (renamed Liberty Cabbage), to Beethoven, to hamburger (renamed Salisbury Steak) were banned or criticized during the war.

Such occurrences prove that Gregory was not exaggerating when he boasted of having "several hundred thousand private citizens . . . keeping an eye on disloyal individuals and making reports of disloyal utterances, and seeing that the people of this country are not deceived." The crusade against dissent in World War I unquestionably benefited from the active encouragement of the central government. But it succeeded because it fed on a broad, popular feeling that deviance in thought as well as deed must be suppressed.

In 1919 the high Court recognized this feeling by sustaining the wartime statutes. The Espionage Act, Justice Holmes held in *Schenck* v. *U. S.* (1919), was justified. "The question in every case," he said, "is whether the words are used in such circumstances and are of such a nature as to create a clear and present danger that they will bring about the substantial evils that Congress has a right to prevent. It is a question of proximity and degree. When a nation is at war many things that might be said in time of peace are such a hindrance to its effort that their utterance will not be endured so long as men fight." The First Amendment, he added, was not absolute, for "the most stringent protection of free speech would not protect a man falsely shouting fire in a theater and causing a panic." In the case of *Abrams* v. *U. S.* (1919) Holmes took a slightly more libertarian view by defending a "free trade in ideas." The "best test of truth," he said, "is the power of the thought to get itself accepted in the competition of the market. . . . we should be eternally vigilant against attempts to check the aggression of opinions that we loathe." But Holmes was outvoted, and the Abrams decision sustained the Sedition Act, seven to two. In reaching such decisions the Court placed its view of the national interest ahead of the Bill of Rights. In doing so it was merely reflecting the majority view of the time.

An intriguing question remains: Why, with little organized opposition to war, did this crusade against dissent occur? One reason is that the centralized state now possessed the resources to assist such a crusade. Another is that the mass nature of the war—the first total conflict in modern history—caused all peoples involved in it (in Europe as well as in America) to become harsh and even hysterical about "slackers" and "seditionists." From this perspective America was no more repressive than other countries caught up in the holocaust. And a third is that the war served as the occasion for "purifying" American life, for restoring to it some of the social harmony that was presumed to have existed in the "good old days"of 1914, or 1890. When these broad forces came together in 1917, they threw the nation into one of the periodic panics of intolerance that have stained American history.

The Red Scare

If peace in November 1918 had brought stability to America, these excesses might have faded from sight. But wartime inflation left many American workers dissatisfied, and they determined to strike for recognition and for better pay. In January 1919, 35,000 shipyard workers in Seattle went on strike. When laborers in other trades joined them, it appeared for a few days that a general strike of 100,000 people might paralyze the region. A series of labor disturbances followed in the spring and summer, culminating that September in a strike of Boston police officers, which Wilson called a "crime against civilization." Some 350,000 steel workers went on strike a few days later, shortly to be emulated by coal miners.

This rash of strikes terrified people of property, who were quick to blame aliens, radicals, and communists. In March 1919 the Bolsheviks, who had secured power in Russia in 1917, proclaimed their dedication to worldwide revolution, and communist revolts erupted in eastern Europe. A few weeks later, homemade bombs, timed to go off on May Day, began appearing in the mail of people like John D. Rockefeller, Postmaster General Burleson, and Mayor Ole Hanson, the Red-baiting mayor of Seattle. On June 2, bombs exploded in eight American cities at the same hour, and one damaged the home of Attorney General A. Mitchell Palmer. The bomb thrower at Palmer's house was blasted to pieces, but evidence suggested he was an Italian alien and an anarchist. And in September 1919 radicals appeared to complete preparations for revolution by forming the American Communist and Communist Labor parties. Though divided along ethnic lines (most of the foreign-language speakers joined the CP), both groups were endorsed by the Third International. Their estimated combined membership totaled between 25,000 and 40,000 people.

These events created a Red Scare of unprecedented proportions. Chief of Staff General Leonard Wood demanded the deportation of Bolsheviks in "ships of stone with sails of lead, with the wrath of God for a breeze and with hell for their first port." Billy Sunday added, "If I had my way with these

---

The so-called sympathetic Seattle strike was an attempted revolution. That there was no violence does not alter the fact. . . . The intent, openly and covertly announced, was for the overthrow of the industrial system; here first, then everywhere. . . . True, there were no flashing guns, no bombs, no killings. Revolution, I repeat, doesn't need violence. The general strike, as practiced in Seattle, is of itself the weapon of revolution, all the more dangerous because quiet. To succeed, it must suspend everything; stop the entire life stream of a community. . . . That is to say, it puts the government out of operation. And that is all there is to revolt—no matter how achieved.

Mayor Ole Hanson of Seattle defines revolution.

Attorney General Palmer reports to Congress on American radicals.

ornery, wild-eyed Socialists and IWW's, I would stand them up before a firing squad and save some space on our ships." The Harvard *Crimson* damned the British Socialist Harold Laski, who had defended the striking policemen, as "Laski de Lenin" and "Ivan Itchykoff," Bolshevik seducer of Radcliffe girls. Elbert Gary, head of U. S. Steel, refused even to recognize the steel union. "The contemplated progress of trade unions if successful," he declared, "would be to secure the control of the shops, then of the general management of business, then of capital, and finally of government."

Attorney General Palmer, an ardent Wilsonian progressive, then brought the full force of the federal government into play. In August he called on J. Edgar Hoover to run a new antiradical division of the Department of Justice. In November Palmer staged raids on radicals in twelve cities, arresting 250 people and recommending 39 for deportation. On December 21, 1919, he deported 249 aliens, including Emma Goldman, to Russia. Few of the 249 were Bolsheviks, many were philosophical anarchists opposed to violence, and most had no criminal records. And on one night in January 1920 Palmer's men arrested more than 4000 alleged Communists throughout the nation. Many of the suspects were kept for days in jail without charges, kicked about or denied food by police, or held incommunicado. The raids were justified, Palmer said, because the country was infested with the "moral perverts and hysterical neurasthenic women who abound in communism."

The Red Scare then subsided almost as quickly as it had started. Cooler heads prevailed in the Department of Labor, and only 600 aliens were ultimately deported. Most of the arrested Communists, having commited no crimes, were released. By midsummer of 1920 labor agitation had been quashed and American radicals had become badly split into warring factions of Socialists, Communists, and Communist Laborites. Most important, Americans relaxed as the threat of bolshevism in Europe subsided. By September

Americans refused to respond to Palmer's proclamation of impending revolution even after a wagonload of bombs exploded on Wall Street, killing 33 and injuring 200 more. Warren Harding, no radical, pronounced the epitaph: "too much has been said about bolshevism in America."

The treatment of dissenters between 1919 and 1920 marked the most wholesale deprivation of civil liberties in American history. It effectively stifled the labor movement for more than a decade. It showed that supposedly progressive public officials, like the people at large, lacked even an elementary understanding of the Bill of Rights or of the distinctions between socialism, anarchism, and communism. It resulted in 1920 in the arrest for murder of Nicola Sacco and Bartolomeo Vanzetti, Italian aliens and anarchists whose ultimately unsuccessful battles to escape execution were depressing reminders of the excesses of intolerance. And it profoundly discouraged people who might otherwise have worked for reform. Frederic Howe, the immigration commissioner who fought against deportations, confessed that his faith in public power as an agent of reform had been misplaced. "My attitude toward the state," he wrote later, "was changed as a result of these experiences. I have never been able to bring it back. I became distrustful of the state. It seemed to want to hurt people; it showed no concern for innocence; it aggrandized itself and protected its power by unscrupulous means. It was not my America, it was something else.''

The fight for the League of Nations

During much of the time that Palmer was conducting his raids Wilson was either at Paris negotiating the peace treaty, on speaking tours defending it, or—after suffering a severe stroke in October 1919—trying vainly to restore his health. Had he succeeded in concluding the peace he sought, he might have been forgiven the excesses of his domestic policies. But the Senate ultimately refused to approve the treaty. In so doing it showed that neither Wilson nor the Senate as yet had a realistic sense of America's role in world affairs.

Prospects for the ''peace without victory'' that Wilson desired appeared excellent in late 1918. ''We expected,'' Lewis Mumford recalled, ''that at the end of that fierce and rancorous conflict, in which other men had been engaged for four searing years, the beat of angels' wings would at once be heard in the sky, and concord and brotherly love would immediately settle over the earth.'' When Wilson went to France after the armistice, he was acclaimed by the European people. One woman wrote, ''Wilson, you have given back the father to his home, the ploughman to his field. . . . You have saved our children. Through you evil is punished. Wilson. Wilson. Glory to you, who, like Jesus, have said: Peace on Earth and Good Will to Men.''

From the start, however, Wilson made tactical errors that did his cause no good in the Senate. The first of these occurred before the midterm elections of 1918 when he asked voters to return loyal Democratic majorities. This ill-advised appeal, which Colonel House regarded as a ''needless venture,'' backfired when the voters sent a Republican majority, angry at Wilson's slurs on their patriotism, to Washington. Wilson then compounded his error by naming himself to head the peace delegation and by including no senators or prominent Republicans on it. ''There is no God but God, and Mohammed is his prophet,'' California Senator Hiram Johnson observed. ''In selecting himself as the head of the American delegates to the conference, President Wilson has named himself five times.''

INTERNATIONAL RELATIONS AND THE PEACE CONFERENCE
AT VERSAILLES

Wilson also faced an almost herculean task at Versailles, for Prime Minister David Lloyd George of Britain and Premier Georges Clemenceau of France were determined to secure economic and territorial aims that they had secretly mapped out early in the war. The Italian delegate, Vittorio Orlando, was

Clemenceau, Wilson, and Lloyd George leave the Palace of Versailles
after signing the peace treaty.

concerned primarily with gaining disputed territory for his country. The
Japanese exerted pressure for further concessions in east Asia. None of these
nations welcomed Wilson's Fourteen Points, which called for "open covenants of peace, openly arrived at," freedom of the seas, free trade, the self-
determination of peoples, just territorial settlements, fair treatment of Germany, and a "general association of nations." "God gave us the Ten Com-
mandments," Clemenceau said, "and we broke them. Wilson gave us the
Fourteen Points. We shall see."

The specter of the Soviet Union also haunted the conference. Wilson,
perceiving himself as the spokesman for capitalistic democracy, was appalled
by Lenin's contrary vision of the future, and he refused to recognize the
Soviet Union—or to admit it to deliberations at Paris. The Allies, furious at
Soviet withdrawal from the war against Germany in February 1918, had sent
in troops to reopen the eastern front. When the conference opened, these
troops were helping Russian counterrevolutionaries try to overthrow the
Bolshevik regime.

To his credit, Wilson refused to engage American troops in the Russian
civil war. But he did decide in the summer of 1918 to dispatch 5,000 men to

1. "Open covenants of peace, openly arrived at" and an end to secret diplomacy.
2. "Absolute freedom of navigation upon the seas . . . alike in peace and in war."
3. "The removal, so far as possible, of all economic barriers" to free trade.
4. Reduction of armaments "to the lowest point consistent with domestic safety."
5. An "absolutely impartial adjustment of all colonial claims" giving equal weight to the interests of the colonial populations and "the equitable claims" of the imperial governments.
6. "The evacuation of all Russian territory" and cooperation to allow Russia "the independent determination of her own political development and national policy and assure her of a sincere welcome into the society of free nations under institutions of her own choosing."
7. German evacuation of Belgium and restoration of full sovereignty.
8. "All French territory should be freed" and Alsace-Lorraine, taken by Prussia in 1871, should be returned to France.
9. "A readjustment of the frontiers of Italy . . . along clearly recognizable lines of nationality."
10. Autonomy for the peoples of Austria-Hungary.
11. Evacuation of Rumania, Montenegro, and Serbia; international guarantee of the political and economic independence of the Balkan states; and Serbian access to the sea.
12. Autonomy for the subject nationalities within the Turkish Empire and free passage through the Dardanelles for ships of all nations.
13. An independent Poland with "free and secure access to the sea."
14. "A general association of nations."

Wilson's Fourteen Points.

northern Russia and 10,000 more to Vladivostok near Manchuria. His motives for sending the expeditions were honorable: to stop supplies from reaching the Germans, to help stranded Czech soldiers get out of Siberia, and to warn the Japanese against overrunning Manchuria. But Wilson did not remove the American troops from northern Russia until June 1919 and from the Manchurian area until April 1920. During this time they did nothing to keep supplies from Germany (Lenin got them out of the way on his own), to evacuate the Czechs, who regrouped and fought the Bolsheviks, or to deter the Japanese, who stayed in Manchuria until 1922. Understandably, the Soviets distrusted Wilson's motives, the more so because he refused to deal with them in Paris. The gulf that developed between Russia and the West cast a measure of unreality over the whole proceedings at the conference.

In the face of so many obstacles Wilson did well to salvage parts of his Fourteen Points. With the help of Lloyd George he successfully resisted the French demand for the cession of the Saar basin. Instead, the Saarland was to be turned over to the League of Nations for fifteen years, after which a

The changed face of Europe after the Treaty of Versailles, 1919

Legend on map:

National boundaries
New nations created from Russia
New nations created from Austro-Hungary
Territories lost by Austro-Hungary
Territories lost by Germany
Demilitarized zone
Plebiscite areas

plebiscite would determine its fate. Wilson and Lloyd George forced Clemenceau to drop his plan for an independent buffer state in the Rhineland and to accept permanent demilitarization of the area and French occupation for fifteen years. The President also resisted Japanese demands to annex the Shantung peninsula, and Italian claims on the port of Fiume. And he secured his primary goal: incorporation of the League of Nations as part of the treaty itself.

These were considerable accomplishments—more than any other statesman could have achieved. But they inevitably fell short of the goals he had outlined during and after the war. The treaty was drafted secretly, and it said nothing about freedom of the seas or the lowering of international economic barriers. It violated the principle of self-determination by turning over land in South Tyrol to Italy, by granting Japan economic rights in the Shantung peninsula, by placing Germans under Polish rule in Silesia, and by handing over German colonies to the British, French, and Japanese. (Wilson, Clemenceau remarked cynically, "talked like Jesus Christ, but acted like Lloyd George.") The treaty also saddled Germany with the "war guilt" clause and with reparations that ultimately amounted to $33 billion. These made the embittered Germans receptive to Hitler in 1933. To assuage French opinion, Wilson and Lloyd George negotiated separate treaties obligating their countries to defend France in case of unprovoked attack by Germany. These treaties were central to the key postwar question of French security. But because the Franco-American treaty conflicted with the principle of no entangling alliances in time of peace, it never had a chance in Congress.

THE VERSAILLES TREATY AND THE SENATE

Well before the conference completed its work in late June it was obvious that Wilson would have to fight hard for Senate approval. On March 5, thirty-nine senators or senators-elect—six more than the one-third necessary to defeat the treaty—signed a so-called Round Robin that declared that "the constitution of the League of Nations in the form now proposed to the peace conference should not be accepted by the United States." The League, these senators agreed, should not be discussed until the terms of peace were agreed upon. Wilson tried to meet such objections by getting the delegates at Versailles to recognize the Monroe Doctrine and by inserting an "escape" clause permitting member nations to withdraw from the League in two years, but he refused to separate the League from the terms of peace. "When that treaty comes back," he declared in New York, "gentlemen on this side will find the covenant not only in it, but so many threads of the treaty tied to the covenant that you cannot dissect the covenant from the treaty without destroying the whole vital structure."

By the summer of 1919, when the struggle for ratification began, the nature of his opposition in the Senate was ominous. His most extreme foes in the Senate were approximately eighteen "irreconcilables" who opposed the treaty in any form. Some of these men, like La Follette, were consistent isolationists who objected to American participation in the League with the same passion they had shown against American involvement in 1917. Some, like Johnson, were violent partisans as well as isolationists. Other irreconcilables, like Medill McCormick of Illinois and James Reed of Missouri, were racist xenophobes. The League, McCormick said, will create a superstate with "economical Japanese operating our street railways . . . Hindoo janitors in our offices and apartments . . . Chinese craftsmen driving rivets, joining timbers, laying bricks in the construction of our buildings." Reed added, "Think of submitting questions involving the very life of the United States to a tribunal on which a nigger from Liberia, a nigger from Honduras, a nigger from India, and an unlettered gentleman from Siam, each have votes equal to the great United States of America."

The strongest tie binding the irreconcilables was a nationalistic fervor that insisted that America retain a free hand. Most of them opposed joining the League because they feared even a moral obligation to engage in collective security. In particular they opposed Article X, which said that members would "undertake to respect and to preserve as against external aggression the territorial integrity and existing political independence of all Members of the League." This clause did not require member states to send troops, but only to "advise upon the means by which this obligation shall be fulfilled." As Wilson explained, Article X was a "moral not a legal obligation." But the irreconcilables, like many other senators, were unconvinced. Their leader, William Borah of Idaho, explained that he would indeed support American intervention abroad, but only on his own terms. "I may be willing to help my neighbor, though he be improvident or unfortunate," Borah declared,

> but I do not necessarily want him as a business partner. I may be willing to give liberally of my means, of my council and advice, even of my strength or blood, to protect his family from attack or injustice, but I do not want him placed in a position where he may decide for me when and how I shall act or to what extent I shall make sacrifice.

A larger and more dangerous group of senatorial opponents were the "strong reservationists" led by Henry Cabot Lodge, a Harvard-educated patrician who chaired the foreign relations committee. Standing between La Follette and Wilson, Lodge opposed both isolationism and utopian internationalism. Instead, like Roosevelt, he believed that American influence must be exerted to maintain a stable balance of power, and he favored guaranteeing French security against the Germans. Lodge's nationalistic stance was reasoned and realistic, and it probably came closer than Wilson's expansive internationalism to expressing the views, however vague, of Americans in 1919.

But Lodge was a partisan politician who was determined to stop men like Borah from bolting the Republican party. He also despised the President. "I never expected to hate anyone with the hatred I feel toward Wilson," he had written Roosevelt in 1915. The phraseology of the League Covenant, he sneered, "might get by at Princeton, but certainly not at Harvard." Holding such views, Lodge misused his key position. Instead of educating Americans to their world responsibilities, he engaged in vituperative partisan debate, packed the foreign relations committee with Wilson's enemies, delayed while foes of the League coalesced, and suggested so many "reservations" that Wilson concluded that Lodge could never be placated. The most controversial of these reservations stated that America was not obliged to act under Article X unless Congress approved in each case.

Lodge's delaying tactics permitted a wide variety of opponents of the treaty to express their positions. Among these were supernationalists who wrote stories with such titles as "Betsy Ross is Forgotten," and "John Paul Jones Is Degraded." Others, including many returning soldiers, wanted to

Breakers Ahead.

forget Europe. "There's no nation in Europe worth a tinker's damn," one complained. "The whole continent is rotten, or tyrannical." More worrisome to Wilson was the stand of people who might otherwise have supported him. These included pacifists like Jane Addams, who feared that the League sanctioned the possibility of war, and progressive purists who could not stomach the compromises he had made at Paris. "THIS IS NOT PEACE," the *New Republic* proclaimed. "The peace cannot last. America should withdraw from all commitments which would impair her freedom of action." Wilson also faced growing hostility from ethnic groups. German-Americans resented the war-guilt and reparations clauses, Italian-Americans the failure of Italy to gain Fiume, and Irish-Americans the inability of the delegates to do anything for Ireland.

The defection of so many people who had formed his electoral coalition in 1916—peace workers, progressive reformers, ethnic leaders—greatly weakened his chances of persuading fence-sitting senators that he had the masses with him. The treaty gave these people another powerful reason—as if inflation, high taxes, and the Red Scare had not been enough—to distrust their government and the Democratic party in particular. In this sense the League issue was a final blow to the chances for a stable reform coalition in the 1920s and to the unity of the Democratic party.

The pragmatic Wilson of 1913 would probably have tried to meet such opponents halfway. But the Wilson of 1919 was too sure of his vision to listen to reason. These opponents, he said in February, were "blind and little provincial people" who reminded him of a "man with a head that is not a head but is just a knot providentially put there to keep him from ravelling out." When Colonel House urged him in June to be conciliatory, Wilson replied, "House, I have found that one can never get anything in this life that is worthwhile without fighting for it." When his Senate floor leader later warned him to compromise, he shot back, "anyone who opposes me in that I'll crush."

When his foes persisted, Wilson set out in September on a cross-country speaking tour. At first his speeches met with mixed reactions, but by the time he reached California he attracted cheering crowds. His schedule, however, was grueling, and the sixty-three-year-old president grew exhausted as he turned east. After giving a great speech in Pueblo, he collapsed in pain and had to cancel the rest of the tour. Four days later his wife found him unconscious on the floor. He had suffered a stroke, which paralyzed the left side of his body. Though his mind still functioned, the stroke left him too weak to carry out his duties properly. During that time—October 1919 to March 1921—the business of the country was in the hands of his wife and a few close aides.

Shortly after Wilson suffered his stroke Lodge reported out the treaty with fourteen reservations. Democratic supporters of the League were willing to accept Lodge's version. Most of the reservations made little difference, they pointed out, and even the modification of Article X was acceptable to the European powers. Had Wilson followed their advice, it is possible that the treaty would have passed. But Wilson did not compromise. Lodge's reservations, he insisted, removed America's all-important moral obligation. Obstinately, he instructed his Democratic followers to hold firm, and on November 19 they joined the irreconcilables in voting against the treaty with reservations, fifty-five to thirty-nine. A vote on the treaty without reservations then fell before a coalition of Republicans and irreconcilables, fifty-three to thirty-eight. These votes showed that 85 percent of the senators accepted the League in some form, and moderates worked toward compromise. When the Senate voted again on March 19, 1920, twenty-one Democrats broke ranks to accept Lodge's reservations, and the treaty in that form secured a majority of forty-nine to thirty-five. But that was seven short of the two-thirds necessary for ratification. Of the thirty-five, twenty-three were Democrats who followed their stricken leader to the end.

Many forces killed the treaty, including xenophobia, ethnic loyalties, isolationism, and party politics. But Wilson deserves much, perhaps most, of the responsibility. As early as the spring of 1917 he had known of the Allied secret treaties, yet he sent American soldiers to fight in Europe without demanding that the treaties be repudiated. He then persisted in proclaiming that the war was being fought for noble ends. When the Versailles treaty proved otherwise, many Americans were shocked. Others, worried about social problems at home, were simply apathetic about the treaty. Even so, Wilson could probably have secured most of the basic terms had he been willing to compromise. That he did not was his personal tragedy.

Was it a tragedy for the world? Probably not. The resistance to Article X, to say nothing of subsequent isolationism in the 1920s and 1930s, suggested that Americans—League or no League—were not yet ready to assume the burdens of collective security. Neither, as later events would demonstrate, were the English or the French: such developments as appeasement and the Maginot Line mentality revealed that isolationism and nationalism were not unique to America, but dominant throughout the Atlantic world before 1939. In this sense the Senate's rejection of the League was neither tragic nor irresponsible. Rather, it reflected the national selfishness that the war of 1914–18 had intensified throughout the West.

It was a fact, nonetheless, that the partisan debate accompanying the Senate's rejection of the treaty was unenlightening. Isolationists and irreconcilables oscillated between xenophobia and the unrealistic belief that America could ignore European developments. Wilsonians proclaimed sweeping visions, preached a *Pax Americana* to the rest of the world, and went out of their way to offend the Soviet Union. Men like Lodge, who appreciated the nation's expanded role in world affairs, spent more of their time conjuring up frightening consequences of collective security than they did in defining the country's international responsibilities. For all these reasons the nature of America's basic strategic interests received little thoughtful discussion. The Great War, it appeared, had taught Americans only that they should stay out of the next one.

Disillusionment with the war and withdrawal

The experience of war meant to a few intellectuals that idealism was just so much cant, that "progressivism" has been a ghastly mistake. Young people, F. Scott Fitzgerald wrote, had "grown up to find all the Gods dead, all wars fought, all faiths in man shaken." John Dos Passos best described this disillusion with idealism—and with the State—that some intellectuals felt in the aftermath of war. "Where his chest ought to have been," he wrote of the Unknown Soldier,

> they pinned the Congressional Medal, the D.S.C., the Medaille Militaire, the Belgian Croix de Guerre, the Italian gold medal, the Vitutea Militara sent by Queen Marie of Rumania, the Czechoslovak war cross, the Virtuti Militari of the Poles, a wreath sent by Hamilton Fish, Jr., of New York, and a little wampum presented by a deputation of Arizona redskins in warpaint and feathers. All the Washingtonians brought flowers. Woodrow Wilson brought a bouquet of poppies.

Few Americans were as bitter as these intellectuals. Indeed, men like Dos Passos were alienated in part because they sensed that thousands of fellow citizens, who had much innocence yet to lose, were not listening to them. By mid-1920 most people simply seemed glad that the heroics were over, that the "Reds" had been suppressed, that the nation was free of foreign entanglements. They were angry about inflation, weary of big government, ready for what Wilson's popular successor, Warren G. Harding, called "normalcy." The wartime suppression of civil liberties, the emotional appeals of the Committee on Public Information, the Red Scare, the race riots, the battle for the League—all were parts of the past, perhaps necessary but best forgotten. It was time to live again as in the supposedly harmonious days before the divisive and dissatisfying experience of war.

Suggestions for reading

A starting point for military history and the effect of war at home is Russell Weigley, *The American Way of War** (1973). A helpful survey is Harold and Margaret Sprout, *The Rise of American Naval Power, 1776–1910* (1939). A general history is Frederic L. Paxson, *American Democracy and the World War* (3 vols., 1936–48). See also Elting Morison, *Admiral Sims and the Modern American Navy* (1942); and John G. Clifford, *The Citizen Soldiers* (1972), on preparedness. Useful books on attitudes are Charles Chatfield, *For Peace and Justice** (1971), which discusses pacifism 1914–41; and Warren Kuehl, *Seeking World Order: The United States and World Organization to 1920* (1969).

   Domestic politics and economic policy are covered in Robert D. Cuff, *The War Industries Board: Business-Government Relations During World War I* (1973); S. W. Livermore, *Politics Is Adjourned* (1968), on politics, 1916–18; and Daniel R. Beaver, *Newton D. Baker and the American War Effort, 1917–1919* (1966). George T. Blakey's *Historians on the Home Front* (1970) shows how wartime passions influenced scholars. The books by Kerr and Urofsky mentioned in the bibliography for chapter 3 cover regulatory policies.

   The effect of the war on civil liberties is the subject of several good studies. Among them are William Preston, *Aliens and Dissenters: Federal Suppression of Radicals, 1903–1933** (1963); H. C. Peterson and Gilbert Fite, *Opponents of War, 1917–1918*

(1957); Zechariah Chafee, *Free Speech in the United States* (1941); and Paul L. Murphy, *The Meaning of Freedom of Speech: First Amendment Freedoms from Wilson to FDR* (1972). See also Donald Johnson, *Challenge to American Freedoms** (1963), the story of the birth and growth of the American Civil Liberties Union; and Joan M. Jensen, *The Price of Vigilance* (1968), which deals with superpatriotism during the war.

For developments in the period 1918–21 the most important studies are William Tuttle, Jr., *Race Riot: Chicago in the Red Summer of 1919** (1970); David Brody, *Labor in Crisis: The Steel Strike of 1919** (1965); Stanley Coben, *A. Mitchell Palmer* (1963); Robert K. Murray, *The Red Scare** (1955); and Burl Noggle, *Into the Twenties: The United States from Armistice to Normalcy* (1974). See also Kenneth Jackson, *The Ku Klux Klan in the City, 1915–1930** (1967); G. L. Joughin and E. M. Morgan, *The Legacy of Sacco-Vanzetti* (1948); and Arthur Waskow, *From Race Riot to Sit-in, 1919 and the 1960's** (1966).

Foreign policy and peacemaking, 1917–21, are covered in Thomas Bailey, *Woodrow Wilson and the Lost Peace** (1944), and *Woodrow Wilson and the Great Betrayal** (1945); N. Gordon Levin, Jr., *Woodrow Wilson and World Politics** (1968); John Garraty, *Henry Cabot Lodge* (1953); Arno J. Mayer, *Politics and Diplomacy of Peacemaking: Containment and Counterrevolution at Versailles, 1918–1919* (1967); John M. Thompson, *Russia, Bolshevism, and the Versailles Peace* (1966); and Ralph A. Stone, *The Irreconcilables: The Fight Against the League of Nations** (1970). See also H. R. Rudin, *Armistice* (1944); George F. Kennan, *The Decision to Intervene: Prelude to Allied Intervention in the Bolshevik Revolution* (1956); and Paul Birdsall, *Versailles Twenty Years After* (1941).

6

The
1920s:
the modern
decade

"The aspirin age," the "roaring twenties," the "era of excess," a time of "Fords, flappers, and fanatics"—these are but a few of the labels pasted on the decade of the 1920s in America. All of them portray a hedonistic populace staggering out of World War I and plunging toward the crash of 1929. The 1920s, it appeared later, were a frenzied interlude between war and depression.

A more accurate way of describing the period is to stress its modernity. Though many people hoped to preserve "normalcy," to reaffirm values of the past, millions of others welcomed the first recognizably "modern" decade in American history. The major forces of twentieth-century life—technological change, bureaucratization, the growth of the middle class, suburbanization—accelerated so rapidly that people thought they were living in a capitalist utopia, or—as it was then called—a "new era."

Avenues to the future

ECONOMIC PROGRESS

The most striking manifestation of the "new era" was economic growth. The per capita GNP in current prices jumped from an average of $719 in the prosperous years of 1917–21 to $857 in 1929. Between 1922 and 1929 the

Economic growth, 1919–1929,
compared to select years before and after this period

	NATIONAL PRODUCT AND INCOME (In billions of current dollars)			PER CAPITA INCOME (In current dollars)
	GNP	NATIONAL INCOME	PERSONAL INCOME	
1900[a]	17.3	14.6	14.3	231
1914[a]	40.3	34.8	33.7	408
1919	78.9	70.2	65.0	755
1920	88.9	79.1	73.4	835
1921	74.0	64.0	62.1	682
1922	74.0	63.1	62.0	672
1923	86.1	74.3	71.5	769
1924	87.6	75.2	73.2	768
1925	91.3	78.2	75.0	788
1926	97.7	83.7	79.5	832
1927	96.3	81.7	79.6	809
1928	98.2	82.8	79.8	815
1929	104.4	87.8	85.8	857
1933	56.0	40.2	47.2	446
1945	213.6	181.2	171.2	1,526

SOURCE: Adapted from *Historical Statistics of the United States*, p. 139
[a]Annual averages, 1897–1901, 1912–16

national income rose from $63.1 billion to $87.8 billion. This was an annual increase in real dollars of 6.2 percent, a rate unmatched for any comparable length of time in modern American history.

At the root of this growth were steady technological advances, many of which had been developed or perfected in the war period. The years between 1917 and 1929 witnessed major industrial breakthroughs, such as the manufacture of continuous strip-sheets in steel and tin, and of machines to make glass tubing, which completely replaced glass blowers by 1925. New machines revolutionizing the construction industry included power shovels, belt and bucket conveyors, pneumatic tools, concrete mixers, and dump trucks. The communications industries developed automatic switchboards, dial phones, and teletype machines. Innovations in chemicals and synthetics included rayon, bakelite, and cellophane. George Washington Carver, a pioneer in developing farm products for industrial use, found ways of turning peanuts into axle grease and shaving lotion, and sweet potatoes into shoe blacking, library paste, and synthetic tapioca.

Ordinary people profited from these technological and economic changes. Real wages for regularly employed factory workers increased by about 11 percent during the decade. Technological advances in industrial production brought about major changes in working conditions: hours for manufacturing workers decreased from 47.4 hours per week in 1920 to 42.1 in 1930. The long-range trend toward enlarging the middle class accelerated. During the 1920s the number of farm workers decreased (from 11.4 to 10.3 million), and the number of manual and service workers increased only gradually—from 20.3 to 24 million. White-collar workers, meanwhile, jumped in numbers from 10.5 to 14.3 million, or from 22 percent to almost 30 percent of the labor force of 50 million. These white-collar workers rarely toiled for longer than 40 hours per week. For the first time in American history a significant percentage of the population was getting the money, and the time, to buy and to enjoy consumer goods.

Reflecting this potential, consumer goods industries boomed as never before. Moderately priced products included radios, wristwatches, cigarette lighters, hand cameras, linoleum, vacuum cleaners, and washing machines. Nine of the top twenty industries in 1930 specialized in consumer goods, compared to one in 1920. The availability of such creature comforts to common people astounded contemporaries. America, the French observer André Siegfried wrote in 1927, "has again become a new world. . . . The American people are now creating on a vast scale an entirely new social structure which bears only a superficial resemblance to the European. It may even be a new age."

Siegfried and others were especially impressed by the revolution in communications—film, radio, and the telephone—in the 1920s. As early as 1915,

Jazz, the music of black America, became a favorite form of entertainment in the 1920s. The small clubs in which jazz was performed became accessible thanks to the automobile.

when *Birth of a Nation* grossed $18 million, the film industry revealed its amazing potential, and in the 1920s movies all but displaced camp meetings and political rallies as essential mass entertainment for Americans. By 1926 every large American city had deluxe theatres seating 2500 to 4000 people. By 1930 the average weekly attendance was 90 million, a figure never exceeded since. In 1929, the first year of "talkies," revenues were $720 million, almost three times the amount spent on books and ten times the sum expended on spectator sports.

The growth of radio was equally spectacular. As late as August 1921, KDKA, which had pioneered in news coverage by broadcasting the 1920 election returns, was the only licensed radio station in America. By the end of 1922, however, there were 508 stations, and 3 million Americans owned sets. In 1926 the National Broadcasting Company began consolidating the stations into a network, and in 1927 the Federal Radio Commission was established to police the industry. By then radio was big business. In 1929 Americans spent $850 million for sets and parts, advertisers paid $10,000 an hour for a national hookup, and NBC's gross income was $150 million.

Easily the most dramatic development was the automobile. Like the movies, cars were prewar innovations: almost 2.5 million were registered in 1915. Yet they did not spread to the masses until after the war, when installment plans and technological advances in production (Ford turned out a Model T every ten seconds by 1925) cut prices to new lows. (Model T's cost $290 in 1925, roughly the equivalent of three months' wages for factory workers, who were offered all sorts of inducements to buy on time.) In 1920 Americans registered 9.2 million motor vehicles, in 1925 20 million, in 1930 26.7 million, or more than two for every three American families.

The impact of the automobile on the American economy was enormous. The car industry in the 1920s absorbed 20 percent of America's steel, 80 percent of its rubber, and 75 percent of its glass. It built oil into a major industry and ultimately created the fateful dependence of the economy on petroleum. Automobiles promoted real estate booms in heretofore distant Florida and California, facilitated the development of consolidated schools, worked wonders for highways (and road builders), prompted the sprawl of roadside restaurants, motels, and service stations, and assured the decline of railroads. Automobiles were to the 1920s what the railroads had been to the nineteenth century—a major force affecting the entire economy.

Automobiles also helped the rapid growth of metropolitan and suburban development. As early as 1920 the census reported that a majority of Americans (51.4 percent) lived in urban areas for the first time, and that the number who lived in places with 100,000 or more people exceeded the number who resided in all smaller cities. Assisted by the automobile, this metropolitan sprawl accelerated in the 1920s: by 1930, 8 million more Americans lived in places with populations exceeding 250,000 than had ten years earlier. It was a decade of revolt against small-town values, of heightened tension between metropolitan and rural styles of life.

Above, a traffic jam in Michigan suggests the "modernity" of the 1920s. The decade was one in which the number of roadside stands, like the one shown below, climbed into the thousands.

These striking economic and demographic changes inevitably provoked sharp controversy and social conflict. Critics estimated that technological developments displaced perhaps 3 million workers in the 1930s, of whom perhaps 1 million remained unemployed. Plays like Eugene O'Neill's *Dynamo* and Elmer Rice's *Adding Machine,* as well as the Czech term "robot," expressed widespread doubts about scientific management and the effects of the assembly line.

Other critics complained that the "modernization" of economic life accelerated corporate concentration. Before 1910, 200 firms had made cars, but by 1930 the Big Three, Ford, General Motors, and Chrysler, with 83 percent of sales, had already established their oligopolistic control. In 1930 there were 25,000 banks, 1 percent of which possessed 46 percent of bank resources. In the same year CBS and NBC, with control over more than 150 transmitters, dominated the field of broadcasting. Chain stores grew spectacularly, with A&P expanding from 400 outlets in 1912 to 15,500 in 1932, and Drug, Incorporated, a holding company, controlling Vick Chemical, Bayer Aspirin, and Bristol-Myers as well as 10,000 Rexall and 706 Liggetts stores. Adolf Berle, Jr., and Gardiner Means, whose *Modern Corporation and Private Property* (1932) treated the subject authoritatively, estimated that of the 300,000 nonfinancial corporations in America approximately 200 had half of the nation's corporate wealth. These top corporations made such unprecedented profits between 1915 and 1929 that they were able to do much of their own financing, without recourse to investment bankers like Morgan. If the turn of the century had been the golden age of the financier, the 1920s saw the triumph of the oligopolistic, self-sustaining corporation.

The 1920s were also an age of managers. In order to expand, the corporations issued thousands of shares of new stock to many more people. The Pennsylvania Railroad, for instance, had 65,000 stockholders in 1910 and 207,000 in 1930. During the same period stockholders of AT&T increased from 41,000 to 567,000 and of U. S. Steel from 28,000 to 145,000. This growth meant that ownership in many corporations was widely dispersed: the twenty largest stockholders of U. S. Steel, AT&T, and the Pennsylvania Railroad owned but 5.1 percent, 4 percent, and 2.7 percent, respectively, of the outstanding shares. The dispersal of ownership did not take place in all companies: Ford, for instance, still kept control of his operations within the family. It did not mean that small shareholders ran big companies. It surely did not promote greater corporate responsibility. It did mean, however, that day-to-day operation of many corporations fell into the hands of managers and highly skilled professionals. The "managerial revolution" directed by the "organization man" was occurring in the 1920s.

It went without saying that these managers varied widely. Some, such as Samuel Insull, presiding manipulator of several hundred electric light and power companies throughout the nation, were buccaneers of the old school. More characteristic of the "new" executive was Alfred P. Sloan, the efficient chief of General Motors after 1923. Unlike William C. ("Billy") Durant, his colorful predecessor, Sloan recognized that "General Motors had become too big to be a one-man show." It had to be decentralized, with expert managers placed in control of functionally organized divisions. Modern methods of marketing helped Sloan understand also that car buyers yearned for new and distinctive models every year—the unchanging black Model T was too commonplace. So GM relied shrewdly, profitably on planned obsolescence. By the end of the decade GM had surpassed Ford as the nation's leading automobile manufacturer. Such is progress.

Another questionable manifestation of "progress" in the 1920s was the booming advertising business, whose earnings jumped from $1.3 billion in 1915 to $3.4 billion in 1929. Such advertising encouraged a six-fold increase in installment buying—to $7 billion—during the same period. Advertising, Calvin Coolidge proclaimed in 1926, "is the most potent influence in adopting and changing the habits and modes of life, affecting what we eat, what we wear, and the work and play of the whole nation."

Many advertisers drew on the rather frightening behaviorist theories of John B. Watson, a psychologist and successful advertising executive. Like Freud, Watson rejected the nineteen-century notion that physiological processes governed man. He also shared Freud's assumption that psychology, properly applied, could ameliorate the human condition. But unlike Freud, who emphasized instinctual drives within man, Watson stressed the power of the environment. Control the environment, he said, and human beings could be shaped at will. "Give me a dozen healthy infants," he proclaimed, " . . . and my own specified world to bring them up in, and I'll guarantee to take any one at random and train him to become any specialist I might select, doctor, lawyer, artist, merchant, chief, and yes, even beggarman and thief, regardless of his talents, tendencies, abilities, vocations and race of his ancestor."

Advertising leaders, like proponents of scientific management, readily accepted this view of manipulable humanity. Kenneth Goode and Harford

> *Advertising does give a certain illusion, a certain sense of escape in a machine age. It creates a dream world: smiling faces, shining teeth, school girl complexions, cornless feet, perfect fitting union suits, distinguished collars, wrinkleless pants, odorless breaths, regularized bowels, happy homes in New Jersey (15 mins. from Hoboken), charging motors, puncture-less tires, perfect busts, shimmering shanks, self-washing dishes—backs behind which the moon was meant to rise.*
>
> Stuart Chase offers a critique of advertising, 1925.

Powel, Jr., wrote in *What About Advertising?* (1927) that the advertiser "must recognize the extreme mental stupidity of the vast majority of his audience, and their pathetic lack of adult mental nourishment. The average normal American, broadly speaking, celebrates his twenty-fifth birthday by shutting up shop mentally and refusing to accept any new ideas. He has then the literate capacity of a twelve- or fourteen-year-old." It followed, Goode and Powel concluded, that people would believe almost anything that kept them up with the Joneses.

This was also the message of Edward Bernays, a nephew of Freud who worked for the Creel Committee in 1918 and who became America's leading public relations man in the 1920s. "The counsel in public relations," he said, "not only knows what news value is, but knowing it, he is in a position to *make news happen.* He is a creator of events." Opinions, he insisted, were developed by groups, not by individuals. The job of the advertiser, the PR man, indeed the political leader, was to appeal to group leaders. Sell new fashions by getting society women to model them. Promote cigarettes by showing debutantes smoking. Sell baseball equipment by telling the people Babe Ruth uses it. And forget progressive nonsense about educating the common people. The American system, he said, "must be a leadership democratically administered by the intelligent minority who know how to regiment and guide the masses." Bernay's elitism echoed that of Walter Lippmann and other gloomy observers of the mass mind. It was adopted by advertisers and political brokers in the decades to come.

Traditionalists viewing these innovations lamented the passing of prewar social patterns. Cars, they complained, were hurting church attendance, taking entertainment from the home to the roadhouse, and inducing young people—roaming far in search of opportunity—to neglect the old folks at home. They grumbled especially that cars, movies, and advertising were intensifying materialism and conspicuous consumption. "The blue dusk of the deluxe house," one critic wrote, "has dissolved the Puritan strictures that . . . [people] had absorbed as children." Ford, Lincoln Steffens explained in 1931, "was a prophet without words, a reformer without politics, a legislator, a statesman, a radical. I understand why the Bolshevik leaders of Russia admired, coveted, and studied him."

This centralizing tendency of the automobile may be only a passing phase; sets in the other direction are almost equally prominent. "Our daughters [eighteen and fifteen] don't use our car much because they are always with somebody else in their car when we go out motoring," lamented one business class mother. And another said, "The two older children [eighteen and sixteen] never go out when the family motors. They always have something else on." "In the nineties we were all much more together," said another wife. "People brought chairs and cushions out of the house and sat on the lawn evenings. We rolled out a strip of carpet and put cushions on the porch step to take care of the unlimited overflow of neighbors that dropped by. We'd sit out so all evening. The younger couples perhaps would wander off for half an hour to get a soda but come back to join in the informal singing or listen while somebody strummed a mandolin or guitar." "What on earth do you want me to do? Just sit around home all evening!" retorted a popular high school girl of today when her father discouraged her going out motoring for the evening with a young blade in a rakish car waiting at the curb. The fact that 348 boys and 382 girls in the three upper years of the high school placed "use of the automobile" fifth and fourth respectively in a list of twelve possible sources of disagreement between them and their parents suggests that this may be an increasing decentralizing agent.

The baneful effect of the car, as seen by Robert and Helen Lynd in *Middletown* (1929).

Steffens's point was well taken, for the economic and technological changes of the 1920s did affect attitudes and behavior. People who went to the movies, who read the ads (or heard them on the radio), and who rode about in cars were bombarded by the variety of the American scene. To some degree, their taste was nationalized, their values urbanized. They became disposed to accept the more centralized direction initiated by New Dealers in the 1930s. And they discovered what others possessed: bathtubs, up-to-date fashions, household gadgets, matching furniture, and, of course, the latest styles in cars. In the process they were groomed for the most "subversive" change of all: the growth of consumerism and leisure-orientation. As one writer observed sadly, Americans were beginning to prefer indulgence to adventure; their travels were marked "not by the whitening bones of pioneers" but "by discarded inner tubes and heaps of salmon cans."

Most important, Americans were readier than ever to believe in the positive virtues of economic progress. Growth, prosperity, and material possessions, it was hoped, would blur ethnic and class distinctions and give everyone a stake in the system. Herbert Hoover, in accepting the GOP presidential nomination of 1928, remarked that "we in America are nearer to the financial triumph over poverty than ever before in the history of our land. The poorhouse is vanishing from among us." Like *Time* magazine, which named Walter Chrysler its "man of the year" in 1929, Hoover was dazzled by technological change and by modern, functional methods of business administration. Millions of Americans welcomed the "new era" that was dawning in the land.

The new era

CHANGING SEXUAL MORES

Another manifestation of modernity in the 1920s was the spread of permissive attitudes toward sex. It was the decade of the "flapper," of flesh-colored stockings, of "petting," of increased divorces (100,000 in 1914, 205,000 in 1929), of daring modern dancers like Isadora Duncan, and of Cecil B. De Mille movies with titles like *Old Wives for New, Women and Lovers*, and *Golden Bed*. Where the reigning goddesses of the screen before World War I had been chaste Pollyannas, those of the 1920s, like Clara Bow (the "it" girl), were sex symbols whom later actresses like Jean Harlow and Marilyn Monroe could only emulate.

Other products of popular culture reinforced this emphasis on sexuality. Songs carried titles like "Hot Lips," "I Need Lovin'," and "Burning Kisses." The "Little Blue Books," five- to ten-cent precursors of paperbacks, featured titles like *Love Letters of a Portuguese Nun, Sex Life in Greece and Rome*, and *One of Cleopatra's Nights*. Popular magazines for men, or "pulps," included *Breezy Stories, Jim Jam Jems*, and *French Stories*. The sociologists Robert and Helen Lynd discovered that the high-school girls of Muncie, Indiana, wore cosmetics (called "paint"), that they checked their corsets in ladies rooms at dances, and that they seemed to spend more time riding around (and parking) with boys than sitting at home.

If I see any more of these passionate fiery movies I will not be able to resist the plan to become a wife before next quarter. These passionate pictures stir such longings, desires, and urges as I never expected any person to possess. Just the way the passionate lover held his sweetheart suggests so many beautiful and intimate relations, which even my reacting a scene does not satisfy any more. I cannot believe myself that I am "I" any more; because when I first entered high school these scenes gave me unpleasant and guilty feelings. I would determine that I would never see them again. And now they come back clearly to me, but in such a different light. I actually want to experience these scenes, and see beauty in them.

An eighteen-year-old girl describes to an interviewer her view of the impact of movies, 1933.

Sigmund Freud, himself a respectable Victorian, became a culture hero to the advocates of the new permissiveness. Distorting his theories, these Americans believed that he advocated the casting off of all sexual restraints. The vogue for Freud led some writers to produce facile psychoanalytic explications of history and literature, and it served to provide justifications for many rebels against convention, including proponents of free schools, surrealist painting, and modern dance. Used as a kind of secular evangelism, Freudianism expressed the progressive faith that human beings have an inalienable right to happiness and the potential to ameliorate their lives.

Taking a different tack, a few feminists campaigned for women's liberation. Thus Dorothea Dix, counsel to the young, advised girls to "learn a trade," for "economic independence is the only independence in the world. As long as you must look to another for your food and clothes you are a slave to that person." Dorothy Canfield Fisher's *The Home-Maker* (1924) made the same point by portraying a woman who was successful in business while her husband did the housework and raised the children. Fisher, like Charlotte Gilman a generation earlier, kept alive the vision of women finding themselves through creative work.

A daring debutante, ready for a swim, tries a cigarette on the beach at Southampton, Long Island.

Sexual permissiveness amused a few urbane observers. "If all the girls at the Yale prom were laid end to end," Dorothy Parker wrote, "I wouldn't be surprised." Others, however, reacted rigidly, exposing yet another division in American society in the 1920s. Self-proclaimed arbiters of public taste imposed censorship on magazines and books and tried—with limited success—to set standards of decency in films. An Ohio legislator introduced a bill outlawing any "garment which unduly displays or accentuates the lines of the female figure" and prescribing that "no female over fourteen years of age shall wear a skirt which does not reach to that part of the foot known as the instep." And the town of Norphelt, Arkansas, actually passed a statute that read:

Sect. 1. Hereafter it shall be unlawful for any man or woman, male or female, to be guilty of committing sexual intercourse between themselves at any place within the corporate limits of said town. . . .
Sect. 3. Section one of this ordinance shall not apply to married persons as between themselves and their husband and wife, unless of a grossly improper and lascivious nature.

As usual, the alarmists exaggerated a little, for the movement for sexual freedom had far to go. In Muncie, for instance, talk of sex in the schools was taboo. Movies featured the wife returning to her husband and the "jazz baby" marrying the small-town boy next door. The wide appeal of *Gentlemen Prefer Blonds,* a popular novel and play of mid-decade, suggested that men—and many women—still expected women to be "feminine" (beautiful, zany, and not too bright). And shorter skirts did not indicate sudden liberation, since hemlines had been rising gradually since the turn of the century.

The stress on sexual liberation also had questionable effects. A few women who cast off traditional restraints undoubtedly experienced emancipation. Many others, however, probably felt confused. And social workers justly complained that sexually liberated feminists worshipped Isadora Duncan, not Jane Addams. The Women's Trade Union League, the National Consumers League, and the League of Women Voters, which tried vainly to make women a force in politics, languished in the 1920s. The Women's Party, the home of radical feminists who sought full social and economic equality for women, attracted only a handful of supporters.

Still, sexual attitudes as well as behavior were changing, at least among the urban middle classes. Though few women embraced sexual license, they did rebel against Victorian prudishness and the double standard. They also popularized the idea that sex was "fun." These attitudes provided a rationale for changes in behavior later documented by Dr. Alfred C. Kinsey and other researchers. Their findings, based on retrospective interviews of middle-class people, revealed that premarital sex was more common among unmarried women in the 1910s and 1920s than previously. To this degree the guardians of conventional morality were correct in complaining that sexual mores were becoming more permissive.

EDUCATION AND SOCIAL SCIENCE

The 1920s witnessed important long-range developments in education. First among these was an acceleration in attendance at all levels. Thanks to urbanization, and such basic developments as the school bus, enrollments in high schools rose from 1.3 million in 1915 to 4.4 million in 1930. The number of high school graduates increased from 240,000 (12 percent of seventeen-year-olds) to 667,000 (29 percent). College enrollments during the same period rose from 404,000 (5.5 percent of eighteen- to twenty-year-olds) to 1.1 million (12.5 percent).

This growth did not bring on the millenium, for 71 percent of American young people, mainly from the lower classes, failed to graduate from high school as late as 1930. There is also little evidence suggesting that schools in the 1920s turned out more enlightened or proficient students. Most parents continued to regard school functionally—as socializing institutions and as training grounds for jobs. Still, the rise in attendance and in per pupil spending for public schools (up from $33.55 in 1915 to $86.70 in 1930) was unprecedented. Schools, like much in American life during the 1920s, were becoming efficient, consolidated, businesslike institutions that reflected the middle-class development of society.

The same practical considerations led to the growth of college enrollments during the decade. Continued support for federal aid to agricultural extension work and vocational training showed that many people conceived of colleges as places for the inculcation of occupational skills (though too often outdated) that earlier generations had received through an apprenticeship system.

Nevertheless, alert students, especially the large body of graduate students who would do much of the university teaching for the next three decades, could not avoid being exposed to new approaches to learning. These approaches drew on the search for empirical verification promoted a decade earlier by men like Dewey and James, and on the pervasive, if dimly understood, theory of relativity propounded by Einstein, which further diminished faith in eternal "truths."

Drawing on these methods and ideas social scientists rejected macrotheories based only on conceptualization. Some stressed the need for quantitative work. Others, including the Lynds, whose *Middletown* (1929) remains a classic of empirical sociology, pioneered in team observation of everyday life. The "Chicago School" of sociology, led by Robert Park, insisted that environment was a key to human behavior and undertook ecological investigations of the city. "Legal realists" like Jerome Frank extended sociological jurisprudence to the point where they argued that judges, utilizing their own observations, could establish new law. One of these legal realists, William O. Douglas, later became a leading liberal judge of the Supreme Court.

Economists and anthropologists also insisted on the necessity for careful empirical study. Rexford Tugwell, Wesley Mitchell, and other made detailed analyses of institutions. Reflecting the belief that social science should be utilitarian, many of these institutional economists, including Tugwell and Adolf Berle, Jr., emerged as "brain trusters" for the New Deal in the 1930s. Cultural anthropologists ranged still farther afield. Melville Herskovits embarked on his influential studies of African survivals in the New World. And Ruth Benedict and Margaret Mead carried the emphasis on empirical study to its logical conclusion by observing American Indians and South Sea Islanders in their native settings. Their findings, like those of the Chicago sociologists, stressed the crucial roles of culture and environment. In the process they further challenged monistic explanations of behavior or immutable laws of human conduct.

These ideas hardly swept the older views from the American scene. If they had, racists would not have received a wide hearing. Moreover, the new social scientists sometimes made questionable claims. William Ogburn, a leading sociologist, argued that he could be "scientific," that research could be value free. Benedict insisted that objective investigators could trace "patterns of culture." The Chicago sociologists appeared to argue that ecological variables explained the nature of cities. And many of the followers of Frederick Jackson Turner implied that careful studies of frontier communities provided the key to the American experience. In their passion for empiricism some of these

> *Under the machine and science, the love of beauty, the sense of mystery, and the motive of compassion—sources of aesthetics, religion, and humanism—are not destroyed. They remain essential parts of our nature. But the conditions under which they must operate, the channels they must take, the potentialities of their action are all changed. These ancient forces will become powerful in the modern age just in the proportion that men and women accept the inevitability of science and the machine, understand the nature of the civilization in which they must work, and turn their faces resolutely to the future.*
>
> Charles Beard, 1928, offers a characteristically optimistic view of the "new era."

scholars became almost as dogmatic as the older theorists they attempted to refute.

Still, they left an important legacy, for many of these social scientists believed in the practical utility of research. Tugwell, a follower of Veblen, believed that empirical studies could assist planners and social reformers. Frank and Douglas conceived of legal realism as an antidote to conservative jurisprudence. Political scientists pioneered in setting up such organizations as the National Institute of Public Administration (1921) and the Social Science Research Council (1924). With many other enthusiastic social scientists they assisted the Committee on Social Trends (1929), President Hoover's attempt to gather data for policy-makers. These people, far from succumbing to postwar disillusionment, believed that they could improve and rationalize American life, that a "new era" was at hand, and that they could bring the progressive movement to full flower. Their students carried this faith in experimentalism and empiricism into the New Deal.

Affirmations of the past

FOREIGN POLICY

These manifestations of the "new era"—economic progress, technological innovation, sexual liberation, educational and intellectual change—were powerful and ultimately triumphant. But they were not pervasive enough to destroy older patterns of life and thought. In many areas of activity—foreign policy, politics, small-town life, religion, race relations—many Americans affirmed the past. Their persistence accounted for considerable conflict and tension throughout the decade.

Statistics on American economic interests abroad in the 1920s suggest the nation's irreversible involvement in world affairs. Exports increased from $2.4 billion in 1914 to $7.03 billion fifteen years later, while private investment overseas jumped during the same period from $3.5 billion to $17.2 billion. The 1920s witnessed rapid Americanization of the western economy. In Latin America, where American investments literally skyrocketed from $800 million in 1914 to $5.4 billion in 1929, military and political intervention continued to follow the dollar. By 1924 the United States was directing the finances of ten nations in the Caribbean area.

This growing economic influence did not lead Americans to commit themselves outside the Western Hemisphere. On the contrary, rejection of the League of Nations was but one manifestation of the broader nationalism and xenophobia intensified by the frustrations of World War I. Other manifestations were America's insistence that the hard-pressed Allies pay their "war debts"; the refusal to guarantee French security; the passage of the high-tariff Fordney-McCumber Act in 1922; the exclusion of Japanese immigrants; and the application of a quota system of immigration that discriminated heavily against southern and eastern Europeans. (It erected no bars against Mexicans, Canadians, or Latin Americans.)

America's military unreadiness was another sign of the country's aversion to foreign entanglements. Demobilization began as soon as the war ended, and the armed services remained poorly supported for the next twenty years. General Billy Mitchell, a flamboyant advocate of aircraft development, proved in 1923 that planes could sink battleships, but the naval brass learned little from this lesson. Throughout the period the army and navy devoted little attention to air power, to amphibious warfare, or to aircraft carriers. Distressed, Mitchell blamed plane crashes in 1925 on the "incompetency, the criminal negligence, and the almost treasonable administration of our national defense by the Navy and War Departments." Court-martialed, he was convicted and resigned from the service. The aftermath of World War I, unlike the years following World War II, was no time for forceful generals or for military expansion.

The Washington Conference, called in 1921–22 by Secretary of State Charles Evans Hughes, clearly revealed American reluctance to get involved beyond the Western Hemisphere. The conferees successfully negotiated three agreements. One, the nine-power treaty, was a pious reaffirmation of the unenforceable Open Door policy regarding China. The second, the five-power treaty, marked one of the few times in world history that large nations agreed to scrap existing naval vessels. They accepted ratios for tonnage of battleships (smaller vessels were not covered) of approximately 5:5:3 for the United States, Great Britain, and Japan, and 1.75 for France and Italy. The four-power treaty (United States, Britain, France, and Japan) declared that the four signatories would consult whenever peace in East Asia was threatened.

When Japan attacked Pearl Harbor in 1941, some writers blamed the five-power treaty for weakening American defenses in the Pacific. To a limited extent they were right, for the agreement forbade the United States to fortify Guam or the Philippines, and it sanctioned the very Japanese hegemony in the area that the nine-power treaty was supposed to have prevented. But in 1922 the five-power agreement seemed satisfactory to the United States, which now matched Great Britain, long the world's primary naval power. It was received poorly by many Japanese, who dubbed the ratio Rolls Royce, Rolls Royce, Ford. Moreover, the parsimony of subsequent Congresses revealed that America would have limited its naval building even in the absence of a treaty. The United States was relatively weak in the western Pacific by 1941 because Japan increased its naval construction in the 1930s and because Congress, reflecting public opinion, consistently refused to authorize a fleet even to treaty strength. America would not back up the Open Door with arms.

The different congressional responses to the treaties also exposed American fears of overcommitment. The five-power and nine-power treaties—affirmations of honorable intent—swept through easily. But the four-power agreement encountered stiff opposition from men like Borah and Johnson, who tacked on a reservation stating that the treaty involved no "commitment to armed force, no alliance, and no obligation to join in any defense." Reassured, the treaty's foes withdrew their opposition, but their strong stand against even the hint of sustained international cooperation reflected widespread feeling at the time. For most Americans in the 1920s foreign affairs were peripheral concerns. It was all right for policy-makers—a distant elite—to assist in the search for overseas markets and to intervene in the Caribbean, but they should otherwise stay clear of commitments abroad. The contrast between the dramatic growth in American economic involvement overseas and the return to prewar visions of international policy provided one of the many instances of the decade's uncertain, transitional character.

POLITICS

American politics in the 1920s revealed a similar contrast between modernizing forces and older attitudes. On the one hand, the exigencies of the war, along with the progressive bureaucratization of life, had greatly increased the size and scope of government at all levels. Federal employees numbered 395,000 in 1915 and 600,000 in 1930 (in 1918 they had peaked at 850,000). Federal spending, only $760,000 in 1915 ($7.60 per capita), leaped to $18.5 billion in 1919 ($170 per capita) and then leveled off at around $3 billion ($24.00 per capita) annually in the 1920s—four times what it had been before the war. State and local spending, only $2.2 billion in 1913, increased just as rapidly, to approximately $8 billion on the eve of the crash of 1929. These statistics suggest the obvious: that government was steadily more capable of influencing the lives of citizens.

Government was also increasingly well equipped to respond to the group orientation of American life. Like large corporations, which were restructuring themselves along functional lines, governments at all levels were becoming more "progressive" in the sense that they were developing the specialized skills necessary to preside over a complex society. The federal government, for instance, adopted an executive budget in 1921 in place of the previous "system" that had left spending to the discretion of congressional appropriations committees. (The budget act, however, limited executive freedom by denying presidents the power of item vetoes and by setting up the Comptroller General's office independent of the White House.) Executive agencies like Herbert Hoover's Commerce Department branched far afield to provide businessmen with data and advice. The Agriculture Department developed close ties with powerful pressure groups representing agribusiness. The Federal Trade Commission (FTC), dominated by conservatives, worked purposefully to assist business groups. The idea of resource management also spread within the government, which created a network of migratory bird sanctuaries and gave aid for flood control projects in the Mississippi River valley. Though conservatives overrode efforts to provide public funds for the development of the Tennessee Valley region, they approved plans for Boulder Dam, the first federally sponsored large-scale, multipurpose river basin development. The influence of such agencies reveals that the 1920s—far from being a time of governmental retrenchment or of break with a "progressive" past—broadened the public sector.

As many reformers realized, however, these structural developments in government did much more to assist well-organized groups than they did to advance the cause of social change. Settlement house workers, labor leaders, advocates of civil rights, spokesmen for ethnic groups, and feminists all complained bitterly about the response of government during the years between 1917 and 1933.

One obstacle to social reform was clear to all: Republican control under presidents Warren Harding and Calvin Coolidge from 1921 to 1929. Harding was flexible, agreeable, and decent. Unlike Wilson, he was popular with Congress, and, contrary to myth, he had ideas of his own. He approved the new budget system, appointed able subordinates like Hughes and Hoover, advocated a federal antilynching law, called for a Department of Public Welfare, intervened to end the twelve-hour day in steel mills, and approved legislation assisting farm cooperatives and liberalizing farm credit. His record in the field of civil liberties contrasted sharply with the repressiveness of Wilson—Harding not only let Eugene Debs out of jail but received him in the White House. His tolerant approach brought Americans a necessary respite from postwar acrimony. When he died, people wept as if they had lost another President Lincoln.

As early as the 1920 campaign, however, Harding was the target for all sorts of gibes about his cliché-ridden oratory. "Keep Warren at home," one cynical Republican boss advised. "Don't let him make any speeches. If he goes out on tour somebody's sure to ask him questions and Warren's just the sort of damned fool who will try to answer them." A Democratic critic sniped that Harding's speeches "left the impression of an army of pompous phrases moving over the landscape in search of an idea." H. L. Mencken concluded that Harding "writes the worst English that I have ever encountered. It reminds me of a string of wet sponges; it reminds me of tattered washing on the line; it reminds me of stale bean soup, of college yells, of dogs barking idiotically through endless nights. It is so bad that a sort of grandeur creeps through it."

Harding's record as president caused few of these critics to change their minds. Though he appointed Hughes and Hoover, he also frequented the company of party hacks, hustlers, and low life. Other appointments appalled reformers. He named Harry Daugherty, a crass party functionary, as Attorney General; former President Taft as chief justice of the Court; James J. Davis, Supreme Dictator and Reorganizer of the Loyal Order of Moose, to Labor; Albert Fall, a reactionary senator from New Mexico, to Interior; and Andrew Mellon, a multimillionaire industrialist, to the Treasury. Daugherty, later charged (though not convicted) with accepting bribes, was a vigorous foe of labor who secured a crushing injunction against the striking United Mine Workers in 1922. Taft presided over a conservative Court that struck down a national child labor law, held minimum wages for women unconstitutional (Taft dissenting), and increased restrictions on boycotts and picketing. The role of the Court, he said, was "to prevent the Bolsheviki from getting control." Davis was an uninformed, complacent official who complained of reformers, "I never knew a theorist who wasn't a sick man." And Fall accepted bribes for turning over valuable mineral reserves to private interests. The resulting Teapot Dome scandal failed to implicate the President directly; compared to the Watergate affair of the 1970s, it was a limited misuse of power. But with other lesser scandals it revealed the corruption of many of Harding's friends. Quite obviously, he was a poor judge of people.

Mellon, who headed the Department of the Treasury until 1932, was the high priest of business-oriented welfare capitalism—the J. P. Morgan of the "new era." Like Morgan, he was domineering and certain that big businessmen could curb "wasteful" competition and promote the capitalist utopia. It followed, Mellon believed, that government must intervene to assist people who had capital. So throughout the 1920s he labored—usually successfully— to cut taxes on the rich and on corporations. These policies widened the gulf between rich and poor, concentrated capital in relatively few hands, and did nothing to broaden consuming power, so necessary to sustain prosperity.

Harding's successor, Calvin Coolidge, was a sour and nasty man who took pleasure in playing practical jokes on aides and secret service men. At the same time, however, he was fastidious, plain, and upright—so reassuring a figure that Americans easily forgave his party the scandals. "Silent Cal," as he was called, had been awarded the vice-presidential nomination in part because people thought that as governor of Massachusetts he had helped settle the Boston police strike of 1919 (actually he had procrastinated and made matters worse), and in part because he seemed a champion of business values. "Governor Coolidge," the Chicago *Tribune* had said approvingly, "is a red, white, and blue American by birth."

The *Tribune* saw Coolidge correctly. He was a safe, do-little president. In part because of metabolic need, he had to have a nap every afternoon as well

Left, Warren Harding's 1920 campaign button. Above, the Coolidge thimble, which was designed to attract women voters in the 1924 election.

as ten hours of sleep a night; he averaged four hours of work per day. He believed firmly in the Jeffersonian dictum: that government is best which governs least. "I am for economy and after that for more economy," he said. "Public administrators," he added, "would get along better if they would restrain the impulse to butt in or be dragged into trouble. They should remain silent until an issue is reduced to its lowest terms, until it boils down to something like a moral issue." No twentieth-century American president had been a more devoted advocate of small government.

This faith was part of a consistent philosophy that enshrined business values. Where Harding was an amiable moderate who wished to please everyone, Coolidge was a dedicated champion of corporations. "The business of America is business," he said. "The man who builds a factory builds a temple. The man who works there, worships there." Mellon had been an ornament in Harding's cabinet; he was Coolidge's major adviser. Coolidge opposed labor unions, tried (unsuccessfully) to turn over government-owned facilities in the Tennessee Valley to private interests, appointed business spokesmen to regulatory agencies like the FTC, and twice vetoed bills aimed at providing government assistance to agriculture. "Farmers," he said characteristically, "have never made much money. I don't believe we can do much about that."

Coolidge's dour expression, his hatchet face, his taciturn nature, and his legendary laziness made him easy to ridicule. Alice Roosevelt Longworth, Theodore Roosevelt's daughter, sniped that he had been weaned on a pickle. Dorothy Parker, informed that Coolidge had died, responded, "How can you tell?" Mencken complained that "Nero fiddled but Coolidge only snored. . . . He had no ideas and was only a nuisance."

Wise observers realized, however, that the business orientation of men like Coolidge commanded widespread public support. In 1920 Harding beat Governor James M. Cox of Ohio, his Democratic opponent, 16,143,407 to

9,130,328; in 1924 Coolidge trounced John W. Davis, 15,718,211 to 8,385,283; and in 1928 Hoover beat Alfred E. Smith, the progressive governor of New York, 21,391,993 to 15,016,169. These were by far the largest margins in modern American history to that date. Moreover, left-wing third parties trailed badly. Debs received only 919,799 votes in 1920 and Norman Thomas, the Socialist candidate in 1928, only 267,835. La Follette, running as a Progressive with socialist and (lukewarm) union backing, received 4,831,289 votes (17 percent) in 1924, an impressive showing when contrasted to that of other third party candidates in American history. But he carried only one state (Wisconsin). These statistics are a little deceptive, for voters did maintain a core of determined, if beleaguered, progressives in Congress. These activists, including new urban liberals like Robert Wagner of New York, showed that progressive politics were not dead in the 1920s. But they remained frustrated by the essential weakness of the left in that decade. People were content to "keep cool with Coolidge."

The presidential elections suggest other parameters of the political universe of the 1920s. One aspect was the division within the Democratic party. Disillusion with Wilson had shattered the coalition the party had been developing since 1916. Amid the wreckage two broad groups struggled for supremacy. One, strong in rural regions of the West and South, rallied behind men like William G. McAdoo, Wilson's secretary of the treasury and son-in-law. The other, which represented the urban ethnic groups, followed Alfred E. Smith, governor of New York, for much of the decade. In the 1924 convention the two men battled for 103 ballots before giving way to Davis, a Wall Street lawyer whom no one much wanted. Until this gap was bridged—by Franklin D. Roosevelt in the 1930s—the Democrats remained too divided to agree on national policy.

Another characteristic of the political scene in the 1920s was the continuing low turnout of eligible voters, especially before 1928. Many forces contributed to this poor showing, including stringent voter-registration laws and the absence of a meaningful two-party system in many states. Another reason, which feminists and idealists deplored, was light voting by women, again before 1928. Whatever the causes, the low turnouts carried on patterns that had developed in the progressive era. In political behavior, as in many other areas of life, the 1920s witnessed considerable continuity with the past.

B-but How Dead Are They?

The politics of the 1920s revealed also that people appeared to care little for debate about "big" national issues—trust busting, tariffs, conservation—that had animated many progressives. They worried instead about ethno-cultural questions like immigration restriction, the Ku Klux Klan, fundamentalism, and prohibition. These ethno-cultural divisions had intensified during the war and the Red Scare, leaving many ethnic voters unhappy with both parties by 1920. Because of apathy or alienation, millions of them did not vote for the next seven years. In 1928 they finally found their champion in Smith, an Irish-Catholic, an outspoken foe of prohibition, and a product of New York City's lower east side.

Though Smith lost badly, he carried America's top twelve cities by 38,000 votes, and he brought millions of ethnics and many women to the polls for the first time. His total vote almost doubled that of Davis, and it was only slightly less than that received by Harding in 1920 or Coolidge in 1924. In strengthening the affiliation of urban dwellers and ethnics with his party he began the

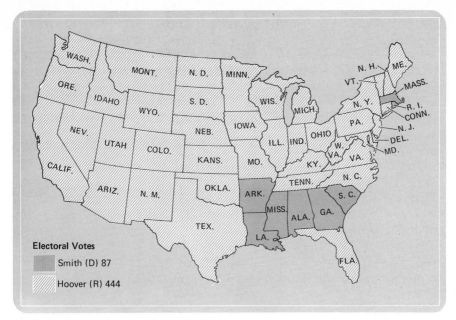

Election, 1928

historic realignment toward Democratic dominance that the depression and the New Deal completed. This movement of ethnic voters (though not of blacks, who remained Republican, disfranchised, or apathetic) was perhaps the most significant long-range political development of the decade. It suggests again that the 1920s were not insulated from the past and the future but in some respects a decade of transition.

BABBITTRY SUPREME

Bohemians, expatriates, alienated intellectuals; F. Scott Fitzgerald, Sinclair Lewis, H. L. Mencken; these were the savage critics of America in the 1920s. If we read only these writers we would have to assume that the decade witnessed a fierce and ultimately successful assault on traditional values.

Their critique, hardly subtle, aimed first at small-town mindlessness and materialism. Mencken dismissed the South as the "Sahara of the Bozart," a "gargantuan paradise of the fourth-rate." Lewis complained that "Main Street is the climax of civilization. That this Ford car might stand in front of the Bon Ton Store, Hannibal invaded Rome and Erasmus wrote in Oxford cloisters."

These critics complained especially of the conformity of American civilization. Following Nietzsche, Mencken yearned for philosopher kings, supermen who could rise above the commonplace. The gulf between the cultivated and the masses, he believed, was unbridgeable. Van Wyck Brooks, influenced by

Pale druggists in remote towns of the Epworth League and flannel night-gown belts, endlessly wrapping up bottles of Peruna. . . . Women hidden away in the damp kitchens of unpainted houses along the railroad tracks, frying tough beefsteaks. . . . Lime and cement dealers being initiated into the Knights of Pythias, the men at lonely railroad crossings in Iowa, hoping that they'll be able to get off to hear the United Brethren evangelist preach. . . . Ticket-choppers in the subway, breathing sweat in its gaseous form. . . . Family doctors in poor neighborhoods, faithfully relying upon the therapeutics taught in their Eclectic Medical College in 1884. . . . Farmers plowing sterile fields behind sad meditative horses, both suffering from the bites of insects. . . . Greeks tending all-night coffee-joints in the suburban wilderness where the trolley-cars stop. . . . Grocery-clerks stealing prunes and ginger-snaps, and trying to make assignations with soapy servant-girls. . . . Women confined for the ninth or tenth time, wondering helplessly what it is all about. . . . Methodist preachers retired after forty years of service in the trenches of God, upon pensions of $600 a year. . . .

Mencken's view of Middle American "Virtue," 1922. From *Prejudices*, 3rd series, 1922.

Freud, concluded that geniuses like Mark Twain had been repressed by American culture. "A vast unconscious conspiracy," he said, "actuates all Americans against the creative spirit." Babbitt, Lewis's unforgettable conformist, seemed so typically American that the word *Babbittry* passed into the language as a synonym for what people in the 1950s called the Organization Man. Americans, it seemed, were crude, conformist, consumption-crazed Philistines whose gods, as Babbitt conceded, were "Modern Appliances."

Disgust with American culture led some critics to glorify youth. Like Randolph Bourne before the war, they hoped the coming generation could sweep away the past. Amory Blaine, the youthful and idealistic hero of Fitzgerald's *This Side of Paradise,* was for many young readers the innocent figure that J. D. Salinger's Holden Caulfield *(Catcher in the Rye)* was in the 1950s. "The older generation had certainly pretty well ruined this world before passing it on to us," a critic commented in 1920. "They gave us this Thing, knocked to pieces, leaky, red-hot, threatening to blow-up; and then they are surprised that we don't accept it with the same attitude of pretty, decorous enthusiasm with which they received it."

The pessimism of such writers was reflected in growing skepticism about the possibility of promoting progressive change. Lincoln Steffens, rejecting reform, observed, "I can't see why everybody is so anxious to save this rotten civilization of ours." In his autobiography (1931) he praised such diverse autocrats as Mussolini, Lenin, and Henry Ford. Walter Lippmann, no longer an ardent progressive, argued the need for an elite governing class. The protagonists of Dreiser's *American Tragedy* (1925) had to surrender to inexor-

> *Now my generation is disillusioned, and I think, to a certain extent, brutalized, by the cataclysm which their complacent folly engendered. The acceleration of life for us has been so great that into the last few years have been crowded the experiences and the ideas of a normal lifetime. We have in our unregenerate youth learned the practicality and the cynicism that is safe only in unregenerate old age. We have been forced to become realists overnight, instead of idealists, as was our birthright. We have seen man at his lowest, woman at her lightest, in the terrible moral chaos of Europe. We have been forced to question, and in many cases to discard, the religion of our fathers. We have seen hideous peculation, greed, anger, hatred, malice, and all uncharitableness, unmasked and rampant and unashamed. We have been forced to live in an atmosphere of "to-morrow we die," and so, naturally, we drank and were merry. We have seen the rottenness and shortcomings of all governments, even the best and most stable. We have seen entire social systems overthrown, and our own called in question. In short, we have seen the inherent beastliness of the human race revealed in an infernal apocalypse.*
>
> "Youth culture," 1920s: the response of John F. Carter, a young journalist, 1920.

able natural forces, while Ernest Hemingway's characters achieve manhood only through self-assertion and physical courage. In 1929 Joseph Wood Krutch wondered if people could ever reconcile traditional beliefs with modern experience. "The possibility of an actual human maturity," he wrote, "is problematic. There impends for the human spirit either extinction or a readjustment more stupendous than any made before."

Many of these writers were also nostalgic, suspicious of technology and of urban growth. Lewis, while ridiculing small towns, cherished their warmth and friendliness, and he made no effort to praise the city. Other writers, like Hemingway and Robert Frost, exalted solitude. Floyd Dell and other bohemians celebrated the virtues of small communities like Greenwich Village. At the root of much cultural criticism in the 1920s was a highly ambivalent attitude toward modernization, and especially toward machine technology.

For these reasons many of the critics of American life in the 1920s were essentially harmless. Relatively few were bohemians or expatriates for long, and fewer still advocated radical changes in sexual behavior or in familial patterns. Only a handful of writers—Dos Passos and Steffens were among them—went beyond a critique of materialism to engage in a serious examination of capitalism itself. The transition from assaults on the "Booboisie" to economic radicalism began in the late 1920s, especially after the executions of Sacco and Vanzetti. But it took the depression to revive the left in America.

Above all, writers like Mencken and Lewis failed utterly to undermine the self-confidence of the dominant business elites. Observe a few statements from businessmen of the time.

On the glories of capitalism:

History shows that the prime motive of capitalism—namely, *selfishness*—merely reflects the conviction, *inborn in every living creature,* that *it is his natural right to keep, own, and control whatever he himself has made, saved, thought out, bought, or fought for;* a conviction which works out broadly not only for *justice* to the individual, but to the common good of all.

(Charles N. Fay, Business in Politics, 1926.)

On Jesus as the archetypal businessman:

So we have the main points of [Jesus's] business philosophy:

1. Whoever will be great must render great service.
2. Whoever will find himself at the top must be willing to lose himself at the bottom.
3. The big rewards come to those who travel the second, undemanded mile.

(Bruce Barton, The Man Nobody Knows, 1925.)

And on the nature of labor:

It is the aim of Scientific Management to induce men to act as nearly like machines as possible, so far as doing the work in the one best way that has been discovered is concerned.

(Frank Gilbreth, successor to Frederick Winslow Taylor as crusader for scientific management.)

Not all business spokesmen were so crude. The larger, wealthier corporations moved further in the direction of welfare capitalism by developing pension plans and providing paid vacations. But even the enlightened capitalists tended to denigrate the masses, to use workers as automated machines, and to welcome the bureaucratization and corporate concentration that undermined the individualism they professed to cherish. They also helped to crush the American labor movement. Thanks primarily to a concerted strike-breaking campaign in 1919–20, union membership declined from 5 million in 1920 to less than 3 million by 1932. The decline of organized labor in the 1920s was the most impressive display of the power of the business ideology of the time.

This business-oriented belief system reflected a broad faith in individualism that was shared by millions of Americans in the 1920s. These Americans worshipped Henry Ford, the churlish epitome of oligopoly, because he made inexpensive cars, but also because he despised unions, constructed a colonial village, and proclaimed loudly that he was a self-made man. They revered Thomas Edison, an originator of team science, because they pictured him as a solitary genius working with his hands. They adored Charles Lindbergh in part because he was the "lone eagle," a lineal descendent of other frontier-breaking pioneers in American history. They heaped praise on sports figures like Babe Ruth, Bobby Jones, and Gene Tunney. They deeply admired Herbert Hoover, the Great Engineer who defended rugged individualism. All these heroes appeared to personify the characteristics that had made America great: solid achievement and self-reliance.

In so believing, Americans conveniently forgot that many of their heroes—Ford, Lindbergh, Edison, and even Hoover—were helpmates of scientism, technological displacement, and collectivization. But these contradictions did not bother them, for they saw what they wanted to see. Like their fathers and mothers, they cherished a world where traditional values of self-reliance would count, where the masses did as they were told, where government minded its own business, and where the capitalistic system could spread its blessings to all who worked to get them. In this sense the business values of the 1920s easily survived the barbs of Mencken and Lewis, the rejections of the expatriates, and the sneers of the bohemians.

THE PERSISTENCE OF PIETISM

Even the casual newspaper reader in the early 1920s had to be struck by the visibility and power of two related groups: prohibitionists and fundamentalists. By 1932, however, the prohibitionists were fighting an obviously futile battle and the fundamentalists seemed all but forgotten. The diminishing visibility of these groups, allied in their pietistic insistence on right conduct, symbolized the apparent decline of village values and the triumph of more "modern" urban and secular beliefs.

On the surface this picture of the decade had much to commend it. Prohibition, for instance, was an obvious failure well before it was repealed in 1933. Though it eradicated the saloon and decreased the alcohol consumption of the lower classes (who could least afford speakeasies or bootlegged stock), it stimulated the illicit sale of awful concoctions. These included Jackass Brandy, which caused internal bleeding, Soda Pop Moon, which contained poisonous alcohol, and Panther Whiskey, which was based on esters and fusel oil. (The joke went around that one customer, suspicious of his bootlegger's stock, sent a sample to a chemist, who replied, "Dear Sir, your horse has diabetes.") The total income of bootleggers, based on annual sales of 150 million quarts of liquor, was $2 billion per year, roughly 2 percent of the Gross National Product.

In gang-ridden Chicago, the failure of prohibition was especially clear. As early as 1920, when vice king "Big Jim" Colosimo was murdered, he was mourned by an estimated 5000 people. His honorary pallbearers included three judges, eight aldermen, an assistant state attorney, and two congressmen. The cavalcade to his burial, the Chicago *Tribune* noted, was "such as moved behind the funeral car of Caesar." Colosimo's death permitted ruthless men like Al Capone to take over, and violence mounted: one article estimated that 1,291 people were murdered in gang warfare between 1926 and mid-1929.

Prohibition alone did not cause the organization of crime in America during the 1920s. Vice rings, like most American institutions, had grown

This Model T, seized by U. S. Customs officers in Marfa, Texas, yielded 110 bottles of Mexican liquors—stowed in the spare tire and under the seats and tied to the chassis.

steadily more centralized in previous decades. Moreover, the economic opportunities offered by syndicated crime provided a ladder to wealth for ethnic groups denied access to more legitimate businesses. "Prohibition is a business," Capone proclaimed. "All I do is supply a public demand. I do it in the best and least harmful way I can." But the very prominence of men like Capone showed that prohibition remained a dreadful mistake. It discriminated against poor people and ethnics. It diverted attention from people who hoped to promote noncoercive remedies for the curse of alcoholism. It disillusioned progressives who had relied on statutes to bring about right behavior. It encouraged stereotypes about knife-wielding Sicilians and crime-ridden cities. It led otherwise respectable people to act in contempt of the law. No wonder it was eventually repealed.

Fundamentalists (many of whom were prohibitionists) also seemed anachronistic to sophisticates during the decade. Billy Sunday, the baseball player turned evangelist, confessed that he didn't "know any more about theology than a jack-rabbit knows about ping-pong," but that "that old bastard theory of evolution" was "jackass nonsense." Aimée Semple McPherson, popularizer of the "Four-Square Gospel," used her good looks, modern showmanship, and claims of faith healing to found the Angelus Temple, capacity 5,300, in Los Angeles. "To visit Angelus Temple," one cynic wrote, "is to go on a sensuous debauch served up in the name of religion." The Reverend J. Frank Norris, head of the First Baptist Church of Fort Worth, Texas, built a 6000-seat church and bathed it in searchlights making it visible for thirty-two miles. A crude, violent man who once shot and killed someone in his office, Norris hotly opposed "that hell-born, Bible-destroying, deity-of-Christ-denying, German rationalism [known as] . . . evolution."

Assertions such as these led to the wide publicity given the trial of John Scopes, a biology teacher in Dayton, Tennessee, for the illegal teaching of Darwinian theories. At the trial William Jennings Bryan defended the state's antievolution law by insisting that "it is better to trust in the Rock of Ages than to know the age of rocks; it is better for one to know that he is close to the Heavenly Father than to know how far the stars in the heavens are apart." He conceded, however, that the "day" of creation might mean a million years. Clarence Darrow, who cross-examined Bryan at the trial, expostulated, "I am examining you on your fool ideas that no intelligent Christian on earth believes."

Because Scopes made no pretense of denying his "guilt," no one was surprised when the court ruled against him. The antievolution law remained on the books for forty-two more years. Yet the case enabled journalists like Mencken to ridicule Bryan (who died immediately after the trial) and pietists generally. A handful of extreme fundamentalists, like Gerald B. Winrod, counterattacked by embracing anti-Semitism, anticommunism, and authoritarianism—beliefs that made them precursors of the post–World War II radical Right. Most fundamentalists, however, nursed their resentments more quietly. Fundamentalism, modernists thought prematurely, was as doomed as prohibition.

In fact, these expressions of pietism remained considerably more vigorous than many people realized. The dry forces, far from renouncing their cause, might have held out longer if the depression had not led people to believe that the legalization of liquor would produce tax revenue. At that point in 1933, the "great experiment" was repealed, but the pietists did not embrace the values of their opponents. Instead, they withdrew into themselves, more conscious as a group than ever before and more certain that the dominant elites— eastern, urban, corporate—were their enemies.

Modernists could not even take solace from assaults on men like Bryan. Convinced of their rectitude, fundamentalists popularized the once radical idea that ordinary people could build their own pipelines to God. In so doing they promised individuals faith amid secularization and group solidarity amid the pressures of migration and rapid social change. As thousands of rural Americans moved to unfamiliar urban surroundings—like McPherson's Los Angeles or Norris's Fort Worth—the fundamentalists increased their strength. From this perspective the fundamentalists offered much to millions of people. Like many other out-groups of the decade, they counterorganized in order to combat the social focus of the age.

THE KU KLUX KLAN

Another manifestation of rural, old-stock pietism in the early 1920s was the Ku Klux Klan, which was resurrected in 1915 by William J. Simmons, an evangelist and insurance salesman from Atlanta. Inspired by the racist film, *Birth of a Nation,* Simmons proclaimed himself Imperial Wizard, burned

A KKK meeting in the 1920s.

crosses, and spread the gospel of native white supremacy. When he enlisted the services of public relations specialists in 1920, his organization blossomed into both a profitable racket and a national movement. Despite the then costly membership fee of $10 (to pay, among other things, for sheets), 4 to 5 million Americans joined the Klan in the next five years.

The new movement was anti-Catholic, anti-Semitic, anti-immigrant, and antiradical as well as antiblack. It represented, with prohibition and fundamentalism, an assertively Christian indictment of urban, ethnic, modern America. It stood for "Americanism," a euphemism for white Protestantism and for God-fearing, law-abiding behavior. It openly sanctioned night-riding, tar-and-feathering, and other acts of physical intimidation. "The Klan is intolerant," bragged Hiram Wesley Evans, a Texas dentist who headed the organization in the mid-1920s, " . . . of the people who are trying to destroy our traditional Americanism . . . aliens who are constantly trying to change our civilization into something that will suit themselves better."

By 1924 the Klan had become a potent political force, not only in the South (where a liberal lawyer like Hugo Black joined it to advance in politics) but in such nonsouthern states as California, Ohio, Indiana, and Oregon. It showed considerable strength in northern cities, especially those to which blacks and immigrants had streamed during the war and postwar years. Though influential in both parties, it was especially powerful in the Democratic party, which refused to condemn it (by one vote) in the divided

> There are three great racial instincts, vital elements in both the historic and the present attempts to build an America which shall fulfill the aspirations and justify the heroism of the men who made the nation. These are the instincts of loyalty to the white race, to the traditions of America, and to the spirit of Protestantism, which has been an essential part of Americanism ever since the days of Roanoke and Plymouth Rock. They are condensed into the Klan slogan: "Native, white, Protestant supremacy!"
>
> The gospel of the KKK by Imperial Wizard Hiram Wesley Evans, 1926.

convention of 1924. The nineteenth-century Klan had never amassed such national support.

The KKK, like the prohibitionists and the fundamentalists, quickly fell from grace after 1925. One blow was publicity given the sordid leadership of David Stephenson, Grand Dragon of the Indiana Klan, who kidnapped and assaulted his secretary on a train to Chicago. When she died from taking poison, Stephenson was sentenced in 1925 to life in prison. When the governor, a Klansman himself, refused to pardon him, Stephenson produced evidence that sent a congressman, the mayor of Indianapolis, and other officials to jail. Elsewhere voters belatedly voted Klansmen out of office. The fall of the KKK after 1925 suggested that Americans were coming to their senses, that the repressiveness that had blighted the country since the early days of the war was declining.

The rise of ethnic consciousness

THE BLACK EXPERIENCE

In fact, the decline of the Klan was at best a surface victory for the champions of racial and religious toleration. The 1920s witnessed the continued subjection of blacks. Peonage on southern farms was so widespread that Secretary of Commerce Hoover had to appoint a "Colored Advisory Committee" in 1927. The committee tried to investigate the situation, but plantation owners intimidated witnesses, and the Red Cross interfered with efforts to publicize conditions. In the North the continuing migrations of blacks made the modern racial ghetto a reality. Chicago's black population increased from 109,458 to 233,903 during the decade, while New York's rose from 152,467 to 327,706. Blacks often had to resort to strike-breaking to find jobs at all. There were two kinds of businesses in New York, the sociologist E. Franklin Frazier commented, "those that employ Negroes in menial positions, and those that employ no Negroes at all." George Schuyler noted later, "the reason why the depression didn't have the impact on the Negroes that it had on the whites was that the Negroes had been in the depression all the time."

Of course, this grim picture was somewhat one-sided. During the 1920s, as in previous decades, the movement of blacks into the middle class continued. Moreover, places like Harlem, for all their horrors, offered blacks more hope than did the rural South. "I can never put on paper the thrill of the underground ride to Harlem," the black poet Langston Hughes wrote. "I went up the steps and out into the bright September sunlight. Harlem! I stood there, dropped my bags, took a deep breath, and felt happy again."

Black intellectuals like Hughes, Alain Locke, Claude McKay, and James Weldon Johnson thought places like Harlem would create what Locke called the "New Negro." Harlem, Locke said, "has the same role to play for the New Negro as Dublin has for the New Ireland or Prague for the New Czechoslovakia." Hughes explained that it was the "duty of the young Negro artist . . . to change through the force of his art that old whispering 'I want to be white,' hidden in the aspirations of his people, to 'why should I want to be white? I am a Negro—and beautiful.'" Artists such as these led the Harlem Renaissance, a flowering of jazz, poetry, and fiction that suggested that blacks were finding authentic expressions outside the white world.

Other black spokesmen offered a more militant form of black pride. W. E. B. Du Bois, despairing of interracial cooperation, not only drifted away from white liberals, but freely confessed his racial prejudice. Hearing of the lynching of a white man in 1923, he wrote, "We're sorry we're glad. We wish we were big enough to be dissolved in tears. . . . But we're not; we're just plain tickled at this blood-soaked land." He also propagandized for Pan Africanism. By this he did not mean that American blacks should migrate to Africa, but that they should establish their kinship with oppressed people throughout the world. "The spell of Africa is upon me," he wrote in 1924. "The ancient witchery of her medicine is burning in my drowsy, dreamy blood. This is not a country, it is a world—a universe of itself and for itself, a thing Different,

If we must die let it not be like hogs
Hunted and penned in an inglorious spot,
While round us bark the mad and hungry dogs,
Making their mock at our accursed lot.
If we must die, o let us nobly die,
So that our precious blood may not be shed
In vain; then even the monsters we defy
Shall be constrained to honor us though dead!
O kinsmen! We must meet the common foe!
Though far outnumbered let us show us brave,
And for their thousand blows deal one deathblow!
What though before us lies the open grave?
Like men we'll face the murderous cowardly pack,
Pressed to the wall, dying but fighting back!

Black militance in the 1920s. A poem by Claude McKay.

Immense, Menacing, Alluring. Africa is the Spiritual Frontier of human kind."

Another form of black militancy came from A. Philip Randolph, a socialist who had cofounded *The Messenger* (subtitled "The Only radical Negro magazine in America") in 1917 and who had been arrested in 1918 for opposing the war. In 1925 he started the Brotherhood of Sleeping Car Porters. Though it was twelve years before the Pullman Company agreed to sign a contract with the union, Randolph's example suggested that blacks could sustain a nationwide, all-black organization. His insistence that blacks fight for themselves proved inspiring to later generations of militants.

The most colorful black leader of the decade was Marcus Garvey of Harlem. Like many prominent blacks (others in the twentieth century included McKay, Stokeley Carmichael, Shirley Chisholm, and Bayard Rustin), Garvey was a West Indian migrant. One of his early inspirations was Booker T. Washington, apostle of black self-help. Unlike Washington, however, Garvey urged blacks to reject everything white. He took as his colors

Marcus Garvey (second from right) and entourage.

Black queen of beauty, thou hast given color to the world!
Among other women thou art royal and the fairest!
Like the brightest jewels in the regal diadem,
Shin'st thou, Goddess of Africa, nature's purest emblem!

Black men worship at thy virginal shrine of purest love,
Because in thine eyes are virtue's steady and holy mark,
As we see no other, clothed in silk or fine linen,
From ancient Venus, the Goddess, to mythical Helen.

A poem by Marcus Garvey.

red (for slave blood), black (for skin color), and green (for African fertility), and he refused to let his newspaper, *Negro World,* accept ads for hair straighteners or skin bleachers. He also called for a back-to-Africa movement, to be assisted by the Black Star shipping line. A master showman, Garvey relied heavily on fancy uniforms, and he rewarded lieutenants with such grandiose titles as the African Virgin Mary, Duke of Uganda, and Knight Commander of the Nile. His flamboyance, together with the pride in color that he evoked, gave his movement an unprecedented mass appeal in Harlem in the early 1920s.

These expressions of militancy showed that blacks were struggling to organize against their foes. But they fell far short of success. The Harlem Renaissance was heavily dependent on white patronage, and venturesome whites who flocked to the night clubs and jazz halls of Harlem transformed black art forms into variations more suitable for mass white consumption. Other whites saw in jazz confirmation of the stereotype that blacks were rhythmic, spiritual, attuned to the beat of the jungle. Robert Park, the nation's leading sociologist, explained that the Anglo-Saxon was essentially "a pioneer and sociologist," while the black was "primarily an artist, loving life for its own sake. His métier is expression rather than action. He is, so to speak, the lady among the races." Most discouraging of all, the Harlem Renaissance failed to assist the black masses. "Some Harlemites," Hughes lamented, "thought the race problem had been solved through Art. They were sure the Negro would lead a new life from then on in green pastures of tolerance. . . . I don't know what made Negroes think that—except that they were mostly intellectuals doing the thinking. The ordinary Negroes hadn't heard of the Negro Renaissance. And if they had, it hadn't raised their wages any."

The spokesmen for black protest also failed to accomplish much in the 1920s. Du Bois, proud and outspoken, did not reach the masses. Randolph's days of influence lay far ahead. Garvey, who denounced Du Bois as "purely and simply a white man's nigger," antagonized blacks as well as whites. Du Bois dismissed him as an ignorant demagogue, and Randolph called him the "Supreme Negro Jamaican Jackass." Garvey's Black Star Line foundered, the victim of poor management and of unscrupulous dealers who sold him aged ships. The federal government then jailed him in 1925 for mail fraud and deported him in 1927. The suddenness of his decline did not mean that his followers disappeared—on the contrary, some of them founded the Black Muslims in 1931. But it did encourage whites to feel they need not respond to mass appeals for racial justice.

Garvey's fall revealed another obstacle in the way of black progress: blacks themselves were divided into subgroups. Some middle-class blacks, penned into the ghettos, tended to blame the lower-class migrants for intensifying white racism. And in Harlem, the presence of some 50,000 West Indian blacks was a constant source of intraracial tension. These migrants were often better educated, more militant, and prouder of their color than the newly arrived southern blacks. Some of them spoke French or Spanish, and even the English speakers had accents different from the southerners. Most West Indians were Episcopalians or Catholics, whereas the southerners tended to be Baptists or Methodists. These differences led native blacks to refer to the West Indians as "monkey-chasers," "ring-tails," and "cockneys." Ditties ridiculed the back-to Africa movement:

> When I get to the other side
> I'll buy myself a mango,
> Grab myself a monkey gal
> And do the monkey tango. . . .
>
> Garvey, Garvey, is a big man
> To take his folks to monkey land.
> If he does, I'm sure I can
> Stay right here with Uncle Sam. . . .
>
> When a monkey chaser dies,
> Don't need no undertaker.
> Just throw him in the Harlem River
> He'll float back to Jamaica.

The largest barrier to racial justice remained the intolerance of whites. It was in 1929 that "Amos 'n Andy," the insulting black-face radio comedy, began and achieved its immense popularity. Contemporary editors of the *Encyclopedia Brittanica* explained that the "Negro" had a "less voluminous brain as compared with the white races," was "on a lower evolutionary plane than the white man," and was "more closely related to the highest anthropoids." "After puberty," the encyclopedia concluded, "sexual matters take the first place in the negro's life and thoughts." Even well-meaning whites inevitably sounded patronizing. "The Negro," one explained in 1923, "has good points that many other races do not. He is a patriot. He loves the South. He loves his white folks. He understands the southern white. He has a genius for religion. . . . Let us be faithful to God and help the southern Negro to work out to wholesome and worthy ends the strange destiny which has placed him here among us." Attitudes such as these showed that in racial

> There is nothing in the make-up of a Negro, physically or mentally, which should induce anyone to welcome him as a neighbor. The best of them are unsanitary, ... ruin alone follows in their path. They are as proud as peacocks, but have nothing of the peacock's beauty. . . . Niggers are undesirable neighbors and entirely irresponsible and vicious.
>
> A passage from the *Property Owners' Journal*, 1920, Chicago, cited in Allan Spear, *Black Chicago: The Making of a Negro Ghetto, 1890–1920.*

matters, as in much else in the 1920s, Americans held to established ideas. So long as these views persisted, it made little difference whether the Kluxers put on their sheets or not.

ETHNIC CONFLICT IN THE MELTING POT

This discrimination against blacks was but part of broader bigotry that manifested itself in many ways during the 1920s. One was anti-Semitism, reflected in the steady popularity of Madison Grant's *Passing of the Great Race,* first published in 1916. "The man of the old stock," Grant explained, "is today being literally driven off the streets of New York City by the swarms of Polish Jews." Kenneth Roberts, a widely read historical novelist, referred to East European Jews as "human parasites." Henry Ford had his car dealers circulate the "Protocol of the Elders of Zion," the spurious creation of a Czarist secret policeman that supposedly "proved" that Jews were engaged in a conspiracy to take over the world. Anti-Semitism led universities and business to impose religious quotas.

Prejudice surfaced in countless other forms. It made many Americans enthusiastic for Mussolini in the 1920s—Italians, everyone knew, needed a strong man to bring (American) efficiency to a disorderly nation. It was an undercurrent in the writings of Mencken, who stereotyped immigrants with sensuality in order to indict the Puritanism of native whites. It sustained psychological tests "proving" that the foreign-born had low IQs. It powerfully reinforced the Americanization movement, at full flower in the 1920s. "We must resolutely set to work," the educator Ellwood Cubberly explained, "to Americanize the foreign-born in our midst. We must abolish illiteracy and make English our one language." It resulted in the discriminatory immigration act of 1924, which only six United States senators opposed. Three years after the decline of the Klan, it flared openly in slurs on Al Smith, whose Catholicism convinced many otherwise thoughtful Americans that he was a stooge for the Pope.

Intolerance also intensified ongoing patterns of counterorganization and fragmentation in the United States. At the turn of the century many immigrant groups had been too new to the American scene to organize effectively.

The steamship companies haul them over to America, and as soon as they step off the decks of their ships the problem of the steamship companies is settled, but our problem has but begun—bolshevism, red anarchy, black-handers, and kidnapers, challenging the authority and the integrity of our flag, and still we find people who want us to have loopholes in the law so that such may continue to come in.

I do not intend to vote for any such proposition. I would like to shut for a time the immigration door. Thousands come here who never take the oath to support our Constitution and to become citizens of the United States. They pay allegiance to some other country while they live upon the substance of our own. They fill places that belong to the loyal wage-earning citizens of America. They preach a doctrine that is dangerous and deadly to our institutions. They are of no service whatever to our people. They constitute a menace and danger to us every day, and I can not understand the seeming indifference that some national lawmakers exhibit upon this serious subject. This very question of immigration is the most vital question that affects us today.

Senator Thomas Heflin (Alabama) on the evils of immigration, 1921.

Blacks had been oppressed in the rural South. By 1930, however, some of these people were joining the host of interest groups in America. Many Jews, including Justice Brandeis, sought to preserve common bonds by embracing Zionism. Militant blacks looked to Garvey or Randolph. Millions of ethnics buoyed the strength of urban political machines. These efforts at counterorganization, in turn, led disaffected fundamentalists, prohibitionists, and Klansmen to tighten their own group loyalties. Thus fragmentation—of city versus country, of pietists versus modernists, of ethnics against Anglo-Saxons, of blacks versus whites, and of subgroups within these categories—exposed the divisions that characterized American life even in the relatively prosperous 1920s. The "new era," it seems, carried forward many of the ambiguities and tensions of the old one.

Suggestions for reading

Three starting points for interpretive accounts of the 1920s are William Leuchtenburg, *The Perils of Prosperity, 1914–1932* * (1958), a skillful, well-written treatment; John Braeman et al., eds., *Change and Continuity in Twentieth-Century America: The 1920s* (1968); and Robert Elias, *Entangling Alliances with None: An Essay on the Individual in the American Twenties* (1973). Books focusing on currents in thought are Roderick Nash, *The Nervous Generation: American Thought, 1917–1930* * (1969); Alfred Kazin, *On Native Grounds* * (1942), on literary trends; Robert Crunden, *From Self to Society: Transitions in American Thought, 1919–1941* * (1972); and the books by Goldman and Hofstadter cited in the bibliography for chapter 2.

For politics, a useful survey is John D. Hicks, *Republican Ascendancy** (1960). Harding is treated in Andrew Sinclair, *The Available Man** (1965); and Robert K. Murray, *The Harding Era* (1969). Donald McCoy, *Calvin Coolidge* (1967), is an excellent study. Important biographies are Richard Lowitt, *George W. Norris: The Persistence of a Progressive* (1971); William Harbaugh, *Lawyer's Lawyer: The Life of John W. Davis* (1973); Matthew and Hanna Josephson, *Al Smith* (1970); and Arthur Mann, *LaGuardia . . . 1882–1933** (1959). George Tindall, *The Emergence of the New South, 1913–1945* (1967), is almost encyclopedic. Donald Swain, *Federal Conservation Policy, 1921–1933* (1963) is an admirable monograph. Important studies of electoral trends are David Burner, *The Politics of Provincialism* (1968), on the Democratic party; and Samuel Lubell, *The Future of American Politics** (1952). J. Joseph Huthmacher, *Massachusetts People and Politics, 1919–1933** (1959) is a first-rate state study. Clarke Chambers, *Seedtime of Reform, 1918–1933* (1963) concerns itself with the ideas and activities of social reformers.

Many books deal with social and cultural trends in the 1920s. They include Robert and Helen Lynd, *Middletown** (1929); John Rae, *The Road and Car in American Life* (1971); William Chafe, *The American Woman: Her Changing Social, Economic, and Political Roles, 1920–1960** (1972); and J. Stanley Lemons, *The Woman Citizen: Social Feminism in the 1920s* (1973). Also Don Kirschner, *City and Country: Rural Responses to Urbanization in the 1920s* (1970); Andrew Sinclair, *Prohibition: The Era of Excess** (1962); Lawrence Levine, *Defender of the Faith: William Jennings Bryan, the Last Decade, 1915–1925* (1965); Norman Furniss, *The Fundamentalist Controversy, 1918–1931* (1954); David M. Chalmers, *Hooded Americanism: The First Century of the Ku Klux Klan** (1965); Paul Carter, *The Decline and Revival of the Social Gospel** (1954); and Ray Ginger, *Six Days or Forever?** (1958), which deals amusingly with the Scopes trial. Otis Pease, *The Responsibilities of American Advertising, 1920–1940* (1958) covers an otherwise neglected subject.

A solid economic history of the decade is George Soule, *Prosperity Decade** (1947). Equally valuable is the briefer account by Jim Potter, *The American Economy Between the Wars** (1974). Milton Friedman and Anna Schwartz, *The Great Contraction** (1965), focuses on monetary problems; see also Elmus Wicker, *Federal Reserve Monetary Policy, 1917–1933* (1966). James Prothro, *The Dollar Decade** (1954), describes business thought. Allan Nevins and F. E. Hill, *Ford: The Times, the Man, and the Company* (1954) and *Ford, Expansion and Challenge* (1957) are thorough. A durable interpretation of corporate trends is Adolf Berle, Jr., and Gardiner Means, *The Modern Corporation and Private Property** (1969). Alfred Chandler's *Strategy and Structure** (1962) is an indispensable guide to changes in corporate structure. The basic book on labor is Irving Bernstein, *The Lean Years** (1960), to be supplemented with Robert Zieger, *Republicans and Labor, 1919–1929* (1969).

Black History receives coverage in E. David Cronon, *Black Moses** (1955), which deals with Marcus Garvey. See also Theodore Vincent, *Black Power and the Garvey Movement* (1971). Other useful studies are Nathan Huggins, *Harlem Renaissance** (1971); Eugene Levy, *James Weldon Johnson* (1973); and the books on Harlem and Chicago by Osofsky and Spear cited in the bibliography for chapter 2.

For judicial trends consult Alpheus Mason, *The Supreme Court from Taft to Warren* (1958); and Paul Murphy's detailed *Constitution in Crisis Times, 1918–1969** (1970). Foreign policy is surveyed in L. Ethan Ellis, *Republican Foreign Policy, 1921–1933* (1968). See also Joan Hoff Wilson, *American Business and Foreign Policy,*

1920–1933 (1971); Thomas Buckley, *The United States and the Washington Conference* (1970); Akira Iriye, *After Imperialism: The Search for a New Order in the Far East, 1921–1931** (1969); and Joseph Tulchin, *The Aftermath of War: World War I and United States Policy Toward Latin America* (1971).

Primary sources include H. L. Mencken, *Prejudices* (6 vols., 1924–27); James Weldon Johnson, *Autobiography of An ex-Colored Man** (1927); Lincoln Steffens, *Autobiography** (1931; John Chamberlain, *Farewell to Reform** (1933); and Joseph Wood Krutch, *The Modern Temper** (1929).

7

Crash
and
depression

1929 - 1939

For millions of Americans who suffered through it, the Great Depression was the most terrifying experience of their lives. It threw millions out of work, disrupted families, fomented class conflict, and inspired sharp criticism of capitalism itself. It threatened the faith in economic growth and business values that had been at the core of twentieth-century American life. It helped cause lasting changes, especially in politics and in attitudes toward the government. "The experience" of depression, the sociologists Robert and Helen Lynd observed in returning to Muncie in the 1930s, "has been more nearly universal than any prolonged recent emotional experience . . . it had approached in its elemental shock the primary experiences of birth and death."

In retrospect, however, it is striking how little was altered in the long run. Most of the major trends of previous decades continued, some at accelerated rates. Bureaucracy spread, the economy centralized, and technology advanced. Interest groups, more self-conscious and insistent than ever, added to the fragmentation of American society. Hard times or no, there was no turning back.

The crash of 1929

Among the many specialized groups that proliferated in the 1920s was the National Association of Credit Men. In 1925 it issued a warning about the rising level of private debt in America. "There has been built up in our country," its resolution said, "a large peak of installment credit, and it is wise for our business people to exercise caution, for undoubtedly in a credit pinch this condition would prove a very disturbing factor."

A year later their fears were borne out in Florida, where a land boom finally collapsed. The immediate reason for the bust was a hurricane, which caused millions of dollars of damage. But the underlying cause was the speculative fever that had led to the blindest sorts of investment and had enabled avid promoters to stake out more house lots in Florida than there were families in the entire country.

But few Americans appeared to pay much attention to the credit men or to the lesson of boom and bust in Florida. On the contrary, net private debt increased from $139 billion in 1926 to $161 billion in 1929. Trading in the stock market jumped from 451 million in 1926 to 1.1 billion in 1929. During the same period brokers' loans—a measure of borrowing for investment—also increased, from $3.5 billion to more than $8.5 billion. Much of this expansion occurred during the summer of 1928, when the Great Bull Market lifted industrial stocks more than 100 points. Thereafter it became more difficult to make a killing. But stock prices continued to rise. Calvin Coolidge, symbol of Yankee frugality, advised that stocks were "cheap at current prices."

Because these increases in stock prices far outran real economic growth, it was but a matter of time before the nation experienced the bust that had afflicted Florida in 1926. That was precisely what happened when the market crashed in September and October of 1929. By November 13, when prices hit their low for the year, industrial stocks had fallen 228 points, or 50 percent, and more than $30 billion in stock values had disappeared. The magnitude and suddenness of the crash dwarfed previous panics in American history.

Most of the early losers were speculators, not ordinary workers or citizens. If the market had stabilized, as it appeared to by mid-1931, the economy itself need not have been seriously harmed. But stock prices then plummeted again until July 1932. So it was that from October 1929 to June 1932 GM fell from 73 points to 8, U. S. Steel from 262 to 21, Montgomery Ward from 138 to 4, and RCA from 101 to 2.5. The index of common stocks dropped from 26 points in 1929 to 6.9 points in 1932, and the market declined by $74 billion, three times the amount spent to fight World War I. The market then stabilized, but despite record-low interest rates for borrowers, investment was sluggish during the 1930s, and stock prices stayed well below 1929 levels.

It was primarily during this second decline, from mid-1931 to March 1933, that the stock market troubles were accompanied by an ever deepening economic depression. Thousands of brokers and investors simply went under, and 31,822 businesses folded in 1932 alone. Schools released teachers, cut the

The New York Times.

NEW YORK, TUESDAY, OCTOBER 29, 1929.

STOCK PRICES SLUMP $14,000,000,000 IN NATION-WIDE STAMPEDE TO UNLOAD; BANKERS TO SUPPORT MARKET TODAY

Sixteen Leading Issues Down $2,893,520,108; Tel. & Tel. and Steel Among Heaviest Losers

A shrinkage of $2,893,520,108 in the open market value of the shares of sixteen representative companies resulted from yesterday's sweeping decline on the New York Stock Exchange.

American Telephone and Telegraph was the heaviest loser, $448,905,162 having been lopped off of its total value. United States Steel common, traditional bellwether of the stock market, made its greatest nose-dive in recent years by falling from a high of 202½ to a low of 185. In a feeble last-minute rally it snapped back to 186, at which it closed, showing a net loss of 17½ points. This represented for the 8,131,055 shares of common stock outstanding a total loss in value of $142,293,416.

In the following table are shown the day's net depreciation in the outstanding shares of the sixteen companies referred to:

Losses in

PREMIER ISSUES HARD HIT

Unexpected Torrent of Liquidation Again Rocks Markets.

DAY'S SALES 9,212,800

Nearly 3,000,000 Shares Are Traded In Final Hour—The

STAGE | BROADWAY | SCREEN

VARIETY

PRICE 25¢.

Published Weekly at 154 West 46th St., New York, N. Y., by Variety, Inc. Annual subscription, $10. Single copies, 25 cents.
Entered as second-class matter December 22, 1905, at the Post Office at New York, N. Y., under the act of March 3, 1879.

VOL. XCVII. No. 3   NEW YORK, WEDNESDAY, OCTOBER 30, 1929   88 PAGES

WALL ST. LAYS AN EGG

Going Dumb Is Deadly to Hostess In Her Serious Dance Hall Profesh

A hostess at Roseland has her problems. The paid steppers consider their work a definite profession calling for specialized technique and high-power salesmanship.

"You see, you gotta sell your personality," said one. "Each we girls has—

Hunk on Winchell

When the Walter Winchells moved into 204 West 55th street, late last week, June Winchell, selected

DROP IN STOCKS ROPES SHOWMEN

Many Weep and Call Off Christmas Orders — Legit Shows Hit

Kidding Kissers in Talkers Burns Up Fans of Screen's Best Lovers

Talker Crashes Olympus

Paris, Oct. 29.

Fox "Follies" and the Fox Movietone newsreel are running this week in Ath—

Boys who used to whistle and girls who used to giggle when love scenes were flashed on the screen are in action again. A couple of years ago they began to take the love stuff seriously and desisted, but the talkers are reviving the osculators.

Economic collapse, 1929–1939

	1929	1933	1939
Population (millions)	122	126	131
GNP (billions of dollars, 1929 prices)	104	74	111
Per capita GNP (dollars, 1929 prices)	857	590	847
Exports of merchandise (billions of current dollars)	5.2	1.6	3.1
General imports (billions of current dollars)	4.4	1.5	2.3
Wholesale commodity prices (1926 = 100)	95	66	77
Farm products price index (1926 = 100)	105	51	65
Wheat price (current dollars per bushel, received by farmers)	1.04	0.38[a]	0.69
Realized gross farm income (billions of current dollars)	13.9	7.1	10.6
Average weekly earnings for production workers in manufacturing (current dollars)	25.03	16.73	23.86
Unemployed (millions, followed by percent of labor force) (estimates only)	1.6(3)	12.8(25)	9.5(17)
Common stocks price index (1941–43 = 100)	260	90	121
Volume of sales on the New York Stock Exchange (millions of shares)	1,125	655	262
Bank suspensions	659	4,004	72

SOURCE: Adapted from Cole, *Handbook of American History*, p. 211
[a]1932

length of terms, or closed down entirely: Georgia shut 1,318 schools with a total enrollment of 170,790. Some 5000 banks, with aggregate deposits of $3.2 billion, folded between October 1929 and August 1932. As cash disappeared, demand slackened, and the prices for farm and industrial products fell off sharply. The resulting deflation staggered debtors, who now had to pay off predepression debts with more valuable dollars. Corporations, which had speculated freely, cut production and slashed wages: regularly employed manufacturing workers were paid an average weekly wage of $25 in 1929, and $16.73 in 1933. Corporations also laid off workers, until 13 million Americans—one-fourth of the work force—were idle in 1933. All these events caused an unprecedented decline in the national income, from $88 billion in 1929 to $40 billion four years later. They culminated in frantic runs on banks,

Run on banks. Americans, afraid that banks would fail, flocked to withdraw their deposits in the early 1930s.

which President Franklin D. Roosevelt was forced to close in March 1933. The world's strongest, most modern economy had ground to a halt.

The human dimension of these statistics is very hard to describe. Testimony before a Senate committee in early 1932 revealed that Philadelphia had 280,000 unemployed, four-fifths of whom received no relief. The other one-fifth got grants of $4.23 per family per week, two-thirds of what they needed for food alone. The diets of these people consisted of bread and coffee for breakfast, and bread and carrots or canned soup for supper. In Chicago, an estimated 11,000 children had to be fed by their teachers (who did not receive all their back pay until World War II). Thousands of families, evicted from their homes, slept outdoors in parks or huddled in shacks and tents on unused land in "Hoovervilles" on the outskirts of cities. The situation in Washington, D. C., was terrifying. "I come home from the Hill every night filled with gloom," a newsman wrote. "I see on the streets filthy, ragged, desperate-looking men such as I have never seen before." Another observer added, "these [unemployed] are dead men. They are ghosts that walk the streets by day. They are ghosts sleeping with yesterday's newspapers thrown around them for covers at night."

American migrants on the road west. This picture was taken by Dorothea Lange.

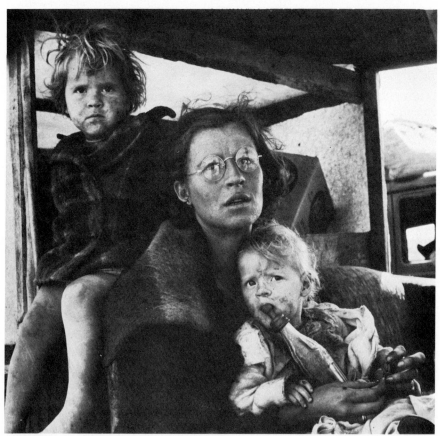

The decay spreads over the State, and the sweet smell is a great sorrow on the land. Men who can graft the trees and make the seed fertile and big can find no way to let the hungry people eat their produce. Men who have created new fruits in the world cannot create a system whereby their fruits may be eaten. And the failure hangs over the State like a great sorrow. . . .

The people come with nets to fish for potatoes in the river, and the guards hold them back; they come in rattling cars to get the dumped oranges, but the kerosene is sprayed. And they stand still and watch the potatoes float by, listen to the screaming pigs being killed in a ditch and covered with quicklime, watch the mountains of oranges slop down to a putrefying ooze; and in the eyes of the people there is the failure; and in the eyes of the hungry there is a filling and growing heavy, growing heavy for the vintage.

John Steinbeck's *Grapes of Wrath* describes poverty amid plenty for migrant workers.

The search for jobs led countless Americans to leave home. *Business Week* reported in 1931 that 100,000 Americans applied for 6000 openings for skilled workers in the Soviet Union. A Missouri Pacific official told the Senate two years later that the number of transients illegally riding trains had risen from 13,700 in 1928 to 186,000 in 1931. Hundreds of thousands rode on other railways, hitchhiked, or gathered their families into an old truck or car and took off. Some communities gave these transients a meal of beans and stale bread in return for a day's work, then herded them to the city limits. Others simply rounded them up, threw them back on the trains or into their trucks, and sent them on their way.

Many of these transients were migratory agricultural laborers. The Farm Security Administration later estimated that 500,000 such workers, with families of 1.5 million, roamed the country during the decade, and that they found employment an average of twenty-one to twenty-four weeks a year for total annual wages of between $110 and $124 per worker. In California, mecca for thousands of "Okies" displaced from the Plains and rural South, such migrants were shunted from town to town, or crowded into unsanitary camps. Many thousands despaired and turned back. Mexican-American workers, who had moved across the border in better times, now encountered violence from fearful local officials. An estimated 500,000, including some American citizens, were deported during the decade. "The Mexicans are trash," one California official declared. "They have no standard of living. We herd them like pigs." Still, the migration northward continued, and by 1940 there were 2.5 million "Chicanos" in America—500,000 more than ten years earlier.

Optimists argued that the situation was not hopeless. Many young people, they pointed out, were finishing school rather than dropping out to look for jobs they knew they couldn't find. The percentage of seventeen-year-olds who finished high school jumped from twenty-nine in 1930 to fifty in 1940, the

In one of the two rooms a six-year-old boy licked the paper bag the meat had been brought in. His legs were scarcely any larger than a medium sized dog's leg, and his belly was as large as that of a 130-pound woman's. Suffering from rickets and anemia, his legs were unable to carry him for more than a dozen steps at a time; suffering from malnutrition, his belly was swollen several times its normal size. His face was bony and white. He was starving to death.

In the other room of the house, without chairs, beds, or tables, a woman lay rolled up in some quilts trying to sleep. On the floor before an open fire lay two babies, neither a year old, sucking the dry teats of a mongrel bitch. A young girl, somewhere between fifteen and twenty, squatted on the corner of the hearth trying to keep warm.

The dog got up and crawled to the hearth. She sat on her haunches before the blazing pine-knots, shivering and whining. After a while the girl spoke to the dog and the animal slunk away from the warmth of the fire and lay again beside the two babies. The infants cuddled against the warmth of the dog's flanks, searching tearfully for the dry teats.

Erskine Caldwell describes the shack of a southern tenant farmer, 1935.

greatest advance in American history. Hard times, optimists added, forced many ruthless employers of child labor out of business. Optimists also pointed to the enormous efforts made by relief officials at all levels of government, especially by New Dealers after 1932. In December, 1934, one of the worst months of the depression, an estimated 19 million Americans received some form of public assistance. Despite impaired diets, they appeared to be getting healthier every year: life expectancy at birth rose from 59.7 years in 1930 to 62.9 in 1940. Such statistics reveal that the depression could not reverse the long-range economic and demographic trends toward modernization.

Other observers were aware that opportunity beckoned in the midst of poverty. J. Paul Getty, who had already grown rich in the 1920s, amassed millions more in the 1930s by buying oil companies cheaply. Norton Simon bought a bankrupt cannery for $7000 in 1931 and scrambled to the top of Hunt Foods, a multimillion-dollar business, by 1942. The actress Constance Bennett earned $30,000 in one week endorsing products, and Maurice Chevalier signed on at a Chicago night club for $12,000 a week. Despite hard times, the tourist business prospered throughout the period, and countless small business people—motel owners, used car dealers, gas station operators—made handsome profits during the decade. So did other people well placed in supposedly "luxury" occupations—cosmetics manufacturers, movie theater and race track owners, cocktail bar managers, major league baseball players. Corporate lawyers and tenured professors were among the professional people who lived fairly well in the 1930s; so did skilled white-collar workers and managers of technologically advanced companies like IBM and AT&T.

The 1930s also witnessed ongoing advances in the products of technology. These included nylon, aluminum, pneumatic tires for tractors, hybrid corn, television, coaxial cables for simultaneous long distance calls, and FM radios. Travelers welcomed completion in the early 1930s of the first coast-to-coast paved road (the Lincoln Highway) and the first uninterrupted air service across the country. (Previously, passengers had had to spend nights in Pullman cars on the ground and fly again by day—a tiring three-day process.) In 1939 alone newspapers reported the introduction of regular air service across the North Atlantic (Long Island to Lisbon in 26½ hours), of the hydraulic clutch, nylon stockings, fluorescent lights, and—ominously—the successful accomplishment of nuclear fission. Some of these advances were promoted by industries that were desperate for marketable new products or for labor-saving devices. Others stemmed from long-range researches begun before the Crash. Either way, it was clear that the technological imperative remained at the essence of modern American life.

These success stories, however, concealed precipitous declines in the opportunities available to most workers, including small farmers and farm laborers, unskilled industrial workers, and employees engaged in all forms of construction, which was paralyzed during the decade. The success stories failed to blot out daily reminders of the misery, malnutrition, family disorder, and hopelessness of millions of Americans. As late as January 1937, with prosperity apparently returning, President Franklin D. Roosevelt admitted that one-third of the nation was still "ill-housed, ill-clad, ill-nourished." In a general way (he had only crude statistics to work with) he was right, for the Great Depression hit America harder and for a longer time than it did other Western countries. And the pockets of wealth amidst poverty made the depression all the more infuriating. The humorist Will Rogers observed: "We've got . . . more of everything in the world than any nation that ever lived ever had, yet we are starving to death. We are the first nation in the history of the world to go to the poorhouse in an automobile."

> Going into the mill was a little like entering a deserted city. There was no movement, no sound. Men worked joylessly at little tasks that had no meaning. The open hearth and rail mills were vast echoing caverns with a single light here and there and a man, sometimes two, puttering around the still machines, the dead furnaces. They looked up eagerly at the sound of a footstep: when they spoke they kept their voices low. But not even the silence and the emptiness were as profoundly disturbing as the all pervading cold, the strange unnatural chill of these places of iron and flame. Leaving there was like worming out of a tomb.
>
> The steel industry in the 1930s, as described by Thomas Bell, *Out of this Furnace*, 1941.

Hard times: above, a bread line providing both food and public humiliation; right, a common street corner scene; below, shacks on a vacant lot housing the unemployed in a Hooverville.

WHY DID IT HAPPEN?

Economists have tried to analyze the forces behind the crash and to explain why the depression lasted as long as it did. They do not agree. Nevertheless, it is possible to offer a few tentative explanations.

One cause of the crash was the jerry-built nature of America's corporate structure by 1929. The most flagrant example was Samuel Insull's utilities empire, a vast complex of holding companies and interlocking directorates that rested on the gullibility of investors. Among other highly vulnerable institutions were investment trusts, which were corporations that used the capital of investors to speculate in the securities of other companies. Some of these trusts, and Insull's holding companies, engaged in stock manipulation and fraud; others were capitalized at levels far above their real value. Either way, they were unable to meet their obligations once stock prices declined. Their fall carried with them thousands of brokerage houses, banks, corporations, and private investors.

The proliferation of investment trusts and holding companies in the 1920s exposed another cause of the crash: the sheer extent of unregulated speculation. Investors were allowed to borrow on large "margins" in order to purchase stock, and to run up still higher debts through installment buying of consumer goods. This runaway speculation also enticed corporations and banks. Indeed, potential profits appeared so alluring in 1928 that corporations borrowed and loaned money on call. These were loans primarily for speculative purposes, and they carried exorbitant rates of interest (as high as 10 to 15 percent, or 5 to 10 percent above normal rates). They were payable on call of the lender. So long as the speculator could get still higher returns from stocks, such loans provided a ready form of capital. But when the market slipped, the lenders (which included corporations and respectable banks) called for their money. If they were lucky, they got it—from corporate borrowers who liquidated their investments, or from speculators who were so desperate to sell securities that they further depressed the market. If they did not get their money, it meant that both the borrower and the lender failed to meet their obligations. This unprecedented involvement of large institutions in the call money market created a vicious circle once prices started to fall.

The instability of banks added to the downward spiral after 1929. Despite efforts by reformers, no federal deposit insurance existed before 1933. Many state banks operated apart from the Federal Reserve system, almost as local capitalists engaged in entrepreneurial ventures. Because banks were not required to separate their banking and investment arms, they used depositors' money for speculative purposes, including call loans. As the economy declined, people pulled out their deposits, either to pay off outstanding debts or to make ends meet. Others, worried that their deposits were not insured, put their money under their mattresses. Caught with huge outstanding liabilities and dwindling deposits, banks foreclosed mortgages, demanded repayment of loans, or went under. To millions of small property owners and depositors nothing was more devastating.

Government policies in the 1920s aggravated these weaknesses. In theory, the Federal Reserve system had the power to prevent violent swings in the business cycle. It could make speculation more expensive, either by increasing the interest rate at which member banks had to borrow, or by increasing the ratio of reserves they had to withhold from investors. In practice, however, important decisions were not made in Washington, but by private bankers with the Federal Reserve bank in New York. These men were slow to act or even to warn against the speculative mania. When they did, by raising rates to 5 percent in 1928 and 6 percent in 1929, they were too late to stop speculators, who turned to the call-money market even at exorbitant rates. If higher interest rates had any effect at all in 1929, they turned the screws on solid investment in plant and equipment and accelerated the uncertainty that often precedes a crash.

Federal Reserve officials also showed an undue concern for the welfare of the English pound, which had been unstable since World War I. Keeping American interest rates low, they realized, might encourage speculation. But raising them might induce English investors to take their money to America, thus draining capital from England and increasing pressure on the pound. Accordingly, the New York bankers kept American interest rates low between 1926 and 1928. This concern for the stability of the pound revealed the extent to which international investments affected the domestic economy.

All these destabilizing forces—investment trusts, holding companies, rampant speculation, shaky banks, counterproductive government policies—were important causes of the crash. But they do not explain the depression. Many of these weaknesses, in fact, were hardly new in 1929. Speculative manias and unstable corporations had always plagued the economy, and American banks had long been decentralized. And monetary policy, while uninformed, was not the panacea that some later economists claimed. In 1929, for instance, higher interest rates failed to prevent speculation, in part because so many corporate investors could employ profits for idle purposes, in part because the psychology of boom made the cost of borrowing almost irrelevant. The reverse psychology in the 1930s meant that record-low rates failed to bring money out of hiding. Investors cannot be moved by interest rates alone.

The depression

What, then, did turn the crash into such a devastating depression?

One cause lay in international economic instability of a peculiarly severe nature. The war had left England and France heavily in debt to America, which insisted on repayment of its loans. But the Allies, even after squeezing Germany dry, were hard-pressed to pay. Until 1928 American investors sustained a circular state of affairs by literally pouring loans into Germany. By 1929, however, they found the fantastic domestic possibilities on the stock market more alluring than European investments. So they began to invest and to speculate at home. As Europe's financial institutions began to weaken, investors throughout the world sought safer places for their money. By September 1931 these forces led to the devaluation of the English pound and the collapse of the Kreditanstalt, Austria's central bank. Frightening withdrawals from banks—what economists call a rush for liquidity—then followed throughout the western world. In America alone 3800 banks failed in 1931 and 1932.

Fundamental domestic weaknesses also made the crash of 1929 more lasting than those in the past. Among these weaknesses were "depressed areas," as they were later called, in mining, textiles, and agriculture. The distress of America's farmers, who had overexpanded during the years of wartime demand, was especially significant, for farmers and farm workers comprised about 10 or 11 million people, or more than one-fifth of the work force. Their plight was contagious, especially in the many towns and small cities sustained by agriculture. (In the "prosperous" years between 1923 and 1929, for instance, banks folded at the appalling rate of two per day. Most of these were in rural areas). For all these people the crash on Wall Street made a difficult situation worse. Their hard times—and loss of purchasing power—were important reasons why the depression lasted as long as it did.

Cyclical downswings in the economy coincided with and intensified these structural weaknesses. The "new era" of the 1920s had been heavily sustained by the automobile and construction industries. As early as 1925, however, residential construction began to level off, and in 1927 auto sales declined. Though the car industry recovered in 1928, construction continued to lag. By the summer of 1929 this "temporary stagnation" began to worry businessmen with large inventories. Their uneasiness, in turn, helped provoke the crash. Thereafter, the sluggishness in these important consumer durables—and the absence of new multiplying innovations in the 1930s—compounded the economic problems of the era.

At the root of this stagnation was the maldistribution of income in America. While the real wages of regularly employed production workers in manufacturing were increasing by 12 percent between 1921 and 1929, corporate profits jumped 62 percent and dividends 65 percent. In 1929 the richest 5 percent of the population received 33.5 percent of disposable income; the richest 1 percent got 19 percent. The 36,000 wealthiest families (less than 1 percent of the total) earned more than the combined income of the 12 million families who got less than $1500 a year, a minimum standard of living.

In some ways this distribution of income was no worse than it had been in earlier decades. The middle classes formed a higher percentage of the population. But therein lay another problem: "new era" prosperity depended as never before on mass purchasing power. Until 1925 or so this consumer power, fueled by gains during the war years, was sufficient to promote growth. People were able to buy cars and houses, and businesses to expand. By 1927, however, most people who could afford to buy such goods had already done so. As this "saturation point" was approached, production leveled off, and payrolls stabilized. If corporations (which had profited immensely since 1915) had lowered prices or raised wages, they could have pumped life into purchasing power. But few producers in the 1920s felt much pressure to do so, for labor unions were weak and price competition (especially in oligopolistic industries like automobiles) was often weak. Fewer still perceived the vital connection between consumption and prosperity. The worker's low wages increased only slightly while industry's high prices remained stable, creating what was in effect concealed inflation. These impediments to increased purchasing power helped make the depression of the 1930s deeper and more severe than any in the American past.

A lack of economic expertise also helped prolong the depression. There was in 1930 no Council of Economic Advisers to assist public officials, and no coherent body of economic theory stressing the need for sustaining purchasing power. Keynesian ideas concerning the uses of compensatory fiscal policy were not fully set out until 1936 or well known among American economists until the end of the decade. Thus it was that government, like private corporations, did little to assist mass purchasing power either in the 1920s or 1930s.

Instead, many Americans persisted in thinking that the "utopia" of the 1920s had rested on rugged individualism and welfare capitalism. The answer to hard times, Andrew Mellon said cavalierly, was to wait for the cycle to hit bottom. "Liquidate labor, liquidate stocks, liquidate the farmers, liquidate real estate . . . enterprising people will pick up the wrecks from less competitive people." Myron Taylor, head of U. S. Steel, added in 1932 that government attempts to stabilize industry would "take out of life its chief elixir, the element of competition, and would eliminate profit, which is the reward for the energetic and patient and far-sighted." Ideas such as these had long prevented Americans from adopting the programs of social insurance that softened the blow of depression in European countries. As late as 1932 these same ideas stopped politicians of both parties from recognizing that positive state intervention can ameliorate hard times.

The deepest cause of prolonged hard times was psychological. Having experienced a "new era" in economics during the 1920s, Americans thought the crash would be short-lived. The market, they told themselves, inevitably falls off from time to time; when it hits bottom, investment will pick up, and growth will resume. But as the downward spiral persisted, surprise turned to shock, panic, and desperation. People who had money refused to risk it, even at the lowest interest rates in history. The shattering sequence of events of 1929–33, following so abruptly on the expectations of the 1920s, created a depression psychology of unprecedented proportions that affected all levels of society.

REPERCUSSIONS

Sexual Mores and Family Life To listen to the moralists in the 1930s, one could easily conclude that hard times were undermining the home and family. Obsession with sex, they added, was corrupting the nation.

These alarmists buttressed their case with seemingly formidable evidence. The depression caused thousands of husbands to move far from home in search of jobs and countless thousands more—no one knows how many—to abandon their families. Many of the jobless who stayed home become morose, took to drink, abused their wives, or lost the respect of their children. Young people leaving home for better opportunities deprived themselves of the security of roots and their parents of companionship and assistance in their old age. Hard times also delayed marriages and sharply depressed the birth rate: the book *Live Alone and Like It* (1936), by Marjorie Hillis, was a best seller. John Steinbeck's epic *Grapes of Wrath* (1939), which portrayed the desperate efforts of the Joad family to stay together under the pressure of poverty and migration, was a fair (if somewhat romanticized) picture of family tensions in the 1930s.

Observers noted that many people turned in on themselves to pursue solitary pleasures. Americans read more, took up stamp collecting, and avidly joined boxtop contests. Other popular pastimes included dance marathons and six-day bicycle races—escape hatches for bored, jobless spectators who lost themselves in the crowd. Above all, people enjoyed themselves by going to the movies or listening to the radio. Some 85 million Americans (65 percent of the total population) saw movies at least once a week. The number of

Radio was not only a popular medium of entertainment in the 1930s, but also a major instrument of communication. Here the humorist Will Rogers talks at a political rally.

Americans who owned radios increased from 10 million in 1929 to 27.5 million a decade later. Each radio, one survey found in 1937, was used for an average of 4½ hours a day.

It also seemed that sexual immorality was spreading in the 1930s. Observing the delay in marriages, the American Association of School Administrators complained of "increases in masturbation, clandestine relations, prostitution, and homosexuality." The Lynds, who were not sexual purists, agreed that the inability of young people to afford marriage, combined with advances in contraception, encouraged premarital sexual relations. They also reported that family tensions caused "a great deal of married women's running around with single men."

As usual, the moralists were unduly alarmed. While many husbands headed off for better opportunity, others, recognizing the futility of migration, clung more firmly than ever to the familiar ties of home and family. The rate of migration to cities decreased during the decade, and, despite the movement of young people, it is probable (statistics are sketchy) that the amount of geographical migration also declined—as it ordinarily does when economic opportunities are limited. The cost of going out also forced many families to entertain at home, and to enjoy simple domestic pleasures like bridge, cookouts, and Monopoly instead of rushing off in their cars. Divorce rates actually decreased in the early 1930s (though the main reason was probably the cost of going through the courts).

The moralists also failed to prove their point about changes in sexual behavior. Organized prostitution probably declined—most businesses did. Alleged increases in masturbation, homosexuality, or adultery simply were— and are—impossible to document. The apparent rise in premarital sexual activity was neither new nor alarming. Rather, it extended a trend which had already surfaced in the 1920s. And sexual attitudes were no more liberated than in the 1920s. The 1930s witnessed the peak in strength of such organizations as the Legion of Decency, the Episcopal Committee on Motion Pictures, and Hollywood censorship under "Movie Czar" Will Hays (who cut the offensive line of Mae West, "I wouldn't let him touch me with a ten-foot pole").

Sexual liberation also seemed trivial in the midst of hard times. As Robert Benchley phrased it, "I am now definitely ready to announce that Sex, as a theatrical property, is as tiresome as the old mortgage . . . I am sick of little southern girls who want to live, . . . I am sick of rebellious youth, and I am sick of Victorian parents, and I don't care if all the little girls in all sections of the United States get ruined or want to get ruined or keep from getting ruined." Even the *Readers' Digest,* the decade's best-selling pacifier, insisted that sex was a normal, useful function. "Marital love," it announced in 1939, "is a creative enterprise. . . . There is profound beauty and even holiness in the act of fecundation. . . . All the resources of science and technique must be used in order to make of marital relations an ever-flowing source of mutual joy."

Statements such as these suggest that feminism had relatively little appeal during the 1930s. Middle-class women, many of whom had tried to enter the professions in the 1920s, seemed ready to welcome marriage and domesticity as primary goals. As if to underline this attitude, women paid little attention to the visible symbols of emancipation like bobbed hair or flattened bosoms. They wore their hair naturally, used practical shoes, and dressed in simple, durable clothes. They submitted to regulations against hiring women as civil servants and even to laws that denied jobs to married women teachers if qualified men could be hired in their place. A Gallup poll revealed that 82 percent of Americans, including 75 percent of women, agreed that wives should not work if their husbands were employed. A women's magazine concluded: "no matter how successful, the office woman . . . is a transplanted posey. . . . Just as a rose comes to its fullest beauty in its own appropriate soil, so does a home woman come to her fullest blooming when her roots are struck deep in the daily and hourly affairs of her own most dearly beloved." The depression years, far from promoting sexual liberation or economic feminism, sustained traditional beliefs in marriage and in the father as head of the household.

Americans felt above all that the family must be preserved. They eagerly read Gasoline Alley, the comic strip about ordinary family problems. They applauded the Hardy family movies, which received a special Oscar in 1942 for "furthering the American way of life." They made big sellers of Clarence Day's *Life with Father* (1935) and *Life with Mother* (1936), and of *Good Housekeeping's Marriage Book: Twelve Ways to a Happy Marriage* (1938). They responded warmly to Steinbeck's heroic Ma Joad, guarantor and preserver of familial unity. While the connection between popular culture and mass values cannot be firmly established, it seems fairly clear that the 1930s made domesticity a primary virtue. It was three decades before "women's liberation" and the "counter culture" of the 1960s popularized an alternative.

Thinkers on the Left   Nothing could be sillier than the notion, spread later by demagogues like Senator Joe McCarthy, that the 1930s were a "Red decade" in America. It is almost as simplistic to apply the term "left wing" to American social thought in the depression years. Writers and thinkers had become too specialized, their audience too diverse to permit such easy categorization. Still, hard times naturally prompted a variety of leftist prescriptions for social action. Other thinkers protested against the behaviorism, elitism, and objectivity of social science as it had developed in the 1920s. The writers and thinkers on the Left had never been more articulate or more relevant.

Unrest in the universities revealed that left-wing ideas generated more interest among the young than they had in the 1920s. College youth joined such leftist organizations as the National Student League and the Student League for Industrial Democracy. Others joined the Young Communist League and led demonstrations against tuition costs or local power elites. In 1934 an estimated 25,000 students went on strike in support of Anti-War Week, and in 1935, 175,000 turned out for a repeat performance. Compared to the demonstrations of the 1960s, those of the 1930s were peaceful and insignificant. Campus life, including fraternities and football, went on as before. But the radical youth of both eras agreed in distrusting the older generation. "A man might be of some use to the community until he was thirty years old," James Wechsler, a young radical, wrote in 1935, "but after that he was automatically aligned with the legions of darkness."

Leaders of the progressive education movement welcomed this turn to the left. Led by George S. Counts, a professor at Teachers College, Columbia, they rejected one monument of progressive educators in the 1920s: the child-centered school. Teachers who concentrated on developing the expressiveness of individual children, Counts argued, were neglecting their social duties. Schools, he said, must "face squarely and courageously every social issue, come to grips with life in all of its stark reality, establish an organic relation with the community, [and] develop a realistic and comprehensive theory of welfare. . . ." The title of his best known book, *Dare the School Build a New Social Order?* (1932), expressed his programmatic orientation. The depression was no occasion for "play schools" or for experiments aimed at enhancing individual creativity; it was the time to indoctrinate people for social change.

The master progressive educator, John Dewey, agreed. In 1934 he helped found, with Counts and others, the magazine *Social Frontier,* which became a forum for leftist intellectuals for the rest of the decade. Though he had long advocated experimentalism, he now emphasized that it must not become an end in itself. "Organized social planning," he said, " . . . is now the sole method of social action by which liberalism can realize its professed aims. . . . Liberalism must now become radical." In stressing the social mission of America's political and educational leaders Dewey revealed a leftist orientation characteristic of many intellectuals of the time.

Influential law school teachers shared this reformist bias. Among them were Jerome Frank and William O. Douglas, who had already spread the gospel of legal realism in the 1920s. Another was Thurman Arnold, a Yale law school professor whose *Symbols of Government* (1935) and *Folklore of Capitalism* (1937) moved from a critique of static jurisprudence into broad-ranging assaults on absolutist dogmas of all kinds. "So long as preconceived principles are considered more important than practical results," he wrote, "the practical alleviation of human distress and the distribution of available comforts will be paralyzed." America, he added, needed "new public attitudes toward the ideals of law and economics" so that a "competent, practical, opportunistic governing class may rise to power." On one level Arnold's plea for "practical results" embraced value-free experimentalism. But his relativism also stemmed from impatience with the existing order. Like Dewey, Arnold hoped to "alleviate human distress" through social engineering.

The planners and relativists did not go unchallenged. Robert Hutchins, the influential president of the University of Chicago, insisted that educators had a duty to provide young people with enduring truths; students at Chicago were required to read the "great books." Walter Lippmann, moving further toward the right, complained of the "aimless and turbulent moral relativity of twentieth-century social thought." Planners, he added, were potential tyrants: "there can be no plan to find the planners: the selection of the despots who are to make society so rational and so secure has to be left to the security of irrational chance." Though these writers differed widely in their politics, they were searching for absolutes more transcendent than social engineering or experimentalism. As the threat of fascism grew in the late 1930s, their call for a return to first principles placed many of their foes on the defensive.

So long as the depression lasted, however, the planners and the experimenters had the advantage of being willing to act. They also could draw on theorists who stressed the social nature of man. One of these theorists was Elton Mayo, an industrial sociologist who performed painstaking studies of the work process in American factories in the 1920s and 1930s. These convinced him that scientific management was unproductive. Workers, he argued, responded best when management recognized the need for "morale" and for "social interrelation." It followed that employers should relieve the boredom of routine labor by inculcating a sense of "belonging" and teamwork in their employees. Mayo's influential writings, notably *Human Problems of Our Industrial Civilization* (1933), were later welcomed by welfare capitalists who adopted personnel gimmicks that were as manipulative as (though more subtle than) those recommended by the proponents of scientific management. For a time, however, his ideas seemed rather more enlightened than those of Frederick Winslow Taylor.

Neo-Freudian psychoanalysts like Karen Horney and Harry Stack Sullivan went further in rejecting individualistic and behavioristic views of humankind. Horney, German born and trained, came to the United States in 1932. In writings such as *The Neurotic Personality of Our Time* (1937) she broke away from the Freudian focus on instinctual forces. The human psyche, she argued, was not predetermined in infancy, but developed through a lifelong interaction with cultural and social forces. Frustration and anxiety, she added, stemmed in part from the pressures within American culture for individual success and material wealth. Sullivan, an American, embarked in the 1920s on careful studies of schizophrenics in mental hospitals and turned to private practice in 1931. Like Horney, he rejected Freudian determinism and stressed the role of society, especially of interpersonal relations, in molding the psyche of humankind. Their conclusions were less mechanistic, less deterministic than orthodox Freudianism, for they held out the hope that human beings had some power over their destiny. Thus was behavioral theory wedded to the cause of social change.

These theorists—Arnold, Mayo, Horney—stopped short of radicalism. Others, however, embraced socialism. Still others turned to the Communist party, which attracted some 50,000 Americans by mid-decade. For such people, socialism was too slow and evolutionary; only proletarian revolution could abolish capitalism. Moreover, after 1933, when Hitler came to power in Germany, many people concluded that the Soviet Union was the only bulwark against the spread of fascism. In the late 1930s, when word of Josef Stalin's ruthless purges reached the West, and especially in 1939, when Russia signed a nonaggression pact with Germany, thousands of American Communists broke with the party. Until then, however, revolutionary rhetoric and Communist sympathy were common among left-wing intellectuals of the 1930s.

Among these Communist sympathizers were established writers like Theodore Dreiser and Lincoln Steffens, younger men like John Dos Passos, Erskine Caldwell, and Lewis Mumford, and rising literary critics like Edmund Wilson, Malcolm Cowley, and Granville Hicks. These sympathizers also included radical playwrights who banded together in collectives like the Group Theatre, or in The Theatre Union, whose motto was "theatre is a weapon in the class struggle." Other young writers, including Richard Wright, joined the John Reed clubs, named after the romantic American radical who had embraced the Bolshevik revolution. Promoting the *New Masses,* the leading Communist organ in America, the John Reed clubs called upon "all honest

The *New Masses,* a Communist magazine, predicts a proletarian revolution. Cover by William Gropper.

writers and artists to abandon decisively the treacherous illusion that art can exist for art's sake, or that the artist can remain remote from the historic conflicts in which all men must take sides." Writers, the manifesto added, must "break with bourgeois ideas which seek to conceal the violence and fraud, the corruption and decay of capitalistic society."

Chief guru of these radical artists was Michael Gold, an editor for the *New Masses* and author of *Jews Without Money* (1930), an unrelievedly grim novel about poverty in New York. Gold angrily rejected the older bohemian left, which he felt spent too much time propagandizing for cultural liberation and sexual freedom. (He called Floyd Dell, a former bohemian, "the historian of the phallic-hunting girls of Greenwich Village.") Gold also insisted that writers and artists employ proletarian themes and advance the inevitable class struggle. This literary theory left nonproletarian writers like Thornton Wilder beyond the pale. Wilder, Gold charged, was the "prophet of the genteel Christ," the "poet of a small sophisticated class that has recently arisen in America—our genteel bourgeoisie. . . . This Emily Post of culture will never reproach them; or remind them of Pittsburgh and the breadlines."

Gold's crudely Marxist approach to literature offended most able writers, including leftists like Wilson and Cowley. It also failed to inspire an outpouring of proletarian writing. But many intellectuals agreed with Gold that writers and artists must be men and women of action and that social criticism was a necessary aspect of true art. These beliefs led social realist painters like Ben Shahn to show the same contempt for expressionist painting that Counts had heaped on free schools. "Is there nothing," Shahn asked, "to weep about in this world any more? Is all our pity and anger to be reduced to a few tastefully arranged straight lines or petulant squirts from a tube held over a canvas? All the wheels of business and advertising are turning night and day to prove the colossal falsehood that America is smiling. And they want me to add my two percent. Hell, no."

Other writers and artists echoed Shahn's faith in the social value of art. Pare Lorentz, a gifted documentary film maker, produced *The Plow that Broke the Plains* (1936) and *The River* (1937), lyrical efforts to propagandize for conservation of natural resources. Warner Brothers films such as *I am a Fugitive from a Chain Gang* (1932) and *20,000 Years in Sing Sing* (1933) reminded audiences of poverty and injustice. Gangster movies featuring tough-guy heroes like James Cagney attempted to show that the lower classes possessed tenderness and human dignity. Folksingers, especially Woody Guthrie, sang the virtues of ordinary working people and Dust Bowl migrants. Playwrights like Clifford Odets composed inspirational dramas such as *Let Freedom Ring, Awake and Sing,* and *Waiting for Lefty* (which stirred audiences to shout "strike, strike, strike" at the end of performances).

Novels of social criticism enjoyed an unprecedented vogue in the 1930s. Dos Passos's *Big Money* (1936), the concluding volume of his massive trilogy, *U. S. A.,* described the pernicious effect of materialism on the ordinary characters who crowded his panorama of twentieth-century American society. Caldwell's illiterate, almost subhuman tenant farmers in novels such as *Tobacco Road* (1934) exposed readers to the poverty of the rural South. James T. Farrell's *Studs Lonigan* (1932–38) chronicled the pathology of Irish-American slum life in the city. Richard Wright's *Native Son* (1940), set in Chicago's black belt, dealt with the evils of racism and capitalism; its most sympathetically drawn character was a Communist lawyer. Steinbeck's *In Dubious Battle* (1939) also included a Communist protagonist, while his socially conscious *Grapes of Wrath* (1939) became a best-selling movie. And Sinclair Lewis wrote *It Can't Happen Here* (1934), a warning cry against fascism.

Even Ernest Hemingway, champion of individual courage, seemed affected by the depression. *To Have and To Have Not* (1937) was the story of a smuggler ruined by society. At the end of the novel, he gasps, "A man ain't got no bloody fucking chance." And in *For Whom the Bell Tolls* (1940), a novel about antifascist heroes in the Spanish Civil War, Hemingway took an openly political stance. His title was taken from a John Donne poem in which also appeared the words, "No man is an island, entire of itself." The depression, it appeared, was provoking a revolutionary change in literature as well as in social theories.

Search for a Usable Past   Appearances, however, were deceptive. Though social consciousness grew in the early 1930s, it was neither pervasive nor lasting. "If you want to hear discussions of the future revolution in the United States," George Soule observed accurately in 1932, "do not go to the breadlines and the mill towns, but to . . . gatherings of young literary men. . . . Searching for actual flesh-and-blood revolutionary proletarians is a thankless task. Most of those who really suffer from the depression are . . . simply stricken dumb by it." These people were shocked by hard times and ashamed to be trapped in them. They blamed themselves, not capitalism, for their troubles. They looked backward for usable values, not forward to revolution. Despite ten years of unparalleled economic hardship, they succeeded in reaffirming much that they had cherished in the years before the Crash.

One manifestation of this search for a usable past was renewed appreciation of small town, rural ways of life. Because of hard times, some Americans self-consciously promoted a Back-to-the-Land movement that romanticized the virtues of self-sufficient living close to the soil. New Dealers, including Eleanor Roosevelt, championed a Subsistance Homestead program. Twelve southern agrarians wrote a manifesto of essays, *I'll Take My Stand* (1930), which combined a quasi-Marxist critique of industrial capitalism with nostalgia for the antebellum South. Thousands of others applauded films like Frank Capra's *Mr. Deeds Goes to Town* (1934) and *Mr. Smith Goes to Washington* (1939), which celebrated the virtues of simple, small-town Americans. Artists such as Lorentz, Guthrie, and Steinbeck, while exposing the excesses of free enterprise, were also composing hymns of praise to the countryside and the agrarian way of life. And many radical intellectuals, including Theodore Dreiser, Edmund Wilson, and Sherwood Anderson, as well as gifted photographers like Walker Evans and Dorothea Lange, traveled the land to record affectionately the everyday scenes they had ignored in the 1920s.

A self-conscious rejection of things foreign accompanied this distrust for urban ways of life. Frederick Jackson Turner's frontier thesis, which apotheosized the rural pioneer, explicitly rejected the "germ" theory tracing American traits to European beginnings. His ideas were widely applauded in the early 1930s. Painters like Thomas Hart Benton and Grant Wood ignored European fashions in art and promoted a Regionalist movement that focused on scenes of the American Plains and Midwest. "No good painting has come out of France since 1890," Benton pronounced with characteristic (and calculated) truculence. Like the nationalistic wing of the isolationists, who also developed imposing influence in the 1930s, the Regionalists sought recompense for hard times by reaffirming their faith in the heartland of America.

Other Americans sought roots far in their past. Van Wyck Brooks, once the harsh critic of American writers, published essays praising a host of second-rate nineteenth-century literary figures. Carl Sandburg wrote an appealing multivolume biography of Abraham Lincoln, who came across as a lovable folk hero. High prices for paintings by primitives like "Grandma" Moses, as well as for antique furniture, suggested that Americans cherished visible reminders of their past. The popularity of tough guys in the movies, of westerns, and of the hard-boiled heroes of detective fiction, revealed that Americans enjoyed being reminded of the good old days when rugged individualists still had a chance against social forces.

Popular and Elite Culture   Other purveyors of popular culture outdid themselves in appealing to this escapist impulse. Popular radio programs included "The Green Hornet," "The Lone Ranger," and the ever-present "Amos 'n Andy." The enormously popular soap operas ("Portia Faces Life," "Life Can Be Beautiful," "Ma Perkins," "Just Plain Bill") almost always featured white, middle-class, small-town Protestants—just plain folks—enduring all manner of minor tragedies before surmounting the forces against them. Housewives, it was assumed, would be relieved to know that ordinary people faced tribulations more trying than theirs, just as they would be reassured by larger-than-life heroines like Ma Perkins, stabilizers of all that was good and holy. Escapist novels included such best sellers as Pearl Buck's *The Good Earth* (1931), Margaret Mitchell's *Gone with the Wind* (1936), and Walter Pitkin's *Life Begins at Forty* (1932). The comics, more popular than ever, featured new strips like *Tarzan* (1929), *Dick Tracy* (1931), and *Terry and the Pirates* (1934). Many of these, like *Tarzan* and *Terry and the Pirates,* reinforced stereotypes about apelike blacks and wily orientals. That may have been part of their appeal. In any event, they were clearly reassuring to Americans who looked for rugged, he-man heroes. Milton Caniff, creator of *Terry and the Pirates,* admitted as much. "The strip started out," he said later, "in October, 1934, and the country was already on its way out of the muddle, but the people were so exhausted by the emotional drain that I used the simple picaresque device of attempting to take them out of their post-depression milieu and at least pretend for a Scheherazade moment that they are somewhere else dreaming Walter Mitty dreams of their position (in the manner of Don Quixote). In the very nature of this a certain order was implied."

Even the leftists—except for self-styled proletarians like Gold—could be understood on different levels. Though members of the Group Theatre submerged their individual personalities in a collective effort, they often did so to experiment with new dramatic forms, not to promote social art. Hemingway's books continued to utilize the time-tested American theme of man against nature and to show masculine heroes larger than life: the difference between *For Whom the Bell Tolls* and his sentimental *Old Man and the Sea* (1952) was much less than it appeared. Caldwell's tenant farmers, like Steinbeck's migrants, cared little for socialism; they wanted only land and meaningful work. Many apparently leftist books—Henry Roth's *Call It Sleep* (1934), Farrell's *Studs Lonigan,* Jack Conroy's *The Disinherited* (1933), Wright's *Native Son*—were autobiographical and existential as much as they were programmatic calls for social change. William Faulkner, the most powerful novelist of the era, devoted much of his work to essentially timeless nonpolitical themes associated with his native Mississippi.

The work of Dos Passos, who had criticized capitalism even in the 1920s, revealed similar ambiguities. Though money corrupted many of his characters, he offered no political solution, and he portrayed Mary French, the leading leftist in his book *U. S. A.,* as a rather pathetic woman trapped in a dreary round of radical activities. His heroes were hard-working, rugged young men like "Vag," the hitchhiker who is kicked about as he wanders—alone—toward some unknown opportunity in the future. A writer, Dos Passos concluded, should resist oppression and injustice. But he "must never, no matter how much he is carried away by even the noblest political partisanship in the fight for social justice, allow himself to forget that his real political aim . . . is [artistic] liberty."

This refusal to surrender artistic sensibility motivated most of the well-known writers of the decade. Intellectuals, Edmund Wilson observed, were free to work for collectivist programs, but should insist on remaining independent custodians of ultimate values. Archibald MacLeish felt that the true artist should never follow the "social and intellectual fashions of the day." And James Agee, coauthor with Walker Evans of *Let Us Now Praise Famous Men* (1941), a photo-poetic attempt to recapture the daily lives of southern tenant farmers, characterized the feeling of many critical intellectuals in the 1930s. "A good artist," he said, "is a deadly enemy of society, and the most dangerous thing that can happen to an enemy . . . is to become a beneficiary." Agee meant that sensitive intellectuals could not help being alienated by the crassness and injustice of American life—he did not defend the status quo. He also meant that artists must remain free to express their alienation as they saw fit.

The Quest for Self-Respect   The Lynds, describing Muncie at mid-decade, were persuaded that the depression did not affect the attitudes of the residents. "In the main," they argued, "a Rip Van Winkle, fallen asleep in 1925 while addressing Rotary or the Central Labor Union, could have awakened in 1935 and gone right on with his interrupted address to the same people with much the same ideas."

The Lynds recognized that it was risky to make such sweeping statements about the attitudes of an entire city. Muncie, in any event, was not necessarily "typical." Yet many clues existed to support their essential argument that the desire for material goods, so sweeping in the 1920s, survived the hard times of the 1930s. Among these clues were the fantastic sums bet on football pools, the proliferation of slot machines, the passion for the game of Monopoly, and the popularity of Dr. Napolean Hill's *Think and Grow Rich,* which sold 5 million copies. The anthropologist Margaret Mead concluded that parents persisted in inculcating such values in their children throughout the decade.

In 1936 *Fortune* magazine offered a slightly different interpretation. Surveying the "present-day college generation," it concluded that it was "fatalistic . . . it will not stick its neck out. It keeps its pants buttoned, its chin up, and its mouth shut. If we take the mean average to be the truth, it is a cautious, subdued, unadventurous generation. . . . Security is the *summum bonum* of the present college generation."

The very success of a magazine named *Fortune*—and the fact that it was part of Henry Luce's magazine empire—might suggest that the Lynds were closer to the mark, that Americans were as hungry as ever for wealth and power. But *Fortune* (which pioneered in the new "science" of polling) was also correct to stress that this hunger had security as the ultimate goal. As

> All profits disappear; the gain
> Of ease, the hoarded, secret sum;
> And now grim digits of old pain
> Return to litter up our home.
>
> We hunt the cause of ruin, add,
> Subtract, and put ourselves in pawn;
> For all our scratching on the pad,
> We cannot trace the error down.
>
> What we are seeking is a fare
> One way, a chance to be secure:
> The lack that keeps us what we are,
> The penny that usurps the poor.

"The Reckoning," a poem by Theodore Roethke, 1941, reveals the desire for security.

Dale Carnegie explained in his best-selling manual, *How to Win Friends and Influence People* (1936), one should not shake the social ladder too hard in climbing to success. One should learn to adjust, to become socialized. If the popularity of Carnegie's book was any indication, the 1930s were the decade when Americans, in William F. Whyte's terms, began to substitute the Social Ethic for the Protestant Ethic of years past.

Such an argument is impossible to document or to apply to millions of people. Yet it is plausible. For a brief time the depression turned many Americans to the left. But as early as 1936, when the worst appeared to be over, many Americans began to long for the old ways. Though some of these people hoped to rise like Horatio Alger characters, from rags to riches, most of them yearned primarily to exorcise the guilt and shame they had felt on losing their jobs, their homes, or their social position. They wanted self-respect, dignity, the security of work, home, and family. They continued to be cautious, scared, and "unadventuresome" long after prosperity returned. No one put it better than Woody Guthrie:

> I don't want your millions mister
> I don't want your damned ring
> All I want's just live and let live
> Give me back my job again
>
> Think me dumb if you wish, mister,
> Call me a green or blue or red.
> There's just one thing that I know, mister
> Our hungry babies must be fed. . . .

Suggestions for Reading

Among the clearest accounts of economic trends in the late 1920s and 1930s are J. K. Galbraith, *The Great Crash** (1955); Robert Sobel, *The Great Bull Market** (1968); Broadus Mitchell, *Depression Decade** (1947); and Charles Kindleburger, *The World in Depression, 1929–1939* (1973). See also works by Friedman and Schwartz and by Potter cited in the bibliography for chapter 6. Other useful books are Murray Rothbard, *America's Great Depression* (1963); Herbert Stein, *The Fiscal Revolution, 1931–1963** (1969); Robert Lekachman, *The Age of Keynes** (1966); Lester Chandler, *American Monetary Policy, 1929–1941** (1971); and Susan Kennedy, *The Banking Crisis of 1933** (1973).

Social trends are covered in Dixon Wecter, *The Age of the Great Depression, 1929–1941** (1948); Robert and Helen Lynd, *Middletown in Transition** (1937); Irving Bernstein, *The Turbulent Years** (1970), on labor; David Conrad, *Forgotten Farmers* (1966); John Shover, *Cornbelt Rebellion* (1965); and Walter Stein, *California and the Dust Bowl Migration* (1970). Other subjects are treated in Robert Angell, *The Family Encounters the Depression* (1936); Mirra Komarovsky, *The Unemployed Man and His Family** (1940); and Abraham Hoffman, *Unwanted Mexican-Americans in the Great Depression** (1974). John Dollard, *Caste and Class in a Southern Town** (1937), is a sociological study. Caroline Bird, *The Invisible Scar** (1965), is a general account of social trends. Sidney Fine, *Sit-Down: The General Motors Strike of 1936–37* (1969), is a thorough account of its subject.

Books dealing with American thought in the 1930s are Richard Pells, *Radical Visions and American Dreams: Culture and Social Thought in the Depression Years** (1973); Charles Alexander, *Nationalism in American Thought, 1930–1945** (1969); Edward Purcell, Jr., *The Crisis of Democratic Theory* (1972); Donald Meyer, *The Protestant Search for Social Realism, 1919–1941* (1960); and David O'Brien, *American Catholics and Social Reform: The New Deal Years* (1965). Barry Karl, *Charles E. Merriam and the Study of Politics** (1974), is an important book dealing with political science at the time; on left-wing and radical thought see Frank A. Warren, *Liberals and Communism: the "Red" Decade Revisited* (1966); Irving Howe and Lewis Coser, *The American Communist Party* (1957); Daniel Aaron, *Writers on the Left** (1961); and Bernard Johnpoll, *Pacifist's Progress* (1970), on Norman Thomas.

For black history consult Raymond Wolters, *Negroes and the Great Depression** (1970); and Dan T. Carter, *Scottsboro: A Tragedy of the Modern South** (1969). Primary sources include twelve southerners, *I'll Take My Stand** (1930), which is a collection of essays by southern agrarians; Thurmond Arnold, *Folklore of Capitalism** (1937); Edmund Wilson, *American Earthquake** (1958); Richard Crossman, ed., *The God That Failed** (1949), essays by disillusioned former communists; Walter F. White, *A Man Called White** (1948), a memoir by the leader of the NAACP; James Agee and Walker Evans, *Let Us Now Praise Famous Men** (1941), a moving account of life among poor farmers in the South; and James Burnham, *Managerial Revolution** (1941). William Stott, *Documentary Expression and the 30s America* (1973) is a very relevant study.

8

Political
modernization
in the
1930s

"Under Franklin D. Roosevelt's New Deal," a conservative complained in the late 1930s, "America took a decisive step toward Caesarism. The remarkable feature of this subtle evolution was that it could take place constitutionally, without any illegal move, simply by stretching the extremely pliable fabric of America's political institutions."

Such talk about "Caesarism" was characteristic of the exaggerated rhetoric of the Right in the 1930s. But the central point about the "stretching" of governmental institutions was accurate. The expansion of public authority—at the local, state, and national levels—began to modernize American governments. That development proved necessary to fight the prolonged depression and to assist the country in the management of World War II. It assisted interest groups in their ongoing effort to broaden their access to the government. Negatively it accelerated the "subtle evolution" toward bureaucratic confusion and presidential aggrandizement. Political centralization was therefore a mixed blessing. No development of the decade was more significant.

The Hoover years

Few Americans seemed better qualified to deal with hard times than Herbert Hoover, who succeeded Coolidge in 1929. Orphaned at eleven, he left his native Iowa to live with relatives in Oregon, then to work his way through Stanford University. On graduating he became a mining engineer, in which capacity he traveled the world. Intelligent and efficient, he moved speedily ahead. By the age of forty he was a millionaire and a recognized expert in streamlining complex operations. Woodrow Wilson then made him director of relief efforts in Belgium in 1914, of the Food Administration during the war, and finally of postwar American relief operations throughout Europe. Impressed by his expertise in these capacities, Franklin D. Roosevelt exclaimed in 1920, "Hoover certainly is a wonder, and I wish we could make him President of the United States. There could not be a better one."

At that time Republican regulars were cool to Hoover, who had worked for a Democratic administration and who had never run for office. But the regulars also recognized that he was too prominent to be ignored. Harding made him secretary of commerce, and Coolidge, while resenting Hoover's activist expansion of the Commerce Department, kept him on. By 1928, Hoover was the obvious choice for the GOP presidential nomination, and he beat Al Smith with ease.

Like most Americans in 1929 and 1930, Hoover assumed that the crash was a temporary dip in the business cycle. But from the beginning he was not prepared—as Coolidge would have been—to sit back and do nothing. On taking office he called a special session to deal with depressed farm prices, and after much wrangling Congress passed a law that provided federal loans to farm cooperatives. In 1930 he asked for and received a tax cut of $160 million. He also engaged in what later presidents called "jawboning"—using his prestige to urge businessmen and labor leaders to cooperate.

When conditions deteriorated in 1931, Hoover moved further in the direction of governmental intervention. In June he called for a moratorium in the payment of war debts to America. He accelerated work on Boulder dam and developed plans for Grand Coulee dam, started in 1933. He signed the Norris–La Guardia Act of 1932, which outlawed "yellow dog" (antiunion) labor contracts and restrictive antistrike injunctions. Acting under pressure from congressional progressives, he approved creation of the Reconstruction Finance Corporation in late 1931. The RFC was authorized to lend some $500 million (later much expanded) to financial institutions, which in turn would direct the "trickling down" of money to the public. In 1932 he agreed, though reluctantly, to let the RFC lend $300 million to states for the relief of unemployment.

Unfortunately, these measures proved to be too little too late. The modest tax cut made little difference, primarily because few Americans in that more

A caricature of Herbert Hoover from *Liberty* magazine. The background suggests his interests—engineering and government.

innocent age paid federal taxes anyway. "Jawboning" helped sustain wage rates until 1931, but only at the expense of the millions of workers who were laid off. The new Agricultural Marketing Administration did not try to control overproduction—the central cause of depressed prices—and its revolving fund to aid cooperatives was quickly exhausted. The belated loans for relief were far too small to combat hard times as they had developed by 1932.

The RFC, though helpful to a few large financial institutions, involved only loans, not grants. It failed to prevent bank panics or to save hundreds of smaller companies that needed massive aid. By following the "trickle down" theory the RFC also became an easy target for critics who wondered why Hoover was willing to earmark federal money for business while denying it to the unemployed. The progressive economist Rexford Tugwell said the RFC's policies were like putting fertilizer in the branches of a tree instead of its roots, and Will Rogers irreverently concluded that the trickle down theory always operated in reverse. "You can drop a bag of gold in Death Valley," he quipped, "which is below sea level, and before Saturday it will be home to Papa J. P. [Morgan]."

Hoover pursued other policies that actually harmed the world economy. One of these was the Hawley-Smoot Tariff, which he signed in 1930 despite the advice of almost all economists. The record-high rates of this tariff probably had little impact on domestic prices or on overseas exporters (who had already found difficulty in cracking the American market). But the tariff did provoke sharp retaliation from other countries: America's exports were cut in half between 1930 and 1932. It also intensified the pessimism spreading through the Atlantic world. The United States, it was clear, was not going to use its immense economic power to be a banker or creditor "of last resort."

Another counterproductive move was the decision of the Federal Reserve Board in October 1931 to increase the discount rate from 1½ percent to 3½ percent. This action, taken after Britain had abandoned the gold standard, was intended to dissuade foreign investors from pulling their gold out of the United States. It probably assisted in preserving the gold standard at home. But it also dampened economic activity by raising the cost of borrowing. In so doing it compounded the already deteriorating conditions of late 1931 and helped provoke the serious problems of 1932–33.

Hoover also resisted congressional efforts toward more substantial farm relief; he vetoed a bill to strengthen the United States Employment Service; and until the summer of 1932 he stopped all congressional appropriations for direct relief of unemployment. His tenacious defense of the gold standard and of balanced budgets (which falling tax revenues nonetheless made impossible) prevented him from devaluing the dollar to promote American exports or from approving inflationary measures to assist debtors.

His stance on all these issues stemmed from a consistent economic philosophy. As a humanitarian he recognized that the government must sometimes intervene: he was not a reactionary social Darwinist. But as a self-made man he believed that America provided equality of opportunity to all who made the effort to advance. And as an old Wilsonian he cherished voluntarism and states rights. It followed that the federal government should try to keep its hands off the economy. "We must not be misled by the claim that the source of all wisdom is in the government," he said. "The way to a nation's greatness is the path of self-reliance, independence, and steadfastness in times of trial and stress."

Hoover's philosophy rested on his understandable faith that American capitalism was essentially sound. This conviction led him to believe that reassuring White House statements could restore public confidence. It caused him also to argue that the root of economic maladjustment lay abroad. European banks, he maintained, were unstable in the aftermath of World War I. When they began to fall in 1931, they forced nations like England off the gold standard. The failures staggered American investors, whose loans had sustained these banks until 1929. This blow to American capital, together with unscrupulous dealings by Wall Street speculators, led to the panicky runs on banks after 1931.

Hoover's belief in the overseas origin of depression was comforting, for it sustained his reluctance to engage in large-scale governmental intervention at home. But his analysis was one-sided. The serious domestic problems—maldistribution of income, depressed agriculture, the collapse of banks—cried out for attention. The centralization of the economy during Hoover's lifetime meant that these problems became widespread and long-lasting.

Hoover also displayed unfortunate personal and political limitations. His background in the world of business and administration had given him little appreciation of the problems faced by congressmen, who found him cold, distant, and unwilling to compromise. The 1930 elections brought scores of

Democrats into power, and when they joined with Republican progressives, Hoover was outnumbered. Sure of his course, the President refused to compromise with these adversaries, and by 1932 no one on the Hill wanted to defend him. "Politics," the journalist William Allen White explained, "is one of the minor branches of harlotry, and Hoover's frigid desire to live a virtuous life and not follow the Pauline maxim and be all things to all men, is one of the things that has reduced the oil in his machinery and shot a bearing."

Because Congress was not only divided but (like all Americans at the time) bewildered by the persistence of economic difficulties, it is questionable whether any president could have led it in fruitful directions. But Hoover made it easy for congressmen to oppose him by doing little to gather public support. "This is not a showman's job," he insisted. "I will not step out of character." The sickness of the economy made him ever more glum, sensitive to criticism, isolated from other people. His Secretary of State, Henry Stimson, remarked after talking with him that "it was like sitting in a bath of ink in his room." Even outside the political arena Hoover's personality was severely criticized. The sculptor Gutzon Borglum added, "if you put a rose in his hand, it would wilt." The story circulated that Hoover asked an associate for a nickel to phone a friend. "Here's a dime," came the reply. "Call all your friends."

Hoover himself admitted late in the year, "all the money in the world could not induce me to live over the last nine months. The conditions we have experienced make this office a compound hell." With the President in such a dark mood it was not surprising that Americans disregarded his optimistic statements or that they shied away from embarking on new investments. No president could have been worse at countering the depression psychology.

His most grievous error was to move against the "bonus army" of 1932. This "army" was actually a ragged bunch of some 22,000 unemployed citizens, most of whom claimed to have been veterans of World War I. By the summer of 1932 they had descended on Washington to lobby for immediate payment of bonuses due them (in 1945) for their service. When the Senate rejected the bonus bill, many of the veterans left for home. Others, however, camped in ramshackle quarters on Anacostia Flats across the river from the Capitol. A daring president might have visited them or at least shown some sympathy for their plight. But Hoover believed in law, order, and efficiency. So he ordered the reluctant police to clear the veterans from the area near the White House. When bricks started to fly, a policeman panicked, and two veterans were killed by gunfire. Hoover then commanded the army to chase the veterans across the river to Anacostia Flats, and the city witnessed the spectacle of four troops of cavalry, four troops of infantry, a machine gun squad, and several tanks proceeding along Pennsylvania Avenue. The troops, under the leadership of General Douglas MacArthur, then charged into the Flats, where they chucked tear gas into tents, plunged, bayonets drawn, into crowds of men, women, and children, burned the shacks, and ran the "army" out of the District. Perhaps 1000 people were gassed, and 63 were injured. Seldom in American history have troops been used with so little cause.

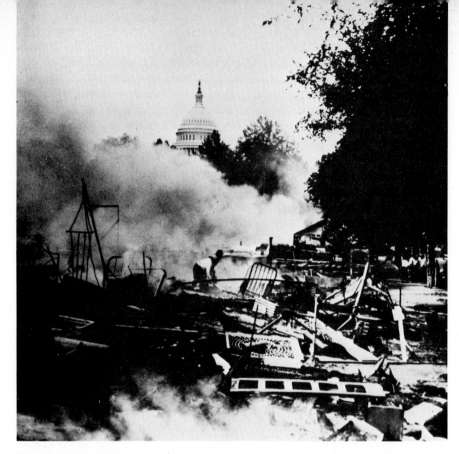

The Bonus 'Army' is burned from Anacostia Flats, 1932.

Hoover is my shepherd; I am in want.
He maketh me to lie down on park benches:
He leadeth me beside still factories.
He restoreth my doubt in the Republican Party:
He leadeth me in the path of destruction for his party's sake.
Yea, though I walk through the valley of the shadow of destruction, I fear evil:
For thou art with me; the politicans, and professors, they frighten me.
Thou preparest a reduction in my salary before me in the presence of my Creditors: Thou anointest my income with taxes; my expenses runneth over.
Surely unemployment and poverty will follow me all the days of the Republican administration: And I shall dwell in a mortgaged house forever.

Hoover and the depression, 1932

Franklin D. Roosevelt and New Deal solutions

THE TRIUMPH OF DEMOCRATIC RHETORIC, 1932

The deterioration of Hoover's presidency made it virtually certain that he would be overwhelmed at the polls in 1932. John N. Garner of Texas, Franklin D. Roosevelt's Democratic running mate, half seriously suggested a do-nothing campaign. "All you have to do," he told FDR, "is to stay alive until election day."

Garner, however, recognized that Roosevelt was too appealing a candidate to stay at home. Over the years FDR had changed from an arrogant, supercilious young aristocrat (product of private tutors in Hyde Park, New York, of Groton School, and of Harvard) into a charming, gregarious, seductively charismatic man. He had begun his political career as a good-government state senator in 1910, and as a fervent admirer of TR, a distant relative. (FDR's wife Eleanor, was also TR's niece.) In 1913 he became Wilson's assistant secretary of the navy, and in 1920 he was the party's popular choice for the vice-presidency. Crippled by polio in 1921, he refused to retire to a life as country gentleman. In 1928 Smith and other Democratic leaders pressed him back into active service by making him the party's nominee for governor of New York. When Roosevelt withstood the Hoover landslide to win—and then to prove himself a vigorous and popular governor—he emerged as a leading presidential contender for 1932. At the convention he had to overcome bids by Smith and Garner. But he ultimately prevailed. The Roosevelt-Garner ticket, by bridging the fatal urban-rural split in the party, united the Democrats as they had not been united since 1916.

Roosevelt waged an energetic, well-organized campaign. Wealthy backers like Bernard Baruch and Joseph Kennedy supplied him with ample financing,

An election poster in the campaign of 1932. It appealed to the strong antiprohibition sentiment in the country.

and "brain trusters" like Raymond Moley and Rexford Tugwell, Columbia professors, offered him ideas and well-written speeches. Savvy politicos like Louis Howe, a newsman who had long counseled Roosevelt, and James A. Farley, the campaign director, provided expert counsel on strategy and tactics. Roosevelt's campaign revealed one of his great assets as president: an ability to attract able associates from diverse backgrounds and political persuasions. Unlike Hoover, he was assuredly all things to all men.

Finally, FDR seemed ready to act. He promised to look after the "forgotten men, the unorganized but indispensable units of economic power." He pledged to end prohibition, to "restore purchasing power to the farming half of the country," and to bring "relief to the small banks and homeowners." Washington, he added, "will assume bold leadership. . . . The Federal government has always had and still has a continuing responsibility for the broader public welfare. It will soon fulfill that responsibility." "I pledge myself," he declared, "to a new deal for the American people. . . . This is more than a political campaign; it is a call to arms."

FDR campaigning in West Virginia, October 1932.

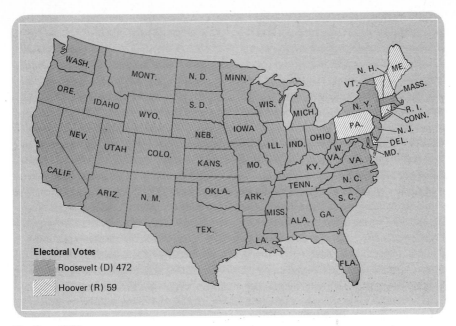

Electoral Votes

Roosevelt (D) 472

Hoover (R) 59

Election, 1932

All these assets, combined with Hoover's obvious liabilities, brought Democratic triumph in November. Roosevelt amassed 22 million votes to Hoover's 15 million. Democrats swept to power in many previously Republican states, and in both houses of Congress, 311 to 119, and 60 to 35. Considering the subsequent power of Democrats in urban areas, it was interesting that Hoover's only important victories were in Pennsylvania and Connecticut. The election marked an astounding reversal in voter preference. After nearly forty years, America had become a Democratic country.

But what would the new president do with his mandate? Speeches suggested he would promote conservation, lower tariffs, regulate public utilities, and curb the excesses of Wall Street. They also revealed that he would try to revive capitalism, "avoiding alike the revolution of radicalism and the revolution of conservatism." America, he said, "demands bold, persistent experimentation. It is common sense to take a method and try it: if it fails, admit it frankly and try another. But above all, try something." This speech indicated his experimental method: unlike Hoover, he would not be bound by a consistent economic philosophy. But it promised nothing specific.

Many observers, however, considered FDR too conservative. Though a few of his speeches suggested he believed in governmental planning, he said nothing about such subsequent programs as the Tennessee Valley Authority, the National Recovery Administration, extensive public works spending, or labor reform. Though he implied he would be willing to unbalance the budget, his focus was on economic orthodoxy. "I regard reduction of federal spending," he said, "as one of the most important issues of this campaign."

Roosevelt was not making idle promises: like Hoover, he wanted very much to avoid deficit spending.

For these reasons the Left was as discouraged by the campaign as was the Republican Right. Both party platforms, one reformer complained, were "rehashes of old proposals, political croquettes concocted from the leftovers of former years and dressed up with a little fresh verbal parsley." Socialists noted gloomily that Norman Thomas, their presidential candidate, received only 880,000 votes, less than Debs had gotten in 1912 or 1920, and but 2.4 percent of the total turnout. William Z. Foster, the Communist candidate, got but 100,000. The weakness of the American Left in such difficult times revealed the vigor of the two-party system and the reluctance of Americans to abandon traditional beliefs about the government's role in the economy.

THE 100 DAYS

The four months between election day and inauguration in March 1933 were among the most dismal in American history. Consistent to the end, Hoover tried to commit Roosevelt to his deflationary program, but the President-elect refused to be trapped into cooperation. The lame-duck Congress managed to send repeal of prohibition to the states for ratification but otherwise debated fruitlessly. It was then that the final wave of panic swept depositors and forced state governors to declare "holidays" lest the banking system collapse altogether.

In the long run, however, the interregnum worked to Roosevelt's advantage, for it left people ready to do almost anything he might wish. As Will Rogers put it shortly after the inauguration, "I don't know what additional authority Roosevelt may ask, but give it to him, even if it's to drown all the boy babies." Senator Arthur Vandenberg of Michigan, a Republican conservative, added, "I think we need a 'dictator' in this particular situation. But a dictator is of no particular use unless he *dictates*. I think the country is crying to heaven for the announcement of a firm, comprehensive banking plan."

The new president's inaugural address hinted that he would seek the sort of power that Rogers and Vandenberg wanted to give him. Though he remained unspecific, he spoke of the need for "national planning" of utilities and transport, for "strict supervision of all banking and credits and investments," and—taking a neo-Populist phrase from Justice Brandeis—"an end to speculation with other people's money." Invoking wartime metaphors, he announced he would call a special session immediately, and would "ask the Congress for the one remaining instrument to meet the crisis—broad executive power to wage a war against the emergency, as great as the power that would be given to me if we were in fact invaded by a foreign foe."

In the "100 Days" that followed Roosevelt kept his promise to act, and an unprecedented volume of important legislation flowed from Congress. After declaring a national bank holiday, he hurried through a bill outlawing hoarding and providing federal assistance to solvent banks. In the next few weeks most of the bigger banks reopened, and when Congress (with Roosevelt's reluctant approval) created the Federal Deposit Insurance Corporation later in the session, it erected a durable barrier against unreasoning banking panics. Indeed, FDIC became a major prop sustaining the role of private banking in a capitalist economy. Roosevelt then honored his pledge to cut government spending by securing passage of an Economy Act cutting $400 million from veterans' payments and $100 million from the salaries of federal employees. The President concluded his early program by dispatching a popular message calling for the legalization of 3.2 beer. Congress approved the measure, and on April 7 beer was legally sold in America for the first time since 1919.

As many progressives noted in anguish, these early measures were far from radical. His original banking act discriminated against smaller institutions and left the system, such as it was, in the control of private interests. The economy bill was deflationary and harsh. The beer bill, which imposed taxes on sales, did nothing to improve purchasing power. It was obvious that fiscal conservatives, especially Budget Director Lewis Douglas, were closest to the President's ear. It was also clear that many congressmen stood to the left of the executive branch.

Subsequent actions were more far-reaching. Reversing Hoover's policy, Roosevelt moved cautiously toward relief of exporters and debtors by taking the nation off the gold standard, by devaluing the dollar, and by encouraging Federal Reserve officials to pursue an easy money policy. He secured passage of the Civilian Conservation Corps, which ultimately gave more than 2 million men useful and remunerative work in camps administered by the army. Congress also approved funds for the Home Owners Loan Corporation, which could buy mortgages from banks and offer owners generous, long-range terms for repayment. With the Securities Act he began to honor his promise to oversee Wall Street. And a new Public Works Administration was authorized an initial fund of $3.3 billion for large-scale projects.

A more momentous act set in motion the Federal Emergency Relief Administration. The FERA began with an initial appropriation of $500 million (the amount FDR had "saved" through the Economy Act) and received millions more before expiring in 1935. Under the direction of Harry Hopkins, a complex, fast-acting humanitarian, it gave grants (not loans) to states on a matching basis of $3 of state money to $1 from Washington. Hopkins further had power to spend as he felt necessary, whether states matched the grants or not. When the FERA failed to meet the needs of the unemployed, Roosevelt set up a temporary work relief program (the Civil Works Administration) during the winter of 1933–34. It is frightening to think of the suffering that would have continued without the FERA and CWA. Perhaps no New Deal programs did more to restore the faith of masses in government, in Roosevelt, and in the Democratic party.

Roosevelt also broke with Hoover's policies by working for passage of a bill creating the Tennessee Valley Authority. Progressives, spearheaded by George Norris of Nebraska, had long urged public development of the backward, poverty-stricken region, but Coolidge and Hoover had stood firmly in their way. The legislation that Roosevelt sponsored not only empowered the Authority to control floods and to provide fertilizer and electric power, but to encourage social reconstruction of the entire valley. An admiring Norris confessed that FDR "plans to go even further than I did." Private utilities in the area protested vigorously that the government would drive them out of business. Still other critics complained that the TVA, the New Deal's most far-reaching intervention into the preserves of private enterprise, was state socialism. But Roosevelt thought not. The TVA, he said with characteristic pragmatism, was "neither fish nor fowl, but . . . it will taste awfully good to the people of the Tennessee Valley."

Subsequent conflicts within the TVA board limited the effectiveness of this great experiment, as did resistance by vested interests, who turned TVA Director David Lilienthal's faith in "grass roots democracy" to their own advantage. Tugwell observed in 1936 that TVA should be called the "Tennessee Valley Power Production and Flood Control Corporation." Even in this somewhat limited fashion, however, TVA did benefit thousands of farmers by providing them with low-cost electricity for their homes. Decades later, it remained overwhelmingly popular in the many states affected by it.

Though some of these measures contributed to economic recovery, their primary purpose was relief—or, as in the case of the TVA, long-range reform. To break the depression, Roosevelt relied on two other creations of the 100 Days, the National Recovery Administration (NRA), and the Agricultural Adjustment Administration (AAA). These agencies, the core of his recovery program, showed the basic philosophy of the early New Deal.

NATIONAL RECOVERY ADMINISTRATION

The central aims of the NRA were to stabilize industrial prices and provide minimal guarantees to organized labor. Like many New Deal measures, it emanated primarily from the executive branch after conferences among brain trusters like Raymond Moley, big business leaders, and labor unionists. Their compromise bill attempted to satisfy everyone by authorizing management and labor within each industry to formulate "codes" of fair competition. These codes were suppose to outline production and pricing policies. Section 7-a of the bill stipulated that the codes guarantee minimum wages, maximum hours, and the right of collective bargaining for unions. While the government could not coerce industrialists into signing a code—Roosevelt shied away from such federal compulsion—it could shame noncooperators by withholding its insignia of approval—a blue eagle—from recalcitrant employers. The Justice Department was also empowered to prosecute violators of the codes. Roosevelt called the NRA "the most important and far-reaching legislation ever passed by the American Congress."

The NRA showed that Roosevelt wished to work with, rather than against, business interests. Indeed, the NRA favored big business by exempting code

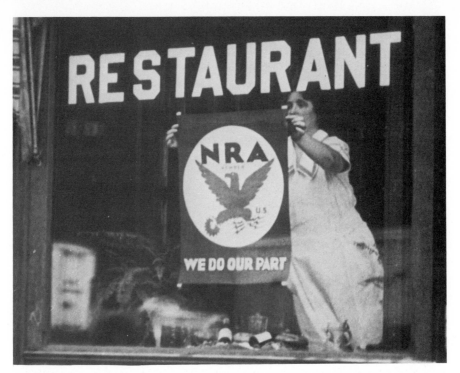

For a brief time in 1933 many American businesses advertised their cooperation
with the NRA.

signers from antitrust prosecution. As Moley put it, "any attempt to atomize
big business must destroy America's greatest contribution to a higher standard
of living for the body of its citizenry—the development of mass production."
Antimonopolistic progressives bitterly opposed this aspect of the plan in
Congress. But Roosevelt applied pressure, and their cause failed. The President, it was clear, placed more faith in the New Nationalism of TR and in the
government-business partnership of World War I than in the trust-busting
philosophy of Wilson's New Freedom.

Thanks to Hugh Johnson, the NRA's super-energetic chief executive, the
recovery program at first seemed assured of success. Working quickly, he
herded reluctant employers and labor leaders into his office, and by midsummer more than 500 industries, including such important ones as shipbuild-
ing, wool textiles, and electrical manufacturing, had signed codes. In all, the
codes covered some 2½ million firms and 22 million workers. Equally heartening was the index of factory production, which nearly doubled between March
and July.

By midautumn, however, the NRA was having serious troubles. Johnson,
who had worn himself out negotiating so many codes (even gravediggers and
strip-tease artists were included), grew snappish and erratic. Antimonopolists
grumbled that big businessmen, best able to survive downturns in the econ-

omy, were negotiating codes that put competitors into bankruptcy. Labor leaders complained that Johnson and FDR were unsympathetic. Critics noted especially that some NRA codes attempted to sustain prices by limiting production. In so doing they inhibited new investment and penalized consumers. This basically deflationary approach, the reverse of what was needed, was intensified by Secretary of the Interior Harold Ickes, the churlish, fiercely honest administrator of the Public Works Administration. Ickes moved so cautiously in approving projects that purchasing power, necessary if production were ever to be increased, developed only slowly.

Opposition from business interests also hurt the NRA. Some major industries, like oil, dragged their heels before signing. Others, like coal, underwent strikes before cooperating. "Rugged individualists" like Henry Ford (who pointed out that working conditions in his factories were superior to those prescribed in the automobile code) simply refused to sign. Leading steel executives, fearing that talk with labor spokesmen would imply union recognition, had to be dragooned by Secretary of Labor Frances Perkins into dicussing a possible steel code.

Small businessmen presented still larger obstacles. Many such operators, often ignored in the code-negotiating process, discovered that they could not comply with pricing and labor provisions. Faced with the alternative of bankruptcy, they resorted to evasion. But Johnson lacked the staff to police so many codes, and violators soon acted with impunity. By mid-1934 the administrative breakdown of the NRA, derisively branded the "National Run Around" by opponents, was apparent to all.

The NRA was not a total failure. However temporarily, it gave people the idea that the New Dealers were trying. Section 7-a, though subject to circumvention by employers, prompted labor leaders to sponsor unionization drives. But the NRA's inability to secure recovery suggested the need for better coordination between spending and industrial policy. Its failure to compel cooperation from private interests showed that centralized planning had to involve stronger government enforcement powers. Recognizing the difficulties inherent in voluntary cooperation between government and business, FDR turned by 1935 to tougher measures against big business.

AGRICULTURAL ADJUSTMENT ADMINISTRATION

Like the NRA, New Deal agricultural policies grew out of prolonged discussion within the executive branch, especially by Milburn Wilson, a Montana professor and farm expert, Secretary of Agriculture Henry A. Wallace, a progressive farm editor from Iowa, and Rexford Tugwell, whom Roosevelt made an assistant secretary of agriculture. Their primary concern was to increase farm income, which had fallen by 60 percent since 1929. Conditions were so desperate in rural areas that conservative, property-owning farmers from the eastern seaboard to the Plains had intimidated lawyers and judges who attempted to foreclose mortgages, and had sponsored "farm holidays" keeping goods from market until prices increased.

To stabilize the farm sector, Wallace and his advisers devised a complex of proposals. These aimed at extending farm credit, assisting cooperatives, and encouraging marketing agreements and export trade. Their key proposal outlined a "domestic allotment" plan to guarantee "parity," prices restoring the favorable ratio with industrial goods that farm products had enjoyed in the prosperous years between 1909 and 1914. This goal was to be achieved through crop controls which would battle the chronic problem of overproduction.

The AAA, which administered domestic allotments, stopped short of full-scale national planning. Because he feared excessive centralization, Roosevelt insisted that farmers growing major crops decide policies themselves. These farmers were to hold periodic referenda that would determine total output and set acreage quotas for each producer. Farmers who reduced their acreage would benefit in two ways: by receiving higher prices for their goods, and by getting government subsidies for cooperating. In this way the government was intervening with a carrot, not a stick, for farmers who thought they could do better without the subsidy were free to grow all they liked. The AAA was also expected to run in the black, for the cost of the subsidies was to be met by a federal tax on agricultural processors. Like the NRA, the AAA was an effort to promote cooperation between government and major producers. Though more far-reaching than anything attempted before, it preserved the principles of voluntarism and decentralization.

Because the extensive droughts of 1933–35 cut output sharply, it is difficult to measure precisely the economic impact of the AAA. But it undoubtedly did much to raise farm income, which doubled between 1933 and 1936. Other farm programs—the Soil Conservation Service, the Rural Electrification Administration, the Farm Credit Administration, and the Commodity Credit Corporation (which offered loans on storable products)—were equally effective in achieving their differing aims. Agricultural radicals, who had capitalized on widespread rural unrest in 1932, found relatively little support four years later.

Drought affected large areas of the United States.

And Democrats made huge inroads in normally Republican rural areas in 1934 and 1936. In all these respects the farm program of the New Deal was successful.

But the AAA exposed many anomalies and contradictions in the New Deal approach. One of the most glaring was the policy of curtailing production—indeed of destroying crops and livestock already planted or born in early 1933—at a time when millions of Americans were desperate for food and clothing. As one critic observed, Roosevelt seemed to be solving the paradox of want amidst plenty by doing away with plenty.

Roosevelt's preference for decentralization also presented problems. It meant that local committees of farmers enjoyed wide discretion. Some of them inflated the value of land taken from production. "It's a miracle," one farmer noted, "how the prospect of getting a little extra cash out of Uncle Sam has improved South Carolina dirt." Worse, decentralization left major policy decisions in the hands of large commercial farmers and of local Agriculture Department officials who echoed their points of view. It was yet another example of Roosevelt's reluctance to upset the power of well-entrenched groups.

George Peek, the AAA administrator, accepted this world as he found it. "No democratic government can be very different from the country it governs," he answered. "If some groups are dominant in the country, they will be dominant in any plan that government undertakes." But subordinates in the Department of Agriculture thought otherwise. Led by General Counsel Jerome Frank, they complained that acreage reductions were displacing thousands of tenant farmers, especially in the South. They also demanded a farm policy that would include social planning as well as price supports. When Wallace, caught in the middle, appeared to back the rebels, Peek resigned in late 1933. But infighting continued to plague the AAA until 1935, when Wallace bowed to the pressures of large commercial farmers and dismissed the rebels. The struggle exposed the administrative hassling that accompanied the rapid growth of bureaucratic power during the New Deal.

Meanwhile, tenants continued to suffer. Perhaps 3 million people were displaced from the land between 1932 and 1935 alone. In 1935 Tugwell and others attempted to deal with the problem through the Resettlement Administration, which aimed at relocating people in garden cities. In 1937 Congress approved loans for further relocation of tenants, and FDR set up the Farm Security Administration to tackle such problems. But conservatives prevented these programs from receiving adequate funding. And even with larger appropriations, it is very questionable whether government aid for small farmers, who had been struggling against economic centralization for decades, was a realistic long-range answer. Opportunity for small farmers depended instead on rapid industrial expansion, and this the New Deal was unable to promote.

Two final problems hurt the long-range effectiveness of domestic allotment. One was continuing technological change, especially in chemical fertilizers, which created dramatic increases in production per acre. To combat this rise in supply, some farmers opted for compulsory quotas in 1934. Others relied on the government to store the excess: by 1939, after six years of subsidies, the carryover of cotton to be stored was 3 million bales greater than in 1932. Though the demand generated by World War II temporarily alleviated this problem, it became obvious in the postwar years that the cycle of subsidies, crop loans, and government storage was costing the taxpayers billions of dollars and that it was enriching an ever smaller number of commercial farmers.

The other problem was that the American agricultural depression was only a part of the larger decline at home and abroad. Limiting domestic production assisted foreign farmers, who acquired a larger share of the world market. At home, increased prices for farmers meant higher costs to consumers for the necessities of life. Moreover, to the extent that the NRA brought about higher prices for industrial goods, it worked against the interest of farmers, who had to buy them. Some reformers concluded that Roosevelt should have combined the best features of the NRA and the AAA into a comprehensive national plan. Others, perceiving the complexity of the national economy, replied that no such plan could work in time of peace. Perhaps they were right—for interest groups throughout twentieth-century American history have proved too strong for government planners. Still, it remained true that the NRA and AAA sometimes worked at cross purposes and that neither did much for purchasing power—the key to recovery.

REMEMBERING THE FORGOTTEN MAN

Any activist administration inevitably confronts hostility before long, and Roosevelt's was no exception. The Securities and Exchange Commission, approved in 1934 to define a federal role in regulating the stock exchange, was particularly controversial. Though it gave the financial community considerable latitude in managing its own activities, it nonetheless infuriated the right-wingers on Wall Street. Some of these joined the Liberty League, which led reactionary opposition to the New Deal in 1934–37. Other conservatives complained loudly about deficit spending. Budget Director Lewis Douglas resigned in August 1934, warning the President that upon a balanced budget "hangs not only your place in history but conceivably the immediate fate of our civilization." Deriding the presidential "royal family," one reactionary wrote,

> The King is in the White House
> Handing out the money.
> The Queen is on the front page
> Looking very funny.
> The knave [their son James] is up in Boston,
> Picking up the plums
> While the country alphabetically
> Is feeding all the bums.

But criticisms such as these made little mark. Though the depression persisted, Roosevelt's measures were obviously popular. Accordingly, Democrats won heartening victories in 1934, the first time since 1902 that the party in power gained seats in an off-year election. Encouraged, Hopkins saw a mandate for further reform. "Boys," he told his aides, "this is our hour. We've got to get everything we want—a works program, social security, wages and hours, everything—now or never!"

Hopkins correctly assessed the activist mood of the new Congress, which in 1935 passed more important laws than in any previous session of modern American history. Heading them were three landmark acts: a relief bill leading to creation of the Works Progress Administration, a social security act, and the National Labor Relations (or Wagner) Act providing unprecedented guarantees to labor. These assisted the so-called forgotten man in ways scarcely dreamed of by many New Dealers themselves during the 100 Days.

WPA The relief program stemmed in part from Roosevelt's unhappiness with the dole. "Continued dependence on relief," he complained, "induces a spiritual and moral disintegration fundamentally destructive of the national fiber." Unlike some conservatives, however, he shrank from throwing the unemployed back on their own. The answer was to require work from the able-bodied unemployed. Congress, after exacting the right to control important relief appointments, then provided an initial fund of $4.8 billion— the largest peacetime appropriation in American history. The newly created WPA, focus of the administration's relief efforts for the next five years, received a substantial portion of the money, and Hopkins set to work spending it.

Right-wing spokesmen quickly assailed the plan. Even work relief, they insisted, would create a nation of parasites, and would plunge the country into everlasting debt. "If the government keeps handling relief, manicuring ladies nails, and giving relief people cars to ride around in," one reactionary state governor lamented, "it will stifle religion in the country." Other right-wingers repeated stale jokes about WPA "workers." "There's a new cure for cancer," one went, "but they can't get any of it—it's sweat from a WPA worker." Southern conservatives grumbled that relief wages assisted "lazy blacks" who would otherwise have increased the supply of farm labor. Leaving nothing to chance, they successfully excluded blacks from coverage

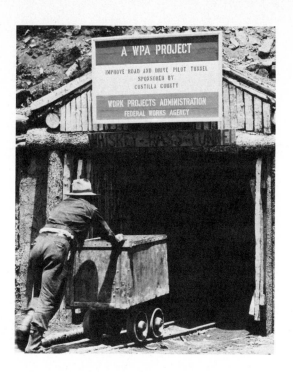

No agency was more important than the Works Progress Administration in providing assistance to the unemployed in the 1930s.

in many regions. Republicans insisted that the WPA was a Democratic racket devised to employ party hacks and to swell the New Deal vote in 1936.

None of these criticisms was based on fact. Though some people may have preferred easy jobs with the WPA to regular work, the vast majority struggled to avoid the stigma of accepting public employment. "I didn't want to go on relief," one said. "Believe me, when I was forced to go to the office of the relief the tears were running out of my eyes." And while a few state relief officials played politics with relief money, the vast majority—under strict orders from Hopkins—acted with remarkable nonpartisanship. Nonetheless, criticisms persisted, for some of the projects were makework in character. Many Americans also wondered when, if ever, such virtues as "rugged individualism" would again become part of the national dream.

Criticism from the Left was more persuasive. Radical spokesmen for the unemployed complained that the appropriation was too small, that millions of people still had to hope for charity from local agencies. Some of these complaints were justified, for the WPA provided an average monthly wage of $52, which was rarely enough for heads of households, and it never employed more than 40 percent of the unemployed. Far from being a lavish expenditure of tax money, it proved that much remained to be done.

But these criticisms could not diminish the great popularity of the WPA, especially during its first two years of operation. During that time it provided relief to between 1.9 and 3.2 million people per month, and by 1941 it had pumped more than $11 billion into the economy. Though most of this money went to unskilled or semiskilled workers, some of it aided artists and writers who enriched the nation's cultural experience. The Federal Theatre Project, sponsored by the WPA, employed 12,500 actors and stagehands, who performed before 350,000 people a week in 1936. The National Youth Administration offered aid to some 2 million students and 2.6 million nonstudents during the 1930s. The WPA, like the FERA and CWA before it, revealed the New Deal at its most humanitarian.

Social Security   Where the WPA tried to offer immediate relief, social security, the other half of Roosevelt's welfare program, promised longer-range protection. The measure featured three forms of aid. The first, pensions for people over sixty-five, was to be financed by a tax on payrolls. The federal "reserve fund" thus built up would provide pensions to all people who had worked long enough in covered occupations to qualify. The second type of aid was unemployment compensation. Such compensation, directed by states, was to come from taxes on employers, who would receive generous federal rebates providing they did not lay off workers. The third form of aid was money given categories of poor people—blind, dependent, and disabled—who could not qualify for WPA work or find other forms of employment. This "categorical assistance," like unemployment compensation, involved federal-state coordination. Funds were to come from federal grants, providing states appropriated matching funds.

Progressives recognized flaws in this "system" from the beginning. The old age pension plan excluded millions of workers who pursued occupations not covered by the original legislation. Moreover, the government would not begin to pay pensions until 1940. Meanwhile, money for pensions would be drawn from employers and employees. It required little imagination to see that the old age pension plan was limited in scope and that it reduced purchasing power at the time the economy most needed stimulation. Like the Economy Act of 1933, it showed that Roosevelt was at heart a fiscal conservative.

A major weakness in the unemployment compensation plan was its federal-state nature, which meant that states, unwilling to penalize business interests within their borders, tended to enact only the minimum federal requirements. The result was stingy, short-lasting benefits for workers. By penalizing employers who laid off workers the plan also reflected the view that irresponsible firms were responsible for unemployment. Given the magnitude of the economic crisis, this was a false assumption. The plan also discouraged employers from hiring workers whom they might have to lay off if conditions failed to improve. Overall, it was ill-formed in conception, faulty in administration, and ungenerous in benefits.

The categorical assistance plans were plagued by their federal-state administration. Many states proved unwilling to spend much money for the programs, and the recipients suffered accordingly. Some states made no provision at all for so-called unemployables, a large group of people covered neither by the WPA nor by the categories. Even the more generous states felt obliged to provide relief on a pay-as-you-go basis. Accordingly, they resorted to sales taxes to find the money. These, like the payroll taxes to support old age pensions, were socially regressive and ultimate impediments to economic revival.

The federal-state nature of categorical assistance also caused wide variations in benefits and prevented establishment of a national "floor" under income. To a degree these variations may have encouraged people to move from the least generous states, in the South, to crowd into the cities of the Midwest and Northeast. Similarly, the act may have induced some employers

Growth of federal services, 1905–1945

SOURCE: Adapted from *Historical Statistics of the United States*, p. 711

Fear and worry based on unknown danger contribute to social unrest and economic demoralization. If, as our Constitution tells us, our Federal government was established among other things "to promote the general welfare," it is our plain duty to provide for that security upon which welfare depends.

These three great objectives—the security of the home, the security of livelihood, and the security of social insurance—are, it seems to me, a minimum of the promise that we can offer to the American people. They constitute a right which belongs to every individual and every family willing to work. They are the essential fulfillment of measures already taken toward relief.

Roosevelt's welfare philosophy, 1934.

to relocate in states with attractively inexpensive compensation plans. In fact, a complex of motives created such migrations and relocations—by themselves, federal provisions probably mattered little. But any law that permitted, indeed exacerbated, such regional variations was obviously inequitable. Both unemployment compensation and categorical assistance would have been fairer had they used funds raised by progressive federal taxation and been administered with an even hand from Washington.

Some of these weaknesses stemmed from Roosevelt's fiscal orthodoxy and from his faith in decentralization and states rights. But FDR was not a social reactionary. On the contrary, his faith in a "cradle to the grave" system of "social insurance" was enlightened for its time in the United States. Roosevelt also recognized that the Supreme Court as then constituted might overturn a law that failed to give states a role in the operation. And he foresaw the vulnerability of any plan that depended for its success on annual congressional appropriations. Hence he defended the payroll taxes on employees. "Those taxes," he admitted, "were never a problem of economics. They are politics all the way through. We put those payroll contributions there so as to give the contributors a legal, moral, and political right to collect their pensions and their unemployment benefits. With those taxes in there, no damned politician can ever scrap the social security program."

In this prediction the President was accurate, for the mixed system enacted in 1935 remained the basis of American welfare for decades thereafter. Subsequent Congresses felt obliged to provide more generous benefits (and to increase payroll taxes) so that social security became virtually unrepealable. The system therefore had the advantage of building a measure of permanence into social legislation. With all its faults, the social security law was a major step forward in the assistance of the "forgotten man." As one social worker wrote, "during the years between 1929 and 1939 more progress was made in public welfare than in the hundred years after this country was founded."

Wagner Act: NLRB The third major accomplishment of the 1935 Congress, the Wagner Act, was demanded by reformers who had chafed under the ambiguities and limitations of NRA's Section 7-a. Their bill called for a permanent, independent National Labor Relations Board, which would have the power to conduct elections determining bargaining units. The NLRB was also to prevent such "unfair" management practices as firing workers for union membership or fostering employer-dominated company unions. Henceforth, the bill stipulated, bargaining agents for workers would be chosen by a majority of employees. These far-reaching provisions—which promised to throw the balance of power toward unions for the first time in American history—were not FDR's doing. Indeed, the squire of Hyde Park was barely informed concerning the intricacies of labor-management relations. Labor Secretary Frances Perkins conceded later that he "never lifted a finger" for the bill. But Wagner and others did not need FDR's expertise, only his benevolent neutrality. And that, he gave them. With the White House offering no comfort to spokesmen for management, the National Labor Relations Act passed both houses in May and June of 1935. In early July FDR signed it into law.

From the beginning the NLRB found itself engaged in one of the most tumultuous periods of labor–management controversy in American history. This conflict had begun to escalate in 1933, when Section 7-a of the NRA had encouraged militant labor leaders like John L. Lewis of the United Mine Workers to conduct organization drives. These drives deeply frightened employers, for they aimed at developing nationwide industrial unions composed not only of skilled craftsmen (many of whom were already members of the AFL) but also of masses of unskilled and semiskilled workers. Such industrial unions, Lewis recognized, would confront employers with one united force; management could no longer deal separately with elitist craft unions. By 1934 these campaigns for new members had led to a wave of strikes involving 1.5 million workers. Some of the strikes erupted in battles between workers and authorities. And in October 1935, only three months after passage of the Wagner Act, the militants forced a break within the labor movement itself. Following a wild AFL convention, Lewis and other industrial unionists split off to form the Committee for Industrial Organization (later renamed the Congress of Industrial Organizations). Free of the inhibiting influence of the AFL, the CIO leaders redoubled their drives for membership.

In this kind of controversy the NLRB could hardly satisfy everyone. AFL unions complained that its decisions favored the CIO. Employers grumbled that the Wagner Act should have enumerated unfair union practices and that the NLRB was riddled with "left-wing bias." William Knudsen, head of General Motors, exclaimed in 1938 that the NLRB was "the largest drawback to good industrial relations." This conservative opposition, frequently savage and unreasoning, revealed the insecurity behind welfare capitalism. It probably impeded investment, so vital for recovery. It led to passage of the Taft-Hartley Act of 1947, an effort to redress the balance of power toward management.

THE RISE OF UNIONS

The NLRB also had to contend with the frightening new tactics of CIO militants in 1937. These militants, acting without Lewis's approval, dramatized their struggle for union recognition by occupying factories, most importantly in the rubber, automobile, and steel industries. Such "sit-down" strikes involved perhaps 400,000 workers. They terrified men of property, and they were later declared illegal by the Supreme Court. But they were hard to combat, for the use of force by management could easily damage valuable plant and equipment. By 1938 such strikes had compelled antiunion strongholds like General Motors and U. S. Steel to bargain collectively with the CIO. By 1940 American unions claimed almost 9 million members, compared to 3.2 million in 1932.

In some ways the benevolent neutrality of the New Deal promoted this growth. In particular, the NLRB proved important in clarifying the rights of labor and in helping to settle disputes. No single reform of the New Deal had greater long-run significance. And ordinary Americans appreciated this new, more sympathetic attitude in Washington. One person said simply, "Mr. Roosevelt is the only man we ever had in the White House who is not a son of a bitch." "Every house I visited," a social worker reported after a tour in South Carolina, " . . . had a picture of the President. These ranged from newspaper clippings (in destitute houses) to large colored prints, framed in gilt cardboard. The portrait holds the place of honor over the mantel; I can only compare this to the peasant's Madonna."

Union members expressed this gratitude at the polls. As early as 1934 industrial wards began developing large voting margins for the Democratic party. In 1936, when Lewis campaigned for FDR, the alliance between the CIO and the New Deal became open. The frank partisanship of the CIO, and the overwhelming support that prolabor Democrats consistently received from working class areas, were among the most significant political developments of the 1930s—and thereafter.

In retrospect, however, it is clear that FDR's services to the labor movement were not as crucial as some people thought. During the controversy over the sit-down strikes, he was benevolent enough not to call out troops, as many of his predecessors would have done. But he also determined not to take sides, and pronounced a "plague o' both your houses." This statement infuriated Lewis, who later defected to the Republican party. Workers, however, continued the strikes without the assistance either of FDR or of the NLRB. In this sense their militancy, and their achievements, owed relatively little to the New Deal.

Moreover, the triumph of industrial unionism in the 1930s was far from complete. As late as 1940 American unions embraced only 28 percent of nonagricultural workers. In 1945, a peak year of union power, they had but 36 percent. Most of the unskilled remained unrepresented and relatively powerless. Companies such as American Tobacco Company and Woolworth, both

Rise of labor unions, 1900–1950						
(In thousands)						
	1900	1910	1920	1930	1940	1950
Total labor force	29,030	37,291	42,206	50,080	56,180	63,858
Total union membership	791	2,116	5,034	3,632	8,944	15,000
Percentage	2.7	5.7	11.9	6.8	15.5	22.3

SOURCE: Adapted from *Historical Statistics of the United States,* pp. 75, 97; U. S. Department of Labor, *Handbook of Labor Statistics: 1973* (Washington, D. C., 1973), p. 345

of which flourished in the 1930s, continued to pay their employees very low wages. Executives like Alfred Sloan of General Motors and Thomas Watson of IBM received huge salaries—$500,000 and $400,000 respectively.

Corporate attitudes showed little improvement also. For every industrial leader like Myron Taylor of U. S. Steel, who recognized the futility of combatting unions at every turn, there were many who battled on. Among

Labor–management conflict erupts in violence at Republic Steel, 1937.

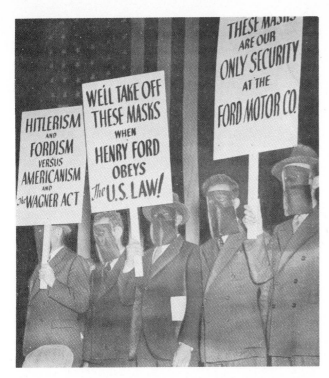

Henry Ford resorted to intimidation in his battle against the unions.

them was aging Henry Ford, who refused to recognize the CIO until the eve of World War II, when the promise of profits through labor peace proved too alluring to resist. Ford entrusted labor matters to thugs who beat up United Auto Workers organizer Walter Reuther and threw him off an overpass. Another recalcitrant employer was James H. Rand of Remington, whose "Mohawk Valley Formula" appealed strongly to antiunion employers. This formula, effective in one-company towns, prescribed that employers brand union organizers as Reds and anarchists, that citizens' committees and local police restore "law and order," and that companies threaten to leave town if strikes were not stopped quickly. Perhaps the most adamant corporate leader of all was Tom Girdler, president of Republic Steel and, by example, of "little steel" companies that resisted the sit-down strikes. "I won't have a contract," Girdler proclaimed, "verbal or written, with an irresponsible, racketeering, violent, communistic body like the CIO, and until they pass a law making me do it, I am not going to do it." Girdler was prepared to fight, and he purchased quantities of billy clubs, shells, rifles, and grenades. Like many such employers, Girdler succeeded: "little steel" was not unionized until the 1940s.

The labor militancy of the mid-30s did not last beyond 1950. As time passed CIO leaders conceded that industries like textiles and tobacco relied heavily on unskilled workers who were hard to recruit into unions, and that still other groups of laborers—farm workers, restaurant help, domestic servants—were too dispersed geographically. They learned that corporations would never surrender control over pricing policies. And they recognized their primary duty to their own rank and file. Thus it was that the CIO passed from a militant defender of the industrial working class to an increasingly self-interested pressure group, which worried little about minority groups, consumers, or workers in nonunionized areas. By 1945 it was securely established as one of the many influential interest groups within the fragmented society, and by the 1950s it differed little, if at all, from the AFL.

Union organizers also came to realize that most blue-collar workers had little interest in the "working class" as a concept. As in the past, American laborers were captivated by the dream of monetary success. They longed for the consumer goods, especially cars, that technological advances had brought within their reach during the 1920s. They wanted security and self-respect, not conflict. When prosperity returned, most of them continued to pay their union dues, to vote Democratic, and to show the boss considerably less deference than in years past. Together, they formed a limited "countervailing power" against employers. But they had as little use as ever for socialism, for proletarian revolution, or for racial equality. The class-consciousness of 1937, half-formed even then, barely outlasted the hard times that created it.

THE OPPOSITION AND NEW DEAL RESPONSES

The passage of landmark social legislation in 1935 earned Roosevelt the support of many members of the Left. But recovery remained as elusive as ever, and disaffected groups grew steadily more impatient. By mid-1935 they had grown so insistent that Roosevelt's political advisers grew alarmed about the prospects for reelection in 1936.

The spokesmen for these groups were a mixed lot. Minnesota Governor Floyd Olson demanded increased federal spending to assist farmers and workers. Mayor Fiorello La Guardia of New York insisted on more generous relief and housing measures to assist the urban, ethnic masses. Congressional progressives Robert La Follette, Jr., and Burton Wheeler of Montana demanded tougher measures against monopolies. Easily the most outspoken critics, however, were three magnificent spellbinders who appealed to disaffected Americans on the Left and Right alike. They were Father Charles Coughlin, Dr. Francis Townsend, and Senator Huey Long of Louisiana.

Father Coughlin of Royal Oak, Michigan, was already a well-known "radio priest" during the Hoover administration, which he flayed with abandon. At first he warmly supported Roosevelt's policies, even asserting that the New Deal was "Christ's deal." But from the beginning Coughlin called for monetary inflation and for the nationalization of banking. Ambitious, vitriolic, anti-Semitic, Coughlin became steadily more extreme. Millions of Americans listened to his broadcasts, and many appeared ready to follow his apparently egalitarian Union for Social Justice. By early 1935 he seemed a threat Roosevelt could not afford to ignore.

Townsend, an elderly California doctor, was a gentler, more decent man than Father Coughlin. But he was no less determined, and his cause of government aid for old people cried out for attention. With the aid of shrewd promoters, Townsend set up Old Age Revolving Pensions, Ltd., and gained hundreds of thousands of converts by 1935. His plan called for the government to provide people over sixty with $200 per month, providing the recipients spent the money within that time and retired if employed. Money for the pensions was to come from a "transactions tax" (essentially a sales tax). Critics were quick to show that the plan would have cost some $20 billion a year for a minority of old people. But to Townsend's impassioned followers that made little difference. Even after passage of social security, agitation for the plan continued.

Long, the self-styled "Kingfish" who was virtual dictator of Louisiana, posed the greatest danger of all to Roosevelt. Like Father Coughlin, he had supported much of the New Deal in 1933. But even then he had balked at the exemption of the NRA codes from antitrust suits, and by 1934 he had broken

Huey Long of Louisiana in action.

with the administration. Roosevelt, he said, differed hardly at all from Hoover. "Maybe you see a little change in the men working in the dining room," he sneered, "but back in the kitchen the same old cooks are back there fixing up the vittles and the grub for us that cooked up that mess under Hoover. There has never even been a change in the seasoning." By 1935 Long was promoting his "Share Our Wealth" plan, which promised to soak the rich and make "every man a king." Shrewd, quick-witted, and fiercely ambitious, Long claimed some 5 million followers. It was obvious that he longed to take FDR's place in the White House.

The Roosevelt of 1933, seeking to promote business–government cooperation, might well have ignored these challenges. Coughlin, Townsend, and Long, after all, had little support among party leaders. But at this very time in late 1934 and early 1935 the Right also began to recover from its shock and despair of 1933. Most alarming, the conservative Supreme Court, which until 1935 had sustained New Deal legislation (sometimes by five to four margins), began to counterattack. Its most momentous decision, *Schechter* v. *US*, unanimously struck down the NRA in May 1935. In doing so it proclaimed what Roosevelt aptly denounced as an outdated "horse and buggy definition of interstate commerce." It also ruled against the delegation of legislative authority to code makers. These were essentially *obiter dicta* stemming from the conservative economic philosophies of the judges. If the TVA, AAA, and other agencies ran into the same biases, the New Deal could be destroyed.

Until the court's decision Roosevelt had continued to hope for cooperation from business interests and economic conservatives. He had accordingly refrained from rhetoric aimed at stealing the thunder of men like Coughlin and Long. But the court now helped him change his course. Acting fast, he supported legislation against special privilege. Some of this legislation, such as an act to establish more centralized control of banking, was already moving through Congress. But the most controversial results of Roosevelt's turn to the left were the public utilities holding company act and the "wealth tax."

The holding company bill clearly reflected the administration's new hostility toward big business. Its drafters, Benjamin Cohen and Thomas Corcoran, were young Washington lawyers who admired Justice Brandeis. Like him, they believed in trying to restore a measure of decentralization and free competition to the economy. Their bill revealed this philosophy by applying a "death sentence" to large integrated holding companies in the utilities field. As Wheeler, its Senate sponsor, put it, the bill was a "federal tax on bigness . . . the only program that can eventually restore to us the reality of that economic and political democracy by which we fondly like to think this nation lives."

The "wealth tax" began as a Treasury bill—aimed at increasing revenue from high income brackets and corporations. By the summer of 1935, however, Roosevelt seized on it to placate followers of men like Long. He wrote a friend that he was "fighting Communism, Huey Longism, Coughlinism, Townsendism. . . . To combat . . . crackpot ideas, it may be necessary to throw to the wolves the forty-six men who are reported to have incomes in excess of one million dollars a year. This can be accomplished through taxation." When Long saw the tax message, he crowed that FDR was "copying my share-the-wealth speeches now that I was writing when I was fourteen years old. So he's just now getting as smart as I was when I was in knee breeches."

Both measures aroused excited protests from conservatives. Wendell Willkie, a leading utilities executive, led a well-organized lobbying campaign against the holding company bill, which John W. Davis, Democratic presidential nominee in 1924, termed the "gravest threat to the liberties of the American citizen that has emanated from the halls of Congress in some time." Hearing of the wealth tax, William Randolph Hearst told his editors to refer to it as "Soak the Successful" and to label the New Deal the "Raw Deal." Walter Lippmann called it the "work of tired brains, relying on their wishes and their prejudices and throwing out suggestions which they are too hot and bothered to think about."

Such vocal opposition was partly successful. Congress softened the holding company bill to permit the continued existence of geographically defensible empires. It amended the wealth tax bill into an innocuous measure that failed either to soak the rich or to produce much additional revenue. Congress's response to conservative pressure showed again that organized interest groups were not to be denied. It also revealed that Roosevelt, while still in command, backed away from fighting Congress for long on such issues. A congressional renaissance was underway.

The battles over the holding company and tax bills suggested further that Roosevelt was an inconsistent economic thinker. Having failed in 1933 to establish business–government cooperation, he had switched—in part for political reasons—to a New Freedom animus against bigness. Given the hostility of businessmen and the gross inequities in wealth, this change of course was understandable. But it was also irrelevant to economic recovery. What the nation required was countercyclical fiscal policy (especially heavier spending), not higher taxes.

Nevertheless, Roosevelt's sally against big business paid political dividends. Though it failed to silence implacable critics like Long, it suggested that he stood for economic and social justice. Roosevelt, the master politician, realized that throwing plutocrats "to the wolves" was almost always popular with the voters.

The second term: programs and frustrations

VICTORY IN 1936

As the 1936 campaign developed momentum, the Right outdid itself in hurling invective at the New Deal. Mark Sullivan, an influential conservative columnist, worried that 1936 might witness the "last presidential election America may ever have. . . . It is tragic that America fails to see that the New Deal is to America what the early phase of Nazism was to Germany." Switchboard operators at the Chicago *Tribune* greeted callers with, "Good morning, Chicago *Tribune*. There are only——days in which to save the American way of life."

Demagogues were equally unhappy. Though Long had been assassinated in late 1935, Gerald L. K. Smith, an anti-Semitic rabble-rouser, moved in to direct Long's followers against the President. Coalescing with Coughlin and Townsend, they nominated William Lemke, a progressive North Dakota congressman, for the presidency on the Union party ticket. "Liberty Bell" Lemke, as he was called, stood for the inflationist, anti–Wall St., quasi-populist platform of Coughlin's Union for Social Justice.

Roosevelt also confronted discontent among militant spokesmen for blacks. The NRA, they maintained, had displaced black workers; its initials represented "Negroes Ruined Again." The AAA had dispossessed thousands of black tenants. TVA towns were for blacks only. The NAACP complained especially about Roosevelt's refusal to endorse a federal bill against lynching, only to be told, "If I come out for the antilynching bill now, they [influential southern congressmen] will block every bill I ask Congress to pass to keep America from collapsing. I just can't take that risk." This was a politically correct assessment, for few Americans paid much attention in the 1930s to the plight of blacks. But it left black leaders unhappy. *Crisis,* magazine of the NAACP, concluded that blacks "ought to realize by now that the powers-that-be in the Roosevelt administration have nothing for them."

The President welcomed the self-defeating rhetoric of the Right. "Economic royalists," he proclaimed, had never "been so united against one candidate as they stand today. They are unanimous in their hatred of me—and I welcome their hatred. . . . I should like to have it said of my second administration that in it these forces met their master." Raymond Moley, who had broken earlier with the President, recalled that "thoughtful citizens were stunned by the violence, the bombast, the naked demagoguery of these sentences.'' Perhaps. But assaults on the privileged few won a great many more votes than they lost.

As the election drew near it became equally obvious that Roosevelt had little to fear from the Union party, which clumsily combined populism, anti-Semitism, and rhetorical excesses. Lemke, though an earnest candidate, suffered from reminders that the Liberty Bell was cracked. Compared to headline-seekers like Coughlin and Smith, he was all but forgotten by election day.

The Republican party also offered little challenge. Its candidate, Governor Alfred M. Landon of Kansas, was a decent, moderate man who had little in common with right-wing extremists. Unlike many Republicans, he was sensible enough not to attack popular New Deal measures such as social security. But he was too restrained and too plain to develop much popular appeal. The ''Kansas Coolidge,'' as he was unfairly labeled, never posed much of a threat.

Roosevelt knew also that most blacks would have to support him. Neither the GOP nor the Union party seemed likely to help them, and the communists were urging their followers to back Roosevelt as part of Moscow's popular front against fascism. Norman Thomas, who had eloquently supported black tenant farmers, seemed such an unlikely winner as the Socialist presidential candidate that few blacks considered wasting their votes on him. Blacks also recognized that many New Dealers sympathized with them. Mrs. Roosevelt often intervened on their behalf, and Harold Ickes secured places in the federal bureaucracy for black spokesmen. Other department heads challenged the Jim Crow practices that Wilson had developed years earlier. Most important, programs like the Civilian Conservation Corps, Public Works Administration, and Works Progress Administration employed thousands of poor blacks, who at last felt the direct benevolent hand of Uncle Sam. Far from antagonizing the black electorate, FDR's policies swung it into the Democratic column. Some 75 percent supported him in 1936, compared to but 21 percent four years earlier.

In this same positive way Roosevelt attracted ethnic voters to his side. New Deal welfare policies pumped millions of dollars into the cities, where the established ethnic machines became the natural distributors and beneficiaries. Roosevelt also spread patronage generously to ethnic leaders. By 1936 most of these leaders, especially Jews and Irish-Americans, were fervent supporters of Roosevelt and the Democratic party. They, too, would retain these loyalties for decades.

With all these advantages Roosevelt scored a spectacular victory on election day. He swept every state but Maine and Vermont, and carried with him into Congress unprecedented Democratic margins of 331 to 89 and 76 to 16. (Progressives and Independents like La Follette and Norris added to his margin of support.) His total vote of 27.8 million swamped Landon's 16.7 million, Lemke's 880,000, and Thomas's 187,000 (700,000 fewer than in 1932). Roosevelt's total, more than 5 million more than he had gotten four years earlier, was swelled by throngs of people who previously had not voted. These people—blacks, ethnics, workers, and poor people—formed an enduring coalition of forgotten men and women for the Democratic party.

STALEMATE

Shortly after the election, Senator Hiram Johnson of California prophesied the future. "I think," he wrote, "that Roosevelt during this next session will give free rein to his imagination. There will be nobody to stop him, and but few to protest. All sorts of experiments we may see, some of which will give us the cold shivers." It is difficult to explain why this did not happen and why the New Deal advanced no further.

One important reason was the "court reform" bill with which Roosevelt polarized the country in February 1937. The reform called for the addition of new judges to the federal courts when the incumbents refused to retire at the age of 70. The Supreme Court (which then had six judges over 70) could be expanded to a maximum of 15. With new blood, the President argued, the courts could stay abreast of their work.

Roosevelt's desire to curb the "nine old men," as progressives called them, was understandable. After overturning the NRA, the judges had proceeded in 1936 to reject the AAA (six to three) and state minimum wage acts (five to four). Justice Harlan Stone, one of the three consistent liberals on the Court (Brandeis and Benjamin Cardozo were the others) called the 1936 term "one of the most disastrous in history." With other key legislation, such as social security and the Wagner Act, soon to reach the high tribunal, New Dealers feared for the worst.

But the President's message badly misjudged popular reverence for the Court and for the sanctity of separation of powers. The New York *Herald Tribune,* a Republican paper, typified this sort of reaction by proclaiming that "it was a French King, Louis XIV, who said: 'L'Etat c'est moi'—I am the state. The paper shell of American constitutionalism would continue if President Roosevelt secured the passage of the law he now demands. But it would only be a shell." Liberals, too, worried about the President's plan. The Court, they agreed, was not falling behind in its work. Aged justices—their hero, Brandeis, was eighty-one—were not the problem. Roosevelt had said nothing about Court reform during the election, nor had he consulted his congressional backers. "The President's plan," Wheeler complained, "is a fake and a sham proposal. It does not accomplish one single thing that the liberals of this country have been fighting for."

Roosevelt professed to be unperturbed by the outcry. "Conservatives," he chortled to a friend, "are running about tearing their hair and using language about me that surpasses even that of the campaign." But during the prolonged hearings on the plan opposition mounted steadily. Charles Evans Hughes, the formidable, white-bearded chief justice, showed conclusively that the Court was fully abreast of its duties. Because he was one of the Court's two moderates, or "swing men," and because he was a widely respected elder statesman, his argument helped demolish the President's case. The Court itself—in a "switch in time that saved nine"—then undermined Roosevelt's effort by sustaining (by votes of five to four) the social security and Wagner acts and by reversing its decision of 1936 on state minimum wage laws. Thereafter, even Roosevelt's most loyal supporters pleaded for an end to the divisive debate. After holding out stubbornly for five months, the President finally gave up the struggle.

In some respects Roosevelt could argue that the Court had appeared to reverse itself under pressure. Moreover, the retirement of one of the conservative judges in May promised to give the New Deal a safer margin of support in the future. (By 1941 four other judges had retired, and Roosevelt had safely assured himself of support for liberal legislation by naming men like Hugo Black, William Douglas, and Felix Frankfurter to the Court.) But such an argument failed to recognize that the Court had frequently divided, five to four, for New Deal laws before 1937, or that the decision sustaining minimum wages, though announced after the release of the President's court-packing announcement, had actually been arrived at beforehand. What motivated the two "swing men," Hughes and Owen Roberts, to change their minds in 1937 was not wholly clear—perhaps the Democratic triumph of 1936—but it was not the plan itself. Instead, Roosevelt's proposal alarmed the country, split the

Democratic coalition, and encouraged congressional moderates, who had previously feared to challenge such a popular president, to resist. From that point on, Roosevelt had to fight for what he could get from an increasingly hostile Congress.

Other developments added to Roosevelt's difficulties in his second term. One was the sit-down strikes, which business spokesmen were quick to blame on the administration's friendliness toward the CIO. Another was the state of the economy. Early in 1937 it seemed that prosperity was returning at last. But Roosevelt, anxious as always to reduce federal spending, cut back on relief. At the same time the Federal Reserve tightened money. Businessmen, perhaps in response to an undistributed profits tax approved in 1936, held back on new investment. For all these reasons one of the most serious recessions in American history descended in late 1937. Within ten months some 4 million people lost their jobs, and unemployment rose to 11.5 million.

Conservatives responded to this state of affairs by saying, "I told you so." Moderates wondered if the New Deal had done any good at all. Keynesian economists and progressives demanded that FDR resume heavy public spending. Caught in a crossfire, Roosevelt procrastinated, agonized, and finally (after sensing trouble ahead in the 1938 elections) supported the spenders. By late 1939 the economy moved sluggishly out of the recession. But Roosevelt's policies (and indecision) had contributed to two more years of hard times. Under such conditions it was not surprising that Republicans made strong inroads on his congressional majorities in 1938.

Despite these setbacks, Roosevelt pressed for further reforms: regional resource development, minimum wages, maximum hours, protection of child labor, assistance to tenant farmers, reorganization of the federal government. Persuaded that big business was holding out on him, he encouraged the antitrust division of the Justice Department to move more vigorously against

Business men have a different set of delusions from politicians; and need, therefore, different handling. They are, however, much milder than politicians, at the same time allured and terrified by the glare of publicity, easily persuaded to be 'patriots,' perplexed, bemused, indeed terrified, yet only too anxious to take a cheerful view, vain perhaps but very unsure of themselves, pathetically responsive to a kind word. You could do anything you liked with them, if you would treat them (even the big ones), not as wolves and tigers, but as domestic animals by nature, even though they have been badly brought up and not trained as you would wish. It is a mistake to think that they are more immoral than politicians. If you work them into the surly, obstinate, terrified mood, of which domestic animals, wrongly handled, are so capable, the nation's burdens will not get carried to market; and in the end public opinion will veer their way.

Lord John Maynard Keynes advises Roosevelt on handling businessmen, 1938. Roosevelt paid him little heed.

monopolies. Contrary to the view of some disenchanted leftist historians, he had neither run out of ideas nor given up the struggle.

But he was unable to translate his personal popularity into legislation. The interest groups that comprised his formidable electoral coalition repeatedly failed to work jointly for legislation unless it directly affected them individually. And the conservative coalition in Congress recognized accurately that the Democratic party had been transformed since 1928 from the largely southern and western bloc it had been in the days of William Jennings Bryan to a predominantly urban agglomeration symbolized by people like Robert Wagner of New York. Angered by the demands of the urbanites—money for relief and housing, assistance for blacks, laws protecting labor—the rural forces determined to mount a strong opposition. With their demoralization of 1933–35 overcome, they were no longer willing to help the New Deal.

The result was stalemate. Between 1937 and 1939 Congress approved laws providing small sums for public housing and tenant farmers. It enacted a second AAA, without the tax on food processors to which the court had objected. In a change which foreshadowed many later moves to expand the White House staff, it authorized Roosevelt to create the Executive Office of the President. Most important, it finally approved a law abolishing child labor in interstate commerce and providing for federal minimum wages and maximum hours. But these laws were heavily amended before passage. Congress also dismissed Roosevelt's requests for regional development, it whittled away at the WPA, it cut off funding for the Federal Theatre project, it rejected an expansion in government lending, and it ushered in a new age of congressional investigatory activity by authorizing a probe into the NLRB and providing generously for the new House Un-American Activities Committee. It was clear that Congress had moved from the left of the White House (where it had usually been between 1909 and 1936) to the right, and that it was resuming the assertive behavior it had demonstrated from 1919 to 1933. Presidential success, it appeared, inevitably bred congressional counterreaction.

The New Deal: an evaluation

Because Roosevelt attempted so much, it is easy to criticize him. Conservatives were correct in complaining about the maze of bureaucratic agencies; even Roosevelt conceded in 1936 that "administration" was his greatest weakness. They were also correct in accusing Roosevelt of inconsistency. And they were wise to be wary about the dangers of executive direction. "The old Jeffersonian emphasis on schools for citizenship and on self-government," one critic observed, "has changed to a Rooseveltian emphasis on response to a heroic leadership."

Other critics focused on what they perceived as the synthetic quality of Roosevelt's personality. The President, they agreed, was flexible, buoyant, charismatic, an eloquent speaker who evoked mass loyalty unprecedented in American politics. But, they added, he was primarily a political animal who concealed a calculating nature behind a façade of good humor and patrician assurance. Worse, he was a drifter and an improviser who lacked the intellectual capacity to understand economics and the courage to act when—as during the recession of 1937–38—decisive responses were required. According to this perspective, Roosevelt was sheer personality—a con artist supreme.

Critics on the Left stressed the economic limitations of the New Deal. Roosevelt, they said, was often cautious and conservative. He refused to nationalize banking, to sponsor laws against lynching, or to work hard for public housing. He was slow to perceive the needs of organized labor and he was virtually blind to those of the city. Before 1942 he barely mentioned such later reforms as federal aid to education, health insurance, or civil rights legislation. Despite his rhetoric against big business, he did little to stem the growth of monopoly, which proceeded apace in the 1930s. After his abortive attempt for a "wealth tax," he left the tax structure as it was. Income distribution in 1940 was much as it had been ten years before.

Other reformers argued that FDR hardly affected the sources of power in America. He remained a firm believer in decentralization and in a responsive approach to interest groups. Large farmers and businessmen expanded their influence, while newer groups, especially labor unions, added to the pressures on government. In theory this state of affairs culminated in a balance of "countervailing powers," bringing rough justice to all groups. In practice, however, it meant that the strongest groups got what they wanted while others—consumers, unskilled workers, women, blacks—got little or nothing.

Finally, critics observed that the New Deal failed to arrest the depression. Even in the "good" times of early 1937 some 7.5 million Americans (out of a work force of 54 million) were unemployed. In the same year gross private domestic investment was only $11.7 billion, compared to $16.2 billion in 1929. Per capita national income did not reach 1929 levels until early 1940.

Why this was so remains in dispute. Some conservative economists main-

President Roosevelt is the first statesman in a great capitalist society who has sought deliberately and systematically to use the power of the state to subordinate the primary assumptions of that society to certain vital social purposes. He is the first statesman deliberately to experiment on a wholesale scale with the limitation of the profit-making motive. He is the first statesman who, of his own volition, and without coercion, either direct or indirect, has placed in the hands of organized labor a weapon which, if it be used successfully, is bound to result in a vital readjustment of the relative bargaining power of Capital and Labor. He is also the first statesman who, the taxing power apart, has sought to use the political authority of the state to compel, over the whole area of economic effort, a significant readjustment of the national income.

No unbiased spectator of the adventure involved can withhold his admiration for the courage such an effort has implied. Success or failure, it bears upon its face the hallmarks of great leadership. Improvised in haste, devised under the grim pressure of crisis, imposed, as no doubt it has been imposed, in an atmosphere of panic and bewilderment, it stands out in remarkable, even significant, contrast to the economic policy of any other capitalist government in the world.

Harold Laski, a British Socialist, offers his view of the New Deal.

tain that more sophisticated monetary policy was the answer—that the Federal Reserve in 1931, and again in 1937, tightened money at the wrong times, thereby deterring potential investors. This view, however, tends to assume that investors venture their money only when interest rates are low. It also downplays the fact that cheap money between 1933 and 1937 had little impact on investment.

A more persuasive argument blames conservative fiscal policy for the persistence of hard times. Federal tax rates, instead of being reduced to stimulate consumption (and investment), were sustained, and new levies (including social security) were added. Though federal spending increased—from approximately $3.3 billion in 1929 to $4.6 billion in 1932–33 to $8.9 billion in 1939—this was still too little too late. Moreover, the modest federal deficits (averaging $3 billion a year between 1933 and 1939) caused by these increased expenditures were counterbalanced by surpluses in state and local budgets throughout the decade. Accordingly, there was no public deficit spending by governments—federal, state, and local—in the 1930s. As public works expenditures in Germany and England during the 1930s were already suggesting, the best remedy for hard times was higher public spending at all levels, and neither Roosevelt nor Hoover ever fully accepted that fact.

These criticisms, however, exaggerated Roosevelt's alleged opportunism. Unlike some of his successors in the White House, he was concerned with more than augmenting his own position (though he cared very much about that). While uninformed about labor organization, he wanted to assist ordinary people, and he expressed their needs in simple language they could understand. In his "fireside chats," his numerous press conferences, his close attention to the avalanche of mail that poured into the White House, he projected the image of a man who cared, and in his dealings with Congress he proved supple, forceful, and—for a time—even charismatic. By his confidence he gave his people hope, and with his vigor he restored faith in democratic institutions. "He showed," one admirer concluded, "that it is possible to be politically effective and yet benevolent and civilized."

Critics also underestimated the obstacles to thoroughgoing reform. The court, which caused him to introduce his ill-fated packing plan, was one. Congress, weighted toward rural conservatism, became another. The federal system was a third, for Roosevelt could not change state fiscal policies, which were regressive, or state political parties, which remained free to sabotage his programs. Roosevelt might have worked harder than he did to place progressives in power at the grass roots. But he did not have time to do everything, and when he attempted (rather hastily) to "purge" conservative Democrats from Congress in 1938, he failed. Roosevelt also had to contend with the essentially partisan, nonideological orientation of voters, who did not vote for "liberals" or "conservatives" but for the nominees of their party. Neither Roosevelt nor any of his successors could alter that.

The largest obstacle to reform remained the economic interest groups. If Roosevelt had chosen to confront them in 1933, when even conservatives yearned for strong leadership, he might have battered them about. Trusts might have been weakened, utilities nationalized, banks and stock exchanges centrally directed. Such policies, if combined with massive spending, might have brought recovery as well as reform. But few political leaders were willing to go that far, even in 1933, and it is highly unlikely that the President could have moved that fast without prompting divisiveness and loss of confidence at the very start of his administration.

Above all, Roosevelt's detractors tend to neglect his accomplishments. In part because of the New Deal, the economy stopped its disastrous slide of 1930–32. Farm prices increased, debtors received relief, banks reopened. The New Deal introduced modest centralization of banking and limited regulation of stock issues. It created landmark achievements such as social security and TVA and pioneered in the federal development of public welfare. The Wagner Act helped unionized workers to receive a hearing. And while Roosevelt rejected deficit spending as a long-range policy, so did most of his contemporaries: his willingness to resort to it at all stamped him as a flexible leader.

These acts were "conservative" in that they maintained the capitalistic system. But they were also reforms and they were partially successful. They resulted—at last—in a measure of political modernization capable of struggling with the economic centralization of previous decades. Compared with what had come before, the growth in the 1930s of the welfare state was considerable.

Suggestions for Reading

Books on the Hoover years include Joan Hoff Wilson, *Herbert Hoover** (1975); Harris Warren, *Herbert Hoover and the Great Depression** (1959); Jordan Schwarz, *Interregnum of Despair* (1970); Albert Romasco, *The Poverty of Abundance: Hoover, the Nation, the Depression** (1965). See also Roger Daniels, *Bonus March** (1971).

The most important general works on the New Deal are William Leuchtenburg, *Franklin D. Roosevelt and the New Deal, 1932–1940** (1963); Arthur Schlesinger, Jr., *The Coming of the New Deal** (1959) and *The Politics of Upheaval** (1960); James M. Burns, *Roosevelt: The Lion and the Fox** (1956); Otis Graham, Jr., *An Encore for Reform** (1963); Paul Conkin, *The New Deal** (1967), a brief interpretation; and the four volumes on Franklin D. Roosevelt by Frank Freidel. These volumes take Roosevelt into 1933. See also Joseph Lash, *Eleanor & Franklin** (1971). Books revealing the impact of the New Deal on politics are Theodore Lowi, *The End of Liberalism** (1969); Grant McConnell, *Private Power and American Democracy** (1966); Bruce Stave, *The New Deal & The Last Hurrah* (1970), on urban politics; and the book by Lubell cited in the bibliography for chapter 7.

Studies dealing with New Deal programs include Randolph Paul, *Taxation in the United States* (1954); John M. Blum, *Roosevelt and Morgenthau* (1970); Ellis Hawley, *The New Deal and the Problem of Monopoly** (1966); Richard Kirkendall, *Social Scientists and Farm Politics in the Age of Roosevelt* (1966); and James T. Patterson, *The New Deal and the States: Federalism in Transition* (1969). Also Roy Lubove, *The Struggle for Social Security, 1900–1935** (1968); Paul Conkin, *Tomorrow a New World* (1959), which deals with community programs; Jane D. Mathews, *The Federal Theater, 1935–1939** (1971); Joseph Arnold, *The New Deal in the Suburbs** (1971); Thomas McCraw, *TVA and the Power Fight, 1933–1939** (1970); Michael Parrish, *Securities Regulation and the New Deal* (1970); and John Salmond, *The Civilian Conservation Corps* (1967).

For Roosevelt's opponents, see Charles Tull, *Father Coughlin and the New Deal* (1965); David H. Bennett, *Demagogues in the Depression: American Radicals and the Union Party, 1932–1936* (1969); Abraham Holtzman, *The Townsend Movement* (1963); and Donald McCoy, *Angry Voices* (1958). Conservatives are covered in James Patterson, *Congressional Conservatism and the New Deal** (1967); John Hudson and George Wolfskill, *All But the People: FDR and His Critics** (1969); and McCoy, *Landon of Kansas* (1966). See also Richard Polenberg, *Reorganizing Roosevelt's Government . . . 1936–1939* (1966); Barry Karl, *Executive Reorganization and the New Deal* (1963). Important biographies include T. Harry Williams, *Huey Long** (1969); Ellsworth Barnard, *Wendell Willkie* (1966); and J. Joseph Huthmacher, *Senator Robert Wagner and the Rise of American Liberalism* (1968). For the Supreme Court consult Leonard Baker, *Back to Back: The Duel Between Franklin D. Roosevelt and the Supreme Court* (1967); Robert Jackson, *The Struggle for Judicial Supremacy** (1941), an account by a New Deal partisan who later joined the Court; and C. Herman Pritchett, *The Roosevelt Court, 1937–1947* (1963).

From
nonintervention
to
war

1929-1941

"There is the most profound outlook for peace today," President Hoover told Secretary of State Henry Stimson in 1930, "that we have had at any time in the last half century." Five years later, *Christian Century* accurately reported that "ninety-nine Americans out of one hundred would today regard as an imbecile anyone who would suggest that in the event of a European war the United States should again participate in it." In 1940 President Roosevelt assured an audience in Boston, "while I am talking to you, fathers and mothers, I give you one more assurance. I have said this before but I shall say it again and again: your boys are not going to be sent into any foreign wars."

Events forced Hoover and *Christian Century* to revise their predictions, and they made a liar out of FDR. By 1945, when World War II finally ended, 50 million people, including 405,000 Americans, had been killed. Yet the three quotations tell much about the movement of American thinking at the time: from optimism for peace, to assertions about the virtues of isolation, to desperate, deceiving assurances about the prospects for noninvolvement.

Hoover and foreign affairs

Hoover was perhaps the most pacifistic of American presidents. During his administration he worked earnestly toward renouncing the Roosevelt Corollary that had justified American military intervention to stop "chronic wrong doing" within Latin America. He attempted—unsuccessfully—to commit the leading powers to a broadening of the naval limitations established in 1922. Though he signed the nationalistic tariff act of 1930, he attempted to lessen international economic tensions by declaring the moratorium on war debt payments in 1931.

Hoover was also a staunch nationalist. At Versailles he had concluded that Europeans were irreparably selfish and quarrelsome. Like most Americans, therefore, he showed little interest after 1920 in the League of Nations. When confronted with demands that America take a hard line against overseas aggression, his instinctive reaction was to refuse. Like George Washington, he believed America should mind its own business.

The Manchurian crisis of 1931 revealed the strengths and limitations of Hoover's pacifistic nationalism. The area had long been a source of conflict between Russia, Japan, and China. The Japanese secured leaseholds and railroad rights there after World War I. Their presence antagonized Chinese nationalists under Chiang Kai-shek, who encouraged local warlords to compete with Japan. In September 1931 the Japanese responded with a well-coordinated assault on the whole of Manchuria. The League called rather vaguely for sanctions. But it lacked an army, and Britain and France, the League's strongest powers, were ill prepared to resist. What, therefore, were Herbert Hoover and the United States prepared to do?

The answer was, very little. Hoover authorized an American to sit in at meetings of the League Council but to speak only if the delegates attempted to utilize the pious Kellogg-Briand Pact of 1928, which "outlawed" aggressive war. He also refused to recognize Japanese conquests in Manchuria. Following this American approach, the League embraced the nonrecognition doctrine. Secretary of State Stimson went further in February 1932 by sending a letter to Senator William Borah, chairman of the Foreign Relations Committee. The letter implied that because Japan was breaking the nine-power agreement concerning the Open Door, America might consider ignoring the five-power treaty on naval limitations.

Stimson hoped the letter might stiffen Britain's resolve, enlighten American public opinion, and assist congressional advocates of rearmament. The Senate, however, paid no attention to the letter. And the Japanese first ignored the League, and then, in February 1933, withdrew from it. When Hoover left office in March 1933, it was obvious to all that no one could halt the Japanese armies, which remained in China and Manchuria until 1945.

This western weakness later encouraged both Germany and Japan to pursue aggressive policies. But what was Hoover (and later Roosevelt) to do? In the depth of the depression it seemed senseless to cut off American trade with Japan, which bought four times as much as China, or to try to resist the well-equipped Japanese armies. It seemed equally unwise to defy the American public, which wanted no part of military involvement in Asia. Indeed, the historian Charles Beard spoke for many in proclaiming that it was not worth "killing American boys in a struggle over the bean crop in Manchuria." If Hoover had used the crisis to assume a consistent stance against foreign aggression, he might have helped—a little—to educate people about the dangers that lay ahead. But he could have done nothing to stop Japan in 1931.

Hoover also asked the broader question: Was it really in America's national interest to defend the Open Door against Japan? Unlike Stimson—and many later "experts" on Oriental behavior—he did not believe the Japanese could be scared into submission. Challenging them, he thought, would be like "sticking pins in tigers." America's only vital interests, he added, lay in the Western Hemisphere. This argument stemmed primarily from his rather narrow nationalism, and it led to appeasement. But in 1931–33 it was sane, restrained, and—given the temper of the times—realistic. Only later, when the aggressive powers banded together, did its limitations become clearer.

The rise of noninterventionism, 1933–1936

Roosevelt's first term witnessed the spread of virtually unchallenged militarism and aggression. In January 1933 Hitler assumed power, and in October France, having failed to secure western guarantees of her borders, pulled out of a European disarmament conference. Using France's action as an excuse, Hitler resigned from the League, and followed by intensifying his persecution of Jews and leftists. In 1935 Mussolini invaded Ethiopia, and Germany started conscription. In 1936 Hitler further violated the Versailles treaty by moving into the Rhineland. Meanwhile, Japan tightened control in Manchuria and refused any longer to be bound by the five-power treaty limiting naval armaments.

On the surface Roosevelt appeared well prepared to deal with such a world. As Wilson's assistant secretary of the navy he had shared Wilson's faith that America must play an active role in world affairs. "Modern civilization," he said in 1920, "has become so complex and the lives of civilized men so interwoven with the lives of other men as to make it impossible to be in this world and not of it." By 1932 such influential forces as the chauvinistic Hearst press had induced him to back away from support of the League. But he never shared Hoover's instinctive suspicion of Europe or his faith that America should go it alone.

During his first years in office he occasionally acted on cautiously internationalist premises, especially where they promised to aid the economy. Following Hoover, he worked toward what he called the "good neighbor" policy in Latin America. In 1934, with a conservative regime protecting American interests, he ended the United States protectorate of Cuba, and by 1940 some harmony (and much increased trade) existed within the Western Hemisphere. FDR also recognized the Soviet Union in 1933, primarily in the misplaced hope of developing trade. And he named as his secretary of state Cordell Hull, an ardent believer in lower tariff barriers as the way to peace and prosperity. Thanks to Hull's efforts, Congress approved the Reciprocal Trade Agreements Act of 1934, which stopped congressional log-rolling by empowering the executive branch to negotiate rates. In the same year Roosevelt established the Export-Import Bank, which extended credit to potential customers abroad. In part because of these efforts, and in part because of returning prosperity in other areas of the world, America's exports grew from $2.2 billion in 1934 to $3.2 billion in 1939.

But neither Roosevelt nor Hull was a profound thinker concerning foreign affairs. Hull, indeed, was a rather rigid moralist obsessed with the vision of free trade. Roosevelt kept many important matters out of Hull's hands, and in so doing reduced morale in the State Department. Worse, FDR occasionally acted as if his charm and adaptability could bring to international relations the same soothing results they brought to domestic affairs. The diplomat George Kennan complained later that some of Roosevelt's problems stemmed from his "superficiality, the forced and often unsuccessful humor, the studied avoidance of every serious issue."

Roosevelt's greatest handicap was the depression, which forced him to place domestic policies above all else. Accordingly, he sent a "bombshell" message to the London Economic Conference that met in June 1933. Efforts to stabilize currencies, he proclaimed, were "old fetishes of so-called international bankers" and were "purely artificial and temporary." The United States must act alone to develop "the kind of a dollar which a generation hence will have the same purchasing and debt paying power as the dollar we hope to obtain in the near future." This nationalistic message was defensible economically, for it promised to free western nations from the inhibitions of the gold standard and to permit expansionary fiscal policies at home. At the same time, the message was blunt and curt. It effectively torpedoed the conference.

This economic nationalism was part of a much broader current of isolationist thinking in the mid-1930s. Abroad isolationism led to the growth of pacifism and "appeasement" in England and France. Both countries felt guilty about the treatment accorded Germany at Versailles, and both shrank from a repetition of World War I. In America isolationism was reflected in books like Charles Beard's *Open Door at Home* (1934), which maintained that overseas adventurism blocked domestic reforms. Nationalism assisted the vogue for the "regionalist" school of painting, which glorified the American heartland. In historical writing it gave support to Frederick Jackson Turner's thesis that the essence of Americanism lay in the country's own frontiers. Among young people it helped promote a rise in pacifism, which led to creation of the mock-serious Veterans of Future Wars (whose members demanded pre-service bonuses) and to a wave of student strikes for peace.

This understandable fear of a World War II also promoted a wave of historical revisionism that blamed Wilson and profiteers for dragging America into World War I. *Merchants of Death* by Helmuth Englebrecht and Frank Hanighen, a tract against munitions makers, became a best seller in 1934. Walter Millis's *Road to War,* which stressed the role of economic motives and of Allied propaganda, became a Book-of-the-Month Club selection in 1935. Robert Sherwood's *Idiot's Delight,* a play featuring an evil arms manufacturer, received a Pulitzer Prize in 1936. As one bitter revisionist put it, "platitude-mongering Wilson, who was willing to have young men die for old men's dividends," was no longer the magnificent idealist who had stirred people's visions in 1919, but the arch villain of his time.

All these strands of thinking—fear of war, hatred of profiteers, distrust of presidential power—were strong on Capitol Hill. As early as 1933, at the height of Roosevelt's popularity, Congress refused to give him discretionary power to apply arms embargoes against nations he labeled aggressors. In 1934 it passed a law prohibiting American loans to nations defaulting on war debts. At the same time it authorized a special Senate committee to investigate munitions-making during World War I. The committee, headed by Gerald P. Nye of North Dakota, discovered only the obvious: that munitions manufacturers made money, and that they engaged in collusive bidding. It did not uncover a conspiracy to get the nation into war, nor did it succeed in implicating Wilson, who was no friend of arms manufacturers like the Du Ponts. But neither Nye nor his wide audience worried much about lack of evidence. It was enough that rich manufacturers (already scapegoats for the depression) had made huge profits while American boys died on European soil. The economic motive for war must not be allowed to develop again.

In mid-1935 Congress took a still more fateful step by debating a "neutrality" law applying the "lessons" of 1914–17. Among the law's provisions was an automatic embargo on American arms and ammunition to all parties at war. Alarmed, Hull sought amendments enabling the President to discriminate between aggressor and innocent. Roosevelt recognized that the bill not only tied his hands but repudiated traditional American shipping rights—which Wilson had gone to war to protect. But FDR's top priority remained domestic legislation against the depression. To challenge Congress over the neutrality bill, he realized, would be futile and counterproductive. So he told Hull to submit. When Congress approved the measure at the close of the session, Roosevelt signed it and called it "entirely satisfactory."

A few weeks later Mussolini launched a long-expected attack on Ethiopia. Roosevelt immediately applied the arms embargo against both sides. His action probably made little difference, for Italy did not need American arms, and Ethiopia could ill afford to buy them. More significant was the failure of the United States to ban the shipment of oil, the key to the success of mechanized armed forces such as Italy's. When American exporters sent oil to Italy, Roosevelt and Hull urged them to apply a "moral embargo." But the hard-hit companies were anxious to make a profit, and they saw little reason to comply with a President who had turned against big business. The shipments proceeded.

American policy was by no means the only obstacle to Ethiopia's cause. Britain and France also shied away from taking a stand that might involve them in war. Both countries shipped oil to Italy throughout the crisis. Nor could Roosevelt have secured repeal of the neutrality act, which had passed the Senate by a vote of seventy-nine to two, and the House without even a roll call vote. Still, the neutrality law showed how far America was willing to go to keep the nation out of war. The "lessons" of 1917 had been learned too well.

The hope for appeasement, 1936–1938

In August 1936 Roosevelt again appealed to isolationist feelings. "I hate war," he proclaimed. "I have passed unnumbered hours, I shall pass unnumbered hours, thinking and planning how war may be kept from this nation."

His hopes for peace were sincere. Whose are not? But in reiterating them he was concealing from the public his own private anger at the aggressors. He was also ignoring the advice of many emissaries abroad, especially William Dodd in Berlin and George Messersmith in Vienna. "The Hitler triumvirate," Dodd warned in 1935, "is . . . far more powerful than the Kaiser was. . . . You may infer . . . that war is their direct and major aim." In 1936 Messer Smith added, "there is only one way to deal with the German regime of today, and that is to meet its brutal, ruthless action by an equally determined stand. It is the only language which that regime understands. . . ."

Congress, of course, would not have permitted Roosevelt to follow such a course in 1936, or even in 1938. Still, he could have begun the process of educating the public for the ordeal that he recognized might lie ahead. That he did not, that he persisted in appeasing the isolationists, revealed him as less than forthright. It marked him also as one of the many, including Britain's Prime Minister Neville Chamberlain, who clung to illusions about the chances for real neutrality in a world being overrun by men like Hitler.

Roosevelt's hopes for peace proved useless against the ever more aggressive behavior of the antidemocratic forces. In November 1936 Germany and Japan signed the Anti-Comintern Pact, forerunner to later agreements that bound the two powers (and Italy) in military defense alliances. Fascists under Franco then revolted against the legitimate republican government of Spain. In 1937 Japan launched a full-scale invasion of China. In 1938 Hitler annexed Austria, and then, after the other western powers bowed to his threats at the Munich conference, he took the Sudetenland of Czechoslovakia.

Confronted with these threats, Congress pursued a still more nationalistic course. In 1936 it prohibited citizens from advancing loans or credits to belligerents. Early in 1937 it hurried through a law extending this ban, as well as an arms embargo, to the civil war in Spain. Progressives, including many who had supported previous neutrality legislation, complained that the act would assist Franco. They were overruled, and America stood by while Hitler used the Spanish war as a testing ground for his weaponry.

In May 1937 Congress, still preoccupied with learning lessons from 1914–17, completed its illusory pursuit of peace by passing a comprehensive neutrality law. It banned American ships from war zones, prohibited Americans from traveling on belligerent ships, and extended the mandatory embargo on arms and ammunition. Making sure that the United States had its cake and ate it too, it placed other vital exports, including oil, steel, and rubber, under the rubric of "cash and carry" for two years. Foreign belligerents could buy such goods only if they paid for them in cash and carried them in their own ships. Cash and carry, Congress recognized, would enable producers to sell their goods abroad, without exposing American ships to enemy submarines and without giving Wall Street any cause to press for defense of its loans. Such legislation, if in force in 1914–17, might have kept America out of World War I. Germany's insatiable aggressiveness, however, made it increasingly irrelevant by 1941.

As in earlier years, Roosevelt wasted little effort trying to dissuade Congress from pursuing a path that obviously commanded popular support. But in the fall of 1937 he appeared to move cautiously away from his hands-off policy. Taking advantage of the fact that no "war" was declared in Asia, he refused to apply an embargo, thus permitting American ships and creditors to deal with China in the years ahead. In October he followed by giving his "quarantine" speech in Chicago. "The epidemic of world lawlessness," he said, "is spreading. When an epidemic of physical disease starts to spread, the community approves and joins in a quarantine of the patients in order to protect the health of the community against the spread of disease. . . . There must be positive endeavors to preserve peace." At last, so it seemed, Roosevelt was moving toward a policy of resistance, especially since Hull announced the next day that America was going to participate in a nine-power conference in Brussels in November, the purpose of which would be to consider joint efforts against Japan.

Having ventured toward activism, Roosevelt failed to follow it up. In fact, it remains unclear what he had expected to do in the first place, for the quarantine speech was equivocal. It talked of action by the "community" and of "positive endeavors," but it offered no concrete suggestions for collective measures, and it reiterated that "America hates war. . . . America actively engages in the search for peace." When a few isolationist newspapers exploded in protest, Roosevelt ignored contrary reactions, and said nothing more. Amid such an atmosphere of caution it was not surprising that the Brussels conference accomplished nothing, or that Japanese planes over the Yangtze felt bold enough in December to sink the American gunboat *Panay,* to strafe its crew, and to kill two American sailors in the process. Though Roosevelt privately considered responding with economic sanctions, he did nothing when Japan apologized: he wanted no part of using such incidents to fan the passions of war.

By 1938 many influential Americans were chafing openly at Roosevelt's temporizing. Former Secretary of State Stimson was one, Harold Ickes another, Secretary of the Treasury Henry Morgenthau, a close advisor of the President, a third. But the House of Representatives grew so alarmed about the *Panay* incident that it nearly approved a constitutional amendment requiring a national referendum before America could go to war, and polls suggested that sizable majorities of the people supported strict neutrality. Ever sensitive to the popular pulse, Roosevelt contented himself with stopping the amendment and with working successfully for more generous naval appropriations.

It was at this point, in mid-1938, that Hitler demanded the Sudetenland of Czechoslovakia. Pursuing appeasement to its logical conclusion, Prime Minister Neville Chamberlain of England and Premier Eduard Daladier of France went to the Munich Conference in October and surrendered to Hitler's demand. Actually, Chamberlain and Daladier had a difficult choice, for their nations did not want war, and even with the aid of the Czech army they would have been hard-pressed to defeat Germany. Chamberlain was nonetheless foolish to proclaim that he had secured "peace in our time." Winston Churchill, a foe of appeasement, was closer to the mark in exclaiming that "Britain and France had to choose between war and dishonor. They chose dishonor. They will have war."

The United States played no direct role in the Munich Conference. ("It is always best and safest," Chamberlain remarked, "to count on nothing from the Americans but words.") Roosevelt also showed little sympathy for Churchill's position. Two days after the conference he told Chamberlain, "I fully share your hope and belief that there exists today the greatest opportu-

nity in years for the establishment of a new order based on justice and law.''
As Hitler prepared for his greatest conquests, the United States remained as
doggedly neutral as ever.

America and Hitler, 1939–1941

When Hitler seized the remainder of Czechoslovakia in March 1939, it became
difficult to doubt his insatiable ambitions. Further German expansion, the
British and French warned, would mean war. Unimpressed, Hitler negotiated
a nonaggression pact with Stalin to protect his eastern front, and in September
the two nations invaded Poland. "Close your hearts to pity," Hitler told his
generals. "Act brutally. Eighty million people must obtain what is their right.
Their existence must be made secure. The strongest man is right. . . .''

Before the invasion Roosevelt asked for and received greatly expanded
funds for defense. He also made a belated effort to get Congress to repeal the
mandatory arms embargo. Congress, however, had refused. So when war
broke out in September 1939, Roosevelt tried again. After prolonged debate,
Congress repealed the mandatory embargo in November, and munitions
began to flow across the Atlantic. At the same time Roosevelt quickly
provided funds to scientists eager to develop an atomic bomb. But he still
insisted that America "will keep out of this war. . . . there will be no blackout
of peace in the United States.'' And Congress persisted in adhering to cash
and carry—the Allies must buy all goods, including munitions, in cash and
transport them in their own ships.

Hitler then overran Denmark and Norway in April 1940 and France and
the low countries in May and June. Only Britain, whose troops fled across the
Channel from Dunkirk, remained to fight the fascist menace. For many
Americans the fall of the French, who had stayed in the trenches for four
years in World War I, was a sobering event. They formed the Committee to
Aid the Allies under the leadership of the veteran publisher William Allen
White. Equally alarmed, Roosevelt began securing certain kinds of weapons
for Britain. At Charlottesville in June he proclaimed "we will extend to the
opponents of force the material resources of this nation, and, at the same time,
we will harness and speed up the use of these resources.''

Other moves in mid-1940 suggested that FDR was ready to pursue a more
resolute course against Hitler. In June he named Stimson, an ardent foe of
appeasement, as secretary of war. He lent passive support to Stimson's drive,
which proved successful, for the nation's first peacetime draft. He received
quick congressional backing for defense spending. After assuring himself that
Wendell Willkie, the Republican presidential nominee, would not attack him,
he agreed in September to the unneutral "destroyer deal,'' whereby America
released fifty aged destroyers in return for leases on British bases in the
Western Hemisphere. Because some of the ships could barely make it to sea,
they were of limited use in Britain's desperate defense against German

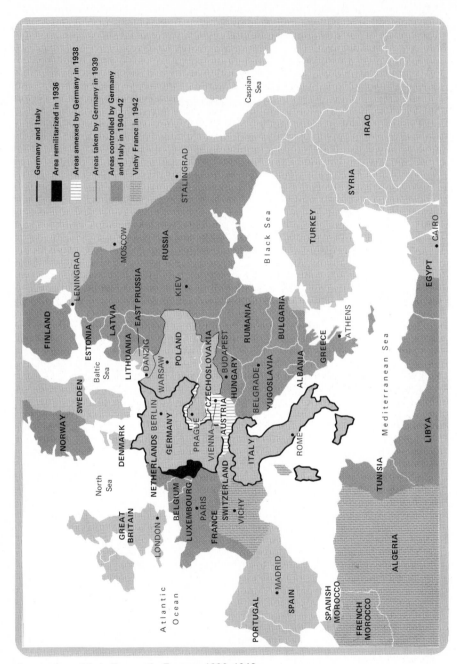

Aggression of Axis Powers in Europe, 1936–1942

submarines. But the deal symbolized America's increasing readiness to get involved.

The drift away from neutrality aroused the anti-interventionists to renewed activity. Many of them joined America First, a broad isolationist front. Others, like Senators Robert Taft of Ohio and Arthur Vandenberg of Michigan, led a Republican onslaught in Congress. Socialists and pacifists, including Norman Thomas, added their voices. So did former President Hoover, flying hero Charles Lindbergh, Progressive Senator Robert La Follette, Jr., Charles Beard, John L. Lewis, Frank Lloyd Wright, Joseph Kennedy, America's ambassador to Great Britain, and spokesmen for German, Italian, and Irish ethnic groups. Though the isolationists were probably outnumbered after the fall of France, they were strong in the Midwest, in a few German-American enclaves, and among nonseaboard Republicans. They attracted enough liberals and progressives to represent a broad political spectrum. It was a formidable coalition of people who believed passionately in their cause.

Some of their arguments were crude and ill informed. Lindbergh, one of the stalwarts of America First, reflected the anti-Semitism that persisted in America in the 1930s and that contributed to a callous policy toward Jewish refugees seeking escape from Hitler. ''The three most important groups which have been pressing this country toward war,'' he said, ''are the British, the Jewish, and the Roosevelt administration.'' His wife, the author Anne Morrow Lindbergh, conceded that fascism was often ''evil and horrible,'' but added with defeatism that it was the ''wave of the future. . . . there is no fighting the wave of the future any more than as a child you could fight against the gigantic roller that loomed up ahead of you.'' These kinds of arguments alienated many people, including some followers of America First.

More thoughtful anti-interventionists worried that the European war was already concentrating power in the presidency and creating a potential threat to civil liberty. If America decided to enter the war, Vandenberg charged

I'll sing you a song, and it's not very long
It's about a young man who never did wrong
Suddenly he died one day
The reason why no one could say
. . . Only one clue as to why he died
—A bayonnet sticking in his side.

Would you like to see the world
Billy boy, Billy boy?
Would you like to see the world
Charming Billy?
No it wouldn't be much thrill
To die for Dupont in Brazil.
He's a young boy and cannot leave his mother.

Two songs by the left-wing antiwar Almanac Singers, 1940–41.

Wake up! Wake up, Uncle!

angrily, "we would get such a regimentation of our own lives and livelihoods . . . that the Bill of Rights would need a gas mask, and individual liberty of action would soon become a mocking memory." Professor Edward S. Corwin, a distinguished specialist in constitutional law, observed that the destroyer deal, an executive agreement negotiated without congressional consent, represented "unrestrained presidential power in the conduct of our foreign relations. . . . No such dangerous opinion was ever before penned by an Attorney General of the United States." Charles Beard observed that the war was giving the President extraordinary powers. "With a political machine, a judicial machine, an industrial machine, and a military machine combined under his control, a President of dictatorial propensities could find ready instruments at hand for extending and entrenching his authority." Though most of these arguments exaggerated Roosevelt's power—and distorted his intent—they were almost prophetic in warning against the long-range constitutional effects of modern war.

Central to the isolationist case was the argument that the European war, like World War I, was none of America's business. As Joseph Kennedy put it, "I do not want to see this country go to war under any conditions whatsoever unless we are attacked. . . . England is not fighting our battle. This is not our war." (Kennedy, Roosevelt complained privately, "has been an appeaser and always will be an appeaser. . . . He's just a pain in the neck to me.") The anti-war wing of the Socialist party reached the same conclusion from a more radical perspective. "The cause for which Hitler has thrown the German masses into war," it concluded in April 1940, "is damnably unholy. But the war of England and France is not thereby rendered holy. . . . The Allied governments have no idealism in the conflict, no war aims worthy of the sacrifice of overthrowing fascism except to replace it by a more desperate and brutal government, if need be. . . ."

Few of the isolationists went so far as did these Socialists. They recognized that Hitler was a barbarian, that only the Allies could claim to be defending democracy. But even after the fall of France they persisted in arguing that Britain could survive and if not, that Hitler posed no direct threat to a well-armed United States. Even with Hitler controlling all of Europe—which they thought impossible in the long run—America had the resources to stand alone as a beacon of freedom and self-sufficiency. Because the enemy powers lacked planes that could attack the Western Hemisphere and return, the isolationist concept of "fortress America" was particularly difficult to contest.

None of these arguments convinced Roosevelt. But he shied away from confronting opposition from such an articulate minority—at least until the

There was considerable opposition to a third term for FDR.

NO CROWN FOR FRANKLIN

I'M AGAINST THE 3rd TERM
WASHINGTON WOULDN'T
GRANT COULDN'T
ROOSEVELT SHOULDN'T

NO THIRD TERM

NO MAN IS GOOD THREE TIMES

OUT! STEALING THIRD!

TWO TIMES IS ENOUGH FOR ANY MAN

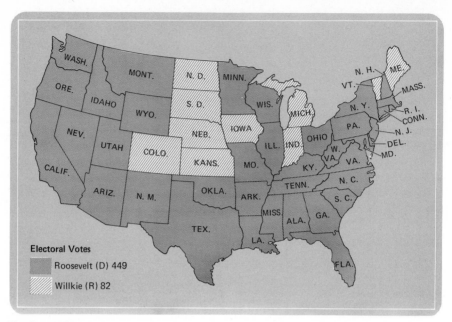

Electoral Votes

▪ Roosevelt (D) 449

▨ Willkie (R) 82

Election, 1940

election was safely behind him. Accordingly, he gave no hint in 1940 that he would request further alterations in the neutrality law. And he uttered his misleading promise that Americans would not "be sent into any foreign wars." With Willkie, an internationalist, proclaiming, "If you elect me I will never send an American boy to fight in a European war," the campaign degenerated into a contest between two charismatic leaders who lacked the courage to admit the probability of war.

After winning the election, Roosevelt moved more directly into the British camp. In December he called for neutrality revision to permit the lending and leasing of American equipment to Britain and her allies. In January he authorized secret staff talks between British and American army officers. In April he negotiated an executive agreement with Denmark permitting the United States to take over bases in Greenland. In July America went still farther into the North Atlantic by occupying Iceland. In the fall Roosevelt belatedly revealed that American destroyers were escorting British convoys across the Atlantic.

These moves infuriated the noninterventionists. Opposing lend-lease, Senator Burton Wheeler called it a Triple A foreign policy that would plow under every fourth American boy. Bitterly, isolationists warned, "when your boy is dying on some battlefield in Europe, and he's crying out, 'Mother, Mother,' don't blame Franklin D. Roosevelt because he sent your boy to war. Blame YOURSELF, because YOU sent Franklin D. Roosevelt back to the White House."

Such rhetoric aside, the isolationists were correct about the President's lack of candor. His supporters numbered the lend-lease bill 1776 and disarmingly entitled it "An Act Further to Promote the Defense of the United States." Roosevelt himself said that extending lend-lease was the same as offering a neighbor an old garden hose to help him extinguish a fire. When the fire was out, the hose would be returned. If the hose were destroyed, the neighbor would provide a new one. Taft remarked pointedly that Roosevelt should have talked about lending chewing gum: after it had been used, no one would want it back. Lend-lease, he added, repealed the "cash" half of cash and carry and exposed American goods to German attack at sea. Inevitably, the administration would respond by dispatching naval vessels on convoy duty. Shooting on the high seas would follow. Vandenberg lamented after the Senate vote, "I had the feeling, as the result of the ballot was announced, that I was witnessing the suicide of the Republic."

As Roosevelt had hoped, lend-lease proved to be of vital assistance not only to Britain but (after Hitler invaded Russia in June 1941) to the Soviet Union; by 1945 it totaled some $50 billion, or four times the amount loaned the Allies between 1917 and 1919. But the isolationists were equally correct in predicting the use of American naval vessels as escorts, which began in late summer. Roosevelt, however, at first concealed this fact from the public. He

Punch, January 1941

A British view of lend-lease.

also resorted to deliberate falsehood when the American destroyer *Greer,* which had been tracking German submarines for the British, was harassed early in September. The *Greer,* the President announced angrily, had been carrying passengers and mail to Iceland when it was attacked without provocation. Henceforth, he added, American naval vessels were authorized to shoot at hostile vessels on sight. As in 1964, when Americans hailed President Johnson's "defense" of Tonkin Gulf, more than 70 percent of Americans reported in a poll that they approved of Roosevelt's course.

Further incidents on the Atlantic followed quickly. Eleven Americans on the destroyer *Kearney* were killed after a submarine attack October 11, and 115 lost their lives on the destroyer *Reuben James* October 31. These assaults led FDR to ask for permission to arm merchant ships, to send them across the Atlantic, and to let them enter European ports in the previously prohibited war zones. When Congress reluctantly agreed, it dismantled the "carry" part of cash and carry and tore down the last important prop in the neutrality legislation it had laboriously erected in the 1930s. Full-scale war with Germany was now but a matter of time.

Roosevelt and Hitler: an evaluation

The case against Roosevelt's European policy was never made better than by the isolationists themselves at the time. The President, they insisted, decided sometime in 1940 (perhaps earlier) that Hitler must be defeated, even if it meant American participation in the war. To that end, he deceived the people. Involvement in the war, critics added, was not necessary to advance United States interests. By March 1941 Britain, without lend-lease assistance, had succeeded in deterring Hitler from invasion, and after June, when Germany invaded the Soviet Union, America could have watched the two dictatorial countries tear each other apart. Even if Hitler defeated the Soviet Union and then overran Britain, he would be too absorbed in managing his far-flung empire to threaten the Western Hemisphere. The administration, isolationists concluded, need not have adopted lend-lease. Or, having done so, it should have been restrained enough to avoid incidents on the Atlantic and patient enough to await European developments.

Some of these arguments were well taken. Though Roosevelt vacillated until mid-1940, it is fairly clear that he thereafter entertained the possibility of entering the war. In the election campaign, in his argument for lend-lease, and in his handling of the convoy question, he did not tell the whole truth. The isolationists may also have been correct in maintaining that Russia and Britain could hold out (though lend-lease was already of some help in 1941), that Germany was overextended, and that Hitler—at least in 1941—had no quarrel to pick with the United States. As late as November, America could have prevented an escalation of hostilities on the Atlantic if it had refrained from arming its ships and sending them into the war zones.

Later critics were persuasive in rejecting the argument that Roosevelt's ends justified his means. Granted that the isolationists had become an increasingly unbending obstacle. Still, he relied much more heavily on deception than on democratic methods of persuasion. Placing the end before the means set precedents for presidential aggrandizement and dishonesty, which later occupants of the White House would emulate for ignobler ends.

Nevertheless, the President's conduct of European affairs after 1939 has to be understood in the context of the times. Unlike some of his opponents, Roosevelt was correct in suspecting that Hitler's ambitions truly knew no bounds. If Hitler had gained control of all of Europe, he would have destroyed Western civilization. He would have been free to exterminate even more of European Jewry and to develop jet planes, rockets, and the A-bombs (on which his scientists were working), to threaten the Western Hemisphere. With Japan and Italy, with whom he had signed the Tripartite Pact in September 1940, he would have controlled most of the industrial world. It so happened, of course, that Britain and Russia still stood in his way in late 1941. But as Germany slashed toward Moscow, the need for all-out aid to Britain and Russia seemed overwhelming. As any head of state must, Roosevelt acted on the basis of his perception of the world at the time, not on speculation about the future.

Roosevelt was also less bellicose than his critics liked to think. Until 1939 he appeared resigned to, if not in fact content with, a policy of appeasement. Thereafter he worked to aid the Allies, but until mid-1941 he still hoped to keep America from the fighting. Even on December 7, with blood coloring the waters of the Atlantic, he desisted from asking for war against Germany. That came on December 11, when Hitler acted first. That Hitler did not have to declare war on the United States (the Tripartite Pact required him to aid his allies only if they were attacked) was final testimony to his ambitions and to his weakening grasp on reality. So long as such a madman existed, no great power could feel safe for long.

Toward war with Japan

One of Hitler's excuses for aggression was the need for *Lebensraum*—space to expand. The military leaders who dominated Japan during the 1930s made the same claim. Japan, they insisted, needed guaranteed access to raw materials and foodstuffs to feed a rapidly growing, highly industrialized population. This was a somewhat specious argument, for expansion into Korea and Manchuria had not benefited the Japanese people. But the military made good use of it nonetheless: only through the Greater East Asia Co-Prosperity Sphere, an empire embracing much of China, Southeast Asia, and the western Pacific, could Japan feel secure in the future.

In contending with this bellicosity, Roosevelt was much freer to act tough

Japanese aggression in Asia and Pacific, 1931–1942

toward Japan than he was in dealing with Europe. One reason for this freedom was that most Americans focused on the more frightening developments in Europe; by contrast, the endless fighting in China seemed unlikely to involve the United States in war. Another reason was the mystique of the Open Door policy, which presumably made the United States the protector of China— and of American economic interests in Asia. Other Americans embraced the vision of Pearl Buck's best selling *The Good Earth* (1937), a sugary glorification of the Chinese peasant. Roosevelt (whose maternal grandfather had made a fortune in the China trade), also sentimentalized the Chinese as a potentially great but exploited people who needed western beneficence to achieve their destiny. It followed that the United States must protect this helpless giant from the predations of foreign powers like Japan.

American images of Japan reinforced these feelings. Compared to the Chinese, they seemed competitive, expansive, militaristic—the "yellow peril" that racist writers had described for decades. Exploiters of labor, they threatened to engulf the West with "cheap Jap goods." For all their energy, they were little people who built top-heavy ships and whose nearsighted pilots were no match for a determined enemy. As Freda Utley implied in her *Japan: Feet of Clay* (1937), Japan would never dare to fight, much less attack, a western nation like the United States.

What little sympathy existed for Japan evaporated in the wake of events after 1937. Japanese forces, uncontrolled by civilian leadership, bombed Chinese cities and pillaged the countryside. In Nanking they slaughtered 100,000 Chinese. When France and Holland fell to Germany in 1940, Japan moved quickly to dominate French Indo-China and the oil-rich Dutch East Indies. By the end of the year the blueprint for the co-prosperity sphere was clear: Japan would conquer China, insist on control of valuable resources in Indo-China and the Indies, and demand that the West mind its own business.

American racist stereotypes about Asia combined with Japanese aggressiveness explain why even the isolationists—so determined to tie Roosevelt's hands in Europe—rather inconsistently approved of a tough policy in the Pacific. Asians (and Latin Americans) were easier—so it was thought—to cow into submission. In July 1939 the United States served notice that in six months it would feel free to impose economic sanctions, and in July 1940, after the Japanese demands on Southeast Asia, America clamped an embargo on shipments of top grades of gasoline and scrap iron to Japan. The embargo left Japan free to buy iron ore and lower grades of oil, which could be refined for military use. But the message to Japan was clear: refrain from expansion or face further reprisals.

When the Japanese refused to budge, even moderates like Joseph Grew, America's experienced ambassador in Tokyo, were disillusioned. "Until such time as there is a complete regeneration of thought in this country," he wrote in September 1940, "a show of force, together with a determination to employ it if need be, can alone contribute effectively to the achievement of such an outcome and to our own future security." This "green light" message, as it was called, was strong grounds for tightening the American noose on exports. When Japan moved its armies into Indo-China on September 24, America responded immediately with an embargo on scrap iron and scrap steel.

America's policy of economic warfare had much to commend it. Restrained, it awaited overt Japanese acts before being applied. Incremental, it gave Japan time to reconsider its course. Roosevelt hoped it would assist Japan's more moderate leaders and deflect the military from its course of conquest. And what else was he to do? With the threat of Hitler to worry about, he could hardly push for war in Asia, nor could he happily provide Japan with the means to overwhelm China and the Indies.

The trouble with economic war was that the Japanese were determined to achieve their co-prosperity sphere. Though moderates occasionally called for caution, they were much too weak, indeed they were intimidated by assassinations, to stand in the way of the armed forces, who pointed out that American reprisals made command over the resources of Southeast Asia that much more essential. FDR's reliance on economic warfare—as so often in world history—proved more provocative than persuasive.

The war of wills then proceeded. Japan's answer to the tightened embargo was to announce the Tripartite Pact with Germany and Italy two days later. In April 1941 it protected its northern flank by negotiating a five-year nonaggression pact with Russia. In July it demanded air bases in southern Indo-China, within range of the East Indies. Hull responded to these demands by agreeing with the Dutch and English to freeze Japanese assets and to impose a total embargo. As Grew observed, "the vicious circle of reprisals and counterreprisals is on. . . . Unless radical surprises occur in the world, it is difficult to see how the momentum of the down-grade movement can be arrested, or how far it will go. The obvious conclusion is eventual war."

In the months of peace that remained several issues divided the two powers. One was Japan's true relationship with Germany. America demanded that Japan reveal its obligations under the Tripartite Pact, which Tokyo refused to do. Another issue was China. Hull clung to the Open Door: Japan must withdraw. The Japanese, however, countered by insisting on retaining troops and economic rights in China. They demanded also that America stop aiding Chiang Kai-shek and that it recognize Manchukuo, the puppet government in Manchuria. A third bone of contention was the status of southern Indo-China, which Roosevelt insisted the Japanese evacuate. Japan said no, and followed by demanding that America end its embargo on oil. Indo-China was already an important pawn in the chess game of international politics.

At times it appeared that compromise might break the deadlock. In August 1941 Prime Minister Fumimoro Konoye, who hoped for peace, proposed a summit conference with Roosevelt. Hull, however, rejected the idea by pointing out that the Japanese promised no concessions and that militarists were insisting on accompanying Konoye to the conference. Two months later Konoye fell and was replaced by War Minister Hideki Tojo. Recognizing the weakness of civilian leadership, Konoye included a heading in his memoirs: "The independence of the Supreme Command and State Affairs from Each Other: The Anguish of Cabinets from Generation to Generation."

Tojo's government then made a final proposal in November. If America agreed to stop helping Chiang, if it assisted Japan to secure access to raw materials in the East Indies, and if it restored economic relations to their status before the freeze in July, Japan would promise to pull its troops out of southern Indo-China. When the war with China was over, Japan would withdraw from Indo-China entirely. After rejecting suggestions that America make concessions, Hull drafted the so-called modus vivendi of November 25. It called on Japan to renounce further expansion in any direction, to reduce her forces in northern Indo-China, and to get out of southern Indo-China immediately. In return America would admit small quantities of Japanese imports and send some cotton and oil (for civilian use only) to Japan.

To American military leaders, who wanted a few more weeks to ferry bombers to the Philippines, the modus vivendi promised at least to buy time. It brought the two adversaries slightly closer on the issue of Indo-China and the related fate of the Indies. But bombers would have been useless without fighter escorts, which were not to be spared for Asia. Hull noted also that America was asked to make economic concessions right away, *after* which Japan would respond. Given past Japanese behavior, he had little trust in such assurances. He knew that a Japanese task force was even then steaming toward the Indies. And he was under strong pressure from China and Great Britain to make no concessions whatever. The modus vivendi was never delivered.

In failing to respond Hull knew that war must follow. "I have washed my hands of it," he told Secretary of War Stimson. "It is now in the hands of you and [Secretary of the Navy] Knox—the Army and the Navy." Four days later, on December 1, Japan secretly reaffirmed its decision for carrier-launched attacks on December 7. (To wait longer would be to risk unfavorable weather patterns and to endanger oil supplies.) Its task forces, already under way, ploughed toward Hawaii and the Indies. Roosevelt toyed with the idea of appealing to Emperor Hirohito, but did nothing about it until December 6, far too late for any impact. That night American experts, who had broken many top Japanese codes, began to decipher a truculent fourteen-part message sent from Tokyo to the Japanese ambassador in Washington. Informed of the first thirteen parts that night, Roosevelt remarked simply, "This means war."

The Japanese attack on Hawaii came at dawn the next day, Pearl Harbor time. Fortunately for the United States, American carriers were out at sea. But Japan's torpedo bombers were otherwise devastating. The raid destroyed or severely damaged 8 battleships, 3 light cruisers, and 188 planes, and inflicted 3,435 American casualties. It was the worst loss in American history.

When the Japanese attacked Pearl, it was about 2:00 P.M. on Sunday in Washington. Cordell Hull, awaiting two Japanese emissaries in his office, already knew from the code-breakers that war was imminent, and Roosevelt had called him with the news about Hawaii. The Japanese, including the ambassador, then arrived and handed Hull an uninformative note. Kept in the dark by the military in Tokyo, they had negotiated in good faith with Hull for months. Now, because their aides were still struggling to read the fourteen-part note, they did not even know of the attack. Hull kept them standing while pretending to read their message. Then he burst forth. "In all my fifty years of public service," he said, "I have never seen a document that was more crowded with infamous falsehoods and distortions—on a scale so huge that I never imagined until today that any Government on this planet was capable of uttering them." The Japanese struggled for words, but Hull cut them off with a nod towards the door.

The USS *Arizona, Tennessee,* and *West Virginia* after the attack on Pearl Harbor, 1941.

The next day Roosevelt called for a declaration of war. With but one dissenting vote (that of Jeannette Rankin, a Montana pacifist who had also voted against World War I), the House agreed. The Senate vote was unanimous. When Germany then joined Japan, America was involved—at last—in World War II.

REVISIONISTS AND PEARL HARBOR

The Japanese success at Pearl Harbor naturally prompted outraged calls for an investigation of "blundering" American officialdom. In later years it also led revisionist historians to lambast the whole course of Roosevelt's diplomacy.

Some of these revisionists were bitter in the extreme. The historian Harry Elmer Barnes charged that "Roosevelt's political ambitions and his mendacious foreign policy" led "some 3000 American boys [to be] quite needlessly butchered at Pearl Harbor." Charles Tansill, in his appropriately entitled book *Back Door to War,* concluded that Roosevelt, having failed to draw Germany into war, deliberately provoked the Japanese. "In 1941," he wrote, "Roosevelt's orchestra of death was anxiously waiting for the signal to begin the new symphony. He had hoped for a German motif but Hitler had refused to open with a few martial notes. Perhaps some Japanese statesman would prove more accommodating? At any rate . . . he turned his eyes toward the Orient and sought new inspiration from the inscrutable East."

Though Tansill went so far as to imply that Roosevelt invited the attack, most revisionists contented themselves with uncovering American blunders. Some of these errors were military. Why had American naval leaders placed the battleships so invitingly close together in the harbor? Why had they not set baffles before the ships in order to protect them against torpedo bombers? Why were planes lined up openly and bunched together on the airstrips? How had a virtual Japanese armada steamed within fighter plane range of Hawaii? Why didn't army chief General George Marshall send his final warning—of the fourteen-part note—by wireless instead of by Western Union? (The message took more than ten hours to reach American commanders in Hawaii, and was delivered by a messenger on a bicycle after the attack had caught the United States by surprise.)

Many revisionists focused on the government's role in the Pearl Harbor debacle. Why had Roosevelt, despite contrary advice from some naval experts, sent the Pacific fleet from the West Coast to the more exposed base in Hawaii? Since America had broken some top Japanese codes, why were the military commanders at Pearl not informed that a rupture in relations was imminent? As early as January 1941 Ambassador Grew had told Washington: "there is a lot of talk around town to the effect that the Japanese, in case of a break with the United States, are planning to go all out in a surprise attack on Pearl Harbor." Why wasn't Hawaii alerted to evidence of this nature?

Some of these questions were well founded. Though short of equipment, the military at Pearl could have done a more thorough job of searching the Pacific west and north of Hawaii. Junior officers and enlisted men could have acted more quickly to report last-minute signals, such as the blips representing Japanese planes found on a radar screen, or the Japanese midget submarine discovered in the harbor itself shortly before the attack. Given the possibility that the Japanese would soon declare war (a Honolulu paper on November 30 had carried the headline, "Japanese May Strike over Weekend"), the military at Pearl should have been better prepared.

These errors, however, were of the human kind that all nations tend to make. There was no conspiracy to tempt the Japanese into attacking. Roose-

Including the movement of aviation now in progress, Hawaii will be defended by 35 of our most modern flying fortresses, 35 medium range bombers, 13 light bombers, 150 pursuit bombers of which 105 are of our most modern type. In addition Hawaii is capable of reinforcement by heavy bombers from the mainland by air. With this force available a major attack against Oahu is considered impracticable.

In point of sequence, sabotage is first to be expected . . .

General Marshall explains to FDR, May 1941, that sabotage, not Japanese attack, is the likely problem at Pearl Harbor.

velt had moved the fleet to Hawaii to warn Japan, not to expose it. The planes were bunched together so that they could be guarded against sabotage, which is what the Hawaiian commanders had been ordered by Marshall to expect. The final warning had gone by Western Union so that the Japanese could not pick it up on the wireless. Washington failed to keep Hawaii fully informed because it had to refrain from sending messages that might tip off the Japanese that their codes had been cracked.

Cultural and racist presuppositions lay at the root of these human errors. Assuming the Japanese to have "feet of clay," Americans doubted that they could develop torpedo bombers capable of sinking large ships in shallow water, or that their "nearsighted" pilots could maneuver so capably. The blips, radar watchers thought, must be American planes circling in for a landing; the submarine must have strayed. Americans dismissed the very idea that Orientals would dare to attack a bastion of western defense like Pearl Harbor. Instead, the attack—if it came at all—would be on British and Dutch possessions in the East Indies, toward which a Japanese task force was known to be heading. (The attack came there, too.) It was these failings—a lack of imagination, of historical perspective, of cultural understanding—and not gross stupidity or conspiracy that made the attack so successful.

ROOSEVELT'S ASIAN DIPLOMACY

The furor over Pearl Harbor obscured three basic questions about Roosevelt's Asian diplomacy.

1. Could America have deterred Japan from its aggressive course without getting involved in war?

2. Could the United States have postponed the impasse?

3. Should the United States have engaged in the war against Japan at all?

The answer to the first question is almost certainly no. The Japanese longing for the Greater East Asia Co-Prosperity Sphere was shared by practically all shades of influential opinion, including Konoye as well as Tojo. It was repeatedly reaffirmed in 1940 and 1941, even though the war in China was already a severe drain on Japanese resources. If America hoped to discourage Japanese ambitions, its best course short of war was the one it pursued:

economic warfare. As it happened, this course drove the Japanese to acts of desperation, including the attack on Pearl Harbor. But the alternative, desisting from economic sanctions, would obviously have played into Japanese hands. So long as the administration made it its policy to deter Japan, armed conflict was highly likely.

America could have tried harder to postpone the impasse. In July 1941 Roosevelt could have thought twice before tightening the economic sanctions that had already proved provocative. If so, Japan might not have felt driven to move so fast. In August he could have stalled for time by agreeing to meet Konoye or by exchanging long notes about the agenda for the conference. Such an exchange might have sustained the Konoye government for a few more weeks and delayed the more aggressive plans of Tojo. In November a secretary of state less rigid than Hull might have delivered the modus vivendi or proposed some other softening of America's economic war. The Japanese might then have paused to consider an answer.

Such possibilities were unlikely, since by August 1941 the Japanese military had set an almost irreversible timetable. It is therefore unlikely that Roosevelt could have done much to postpone the war beyond very early 1942. Still, it is sad that America did not exhaust all hopes for postponement. And to secure time to prepare, it is unfortunate that Hull did not try harder to coordinate diplomatic responses with the needs of the army and the navy. If he had, such disasters as Pearl Harbor, and the defeats at Bataan and Corregidor, might have been less severe.

Should America have fought the war at all? The tempting answer to this question is no, for America's real interests in Asia, except for Guam and the Philippines (which were due to be set loose in 1946), were limited. Despite the rhetoric about the Open Door, China was of little value economically or

I recall talking to the President many times in the past year and it always disturbed him because he really thought that the tactics of the Japanese would be to avoid a conflict with us; that they would not attack either the Philippines or Hawaii but would move on Thailand, French Indo-China, make further inroads on China itself and possibly attack the Malay Straits. He also thought they would attack Russia at an opportune moment. This would have left the President with the very difficult problem of protecting our interests.

He always realized that Japan would jump on us at an opportune moment and they would merely use the 'one by one' technique of Germany. Hence his great relief at the method used. In spite of the disaster of Pearl Harbor and the blitz-warfare with the Japanese during the first few weeks, it completely solidified the American people and made the war upon Japan inevitable.

Harry Hopkins, six weeks after Pearl Harbor, reveals that FDR was "relieved" by the attack.

militarily to the United States. Nor were Indo-China and the atolls of the western Pacific. Even the tin and rubber of the East Indies could have been dispensed with or replaced by synthetics and alloys. To go to war in defense of these areas was to aid British, Dutch, and French imperialism and to tie up American forces needed for the fight ahead against Hitler.

In retrospect it is not clear whether the war did much to advance long-range western interests in Asia. The turmoil unleashed anti-Western feelings that all but destroyed British, Dutch, and French power in the area. It permitted the Soviet Union to move into the vacuum left by Japan. It assisted the growth of communism in China and Indo-China. As John MacMurray, the former chief of the Far Eastern division of the State Department, phrased it in 1939, "the defeat of Japan would not mean her elimination from the problems of the Far East. . . . It would merely create a new set of stresses and substitute for Japan the USSR as the successor. . . . Nobody except Russia would gain from our victory in such a war."

But these arguments, like those that criticize American toughness toward Hitler, fail to appreciate the crisis atmosphere of the time. Japan had been molesting China, land of the supposed Open Door, for years, and by 1941 Americans were understandably impatient. Why, they asked, should America keep on sending vital supplies to such an aggressor? Why also should Japan be permitted to take over the rich resources of the Indies? China asked the same questions, as did England, which in 1941 desperately needed American support in Asia. It would have been politically hazardous for FDR to refrain from retaliatory economic measures—the only ones he could employ—against the accelerating Japanese advance.

This is another way of saying that Roosevelt, far from seeking a "back door to war" in Asia, wanted very much to avoid it. But the Japanese, like Germany in 1917, had determined on a course that narrowed his choice of policy. In so doing, they invited war against a nation they knew they could never conquer. Indeed, their great "success" at Pearl Harbor, which they hoped would neutralize the United States long enough to solidify their conquests in Southeast Asia, was their greatest blunder of all, for it united America as nothing else could have. Senator Wheeler, an avid isolationist, commented, "The only thing to do now is to lick hell out of them." The *Chicago Tribune* changed the slogan on its masthead from "Save our Republic" to "Our Country Right or Wrong." Others, "remembering Pearl Harbor," later thought nothing of demanding unconditional surrender, of fire-bombing Japanese cities, and of obliterating Hiroshima and Nagasaki.

The intractability of Japan had the still more fundamental effect of nearly demolishing pacifism and anti-interventionism in America. As Vandenberg put it, "that day [December 7] ended isolationism for any realist." Vandenberg meant that the dawn of air power ended America's historic safety from foreign attack. Like his contemporaries he also meant that America must never again be caught unprepared. There must be no more appeasement, no more "Munichs." The United States must stay armed and ready to meet potential threats all over the globe. Like a sleepy giant, America staggered to its feet in 1941, battered its enemies for four years, and kept on swinging in all directions until the strain of ten years in Vietnam took its toll.

Suggestions for reading

The major books covering foreign policy in the Hoover era are Robert Ferrell, *American Diplomacy in the Great Depression: Hoover-Stimson Foreign Policy, 1929–1933* (1957); Elting Morison, *Turmoil and Tradition: A Study of the Life and Times of Henry L. Stimson** (1960); and Richard Current, *Secretary Stimson: A Study in Statecraft* (1954). For the 1930s consult John E. Wiltz, *From Isolation to War, 1931–1941** (1968), an excellent brief interpretation; and Julius Pratt, *Cordell Hull*, 2 vols. (1964). Bryce Wood, *Making of the Good Neighbor Policy** (1954) expertly covers its subject. Lloyd Gardner, *Economic Aspects of New Deal Diplomacy* (1964) emphasizes economic considerations.

Four excellent books deal with isolationism and its manifestations in the 1930s. They are: John E. Wiltz, *In Search of Peace: The Senate Munitions Inquiry, 1934–1936** (1963); Robert Divine, *The Illusion of Neutrality** (1962), which focuses on congressional battles; Manfred Jonas, *Isolationism in America, 1935–1941** (1969), a study of ideas; and Wayne S. Cole, *America First* (1953). Coverage of America's response to the Spanish civil war is provided in Allen Guttmann, *The Wound in the Heart: America and the Spanish Civil War* (1962); and Richard P. Traina, *American Diplomacy and the Spanish Civil War* (1968). Beatrice Farnsworth, *William C. Bullitt and the Soviet Union* (1967), and Edward E. Bennett, *Recognition of Russia** (1970), deal with Soviet-American relations in the 1930s.

For American involvement in World War II, consult first the detailed volumes by William Langer and S. Everett Gleason, *Challenge to Isolation, 1937–1940** (1952), and *The Undeclared War, 1940–1941** (1953). See also Theodore A. Wilson, *The First Summit: Roosevelt and Churchill at Placentia Bay, 1941* (1969); Arnold Offner, *America's Appeasement of Germany* (1968); and Robert Dallek, *Democrat and Diplomat: The Life of William E. Dodd* (1968) about America's ambassador to Germany. An excellent brief interpretation is Robert A. Divine, *Franklin D. Roosevelt and World War II** (1969). Books that criticize the way in which Roosevelt maneuvered the country into war include Charles A. Beard's older revisionist accounts, *American Foreign Policy in the Making, 1932–1940* (1946) and *President Roosevelt and the Coming of War, 1941* (1948); and a provocative brief interpretation by Bruce Russett, *No Clear and Present Danger** (1972). An iconoclastic account of European diplomacy is A. J. P. Taylor, *Origins of World War II** (rev. ed., 1968). See also Alan Bullock, *Hitler** (1952); and Alton Frye, *Nazi Germany and the Western Hemisphere, 1933–1941* (1967).

Diplomacy involving Asia is covered in Dorothy Borg, *The United States and Far Eastern Crises of 1933–1938* (1964); Herbert Feis, *Road to Pearl Harbor** (1950); Waldo H. Heinrichs, *American Ambassador: Joseph C. Grew and the Development of the United States Diplomatic Tradition* (1966); Charles E. Neu, *The Troubled Encounter: The U.S. and Japan** (1975); Robert Butow, *Tojo and the Coming of the War* (1961); and Paul Schroeder, *The Axis Alliance and Japanese-American Relations* (1958). For Pearl Harbor see Robert Wohlstetter, *Pearl Harbor** (1962), a brilliant study of intelligence problems; and Walter Lord, *Day of Infamy** (1957), a popular account.

10

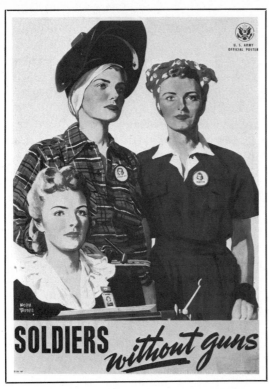

SOLDIERS *without guns*

World War II: the great divide

Beginning around 1939, the social historian John Brooks concluded, America began a "Greap Leap" toward the future. The critic Irving Kristol added that the 1930s were the "last amateur decade." Both writers properly stressed the incalculable impact of World War II on American life. In every area—military and diplomatic affairs, politics, social and economic relations—the war greatly accelerated the processes of economic change, political centralization, and international involvement that were the grand themes of American twentieth-century life. More than ever before, there was no turning back.

The military effort

America's primary task after the attack on Pearl Harbor was of course to settle on the quickest, most effective way of defeating the enemy. This problem, in turn, raised four major questions, all of which had profound long-range implications.

Which adversary, Germany or Japan, was to be concentrated on first? Should the enemy be totally defeated or, as in 1918, be permitted to reach an armistice? What emphasis should Britain and the United States place on strategic bombing, thought by some to be a way of avoiding the bloodbath of World War I? Where, and when, should Allied ground forces actually attack Germany and Japan?

The answer to the first question aroused little controversy at the time. At least as early as the fall of France, Roosevelt and his advisers considered Germany the number one enemy, and in March 1941 British and American military leaders agreed. After the attack on Pearl Harbor, Prime Minister Winston Churchill came to the United States for the first of many summit conferences, and the agreement became official policy.

At times during the war Roosevelt appeared to depart from this position. In mid-1942, American naval forces scored unexpectedly quick victories at the battles of Midway and Coral Sea, and Admiral Chester Nimitz, commander in the central Pacific, was authorized to mount offensives against Japanese-held islands. By October America had more forces deployed against Japan than against Germany; by the spring of 1943 Nimitz's forces had captured the Solomon Islands; and by October 1944, after desperate island battles, American soldiers were invading the Philippines. This military progress in the Pacific caused a few critics to argue later that America should have concentrated its efforts against Japan, thereby leaving Hitler and Stalin to destroy each other in the West.

Roosevelt refused to go that far. The offensives against Japan were expropriating landing ships needed for a full-scale amphibious assault on the European continent. Roosevelt recognized that any American invasion of Japan's home islands would encounter fanatical resistance. He also had to

---

Whether nations live in prosperity or starve to death interests me only so far as we need them for slaves for our Kultur; otherwise it is of no interest to me. Whether 10,000 Russian females fall down from exhaustion while digging an anti-tank ditch interests me only in so far as the anti-tank ditch for Germany is finished. We shall never be rough and heartless when it is not necessary, that is clear. We Germans, who are the only people in the world who have a decent attitude toward animals, will also assume a decent attitude toward these human animals. But it is a crime against our blood to worry about them and giving them ideals, thus causing our sons and grandsons to have a more difficult time with them. When someone comes to me and says: "I cannot dig the anti-tank ditch with women and children, it is inhuman, for it will kill them," then I have to say "You are the murderer of your own blood, because if the anti-tank ditch is not dug German soldiers will die, and they are the sons of German mothers. They are our own blood."

Heinrich Himmler, head of the Nazi SS, explains the nature of modern war.

respond to the incessant pleas of Josef Stalin, his wartime ally, for aid against Germany. And like most of his contemporaries, the President was anxious to destroy the scourge of Hitler first and forever. For all these reasons he paid little attention to the "Asia-firsters" (whose counsel might have left Stalin free to overrun all of Europe). Under the circumstances Roosevelt's decision for "Europe first" was both unavoidable and sensible.

The second question was answered formally at the Casablanca conference in January 1943, at which Roosevelt, with Churchill's apparent approval, proclaimed the policy of unconditional surrender. Later, America deviated slightly from it: Italy was permitted to lay down its arms in 1943, and Japan was ultimately allowed to retain its emperor. But the total defeat of the enemy remained at the heart of Roosevelt's thinking. "I do not want them to starve to death," he said of the Germans, "but, as an example, if they need food to keep body and soul together, they should be fed three times a day with soup from army soup kitchens." In late 1944 he even initialed the unrealistically harsh Morgenthau Plan aimed at "converting Germany into a country primarily agricultural and pastoral in character." Though he quickly dropped the plan, he adhered consistently to the central goal, that of beating the enemies so thoroughly that they could never again threaten the peace.

To many postwar critics the policy of unconditional surrender seemed a tragic mistake. Supposedly, it steeled the resolve of the enemies, discouraged leaders of the resistance in Germany and Japan, and practically invited Russia to move into the power vacuum in central Europe and Manchuria. Roosevelt, it appeared, forgot the fundamental maxim that wars are fought for political as well as military objectives.

Some of these criticisms were well taken. American insistence on Japan's unconditional surrender proved a stumbling block (though not the only one) to peace in July 1945, before the dropping of the atomic bombs on Hiroshima and Nagasaki. Otherwise, however, the critics were unfair. No policy, no matter how generous, could have swayed the leaders of Germany and Japan from their destructive course. The threat of unconditional surrender did not prevent dissidents in Germany from attempting to overthrow Hitler—an officers' plot almost succeeded in 1944. And Russia charged into central Europe because its armies were powerful, not because of the policy of unconditional surrender. If Roosevelt had shown the slightest tendency to negotiate a truce with Hitler—which he did not—Stalin would probably have kept on fighting—and have ended up with more territory than he did.

The critics of unconditional surrender also forgot the ruthless nature of modern war. In 1917 it was possible for "Yanks" to believe that they were fighting a war to save democracy; there were ideals to be achieved. In 1941, however, American soldiers were "GIs"—"government issued" machines sent abroad by a much more organized society that remembered Pearl Harbor and loathed Hitler. Like Willie and Joe, cartoonist Bill Mauldin's dirty, unshaven infantrymen, they fought because they had to, and they had few aims save destroying the enemy quickly and coming home. General Lesley J.

McNair, director of the training program for all American ground forces, put it this way to a radio audience in 1942: "We must lust for battle; our object in life must be to kill; we must scheme and plan night and day to kill." What McNair meant, and what every American understood, was that Germany and Japan must be totally defeated. No Allied leader in World War II could have pursued a policy that promised otherwise.

The quest for total victory helps explain Roosevelt's support of scientific research into the development of atomic weaponry. This effort began in October 1939, when Leo Szilard, Enrico Fermi, and other emigré scientists, worried about Nazi progress in the field of atomic physics, persuaded Albert Einstein to write a letter to Roosevelt. The letter urged the President to engage the United States in the race to harness atomic energy. Though responsive to the scientists' pleas, the President moved slowly, and it was not until the summer of 1941 that the administration established a "uranium section" in the National Defense Research Committee.

The attack on Pearl Harbor gave renewed urgency to the program, and in 1942 Secretary of War Henry Stimson placed General Leslie Groves, a tough, secretive administrator, in charge of the Manhattan District Project, code name for bomb development. The project's purpose was to beat the Nazis. Japan, concentrating on more conventional weapons, was never seriously engaged in the race.

From 1942 on, American and emigré scientists working on the program received more than $2 billion in federal funds. All of it was appropriated for unspecified military purposes by a Congress that heeded Stimson's requests not to probe closely into how it was going to be used. Top military leaders, including generals Douglas MacArthur and Dwight Eisenhower, America's army commanders in the Pacific and Atlantic, were kept almost as much in the dark. Working rapidly, scientists at the University of Chicago succeeded in setting off a controlled atomic reaction in December 1942. Other scientists and technicians at secret places like Oak Ridge, Tennessee, and Hanford, Washington, prepared material to be used in the bombs, while J. Robert Oppenheimer headed a bomb manufacture laboratory at Los Alamos, New Mexico. In all, some 540,000 people worked on the project during the war.

This incredibly vast, secret operation enabled the United States to pass Germany, which diverted much of its expertise to jet planes and rocketry and failed to test a bomb before the end of the European war in May 1945. The Manhattan project also testified amply to America's desire to win the war by whatever means necessary, and to the willingness of the nation's elected representatives to turn over authority, no questions asked, to the executive branch. This delegation of responsibility, justified at the time by the need for security, was both unprecedented and frightening.

The passion for total victory also helped to sustain the argument for strategic bombing—mass raids against enemy cities, factories, storage facilities, military bases, and transportation complexes. Theoretically, these raids would do such a thorough job of weakening enemy strength (and morale) that ground forces could complete the job with minimal loss of American life. "Strategic air power," General Henry ("Hap") Arnold claimed, "is a war-winning weapon in its own right, and is capable of striking decisive blows far behind the battle line, thereby destroying the enemy's capacity to wage war."

Though Arnold did not get all the planes he wanted until late in the war, he could hardly complain about the administration. As early as 1940 Roosevelt astounded Congress by asking for production of 50,000 planes per year. By 1942, B-17's and B-24's were already being flown over to Great Britain; by 1943 they were taking off on steady raids against the enemy; and by late 1944 they were smashing the Japanese home cities. Before the end of the war the strategic bombing attacks had leveled many industrial cities in both nations.

Whether strategic bombing was as effective as Arnold claimed was another matter. Undoubtedly, it forced the enemy nations to divert manpower and equipment to reconstruction. In crowded, urban Japan it was so effective that neither the atomic bombs nor an invasion may have been necessary. But until late 1944 it was also terrifically costly to the United States. Only 28 of 120 bombers that took off for a raid on Berlin in July 1943 made it to the target. A month later 60 of 560 B-17's were destroyed in the course of an attack on Regensburg and Schweinfurt. Between February 20 and 26, 1944, America lost 226 bombers, 28 fighter planes, and 2600 crewmen. Only in the last year of the war, when American fighter planes finally gained air supremacy, did these raids become reasonably safe for planes and crew.

Strategic bombing enthusiasts were also far too optimistic about the possibility of "pinpoint" bombing. The British bombed mostly at night and could not be too precise about their targets. Americans were scarcely more accurate. Often it was too overcast to see much; often German fighters or antiaircraft artillery forced American pilots to hurry in and off. Either way, the bombs all too frequently blasted civilian areas. And the British and Americans sometimes resorted to indiscriminate firebombing. One raid against Tokyo killed an estimated 84,000 people and left a million homeless. The city, said one observer, was a "midden of smoking flesh." Another attack by the British and Americans, against nonindustrial Dresden in 1945, killed more than 100,000 people.

Even when the bombs hit their targets, they caused much less disruption than many strategists supposed. Against Japan in 1945 they were devastating, for by then many key targets were defenseless. Germany, however, always maintained surplus factory space and labor, and the bombers caused more inconvenience than crisis. Die-hard enthusiasts of bombing argued later that America's mistake was only in not staging enough raids against German oil reserves, necessary for most forms of production. Perhaps so. But because that was not done, it cannot be proved that bombing the oil reserves would have made a significant difference. What is known is that Germany's productive capacity increased until the last weeks of the war.

These limitations of bombing should have suggested that modern war requires great flexibility in response, that not only bombers but also fighters,

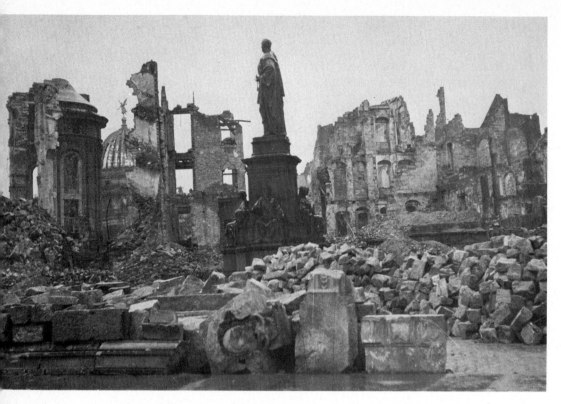

Dresden, Germany, after Allied bombing.

tanks, and—as ever—infantry are essential to victory. Unfortunately, however, strategic bombing continued to offer an almost fatal allure after the war. To many people anxious for quick solutions to complex international problems it seemed a "surgical" way to dispose of troublesome opponents. So President Truman thought in authorizing the incineration of Hiroshima; so General Douglas MacArthur thought in advocating the blasting of Manchuria in 1951; so Secretary of State John Foster Dulles thought in talking about "massive retaliation" against Russia in 1954; and so America's "best and brightest" leaders thought during a decade of war in Vietnam.

The fourth military question—where and when to attack the enemy—was ultimately avoided in the Asian theater, where a land invasion of Japan's home islands proved unnecessary. Regarding Europe, however, it sparked heated debate.

At first it was assumed that Britain and the United States would attack Germany's western front as soon as possible. Stalin, whose people were suffering horribly, insisted on help right away. He was supported by American army leaders like Marshall and Dwight D. Eisenhower, commander of the war plans division. "We've got to go to Europe and fight," Eisenhower said in

January 1942, "and quit wasting resources all over the world—and still worse, wasting time."

With men like Marshall so optimistic, Roosevelt led Stalin to believe that America would stage a second front before the end of 1942. But he then had to confront Churchill, whose cooperation was essential to the success of a cross-Channel invasion. Churchill vividly remembered the frightful British losses in World War I, especially in the disastrous amphibious assault at Gallipoli, which he had engineered himself. He was also persuaded, probably correctly, that the Allies lacked sufficient men and equipment, especially landing ships for vehicles. Accordingly, he insisted on smaller attacks against Germany's periphery in the Mediterranean. Roosevelt had no choice but to postpone the invasion to 1943.

Churchill's stand infuriated American army leaders. Stimson dismissed it as "pin-prick warfare," and Eisenhower suggested concentrating on Japan. Roosevelt, however, replied no—"that would be like taking up our dishes and going home." FDR realized that Stalin, to say nothing of the American public, would expect the army to fight somewhere against the Germans in 1942. So he accepted Churchill's plan for an offensive in November in North Africa, where Britain had historic interests. "In wartime," Marshall observed sourly, "the politicians have to do *something* important every year. They could not simply use 1942 to build up for 1943 or 1944: they could not face the obloquy of fighting another 'phony war.'"

When the North African campaign proved successful, Marshall and Eisenhower hoped for a cross-Channel invasion in 1943. Churchill, however, still posed objections, and at Casablanca in January he persuaded Roosevelt to agree to "pin-prick warfare" against Sicily and Italy. Marshall observed angrily that "we lost our shirts . . . we came, we listened, and we were conquered." Moreover, the Italian campaign proved costly: at war's end in 1945 Allied troops were still battling their way up the peninsula. So the months slipped by without the long-anticipated invasion. Not until the Teheran summit conference of November 1943 did the Russians receive a guarantee for an attack early in 1944.

Churchill's fear of an English Channel "running red with the blood of British and American boys" also caused him to suggest the so-called soft-underbelly strategy. This called for an Allied invasion of the Adriatic coast, to be followed by an offensive into southeastern Europe, where Stalin's onrushing armies would join in the attack. To this idea, however, Americans sensibly objected. Such an invasion would have been difficult to stage so far from the main Allied bases in Britain. It would have committed soldiers to very difficult mountainous terrain that was not "soft" at all. At war's end it might have given Russia some claim to occupy parts of western Europe. Churchill's advocacy of the soft-underbelly idea revealed him to be an imaginative but not very sound armchair strategist.

Churchill was probably right in arguing that a second front in 1943, when the Allies lacked full control of the air, would have been costly. But the

FDR visits Sicily in late 1943 accompanied by his commander of the European theater of operations, General Dwight D. Eisenhower.

political ramifications of postponing "D day" to June 1944 were equally unfortunate, for Stalin, having been assured of aid in 1942 and again in 1943, grew ever more suspicious of his English-speaking allies. And when the front finally materialized, his armies were already poised on Germany's eastern borders. At war's end he had little reason to be trustful of the "friends" who were so slow to help in his time of trial.

Roosevelt's handling of these military questions subjected him later to complaints that he was the same short-sighted opportunist during the war that he had sometimes been during the New Deal. If he had thought more often about the postwar world, critics argued, he would have insisted on a second front in 1943 and done all he could to build up ground forces capable of getting into eastern Europe before the Russians. Barring that, he should have agreed to a conditional surrender before the Russians moved into Germany. These arguments ask the impossible. Neither the American public nor Roosevelt's allies would have tolerated conditional surrender, and Churchill stood in the way of a harmoniously organized invasion prior to 1944. In acting to safeguard military victory and to keep the voters behind him in a long and bloody struggle, FDR did what any democratic leader in war has to do.

Wartime diplomacy

Complaints about Roosevelt's military leadership were but part of broader attacks on his diplomacy. Left-wing critics later charged him with refusing to stand up to imperialists like Churchill and with cooperating with decadent forces in China and France. Right-wingers countered by accusing him of naiveté concerning the Soviet Union. Whatever he did, it seemed he could not win.

The left-wing critics focused first on Roosevelt's dealings with Vichy France, the pro-Nazi collaborators who controlled much of France following Hitler's victory in 1940. First he recognized the puppet regime. Then, in planning the North African invasion he (and Eisenhower) worked carefully with Admiral Jean Darlan, head of the Vichy fleet. The "deal" secured Darlan's noninterference with the Allied invasion. But it also annoyed General Charles de Gaulle, the super-sensitive leader of the French resistance forces, and it outraged many American progressives. The United States, they thought, was tainted by association with fascists.

The American Left also disliked his handling of China. During the war Chiang Kai-shek, the Nationalist leader, antagonized American officials by fighting harder against the communist Chinese than against the Japanese. Corruption and mismanagement within Chiang's regime were undermining what little hold he retained on the peasantry. By 1943, General Joseph ("Vinegar Joe") Stilwell, America's military commander in China, was so disgusted that he referred to Chiang as "Peanut." Roosevelt urged Chiang to mend his ways. Chiang, however, ultimately responded by demanding Stilwell's recall. Roosevelt acceded. When he named General Patrick Hurley, a Republican anticommunist with little knowledge of China, as ambassador in 1944, he played further into Chiang's hands.

Other liberals grumbled that FDR failed to appreciate the anticolonial stirrings of the nonwhite world. Why didn't the President make it clear to Churchill, who had been so anxious for American aid in 1941, that the price was surrender of India, Malaya, and other colonial possessions? Roosevelt did not, his biographer James MacGregor Burns concluded, because he was too "soft and pasty" to risk unpleasantness in negotiations, and because he was content to let occasional rhetorical outbursts against colonialism substitute for the effective use of American power.

These critics agreed with spokesmen of the Right (and the center) that Roosevelt possessed many traits ill suited for the business of diplomacy. One of these was his legendary reliance on his own charm. Though very effective in his early dealings with Congress, it failed to impress no-nonsense administrators such as Stimson, who described wartime Cabinet meetings as "solo performances by the President interspersed with some questions and very few debates." It led him, critics charged, to jolly his way through conferences

Though I enjoyed these conversations, the exercise of the President's charm and the play of his lively mind, they were also perplexing. Roosevelt was familiar with the history and the geography of Europe. Perhaps his hobby of stamp collecting had helped him to this knowledge. But the academic and sweeping opinions which he built upon it were alarming in their cheerful fecklessness. He seemed to see himself disposing of the fate of many lands, allied no less than enemy. He did all this with so much grace that it was not easy to dissent. Yet it was too like a conjurer, skillfully juggling with balls of dynamite, whose nature he failed to understand.

Anthony Eden, Britain's Foreign Secretary during the war, recalls FDR's handling of foreign affairs (1965).

instead of standing up to Stalin or Churchill. Worst of all, FDR's detractors pointed out, it caused him to rely on summit meetings and on personal emissaries like Hopkins instead of on briefings by experts. "I know you will not mind my being brutally frank," he told Churchill in 1944, "when I tell you that I think I can personally handle Stalin better than either you or your Foreign Office or my State Department. Stalin hates the guts of all your top people. He thinks he likes me better, and I hope he will continue to do so."

These habits appeared to make Roosevelt into a Great Procrastinator who preferred to keep everyone happy by committing himself to nothing. Unlike Wilson, he gave little encouragement before 1945 to supporters of a United Nations organization. He refused to be specific about America's postwar commitments, except to imply that the United States would win the war and go home. At the Teheran conference he even told Stalin that the American people would chafe at stationing soldiers in Europe after 1947. And in early 1944 he wrote, "I do not want the United States to have the post-war burden of reconstituting France, Italy, and the Balkans. This is not our natural task at a distance of 3500 miles." Attitudes such as these caused some observers to wonder if the President had any purposeful postwar goals at all.

Critics on the Right insisted that Roosevelt's desire to avoid unpleasantness led him to be "soft on the Soviets." If Roosevelt had not been such a procrastinator, they argued, he could have exacted promises from the Russians in 1942, when they were calling anxiously for American assistance. If he had understood the peculiar ruthlessness of Stalin's regime, he would have seen the futility of dealing with him. If he had not been so anxious to win friends at the conference table, he would have refused to make damaging and unnecessary concessions.

In making such criticisms Roosevelt's foes on the Right pointed out that Averell Harriman, America's ambassador to Russia during the later years of the war, had given ample warning of Soviet postwar ambitions. In January 1945 Harriman wrote, "the Soviets are employing the wide variety of means at their disposal—occupation troops, secret police, local communist parties, labor unions . . . and economic pressure . . . to assure the establishment of regimes which, while maintaining an outward appearance of independence and broad popular support, actually depend for their existence on . . . the Kremlin." Instead of heeding Harriman's advice, Roosevelt supposedly went on his feckless way. "Stalin doesn't want anything but security for his country," FDR said, "and I think if I give him everything I possibly can and ask for nothing from him in return, *noblesse oblige,* he won't try to annex anything and will work with me for a world of democracy and peace."

The culmination of this foolish approach, critics grumbled, was at the Yalta Conference of February 1945. There, Roosevelt allegedly betrayed American interests by permitting Russia three seats in the UN General Assembly, by settling for a vague agreement on reparations (which later permitted Russia—when denied American economic aid—to paralyze eastern Germany), by doing nothing to assist Polish boundary claims, and by failing to secure a noncommunist Polish government. Without consulting China, Roosevelt also reached a secret accord with Stalin that gave the Soviets Southern Sakhalin, the Kurile Islands, joint operation of the Chinese-Eastern and Southern Manchurian railways, and which recognized Russia's "preeminent interests" in Manchuria. In return for these concessions Roosevelt secured only the vague Soviet promise to hold free elections in eastern Europe, and the assurance that Russia would enter the war against Japan within three months of Germany's surrender.

Many of these complaints, from both the Left and the Right, were partly justified. Roosevelt placed far too much faith in Chiang Kai-shek, and he overestimated the value of personal diplomacy. His hopes for the democratic governments in eastern Europe were misplaced: by 1948 all of them had fallen under the thumb of the Kremlin. His failure to secure precise guarantees of access routes to western zones in postwar Berlin caused no end of conflict later on. And successful development of atomic energy later made the Asian deal at Yalta unnecessary.

But FDR's options were restricted. As commander-in-chief his first concern, properly enough, was to win the war with as little suffering to America as possible. The deal with Darlan, therefore, seemed necessary; the alternative might have subjected Allied forces to substantial fighting against the French. Playing along with Chiang was less wise. But cutting off aid to Chiang, who threatened to quit the war unless America kept the dollars flowing, would have been politically hazardous. The middle of a world war, in any event, was no time to attempt the impossible task of "saving" China. And what was the President to do with Churchill, who proudly proclaimed, "I did not become the King's first minister in order to preside over the liquidation of the British empire"? If preserving wartime unity was the primary goal—as it had to be—it made little sense for America to issue demands on such a cooperative ally. In assuming that the United States could have forced its will,

Roosevelt's detractors presumed an omnipotence that America has never possessed.

Complaints about the President's Russian diplomacy falsely assumed that Soviet designs were both evil and clear at the time. In fact, Roosevelt heard not only from hard-liners like Harriman but from much more conciliatory men like Hopkins, Hull, and Eisenhower, who reported that "nothing guides Russian policy so much as a desire for friendship with the United States." The critics also exaggerated America's potential to influence events. The Soviets overran eastern Europe by force of arms, just as the United States and Great Britain took France and the low countries. Recognizing the American sphere of influence, Stalin expected the United States, which had historically shown little concern for the fate of eastern Europe (witness the Munich accord, or the division of Poland in 1939) to leave him alone in his sphere of interest. This meant letting Russia protect itself against unfriendly governments on its borders. And it meant permitting Stalin to subjugate the East Germans, who had invaded Russian territory twice since 1914. In this sense Roosevelt did well to get Russia to make any "promises" whatever about eastern Europe. Americans at the time applauded his "success" at Yalta.

Roosevelt was right also in recognizing that America could secure free elections in eastern Europe only by force, which he had neither the will nor the power to apply. His attitude was best expressed in an exchange with Admiral William Leahy, his top military aide. Leahy complained that the Polish accord was so vague that Russia could "stretch it all the way from Yalta to Washington without ever technically breaking it." Roosevelt nodded, but replied, "I know it, Bill—I know it. But it's the best I can do for Poland at this time." This was not naiveté, but an accurate appreciation of military reality in Europe.

Roosevelt could even be forgiven his concessions to the Soviet Union in Asia. In February 1945 the Japanese were obviously doomed, with or without Russian intervention. But no one could be sure at the time that the atomic bomb, untested until July 1945, would work. What Roosevelt did know was that Japan was fighting fanatically to hold all its possessions. He was further advised (probably wrongly) that America might suffer as many as a million

> We really believed in our hearts, that this was the dawn of a new day we had all been praying for and talking about for so many years. We were absolutely certain that we had won the first great victory of the peace, and by 'we' I mean ALL of us—the whole civilized human race. The Russians had proved that they could be reasonable and farseeing, and there wasn't any doubt in the minds of the President or any of us that we could live with them and get along with them peacefully for as far into the future as any of us could imagine.
>
> Harry Hopkins reflects American hopes for postwar cooperation, after Yalta (1945).

casualties in an invasion of the home islands. To avoid such a catastrophe he determined to secure Russian help, which Stalin would have given grudgingly, if at all, without securing concessions for himself.

In these ways Roosevelt's Russian diplomacy revealed not softness but the realism born of perceived military necessity. Despite strains over the second front (and over the Russian use of lend-lease supplies), his policies managed to sustain Allied cooperation. Roosevelt may also have been correct in assuming that Stalin was more concerned for his nation's security (and for traditional Russian territorial gains) than in fomenting world-wide communist revolution. Stalin gave little support to communist forces under Marshal Tito of Yugoslavia; he recognized Chiang in China (then, as always, Stalin was ambivalent about Mao Tse-tung); and he kept a bargain made with Churchill in the fall of 1944, by which Britain recognized Russia's paramount interests in much of southeastern Europe in return for a Soviet hands-off policy in Greece (which became scarcely more "democratic" than Poland). Stalin also cruelly disappointed the communist parties in Italy and France, which had hoped for Russian postwar aid in the West.

All these Soviet actions suggested that Stalin's ambitions—at least to 1945—were limited, and that postwar cooperation was possible. In making such assumptions FDR took risks. But he was operating according to a higher realism, which perceived that Soviet-American détente in the postwar world was a *sine qua non* for world peace. Compared to Wilson's milennial visions, this faith struck many Americans as amoral and unfeeling, but it was in fact responsible, flexible statesmanship.

The expansion of government

FROM WELFARE PROGRAMS TO WARTIME POWERS

In December 1943 Roosevelt explained that he was no longer "Dr. New Deal," but "Dr. Win the War."

His remark confirmed that the exciting days of domestic reform were past. Though Roosevelt continued to work for his programs, he was necessarily preoccupied with military problems. And Congress grew even more obstructive than it had been in his second term, especially after the Republicans made further inroads in 1942. The conservative coalition of Republicans and rural Democrats killed the WPA, the CCC, and the National Resources Planning Board. It defeated bills for federal aid to education, national health insurance, and public power development, and it ignored groups crusading for civil rights. As responsive as ever to well-organized interest groups, it approved legislation granting farmers 110 percent of parity and exempting many agricultural laborers from the draft.

The conservatism of the wartime Congresses was most pronounced in the areas of labor legislation and taxation. In 1943 Congress approved, over Roosevelt's veto, the Smith-Connally Act, which authorized the President to seize strike-bound defense plants and to impose thirty-day "cooling off" periods before labor could go on strike. In the same year it enacted a plan that introduced the principle of withholding taxes, but at the cost of forgiving taxpayers an estimated 75 percent of 1942 taxes. The plan especially benefited high-income people in the good year of 1942. Then in 1944 Congress passed a tax bill that raised only $2 billion more than before. FDR, who had called for an increase of $10 billion, snapped publicly that it was "not a tax bill, but a tax relief bill providing relief not for the needy but for the greedy." His blunt remark angered even his congressional supporters, who helped to pass the bill over his veto. Long before FDR's death in 1945, relations between Capitol Hill and the White House were cold indeed.

The balance of power within the parties also shifted toward the Right during the war. In 1944 the GOP nominated New York governor Thomas E. Dewey as its presidential candidate. Though Dewey accepted much of the New Deal, he waged an abrasive campaign. Other Republican orators engaged in a demagogic effort to link the Roosevelt administration with communism. The Democrats, meanwhile, refused to renominate the liberal Henry Wallace for the vice-presidency. Instead, Harry Truman, a dependable middle-of-the roader from Missouri, received the prize. Thanks to the power of the Democratic voting coalition, and especially to the efforts of organized labor (which provided $2 million to party funds), Roosevelt and Truman won handily. But their margin of 3.6 million votes fell well short of the Democratic lead of 5 million votes in 1940 and 11 million in 1936. Republicans understandably looked forward to 1948, when they expected to triumph at last.

Despite these blows against the New Deal, the war years did not witness any triumph for reaction. Many of the defeated programs, such as the WPA or the CCC, truly seemed unnecessary in the midst of a revived wartime economy. More important reforms—TVA, social security, the minimum wage, even the NLRB—emerged intact. Nondefense spending actually increased during the war from $7.2 billion to $17 billion, thus remaining at about 8 percent of the Gross National Product. Having helped to build a partial welfare state, Congress was not about to dismantle it.

The growth in domestic expenditures was but one manifestation of a virtual explosion in the size of government during the war. Thanks primarily to defense spending, the federal budget jumped from $9 billion in fiscal 1940 to $98 billion in 1945, or from 9 percent to 46 percent of the GNP. The number of civilian employees of the federal government increased during the same period from 1 to 3.8 million. Federal taxes leaped ahead from $5 billion to $44.5 billion, and millions of Americans felt the bite of the Internal Revenue Service for the first time. With so much money at its command, and with virtual armies of bureaucrats staffing such new agencies as the Office of Price Administration, the War Production Board, the War Labor Board, and Selective Service, the federal government enjoyed more power than the most avid New Dealers ever envisioned in the 1930s.

The impact of this expansive fiscal policy was little short of revolutionary. By increasing federal spending more than tenfold within six years, the government ran up deficits averaging more than $30 billion per year, or ten times the average deficits during the New Deal. Chiefly because of this spending, the economy finally surged back. Unemployment virtually disappeared (thanks in part to the draft), and the GNP (in 1929 prices) shot forward from $121 billion in 1940 to $181 billion in 1945. Few politicians dared to endorse this Keynesian approach as a matter of regular policy, and deficits were modest (except during war) from 1946 through 1963. Still, the power of public spending had been demonstrated beyond doubt. Thereafter all but the most hardened fiscal conservatives admitted that a little pump priming in times of recession was desirable.

The war witnessed an almost equally revolutionary growth in the power of the presidency. Only the White House seemed able to carry on the war and manage the nation's more complex international responsibilities. As Professor Edward Corwin noted ruefully, phrases describing the presidency as the "great engine of democracy" and "the American people's one authentic prophet" began appearing in textbooks. The diplomatic historian Thomas Bailey spoke for many scholars in 1948 by stressing the need for a strong presidency. "Just as the yielding of some of our national sovereignty is the price we must pay for effective international organization," he wrote, "so the yielding of some of our democratic control of foreign affairs is the price we may have to pay for greater physical security." If TR began the twentieth-century American infatuation with the presidency, World War II transformed it into a long-lived affair.

BIG GOVERNMENT: BLESSING OR CURSE?

Most reformers welcomed this explosion in the power of the presidency. Congress, after all, was in the hands of conservatives, and the Court had until

1937 stood in the way of social legislation. By 1945 belief in an activist central administration was a cardinal tenet of modern American liberalism.

Even during the war, however, some people worried about the concentration of enormous power in the hands of a few. One concern was the Office of War Information, which was formed to apprise the public of the course of the war. The *New York Times* observed that it was "feeding us bad news when it was thought we could stand it and good news when it was thought we needed it." Even Elmer Davis, the experienced newsman who headed the agency, fought regularly with military brass who refused to give him accurate, up-to-date information. Admiral King's idea of war information, Davis complained, "was that there should be just *one* communique. Some morning we would announce that the war was over and that we won it." Though these charges were a little exaggerated, they were accurate in complaining about the government's close-mouthed monopoly on sources of important news. They suggested also that Americans had become more conscious of the damages of government manipulation—and of the need to protect civil liberties—than they had been during the days of the Committee on Public Information in World War I.

The administration's handling of civil liberties during the war was equally unsettling. The 12,000-odd conscientious objectors who refused to accept noncombatant military service were placed in so-called Civilian Public Service camps, where the courts refused to extend the protection of the first and fifth amendments. They did not receive pay. The administration imprisoned some 5500 other conscientious objectors, including Jehovah's Witnesses, who claimed exemptions as ministers. Roosevelt also showed himself capable of harshness in handling allegedly profascist dissenters. In 1942 the Justice Department charged twenty-six "native fascists" with conspiring against the government. The accusations were based in part on the arbitrary Smith Act of 1940, which made it an offense even to advocate the overthrow of the government. After much legal wrangling, which revealed no evidence of conspiracy, the government finally had to drop the cases in 1944.

Defenders of the administration rightly pointed out that Roosevelt treated dissenters more even-handedly than Wilson had in World War I. But this improvement did not necessarily signify that America was growing more tolerant or more mature. Rather, it reflected the relative absence of dissent in a war precipitated by the "sneak attack" on Pearl Harbor. As one congressman phrased it a week after the attack, "This war had to come. It is a war of purification in which the forces of Christian peace and freedom and justice and decency and morality are arrayed against the evil pagan forces of strife, injustice, treachery, immorality, and slavery. . . ."

This kind of passion erupted quickly in open racism against Japanese-Americans. A California barber advertised "free shave for Japs," but "not responsible for accidents." A funeral parlor proclaimed, "I'd rather do business with a Jap than with an American." A poll in 1944 that asked Americans

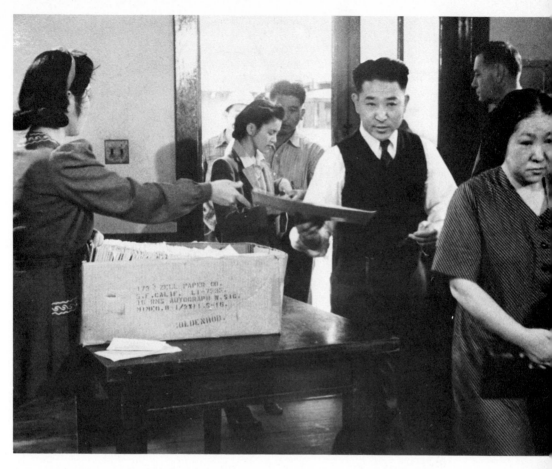

Japanese-Americans start the relocation process at detention camps in World War II.

to say which enemy, Germany or Japan, the United States could "get along with better after the war" revealed that only 8 percent picked Japan.

This kind of thinking led to unjust policies. Though the government treated German- and Italian-Americans well, in 1942 it began systematically to round up Japanese-Americans and to place them in detention centers. These were really concentration camps guarded by soldiers and situated in remote areas of the West. In all, they contained some 112,000 people for the duration of the war. Most of these (perhaps 70,000) were second-generation Nisei who were American citizens. Though a few brought suit, the Supreme Court sanctioned the government's action (during wartime) in 1944. Only later, when passions had subsided, did Americans realize the truth of Justice Frank Murphy's dissent labeling the evacuations "one of the most sweeping and complete deprivations of constitutional rights in the history of this nation."

> *The Japanese, because they are unassimilable, because the aliens have been denied the right to own real property in California, because of the marked differences in appearance between Japanese and Caucasians, because of the generations of training and philosophy that makes them Japanese and nothing else—all of these contributing factors set the Japanese apart as a race, regardless of how many generations have been born in America. Undoubtedly many of them intend to be loyal, but only each individual can know his own intentions, and when the final test comes, who can say but that "blood will tell"?*
>
> Los Angeles Mayor Fletcher Bowron arouses passions against Japanese-Americans, Feb. 1942.

Those who feared the excesses of big government could content themselves with the hope that ominous wartime developments like the Office of War Information and detention centers were temporary phenomena. The administration's handling of defense contracting, however, led first to bureaucratic confusion and then to the development of a military-industrial complex. Together these exposed the dangers of the governmental expansion produced by modern war.

Bureaucratic confusion began as early as 1939, when Roosevelt created the War Resources Board to oversee defense needs. It received only limited support from the administration before being replaced after the fall of France by the Advisory Commission of the Council of National Defense. This, in turn, gave way in 1941 to the Office of Production Management. All these agencies had to contend with other sources of power, such as Secretary of the Interior Harold Ickes, who was also oil administrator, and Jesse Jones, the imperious banker who headed the Reconstruction Finance Corporation. Critics demanded that Roosevelt create a more permanent agency and give it real authority.

When the President established the War Production Board in January 1942, it appeared that he recognized the need for centralization. But he still refused to make Donald Nelson, the WPB chief, a "czar" over production. His stand was deliberate. As he told Labor Secretary Frances Perkins, "there is something to be said . . . for having a little conflict between agencies. A little rivalry is stimulating. . . . the fact that there is somebody else in the field who knows what you are doing is a strong incentive to strict honesty." The President also did not want to turn over such power to someone else. So he gave only sporadic support to Nelson's efforts at concentrating authority in the WPB. Important pricing matters were handled by Chester Bowles, head of the Office of Price Administration, while James Byrnes, who ran yet another agency, the Office of Economic Stabilization, possessed more power than Nelson himself. From the beginning Nelson, like almost all later civilian officials in charge of defense planning, was unable to override the military whom Roosevelt permitted to control the crucially important matter of procurement.

The WPB needed most the authority to establish priorities for the allocation of scarce commodities. Without such power, it could not assure that contractors and subcontractors would receive necessary supplies. The result was shortages, serious delays in production, and, most ominously, so-called priorities unemployment. In 1943 the WPB at last began applying the Controlled Materials Plan, which required defense contractors to submit quarterly estimates of their needs. This plan removed bottlenecks, but it came too late to help businessmen who, for lack of materials, had been unable to convert to war production. It also led many producers to exaggerate their needs and forced the government to supervise more closely the manifold activities of American manufacturing. The process created considerable bureaucratic growth, red tape, and hard feelings.

Despite these problems, American production leaped ahead with astonishing speed. Confusion, in fact, was less prominent than it had been in World War I. After procrastinating in 1940 and 1941 to assure themselves of markets, American manufacturers converted rapidly to war production. Many assumed direction of plants built almost overnight with public funds. The enormous airplane manufacturing facilities at Willow Run, Michigan, were larger than the combined prewar plants of Boeing, Douglas, and Consolidated Aircraft. More than a mile long, they included 1600 machine tools and 7500 jigs and fixtures. The story of rubber production was equally amazing. The government built fifty-one synthetic rubber making plants, which by 1944 made close to a million tons per year. (The German peak, in 1943, was 109,000 tons.) These fantastic increases in output created a virtual overabundance of weaponry by late 1943. Thereafter many contractors began scrambling for the privilege of reconverting to civilian production.

The production miracle unfortunately led many people to believe that America was all but omnipotent, that it could move with lightning speed to demolish enemies all over the world. It also caused businessmen to praise

A ship is launched at one of Henry Kaiser's seven shipyards. At its peak, this yard turned out a ship a day.

themselves for accomplishing so much. Conveniently overlooking the role of government spending, they extolled the virtues of capitalistic free enterprise, and they rejected arguments that more government supervision might have secured better results. To a degree this claim may have had merit, for even a "czar" might have found it impossible to manage an economy so huge and complex as America's. Businessmen may have been equally correct in asserting (Roosevelt agreed) that a degree of voluntarism was necessary for morale in such a long war. For social reformers, however, the self-assured hostility of many businessmen to government "interference" proved a formidable obstacle to change in the 1940s and 1950s.

Reformers worried also about the lasting connections developed in wartime between big business and the military. For it was the big operators to whom the army, the navy, and the newly created Office for Scientific Research and Development turned for help. These large organizations had the capital, the research potential, and the equipment to produce quickly. They could free middle management specialists and white-collar workers to handle government red tape. Above all, big institutions could be dealt with quickly. Government officials liked to work with a handful of experienced operators instead of with a host of smaller entrepreneurs unfamiliar with the labyrinth of federal bureaucracy.

Top government officials made sure that big business was at home in its developing relationship with Washington. Many of them had been recruited, by the supposedly "radical" New Deal, from corporations, and they agreed that producing for defense ought to bring a handsome profit. "If you are going to . . . go to war, . . . in a capitalist country," Stimson observed, "you have got to let business make money out of the process." Stimson and others offered contractors cost-plus contracts and generously renegotiated deals when businesses complained. The government also provided low-interest federal loans for plant expansion and easy tax write-offs. Patents for processes developed with government aid generally reverted to the manufacturer. Such massive assistance assured big corporations of commanding positions in areas formerly handled by subcontractors. Similarly, scientists engaged in practical military research, especially in atomic physics, reaped great rewards from government grants while scholars in the humanities and social sciences had to plug away as in the past.

There was no easy way for government to reverse the long-range movement toward concentration, whether in business or in universities. Still, progressives correctly complained about government's enthusiastic hand on the tiller. They astutely observed that big business and the military, eclipsed by other contenders for federal favor in the 1930s, had now surpassed in influence other interest groups like big labor and big agriculture. They prophesied also that the military-industrial complex, as it came to be known, could lock the nation on a martial course. Among the baneful results of political centralization, the military-industrial nexus perhaps was the most frightening of all.

The war and American society

Stuart Chase, a liberal economist, surveyed American society at the end of the war and concluded that prosperity had worked wonders that all the measures of the New Deal had failed to bring about. "The facts," he said, "show a better break for the common man than liberals in 1938 could have expected for a generation."

Almost every economic indicator supported Chase's conclusion. Despite rationing of gasoline, coffee, tin, and other goods, few Americans suffered much at home. National income jumped from $81 billion in 1940 to $182 billion five years later, or from $573 to $1,074 per capita. Improvements in diets and health care during the same period caused life expectancy to increase by three years to sixty-six. (However, poor teeth and eyes, symptoms of malnutrition, still caused more than 50 percent of young men in some regions to fail preinduction physicals.) Thanks in part to the GI Bill, 8 million young people learned a trade or attended college after the war, while bonuses for American veterans totaled more than $2 billion.

The war even improved the distribution of income. This was not because the rich were getting poorer, but because workers were regularly employed and drawing extra pay for overtime. Accordingly, the share of income earned by the bottom fifth of wage-earners rose during the war by 68 percent, compared to 20 percent for the top fifth. These modest gains in income redistribution were the only such advances in modern American history.

Important social changes accompanied this return to prosperity. One was even greater movement of an already mobile people. Those who moved included 12 million men in uniform, dependents who pulled up roots to follow, and millions more who left their homes to work in war plants. Though it is impossible to know exactly how many people moved, the migrations clearly accelerated the trend toward urbanization, which had slowed during the depression years. The number of people living in urban areas increased from 74 million in 1940 to 89 million in 1950, while the total classified as "rural farm" actually decreased during the decade, from 30 to 23 million. A few states, well-favored in the granting of war contracts, virtually exploded in population. California alone gained 2 million people during the four years of war.

The status of women also changed considerably during the war. In 1940 only 14 million American women (26 percent of the total work force) were employed; by 1945, 19 million (or 36 percent) were. Moreover, 22 percent of these working women in 1945 were married, as opposed to 15 percent five years earlier. Contemporaries thought these trends were temporary, for the numbers of regularly employed women dipped in 1946. Polls also suggested that Americans considered it unnatural for women to enter the labor force: a

This is the last time
This time we will all make certain
That this time is the last time!
For this time we are out to finish
The job we started then
Clear it up for all time this time
So we won't have to do it again

The words to a wartime song by Irving Berlin suggest the no-nonsense thoroughness with which Americans approached the war.

The home front. Above, a massive bond drive in Times Square, New York. Above right, ration stamps restricting consumption. Bottom right, a woman contributing a garment to the war effort.

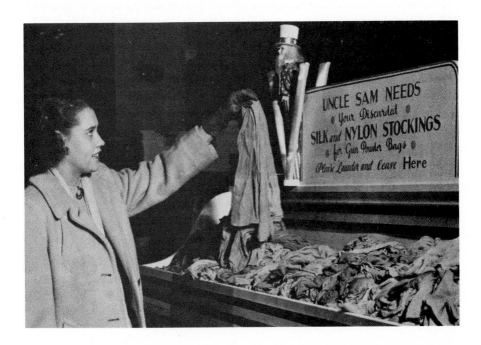

woman's place, the ladies' magazines added, was at home. But increasing numbers of women disagreed, and by 1951 the number of women in the work force was already higher than at any time in World War II. These trends provided an economic underpinning to movements for women's liberation in the late 1960s.

Wartime developments led to yet other changes in the American family. Thousands of young people who had postponed marriage or family in the depression refused to wait in the 1940s. Thousands more, confronted with the draft and overseas service, did the same. The result was a trend toward younger marriages and a baby boom that began in 1940 and rose irregularly throughout the war. Demographers who assumed the increase in birth rates would end with the war were wrong, for the baby boom lasted until the mid-1950s. Rising birth rates helped stimulate demand in a host of consumers goods industries; they prompted great growth in home-building and in suburban development; and they all but swamped educational institutions until the 1970s. By 1965, when these war and postwar babies had reached their late teens or early 20s, the baby boom culminated in the growth of a "youth culture," which baffled and frightened older generations.

To many observers during the war (and since) these developments were unfortunate. Young people, it seemed, were hurrying irresponsibly into marriage and parenthood. They were pulling up roots to live in ill-constructed housing developments without proper socializing institutions for children. Some women were "abandoning" their children in order to enter the work force, while others—"allotment Annies"—deserted their soldier husbands as soon as their dependence allowances stopped coming. A rapidly increasing divorce rate appeared to be one unhappy result of these patterns of behavior. Juvenile delinquency involving "wolf packs" in housing developments and "zoot suit" gangs in large cities appeared to be another. Some people foresaw a new "Lost Generation."

These Cassandras oversimplified a complex set of developments. The increase in divorce, for instance, was assisted by more tolerant attitudes and by more permissive legislation. The rise in juvenile crime is harder to explain, or even to document, because statistics for the period are not very reliable. But it seems to have stemmed from a variety of causes: increasing racial tensions; laws that banned child labor and required bored young people to stay in schools until the age of sixteen; and the broadening areas for petty crime, especially car theft, available in an urban, technological society.

Above all, the war prompted anxieties about the future. Having survived ten years of depression, Americans entered the 1940s already searching for security. With regular employment, they seemed at last to have found it. But would it endure? Many felt certain that depression would recur, that hard-earned gains would be wiped out, that the status of other groups would rise at the expense of their own. The writer Bernard de Voto observed that this anxiety rarely received "public expression, and little direct expression even in private." But "it exists and it may well be the most truly terrifying phenomenon of the war. It is a fear of the coming of the peace."

One group that clearly displayed this anxiety was organized labor—in part because it had gained so amazingly much. In a strong bargaining position at the start of the war, unions received government support of a "maintenance of membership" clause in contracts. This required members to stay in the union for the duration of the war. Unions then drove ahead to recruit the seven million new workers who found jobs between 1940 and 1945. Accordingly, union membership increased from 9 million in 1940 to almost 15 million in 1945, a growth more rapid than at any time in American history. Management generally acquiesced in this union activity: with great profits to be made and a war to be won, it did not seem wise to goad militant workers into strikes. This relative harmony between labor and management foreshadowed a development that was later to become an exploitative reality: both sides cooperating to raise wages and prices, while nonunion wage earners (who still comprised 65 percent of the nonagricultural work force in 1945) paid the bills.

Despite these gains, unions remained uneasy about the future. John L. Lewis and other leaders led dramatic walkouts for better pay during the war. Work stoppages, though usually short-lived, increased from 2,968 in 1942 to 4,956 in 1944. In 1945, 4,750 stoppages affected 12.12 percent of the labor force and involved 3.4 million workers. And 1946, when wartime frustrations could finally be expressed, witnessed a record 4,985 stoppages involving 4.6 million laborers. Unionists, having begun to taste power and increased income, were insisting upon more in the future.

A similar revolution in expectations affected blacks, who made unprecedented gains during the war. Some of these advances were essentially symbolic—in 1943 the first black joined the American Bar Association; in 1944 the first black was admitted to a presidential press conference. Other changes were vitally important. The number of blacks who secured jobs in the federal government increased from 50,000 in 1939 to 200,000 six years later, and the appeal of jobs in northern and western cities pulled more than a million blacks out of the South. This mass migration, one of the greatest of its kind, persisted in the postwar period.

As in the years between 1914 and 1919, this combination of migration and relative prosperity created mounting militancy among black leaders. The Congress on Racial Equality, an interracial organization devoted to pacifism as well as to civil rights, was founded in 1942. The NAACP, the largest of the interracial organizations, increased its membership during the war from 50,000 to 500,000. Most alarming of all to whites was the black power shown by A. Philip Randolph, the porters' union leader who threatened to call for a mass march on Washington in 1941 unless Roosevelt acted to prevent racial discrimination in employment. After much procrastination (for Roosevelt still hesitated to offend southern Democrats), the President relented far enough to issue an executive order setting up a Fair Employment Practices Commission. Easily his most significant contribution to racial justice, it stemmed entirely from black pressure. The lesson was not lost on later leaders of the black cause.

These advances merely reminded blacks how far America had to go. The poorly financed, understaffed FEPC was able to resolve only one-third of the 8000 complaints it had time to hear. Of its forty-five compliance orders, thirty-five were ignored. Despite a Supreme Court ruling against white primaries,

EXECUTIVE ORDER 8802

FAIR EMPLOYMENT PRACTICE
IN DEFENSE INDUSTRIES

. . . . . . I do hereby reaffirm the policy of the United States that there shall be no discrimination in the employment of workers in defense industries or Government because of race, creed, color, or national origin, and I do hereby declare that it is the duty of employers and of labor organizations, in furtherance of said policy and of this order, to provide for the full and equitable participation of all workers in defense industries, without discrimination because of race, creed, color, or national origin . . . . . *

THE PRESIDENT OF THE UNITED STATES OF AMERICA

THE WHITE HOUSE
June 25, 1941

> *While the March on Washington Movement may find it advisable to form a citizens committee of friendly white citizens to give moral support . . . it does not imply that these white citizens . . . should be taken into the March on Washington Movement as members. The essential value of an all-Negro movement such as the March on Washington is that it helps to create faith by Negroes in Negroes. It develops a sense of self-reliance with Negroes depending on Negroes in vital matters. It helps to break down the slave psychology and inferiority-complex in Negroes which comes and is nourished with Negroes relying on white people for direction and support. This inevitably happens in mixed organizations that are supposed to be in the interest of the Negro.*
>
> A. Philip Randolph promotes black power, 1942.

most blacks in the South continued to be disfranchised through poll taxes, literacy tests, and other ruses. Jim Crow laws segregating southern blacks in trains, buses, hotels, schools—even bathrooms and drinking fountains—were daily reminders of injustice. The armed forces, which were under federal control, flagrantly discriminated against blacks. The marines and army air corps simply excluded them, the navy gave them menial tasks, and the army segregated them under white officers. "Leadership," Secretary of War Stimson explained, "is not imbedded in the negro race yet, and to try to make commissioned officers to lead men into battle—colored men—is only to work a disaster to both." It was not until 1944 that the navy integrated the crews of a few of its ships or that the army sent blacks into combat.

Though most blacks supported the war, these humiliations inevitably created conflicts. In 1943 blacks in Harlem rioted against discrimination. A race riot in Detroit the same year killed 34 and injured more then 700. The antiwhite Black Muslims began to make modest gains among the dispossessed. CORE leaders experimented with sit-ins (only in the North) and other forms of direct action. And countless blacks expressed themselves bitterly against a society that fought fascism abroad while ignoring injustice at home. One told Gunner Myrdal, the Swedish social scientist investigating race relations, "just carve on my tombstone, here lies a black man killed fighting a yellow man for the protection of a white man." A "Draftee's Prayer" in a black newspaper added,

> Dear Lord, today
> I go to war:
> To fight, to die,
> Tell me what for?
> Dear Lord, I'll fight,
> I do not fear
> Germans or Japs;
> My fears are here.
> America!

Such attitudes among organized workers and blacks captured one essential aspect of life on the home front. So long as the enemy fought on the field, Americans would try to suppress their frustrations and concentrate on winning the war. The common fear of fascism promoted more unity than in World War I. But it was an increasingly impatient, factious unity. Blacks and workers, like farmers, businessmen, veterans, even specialized groups like educators, had caught the scent of prosperity, and they wanted desperately to taste it once the war was over. More organized than ever, they sought to advance their own interests with the same grim single-mindedness that they showed in battle. This militancy amid plenty, this revolution of expectations, this scramble not only for security but for slices of an ever larger pie—all these were among the major social developments of the "Great Leap" of World War II.

Suggestions for reading

The key books covering American politics and diplomacy in World War II are James M. Burns, *Roosevelt: Soldier of Freedom** (1970); and A. Russell Buchanan, *The United States and World War II*, 2 vol.* (1964). See also W. H. McNeill, *America, Britain, and Russia* (1953); Gaddis Smith, *American Diplomacy During the Second World War, 1941–1945** (1965); John Snell, *Illusion and Necessity: The Diplomacy of World War II** (1963); Herbert Feis, *Churchill, Roosevelt, Stalin** (1957); and the revisionist account by Stephen Ambrose, *Rise to Globalism: American Foreign Policy Since 1938** (1971). Gabriel Kolko, *The Politics of War: The World and U. S. Foreign Policy, 1943–1945* (1969) stresses economic motives.

Other relevant studies are Raymond O'Connor, *Diplomacy for Victory: FDR and Unconditional Surrender** (1971); Trumbull Higgins, *Winston Churchill and the Second Front, 1940–1943* (1957), and *Soft Underbelly: The Anglo-American Controversy over the Italian Campaign, 1939–1945* (1968); Diane Shaver Clemens, *Yalta* (1970); and Robert Divine, *Second Chance: The Triumph of Internationalism During World War II* (1967). Important books on military policy are Kent Roberts Greenfield, *American Strategy in World War II: A Reconsideration** (1967); and Louis Morton, *Strategy and Command* (1962). For science policy consult James P. Baxter, *Scientists Against Time** (1946); Richard G. Hewlett and Oscar E. Anderson, *The New World* (1962), and *The Atomic Shield* (1969), on atomic development; and the highly readable narrative by Robert Jungk, *Brighter Than a Thousand Suns: A Personal History of the Atomic Scientists** (1958).

Books dealing with Asia are John Toland, *The Rising Sun** (1970); Robert Butow, *Japan's Decision to Surrender* (1954); Tang Tsou, *America's Failure in China, 1941–1950** (1963); and Barbara Tuchman, *Stilwell and The American Experience in China, 1911–1945** (1971). Important books on wartime sources of the Cold War include John Gaddis, *The United States and the Origins of the Cold War, 1941–1946** (1972); and George C. Herring, Jr., *Aid to Russia, 1941–1946* (1973).

The starting point for life in the United States during the war is Richard Polenberg, *War and Society: The United States, 1941–1945** (1972). See also John M. Blum, *V Was for Victory* (1976). Other surveys are Richard Lingeman, *Don't You Know There's a War On?* (1970); Geoffrey Perrett, *Days of Sadness, Days of Triumph* (1973);

and William Ogburn, ed., *American Society in Wartime* (1943). For economic policy consult Eliot Janeway, *Struggle for Survival* (1951); John M. Blum, *From the Morgenthau Diaries: Years of War, 1941–1945* (1967); and Bruce Catton, *War Lords of Washington* (1948). See also David Ross, *Preparing for Ulysses* (1969), which deals with manpower and military policies; Walter Wilcox, *The Farmer in the Second World War* (1947); and Joel Seidman, *American Labor from Defense to Reconversion* (1953). Useful biographies of labor leaders include Saul Alinsky, *John L. Lewis* (1949); and Matthew Josephson, *Sidney Hillman* (1952). William Chafe's book on American women, cited in the bibliography for chapter 6, is indispensable.

The experiences of blacks during the war is detailed in Richard Dalfiume, *Desegregation of the Armed Forces, 1939–1953* (1969); August Meier and Elliott Rudwick, *CORE . . . 1942–1968* (1973); Robert Shogan and Thomas Craig, *The Detroit Race Riot* (1964); and Gunnar Myrdal, *An American Dilemma** (1944, rev. ed. 1962), a classic sociological account. The fate of Japanese-Americans is well told in Jacobus ten Broek, et al., *Prejudice, War, and the Constitution* (1945); and in Roger Daniels, *Concentration Camps** (1971). Lawrence S. Wittner, *Rebels Against War: The American Peace Movement, 1941–1960* (1969) covers its subject sympathetically. For constitutional developments see Edward S. Corwin, *Total War and the Constitution** (1947); Francis Biddle, *In Brief Authority* (1962), by Roosevelt's wartime attorney general; and J. Woodford Howard, *Mr. Justice Murphy* (1968).

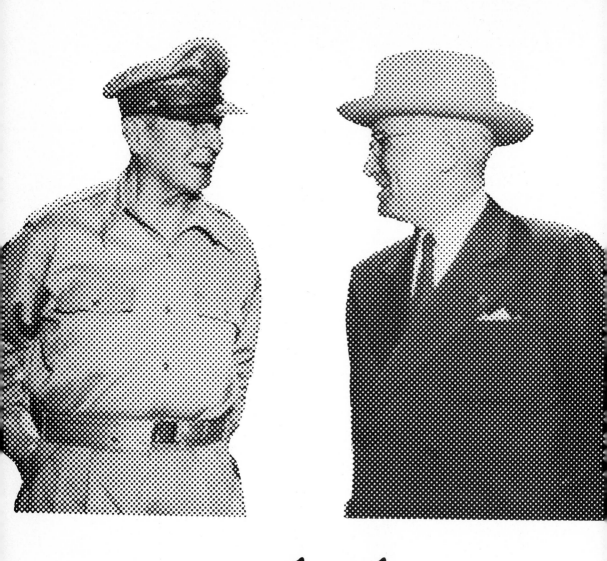

11

Acrimony, home and abroad

1945 - 1952

When Roosevelt died in April 1945, liberals were distraught. TVA director David Lilienthal shuddered to think of "that Throttlebottom Truman. The country and the world doesn't deserve to be left this way." Worrying about Truman's rise in the corrupt politics of Kansas City, the journalist Max Lerner asked, "can a man who has been associated with the Pendergast machine be able to keep the panting politicians and bosses out of the gravy?"

Millions of Americans appeared to share this anxiety. After all, Roosevelt had been president for as long as many people could remember. Yet now, with the Germans still fighting, with Japan to be invaded, and with postwar problems yet to be tackled, the country was saddled with an uninspiring border state senator whom the party had plucked from relative obscurity. Even Truman himself seemed frightened about the responsibilities ahead. "Boys," he told reporters, "if you ever pray, pray for me now. I don't know whether you fellows ever had a load of hay fall on you, but when they told me yesterday what had happened, I felt like the moon, the stars, and all the planets had fallen on me."

Actually, people worried too much, for past events—assassinations, divisive wars, corruption in high office—had demonstrated, as they would again, that the American political system was stable enough to withstand sudden shocks to the presidency. While Truman groped to master his office, delegates in San Francisco completed the task of devising a United Nations charter, which the Senate adopted by a vote of eighty-nine to two in July. In Europe, Allied forces mopped up the Germans, who surrendered on May 8. And in Asia, Americans pressed forward into Iwo Jima and Okinawa. The country's awesome military-industrial machine surged ahead, largely unaffected by personalities in the White House.

Truman also showed himself capable of acting firmly when necessary. His most far-reaching decision in these early months was to authorize the dropping of atomic bombs on Hiroshima (August 6) and Nagasaki (August 9). Later, critics argued persuasively that in reaching this decision he did not ask advice on *whether* the bomb should be used but *how,* and that he listened only to scientists and government officials who could have been expected to favor its use in war. In the process he ignored the pleas of scientists who urged him to warn the Japanese or to demonstrate the bomb in an uninhabited area. Instead, Truman merely told the Japanese on July 26 to surrender unconditionally or face "prompt and utter destruction." Since this was what they had already been receiving from fire raids, it was not surprising that they kept on with the war.

The use of the bombs may have been unnecessary. By July 1945 the Japanese knew they were doomed, and their moderates were exploring avenues to peace. If Truman had told them that they could retain their emperor, they might have agreed to surrender, particularly after Russia joined the war against them on August 8. At least, he could have awaited the impact of the Russian declaration, and of further fire bombings, which many later observers felt would have won the war without an American invasion. He definitely should have paused after incinerating close to 100,000 people in Hiroshima, instead of authorizing the air force to go ahead on its own and kill 40,000 to 75,000 more at Nagasaki. Truman's actions showed that he was more decisive—more impetuous, even—than reflective.

Truman never wavered in defending his decision. Warning the Japanese or demonstrating the bomb seemed risky. The Japanese, he reasoned, would ignore the warning and concentrate their remaining defenses against air

Victims of the atomic blast at Hiroshima await aid a few hours after the explosion.

Seven weeks later I returned to Alamogordo after I had watched the same model of the A-bomb devastate the city of Nagasaki. On that return visit I saw for the first time what the bomb had done to the desert. Over a radius of four hundred yards the ground had been depressed to a depth ranging from ten feet at the periphery to twenty-five feet in the center. All life within a mile, vegetable as well as animal, had been destroyed. There was not a rattlesnake left in the region, nor a blade of desert grass. The sand in the depression had been fused into a glasslike substance the color of jade, all of it radioactive. Eight hundred yards away a steel rigging tower weighing thirty-two tons had been turned into a twisted mass of wreckage. The one-hundred-foot-high steel tower at the top of which the bomb was exploded was completely vaporized. A herd of antelope that had been grazing several miles away had vanished. It was believed they had started on a mad dash for the wilds of Mexico. A number of cows at a similar distance developed grey spots from deposits of radioactive dust. These radioactive cows and their progeny became the nearest equivalent to "sacred cows" in the United States, being carefully studied for the effects of radiation.

William Laurence, a leading American reporter, recalls the power of the first atomic bomb, detonated in Alamogordo, New Mexico, in July 1945.

attacks. Japan might even succeed in shooting down the plane carrying such a bomb. Moreover, there was the chance that a bomb dropped in a demonstration might not work. How foolish the United States (and Truman) would look if that happened, especially as there were only two bombs to go in early August! For Truman, therefore, the decision involved little soul-searching. The United States had spent six years and billions of dollars developing the weapon, and once it had been successfully tested, he thought, it was silly not to use it.

A few later critics contended that Truman authorized use of the bombs to demonstrate America's power to the Soviet Union and to end the war before the Russians could join it. Such concerns did influence men like James Byrnes, who became secretary of state in 1945. They also moved General Leslie Groves, head of bomb development, who recalled, "Russia was our enemy . . . and the project was conducted on that basis." But if America had wanted to keep Russia from entering the war, the most direct way would have been to negotiate in earnest for Japan's conditional surrender in June and July. Moreover, Truman himself was focusing single-mindedly on Japan, not on the Soviet Union. Like Roosevelt, he was more preoccupied with short-run military necessity than with postwar diplomacy. At the time, the Japanese seemed prepared to fight to their last man, and in Okinawa they lost 110,000 men in eighty-three days, while killing 12,500 Americans, or 150 per day.

American soldiers celebrate V-J Day, the day Japan surrendered, in 1945.

(Later, in Vietnam, it was a bad *week* when 200 Americans died.) It was primarily to stop such losses as these, and to prevent the still more unthinkable bloodletting anticipated in an invasion of the home islands, that Truman did what he did.

At the time, Americans had no chance to debate the alternatives and no idea of Truman's options. But they did know that the bombs had worked and that Japan had finally surrendered. So they reacted not with horror at what had been done but with profound relief that the war was over. In this way Truman's popularity was further enhanced, his judgment seemingly vindicated. For the time being, there appeared little question of Truman's capacity to rule.

Domestic controversies

1945–1946

With characteristic briskness, Truman wasted little time after Japan's surrender before turning to problems at home, and on September 6, four days after V-J Day, he asked Congress to enact a "second Bill of Rights" for the American people. Among these rights, Truman declared, were "useful and remunerative" jobs for all, government assistance to farmers, protection for small businessmen against monopoly, decent housing for every family, "adequate medical care," "protection from the economic fears of old age, sickness, accident, and unemployment," and the "right to a good education." These rights, he said, echoing Roosevelt, "spell security."

Truman's requests, to be known as the Fair Deal, aimed at consolidating the partial welfare state built during the Roosevelt years. Indeed, in calling for such measures as national health insurance he went beyond the New Deal. Inevitably his requests provoked controversy. To secure them from a conservative Congress the new president would need all the skill he could muster.

As the struggle developed, it was clear that Truman possessed some of the qualities necessary to win. One of these was his awareness that the president must lead. As he liked to say, "the buck stops here." Another was his initially friendly relations with congressmen of both parties. A senator for ten years, he had pleased New Dealers by supporting most of Roosevelt's policies, while his impartial chairmanship of a wartime committee investigating defense contracting had made him acceptable to moderates and conservatives.

Truman made gestures to improve congressional-executive relations, which had deteriorated badly under Roosevelt. To placate the GOP he named Senator Theodore Burton, an Ohio Republican, to the first vacancy in the Supreme Court. He resurrected Herbert Hoover by having him head a commission studying governmental reorganization. His appointment of Byrnes, a former congressman and senator from South Carolina, as secretary of state and of Fred Vinson, a popular Democratic congressman from Kentucky, as secretary of the treasury (and in 1946 as chief justice) were especially well received on the Hill. More than FDR, Truman appeared to appreciate congressional advice and counsel.

But Truman also left himself open to criticism. In making lesser appointments he showed a tendency to favor old friends from his days in the national guard (he had been a captain in World War I) and in Missouri politics, where he had moved forward through the malodorous Pendergast machine of Kansas City. Most of these appointees, like his military aide Harry Vaughn, enjoyed no real power. But to observers used to the intellectuals and brain trusters who had flourished under Roosevelt they seemed an undistinguished lot. "The composite impression," the journalist I. F. Stone wrote, "was of big-bellied, good-natured guys who knew a lot of dirty jokes, spent as little time in their offices as possible, saw Washington as a chance to make 'useful' contacts, and were anxious to get what they could for themselves out of the experience. . . . The Truman era was the era of the moocher. The place was full of Wimpys who could be had for a hamburger."

The liberal admirers of FDR were especially offended by some of Truman's conservative appointees to important positions. These included Charles Snyder, a Missouri banker who held several major jobs before becoming secretary of the treasury in 1946, and Tom Clark, a conservative Texan who became attorney general and then a Supreme Court justice. By the end of 1946 almost all the important New Dealers whom Truman had inherited—Frances Perkins, Harold Ickes, Henry Wallace, Attorney General Francis Biddle— had resigned or been fired.

These changes were not wholly surprising. The new president, after all, was entitled to his own team of advisers. But Truman alienated many people, who wondered—with good reason—if he was really a sincere New Dealer. Roosevelt's intimates, he told a friend, were "crackpots and the lunatic fringe." He added, "I don't want any experiments; the American people have been through a lot of experiments, and they want a rest." Harry Dexter White, assistant secretary of the treasury under FDR and Truman, explained that when Roosevelt was alive, "we'd go over to the White House for a conference on some particular policy, lose the argument, and yet walk out of the door somehow thrilled and inspired to go on and do the job the way the Big Boss had ordered." Now, he added, "you go in to see Mr. Truman. He's very nice to you. He lets you do what you want to, and yet you leave feeling somehow dispirited and flat."

In addition to discouraging imagination, Truman failed to maintain order within his administration during his first two years in office. Perhaps no one could have done so very well, for the transition from war to peace inevitably caused confusion. But Truman, still feeling his way, too often failed to let conflicting bureaucrats know where he stood. Internal battles, which might have been cleared up quickly, were allowed to fester. Wilson Wyatt, his expeditor for housing, fought a host of rival agencies in his efforts to get much-needed building materials and finally resigned in disgust at the end of 1946, never having received the backing he had been led to expect from the White House. Chester Bowles, who was supposedly in charge of price control, faced the similarly discouraging task of getting presidential support against more conservative competitors in government. He too failed and finally resigned. Harold Smith, Truman's budget director, expressed the dismay of many government officials. "I don't know what goes on around here," he confided to his diary in February 1946, "and that is a rather dangerous situation for all of us to be in. . . . The top people in government are solving problems in a vacuum, and the vacuum is chiefly in their heads."

Moreover, Truman's approach to Congress lacked finesse. Instead of working purposefully for one or two goals at a time, he outlined grandiose programs and left Congress to its devices. "What the country needed in every field," he said, "was up to me to say . . . and if Congress wouldn't respond, well, I'd done all I could in a straight-forward way." To conservatives like House Minority Leader Joseph Martin, however, Truman was "out New Dealing the New Deal." Offended by his demands, they sat back and picked off his programs one by one.

Liberals became even more disenchanted. Truman, they said, should devote less rhetoric to demanding the impossible and more time to working hard behind the scenes. One advocate of civil rights complained that Truman's strategy was "to start with a bold measure and then temporize to pick up the right-wing forces. Simply stated, backtrack after the bang." TRB, the progressive columnist for the *New Republic,* later saw a disturbing pattern: "Truman would ask Congress for about 120 percent more than he expected. Congress, with a great show of indignation, would slash it to 75 percent. Truman would smile his little-man smile and bounce back with something else. It's a funny way to run a country."

Piecing these criticisms of Truman together made a most unflattering portrait. The new president, it appeared, was a poor judge of people, an anti-intellectual, a sloppy administrator, a rhetorical liberal, a heavy-handed manager of Congress. Possibly, he felt unprepared and insecure in the White House and overcompensated by sounding tough and decisive. Perhaps so. In any event, he possessed little of the deftness and none of the charisma that had characterized Roosevelt at his best.

In retrospect it is equally clear that Truman (like most of his contemporaries among leading politicians) lacked vision. Though he carried liberalism slightly beyond the bread and butter issues of the Roosevelt era—as in his support of civil rights—he was blind to the prevalence of poverty and the continuing maldistribution of income. Instead, he concentrated on meeting the presumed threat from the Soviets. To a degree, of course, any president in the late 1940s would have had to do the same. With Truman, however, the focus on foreign affairs meant that many domestic problems received low priority.

But most of the progressives who blamed Truman for the nation's troubles had to concede that he faced formidable obstacles. By 1945 the Democratic party was almost as sharply divided between its northern-urban and southern-

America's mood:
the public's view
of the most important problem
facing the country,
according to Gallup Poll results,
1949–1952

1949	High cost of living
1950	War and the threat of war
1951	War and foreign policy
1952	Korean War

SOURCE: Marian Irish and Elke Frank,
U. S. Foreign Policy (New York, 1975), p. 107

western-rural wings as it had been in the 1920s. Though outnumbered, the rural wing, which opposed the urban liberalism of the New Deal, coalesced successfully with Republicans to dominate both houses of Congress. For example, Joseph Martin and Charles Halleck, his right-hand man from Indiana, worked closely with southern conservatives like Howard Smith of Virginia, a rural reactionary who was a power on the House Rules Committee. The Senate was dominated by southern conservative Democrats, among them Harry Byrd of Virginia and Richard Russell of Georgia, and by Republican leaders like Robert Taft of Ohio.

A still greater barrier to domestic reform was the national mood. Having sacrificed during four years of war (and ten years of depression), Americans demanded the good life. They chafed at shortages, and they yearned for material goods. In doing so they helped build up enormous demand for a host of products that had barely existed, if at all, in 1940: television, heat-and-serve dinners, automatic transmissions, tubeless tires, airconditioning, hi-fis, filter cigarettes, dishwashers, freezers, detergents, tape recorders, and fiberglass. Americans began to fly in four-engine planes, to drive on superhighways, to live in ranch-style homes, to shop in supermarkets. With such a shiny, packaged world spreading out before their eyes it was easy, as it had been in the 1920s, for Americans to turn to their own private concerns.

This mood, however, was different from the "normalcy" of the 1920s, when people praised the virtues of rugged individualism. By 1945 the modest welfare state of FDR had come to stay, and special interest groups fought single-mindedly to broaden their share of it. Veterans demanded benefits, farmers higher prices, unions better wages and working conditions, consumers more goods and lower prices. Where Harding and Coolidge could win acclaim by leaving people alone, Truman (and his successors) had to act to sustain these groups in a standard of living that no society in world history had ever enjoyed before. He was confronted with the full force of the revolution in expectations.

Like Roosevelt, Truman had to rely on an essentially nonideological, indeed almost apathetic, electorate. As studies of voters were beginning to show, most Americans did not act as "liberals" or as "conservatives." Rather, they voted as their parents or their peers did. Millions (some 40 percent of the eligible electorate) failed to vote at all even in presidential elections. It was therefore difficult for Truman (and for reformers in the next fifteen years) to mobilize a mass following or a Democratic party that would consciously demand enactment of a "liberal" program. Instead, he had to work with constituency-oriented congressmen and senators, few of whom felt much pressure from home for progressive legislation.

THE ISSUES

These obstacles, with Truman's own limitations, combined to defeat all of the Fair Deal goals in 1945–46. Congress brought an end to the wartime Fair Employment Practices Commission and filibustered to death efforts to create a new one. It failed to pass measures against poll taxes. It ignored or defeated bills for public housing and federal aid to education. It passed the antilabor Case bill, which was vetoed by Truman. Though it approved the Employment Act of 1946 (which established a Council of Economic Advisers and proclaimed the government's responsibility to step in against economic declines), it rejected amendments that would have committed the government to using Keynesian fiscal policies.

The most pressing issues of Truman's first two years barely touched on his Fair Deal proposals. Rather, they concerned the economic consequences of the war. In trying to deal with them Truman received little but blows for his pains.

The pressures for a return to civilian life were overwhelming by mid-1945. Business interests demanded lower taxes, immediate demobilization, and the end of lend-lease and other measures assisting other foreign competitors in international markets. Soldiers insisted on being allowed to come home, and office-holders were swamped with postcards from Asia labeled, "No boats, no votes." Under such pressure the politicians of both parties simply collapsed. In November 1945 Congress approved a $6 billion tax cut, even though it would obviously contribute to inflation. The administration quickly disposed of most of its war plants, usually by turning them over to private interests on very generous terms. It let business move ahead quickly into civilian production. Given no choice by Congress, it cut lend-lease shipments. And—feeling secure with an atomic monopoly—it brought the boys home. The armed forces, 12 million strong in 1945, had only 3 million by mid-1946 and but 1.6 million by mid-1947.

This rapid demobilization was popular enough at first. But by the end of 1945 its costs were already becoming apparent. The return of so many soldiers to the domestic scene created great competition for jobs and enormous demand for housing. One veteran complained, "six months ago I was piloting a B-29 against the Japs. Now I am trying to build a home in my home town. The first fight was easier. . . .'' Though the economy opened up quickly enough to provide most veterans with jobs, the housing market, depressed since 1928, fell far short of demands, and Americans crowded into urban slums or shacks scattered in the countryside.

Truman tried to alleviate the housing shortage. Through existing agencies such as the Federal Housing Agency he (and his successors) helped millions of Americans get government-insured mortgages at moderate rates of interest. He also called for more generous appropriations for public housing, but even the backing of Robert Taft failed to stop a predominantly rural coalition from blocking the proposal until 1949. Meanwhile, Truman made matters worse by authorizing John Snyder, his director of reconversion, to remove federal controls on building materials. This action, one of many that attempted to placate private interests, made it impossible for Wyatt and other experts to offer central direction to housing policy. It also meant that materials flowed into the areas that would bring builders immediate profit. These areas, as often in the construction business, were commercial, not residential or industrial.

The housing crisis, though serious, seemed almost trivial compared to the problem of inflation. To a large degree this too was inevitable after the war, because demand for consumer goods had been pent up since 1941, during which time Americans had saved unprecedented sums. The baby boom and the sudden return of so many soldiers made this demand still more formidable. Following the end of the war in September 1945, the consumer price index jumped almost 25 percent in the next year and a half. This was a rate of increase greater than at any time since World War I. It seemed destined to wipe out all the hard-earned gains of war.

Truman, of course, could hardly bring prices down. That would happen on a broad front only when supply caught up with demand—in 1948. Moreover, he was again stymied by the conservative coalition in Congress, which passed a law extending price controls in only very weak form after June 30, 1946. Truman vetoed the measure, and the country was without controls at all. Congress then passed another weak bill, but the damage had already been done, and prices rose almost uncontrollably during the summer. By November 1946 Truman removed the few controls that remained.

Truman's handling of inflation made this difficult situation worse. Instead of demanding strong controls from the start, he did little to assist Bowles's congressional supporters. Then, belatedly, he stepped in with a ringing veto of the price control bill. This procedure revealed him to be better at rhetorical outbursts than at the necessary process of day-to-day congressional bargaining. It angered not only conservatives but some of his own party leaders, who had advised him to accept the bill as the best to be had under the circumstances. "The government's stability policy," Bowles complained, "is not what you have stated it to be, but is instead one of improvising on a day-to-day, case-by-case method, as one crisis leads to another—in short . . . there is really no policy at all."

In dealing with labor–management problems Truman again helped exacerbate an already acrimonious situation in which unions tried to make up for wartime restraint by demanding sizeable wage increases. Management refused, and millions of American workers went out on strike in late 1945 and early 1946. Both sides then turned to Truman, who had the power (stemming from the war) to authorize price increases. After a show of firmness, Truman gave way under business pressure by permitting price hikes of approximately 19 percent. Management then granted workers pay increases of 18 to 19 percent. Truman's actions settled some of the strikes, but only by encouraging the first of many postwar rounds of inflationary wage-price agreements between powerful interest groups. Nonunion workers and their families, a majority of Americans, paid the bill in higher prices for basic consumer goods.

John L. Lewis then led the soft coal miners out on strike April 1, 1946. American industry, very dependent on coal, seemed threatened by what promised to be a long and divisive confrontation. At the same time railway engineers and trainmen also served notice of their intention to strike. Furious, Truman went before a joint session of Congress to demand emergency powers. As he was reading his message, he was handed a note advising him that the railwaymen had come to terms. But he went on with his address, which

John L. Lewis, the defiant,
outspoken leader
of the
United Mine Workers,
inspecting
mine conditions.

called on Congress to give him power to order federal troops into strike-bound industries, and even to draft strikers into the armed services.

It was a sign of the hysteria of the times that the House quickly approved this violation of labor's civil liberties. The Senate, however, ultimately listened to calmer men like Taft, the supposed enemy of organized labor, and rejected Truman's appeal. The episode showed how hard it was for Truman (and later presidents) to impose their will on organized labor. It revealed that he could be hot-tempered to the extent of endangering the liberties of working people. Few of his actions were more ill-considered or counterproductive.

By the fall of 1946 these struggles over reconversion, controls, and labor policy had badly damaged Truman's standing with the voters. Gleeful opponents circulated cruel jokes about the President's blundering. One conjectured how Roosevelt would have handled matters by asking, "I wonder what Truman would do if he were alive." Republicans proclaimed that "to err is Truman" and repeated, "Had Enough?" In November, with meat shortages provoking fury among consumers, they succeeded in winning control over Congress for the first time since 1930. With liberals in disarray and with the conservative coalition riding high, Truman seemed doomed to electoral extinction in 1948.

THE 80TH CONGRESS

During the 1948 campaign Truman sounded one theme almost endlessly: the Eightieth Congress of 1947–48 had been "good-for-nothing." Like most politicians at election time, he distorted the past, for the Congress had actually compiled a significant list of foreign policy legislation, including military assistance to Greece and Turkey, the Marshall Plan of foreign aid to Europe, and the National Security Act, which attempted to reduce interservice rivalries by setting up the Joint Chiefs of Staff and the Defense Department. The law also established the National Security Council and the Central Intelligence Agency. These agencies vastly increased the role the military and intelligence services would play in subsequent decision-making.

In giving the impression that the Eightieth Congress was totally obstructive, Truman also distorted the truth. What he should have said was that the majority of congressmen opposed labor union power, deficit spending, high taxes, and wage and price controls—that is, progressive fiscal policy and state regulation of private enterprise. Otherwise, they were often conciliatory. In the 1940s and 1950s most of them supported, though often belatedly, increases in social security and the minimum wage. In battling for tax cuts many of them were in effect conservative Keynesians who agreed that federal policies could and should promote consumer spending. Taft, the conservative leader, spearheaded the battle for aid to education and public housing, both of which passed the Republican Senate in 1948, only to fail in the House. Not just a brave and lonely Harry S. Truman but also conservatives and moderates helped sustain the partial welfare state of the New Deal in the 1940s: it offered too much to too many groups to be abolished.

Truman also conveniently overlooked his own equivocations in 1947–48. After doing little for civil rights in the first two years of his presidency, he used the election campaign to outline (but not work hard for) a broad program which he knew Congress would never pass. He demanded national health insurance, which he had said little about during Democratic control of Congress in 1946. To appear forceful concerning inflation he called for presidential power to control prices—authority he did not really want and knew he could not get. Overreacting to fears about communist subversion, he established loyalty boards, which had the power to ignore civil liberties of governmental employees. It was not surprising that many people thought that Truman cared less about broadening human rights than about getting himself reelected in 1948.

Still, Truman was correct in claiming that the Eightieth Congress was both conservative and partisan. Among its new members—the "infamous class of '46"—were such Red-hunters as Richard Nixon of California and William Jenner of Indiana, opportunists like Joseph McCarthy of Wisconsin (who replaced Robert La Follette, Jr.), and conservatives like John Bricker of Ohio and William Knowland of California. Led by Taft, one of the hardest-working, best-prepared Senate leaders of the postwar era, they were formidable foes to the administration.

In this frame of mind they joined with conservative Democrats to defeat the entire Fair Deal program. The Eightieth Congress rejected public housing, aid to education, and Truman's appeal for universal military training. It refused to relax immigration quotas or to aid displaced persons. Though it did not challenge well-established interest groups such as farmers or veterans or dismantle the social welfare programs of the New Deal, it complained loudly (and most unfairly) about Truman's "lavish" spending. To insure there would be no more four-term presidents, as Roosevelt had been, it set in motion a constitutional amendment limiting presidents to two terms that was later ratified in 1951.

Congress reserved its heaviest ammunition for tax and labor policies. Twice in 1947 it passed tax cuts, only to watch Truman veto them with the claim that they favored the wealthy and imperiled the budget. In the election year of 1948, however, enough of Truman's supporters deserted him to override a third presidential veto. In the area of labor law Congress approved, again over Truman's veto, the Taft-Hartley Act of 1947. The measure enumerated unfair labor practices, outlawed the closed shop, required union officers to sign noncommunist oaths to secure access to the NLRB, and authorized the president to impose eighty-day "cooling off" periods before workers could start strikes threatening national health or safety. Furious, the unions called the act a "slave-labor law."

Neither the tax cut nor the Taft-Hartley law was as retrogressive as Truman and his supporters claimed. The tax cut, which administration economists had thought would be inflationary, helped sustain purchasing power during a recession in 1949, while the labor law proved a workable, if clumsy, measure that Truman himself employed in attempts to head off strikes in key industries. For all their complaints, unions were able to live with Taft-Hartley for decades thereafter. The limited impact of both statutes suggests that the conservatives in Congress were unable (and in part unwilling) to alter the basic realities of income distribution or labor-management relations. Federal legislation, it appeared, made less difference than the politicians claimed.

But the struggles of the Eightieth Congress, and especially over Taft-Hartley, did make a difference in American politics. In 1945–46 Truman had often seemed aimless and complacent. In battling against Taft-Hartley and the tax bills, his combative, partisan spirit arose. Progressives, though remaining suspicious of his motives, cheered him on. "Let's come right out and say it," one exulted. "We thought Truman's labor veto message thrilling." If it did nothing else, the strife of the Eightieth Congress enabled Truman to strike a pose—for that in part is what it was—for the "people" against the "interests." This fighting image, which gained him the support of many New Dealers, was valuable in an election year.

Cold war, 1946–1948

The closing months of 1945 brought no respite from the tension that had been gathering between the United States and the Soviet Union. For the next three years, indeed for the next two decades, this Cold War, as it became known by 1947, was the paramount issue not only of international relations but of domestic politics.

Of the many forces that helped to foment tensions, the most important was Stalin's determination to safeguard Russian interests. By the end of 1945 it was clear that he had no intention of relinquishing his hold on eastern Europe. At the same time he systematically stripped East German industrial potential, and shipped thousands of German citizens—Nazis, Stalin claimed—to forced labor camps in Russia and its "satellites." He pressured Turkey for control of the straits leading from the Black Sea to the Mediterranean, and Iran for oil rights in Azerbaijan. In February 1946 he alarmed American observers by proclaiming that communism and capitalism were incompatible. Eric Sevareid, a progressive journalist, concluded that the speech made it "clear as daylight that the comintern, formalized or not, [was] back in effective operation. If you can brush aside Stalin's speech . . . you are a braver man than I."

These events led western leaders to stiffen their response to Stalin. In a timely cable sent two weeks after Stalin's speech, George Kennan, a top American diplomat in Moscow, argued that Stalin was "only the last of that long succession of cruel and wasteful Russian rulers who have relentlessly forced their country on to ever new heights of military power. . . ." Churchill,

Churchill, Truman
and Stalin
at Potsdam, Germany,
July 1945.

out of power but widely admired in America, spoke two weeks later in Missouri of an "iron curtain" descending around eastern Europe. The Soviets, he declared, sought the "indefinite expansion of their power and doctrines." An approving Truman sat on the platform as Churchill delivered this speech. The President also acted firmly. By dispatching an American battleship to the eastern Mediterranean, he warned against further Russian pressure on Turkey, and by sending stiff notes protesting against Soviet behavior in Iran, he helped stave off Russian encroachment. The American people obviously supported this get-tough policy: 71 percent said they disapproved of Russia's international conduct, and 60 percent thought America "too soft" in dealing with Moscow.

American leaders reflected this hardening of opinion in 1946. In September Secretary of State Byrnes proclaimed that the United States would henceforth forget about trying to secure Russian cooperation in the occupation of Germany. America would unilaterally strengthen its own zone. Russia, with good reason to fear a revitalized Germany, was understandably alarmed. Within a year and a half of the end of the European war, Germany, once the scourge of the world, was becoming the front line of western defense, while Russia, one of the Big Three, became the enemy.

In the same month Truman blundered into an impasse that resulted in the firing of Secretary of Commerce Henry Wallace. While Byrnes was negotiating with the Soviets in Paris, Wallace gave a speech that said the Russians

Division of Europe, 1945–1955

were trying to "socialize their sphere of interest just as we try to democratize our sphere of interest. . . . Only mutual trust would allow the United States and Russia to live together peacefully, and such trust could not be created by an unfriendly attitude and policy." Truman had looked at the speech beforehand, but too perfunctorily to realize how sharply it contradicted his own position. Senator Arthur Vandenberg, with Byrnes in Paris, cabled "we Republicans can cooperate with only one secretary of state at a time." Having maneuvered himself clumsily into a corner, Truman thereupon fired Wallace. In so doing he cut an important tie with left-wing American opinion on foreign policy.

Truman proved especially unbudging on the crucial question of atomic energy. Moderates such as former Secretary of War Stimson had been arguing that Russia would soon be able to develop the bomb on its own and that America ought to earn Soviet good will by sharing scientific secrets. Having done so, the United States and the Soviet Union could develop plans for international supervision and inspection. "The chief lesson I have learned in a long life," Stimson said, "is the only way you can make a man trustworthy is to trust him; and the surest way you can make a man untrustworthy is to distrust him and to show your distrust."

Even during the war, however, America had withheld atomic secrets not only from Russia but from England—in part to secure industrial advantages in the postwar world. Truman, who reflected this attitude, ignored Stimson and listened instead to anticommunist advisers like financier Bernard Baruch and future Secretary of State Dean Acheson. They called for international inspection and for the gradual sharing of scientific information (which could not be kept secret anyway). But they opposed letting the Soviet Union in on American technical expertise. Russia, in short, was to be subjected to prying into her military installations while the United States retained a monopoly of bomb manufacture. Stalin, demanding that America begin by destroying its stockpile, rejected the American proposal, and by the end of 1946 chances for international control of atomic weapons had disappeared.

A series of crises in the next year and a half intensified the Cold War. Indigenous communist guerillas in Greece threatened British influence in the eastern Mediterranean, and communist parties capitalizing on severe economic discontent seemed about to gain office in France and Italy. Responding quickly, Truman called in March 1947 for $400 million in military aid to Greece and Turkey. This Truman Doctrine stated that "it must be the policy of the United States to support free peoples who are resisting subjugation by armed minorities or by outside pressures. . . . we must assist free peoples to work out their own destinies in their own way." In May the same Republican Congress that was blocking Truman's domestic program granted his request.

A month later George Marshall, who had replaced Byrnes as secretary of state in January, called for massive aid to Europe. Seeking to deflect criticisms that America focused on providing military aid to shore up nations against communism, Marshall explained that his aid program was "directed not against any country or doctrine but against hunger, poverty, desperation, and chaos." But the President admitted that the Truman Doctrine and the Marshall Plan (both of which bypassed the United Nations) were "two halves of the same walnut." Marshall himself observed that American economic aid was aimed at permitting the "emergence of political and social conditions in which free institutions can exist." He also made European cooperation (and sharing of information about resources) a condition of getting aid—a requirement that inevitably discouraged Russian and eastern European participation in the plan. And Kennan, whose memorandums had influenced Marshall's thinking, published an article in July (written in January) that urged America to embark on "long-term, patient but firm and vigilant containment of Russia." The Marshall Plan, like the Truman Doctrine, embraced this doctrine of containment.

Congress moved slowly in considering Marshall's request, but the Soviets played into the administration's hands by communizing Czechoslovakia in early 1948. In June they reacted to western plans to create a more autonomous Federal Republic of Germany by blockading West Berlin. Truman, Secretary of Defense James Forrestal, and other ardent hawks in the administration responded with alarmist talk about a Russian takeover of western Europe—and with an airlift to relieve West Berlin. Congress then acquiesced by approving a peacetime draft—which lasted until 1973—and by passing the first of many authorizations for foreign aid.

These grants, so sharp a contrast to America's stinginess after World War I, helped restore European economic health. They showed how far the Cold War had dragged the country from isolation. But they were not altruistic. On the contrary, recipients of aid (which totaled some $100 billion in the next quarter century) were required to buy American goods in return. For Truman and his successors, preserving "free" institutions meant assisting American "free" enterprise. It also meant circling the Soviet Union with military force to ensure that such "freedoms" would thrive.

THE SOURCES OF AMERICAN ANTICOMMUNISM

To a degree, Russian-American rivalry was inevitable. As Alexis de Tocqueville had pointed out more than a century earlier, Russia and the United States were becoming the "two great nations in the world. . . . each seems marked out by the will of heaven to sway the destinies of half the globe." By 1945, with power vacuums in Europe and Asia, Tocqueville's prophecy came true, for the two superpowers found themselves head-to-head for the first time in history. Conflict between such different societies was to be expected.

As Wallace pointed out at the time, however, America's attitude toward the Soviet Union after 1945 was unusually truculent, especially in contrast to its patience with Hitler from 1933 to 1940. Though dictatorial, suspicious, often ruthless, Stalin was not bent on world conquest, or even (as French and Italian communists discovered to their dismay) on controlling western

American enterprise abroad, 1925–1955

| | FOREIGN TRADE (In millions of current dollars) | | | | | INTERNATIONAL INVESTMENTS (In billions of current dollars) | | |
| | EXPORT | | IMPORT | | | | | |
	AMOUNT	% OF GNP	AMOUNT	% OF GNP	BALANCE (+ OR −)	U. S. INVESTMENTS ABROAD	FOREIGN INVESTMENTS IN U.S.	NET INVESTMENT POSITION (+ OR −)
1925	5,272	5.4	4,419	4.6	+ 852	10.9[a]	3.9[a]	+ 7.0
1930	4,013	4.2	3,500	3.4	+ 514	17.2	8.4	+ 8.8
1935	2,304	3.1	4,143	5.7[b]	−1,839	13.5	6.4	+ 7.1
1940	4,030	4.0	7,433	7.4[b]	−3,403	12.3	13.5	− 1.2
1945	10,097	4.9	4,280	1.9	+5,816	16.8	17.6	− 0.8
1950	10,816	3.6	9,125	3.1	+1,691	32.8	19.5	+13.3
1955	15,563	3.9	11,562	2.9	+4,001	44.9	29.6	+15.3

SOURCE: Adapted from *Historical Statistics of the United States,* pp. 537, 542, 564
[a]Data for 1924   [b]Percentages recomputed from Census data

Europe. Despite Truman's assertions, the USSR did little to assist the Greek communists. Rather, Stalin seems—Soviet secrecy makes his ambitions unclear—to have sought traditional Russian goals: expanded influence in Iran to the south, in Manchuria to the east, in Turkey in the southwest. Above all, he hoped to preserve Russian power in eastern Europe as protection against a rearmed Germany. In this sense Wallace was probably correct in stating that Russia wished to protect and communize its sphere of influence in much the same way that the United States wished to expand its interest in Latin America and western Europe.

Why then did America act with such a show of energy and determination against the Soviet Union? The answer lay not only in Russian behavior, but also in domestic tensions and pressures within the United States.

Some of these stemmed from America's historical experience as the world's leading democratic nation. Until 1917, when Lenin led the Bolshevik revolution, Americans had confidently cherished their experience; it was their "manifest destiny" to serve as an example to the world. The rise of communism in Russia, however, was a frightening specter—so much so that America refused even to recognize the new regime until 1933. Like fascism, communism threatened democratic government and individual freedom. It also struck at private property. It possessed a prophetic strain in its ideology—worldwide proletarian revolution—which lent credence to the notion that communism and aggression were much the same. Americans, once so sure of their revolutionary appeal, now felt insecure and defensive, for they had to contend not only with Russian power but with a rival ideology of enormous appeal. Insecure nations, as both Russia and the United States revealed, often act impatiently and provocatively.

Americans especially feared communism's threat to capitalism. Already, it had cut off the markets (such as they were) of eastern Europe. What would happen if it crept into Asia, Latin America, or—as seemed possible in 1947—into Greece and western Europe? The answer, Truman's advisers thought, was that America's exports would suffer. A communistic world would therefore undermine America's dearly loved standard of living. This is not to say that economic motives dominated Truman's policies. But it was true that Truman, his advisers, corporate leaders, labor unions, Americans generally, sought the widest possible "Open Door" for American enterprise abroad. After all, capitalism and democratic government had expanded almost as one; the decline of one might mean the ultimate collapse of the other.

The presumed threat from Russia also aroused what Kennan later called the "American urge to the universalization or generalization of decision." By this he meant that the United States, with a history of relative security, had frequently talked in sweeping, moralistic terms. Now that America had the power to gain its goals, its leaders argued that cherished principles—of constitutional government, individual liberty, and capitalistic free enterprise—were universally good. From this perspective communism was universally evil, and Stalin loomed as the head of a united, worldwide conspiracy against the visions of the Founding Fathers. It followed that the United States must think in equally cosmic ways and spread the blessings of capitalism and democracy around the world. This "globalism" was at the root of Truman's doctrine supporting all "free peoples." By late 1948 it virtually silenced people who sought a more sensitive, limited response to international problems.

As in the past, the "lessons" of history affected policy. In the 1930s, Truman now thought, appeasement had encouraged aggressors to provoke a war. There must be no more "Munichs." Moreover, World War II had disposed people to think in all-or-nothing terms. Coexistence, to use a term the hard-liners hated, had been impossible with Hitler; Stalin, too, had to be battled at every turn until he was driven from the world stage. Some Americans even demanded a "preventive war" with the Soviet Union. Though responsible leaders never endorsed such a plan, their rhetoric grew almost as apocalyptic by the mid-1950s.

Domestic politics in America added to these pressures for firmness. Many of the most outraged anticommunists, including Polish-Americans, were Democrats whom Truman had to satisfy. So were many Catholics, who loathed the atheistic anticlericalism of bolshevism. Moreover, isolationism virtually vanished, a casualty of war. German-Americans, silenced by Hitler's atrocities, were anxious to prove their patriotism by standing up to the Bolsheviks. Republicans like Vandenberg wondered if America could be isolated in the age of air power. Others feared to sound like appeasers. And conservative Republicans were quick to oppose left-wing ideologies whether at home or abroad. The defection of such groups from the isolationist cause meant that Truman, unlike Roosevelt in the 1930s, was safer politically when he struck back at the Soviet Union than he was when he turned the other cheek.

But Truman was no simple prisoner of public opinion. On the contrary, he had displayed his feelings toward Stalin as early as July 1941, when he said, "if we see that Germany is winning we ought to help Russia, and if Russia is winning we ought to help Germany." In office only a few weeks in 1945, he took such a firm line that Foreign Minister Molotov complained that he had never been spoken to so harshly in all his life. "Carry out your agreements," Truman snapped undiplomatically, "and you won't get talked to like that." Once America became the sole possessor of the A-bomb, he felt safer than ever in adopting an unbending line. Thereafter Truman made little effort to carry on Roosevelt's earlier policy of cooperating with the Russians.

These preconceived notions helped Truman to talk tough without qualms. They made him unreceptive to Soviet requests for economic aid. They enabled him to talk of "saving" eastern Europe, an area traditionally outside America's national interest. They induced him to overlook the fact that the bomb, which was of limited value except to blast Soviet cities, was not a credible deterrent in case of military clashes in western Europe. As the historian John Gaddis put it, the bomb represented the Impotence of Omnipotence. Truman's anticommunism also led him deliberately to exaggerate the Soviet threat. This was the approach—"scaring hell out of the country," Senator Vandenberg said approvingly—that he used in 1947 in getting Congress to approve the Truman Doctrine. Far from trying to change the contours of public opinion, Truman exploited the prevailing anticommunist fears of most Americans. In so doing he helped escalate the Cold War.

Truman could have employed much subtler ways of serving his ends. Indeed, the containment policy of the world's only nuclear power made Stalin even more suspicious than he already was. If Truman had really hoped to defuse the Cold War (and after 1946 there is no evidence that he did), he might have spent less time in futile talk about getting the Russians out of eastern Europe. He might have recognized the foolishness of trying to keep knowledge of atomic energy from Russian scientists. He might have conceded the truth of the argument that the Truman Doctrine shored up undemocratic regimes in Greece and Turkey.

America might also have made better use of economic policy. This would have involved providing Stalin with aid as a carrot to induce Soviet cooperation. Because World War II had devastated Russia, Stalin very much wanted such help. Considering Russian sacrifices, he felt he deserved it. If he had gotten it, he would still have insisted on controlling eastern Europe: there was no way to avoid tensions altogether. But economic assistance might have made him feel more secure, less suspicious, much less resentful. It might even have induced him to moderate his pillage of East Germany—one of the most divisive issues of the Cold War. In any event, the carrot of economic assistance would have been better than no carrot at all.

Truman's failure to follow these potential avenues to détente attracted relatively little notice at the time. Instead, he and his fellow warriors struck most Americans as patriots combatting a worldwide communist conspiracy that was as "immoral" as that of fascism a few years before. Blunt, moralistic, and anticommunist, Truman reflected the sentiments of most of his countrymen. As the election campaign approached, his determined foreign policy was an asset, not a liability.

Truman's second term

TRUMAN IN 1948

In early 1948 many liberal Democrats rebelled at the thought of renominating Truman for the presidency. Franklin D. Roosevelt, Jr., Hubert H. Humphrey, the young, progressive mayor of Minneapolis, and others backed General Eisenhower. The *New Republic* editorialized, "As a candidate for President Harry Truman should quit." "If Truman is nominated," the columnists Joseph and Stewart Alsop wrote, "he will be forced to wage the loneliest campaign in history."

After the conventions Truman's chances seemed little better. Though he secured the Democratic nomination (Eisenhower refused to be considered), many left-wing leaders gave their support to Henry Wallace, who broke away to form the Progressive party. Their defection appeared likely to hurt Truman in key urban areas. In addition, Truman had to contend with southerners who bolted in protest against a liberal Democratic civil rights plank. They named Governor J. Strom Thurmond of South Carolina as their candidate on the States Rights Democratic (Dixiecrat) ticket. And Republicans, rejecting Taft, named what appeared to be a strong ticket composed of the popular vote-getting governors Thomas Dewey of New York and Earl Warren of California. The derisive slogan "We're Just Mild About Harry" appeared an accurate description of Truman's appeal to voters.

Until election day the public opinion polls showed Dewey with a strong lead. But it turned out they were wrong. The Dixiecrats failed to gain much support outside the Deep South. Indeed, their very presence in the campaign forced blacks and other civil rights advocates to recognize Truman's efforts, however limited, in their behalf. In November Thurmond won only four states, while Truman ran up large margins in black wards in the North.

Wallace's campaign disintegrated just as rapidly. Some observers, including many who backed his policies, found him vague and mystical. Others worried that he had become a tool of the communists and that many top Progressives were party members or fellow travelers. Labor leader Walter Reuther, a committed reformer, spoke for many anticommunist liberals in concluding that "Henry is a lost soul. . . . Communists perform the most complete valet service in the world. They write your speeches, they do your thinking for you, they provide you with applause, and they inflate your ego." Wallace's pro-Soviet line at the height of the Cold War ultimately left most liberals with no one to turn to save Truman.

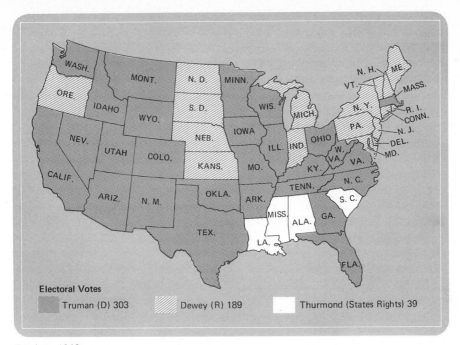

Electoral Votes
Truman (D) 303 Dewey (R) 189 Thurmond (States Rights) 39

Election, 1948

Dewey, too, failed to excite the voters. A trim, dapper little man, he struck one critic as a "certified public accountant in search of the Holy Grail." Others found him cold, curt, and aloof—it was said that "you have to know him really well to dislike him." Certain of victory, Dewey ran a bland campaign aimed at offending the smallest possible number of people. In the process he was vague and unclear on the issues, and he ignited little grass roots enthusiasm. Fewer Republicans came to the polls in 1948 than in either 1940 or 1944.

Finally, Truman himself proved a feisty, opportunistic campaigner. At the convention he electrified the faithful by calling the "do-nothing" Eightieth Congress back into special session to act on Fair Deal legislation. His motives

No presidential candidate in the future will be so inept that four of his major speeches can be boiled down to these historic four sentences. Agriculture is important. Our rivers are full of fish. You cannot have freedom without liberty. The future lies ahead. (We might add a fifth . . . the TVA is a fine thing and we must make certain that nothing like it ever happens again.)

The Louisville *Courier Journal* (November 1948) ridicules Dewey's passive campaign.

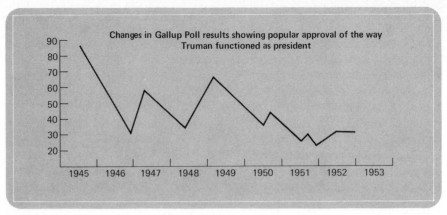

Changes in Gallup Poll results showing popular approval of the way Truman functioned as president

SOURCE: Adapted from Irish and Frank, *U.S. Foreign Policy*, p. 104

Truman started out at the peak of his popularity in 1945, when 87 percent of respondents approved of his presidency, and he consistently moved downward in popular esteem to reach a low in late 1951 when only 23 percent approved of the way he was handling the presidency.

kept up the offensive. Republicans, he charged, were "just a bunch of old mossbacks . . . gluttons of privilege . . . all set to do a hatchet job on the New Deal." He then set off on a series of whistle-stop tours, always on the attack. This partisan strategy developed by his aide, Clark Clifford, was both abrasive and extreme, but it had the virtue of placing the GOP on the defensive. It exploited to the most Democratic ties with labor and the "have-not" coalition that had four times elected Roosevelt.

For all these reasons Truman surprised almost everyone by winning in November, with 24.1 million votes to Dewey's 22 million. Thurmond got less than 1.2 million, and Wallace only 1,157,000 and no electoral votes. Perhaps because of his liberal record as governor of New York, Dewey actually did better in urban states than the Republicans had in 1944, carrying New York, Pennsylvania, Michigan, and New Jersey. But Truman scored well in farm areas, where he had misleadingly accused the Republican Congress of withholding funds for storage facilities. He did sufficiently well in other urban states—narrowly carrying California, Illinois, and Ohio—to pile up a substantial margin in the electoral college of 303 to 189 and to carry with him Democratic majorities in both houses of Congress. Among those who were elected for the first time to the Senate were such important liberal Democrats as Hubert Humphrey of Minnesota, Paul Douglas of Illinois, and Estes Kefauver of Tennessee, as well as the more conservative Lyndon Johnson, who won in Texas. The remarkably low turnout, more than a million less than in 1940, suggested that voters did not find either Truman or Dewey particularly attractive. Truman, in fact, failed to get 50 percent of the vote. But it also showed that the Democratic voting coalition forged during the depression remained intact and that the reforms of the New Deal were safe from attack.

These were impressive reminders of the chronic weakness of the GOP and of the stability of American politics.

PROBLEMS, HOME AND ABROAD, 1949

President in his own right, Truman determined to make up for lost time, and in January 1949 he called on Congress to enact a broad-ranging program. It included health insurance, repeal of Taft-Hartley, extension of social security, increases in the minimum wage, civil rights legislation, federal aid to education, and larger appropriations for public housing. In foreign policy he broached the idea of supplying underdeveloped nations with technical assistance. Point Four, as it was called, suggested that the administration was beginning to worry not only about communism in western Europe but throughout the uncommitted world.

Truman also lent his support in 1949 to the Brannan Plan for farmers. Named after Charles Brannan, his progressive secretary of agriculture, the plan was a dramatic effort to revise the New Deal farm program. Brannan argued correctly that price supports were expensive to the government and a burden on consumers. He insisted that they helped a few large farmers at the expense of small producers, that they encouraged overproduction in crops eligible for federal subsidies, and that other produce—including meat and dairy goods—was often so short in supply that prices escalated and diets suffered. Brannan's answer to these problems was complex. To assist consumers he demanded an end to price supports. Farmers would sell their goods for whatever price they commanded in the open market—prices that would ordinarily be considerably lower than in the past. To help farmers who suffered from the withdrawal of price supports, he called for income supports instead. These income supports, available only in limited amounts per crop, would provide a basic floor under income for all farmers. The package, Brannan thought, would limit the power of agribusiness, assist small farmers, rescue consumers, and save the government money.

During the next two years Truman secured a few of these goals. Some of them, such as progress toward desegregation of the armed forces, came by executive order. Truman also strengthened the Civil Rights Division of the Department of Justice, which brought important suits against Jim Crow practices in education, transportation, and housing. Other reforms actually broke through the bottleneck on Capitol Hill. Congress passed a housing act including funds for public housing. It increased the minimum wage from forty cents to seventy-five cents, extended rent controls through 1950, and approved a displaced persons act admitting some 400,000 refugees to the United States. It raised social security benefits and broadened the program to cover 10 million new Americans. These were the most liberal measures passed by any Congress since 1935.

But the conservative coalition, though weaker than at any time since 1938, still held its own. It fought Truman's requests for civil rights legislation, health insurance, and federal aid to education. It proved slow in providing funds for Point Four. It showed itself willing to revise Taft-Hartley, but when Truman insisted on repeal, Congress balked, and the act remained as it was. After 1949 it proved very stingy in appropriating funds for the public housing program, which never even approached the expectations of reformers. And the Brannan Plan fell under the onslaught of well-organized interest groups. Business people opposed the very idea of income supports, which they insisted would drain the Treasury. Labor unions, seeing nothing in the plan for themselves, were lukewarm. Large commercial farmers opposed the abolition of price supports. Like any proposal lacking the endorsement of entrenched groups, the Brannan Plan was doomed to defeat.

In the area of foreign policy Truman secured a major goal when Congress approved American participation in the North Atlantic Treaty Organization, a mutual defense pact that bound twelve signatories to fight against aggression. It was the first time in American history that Congress had ratified a military alliance with European nations. Later in 1949 Congress added teeth to the pact by authorizing money for military aid to member nations. Because Stalin had no plans to attack western Europe, the NATO pact was of questionable military value. The military assistance plan, still more provocative, propelled America further into the business of supplying arms to other nations. At the time, however, both NATO and military aid were described as essential to sustain the morale of western Europe. They proved highly popular measures during the struggle to win the Cold War.

Events in Asia all but obscured Truman's successes in Europe. Since 1945, when American marines had helped Chiang Kai-shek strengthen his claims on North China, Truman had pursued Roosevelt's illusory hope for a peaceful, noncommunist China. But Chiang's corruption, and his failure to fight hard against the Japanese during the war, had already damaged his claim to rule, and Communist forces under Mao Tse-tung pressed forward. In 1946 Truman dispatched General George C. Marshall to China in an attempt to bring American influence to bear on the situation. Marshall, like other emissaries before him, sought to reconcile Chiang and Mao. When the two sides agreed to a truce, it seemed that his patient efforts had succeeded. But by late 1946 the truce had broken down. Mao's forces pushed on, and Marshall returned home to become secretary of state.

Truman then requested a report from General Albert Wedemeyer, America's chief military emissary in China. Wedemeyer's advice, to escalate aid to Chiang and to send 10,000 American military "advisers" to China, received a cool reception from Marshall and others in the State Department, and Truman not only rejected Wedemeyer's report but kept it from Congress. Within a year and a half, in 1949, Chiang's forces collapsed, and in December he fled to Formosa. China, land of more than 500 million people, was now a communist country.

Truman responded calmly to the "fall of China." His secretary of state after 1948, the tough, aristocratic Dean Acheson, spoke for the administration in defending what had been America's policy since 1945. Sending in "advisers," he pointed out, would lead only to unnecessary loss of American life. Defeating Mao would require a major land war on the Asian continent, a war that the United States had neither the men nor the will to fight, especially at a time when Stalin seemed to pose a threat in Europe. Chiang's own maladministration, not American neglect, had led to the Communist victory. "Nothing this country did or could have done within the reasonable limits of its capabilities," Acheson argued, "would have changed the result, nothing that was left undone by this country has contributed to it."

The Truman-Acheson argument was irrefutable. Few Americans before 1949 had demanded any sizeable commitment to Chiang, and the administration, which was focusing its attention on Europe, would have had serious trouble trying to mobilize support for massive aid in China as well. Moreover, almost no one at the time expected economic or military aid to do much good. Even Wedemeyer had conceded that Chiang was losing because of corruption and "lack of spirit, primarily lack of spirit. It was not lack of equipment. In my judgment they could have defended the Yangtze if they had had the will to do it." In opting for limited aid to Chiang between 1945 and 1949 the Truman administration followed Roosevelt in backing the wrong horse. But it had sense enough not to waste more money than it did (perhaps $2 billion by 1949), and to keep American men out of what would have been an endless bloodbath.

The fall of so much territory to communism was not easy for Americans to accept. The United States, the history books said, had never lost a war. It had beaten both the Germans and the Japanese. It had sole possession of the bomb. Why then had it "lost" China? Why had it not acted to preserve the Open Door policy? Sensible observers replied that China was an ancient civilization that had never been America's to lose. They explained that the Open Door doctrine did not apply, for Mao had triumphed on his own, with little aid indeed from Stalin. But many people refused to listen to reason. Deluded by the illusion of American omnipotence, they continued to ask where and how Truman had gone wrong.

Some of Truman's critics concluded that he had merely made mistakes. Others were "Asia-firsters" or members of the so-called China lobby. Many of these people, especially partisan Republicans, grew nasty. Truman, they charged, had been duped by procommunist sympathizers in the State Department. Moreover, the Russians exploded their own atomic bomb in September 1949: perhaps procommunist scientists working for America had turned over secrets to help Stalin on his way? By 1950, Truman had to confront a resurgence of popular fears about the spread of communism.

MC CARTHYISM

Senator Joseph McCarthy of Wisconsin, the demagogue who capitalized on these fears, began his Red-hunting campaign in February 1950 by claiming in a speech in Wheeling to hold in his hand the names of 207 (or 57—he was not clear) communists in government. Though few people paid him much notice at first, he repeated, expanded, and varied his charges in succeeding speeches, and by March he was front-page news across the country. At last, it seemed to Truman's critics, a responsible person had evidence not only of procommunist sympathy in high places but of disloyalty and treason.

Before McCarthy and fellow Red-haters overreached themselves in late 1954 they broadened their cause into a powerful witch hunt that swept into every corner of American life. McCarthyism destroyed morale in the State Department, cowed the Department of the Army, and exposed America's hysterical anticommunism to the scorn of civilized people throughout the world.

McCarthyism reached deeply into the fabric of American government. The Supreme Court in 1951 upheld the Smith Act of 1940, which had made it a crime even to advocate revolution. Its decision, in *Dennis* v. *U. S.,* resulted in the conviction and imprisonment of eleven top Communists and encouraged the Justice Department to proceed with further prosecutions. Ordinarily decent conservatives, such as Taft, also jumped on the anti-Red bandwagon.

Senator Joseph McCarthy with his aide, Roy Cohn, on his right and Cohn's friend G. David Schine, on McCarthy's left.

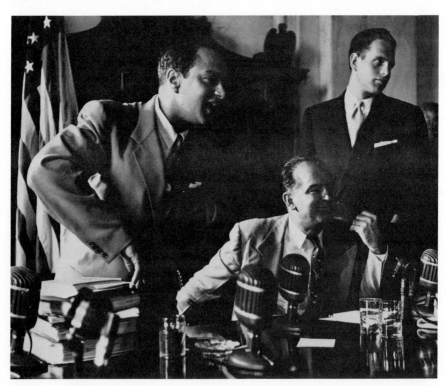

McCarthy, he said, was a "fighting Marine who risked his life to preserve the
liberties of the United States." If accusations proved unfounded, Taft
advised, McCarthy should keep trying. Liberals joined conservatives to
approve the Internal Security Act of 1950. It required Communists to register
with the Attorney General, and it set up the Subversives Activities Board to
review the loyalty of government employees. In vetoing it Truman correctly
contended that the act was obscure, unfair, and unworkable. But 1950 was an
election year, and practically no one dared to oppose the anticommunist
onslaught. Congress quickly passed the act over Truman's veto.

Heartened by such responses, the Red-baiters became almost unbelievably extreme in 1951–52. McCarthy charged that the Democratic party was
"the property of men and women . . . who have bent to the whispered pleas
from the lips of traitors . . . who wear the political label stitched with the
idiocy of a Truman, [and] rotted by the deceit of a Dean Acheson." Marshall,
he added, was "a man steeped in falsehood . . . who has resorted to the lie
whenever it suits his convenience . . . [and who was part of a] conspiracy so
immense and an infamy so black as to dwarf any previous venture in the
history of man." Not to be outdone, Senator William Jenner of Indiana
concluded that America was "in the hands of a secret inner coterie which is
directed by agents of the Soviet Union. . . . Our only choice is to impeach
President Truman and find out who is the secret inner government."

These statements were wholly undocumented. The Red-baiters produced
no evidence to support their accusations, and they never exposed a communist in government. Indeed, McCarthy himself made little effort to follow up
his scattershot accusations. On the contrary, he remained a profane, often
unshaven, half-sober individualist whose crusade against communism was
aimed at securing the recognition he would need for his reelection campaign in
1952, and for higher political ambitions to follow. "That's it," he told friends
who suggested anticommunism as an issue. "The government is full of
communists. We can hammer away at them."

McCarthy's charges were as unnecessary as they were irresponsible, for
Communists in America were weaker in 1950 than at any time since the 1920s.

Anticommunist labor leaders had deprived them of positions of strength that they had enjoyed in the CIO. The government, especially after Truman created loyalty boards in 1947, had launched systematic (and often unconstitutional) security checks on federal employees. Russian moves such as the coup in Czechoslovakia and the blockade of West Berlin had driven all but the avid Stalinists out of the party. By the time McCarthy started his crusade the Communist party had already fallen into the decline that cut its membership from a high of around 80,000 in 1945 to less than 3000 in the late 1950s.

Because McCarthy himself was so crude and reckless, and because communism at home was dwindling, it was hard for contemporary defenders of civil liberties to explain his appeal. In retrospect, however, it is clear that several forces combined to make him the dangerous demagogue that he was.

Among these was McCarthy himself. His very irresponsibility made him a frightening foe, for he thought nothing of charging his critics with communist sympathies. Politicians, therefore, were careful not to antagonize him. McCarthy was also a master at using the press, which had treated his sensational charges as page-one news. Shrewdly, he would call press conferences early in the morning to tell reporters that earth-shaking disclosures were soon to be announced. Alerted, the afternoon papers would print banner headlines, ''McCarthy New Revelations Expected Soon.'' Newsmen for morning papers would then besiege him for the latest developments, and McCarthy obliged by leading them to believe a key witness was about to be found. Hence the morning headlines, ''Delay in McCarthy Revelations: Mystery Witness Sought.'' Tactics such as these brought McCarthy maximum publicity.

McCarthy was also fortunate in his timing. Just as he inaugurated his campaign, Alger Hiss, a former State Department offical accused of espionage, was convicted of perjury—after two widely publicized trials. His conviction, which followed on a congressional investigation spearheaded by Representative Richard Nixon of California, appeared proof that communists infested the government. McCarthy was further helped by the revelation that Klaus Fuchs, a British physicist, had passed American atomic secrets to the Soviets. Legal proceedings stemming from the Fuchs case culminated three years later in the conviction and execution for espionage of Julius and Ethel Rosenberg, American Communists allegedly involved in the atomic plot. Actually, these cases did not prove much. If Hiss was a communist agent— which he steadfastly denied—he appears to have given the Russians nothing of value. Fuchs helped the Russians along on research that they were mastering on their own. The Rosenbergs, whose guilt was still being hotly debated many years later, were in no way associated with the government. Still, the Fuchs case was proof of the need for security. McCarthy, many Americans told themselves, might be a little rough in his methods, but his goals were noble. If permitted to continue, he would uncover the ''traitors'' in government.

Powerful interest groups further assisted McCarthy's campaigns. Among these were defense contractors and the military forces that had suffered from demobilization. Not all these groups thought well of McCarthy's methods—indeed, he later infuriated the army brass by accusing it of harboring Communists. But his virulent campaign obviously assisted their demands for defense spending. With such potent forces supporting McCarthy's goals, or at least acquiescing in them, he had advantages lesser demagogues would have lacked.

McCarthyism also seemed to offer simple answers to the complex questions of the Cold War. China went Communist, he explained, because State Department "traitors" willed it so. Russia developed the A-bomb because people like Fuchs told them how to do it. Capitalism and democracy would have nothing to fear if the "commies" were rooted out of American life. This conspiratorial approach to the world prevented the country from engaging in the debate necessary to develop flexible policies. But because McCarthy's road to salvation seemed so quick and easy, it exercised an appeal that more complex, more accurate explanations failed to provide.

This conspiracy theory appealed in particular to superpatriotic Americans who responded warmly to McCarthy's attacks on intellectuals, left-wing sympathizers, New Dealers, and well-educated, upper-class easterners like Acheson. "I watch his smart-aleck manner and his British clothes and that New Dealism," Senator Hugh Butler of Nebraska exclaimed of Acheson, " . . . and I want to shout, Get out. Get out. You stand for everything that has been wrong with the United States for years." Butler, a Republican, had partisan reasons for welcoming assaults on the "striped-pants boys" in the State Department. An economic conservative, he would have shuddered at the thought of being linked with populism or with Nebraska's "Great Commoner," William Jennings Bryan. But like many Americans he was at one with Bryan in suspecting the worst of the Eastern Establishment. In this way McCarthy had the best of two worlds: by hammering at communism he could appeal to conservatives, and by slashing at intellectuals and the Eastern Establishment he could win the approval of ordinary people.

Others who reacted positively to McCarthy included many ethnic Americans, especially blue-collar Catholics. By 1950 most of these people were second- or third-generation Americans. Many had fought in World War II. But as ethnics and Catholics they frequently suffered discrimination, and they were rarely accepted as "100 percent Americans." McCarthy, himself a Catholic, seemed one of them. By supporting his movement, ethnics could prove their patriotism, indeed their super-patriotism. Catholics could demonstrate their support of a movement directed against atheistic communism. For these reasons McCarthyism was strong in many heavily Catholic urban areas and in Catholic states like Massachusetts, where some politicians shared his concerns. "McCarthy," said John F. Kennedy, "may have something."

Not all political figures acted like Kennedy. Some, especially those who represented rural, Protestant states, felt freer to speak out in defense of civil liberties. These included senators George Aiken, a Vermont Republican, Margaret Chase Smith, a GOP colleague from Maine, and J. William Fulbright, a Democrat from Arkansas. But most office-holders, including many liberals, were almost as anticommunist as McCarthy himself. They might deplore his methods, but they were committed to a hard-line Cold War policy. This is not to suggest, as some historians have, that Truman's exaggerations about Soviet designs made McCarthyism inevitable. But it is to say that the Cold War that the administration waged after 1945 helped sustain the atmosphere of fear in which McCarthy thrived. To this extent McCarthyism was a broad-based (though unorganized) phenomenon, urban-ethnic as well as rural, and promoted by the rhetoric of liberals as well as conservatives.

In this sense McCarthyism was but the latest of many eruptions of intolerance in American history. Federalists had tried to silence their "radical" Jeffersonian foes by introducing the Alien and Sedition acts of 1798. Know-Nothings, nativist politicians of the 1850s, had developed considerable support in their campaign against Catholics and foreigners. Waves of prejudice against aliens had swept the country in tense periods since the 1870s. The Red Scare of 1919, the sharpest explosion of all, had broken out against foreigners as well as leftists. By the early 1950s the "hyphenated-Americans" no longer seemed much of a threat. But the communists did. In such turbulent times, it was easy to make them a scapegoat for the nation's problems.

McCarthyism was above all the product of partisan politics at midcentury. For years American politicians had courted favor by preaching against the evils of communism. Some, such as Nixon, had built political careers by doing it. Like McCarthy, these people wanted desperately to run the Democrats out of the White House, and anticommunism, by 1950, seemed the most effective issue to employ to that end. Thus it was that when McCarthy ran again in 1952 he scored best in areas that had traditionally been Republican. This connection between McCarthyism and Republicanism was important in giving purpose and direction to the anticommunist crusade.

To counter such implacable opposition Truman might have been well advised to take it seriously. This would have involved giving a bipartisan congressional committee access to classified executive documents concerning alleged security risks. Without publicizing information about individuals, the committee might have established the facts concerning McCarthy's charges. Deprived of the claim that Truman was hiding pertinent data, McCarthy would have had to quiet down, or to watch his accusations be torn to shreds.

Truman, however, hardly considered such a strategy. McCarthy, of course, would have insisted on being named to such a committee. If Democrats in Congress had refused to grant his demand, McCarthy would have shouted that he had been excluded. If they had agreed to it, they chanced having McCarthy give classified (and probably misleading) evidence to the press. Either way, the administration—to say nothing of the alleged security risks—might suffer.

Accordingly, Truman resorted to the doctrine of executive privilege: McCarthy would get no documents from him. He stepped up his campaign to rid the government of alleged security risks. Henceforth employees had to furnish proof, beyond a "reasonable doubt," of their loyalty. He encouraged Democrats in Congress to pursue their own counter-investigation of McCarthy's charges. But these approaches merely suggested that Truman had something to hide. And in November 1950, Senator Millard Tydings of Maryland, the conservative Democrat who had chaired the investigation, went down in defeat before a Red-baiter who came close to outdoing McCarthy himself. Thereafter few Democrats wanted to sling stones at the Goliath of American politics. From February 1950 until the end of his tenure in the White House, President Truman had to endure his Wisconsin tormenter.

THE TRAVAIL OF KOREA

On June 25, 1950 communist forces from North Korea poured across the thirty-eighth parallel and attacked the prowestern government of South Korea. Acting quickly, Truman authorized American forces under General Douglas MacArthur to go to South Korea's aid. At first it seemed as if MacArthur's troops might be destroyed. But the Americans and South Koreans held on until September, when MacArthur engineered a brilliant amphibious counterattack north of the enemy's lines. His forces then drove across the thirty-eighth parallel and smashed northward until they came within reach of the North Korean border with China.

If MacArthur's counteroffensive had stopped near the parallel, or if it had moved less precipitously toward China, the war might have ended there and then, a glorious triumph for Truman and for the anticommunist cause. As it was, the Chinese threw masses of men into battle, and American soldiers fled back into South Korea. General Matthew Ridgway, who replaced MacArthur in April 1951, restored order, but the conflict dragged on until a truce was arranged in July 1953. It divided the country along lines similar to those in force before the 1950 invasion and sustained in power Syngman Rhee, the anticommunist ruler of South Korea. For the West, therefore, the war had succeeded in preventing communist gains; Truman's intervention had not been wasted. It also resulted in a huge escalation of defense spending from approximately $14 billion in 1949 to $44 billion in 1953. This figure, some 60 percent of the federal budget, sparked a boom in the economy lasting until 1954. But the conflict left 54,000 Americans dead and 103,000 wounded. It wholly diverted attention—and funds—from domestic reforms. It greatly strengthened the role of the military and of defense contractors in American society. And because Truman refused to escalate the war still faster, he played readily into the hands of McCarthyites. The war applied the *coup de grace* to the administration's standing with the electorate.

Such a protracted war naturally prompted sharp debate over the wisdom of Truman's actions. Some critics complained that American policies had helped provoke the war in the first place. Others questioned his decisions to involve the United States in the fighting and then to press on over the thirty-eighth parallel. Many others denounced him for refusing to broaden the war once the Chinese had jumped into it.

The complaint that America helped to provoke the war was favored by right-wing critics at the time. Truman, they argued, had practically invited a North Korean invasion by removing American occupation troops from South Korea in 1949 and by leaving Rhee's government almost defenseless against the well-drilled forces of the North. Dean Acheson, they emphasized, had outlined an American "defense perimeter" in Asia that appeared to exclude Korea. With such a "soft spot" exposed, the communists, supplied by the Soviet Union, naturally pounced on it in June, 1950.

Later left-wing critics, revisionists who renewed the debate over Korean policy in the 1960s, challenged Truman's policies from a different perspective. Rhee, they argued, was a dictatorial nationalist who had regularly vowed his intention to reunite Korea, by force of arms if necessary. His very presence antagonized the North. When he lost support in the May 1950 elections, revisionists suggested, he determined to provoke border incidents to reestablish his image and perhaps to force the United States to defend his regime. Other revisionists argued that America provoked an attack from the North by announcing plans in the spring of 1950 to negotiate a bilateral defense pact with Japan. To prevent such a development, revisionists surmised, North Korean leader Kim Il Sung attacked before the United States had the power to respond. Other revisionists went still further in chastising the Truman administration. Pointing to a position paper of the National Security Council (NSC-68), they showed that Truman's leading defense planners had agreed early in 1950 to seek enormous increases in American military might. How better to get the money out of Congress than by tempting or provoking the North Koreans to attack?

Because the relevant documents are unavailable to historians it is impossible to know why North Korea attacked in June 1950. It is therefore hazardous at best to evaluate the critiques of Truman. But some facts seem clear. Obviously, the United States was unwise in leaving Rhee's forces so weak and in implying that South Korea lay outside America's primary lines of defense. America could also have moved less threateningly toward a rapprochement with Japan. Conceivably, it could have assisted moderate factions to take over in South Korea. Such a policy—military preparedness allied to political and diplomatic moderation—might have preserved peace on the peninsula.

Still, Truman and Acheson had sound reasons for their prewar policies. The President's military advisers, including General MacArthur, had regularly called for the removal of American troops from South Korea, a place they considered costly to defend and of little strategic value. The military also needed all the strength they could find to bolster NATO. Moreover, arming Rhee properly seemed impossible—Congress would not have supplied the funds—and unwise, for Rhee might then have staged his own attack on the North. And though Truman might have worked to dispose of Rhee, whose

Korean War, 1950–1953

power was slipping in early 1950, North Korea acted first. For better or worse, America and Syngman Rhee were thrust together against a common foe.

The revisionist case distorts two other essential points. First, for whatever reasons, it was not South Korea but North Korea that mounted the attack, which was too well planned and coordinated to pass as a mere border incident. Second, though many American military leaders wanted to increase defense spending, there is no evidence to suggest that they yearned for a war in Korea, which they continued to dismiss as of little importance. Indeed, such a war would drain western defenses in Europe, which was Washington's major concern. The Korean War was a conflict that few people in America had expected and that fewer still were very happy to be involved in while it dragged on to 1951.

Truman's decision to resist the North Korean invasion prompted other criticisms. If Korea was hard to protect and of little military value, why bother to defend it? Key senators like Taft demanded to know why Truman did not consult Congress or ask for a formal declaration of war. Instead, Truman merely secured United Nations sanction (possible because the Soviets were boycotting the Security Council at the time), for common "police action" against the aggressor. Later, when the war deteriorated into an apparently endless stalemate, Truman's failure to consult Congress cost him dearly. Still later it offered an excuse for President Kennedy and Johnson to send American troops to Vietnam without congressional sanction.

In June 1950, Truman easily brushed aside complaints. The North Korean invasion, he declared, was part of a communist design to test America's will in the Cold War. The United States must fight to show that it would hold the line, that it would not repeat the disastrous appeasement policy of the 1930s. There must be no more Munichs. He added that he had to act quickly. If America waited for Congress to debate the issue, the North Koreans would overrun the peninsula.

Truman's arguments were a little self-serving, for no one could prove that the North Korean invasion was part of a broader communist design, or even that it had been encouraged by the Soviet Union. And while it was true that Truman had to act quickly, he could still have requested congressional approval at any time in the early weeks of the war. But the blatancy and the speed of the invasion made his arguments so hard to refute at the time that even critics like Taft grudgingly supported American intervention. In responding as he did Truman acted decisively, even courageously. Years later it is possible to fault his disregard of Congress, but harder to question the wisdom of the basic decision itself.

Truman's most controversial decision was authorizing MacArthur to push on toward the Yalu River, North Korea's northern border with China. His action seemed sensible at the time, for MacArthur had the enemy on the run. It also reflected the almost unanimous counsel of his top military and diplomatic advisers and of Allied leaders. There should not be South Koreans and North Koreans, British Foreign Secretary Ernest Bevin declared, only Koreans. The Chinese, Truman was reassured, were too tired to get involved in Korea. Moreover, Asian peoples were no match for America's technological superiority. "We are no longer fearful of their [Chinese] intervention," MacArthur told Truman at a special meeting on Wake Island in October. "The

United Nations soldiers retreating in Korea, January 1951. This was a low point for the allied forces in South Korea.

Chinese have 300,000 men in Manchuria. . . . Only 50,000 to 60,000 could be gotten across the Yalu River. They have no air force. Now that we have bases for our air force in Korea, if the Chinese tried to get down to Pyongyang [the North Korean capital near the thirty-eighth parallel] there would be the greatest slaughter.''

The astonishingly successful intervention of the Chinese in November 1950, of course, quickly proved the tragic foolishness of such advice. Truman's advisers, including not only MacArthur but also the Central Intelligence Agency, deserved to be condemned for predicting that the Chinese would stay out. But Truman himself might have paused before accepting such counsel, for the Chinese had implied through diplomatic channels that they would attack UN forces that pushed north of the thirty-eighth parallel. In ignoring such a possibility Truman and his advisers displayed exaggerated faith in western technology and contempt for Oriental military potential. As George Kennan pointed out at the time, Truman and his aides were also bemused by the insidious belief, another product of the modern age, that total victory is the purpose of war. In urging MacArthur to drive toward the Yalu, Truman went beyond containment to seek what later became known as a policy of liberation. Nothing could have been more disastrous.

The conflict with China accelerated the war's most dramatic clash of wills—between Truman and MacArthur. As the Chinese advanced, the general became progressively more restive and querulous. Truman, he complained, should escalate the war. The administration must blockade mainland China, "unleash" Chiang Kai-shek for raids in Korea or South China, and authorize air-sea attacks on Chinese "sanctuaries" in Manchuria. Without such steps, MacArthur insisted, America could never win the war.

Truman, however, shrank from embarking on such a course. He recognized that any attempt to blockade China's long coastline would tie up a substantial part of America's navy, which was needed elsewhere. A blockade might also lead to confrontation with other nations, including Russia. In any event, a blockade could do nothing to stop the flow of supplies that came overland from the Soviet Union.

With similar prudence, Truman rejected the idea of helping Chiang raid China. Contrary to MacArthur's assumption, such attacks would not have prompted native uprisings against the communist regime—Chiang remained too unpopular for that to happen. Rather, Nationalist incursions, to be at all effective, would have required an enormous American commitment. The United States might have become involved in a renewal of the Chinese civil war, an eventuality that MacArthur himself shied away from.

Truman was equally wise to refrain from bombing Chinese "sanctuaries." Strategic bombing during World War II had suggested that such attacks rarely worked wonders. In Korea, they would have done nothing to stop China's major asset, masses of foot soldiers who needed only the most meager rations to keep pressing toward the south. Employing bombers would also have frightened America's western allies, who needed no reminding that Russian territory touched the Yalu. Suppose the bombers caused damage to Soviet installations: what then? At the very least Russia would have been free to attack American "sanctuaries" in Japan. Stalin might even have taken advantage of America's commitment in Korea to push his way into western Europe. Either response might have promoted nuclear war. For all these reasons Truman resisted MacArthur's entreaties. As General Omar Bradley, the army

General Douglas MacArthur in Korea, 1950.

chief of staff, put it, they would have involved the nation in "the wrong war, at the wrong place, at the wrong time, and with the wrong enemy."

MacArthur, however, was an imperious, egotistic adversary who could barely conceal his contempt for the likes of people such as Truman. Having served in the Pacific for more than a decade, he failed to comprehend the administration's primary concern for Europe. He had equally little understanding of the sensitivities of the western allies, whom he considered unreliable. He was a passionate globalist who believed that the United States, all by itself, should protect the world against the tide of Marxism. "I believe we should defend every place from communism," he declared. "I believe we are able to. . . . I don't admit that we can't hold communism wherever it shows its head." For all these reasons he was among the most sincere of the Asia-firsters. "It seems strangely difficult for some to realize," he wrote House Minority Leader Martin in April 1951, "that here in Asia is where the Communist conspirators have elected to make their play for global conquest . . . that here we fight Europe's war with arms while the diplomats there still fight it with words; that if we lose the war to communism in Asia the fall of Europe is inevitable; win it and Europe would probably avoid war and yet preserve freedom." With characteristic flourish, MacArthur closed his letter by proclaiming, "there is no substitute for victory."

As MacArthur had intended, Martin made public the letter. A classic confrontation then ensued between civilian and military authority. Truman had already tired of MacArthur's insubordination. He had also doubted MacArthur's handling of the war. The general had overconfidently split America's forces in the fall of 1950, and the Chinese had driven speedily down the middle to the south. Now MacArthur had gone the limit, ignoring presidential orders to keep quiet and challenging the very essence of administration policy. Certain of the course he had to follow, Truman nonetheless requested the advice of his chiefs of staff, who agreed that MacArthur had to go. The President then relieved him from command. If he hoped to preserve civilian rule, he could hardly have done otherwise.

The news of MacArthur's dismissal prompted critics to heap abuse on Truman's head. The GOP National Committee proclaimed that the President had perpetuated a "super Munich." McCarthy grumbled, "the son of a bitch [Truman] ought to be impeached." MacArthur then began a triumphal return to the United States, where throngs of people crowded to sing his praises. To an emotional session of Congress he pulled out all the stops: "I still remember the refrain of one of the most popular barracks ballads of that day which proclaimed most proudly that 'Old soldiers never die; they just fade away.' And like the old soldier of that ballad, I now close my military career and just fade away—an old soldier who tried to do his duty as God gave him the light to see that duty. Good-bye."

Truman wisely did not attempt to counter such theatrics. But he did work to strengthen America's military posture in Asia and elsewhere. In 1951 America signed separate bilateral defense pacts with Japan and with the

Philippines. It agreed to the so-called ANZUS treaty, a mutual defense pact involving Australia and New Zealand. In part to secure French agreement to the inclusion of West Germany in NATO, it stepped up aid to French forces in Indo-China. By 1954 the aid had totaled $1.2 billion in a losing cause.

Truman also called upon loyalists in Congress to expose MacArthur's bombast. Led by Senator Richard Russell, they brought out the fact that all three chiefs of staff had rejected MacArthur's argument. They then exposed the inconsistency of the GOP partisans who were supporting escalation. Taft, for instance, was hardly a globalist like MacArthur, and in early 1951 he had led a "Great Debate" against Truman's plan to commit American troops to a NATO army in Europe. Taft had also criticized America's commitment in Korea, and after the Chinese intervention he had joined other partisans in suggesting that America cut its losses and get out. Yet when Truman dismissed MacArthur, Taft—and many Repulicans with similar beliefs—leaped to the general's defense. The GOP partisans had placed political expediency ahead of ideological consistency.

By the summer of 1951 Truman's patience began to bring modest results, and MacArthur disappeared to the back pages. But MacArthur's dismissal had served as a public acknowledgment that total victory was impossible, that "limited war" would continue to be the policy of the administration. And limited war, as one writer put it, was like a slight case of pregnancy. In their heads Americans might understand the necessity for restraint; in their hearts they wanted to win, as their country always had. Or they wanted to get out. Unless the administration could find an honorable way to end the fighting, it would suffer dearly at the polls in 1952.

Reversal in 1952

Early in 1952 Truman announced he would retire at the end of his term. He could hardly have done otherwise, for almost no one in his party wanted him to run again. Since 1950 he had suffered not only at the hands of McCarthyites and MacArthurites but also from corruption among some of his own friends and aides. Only 23 percent of the American people, a record low, signified their approval of his administration in late 1951.

With their albatross out of the way, the Democrats turned to Governor Adlai Stevenson of Illinois. Though a relative newcomer to electoral politics, Stevenson had already captured the affection of many reporters and intellectuals, who deeply admired his intelligence, his liberalism, and his patrician cultivation. Urban bosses liked his stand on labor and welfare issues and noted his apparent strength at the polls in Illinois. Upright, witty, articulate, Stevenson could be expected to carry on the New Deal–Fair Deal tradition and to defend Truman's internationalist policies. Though Stevenson was perhaps too intellectual for mass taste, he seemed a fresh contrast to the tired

Adlai Stevenson consulting with his friend and supporter Eleanor Roosevelt.

old regulars who had surrounded Truman. To the columnist Marcus Childs, the governor was "Lincolnian"; to David Lilienthal he was a tower of "wisdom and wit and strength"; to Max Lerner, a liberal writer, he was the "first figure of major stature to have emerged since Roosevelt."

Republicans, meanwhile, took no chances. Rejecting Taft, the controversial favorite of the Right, they selected General Eisenhower as their nominee. "Ike" was genial, nonpartisan, and widely admired as a war hero; he was expected to offend no one. As Truman's appointee to develop a NATO army, he was clearly a "Europe-firster," whom no one could accuse of being an isolationist or a McCarthyite. Only the nomination of Richard Nixon as Eisenhower's running mate—creating a ticket that one critic likened to an

It would be very very fine if one could command new and amusing language—witticisms to bring you a chuckle. Frankly, I have no intention of trying to do so. The subjects of which we are speaking these days, my friends, are not those that seem to me to be amusing. . . . Is it amusing that we have stumbled into a war in Korea; that we have already lost in casualties 117,000 of our Americans killed and wounded; is it amusing that the war seems to be no nearer to a real solution than ever; that we have no real plan for stopping it? Is it funny when evidence was discovered that there are Communists in government . . . ?

Eisenhower, stepping up his crusade against Korea and communism, slashes at Stevenson's attempts at humor.

The Eisenhowers and the Nixons receiving the GOP nomination, July 1952.

alliance between Ulysses S. Grant and Dick Tracy—suggested that the GOP had pursued an abrasively partisan line for the past four years.

As the campaign developed, Eisenhower edged closer to his party's right wing. At the so-called Surrender on Morningside Heights in New York City, he met Taft, who had been nursing his grievances in silence, and agreed to support a conservative domestic policy if elected. He endorsed (with some qualifications) the party's platform calling for the "liberation" of countries under communist control. With other partisan orators he stressed the anti-Truman slogan of K_1C_2—Korea, Communism, and Corruption. Nixon denounced Stevenson as "Adlai the appeaser," who "carries a PH.D. from Dean Acheson's cowardly college of communist containment." Leaving nothing to chance, Eisenhower tried to secure McCarthyite support by deleting a paragraph from a Wisconsin speech praising his old boss, General Marshall. He closed the campaign by promising to go to Korea if elected. Ike, it appeared, would get the country out of the "mess" that Truman had caused in Asia.

Stevenson countered Eisenhower's attacks with wit and energy. But as a Democrat he was inevitably associated with Truman's policies. No one, therefore, was surprised when he was overwhelmed in November. Though he got 27.3 million votes, 3.2 million more than Truman received in 1948, he still trailed Eisenhower, who attracted a record 33.9 million voters, 12 million more than Dewey's total four years earlier. Breaking deeply into the Democratic coalition, Eisenhower swept all the big urban states and carried four states in the ordinarily Democratic South. Republicans even won majorities in both houses of Congress, for the second time since 1930. The result not only ended twenty years of Democratic dominance; it appeared to be a virtual revolution overthrowing the electoral universe that Al Smith and Franklin D. Roosevelt had forged in the previous generation.

Democratic gains in congressional elections throughout the 1950s revealed that no such revolution had taken place. Republicans, weakened in the depression years, remained the minority party. But the election of 1952 suggested the enormously important effect that an attractive candidate could have, and the degree to which formerly partisan voters were prepared to split their tickets. It also showed that the South, which had begun to rebel against Truman in 1948, was heading toward the Republican column. These trends toward electoral independence and discontinuity were to expand in the 1960s. Above all, the election of 1952 left little doubt that voters wanted a change in the White House and that Trumanism was almost a dirty word. Like Hoover

Election, 1952

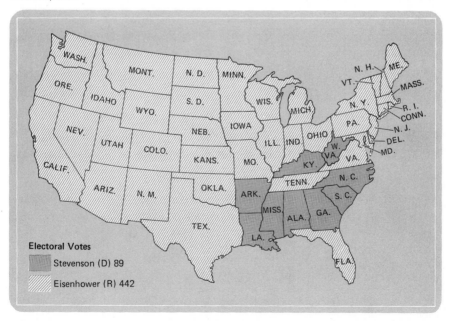

Electoral Votes

Stevenson (D) 89

Eisenhower (R) 442

in 1933, Johnson in 1969, and Nixon in 1974, Truman joined the group of modern American presidents who left office under clouds of disapproval.

Such a verdict, if that is what it was, was unfair, for Roosevelt's "Throttle-bottom" had proved a competent if uninspiring leader. Though partisan in dealing with Congress, he had managed to broaden the partial welfare state of the New Deal. Though inflexible and unsophisticated in diplomacy, he had occasionally proved enlightened, as in his support of foreign aid for Europe, and sometimes decisive as in his intervention in Korea. Given the domestic and international tensions of the time, to say nothing of the constraints imposed by the bureaucracy, by organized interest groups, and by the partisan atmosphere of domestic politics, he did a creditable job. As he left office in early 1953, it remained to be seen whether the GOP could do much better.

Suggestions for reading

Among the many accounts of foreign policy in the Truman years are Herbert Feis, *From Trust to Terror: The Onset of the Cold War, 1945–1950* (1970); Louis Halle, *The Cold War as History* (1967); and the revisionist interpretation by Walter LaFeber, *America, Russia, and the Cold War, 1945–1971** (1972). See also the books by Gaddis and Ambrose mentioned at the end of chapter 10. Revisionist accounts include Thomas Paterson, *Soviet-American Confrontation* (1974); Lloyd Gardner, *Architects of Illusion . . . 1941–1948* (1970); and Thomas Paterson, ed., *Cold War Critics** (1971). Important memoirs are George Kennan, *Memoirs, 1925–1950** (1967); and Dean Acheson, *Present at the Creation* (1969). Gaddis Smith, *Dean Acheson** (1972), is a useful biography. A revisionist account of the decision to drop the atomic bomb is Gar Alperovitz, *Atomic Diplomacy: Hiroshima and Potsdam** (1965). But see also Herbert Feis, *The Atomic Bomb and the End of World War II** (rev. ed., 1966), which refutes Alperovitz. A general study of Soviet-American relations is Adam Ulam, *The Rivals: America and Russia Since World War II** (1971).

Books on more specialized aspects of foreign policy include R. N. Gardner, *Sterling-Dollar Diplomacy* (1956); Tang Tsou, *America's Failure in China, 1941–1949** (1963); Herbert Feis, *The China Tangle* (1953); James Jones, *Fifteen Weeks** (1955), on the Truman Doctrine and the Marshall Plan; Robert Osgood, *NATO: Entangling Alliance* (1962); and Harry B. Price, *The Marshall Plan and Its Meaning** (1955). For the Korean War, consult David Rees, *Korea** (1964); and Ronald Caridi, *The Korean War and American Politics* (1968).

The most balanced book on the Truman administration is Alonzo Hamby, *Beyond the New Deal: Harry S. Truman and American Liberalism* (1973). Bert Cochran, *Harry S. Truman and the Crisis Presidency* (1973) is critical. Cabell Phillips, *The Truman Presidency** (1966) is laudatory. Barton Bernstein and Allen Matusow, eds., *Politics and Policies of the Truman Administration** (1970), is revisionist. Also, Richard Kirkendall, ed., *The Truman Period as a Research Field: A Reappraisal* (1974), offers conflicting interpretations. Richard Neustadt, *Presidential Power** (1960), includes case studies from the Truman administration. For political trends see V. O. Key, Jr., *Southern Politics* (1949); and the book by Samuel Lubell cited at the end of chapter 6. For the 1948 campaign consult Allen Yarnell, *Democrats and Progressives* (1974); Norman Markovitz, *Rise and Fall of the People's Century* (1973);

and Irwin Ross, *The Loneliest Campaign** (1968). James T. Patterson, *Mr. Republican: A Biography of Robert A. Taft** (1972) is a recent biography. Susan Hartmann, *Truman and the 80th Congress* (1971), competently covers its subject.

Books dealing with aspects of domestic policy are Edmund Flash, Jr., *Economic Advice and Presidential Leadership* (1965), on the Council of Economic Advisers; R. Alton Lee, *Truman and Taft-Hartley* (1967); Allen Matusow, *Farm Policies and Politics of the Truman Administration* (1967); Richard O. Davies, *Housing Reform During the Truman Administration** (1966); and A. E. Holmans, *United States Fiscal Policy, 1945–1959* (1961). For civil rights see William Berman, *The Politics of Civil Rights in the Truman Administration* (1970); and Donald McCoy and Richard Ruetten, *Quest and Response* (1973).

The subject of anticommunism has attracted many writers. Among the important books are David Shannon, *The Decline of American Communism* (1959); Earl Latham, *The Communist Conspiracy in Washington** (1966); Alan D. Harper, *The Politics of Loyalty, 1946–1952* (1969); Richard Rovere, *Senator Joe McCarthy** (1959), a brilliant study; and Robert Griffith, *The Politics of Fear** (1970), which focuses on the role of the Senate. Books highly critical of the Truman administration's anticommunism are Athan Theoharis, *Seeds of Repression: Harry S. Truman and the Origins of McCarthyism* (1971); and Richard Freeland, *The Truman Doctrine and the Origins of McCarthyism* (1971). Daniel Bell, ed., *Radical Right** (1963), includes essays stressing the role of social tensions in causing anticommunist hysteria. Michael Rogin, *The Intellectuals and McCarthy* (1967), criticizes the Bell volume and focuses on the impact of domestic politics.

12

The
middle-class
world
of the
1950s

"We've grown unbelievably prosperous and we maunder along in a stupor of fat," the historian Eric Goldman wrote in 1960. "We live in a heavy, humorless, sanctimonious, stultifying atmosphere, singularly lacking in the self-mockery that is criticism. Probably the climate of the late 1950s was the dullest and dreariest in all our history." The journalist William Shannon agreed. The decade, he wrote, was one of "flabbiness and self-satisfaction and gross materialism. . . . The loudest sound in the land has been the oink and grunt of private hoggishness. . . . It has been the age of the slob."

Many liberals echoed Goldman and Shannon. The decade of the 1950s, these critics recognized, was a period of unprecedented prosperity. It was like the 1920s, they said: materialistic, self-satisfied, conformist, politically conservative, and apathetic.

The case against the 50s

Primary targets of such criticism were the suburban middle classes, which expanded dramatically in the postwar years. In 1940, 74.4 million of America's 132 million people (57 percent) had lived in cities, then defined by the census as places with 2500 or more people. By 1950, the Census Bureau recognized that this arbitrary definition excluded millions who lived in suburbs; so it broadened its definition of cities to include "densely settled urban fringes . . . around cities of 50,000 inhabitants or more." The number of urbanites then rose to 96.5 million in 1950, 124.7 million in 1960, and 149.3 million in 1970— 73.5 percent of America's much-expanded population of 203 million. Meanwhile the number classified as "rural farm" dropped precipitously, from 30 million in 1940 to 23 million in 1950 to only 13.4 million in 1960.

These figures did not mean that central cities were growing. Quite the contrary, many of America's largest cities lost people between 1950 and 1960. The density of urban places during the same period declined from 5,408 inhabitants per square mile to 3,376. These one-time city people, plus millions more from the countryside, were flocking to the "settled urban fringes," which—thanks to the ubiquitous automobile—grew three times as rapidly as the overall population. By 1960 a "megalopolis" stretched much of the way between Boston and Washington. Cities, once thought of as concentric, self-contained areas, were now seen as linking up with one another in linear patterns sprawling along new roads and highways. Suburban areas around newer cities—Los Angeles, Dallas, Houston, Phoenix, San Diego—expanded fantastically. By 1970 some 80 million Americans lived in "suburbs." This was approximately 15 million more than lived in central cities, and more than the nation's entire population in 1900.

Naturally, the motives that inspired so many migrants varied widely. Millions fled the urban cores to escape countermigrations of blacks: in the 1950s alone America's twelve largest cities lost 2 million whites while gaining 1.8 million nonwhites. Millions more moved from the country to the city or from suburb to suburb in an apparently unceasing drive to better their social and economic status, to improve educational opportunities for their children, and—probably most important—to secure space and privacy. Some of these migrants were wealthy business and professional people who found open spaces many miles from downtown sections. Others were blue-collar workers of limited means—people who borrowed heavily to buy tiny houses or to rent flats in hastily constructed apartment houses. Such suburban areas, often heavily industrial, offered few of the amenities ordinarily associated with life outside the central city. The variety of suburbs, and of the motivations of the people who caused them to grow, almost defy description.

Generally, however, it is fair to identify most of the suburbanites as members of the white middle classes, which grew rapidly during the postwar era of bureaucratization, specialization, and technological change. As the number of farmers declined, and that of manual workers increased only slightly, the number of Americans classified as white-collar workers rose rapidly throughout the decades since 1940. By the mid-1950s such people outnumbered blue-collar laborers for the first time in American history. By 1970 they were close to 40 million strong, compared to 28.5 million blue-collar workers, 11 million service workers, and 3 million farm workers. Having

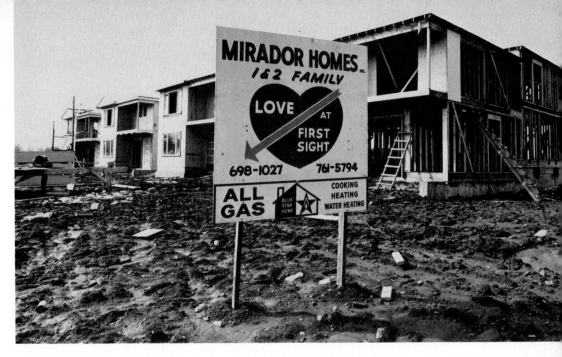

Surburban housing, often constructed of modular units, was built at a great rate
during the 1950s.

escaped blue-collar status, many of these "new" white-collar families sought
the space, the privacy, and the life-styles of the middle classes. In this way
suburbanization and the process of becoming middle-class tended to develop
together, as they already had in earlier decades, and to establish themselves as
the most significant demographic movements of the 1950s.

These middle-class suburbs distressed many observers in the 1950s. Places
like Levittown, Pennsylvania, one of many mass-produced communities
catering to lower- and middle-income groups, received special criticism. So
did more costly but aesthetically dull developments plastered on the once
rural landscape. John Keats, author of the antisuburban book *The Crack in
the Picture Window* (1961), dismissed them as "developments conceived in
error, nurtured by greed, corroding everything they touch." To him as to

> *Little boxes on the hillside*
> *Little boxes made of ticky-tacky*
> *Little boxes on the hillside.*
> *Little boxes all the same.*
> *There's a green one and a pink one*
> *And a blue one and a yellow one*
> *And they're all made out of ticky-tacky*
> *And they all look the same.*
>
> The folk singer Malvina Reynolds describes American postwar life.

other critics it seemed almost criminal that once picturesque countrysides should be bulldozed for houses or apartments, each with a TV antenna scarring a treeless sky. It seemed that a conspiracy of mercenary builders and ignorant architects was fastening a noose of vulgarity around the nation's cities.

Critics worried also about the human values nurtured by such humdrum surroundings. The "heroes" of Keats's book were John and Mary Drone— dull, purposeless materialists. Richard and Katherine Gordon, authors of *The Split-Level Trap* (1961), thought that the monotony of suburban existence promoted mental anguish and "Disturbia." And William H. Whyte, Jr.'s, widely discussed *Organization Man* (1956) bemoaned the fate that met the middle-class suburbanites of Park Forest, Illinois. Though Whyte considered Park Forest a pleasant, friendly place where newcomers were made to feel at home, he concluded that it was hell for people who valued privacy and nonconformity. The middle classes, Whyte implied, were losing themselves in a vast suburban sprawl (what others called "slurbs") of mediocrity and conformity.

The sociologist David Riesman made many of the same points in his book *The Lonely Crowd* (1950), which described the growth of conformist pressures not only in suburbia but in all areas of middle-class life. To Riesman, America had moved from an "inner-directed" culture in which people (through parental guidance) developed individualized goals to an "other-directed" society molded by peer-group pressures. Such a society, Riesman realized, could be more stable and even more tolerant than one composed of self-made men. But it helped create unventuresome little people like the boy who was asked, "Would you like to be able to fly?" and who answered, "I would like to be able to fly if everybody else did."

The alleged conformity of suburbia.

Drawing by Claude, © 1956 The New Yorker Magazine, Inc.

> *Whereas the inner-directed middle-class boy often had to learn after twenty to adjust, to surrender his adolescent dreams and accept a burgher's modest lot, the other-directed boy never had such dreams. In a profound sense he never experiences adolescence, moving as he does uninterruptedly with the peer-group, from the nursery years on. He learns to conform to the group almost as soon as he learns anything. He does not face, at adolescence, the need to choose between his family's world and that of his own generation or between his dreams and a world he never made.*
>
> David Riesman laments the passing of "inner direction."

To writers like Dwight Macdonald the alleged deadness of contemporary life was especially clear in the arts. Unlike Great Britain or other western societies, Macdonald thought, America could not sustain a High Culture. Instead, it had purely commercial television and radio, comic books and cartoon strips that sold by the millions, and "masscult," a parody of High Culture that featured sentimental painters like Norman Rockwell and pseudo-theologians like Norman Vincent Peale. Worst of all, America was becoming swamped by "midcult," which Macdonald thought "watered down and vulgarized" the standards of High Culture. Examples of midcult were Hemingway's *Old Man and the Sea* (1952), Thornton Wilder's nostalgic *Our Town,* and selections by such purveyors of "culture" as the Book-of-the-Month Club. So long as readers preferred *The Saturday Evening Post* and *Readers Digest* to serious literature, America would remain a nation of cultural philistines.

Many of these critics focused on what they saw as the self-indulgence, purposelessness, and lack of discipline in American socity during the 1950s. The United States, wrote the novelist John Updike, "is like an unloved child smothered in candy. God doesn't love us any more. He loves Russia. He loves Uganda. We're fat and full of pimples and always yearning for more candy. We've fallen from grace." The economist John Kenneth Galbraith, in his book *The Affluent Society* (1958), showed that Americans spent billions on consumer goods—TV sets, home freezers, household gadgets, above all, automobiles—while scrimping on necessary public services. Conservatives worried that the consumer society of the 1950s was inducing national flabbiness. "If you ask me," George Kennan wrote, " . . . whether a country that is in the state this country is in today: with no highly developed sense of national purpose, with the overwhelming accent of life on personal comfort and amusement, with a dearth of public services and a surfeit of privately sold gadgetry . . . if you ask me whether such a country has, over the long run, a good chance of competing with a purposeful, serious, and disciplined society such as that of the Soviet Union, I must say that the answer is 'No.'"

Observers of many persuasions shared Kennan's concern over the nation's spirit. Mort Sahl, the comedian, put it simply by mocking the confusion of American "turncoats" in Korea. "The turncoats were steadfast," he quipped. "They refused to give anything except their name, rank, and the exact position of their unit." Paul Goodman, a radical critic, complained that productive work was no longer important, that far too many people shuffled papers or tried to "beat the system." Young people, "growing up absurd," wanted to be movie stars instead of useful adults. And other critics, including Pitirim Sorokin, a distinguished Harvard sociologist, worried that Americans, lacking a sense of purpose, were wallowing in sex. He concluded: "Unless we develop an inner immunity against these libidinal forces, we are bound to be conquered by the continuous army of omnipresent sex stimuli."

Sorokin's worries were exaggerated. Though Alfred Kinsey, an Indiana University researcher, published tomes (*Sexual Behavior in the Human Male* [1948] and *Sexual Behavior in the Human Female* [1953]) that suggested large numbers of young people were indulging in premarital sex (and breaking outdated laws in the process), he scarcely supported the notion that sexual immorality was sweeping the nation. His researches also suggested that American sexual behavior had changed primarily in the 1910s and 1920s, not in the supposedly degenerate postwar years. Scott Donaldson, a balanced observer of suburban trends, added that young people "talked a great deal about sex, but it's all rather clinical, and outside of the marriage no one seems to do much about it." The very alarm displayed at the publication of Kinsey's "statistical filth" underlined the continued power of conventional ideas concerning sex, indeed of prudery, in the American consciousness.

The broadsides against philistinism were equally exaggerated. Scores of previous observers had lambasted America's material greed and cultural crudity. Like Macdonald, they tended to be elitists who would not accept the simple fact that people in most societies prefer personal comfort to High Culture. As one sensible writer pointed out, "the critic waves the prophet's long and accusing finger and warns: 'You may *think* you're happy, you smug and prosperous striver, but I tell you that the anxieties of status mobility are too much; they impoverish you psychologically, they alienate you from your family'; and so on. And the suburbanite looks at his new house, his new car, his new freezer, his lawn and patio, and to be sure, his good credit, and scratches his head, bewildered." Postwar Americans were not more materialistic than earlier generations—just incomparably richer. They were able to buy and to enjoy things that their parents could only dream about.

As careful critics recognized, it was also simplistic to paste labels on a society as diverse as the United States. What might apply to the corporate middle class (or some part of it) did not necessarily describe farmers, blacks, ethnics, blue-collar people, or many others in the enormously varied middle classes. What may have been true of some suburbanites was not in the least true of others—who resembled each other (if at all) primarily in their dependence on the automobile, their geographical mobility, and their lack of attachment to place. It was equally hazardous to contend that "other-directedness" was new or on the upswing. Indeed, peer group pressures in nineteenth-century American towns may have been more formidable than in the ever changing suburbs of the 1950s. Those who perceived only conformity also overlooked the continuing stress on personal achievement and—especially in the prosperous postwar years—the yearning for self-growth and psychological inner development. The very attention accorded such books as *Organization Man* suggested that many Americans, including the middle classes who were supposedly so mindless, were as anxious as their ancestors had been to surmount the homogenizing pressures of life.

A similar yearning for self-expression prompted some of the major trends in art forms during the decade. The "method" style of acting associated with young stars like James Dean and Marlon Brando attempted to approach "reality" through the emotions of the individuals on stage, not through rational speech or dialogue. Poets and dramatists reacted against the social realism of the 1930s and insisted on writing for themselves, not for causes. "A successful poem," the writer Leslie Fiedler explained, "is a complete and final act; if it leads outward to other action, it is just so far a failure." The director Alan Schneider later added, "we all have got to stop looking at all our plays as though they were socialist realism. . . . We can no longer go back to the well-made play because we haven't got a well-made world."

In the same way young painters like Jackson Pollock developed a wholly nonrepresentational style variously called Abstract Expressionism and Action Painting. Reflecting existentialist beliefs, they argued that a work of art must reflect the spontaneous, individual emotions of the creator. Art was a process of expression, not a static final product. Pollock, indeed, came to stand on his canvasses, flinging paint on them with apparently reckless abandon. "What was to go on the canvas," the critic Harold Rosenberg explained approvingly, "was not a picture but an event. . . . It is the artist's existence . . . he is living on the canvas. . . . What gives the canvas meaning is . . . the way the artist organized his emotional and intellectual energy as if he were in a living situation."

This desire to be one's self, to overcome organizational constraints, helped to explain the critical acclaim bestowed in the 1950s on novelists otherwise as diverse as J. D. Salinger, Saul Bellow, and John Updike. In *Catcher in the Rye* (1951) Salinger's "hero" is Holden Caulfield, a supersensitive adolescent bent on preserving innocence against "perverts" and "phonies" who wanted him to conform. Most of Bellow's protagonists, in books such as *Dangling Man* (1946), *Adventures of Augie March* (1949), and *Herzog* (1961), are bemused men who revolt against what Augie called the "shame of purpose-lessness." Like Huckleberry Finn (who also had "adventures"), they tried to be true to themselves. Updike's Rabbit Angstrom in *Rabbit Run* (1961) is a similarly confused young man who looks desperately—and unsuccessfully—for ways to bring back the excitement and meaning of his high school days. Characters like these were hardly tough like John Wayne or Gary Cooper,

> The quest, I am beginning to think, whether it be for money, for notoriety, reputation, increase of pride, whether it leads us to thievery, slaughter, sacrifice, the quest is one and the same. All the striving is for one end. I do not entirely understand this impulse. But it seems to me that its final end is the desire for pure freedom. We are all drawn toward the same craters of the spirit—to know what we are and what we are for, to know our purpose, to seek grace. And, if the quest is the same, the differences in our personal histories, which hitherto meant so much to us, become of minor importance.
>
> Saul Bellow's character Joseph in *Dangling Man* (1946) expresses a feeling later echoed by many of the most memorable characters in post war American fiction.

> ... we get a clear but exaggerated picture of our American society. It has: slums of engineering—boondoggling production—chaotic congestion—tribes of middlemen—basic city functions squeezed out—garden cities for children—indifferent workmen—underprivileged on a dole—empty "belonging" without nature or culture—front politicians—no patriotism—an empty nationalism bound for a cataclysmically disastrous finish—wise opinion swamped—enterprise sabotaged by monopoly—prejudice rising—religion otiose—the popular culture debased—science specialized—science secret—the average man inept—youth idle and truant—youth sexually suffering and sexually obsessed—youth without goals—poor schools.
>
> Paul Goodman, in *Growing Up Absurd* (1957), expresses a radically unhappy view of American society.

masculine heroes of film. They had none of the rebellious individuality of James Dean. Rather, they were fearful, confused, buffeted about—passive victims of larger forces. But they did not surrender. They were existentialist antiheroes who at least survived.

These thrusts against conformity led in the late 1950s to a vogue among more radical students for books like C. Wright Mills's *Power Elite* (1956), Jack Kerouac's *On the Road* (1956), and Paul Goodman's *Growing up Absurd* (1957). The three men held differing social philosophies: Mills was a Marxist sociologist, Kerouac a "beat" novelist who celebrated free-wheeling nonconformity, Goodman a philosophical anarchist who combined Veblen's passion for productive labor, Freud's stress on the need for physical love, and the urban planner Ebenezer Howard's vision of decentralized communities and garden cities. Yet all three men agreed that America—in Goodman's words a "rat race," in Mills's a "great salesroom, an enormous file, an incorporated brain, a new universe of management and manipulation"—stifled creative talent. For them, as for many less radical thinkers, large-scale organization was the enemy. Their appeal to young nonconformists suggested that the 1950s were less serene and complacent than they sometimes appeared.

CAUSES FOR ALARM

Still, there was no denying that many aspects of American life in the 1950s supported the critics of conformity and materialism. One of these was the growth of the huge, bureaucratic corporation. As Adolf Berle and Gardiner Means had pointed out in the early 1930s—and as James Burnham had stressed in his *Managerial Revolution* (1939)—"faceless" bureaucrats were dominating the ever growing corporations. These early writers had worried more about the power of such organizations than about the psyches of their employees. But by the 1950s it was clear that many corporations (to say nothing of government, the biggest bureaucracy of all) stressed "teamwork"

These schools were not only to teach general management, but—most important—they were to give our managers a feeling for IBM's outlooks and beliefs. After a time we found that the schools tended to put too much emphasis on management, not enough on beliefs. This, we felt, was putting the cart before the horse. We felt that it was vital that our managers be well grounded in our beliefs. Otherwise, we might begin to get management views at odds with the company's outlook. If this were to happen, it might possibly slow down our growth and change our basic approach to the management of our company.

The head of IBM defends his company's schools of indoctrination.

and frowned on mavericks. Some, such as IBM, even outlined acceptable standards of dress and decorum. Alarmed, Mills perceived the coming of a "white collar" society in which people would be "estranged from community . . . in a context of distrust and manipulation, alienated from work and, in the personality market, from self, expropriated of individual rationality, and politically apathetic." Mills was wrong to assume that organizations could wholly transform people's minds. But he was perceptive in pointing to the growth of propagandists for "togetherness" and the "need to belong."

The call for togetherness also helped sustain a Cult of Domesticity in the 1950s. More than over before—or so it seemed—Americans yearned to enmesh themselves in the "tender trap" of marriage, parenthood, and the nuclear family. During the late 1940s and early 1950s people continued to marry young and to have children quickly. As a result the baby boom, which demographers had expected would decrease shortly after World War II, continued until the mid-1950s. The nation's population increased from 151 million to 180 million people between 1950 and 1960. This was the largest growth in any decade of American history (before or since). The rate of increase (19 percent) was the greatest since 1910, when heavy immigration had helped to swell the pace of growth.

Few people during the 1950s expressed much alarm about the ecological results of such expansion. The baby boom, they said, helped to sustain prosperity, especially in the construction industry, which was kept busy building approximately 1 million new homes per year throughout the 1950s. By 1960 more Americans owned their homes (with mortgages) than rented, for the first time in the twentieth century. The majority of such homes had the creature comforts that the media promoted as the joys of domesticity and parenthood.

The presumed blessings of domesticity helped to weaken feminism in the 1950s. Feminists, the Women's Bureau of the federal government had announced a few years earlier, were a "small but militant group of leisure class women [giving vent] to their resentment at not having been born men."

Adlai Stevenson added, "the assignment for you, as women and mothers, you can do in the living room with a baby in your lap or in the kitchen with a can opener in your hand. . . . there is much you can do about our crisis in the humble role of housewife. I could wish you no better vocation than that." Dr. Benjamin Spock, whose *Baby and Child Care* (1946) was a huge seller in the 1950s and 1960s, urged the government to pay mothers so they would not leave the home for employment.

Such defenders of domesticity overlooked continuing growth in female employment, a profound demographic development that helped sustain the movement for women's liberation a decade later. But movies and magazines undercut feminism. Hollywood glorified sweet types like Doris Day and Debby Reynolds or sex objects like Marilyn Monroe. Fashion designers popularized spike-heeled shoes, crinolines, and the "baby doll" look. The "ladies" magazines extolled the satisfactions of motherhood and home management. Women, like men in the apparently unventuresome postwar era, seemed to know and accept their status.

There was cause also to worry about the impact of the mass media, particularly television, which one critic labeled the "cheekiest, vulgarest, most disgraceful form of entertainment since bear-baiting, dog-fighting, and the seasonal Czarist Russian pogrom." Like others, he lamented the omnipresence of violence, the virtual absence of serious drama or music, above all the pandering to the commercial nature of the medium. Like the mass circulation magazines and newspapers, TV constantly flashed expensive luxury goods before the consumer. No one, of course, could prove that TV or the other media actually caused people to buy certain goods, much less to become conformists. Indeed, it was possible that the bombardment of images undercut the last vestiges of provincialism and broadened the experience, and the vision, of millions. But by 1960 it was also clear that TV, by invading practically every American home for several hours a day, was projecting a peculiarly middle-class world and stifling dissent. It was also ignoring (or stereotyping) the millions who belonged to minority groups. At best, the mass media were promoting the status quo.

Another sign of blandness in the 1950s was what some contemporaries labeled the "new piety." By 1960 this was reflected in a rise in the percentage of Americans (95%) who identified with a religious denomination. Lesser manifestations of this trend abounded: a new stamp issue proclaimed "In God We Trust"; "Under God" was added to the pledge of allegiance; the practice in Eisenhower's administration of opening meetings with a prayer. Subway posters proclaimed, "Go to church. You'll feel better. Bring your troubles to church and leave them there." Capitalizing on this search for faith, the evangelist Billy Graham "converted" millions during the postwar era, while Bishop Fulton J. Sheen and the Reverend Norman Vincent Peale reached out to the middle classes over the radio and in magazine columns. "Flush out all depressing, negative, and tired thoughts," Peale told his readers in *Look* magazine. "Start thinking faith, enthusiasm, and joy."

This kind of exhortation was nothing new in the American experience, where faith in faith had long enjoyed support. Peale's "power of positive thinking" was a modernized version of Christian Science. Nor was the search for piety hypocritical: the rapid growth of fundamentalist churches during the postwar era suggested that millions of Americans, including many migratory blacks and poor whites, earnestly sought comfort against the forces of urbanization and technological change. But the theologian Will Herberg was correct in stressing, in *Protestant Catholic Jew* (1956), that for most Americans religion had lost its theological meaning. Instead, the churches supported a "civic religion," which sustained the status quo and the "American Way of Life." Far from promoting a Great Awakening, the search for piety revealed a quest for social status and identity.

Like the churches, schools reflected this concern for helping people find their place in mass society. Such a note had been sounded as early as 1939 by Charles Prosser, a leading advocate of vocational education. "The important thing," Prosser said, "is not to teach students how to generalize but to supply them directly with the information they need for daily living." By the early 1950s this focus on "life adjustment" challenged many earlier pedagogical theories, including the stress on the Three R's, Dewey's idea that schools could promote social reform, or the progressive hope that teachers would stimulate the latent creativity of children. Instead, schools offered subjects like "How can I keep well?" "How can I look my best?" "How can I get along better with others?" and "How can hobbies contribute to my social growth?" The historian Richard Hofstadter complained that one New York community required a course in "Home and Family Living" for all children in grades seven through ten. The course featured such topics as "developing school spirit," "clicking with the crowd," "how to be liked," and "what can be done about acne?" Other reformers complained that college youth in the 1950s had become the "Silent Generation," interested in football, fraternities, and, upon graduation, in well-paid security with General Motors, Wall Street, and Madison Avenue. Campus radicalism was so hard to detect that Kenneth Keniston, an acute observer of American youth, complained as late as 1962, "I see little likelihood of American students ever playing a radical role, much less a revolutionary one, in our society."

Hofstadter and others exaggerated the staying power of "life adjustment" in the curriculum. Indeed, traditionalists (who complained that students weren't "learning" anything) successfully counterattacked in the late 1950s, especially after the Soviet Union beat the United States in the race to outer space. Diatribes against campus complacency were short-sighted, for American university students, sons and daughters of the more affluent classes, had rarely shown sustained interest in social reform. It is also clear that some critics of American education placed too much faith in the potential of schools to transcend environmental forces. Schools, after all, are rarely much different from society at large. But that was partly Hofstadter's point: schools, like churches, like corporations, seemed bent on preserving the existing order.

So, too, were many people who had been sharp critics of American life in the 1930s. These included such one-time foes of big business as Adolf Berle and David Lilienthal, both of whom changed their minds in the 1950s. Large corporations, they pointed out, were better able to preserve job security, to pay decent wages, to promote research and development. Labor leaders seemed equally tame in the 1950s. Though they grumbled loudly about Taft-Hartley, they eschewed the militant tactics of the late 1930s. With a few exceptions, such as auto workers' leader Walter Reuther, they neglected the problems of nonunion workers, of blacks, or of other minority groups. The reality of the 1950s for most union spokesmen was unprecedented affluence. In such an age it was foolish to promote class divisions, to talk about trust-busting, or to "spout Marxist clichés."

This moderation found approving interpreters among America's leading intellectuals of the 1950s. These included the historian Daniel Boorstin and the sociologist Daniel Bell. Both welcomed what they considered the stability and consensus of American society. In *The Genius of American Politics* (1953) Boorstin described the national experience as one in which compromise and practicality overcame ideologies and class conflicts. Bell, a prolific writer, gathered many of his essays into a volume entitled *The End of Ideology* (1960). America, he said, was a flexible, pluralistic nation in which many groups vied for position. It was a much more humane, stable society than the Soviet Union, which vividly exposed the dangers of absolutist ideology. These defenders of "consensus" underrated the degree of ethnic, racial, and class conflict in the American past, and they falsely assumed that ideology—or at least activism—was dead. "It's like an old man proclaiming the end of sex," one youthful rebel later sneered. "Because he doesn't feel it anymore, he thinks it has disappeared."

Bell was right, however, in arguing that leftist thinkers made little headway in the 1950s. Thanks to the Cold War, and especially to Korea, Communists and Socialists virtually disappeared. The Progressive party lost what little hope it had had for survival as a political force when Henry Wallace deserted it to back the Korean War. Liberal groups such as the Americans for Democratic Action continued to press for progressive domestic reforms, but they remained on the defensive against McCarthyites who branded intellectuals as "parlor pinks" or communists. As if to prove otherwise, the ADA insisted loudly that it, too, hated the Reds. The weakness of the Left in the 1950s revealed the pervasive impact of the Cold War, the intimidating force of McCarthyism, and the dominance of "middle American" values.

The primary support for such attitudes was the unparalleled affluence of the decade. In constant prices the GNP had already jumped from $205 billion in 1940 to $318 billion in 1950. During the 1950s it leaped again, to $440 billion in 1960. In per capita terms this meant an increase from $1,550 in 1940 to $2,100 in 1950 to $2,435 in 1960. It meant striking advances in life expectancy, education levels, and in disposable income. In the 1950s, consumer credit leaped from $8.4 billion to $45 billion. Workers, who had averaged forty-five

Economic growth, 1950–1960, compared to select years before and after this period

	NATIONAL PRODUCT AND INCOME (In billions of current dollars)				PER CAPITA DISPOSABLE INCOME (In current dollars)
	GNP	PERCENT CHANGE FROM GNP OF PRECEDING YEAR (+ OR −)	NATIONAL INCOME	DISPOSABLE PERSONAL INCOME	
1929	103.1	n.d.	86.8	83.3	683
1933	55.6	− 4.2	40.3	45.5	362
1940	99.7	+10.2	81.1	75.7	573
1944	210.1	+ 9.7	182.6	146.3	1,057
1946	208.5	− 1.6	181.9	160.0	1,132
1950	284.8	+11.0	241.1	206.9	1,364
1951	328.4	+15.3	278.0	226.6	1,469
1952	345.5	+ 5.2	291.4	238.3	1,518
1953	364.6	+ 5.5	304.7	252.6	1,583
1954	364.8	+ 0.1	303.1	257.4	1,585
1955	398.0	+ 9.1	331.0	275.3	1,666
1956	419.2	+ 5.3	350.8	293.2	1,743
1957	441.1	+ 5.2	366.1	308.5	1,801
1958	447.3	+ 1.4	367.8	318.8	1,831
1959	483.7	+ 8.2	400.0	337.3	1,905
1960	503.7	+ 4.1	414.5	350.0	1,937
1970	977.1	+ 5.0	800.5	691.7	3,376
1973	1,294.9	+11.8	1,065.6	903.7	4,295

SOURCE: Adapted from Council of Economic Advisers, "Annual Report, January 1975" in *Economic Report of the President* (Washington, D.C., 1975), pp. 249, 267, 269

hours a week in the 1920s, enjoyed work weeks averaging less than forty hours by 1960, plus annual vacations of at least two weeks. The simplest way to describe the affluence of the 1950s is to note that the average American had twice as much real income to spend (and more time to spend it in) in the mid-1950s than in the supposedly boom times of the late 1920s.

Many forces produced this growth. Among them was the willingness of the private sector to risk funds for investment. Between 1946 and 1958, when a slump hit the economy, Americans pumped an average of $10 billion per year into new plant and equipment. Another was technological change including computers, which became important by the early 1960s. Labor-saving devices understandably alarmed many people, especially in agriculture and in such industries as textiles, where the labor force declined by more than 30 percent between 1945 and 1960. But technological advances also created jobs, especially for white-collar "service" workers. Such areas as electronics and plastics expanded phenomenally during the years between 1945 and 1960.

The public sector played an indispensable role in promoting this prosperity. Much of the economic growth of the period stemmed directly from governmental expenditures for World War II and Korea. Military spending, which approached $40 billion per year in the peacetime years of the 1950s, accounted for approximately 60 percent of federal budgets and 10 percent of the GNP. Overall public expenditures—federal, state, and local—had amounted to only 10 percent of the GNP in 1929; by the mid-1950s they accounted for more than 25 percent. Governments directly employed more than 8 million people by 1957, double the number in 1940. Government work, overwhelmingly white-collar, was the fastest growing area of the economy.

Books like Galbraith's *Affluent Society* accurately exposed many limits to this affluence: technological unemployment, depressed areas, slums, inadequate health care, decaying urban schools, racial injustice. The distribution of income remained inequitable, and poverty was much more widespread than people realized. Almost 13 million families earned less than $4000 per year before taxes in 1955. In the same year, the poorest fifth of American families earned 4.8 percent of the national income, while the top fifth earned 20.3 percent. Also, the rate of economic growth slowed down considerably late in the decade. The affluence of the 1950s did not reach as far or last as long as most people thought.

In history, however, what people think is often more important than reality. Sure that ever greater prosperity lay ahead, Americans remained blind to the signs of poverty and stagnation. Moreover, there was no denying the fact of economic growth or of the boundless supplies of gadgetry available (on credit) to the majority of people. The United States, the richest nation in world history, was wealthier than it had ever been and incomparably more prosperous than in the 1930s. In such a world it was not at all surprising that self-satisfaction and materialism seemed stronger than in many periods of the American past.

THE ASCENDANCY OF THE RIGHT

Those who hoped for social reform found this complacency ominous indeed. As progressives were forced to recognize, people were tired of the Korean War and of partisan controversy. They wanted to be left alone to enjoy their material rewards. Though Americans voted Democratic in congressional elections (even in 1956), they showed little taste for progressive legislation. Like the 1920s, the decade was the despair of reformers.

In such an atmosphere Senator McCarthy continued to thrive. Because the GOP controlled the Congress in 1953, he became chairman of his own investigating committee, which he used to step up his accusations of communist subversion in government. His top aide, Roy Cohn, and Cohn's friend, G. David Schine, toured American embassies in Europe, where they searched for leftist books in government libraries and made a laughing stock of the State Department. A few books were actually burned. McCarthy even cowed the new administration into permitting endless security checks on high-ranking employees, some of whom were forced to resign not because they were disloyal but because they were what the government now vaguely termed "security risks." Among these, amazingly enough, was J. Robert Oppenheimer, "father of the atomic bomb," whose security clearance was taken away in December, 1953, on the grounds that he opposed development of the H-bomb and had associated with left-wingers in the 1930s. A newsman who returned to Washington after an extended absence in 1954 was appalled. "I let myself into the State Department," he wrote, "and there encountered a few 'Acheson holdovers' cowering in their corners. They were aged and their voices were low. But oddly enough, some of the new Republican appointees whom I met seemed to have muffled voices too. . . . it was like Vienna all over again, where we had learned to beware of eavesdroppers."

McCarthy then turned his guns on the army, which had refused to give preferential treatment to Schine, a draftee. During the course of his investigation McCarthy discovered that a left-wing dentist, Dr. Irving Peress, had been permitted to resign from the service with the rank of major. Probing further, he demanded that army brass disclose the names of officers involved in the affair. When the army proved slow to cooperate, McCarthy exploded. "You are a disgrace to the uniform," he told Brigadier General Ralph Zwicker. "You're shielding communist conspirators. You're not fit to be an officer. You're ignorant." Attacks such as these made the hearings, which were televised in the spring of 1954, the most compelling entertainment of the year.

In making such accusations, McCarthy overreached himself. Seeing McCarthy on TV, many Americans began to realize what a barbarian he was. Conservative supporters of the military establishment stiffened. As his appeal ebbed, the Senate roused itself against his insults. (He had described Senator Robert Hendrickson of New Jersey as a "living miracle in that he is without question the only man who has lived so long with neither brains nor guts.") In December 1954 the Senate at last voted, sixty-seven to twenty-two, to "condemn" McCarthy for bringing the Congress into disrepute. McCarthy remained in the Senate, but he was burned out, a casualty of his exaggerations, his alcoholic tendency, and his tiresome repetitions. Three years later, at the age of forty-eight, he died.

McCarthy's downfall, however, did not deter the extreme right wing, which became ever more shrill as the decade progressed. It included members of such superpatriotic groups as the John Birch Society and the Christian Anti-Communist Crusade. One of the right-wing leaders, Fred Schwartz, announced that the communists planned to take over in 1973. "When they come for you, as they have for many others, on a dark night, in a dank cellar, they take a wide-bore revolver with a soft-nose bullet, and they place it at the nape of your neck." Robert Welch, founder of the John Birch Society, insisted that the Soviets were proceeding against America "on the soundest of strategy. It calls for paralyzing their enemy and their enemy's will to resist by internal subversion before ever striking a blow." Eisenhower, Welch concluded, was a "dedicated, conscious agent of the communist conspiracy."

This "Radical Right," as it was called, was much too extreme to be taken seriously by the voters. Unlike McCarthyism, which had a mass base, it appealed primarily to superpatriots and reactionaries who had been ranting against "big government" since 1933. Still, by 1961, a Gallup poll reported that the goals of the John Birch Society were approved by 7 million Americans. The far Right's hostility to big government also had the support of aggressive conservatives in Congress. Among these were Pat McCarran, an obsessively anticommunist Democratic senator from Nevada; conservative Democratic colleagues such as John McClellan of Arkansas and James Eastland of Mississippi; and reactionary solons like William Jenner of Indiana and Barry Goldwater of Arizona.

By mid-decade many of these men were focusing their attacks on the Supreme Court, which they said was "coddling" communists and other undesirables, including blacks. Led by Chief Justice Earl Warren, whom Eisenhower appointed to the court in 1953, the judges revealed their liberal orientation in 1954 by ruling unanimously (in *Brown* v. *Board of Education*) against school segregation. "Separate educational facilities," the Court said in reversing precedents dating from *Plessy* v. *Ferguson* (1896), "are inherently unequal . . . segregation is a denial of the equal protection of the laws." The Court in 1955 then called for school desegregation with "all deliberate speed." Outraged, Senator Eastland denounced the Court's "monstrous crime. . . . These antagonistic decisions are . . . bent upon the destruction of the American form of government and the mongrelization of the white race." Led by Eastland, nineteen southern senators and seventy-seven representatives signed a manifesto in 1956 that bound them to "use all lawful means to bring about a reversal of this decision which is contrary to the Court and to prevent the use of force in its implementation." Among southern senators only Lyndon Johnson of Texas and Estes Kefauver and Albert Gore of Tennessee refused to sign.

Having infuriated the South, the Court then asked for trouble with Red-haters and advocates of what President Nixon was later to celebrate as "law and order." In *Jencks* v. *U. S.* (1956) it ruled that a labor leader had been unfairly tried because he had not been permitted to see prosecutors' files. In *Service* v. *Dulles* (1957) it reinstated John Service, a State Department expert on China who had been dismissed in 1951 after six loyalty clearances. The decision forced the administration to clarify its procedures concerning so-called security risks in government. In *Mallory* v. *U. S.* (1957), it ruled that an accused rapist had been illegally charged because he had been held too long before being brought before a magistrate. Alleged criminals, the Court ruled, must be arraigned "without unnecessary delay." And in *Yates* v. *U. S.* (1956) the Court reversed the conviction of fourteen Communists jailed under the Smith Act of 1940. Mere advocacy of revolution, the Court stated, did not constitute grounds for convictions. The government must prove that defendants had "organized" revolution and that they had succeeded. The ruling caused the government to drop plans for further prosecutions of Communists.

These decisions began a judicial trend, much accelerated in the 1960s, toward greater federal guarantees for accused criminals and subversives. They showed that the Court had moved beyond the paralyzing anticommunism of the McCarthy era. The Bill of Rights, it seemed, meant what it said. But the decisions also prompted right-wingers to finance "Impeach Earl Warren" billboards along the nation's highways. A Cleveland paper intoned (after the *Jencks* decision) that the FBI might as well "close up shop, for the Court had opened their files to the criminal and thus afforded him a Roman holiday for rummaging through confidential materials as well as vital national secrets." Edward Corwin, professor of constitutional law at Princeton, wrote *The New York Times* to complain that the Court had gone on a "virtual binge" and "should have its aforesaid nose tweaked." Most alarming to friends of the Court, a bipartisan congressional coalition almost put through legislation in 1958 that would have stripped the Court of its appellate jurisdiction in cases dealing with loyalty programs, contempt of Congress, state sedition statutes, regulations of employment and oaths of allegiance in schools, and admission to state law practice. Only careful maneuvering by Majority Leader Lyndon Johnson managed the forty-nine to forty-one vote that prevented the law from passing the Senate.

A handful of liberal Democratic senators struggled against these right-wing pressures of the 1950s. They included Hubert Humphrey of Minnesota, a crusader for civil rights; Estes Kefauver of Tennessee, who battled for curbs on monopoly and false advertising; and Paul Douglas, an innovative reformer who developed in the 1950s much of the economic legislation of Kennedy's New Frontier and Johnson's Great Society. Still powerful in the national party, these liberals nominated a progressive ticket composed of Stevenson and Kefauver in 1956. (Senator John F. Kennedy, less experienced and less liberal than Kefauver, sought the vice-presidency and failed.) The prominence of such men suggested that liberalism was neither dead nor dying in the 1950s.

But it remained on the defensive. Bowing to the anticommunist hysteria, liberals like Humphrey and Douglas joined moderates like Kennedy in backing legislation in 1954 to outlaw the Communist party. In 1956 Democrats feared to mention national health insurance in their platform. Stevenson, attempting to placate the South, exclaimed during his campaign that the federal government must not send in money or troops to enforce desegregation. "I think that would be a great mistake," he said. "That is exactly what brought on the Civil War. It can't be done by troops, or bayonets. We must proceed gradually, not upsetting habits or traditions that are older than the Republic."

Stevenson lost more heavily to Eisenhower in 1956 than he had in 1952, even though his foe had suffered a heart attack in 1955. But if he had won, he would have had no chance of putting a liberal program through Congress.

There the power lay, as it had since the Democrats won majorities in 1954, with moderates led by Johnson in the Senate and by his Texan friend, Sam Rayburn, Speaker of the House. Shrewd and tireless, both men were cool to liberals like Humphrey or Douglas. They feared to provoke the right-wingers on both sides of the aisle. And like most Americans in the 1950s, they did not want to rock the boat. Even in 1959, when a band of young liberals entered Congress, and in 1961, when President Kennedy launched his New Frontier, these moderates remained in control. This "Four-Party Government," as political scientist James Macgregor Burns described the coexistence of the more conservative congressional wings of both parties with their more liberal national wings, remained a basic reality of American politics in the 1950s.

President Eisenhower

Dwight D. Eisenhower, who presided over most of the 1950s, was the nation's most admired war hero in 1945. Decent, democratic, decisive, he had seemed a nonauthoritarian officer as well as a just and likeable man. Truman had told him at Potsdam, "General, there is nothing that you may want that I won't try to help you get. That definitely and specifically includes the presidency in 1948."

By that time, of course, Truman had changed his mind. But politicians of both parties yearned to nominate their hero, both then and in 1952. Like the American people, they were taken by his presence, his air of command, by what the reporter Robert Donovan called his "leaping and effortless smile." People responded also to his moderation, his balanced judgment, and his apparent aloofness from the intrigue of politics. The new president, it appeared, was heaven-sent to deliver the nation from the acrimony of the early 1950s. Like a benign father bringing peace to a quarrelsome tribe, Eisenhower seemed untouchable at the polls.

Even liberals were prepared to accept him at first. Though to the right of Stevenson, he seemed to provide a sharp contrast to the conservatives in his party who had supported Taft. This image was more appearance than reality, for the new president considered Taft socialistic on such issues as public housing and aid to education. Nevertheless, Eisenhower was apparently willing to maintain the government's active role in the economy. "Never again," he said during the campaign, "shall we allow a depression in the United States." As soon as we "foresee the signs of any recession and depression . . . the full power of private industry, of municipal government, of state government, of the Federal Government will be mobilized to see that that does not happen." This "Modern Republicanism," as his liberal supporters in the eastern wing of the party liked to call it, suggested that the GOP had left Hooverism far behind.

In the late 1960s and 1970s historians of his administration began to appreciate still another of Eisenhower's virtues. This was his shrewdness. Far

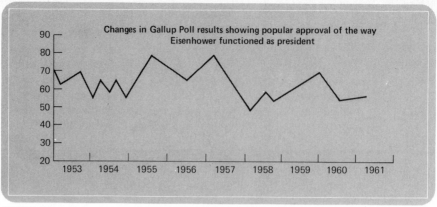

Changes in Gallup Poll results showing popular approval of the way Eisenhower functioned as president

SOURCE: Adapted from Irish and Frank, *U.S. Foreign Policy*, p. 104

The peak of Eisenhower's popularity was reached in mid-1955 and early 1957 when 79 percent of respondents approved of his handling of the presidency. He reached a low in early 1958 when only 49 percent approved.

from having been a placid father figure (a "counterrevolutionist entirely surrounded by men who know how to profit from it," the journalist Elmer Davis had complained in the 1950s), he seemed in retrospect to have been in purposeful control of his administration at all times. Even his convoluted syntax, which had been laughable at the time, seemed part of a deliberate plan. "Don't worry, Jim," he allegedly told his press secretary James Hagerty, who was nervous about an imminent session with reporters. "If that question comes up, I'll just confuse them." As the liberal writer Murray Kempton put it (with some exaggeration) in 1967, Ike "was the great tortoise upon whose back the world sat for eight years. We laughed at him; we talked wistfully about moving; and all the while we never even knew the cunning beneath the shell."

Even writers like Kempton, however, could not ignore qualities that prevented Eisenhower from making maximum use of his personal popularity. Among these was a passivity and lack of sophistication that astonished veteran observers in Washington. The best way to prevent selfishness in labor unions or management, he told the cabinet at one point, was to appeal to their sense of fair play. The way to deal with McCarthy was to ignore him. "I will not get into the gutter with that guy," he remarked, as if keeping himself pure

> *I haven't checked these figures, but eighty-seven years ago, I think it was, a number of individuals organized a governmental setup here in this country, I believe it covered eastern areas, with this idea that they were following up based on a sort of national independence arrangement and the program that every individual is just as good as every other individual.*
>
> One of many parodies in the 1950s of Eisenhower making Lincoln's Gettysburg address.

With the greatest of ease.

Herblock of the Washington Post summarizes
the 1956 election. Although Ike won easily, his
coattails were not strong enough to gain G OP
majorities in both houses of Congress.

would cleanse the country. Eisenhower also told political aides that he would
not descend into making "idiotic promises or hints about elect-me-and-I-will-
cut-your-taxes-by-such-and-such-a-date! If it takes that kind of foolishness to
get elected, let them find someone else for the job." In fact, Eisenhower was
neither so unsophisticated nor so nonpartisan as he sounded. Even his handling of McCarthy—as he may have suspected—had the virtue of letting his
adversary find the rope to hang himself. His passive approach to important
questions, however, was hardly purposeful leadership.

This approach rested on his view that the presidency must not become too
expansive. "I am not one of those desk-pounding types," he explained, "that
likes to stick out his jaw and look like he is bossing the show. I don't think it is
the function of a President of the United States to punish anybody for voting
as he likes." He told his cabinet appointees, "you have full authority. I expect
you to stand on your own two feet. Whatever you decide goes. The White
House will stay out of your hair." Because big government, like large corporations, had to rely on bureaucrats and managers, his approach had the virtue of
freeing him from details. But the deliberate dispersal of power led also to
inertia and procrastination. Eisenhower, in I. F. Stone's words, would be a
"president in absentia, with a sort of political vacuum in the White House
which other men will struggle among themselves to fill." Delegating authority
meant also that he could not secure compliance with his own commands, for

Washington politicians had to feel the whip hand of the president before doing anything. "He'll sit there," Truman said of his successor, "and he'll say, 'Do this! Do that!' And nothing will happen. Poor Ike—it won't be a bit like the army."

Eisenhower's administration reflected his instinctive distaste for involving himself in the legislative process. He rarely applied pressure, and he often sounded ignorant even of important matters. After a Senate committee unanimously reported out to the floor a significant education bill in 1954, he blurted to newsmen, "I do not know the details of that particular legislation. . . . I'd suggest you go to [HEW] Secretary [Oveta Culp] Hobby to find out where we stand." At a press conference following introduction of his Justice Department's civil rights bill in 1957 he told reporters, "I was reading part of that bill this morning, and I—there were certain phrases I didn't completely understand. . . . I would want to talk to the Attorney General." No president since Coolidge had been more poorly informed about what was happening on the Hill.

His practice of paying little attention to details let aides like Sherman Adams, his chief assistant, and top cabinet officials handle many important decisions. Adams, a former governor of New Hampshire, was a "Modern Republican" who conceded the desirability of some activist policies. But he was also abrupt, flinty, as cold to self-important officials as New Hampshire stone in the winter. Until 1959, when ruffled politicians drove him from power by showing that he had used his influence for personal gain, he made more enemies for Eisenhower than friends. On presidential orders, he kept many important questions from receiving the top-level discussion and debate they ought to have had. If the "buck" stopped in the oval office under Truman, it floundered in the anterooms from 1953 to 1959.

Other important decisions were left in the hands of conservative businessmen more notable for their wealth than for their political experience. Democrats, indeed, cracked that Eisenhower's cabinet consisted of eight millionaires and a plumber (union leader Martin Durkin, who lasted less than a year as secretary of labor). Newsman James Reston added that "there is scarcely a member of the cabinet who can make a moving extemporaneous speech. It is humorless, obvious, unintellectual (almost anti-intellectual), and lacking in the one thing it has talked so much about—a crusading spirit."

Chief among these men, especially during the first term, were Secretary of Agriculture Ezra Taft Benson, Treasury boss George Humphrey, and Charles E. Wilson, who assumed command of the Defense Department. Benson, who served for the entire eight years of Eisenhower's presidency, was a devout Mormon who opened cabinet meetings with a prayer. He was an equally devout economic reactionary who vowed to get the government out of the business of supporting farm prices. In so doing, he hoped that marginal farmers would quit the land, overproduction would cease to be a problem, and federal aid would be unnecessary. This approach infuriated all farmers, marginal or otherwise, who demanded government assistance to 90 percent parity or more. The aroused Farm Bloc in Congress coalesced to defeat most of his efforts. For all Benson's persistence, overproduction escalated during the decade, and prices sagged. To keep pace, federal spending for agriculture rose from $1 billion in 1952 to $5.1 billion in 1961. Benson, like his predecessors, failed utterly to change the course of American farm policy.

George Humphrey was an old-fashioned fiscal conservative who considered it his job to reduce spending. "We have to cut one-third out of the budget," he said in 1953, "and you can't do that just by eliminating waste. This means, wherever necessary, using a meat axe." Later he added, "If you're going to live a good life, you've got to live within your income. A good wife can be a helluva good secretary of the treasury because that's all she needs to know." In 1957, when Eisenhower announced a mildly expansionary budget for the coming year, Humphrey bluntly called for restraint, saying that without it "we're gonna have a depression which will curl your hair." This contradiction created total confusion over the administration's economic program until 1958.

Wilson was equally anxious to cut back governmental expenditures. During the congressional elections of 1954 he went to Detroit, where thousands of unemployed were clamoring for aid, to celebrate individual initiative. "I've got a lot of sympathy for people where a sudden change catches them," he said, "but I've always liked bird dogs better than kennel-fed dogs myself. You know, one who'll get out and hunt for food rather than sit on his fanny and yell." As this remark suggests, Wilson had an affinity for gauche statements. One, in 1953, expressed his economic philosophy: "What was good for our country was good for General Motors, and vice versa." In short, the nation had no interests other than those of GM. Another avowed his belief in nuclear weaponry, chiefly because it cost less than large standing armies. "We cannot afford to fight limited wars," he said. "We can only afford to fight a big war, and if there is a war, that is the kind it will be." Appalled by such remarks, James Reston suggested that Wilson had invented the automatic transmission so he would have one foot free to put in his mouth.

Men like Wilson and Humphrey were not out of place in Eisenhower's administration. On the contrary, they reflected the President's fiscal conservatism. Ike once told the cabinet, Sherman Adams reported later, that "if he was able to do nothing as President except balance the budget he would feel that his time in the White House had been well spent." Eisenhower added, citing Lincoln, "in all that the people can do as well for themselves, the government ought not to interfere." He waited a month and a half before getting around to naming Arthur Burns, a conservative economist, as his top aide on economic policy, then told him, "I want you to be my adviser but I don't want to have to sit at a table and listen to a lot of talk." During his eight years as president, federal spending rose by only $8 billion, or 11 percent, while the population as a whole increased by approximately 18 percent.

This reluctance to pursue an expansionary fiscal policy cost him dearly by the late 1950s, when his attempts to limit spending helped to promote the deepest recession since the 1930s. Unemployment, which had remained at approximately 4 percent in the peacetime years of 1955 to 1957, suddenly jumped to 6.8 percent in 1958, a figure that involved close to 5 million people. Eisenhower responded by accelerating spending for highways, by relaxing monetary policies, and by liberalizing unemployment compensation. But he refused to consider heavy public spending for welfare or public housing, he vetoed bills to provide aid to depressed areas, and he rejected out of hand Douglas's call for a tax cut. The economy continued to flounder until 1961, so badly that it caused large drops in tax revenue—which in turn created huge budget deficits. Not surprisingly, Democrats insisted that only they could "get the country moving again." Eisenhower's conservative fiscal policy did more than anything else to harm his party in the election of 1960.

Random quotations from Eisenhower during the decade suggest his conservative views on other issues. On welfare: "If all Americans want is security, they can go to prison." On national health insurance: "I have been against compulsory insurance as a very definite step toward socialized medicine. I don't believe in it, and I want none of it myself." On federal aid to education: "I do not believe the Federal Government ought to be in the business of paying a local official. If we're going into that, we'll have to find out every councilman and every teacher and every other person that's a public official of any kind . . . and try to figure out what his right salary is." On the appointment of Warren as chief justice: "biggest damn fool mistake I ever made." On the TVA (privately): "I'd like to sell the whole thing, but I suppose we can't go that far." On the *Brown* v. *Board of Education* ruling (publicly): "I think it makes no difference whether or not I endorse it. What I say is the—the Constitution is as the Supreme Court interprets it; and I must conform to that and do my very best to see that it is carried out in this country;" and (privately): "I personally think the decision was wrong."

Occasionally, of course, Eisenhower proved flexible enough to accommodate pressure groups. Reactionaries like Goldwater, in fact, grumbled that he was promoting a "Dime Store New Deal." Despite Benson's appeals, Eisenhower signed the expensive farm bills of the decade. He assented to modest increases in welfare payments and in the minimum wage, and to small appropriations for public housing. In 1958 he approved the National Defense Education Act, which Congress hurried through in response to Russia's successful satellite, the Sputnik. The NDEA program provided federal aid for science and language training. In 1960 Eisenhower signed the Kerr-Mills Bill, which offered federal matching money to states that enacted their own health insurance plans for the elderly poor. And in perhaps the most important measure of his administration he readily signed a multibillion-dollar federal highway construction act in 1956. The measure passed because it satisfied all the important interest groups: state highway officials, who sought federal money; trade unions, who needed jobs for their members; farmers, who wanted better roads to market their goods; and city officials, who yearned for faster links with other urban centers. Unlike social welfare legislation, it

> *I am convinced that the Supreme Court decision set back progress in the South at least 15 years. . . . It's all very well to talk about school integration—if you remember that you may also be talking about social disintegration. Feelings are deep on this, especially where children are involved. . . . You take the attitude of a fellow like Jimmy Byrnes. We used to be pretty good friends, and now I've not heard from him in the last eighteen months— all because of bitterness on this thing. . . . We can't demand perfection in these moral things. All we can do is keep working toward a goal and keep it high. And the fellow who tries to tell me that you can do these things by force is just plain NUTS.*

Eisenhower expresses himself on the issues of school desegregation and civil rights.

commanded bipartisan majorities, for everyone thought well of the automobile. It passed Congress with ease.

Both Kerr-Mills and the highway act proved faulty. The Kerr-Mills approach ignored all except poor people over sixty-five. Worse, it resulted in widely differing standards for care. Many states provided little or no money, and their residents suffered accordingly. The impact of the highway law was also controversial. As expected, it provided a much-improved road network and jobs for thousands of workers. But planners thought nothing of running highways through scenic regions or of ripping up residential areas occupied by the voiceless urban poor. A consultant complained, "an aerial photo of any American city reveals devastation as obvious as that resulting from the London blitz. Saturation bombing is the only adequate comparison."

The quest for civil rights, much accelerated in the 1950s, was the most revealing test of Eisenhower's philosophy. After the Court's rulings in 1954-55 reformers thought optimistically that a new era of race relations was at hand. But the Deep South refused to change. Some areas ignored the decision; others bypassed it with "pupil placement" laws, which confirmed segregation in the schools. Jim Crow statutes continued to enforce racial discrimination in housing, transport, and public accommodations. And overtly racist organizations—Citizens Councils, White Americans, Incorporated, the Society for the Preservation of White Integrity—sprang up throughout the South. As early as 1955, when the Reverend Martin Luther King, Jr., attracted nationwide attention by leading a nonviolent boycott against segregation in buses in Montgomery, Alabama, it was clear that blacks were restless and angry and that a civil rights revolution was at hand.

The President was not wholly blind to these developments. In a series of executive actions he moved to improve conditions in the District of Columbia and in military camps. In 1957, when Governor Orval Faubus of Arkansas directly defied federal authority, he sent in troops to sustain token desegregation of a high school in Little Rock. He signed civil rights acts in 1957 and

1960, the first passed since Reconstruction. These laws established a federal commission on civil rights. They also gave the government added powers to promote equal voting rights in the South.

But Eisenhower honestly believed that only changing attitudes, not government, could alleviate racial tensions. Accordingly he did nothing to deal with the racial problems in the North. His refusal to applaud the Court's decisions also encouraged the southern resistance. Faubus, indeed, acted defiantly because he assumed that the White House would do nothing to stop him. In 1958 and 1959 the governor closed Little Rock's high school altogether rather than submit again to the law of the land. As reformers had warned, the Deep South easily circumvented the civil-rights acts of 1957 and 1960, which Eisenhower did nothing to promote. In his attitude toward civil rights the President revealed that he, like many contemporaries, failed to perceive the revolution in expectations that had been growing among blacks since World War II.

Popular complacency, to say nothing of the barriers posed by the Right and by Congress, would have prevented even the most charismatic of leaders from accomplishing very much during the 1950s. Eisenhower, therefore, was not to blame for the decade's rather barren legislative record. Moreover, he proved responsible in his use of presidential power. No postwar president was as respectful of the constitutional prerogatives of Congress. Particularly in his second term, however, he failed to respond to economic stagnation, to urban blight, and to racial confrontation. For this essential lack of vision—the product of his administrative style, his social philosophy, and perhaps his age (he was seventy in 1960, the oldest president in American history)—he failed in his responsibility to educate and to enlighten the people, whose support was necessary before momentum for change could develop. By contrast, both his predecessor, Harry Truman, and his successor, John F. Kennedy, at least tried to deal with the nation's social problems.

The Cold War continues, 1953–1961

Containment, the Republican platform announced in 1952, was "negative, futile, and immoral." It abandoned "countless human beings to a despotism and Godless terrorism." The United States, the party implied, must take steps to "liberate" these downtrodden masses from their oppressors.

The atmosphere in Moscow was hardly more promising for détente. When George Kennan arrived in May 1952 to take up his duties as ambassador, he found Soviet personnel at the embassy too terrified even to help him with his bags, much less talk with him. He discovered that five guards had been assigned to follow him, that he was prevented from talking privately with people, and that his residence was electronically bugged. When he complained of such treatment, he was declared *persona non grata* by the Soviet government. Not until the spring of 1953, when Charles ("Chip") Bohlen was finally confirmed as the new ambassador, did America get around to replacing him.

During Eisenhower's years in the White House several developments promised to soften this frigid state of affairs. Most important of these was the death of Stalin in March 1953 and his replacement by more conciliatory figures, including Nikita Khrushchev, who became the major power in Russia by 1956. Another was the Korean armistice in July 1953. Most important, though little realized at the time, both China and western Europe were developing into powers in their own right. By the 1960s the bipolar confrontation between Russia and America was giving way to a multiplication of power blocs.

Both nations acted sporadically to take advantage of these forces for coexistence. In 1953 Eisenhower startled hard-liners by calling for disarmament, and in 1955 he appealed for a condition of "open skies" over Russia and the United States, a proposal he hoped would lead to meaningful arms control. In 1955 Russia attended a summit conference at Geneva—the first between Soviet and American heads of state since the meeting at Potsdam ten years earlier. Though the conference settled nothing, it showed that the Russians were willing to mingle with American diplomats. In 1956, when Khrushchev denounced Stalin as a "distrustful man, sickly and suspicious," and recounted his "crimes" and "tortures" while head of state, it seemed certain that the Soviet Union was taking a more conciliatory course.

Despite this potential for mutual understanding, relations between Russia and the United States remained cold throughout the 1950s. The Soviet suppression of the Hungarian revolution in 1956, its continuing pressures on the Middle East, its threats to isolate West Berlin, and finally its apparent

© 1956, cartoon from *Herblock's Special for Today*, Simon & Schuster, 1958.

I'll be glad to restore peace in the Middle East too.

support of revolutionary activity in Cuba and other parts of Latin America, all antagonized the western powers. America's containment policy, which encircled Russia with naval and military bases and which included the use of high-level reconnaisance planes to spy on Soviet territory, kept the Russians uneasy and resentful. Persistent talk about liberating eastern Europe was more provocative still. As both sides developed hydrogen bombs and intercontinental missiles, the tension mounted.

Assigning blame for these tensions to individuals is neither easy nor especially helpful. Eisenhower and Khrushchev led societies whose fundamental differences prompted widespread feelings of insecurity and mutual distrust. Neither man had the freedom of action to end the Cold War. Indeed, as McCarthy's influence suggested, domestic obstacles to changing American attitudes were stronger than ever. The military, defense contractors, and the leading labor unions continued to promote a tough line. Influential politicians, including Republican Senate Leader William Knowland, constantly demanded that the administration act more firmly than it did. By contrast, advocates of détente were weak and scattered, and disarmament groups such as the Committee for a Sane Nuclear Policy (SANE) seemed almost subversive. In foreign affairs, as in domestic policy, Eisenhower had to operate under popular, institutional, and political constraints.

In contending with these forces, however, Eisenhower named as his secretary of state John Foster Dulles, one of America's most convinced anticommunists. The nephew of Robert Lansing, Wilson's secretary of state, and the grandson of John Foster, secretary of state under Benjamin Harrison, Dulles had been intimately involved in the making of foreign policy since 1907, when as a Princeton undergraduate he served as secretary to the Hague Peace Conference. In 1919 he had been at Versailles. Since then he had worked as an international lawyer based in New York City, as an adviser to Thomas Dewey and to the State Department under Truman, and as negotiator of the pact with Japan in 1951.

If Eisenhower seriously hoped for détente, he would have done well to choose someone else. For it was Dulles who drafted the "liberation" plank for the party in 1952. A stern Presbyterian, Dulles loathed "atheistic communism," and he took a moralistic approach to foreign policy. A skilled lawyer, he handled negotiations like a prosecutor in a criminal trial, not like a diplomat hoping for compromise. His rigid, humorless approach made him the butt of wits, who dubbed him "Dull, Duller, Dulles." It earned him the cordial dislike not only of the Soviets, but of many French and British statesmen of the period. He was hardly the man to promote international good will.

Consistent with his background, Dulles was ambitious for himself and his party. He was acutely aware of the fate that had befallen Acheson, his predecessor, at the hands of men like McCarthy. He resolved therefore to give the Right no cause for suspicion. This meant actively supporting self-styled security experts, who terminated the appointments of some 5000 State Department employees by August 1953, and by ignoring officials—no matter how expert—who might appear to be at all "soft" on communism. Among those who were not reassigned, and who therefore retired early, was Kennan, America's foremost expert on the Soviet Union. Sherman Adams, who tried to be objective, later conceded that Dulles's "point of view was often negative" and that he had induced a "strong aversion among foreign service career men to anything imaginative and original." Quite obviously, Dulles intended to captain a ship with a wholly submissive crew.

While purging the State Department, he also acted to commit the new administration to hard-line policies. In January he succeeded in getting Eisenhower to insert a section in his state of the union message calling in effect for the "unleashing" of Chiang Kai-shek. Such a policy appeared to be aimed at promoting the "liberation" of mainland China from communism. In March Dulles made no effort to work for détente following the death of Stalin. At the same time he let the Chinese Communists know, again with Eisenhower's blessing, that the United States might use nuclear weapons in Korea if they did not soon agree to an armistice. When China backed off in July, it appeared that his nuclear blackmail (undoubtedly assisted by a more moderate Soviet line following the death of Stalin) had helped to end the war.

By 1954, when he enjoyed Eisenhower's full confidence, it was clear that Dulles would rely on two related policies to sustain his anticommunist world view. One, which he spelled out in April, was already implicit in Secretary of Defense Wilson's policy of the "new look"—heavy dependence on nuclear weapons and strategic bombing. A potential aggressor, Dulles explained, "should know in advance that he can and will be made to suffer for his aggression more than he can possibly gain by it. This calls for a system in which local defensive strength is reinforced by more mobile deterrent power. . . . the main reliance must be on the power of the free community to retaliate with great force by mobile means at places of its own choice." In simpler language this policy of "massive retaliation" meant "more bang for the buck," an approach that Russia emulated in policies dubbed "more rubble for the ruble."

Dulles waited until January 1956 to define the related policy, which critics labeled "brinkmanship." Like massive retaliation, however, it was part of the Eisenhower–Dulles approach from the time it was first used against the Chinese concerning Korea. Its central assumption was that potentially unfriendly nations understood nothing but force, especially nuclear force. Therefore, the United States must be prepared to threaten war. "The ability to get to the verge without getting into the war," Dulles wrote, "is the necessary art. If you cannot master it, you inevitably get into war."

In applying these doctrines Dulles and Eisenhower paid particular attention to Asia. It was there that Republican stalwarts like Senator Knowland demanded firmness. It was there, too, that threats seemed worth making, for Asian communists lacked the nuclear might of the Soviet Union. The first test was in Indo-China, where rebels were gaining in their long war against French colonialism. Responding to French pleas, the Truman administration had already pumped millions of dollars into the area. But the forces of Ho Chi Minh, a Communist who led a broad-based nationalist coalition, trapped the French at Dien Bien Phu in May 1954 and threatened to drive them out of the country.

Many high-ranking members of the Eisenhower administration joined Dulles in recommending the use of American naval and air power—perhaps including atomic weapons—to assist the French. These included Admiral Arthur Radford, chairman of the joint chiefs of staff, and Vice-President Nixon. Eisenhower, too, believed that the loss of Indo-China to communism would be contagious. "You have a row of dominos set up," he observed, "and you knock over the first one, and what will happen to the last one is the certainty that it will go over very quickly. So you have a beginning of a disintegration that would have the most profound influences." Before acting, however, Eisenhower insisted that Dulles consult congressional leaders and the Allies. As he might have suspected, they rejected the idea of using American force against a popular revolutionary movement on the other side of the globe. Bowing to the inevitable after the ensuing fall of Dien Bien Phu, the United States accepted (but refused to sign) an accord worked out at Geneva. It created the Countries of Laos, Cambodia, and Vietnam, the last to be divided temporarily at the seventeenth parallel pending elections in 1956 that would determine the government of a unified nation.

To counter this loss to the West, Dulles embarked on what later critics would term "pactomania": formation of the South East Asia Treaty Organization later in 1954. Its signatories, the United States, Great Britain, France, Australia, New Zealand, the Philippines, Pakistan, and Thailand, contracted to consult in the event of a communist attack on one of them. A separate protocol covered Laos, Cambodia, and Vietnam. SEATO, however, did not include such important Asian nations as India, Indonesia, and Burma; it set up no military force like that which was being developed under NATO; and it required the members only to consult, not to fight. It became little more than a convenient excuse for American participation in Asian affairs.

The next test of administration policy in Asia involved China, where the Nationalists, who had fled to the island of Formosa, and the mainland Communists had been threatening each other since 1950. The administration continued the futile policy of nonrecognition of Communist China. In 1954 Dulles also negotiated a treaty that committed the United States to defend Formosa and the neighboring Pescadore Islands against attack from the mainland. The Communists responded by lobbing shells at Quemoy and Matsu, two Nationalist-held islands close to the mainland. Eisenhower then asked Congress for blanket authority to use force in the area as he, the commander in chief, saw fit. This was a shrewd maneuver, for it left him armed in advance—as Truman never had been in Korea—with congressional sanction. Nine years later President Johnson would employ a similar tactic following alleged attacks on American ships in the Tonkin Gulf. As the more avid Asia-firsters complained, however, Eisenhower's action stopped short of "unleashing" Chiang Kai-shek or of adopting massive retaliation against the Communists. Mao Tse-tung's forces bombed the islands sporadically throughout the 1950s and took the Tachens, a small group of islands north of Quemoy and Matsu, without any countermove from the United States. As in Indo-China, Eisenhower stopped short of getting America's military involved.

The failure to dislodge Mao Tse-tung in China revealed the inappropriateness of the "liberation" policy proclaimed in 1952 and reasserted thereafter by the right wing. Liberation proved equally futile in eastern Europe, where the Soviets tightened their control throughout the 1950s. When Poland and East Germany rebelled against Russian rule, America did nothing. In 1956, when Russian tanks quashed a revolution in Hungary, the Eisenhower administration again stood by helplessly. Liberation, like massive retaliation, was useful for domestic political consumption. But it was too extreme to receive widespread endorsement either at home or among America's allies. And in the absence of large ground forces, which Eisenhower was cutting back, it was too incredible to be believed by the communists.

Moving into Hungary would have geen particularly difficult, for two days before Soviet tanks rolled into Budapest, the western allies broke openly over policy in Egypt. Here, too, Dulles's moralistic style contributed to America's difficulties. In 1954, General Gamal Abdel Nasser, the nationalistic strong man who had taken over in Egypt, induced Great Britain, which controlled the Suez Canal, to remove its troops from the area by 1956. Nasser then turned to the United States, Britain, and the World Bank for a loan to build the High Aswan Dam to harness the Nile River. At first Dulles encouraged the project, which appeared settled at the end of 1955.

Nasser, however, made threatening statements to Israel, which had relied on America for its sustenance ever since Truman proffered it instant recognition in 1948. In May 1956 Nasser recognized Communist China. He also negotiated an arms deal with Czechoslovakia, one result of which was to permit the arrival in Egypt of hundreds of Soviet technicians. The prospect of communist infiltration was disturbing enough, but Nasser also mortgaged Egypt's cotton crop—the nation's primary source of revenue—to pay for the arms. How, Americans asked, was Egypt to repay the loan for Aswan? Southern senators in particular grumbled that the United States was promoting foreign competition against American cotton. Their complaints revealed the thrust of economic considerations in postwar foreign policy. All these developments caused the United States to procrastinate in authorizing the loan. Egypt, impatient, then let it be known it would turn to the Soviet Union. This form of blackmail infuriated Dulles. Without consulting experts in the State Department, the western allies, or World Bank officials, he simply announced that the loan was off. He hoped his action would call Russia's bluff and show have-not nations they could not push the United States around.

His decision merely infuriated Nasser, who immediately nationalized the Suez Canal and closed it to Israeli shipping. Tolls, Egypt said, would help pay for the dam. The Soviet Union then came through with the aid that Dulles had refused. And two months later, after communications between Dulles and the western allies had all but broken down, Israeli troops stormed into the Sinai Peninsula. Britain and France, in what was obviously a well-planned move, assisted Israel.

When Russia stood behind Egypt, it looked as if World War III was on the horizon. Even before the Soviets rattled their rockets, however, Eisenhower had determined not to aid the western allies, and America sponsored a United Nations resolution condemning Israel, Britain, and France, and proposing that UN forces be dispatched to stabilize the situation. Without American backing, the invaders had no choice but to pull out.

Eisenhower's action revealed his essential good judgment concerning military affairs. Fighting a war, even a limited one, to promote western colonialism in Egypt would have been unwise. But the confrontation exposed the rifts in the western alliance that Dulles's cavalier diplomacy had helped to develop. In the Arab world it enormously expanded the popularity of Nasser, who resented his treatment at the hands of the West. And it enabled Russia to claim that it had come to the aid of anticolonialism in the Middle East. With more patience, Dulles might have avoided the whole damaging episode.

The Suez crisis also exposed the Eisenhower administration's lack of understanding of the forces animating the Third World. To Dulles, as to most Americans at the time, nations like Egypt were important only in terms of the Cold War. "Neutralism," he said, "was immoral." America's task was to prop up prowestern regimes, whether dictatorial or not—not to work for social reforms. Governments that turned to the Left, as Egypt's did under Nasser, must be restrained or, like Iran's in 1953 or Guatemala's in 1954, overthrown with the aid of the CIA. Reflecting this attidue, the administration attempted to preserve its influence in the Middle East by proclaiming the so-called Eisenhower Doctrine, approved by Congress in 1957. This promised military aid to friendly governments, thus helping to promote arms sales in that already explosive region. It also authorized Eisenhower to dispatch troops to counter communist advances. Using this authority, the President helped preserve anticommunist factions in Jordan in April 1957. In the summer of 1958 he went still further, by sending marines into Lebanon to preserve a right-wing government that was unconstitutionally clinging to power. These actions sustained western influence in the area. But they did nothing to come to terms with the forces of nationalism and reform in the Middle East.

This is not to say that Eisenhower's neglect of the third world reversed previous American policy. The Truman administration had paid equally little attention to the impoverished masses of Latin America, Africa, and Asia. But in Truman's time the forces of nationalism were not quite so evident as they became by the mid-1950s. By that time Eisenhower's administration should have developed more sensitivity than it did. It was not surprising that Vice-President Nixon, visiting Venezuela in 1958, was stoned as his car drove through the streets of Caracas, or that Cuba's Fidel Castro, relying heavily on anti-American diatribes, overthrew the dictatorial regime of Fulgencio Batista in 1959. "Revolution," the president's brother Milton Eisenhower concluded in 1960, "is inevitable in Latin America. The people are angry. They are shackled to the past with bonds of ignorance, injustice, and poverty. And they no longer accept as universal or inevitable the oppressive prevailing order. . . ."

These events in Latin America symbolized the Eisenhower administration's troubled life in foreign affairs during the second term. In 1957 the Soviets electrified the world by being the first to fire a satellite into space. Americans, once secure and arrogant in their presumed scientific superiority, reacted with surprise and shock. In 1958 Dulles grew ill (he died of cancer in 1959), and Eisenhower assumed more direct control of policy, working harder than before for détente; in 1959 Khrushchev even paid a celebrated visit to the United States, and another summit conference was scheduled for Paris in May 1960. On the eve of the conference, however, the Soviets shot down an American U-2 reconnaisance plane that had been photographing Russian installations. Khrushchev placed the plane on display in Moscow and induced the pilot to tell all. In the process he tricked Eisenhower into several easily exposed lies and finally into an admission of America's illegal peacetime

Khrushchev, Eisenhower, Mrs. Khrushchev, and Soviet Foreign Minister Andrei Gromyko, during Khrushchev's visit to the United States, 1959.

espionage. In this atmosphere the summit conference broke up on the very first day, and the Soviets withdrew an invitation for Eisenhower to visit Moscow later in the year. For the remainder of Eisenhower's presidency Soviet-American relations were more frigid than ever.

Actually, the U-2 affair was not so shocking as Khrushchev made out. He well knew that America had been making such illegal flights for some time. Having hit the plane, he could have crowed about Russia's obviously improved technology, and played the incident down. Instead, he used it to force a break between Russia and the United States, and he carried on his uncompromising behavior into the early Kennedy years. Why he did so was not wholly clear, for Soviet decision-making remained all but impenetrable to western eyes. Perhaps he, too, was under pressure from hard-liners at home. In any event, he was hardly the fun-loving, quasi-democratic figure that some American observers tended to extol.

The most frightening aspect of the U-2 affair, therefore, was not that America was involved in espionage. Rather, it was that such a flight should have been authorized when it was—on the eve of the conference. It was not clear why such a risk was taken, though Eisenhower properly assumed full responsibility for doing so. But evidence suggests that top military and intelligence officials opposed the idea of détente with the Soviet Union and that they pressed the President to go ahead with the flights. If so, the U-2 affair was an especially clear example of the role played by the military-intelligence community in the hardening of the Cold War. It was not for nothing that Eisenhower himself warned of the influence of a military-industrial complex in his farewell speech to the country in 1961.

A summary judgment of the Eisenhower administration's foreign policy must begin by reiterating the constraints under which he had to operate: unreasoning anticommunism among the public, economic pressures against détente, the power of the military-industrial complex, and, not the least important, Russian provocations such as the suppression of the Hungarian revolt. Moreover, Eisenhower himself ordinarily showed balanced judgment—in Vietnam, over Quemoy and Matsu, over Suez. To his credit, he secured peace in Korea, and he kept the country from war for the next seven and a half years. Rhetoric aside, he continued, rather than reversed, the major policies of the Truman administration. As revisionists have rightly observed, he seems the least bellicose of America's postwar presidents.

But questions remain. What if he had consistently pursued détente in the aftermath of Stalin's death? Suppose he had never named Dulles secretary of state, or, having named him, had taken command himself, as he began to do in 1958? Suppose he had pursued the suggestions of people like Kennan that America seek "disengagement" in central Europe. And suppose further that he had appreciated the strivings of China and the Third World? If he had done these things, he might have left behind a calmer world when he stepped down in 1961. He might also have succeeded in educating the citizenry about the dangers of rocket-rattling in the nuclear age. If so, Americans (and perhaps the Soviets) might have behaved with more restraint in the years to come.

In the councils of Government, we must guard against the acquisition of unwarranted influence, whether sought or unsought, by the military-industrial complex. The potential for the disastrous rise of misplaced power exists and will persist.

We must never let the weight of this combination endanger our liberties or democratic processes. We should take nothing for granted. Only an alert and knowledgeable citizenry can compel the proper meshing of the huge industrial and military machinery of defense with our peaceful methods and goals, so that security and liberty may prosper together.

Eisenhower warns against the military-industrial complex, 1961.

The end of the Eisenhower order

John F. Kennedy's victory over Richard Nixon in the presidential election of 1960 appeared a striking repudiation of the past. After all, Kennedy was only forty-three when he took office—the first president to be born in the twentieth century, and the second youngest (next to TR) in American history. He was the first Roman Catholic to be elected president: Americans, it seemed, had progressed far since repudiating Smith in 1928. Most important, he imparted an air of vigor and purpose to the country. By struggling for a progressive program of domestic policies, he would get the country moving again. He would help the nation cross a "New Frontier."

People who expected wonders from the new president, however, would have done well to record several aspects of the campaign. Kennedy was not the liberals' favorite—that had been either Humphrey or Stevenson, who still commanded widespread support in a third bid for the nomination. In selecting Lyndon Johnson as his running mate, Kennedy merely underlined the political caution he had displayed in four years as a representative and eight years as an uninfluential senator from Massachusetts. "I'm not a liberal at all," he told an interviewer. "I never joined the ADA [Americans for Democratic Action] or the American Veterans Committee. I'm not comfortable with those people." Reassuring conservatives, he added, "I believe in the balanced budget," except in a "*grave* national emergency or *serious* recession." Eleanor Roosevelt, speaking for many liberals who distrusted Kennedy, explained, "I would hesitate to place the difficult decisions that the next President will have to make with someone who understands what courage is [Kennedy had written short biographical essays entitled *Profiles in Courage* in 1956] and admires it, but has not quite the independence to have it."

People like Eleanor Roosevelt were especially critical of some of Kennedy's statements. In 1949 he had said that Truman had "lost" China. "Those responsible for the tragedy of China must be searched out and spotlighted," he proclaimed. " . . . What our young men had saved, our diplomats and presidents had frittered away." Pursuing this anticommunist line during the campaign in 1960, he berated the Eisenhower administration for its "softness" regarding Quemoy and Matsu, and he appealed shamelessly to Cold War passions. "The enemy," he told an audience in Salt Lake City, "is the communist system itself—implacable, insatiable, unceasing in its drive for world domination. For this is not a struggle for the supremacy of arms alone— it is also a struggle for supremacy between two conflicting ideologies: Freedom under God versus ruthless, godless tyranny."

During his unprecedented television debates with Nixon—debates that probably enhanced his appeal with millions of voters who did not know him as well as Nixon—Kennedy also adopted a bellicose stance regarding Cuba's Fidel Castro, who was pursuing an anti-American line. When Eisenhower clamped an embargo on Cuba, Kennedy complained that it was "too little too

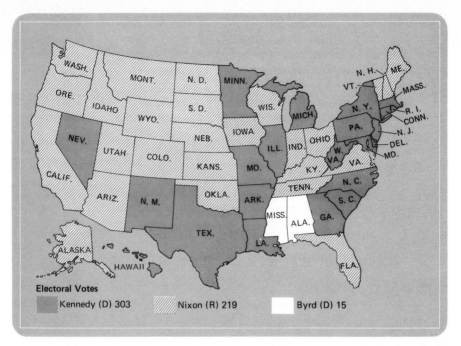

Electoral Votes

Kennedy (D) 303   Nixon (R) 219   Byrd (D) 15

Election, 1960

late" and that it followed an "incredible history of blunder, inaction, retreat, and failure." The United States, he proclaimed, must "strengthen the non-Batista exiles in the United States and in Cuba itself." This was an incendiary and demagogic statement, for he knew that anti-Castro exiles were even then being trained by the Eisenhower administration. In making it he exposed the passion for winning that critics perceived in the Kennedys. He showed that Cold War rhetoric was not the preserve of Nixon alone.

The campaign showed further that religious bigotry, though less overt than in 1928, remained very much alive. The election results revealed that Kennedy fared as well among Protestants as Stevenson had done in 1956. But in that year Stevenson had trailed badly among all groups. Compared to 1958, when Democrats made large gains in congressional races, Kennedy did poorly in Protestant sections, where the political scientist V. D. Key detected "massive shifts" away from the Democratic ticket. Overall, his Catholicism hurt him more than it helped.

The results of the election failed also to produce much of a mandate for anyone. Kennedy's total vote of 34.2 million exceeded Nixon's by only 118,000. It was a "tremendous landslide," the young president observed wryly, "that swept the Vice President and I [sic] into office by one-tenth of one per cent." Without very narrow victories in crucial states such as Pennsylvania, Missouri, and Illinois (where vote frauds in Democratic Cook

County may have made the difference), Kennedy would have lost the election. And his new Congress, while nominally Democratic, had twenty more Republicans in the House to bolster the conservative coalition.

It is hazardous to speculate on the major reasons for Kennedy's victory. Among them, however, was probably Nixon himself, who proved an energetic but unattractive candidate. Kennedy benefited also from Eisenhower's foreign policy setbacks, especially the U-2 affair. His constant focus on the nation's economic stagnation probably helped him most of all. He scored well—like many northern Democrats since the 1930s—in the populous black, ethnic, and industrial wards of urban America. He carried twenty-seven of the nation's forty-one largest cities, including all the biggest ones, where he rolled up a plurality of 2.7 million votes. This continuity in voting patterns reveals that Eisenhower's triumphs in 1952 and 1960 had been aberrations attributable to his unique personal appeal, and that Kennedy won because normally Democratic America reverted to form.

For these reasons the election suggests that voters in 1960 harkened as much to the past as to the future. The nation remained essentially Democratic, as it had since Franklin D. Roosevelt perfected the art of blaming Hoover for the world's problems. It remained divided, though less so than in the past, along religious lines. It responded, or so it seemed, as strongly as ever to appeals for fiscal conservatism, and to candidates of the political center. And it listened as attentively as before to inflammatory Cold War rhetoric. For all the talk about a New Frontier, it was fair to say in 1960, as it had been in 1952, that America, affluent and middle-class, still yearned as much for stability and consensus as for dramatic change.

Suggestions for reading

An important aid in understanding American life since 1945 is William Leuchtenburg, *A Troubled Feast** (1973). Books covering economic change in the 1940s and 1950s include John Brooks, *The Great Leap** (1966); H. P. Miller, *Rich Man Poor Man** (1964), a study of income distribution; Michael Harrington, *The Other America** (1962), a vivid account of poverty; David Potter, *People of Plenty** (1954), a far-ranging book concerning the effect of abundance on the American character; and E. L. Dole, *Conservatives in Power* (1960), which deals with government budgetary policy. Two books by John Kenneth Galbraith offer challenging interpretations of economic life: *American Capitalism** (1952) and *The Affluent Society** (1958).

Social trends are the subject of S. M. Lipset and Reinhart Bendix, *Social Mobility in Industrial Society* (1959); Peter M. Blau and Otis D. Duncan, *The American Occupational Structure* (1967); Robert C. Wood, *Suburbia** (1959); Scott Donaldson, *The Suburban Myth** (1969); William Dobriner, *Class in Suburbia** (1963); and William H. Whyte, *Organization Man** (1956). Like Whyte and Potter, David Riesman discusses the American national character in his widely read *Lonely Crowd** (1950). See also Thomas Hartshorne, *The Distorted Image: Changing Conceptions of American Character Since Turner* (1968); and Seymour Lipset and Leo Lowenthal, eds., *Culture and Social Character* (1961). Books covering aspects of thought in the 1950s also include Lawrence Lipton, *The Holy Barbarians* (1959), on the "beats"; Sam Hunter and John Jacobus, *American Art of the Twentieth Century* (1974); and Richard Kostelanetz, ed., *The New American Arts* (1967).

For religious trends see Will Herberg, *Protestant Catholic Jew** (2nd ed., 1960), a challenging sociological analysis; and Digby Baltzell, *The Protestant Establishment: Aristocracy and Caste in America** (1964). C. Wright Mills offers sharp critiques of American society in *White Collar** (1951), and *The Power Elite** (1956). Edward Banfield, *The Unheavenly City Revisited** (1974), gives a provocative critique of policies to aid the cities. So do Martin Anderson, *The Federal Bulldozer* (1967), and Herbert Gans, *The Urban Villagers** (1962), both of which show the unhappy results of urban renewal. For the role of the military see Edward B. Glick, *Soldiers, Scholars, and Society* (1971); and Samuel Huntington, *The Soldier and the State* (1957). A critique of the military-industrial complex is Seymour Melman, *Pentagon Capitalism* (1970).

Books on politics in the 1950s are Peter Lyon, *Eisenhower** (1974); Herbert Parmet, *Eisenhower and the Great Crusades* (1972); and especially James Sundquist, *Politics and Policy: The Eisenhower, Kennedy, and Johnson Years** (1968). Useful accounts by members of the Eisenhower administrations are Arthur Larson, *Eisenhower: The President Nobody Knew** (1968); Emmet John Hughes, *The Ordeal of Power* (1963), which is unflattering; and Sherman Adams, *First-Hand Report* (1961). I. F. Stone, *The Haunted Fifties** (1964), contains articles highly critical of the Eisenhower administration. Political trends are surveyed in Samuel Lubell, *The Revolt of the Moderates* (1956); and Heinz Eulau, *Class and Party in the Eisenhower Years* (1962). Special studies are Aaron Wildavsky, *Dixon-Yates* (1962), which covers electric power policy; and Alan K. McAdams, *Power and Politics in Labor Legislation* (1964). Biographies are Kenneth Davis, *Adlai Stevenson** (1957); and Joseph Gorman, *Kefauver: A Political Biography* (1971).

For the civil rights revolution see Anthony Lewis and *The New York Times, Portrait of a Decade: The Second American Revolution* (1964); and David Lewis, *King: A Critical Biography** (1970). Excellent on the status of blacks is Talcott Parsons and Kenneth Clark, eds., *The Negro American** (1966). J. W. Anderson, *Eisenhower, Brownell and the Congress* (1964), and Walter Murphy, *Congress and the Court* (1962), describe congressional opposition to decisions such as *Brown* v. *Board of Education*. Southern resistance is described in Numan Bartley, *The Rise of Massive Resistance* (1966); and Neil R. McMillen, *Citizens' Council . . . 1954–1964* (1971). Other books dealing with the Supreme Court are G. Theodore Mitau, *Decade of Decision . . . 1954–1964** (1968); Alexander Bickel, *The Supreme Court and the Idea of Progress** (1970); John D. Weaver, *Warren* (1967); and Paul Murphy, *The Constitution in Crisis Times, 1918–1969** (1972).

Useful books on foreign policy include Seyon Brown, *Faces of Power: Constancy and Change in U. S. Foreign Policy from Truman to Johnson** (1968); Townsend Hoopes, *The Devil and John Foster Dulles* (1973); Richard Goold-Adams, *The Time of Power* (1962), also on Dulles; and the books on the Cold War cited at the end of the previous chapters. See also Norman Graebner, *The New Isolationism* (1956); Hugh Thomas, *The Suez Affair* (1966); David Wise and T. B. Ross, *The U-2 Affair* (1962); J. C. Campbell, *In Defense of the Middle East* (1960); Milton Eisenhower, *The Wine is Bitter* (1963), on Latin America; and Henry Kissinger, *The Necessity for Choice** (1961), on military policies. Two books dealing with the CIA are L. B. Kirkpatrick, *The Real CIA* (1968); and the less flattering account by David Wise and T. B. Ross, *The Invisible Government** (1964).

13

The 1960s:
from
altruism
to
disenchantment

Many idealists found the early 1960s the most exciting time in modern American history. Young civil rights activists were staging interracial sit-ins and freedom rides. The Reverend Martin Luther King, Jr., was dramatizing the crusade for racial justice. The folk singer Bob Dylan was composing memorable ballads for peace and justice. Chief Justice Earl Warren was leading the Supreme Court toward breakthrough decisions broadening the Bill of Rights. And John F. Kennedy, youthful, energetic, articulate, was in the White House. Despite his assassination in November 1963, many progressives kept the faith, and under Lyndon Johnson's leadership they enacted a remarkably wide-ranging body of reforms in 1964 and 1965. The 1960s, it seemed, would witness the triumph of social justice in America.

The new frontier

Kennedy's upbringing offered clues to anyone who wished to predict his behavior as president. His maternal grandfather had been a colorful mayor of Boston, his paternal grandfather a politically active saloonkeeper. Both had been upwardly mobile Irish Catholics anxious to gain acceptance in America. Kennedy's father, Joseph, made millions in a variety of speculative endeav-

411

John and Robert Kennedy discussing problems awaiting decision, 1960.

ors, contributed generously to the Democratic party, and was rewarded with the coveted ambassadorship to Great Britain. Fiercely competitive, Joseph instilled his own energy and ambition in his children. As president, Kennedy was to exalt activity and vigor almost as ends in themselves and to insist that the United States compete strenuously against its enemies. Though fatalistic in many ways—he thought of himself as an "idealist without illusions"—he clothed his doubts in an altruistic rhetoric that captured the mood of the time. "Ask not what your country can do for you," he proclaimed. "Ask what you can do for your country."

In seeking to implement his goals Kennedy deliberately rejected Eisenhower's low-key approach. He revealed—at least in his rhetoric—that he would use all the tools at his command and that opponents could expect retaliation from the White House. Kennedy replaced Eisenhower's businessmen with a corps of academicians, intellectuals, and dynamic younger executives, and he rejected the staff system. "Whereas Eisenhower wanted decisions brought to him for approval," one political scientist has written admiringly, "Kennedy wanted problems brought to him for decision."

Such an administrative style had obvious pitfalls. As the newsman Merriman Smith pointed out, some of the New Frontiersmen had "moments of short-sightedness, bias, prejudice, and needlessly argumentative verbosity."

The reporter Joseph Kraft added that Kennedy, like Truman, was rather too fond of action for action's sake. The President's "bang-bang" style, he complained, "favors people who know exactly what they want to do. It is tough on people who have dim misgivings—even if those misgivings happen to be very important." But most observers praised the new president's methods. Under Eisenhower, I. F. Stone wrote, "teamwork was conducted much in the manner of a football game—frequent huddles, great attention to coordinating everybody, and interminable periods spent catching breath between plays." Kennedy's approach, by contrast, resembled basketball. "Everybody is on the move all the time. . . . The President may throw the ball in any direction, and he expects it to be kept bouncing."

Reporters responded especially favorably to Kennedy's sense of humor. Told of Vatican complaints about his secular approach to politics, the President quipped, "now I understand why Henry the Eighth set up his own church." When people grumbled that his brother Robert was too young to be Attorney General, he joked that Bobby might as well get some experience before practicing law. Reporters also welcomed his articulateness and his accessibility, and people who saw him on television were immediately struck by his poise and good looks. In the TV age of the 1960s, when style and image frequently counted for as much as substance, Kennedy enjoyed great advantages.

These assets appeared to help in his dealings with a still conservative Congress. In early 1961 his followers in the House succeeded, by the narrow margin of 217 to 212, in liberalizing the obstructive Rules Committee. Later, Congress increased the federal minimum wage, set aside funds for manpower training and area redevelopment, and passed a trade expansion act that promised to lower traiffs throughout the industrialized noncommunist world.

Kennedy's popularity in office reached a peak in mid-1961 when 83 percent of respondents approved of his presidency. He reached a low of 57 percent shortly before his assassination in 1963.

Changes in Gallup Poll results showing popular approval of the way Kennedy functioned as president

SOURCE: Adapted from Irish and Frank, *U.S. Foreign Policy*, p. 104

Before his death the House approved a multibillion-dollar tax cut, which the Senate passed early in 1964. This was a Keynesian measure that deliberately risked short-term budgetary deficits in the hope of promoting purchasing power. Kennedy's willingness to embrace this "New Economics" was the most striking manifestation of his gradual receptiveness to unorthodox ideas.

Kennedy also kept his promise to pull the country out of its economic slump. Increases in defense spending pumped new billions into the economy. So did his program to place a man on the moon: by 1969, when Neil Armstrong got there, the government had spent some $25 billion on space exploration. Primarily because of these expenditures, an upswing in the economy developed in 1961 and lasted until the early 1970s—the longest uninterrupted period of growth in modern American history. During this time some 15 million of 40 million American poor rose above the "poverty line" established statistically by the government, and median family income increased from $4000 to $8000, a jump in real dollars of more than 80 percent. Though these unprecedented advances did not significantly change the maldistribution of income, they were widely hailed. By developing faith in the government's ability to promote socioeconomic change, these impressive gains smoothed the way for Johnson's Great Society programs in 1964–65.

Though most liberals favored the tax cut, they observed that it was part of a generally cautious economic policy. During his tenure Kennedy made no serious effort to improve the distribution of income or to plug notoriously large loopholes in the tax laws. He worked harder for increases in defense spending than for social welfare. He encouraged Congress to enact tax breaks for big business. Even the tax cut, John Kenneth Galbraith grumbled, was "reactionary Keynesianism" that helped people spend more on unnecessary gadgetry. "I am not sure what the advantage is," he said, "in having a few more dollars to spend if the air is too dirty to breathe, the water too polluted to drink, the commuters are losing out on the struggle to get in and out of the cities, the streets are filthy, and the schools so bad that the young, perhaps wisely, stay away, and hoodlums roll citizens for some of the dollars that they save in taxes."

By late 1963 reformers were recognizing the limitations of other New Frontier laws. Efforts for tariff reduction, for instance, foundered amid disagreements among the western allies. The manpower training program could barely keep pace with technological change, and it made no attempt at all to attack hard-core poverty—a problem neglected until the end of Kennedy's presidency. Area redevelopment encountered opposition from business interests, which protested the granting of aid to potential competitors, and from labor leaders, who complained when money went to nonunion employers. In 1963, only two years after passage of the act, these pressure groups succeeded in killing a proposed increase in funds for the program.

Congress prevented many other measures from passing at all. These included medicare, aid to education, funds for mass transit, and creation of the Department of Urban Affairs. Some people thought that the lawmakers would have to be more responsive in 1964, an election year. But at the time of Kennedy's death the legislative logjam seemed as imposing as in the 1950s. *The New York Times* commented: "Rarely has there been such a pervasive attitude of discouragement around Capitol Hill and such a feeling of helplessness to deal with it. This has been one of the least productive sessions of Congress within the memory of most of its members."

Those who blamed Kennedy for this unproductive record were a little unfair. Like Truman before him, he lacked three advantages necessary for success on Capitol Hill: reliable progressive majorities, the support of pressure groups, and a popular mandate as expressed at the polls. Congressmen, accordingly, paid more attention to well-organized constituents than to presidential persuasion. "You can twist a fellow's arm once or even twice," a Kennedy aide explained. "But the next time he sees you coming he starts to run."

Kennedy's efforts for an aid to education bill revealed the power of these forces to sustain the status quo. As Kennedy well knew, opponents included many Republicans and Southern Democrats. Some of them objected to spending large sums of money for social programs; others feared that government aid would lead to federal dictation of curricula. In packing the House Rules Committee in early 1961, the President weakened these conservatives at their main bastion of defense. He also succeeded in dissuading Representative Adam Clayton Powell, a Harlem congressman, from attaching his antisegregation amendment to the bill. A similar provision, which denied aid to segregated schools, had forced almost all southerners, liberal or conservative, into opposing aid to education in the 1950s.

With these obstacles surmounted, Kennedy ran into yet another pressure group: the Catholic Church. As a Catholic, he felt he had to deny aid to parochial and private schools. Otherwise, angry Protestants would have accused him of religious favoritism. This decision, however, led prominent Catholic churchmen to oppose the bill. After much maneuvering, the measure sank under such pressure. Only later, in the more ecumenical spirit of the mid-1960s—and under a Protestant president who favored aid to parochial schools—did the bill command sufficient support to pass.

Kennedy's relations with influential spokesmen for big business provided another example of the way in which pressure groups could stymie presidential power. The President took office hoping to conciliate corporate leaders. "I'm not against business," he said, "I want to help them if I can." To prove his point he named Douglas Dillon, a prominent banker who had been under secretary of state in the Eisenhower administration, as secretary of the treasury, and Robert McNamara, head of the Ford Motor Company, as secretary of defense. But many business leaders remained uneasy, and when prices dipped on the stock market, they were quick to blame the White House. Annoyed, Kennedy commented, "I understand every day why Roosevelt, who started out such a mild fellow, ended up so ferociously antibusiness. It's hard as hell to be friendly with people who keep trying to cut your legs off."

His struggle with steel executives in 1962 merely intensified this hostility. This controversy began when Roger Blough, head of U. S. Steel, raised prices in defiance of an understanding previously reached with the White House. Other large steel companies followed Blough's example. Angry, Kennedy bared the weapons of the modern presidency. Antimonopolists in Congress, led by Kefauver, threatened an investigation. The Federal Trade Commission announced it would look into price agreements among large producers. McNamara implied that the Defense Department might deny contracts to corporations that refused to cooperate with Washington. The FBI appeared to be using its formidable powers to gather information against Blough's allies. Kennedy himself made it clear that he would have to review his policies favoring generous tax allowances to business. He observed, "my father always told me that all businessmen were sons of bitches, but I never believed it 'til now." Shortly after this display of strength Blough backed down slightly.

Kennedy's actions were not so potent as they appeared. Blough's retreat stemmed less from fear of the administration (though that mattered) than from the decision of Inland Steel, a dangerous competitor, to keep its prices at existing levels and therefore to bid for a larger share of the market. Inland's action showed that competitive pressures existed even in an industry as oligopolistic as steel. Simplistic talk about a monolithic "power elite" overlooked these fissures within the business community. But Inland's decision also revealed that leading business executives often possessed more power than Big Government or the presidency. Few confrontations offered a clearer example of the institutional obstacles facing elected officials.

As if these obstacles were not burden enough, Kennedy had personal liabilities that hurt his chances on the Hill. Some congressmen remembered him as a former colleague who had spent as much time socializing and promoting his personal ambition as he had fulfilling the duties of committee work. For these reasons he had never been an "insider" in Congress. Others sensed correctly that he was much more interested in foreign affairs than in domestic policy and that he found many congressmen long-winded and boring. As James Reston pointed out, Kennedy disliked "blarneying with pompous congressmen and simply would not take the time to do it." Still others were put off by the elitist tone of his administration. "All that Mozart string music and ballet dancing down there," one congressmen remarked, "and all that fox hunting and London clothes. He's too elegant for me." This populistic reaction to Kennedy's style showed that hostility to the Eastern Establishment—an ill-defined entity—remained a force in American politics. It suggested further that the very traits that assisted the president in his dealings with the media and with what the historian Eric Goldman called "Metro-America," the eastern urban elites, could become liabilities in managing Congress.

Kennedy also showed rather less forcefulness than he had led some progressives to expect. Always a pragmatic politician, he shied away from

America's mood:
the public's view of the most important
problem facing the country,
according to Gallup Poll results,
1961–1963

1961	Prices and inflation
1962	War, peace, and international tensions
1963	Racial problems

SOURCE: Irish and Frank, *U. S. Foreign Policy*, p. 107

promoting controversial programs. "There is no sense in raising hell and then not being successful," he said. This caution led him to rely on congressional magnates like Speaker of the House Sam Rayburn or senators Richard Russell of Georgia and Everett Dirksen of Illinois, the GOP leader. By avoiding confrontations, he hoped he might win the massive victory in 1964 that would give him the mandate he needed.

Progressives found Kennedy particularly cautious in the area of civil rights, where events were rapidly outdistancing the politicians. In February 1960 young people popularized direct action tactics by staging sit-ins at segregated lunch counters in the South. Two months later the Student Nonviolent Coordinating Committee (SNCC) joined the rapidly growing Congress on Racial Equality (CORE), King's Southern Christian Leadership Conference, and older organizations such as the NAACP in the battle for equal rights. By May 1961 CORE workers were staging integrated "freedom rides" into the South in order to desegregate transportation terminals—and getting beaten by angry mobs in the process. In 1962 James Meredith, a black man, tried to enroll in the University of Mississippi, only to be challenged by Governor Ross Barnett and by angry crowds. In a night of campus violence 2 people were killed and 375 injured, including 166 federal marshals. In April 1963, when King led nonviolent demonstrators in Birmingham, Alabama, police under Eugene "Bull" Conner repelled them with electric cattle prods, water hoses, and dogs. The melee, shown to shocked Americans on nationwide television, unleashed a wave of sympathy in the North for King's cause.

Many forces combined to encourage the adoption of these direct action tactics. Among them was the dramatic TV coverage that such methods attracted. More basic was the idealism and fearlessness of the young demonstrators, who were impatient with what they considered the calculations of the politicians and the legalism of groups such as the NAACP. The civil rights movement among young activists owed much to King, a spellbinding speaker whose deep Christian faith evoked ready responses among blacks in the South. Whites, too, found him "safe," for his doctrine of nonviolence suggested they need not fear race war.

The Birmingham, Alabama, police use dogs against civil
rights demonstrators, 1963.

For blacks there was also a revolution of rising expectations. Since 1940
millions had either joined the armed forces or moved to the North. There they
began to escape the poverty, isolation, and relative ignorance that had prevented collective actions in the past. There, too, they encountered a subtler
brand of racism that exposed with even greater clarity the Jim Crow system of
the South. In the 1950s these blacks had hoped, though briefly, that Supreme
Court decisions like *Brown* v. *Board of Education* would bring on the
revolution. By 1960, it was all too obvious that legal protection was not
enough; only direct action could promote social justice.

Kennedy seemed to sympathize with the movement. During the 1960
campaign he had insisted that a presidential "stroke of the pen" could wipe
out racial discrimination in federally supported housing. He had helped get
Martin Luther King out of jail in Georgia—an act that solidified his vote
among blacks in the North. Once in office, he appointed blacks to important
offices—such as Robert Weaver as head of the Housing and Home Finance
Agency, and Thurgood Marshall, a top NAACP lawyer, to a judgeship on the
United States Circuit Court. When confronted by recalcitrant governors like
Ross Barnett and George Wallace of Alabama, he used federal authority. The
Justice Department, under his brother Robert, successfully attacked segregation in southern airports, and it brought more suits in support of voting rights
than the Eisenhower regime had done since passage of the Civil Rights Act of
1957.

Martin Luther King, Jr., tells the throngs attending the march on Washington (1963), "I have a dream . . ."

But the Kennedys remained too cautious to suit the activists. Forgetting the rhetoric of the 1960 campaign, the President waited until after the midterm elections of 1962—by which time hundreds of pens had been sent to him through the mail—to issue his order against discrimination in housing. The order, carefully limited and gently applied, had little impact. Bowing to men like James Eastland of Mississippi, chairman of the Senate Judiciary Committee, he appointed several segregationists to southern judgeships. And he disappointed activists by refusing to introduce a civil rights bill. "When I feel that there is a necessity for a congressional action, with a chance of getting that congressional action," he said in early 1961, "then I will recommend it to the Congress." For the next two years he adhered to this opportunistic course.

By mid-1963 the actions of segregationists like "Bull" Connor forced him to move more purposefully than he had before. Aroused to action, Kennedy called for passage of a civil rights law. When Congress dawdled, Kennedy acquiesced in a plan by activists for a march on Washington in August. To everyone's immense relief, the march, which attracted some 200,000 supporters, went off peacefully. King, the featured speaker, told the throngs (and millions more watching on TV) that he had a "dream, chiefly rooted in the American dream." "One day on the red hills of Georgia," he prophesied, "the sons of former slaves and the sons of former slave-owners will be able to sit at the table of brotherhood."

Even in these last months of his life, however, Kennedy failed to grasp the intensity behind the drive for racial justice. His proposed civil rights bill was moderate. It contained no provision for a commission on fair employment practices, and it limited the Justice Department's injunctive powers against racial discrimination to the area of schools. Its public accommodations section affected only those enterprises having a "substantial" impact on interstate commerce. Recognizing these loopholes, progressives in the House toughened the bill by adding the Fair Employment Practices Commission and by authorizing the Attorney General to intervene in any civil rights suit initiated by private parties. It was this tougher bill, not Kennedy's milder version, that the House passed in January 1964, two months after the assassination in Dallas.

It is all too easy, of course, to criticize Kennedy for his caution concerning civil rights and other domestic reforms. He had considerable obstacles to contend with, for Congress did not share the protesters' views. As late as March 1963—before the demonstration at Birmingham—almost everyone agreed that Congress would have ignored civil rights proposals. Even in 1964 the Senate seemed prepared to filibuster the bill to death. In moving cautiously Kennedy remained flexible enough to take advantage of the changing climate of opinion. Had he lived, he could justifiably have argued that his New Frontier rhetoric assisted in the passage of a range of reforms, including civil rights, by 1965.

Of course, he never got the chance to prove what he might have done in a second term. Moreover, it was not surprising that activists grew impatient. Kennedy, they said, was not so much altruistic as manipulative. He displayed more style than substance, more profile than courage. His rhetoric, other critics added, aroused exaggerated hopes and ultimately weakened the credibility of government. Though these criticisms were harsh, they revealed the disenchantment of many people late in 1963. Kennedy, James Reston concluded, had "touched the intellect of the country but not the heart."

NEW FRONTIERS ABROAD

Perhaps no twentieth-century president had been readier than Kennedy to engage the nation in world affairs. "Let every nation know," he proclaimed, ". . . that we shall pay any price, bear any burden, . . . support any friend, oppose any foe to assure the survival . . . of liberty." Confident about his expertise in the realm of foreign policy, he accelerated the centralization of policy-making in the White House, where McGeorge Bundy, a former Harvard dean, played an important role as national security adviser. Kennedy's secretary of state, Dean Rusk, was expected to have a lesser part. Bundy and Rusk, like Kennedy himself, tended to approach the world in the dualistic terms of the Cold War. "Our first great obstacle," Kennedy said, "is still our relations with the Soviet Union and China. We must never be lulled into believing that either power has yielded its ambitions for world domination."

Kennedy's globalism, his anticommunism, and his self-assured activism led him into one of the greatest blunders in the history of American foreign relations: the attempt in April 1961 to overthrow Fidel Castro in Cuba. The reasons for this decision seemed compelling enough beforehand. By 1961 Castro was welcoming Soviet aid and influence. Eisenhower's administration had been training anti-Castro exiles in Guatemala—something, it seemed, had to be done with them. The Central Intelligence Agency under Allen Dulles (John Foster's brother) warned that it was "now or never" in the struggle against Castro's growing power in Latin America. Procrastination, the CIA expostulated, would give Castro time to train pilots for the jet fighters Russia was supplying. Dulles and his top deputy, Richard Bissell, Jr., outlined a plan calling for American logistical support of an invasion by the exiles. Anti-Castro guerillas in Cuba, they implied, would rise in support of the invasion and topple the regime. When the Joint Chiefs of Staff supported the CIA's argument, the administration had every reason to anticipate success.

A few people expressed doubts about the wisdom of the plan. Among them were Senator J. William Fulbright, head of the Senate Foreign Relations Committee, and Marine Commandant David Shoup. Castro, Fulbright said, was a thorn in the flesh but not a dagger in the heart. American support of an invasion would destroy the remnants of good feeling for the "Yanquis" that existed among the people of Latin America. Shoup was more dramatic. He prepared an overlay map of Cuba and laid it on one of the United States. To the surprise of all, Cuba stretched some 800 miles, from New York to Chicago; clearly, it would not be conquered quickly. Shoup then placed a second overlay on the others. It was of a tiny island. What is that? he was asked. "That, gentlemen," he replied, "represents the island of Tarawa [where Shoup had won a Medal of Honor in World War II] and it took us . . . 18,000 marines to take it." The military lesson could not have been more obvious.

Kennedy's top people, however, were activists by temperament. Placing great faith in America's superior technological capacity, they assumed that a preinvasion air strike would wipe out Castro's defenses and assure the success of the landing. They also thought that an invasion would unleash popular discontent with the government. These characteristically American attitudes—exaggerated faith in technology, blindness to nationalism in the Third World—left Fulbright and Shoup without significant support. With remarkably little hesitation, the National Security Council approved the plan on April 4.

The invasion—at the Bay of Pigs on April 17—was an unrelieved disaster. The open movement beforehand of exiles both in Guatemala and Florida made it easy for Castro to anticipate the attack. Moreover, the air strike failed to destroy Castro's air force. With only six operational fighters he was able to knock out five of twelve planeloads of paratroopers, to strafe ground troops, and to disable a munitions ship loaded with exile soldiers. Richard Bissell and others then tried to persuade Kennedy to authorize the use of American planes as air cover. Kennedy refused, for he knew it was too late to salvage success. Castro then mopped up the remaining invaders. In trying to intervene, the New Frontiersmen revealed that they shared the Eisenhower administration's anticommunism—without possessing the General's military know-how or sense of restraint.

The New Frontiersmen showed better judgment on other foreign questions in 1961 and 1962. Greatly expanding initiatives begun under Eisenhower, the Kennedy administration promoted the Alliance for Progress in the Western Hemisphere. The Alliance promised to outlay some $20 billion by 1970 in American aid for social and economic programs. Other priorities, notably the war in Vietnam, later prevented the program from accomplishing much. But Kennedy's apparent hostility to right-wing elites in Latin America suggested that he sympathized with progressive forces. His support of the Peace Corps, which promoted educational, technological, and social change in the area (and in underdeveloped regions throughout the world), further enhanced his reputation abroad. By 1964 America's relations south of the border were temporarily warmer than they had been in 1960.

Elsewhere in the Third World Kennedy showed more restraint than he had in Cuba. In Laos, where communists, moderates, and right-wing forces struggled for control, he resisted the temptation to involve American manpower and supported instead a neutral coalition. After extended talks in Geneva, Averell Harriman, America's chief negotiator, worked out such an arrangement in 1962. The Pathet Lao, the native communist forces supported by Russia and North Vietnam, soon resumed the fighting, and Laos remained a war-torn land. But Kennedy had at least avoided direct American participation. His toleration of neutralism in the Third World, while limited, contrasted sharply with Dulles's hostility in the 1950s.

Kennedy also exhibited toughness with Khrushchev, who treated his young American adversary contemptuously at a brief meeting in Vienna in June 1961. America, the Soviet leader warned at the time, must agree to a German peace treaty by December. Otherwise, Russia would sign a separate agreement permitting East Germany to control access routes into West Berlin. Kennedy responded by reaffirming America's commitment to Berlin, by mobilizing reserve units, and by using the confrontation to get higher defense appropriations from Congress. He even endorsed, though only temporarily, erection of fallout shelters. Russia reacted by raising barriers (later to become the Berlin Wall) preventing the flow of East German refugees to the West. Suddenly, American and Russian tanks faced each other at the line between the zones. Fighting, perhaps leading to nuclear war, appeared at hand. But the military forces avoided incidents, Khrushchev let his deadline pass without further action, and tensions gradually subsided. Kennedy's management of the confrontation showed that he was tough and that he would employ brinkmanship to secure his ends.

The young president's handling of the Cuban missile crisis in 1962 revealed even more clearly his tendency to toughness and brinkmanship. The crisis

Wright, *The Miami News.*

See how many are staying on our side.

One cartoonist's view
of the Berlin Wall, 1961.

began in October when U-2 planes discovered that the Soviets were emplacing offensive missiles on Cuban soil. Many angry American officials counseled for an air strike to prevent completion of the missile sites, and for a time it appeared that the President would authorize it. After tense discussions, however, this option was postponed. Such a strike, Robert Kennedy recalled, would have made his brother the Tojo of the 1960s. Instead, the administration proclaimed a ''quarantine,'' or blockade, of the island. For two days Russian ships headed for the blockade, and the United States stood ''eyeball to eyeball'' with the Soviet Union. It was the most frightening confrontation of the Cold War. Khrushchev, however, proved wise enough to avoid naval engagements thousands of miles from Russian territory. On October 24 he ordered the ships to turn about, and on October 26 he promised to remove the missiles if the United States ended the blockade and renounced any intention of invading Cuba. The next day he changed his mind and sent a much more hostile message. Kennedy, however, shrewdly pretended that the second cable had never arrived. America acceded to Khrushchev's initial deal, and the crisis was over.

The President's defenders have emphasized his restraint during this confrontation. Kennedy, they point out, resisted pleas for an immediate air strike, then had the cunning to ignore the second Soviet note. Moreover, the President's admirers add, he showed wisdom as well as restraint. Permitting the installation of offensive missiles in Cuba, they insist, would have altered the balance of power by giving the enemy greater "first strike" potential. They argue also that JFK had to prove his toughness to Khrushchev, who had (presumably) found him indecisive at Vienna and during the Bay of Pigs fiasco. Kennedy, they conclude, had to act firmly or risk more provocative Soviet behavior concerning Berlin and western Europe.

These arguments are difficult to disprove—for Khrushchev's behavior seemed both antagonistic and erratic. But it is rather frightening to think of world leaders like Kennedy risking the destruction of Western civilization in order to establish *machismo*. It is equally frightening to learn—from later accounts—that Kennedy was very conscious at the time that toughness would assist his party in the imminent congressional elections. And it is questionable whether his brinkmanship was necessary. Though Khrushchev acted provocatively, his policy in Cuba would have made little difference in the existing military situation: offensive missiles were already well emplaced on Soviet soil. Indeed, in one sense Khrushchev was merely emulating the United States, which had missiles pointing at the Soviet Union from nearby Turkey.

Recognizing this parallel, Adlai Stevenson, who was Kennedy's ambassador at the UN, had recommended tentatively during the crisis that America avoid confrontation by suggesting an exchange. Russia would pull its missiles out of Cuba, and the United States would dismantle its bases in Turkey. Because the Turkish installations were not needed—Kennedy had previously ordered them removed, only to be disobeyed by the Pentagon—Stevenson's idea seemed a more measured response than a blockade. In any event, as Stevenson and others pointed out at the time, there was little to lose by trying to negotiate first. If Russia proved obdurate, there was still time for sterner stuff. But though the Russians were led to believe that the Turkish bases would be dismantled once the crisis was over, the administration's main—and public—response was the blockade. People like Stevenson, White House aides implied, lacked backbone.

Ironically the missile crisis had the unanticipated effect of sobering both sides in the Cold War. Shaken, both Kennedy and Khrushchev paid more attention to nuclear disarmament, and in the summer of 1963 Averell Harriman succeeded in negotiating a Russian-American ban on nuclear testing on land, on the seas, and in the atmosphere. The measure did not permit on-site inspection, nor did it prohibit underground testing, which continued virtually unchecked. Would-be nuclear powers like France and China refused to ratify it. But Kennedy properly called it "an important first step toward peace, a step toward reason, a step away from war." At his assassination in Dallas a few months later Russian-American relations were more relaxed than they had been since the end of World War II. For this improvement Kennedy's administration could take some of the credit. George Kennan was one of many who praised him accordingly. "I am full of admiration, both as an historian and as a person with diplomatic experience,'' he wrote before Kennedy's death, ''for the manner in which you have addressed yourself to the problems of foreign policy. . . . I don't think we have seen a better standard of statesmanship in the present century.''

Kennan, however, did not foresee the legacy of Kennedy's administration in two key areas of foreign policy: defense planning and Vietnam. In the former Kennedy was both opportunistic and demagogic. He came to office having argued on insufficient evidence that America was on the short end of a ''missile gap.'' By February 1961 he knew otherwise. The United States, in fact, had an edge over the Soviets. Yet he acted immediately to improve America's airlift capacity, to speed up Polaris submarine development, and to ''accelerate our entire missile program.'' Using the Berlin stalemate as an excuse, he asked for and received $6 billion in additional defense appropriations in the next six months alone. Russia's response, naturally enough, was to accelerate the production of its own weaponry.

Throughout his administration Kennedy harped on the necessity of balanced defenses—which meant readying America for guerilla warfare as well as nuclear conflict. It was with such wars in mind that he created, over Pentagon protests, the Green Berets, and that he flew himself to Fort Bragg to pick their special equipment. Given these actions, it was ironic that his admirers praised Secretary of Defense McNamara for restoring civilian control over military policy. McNamara's feat, a triumph of managerial expertise, could make a difference only if the ''civilians'' approached the Cold War differently from the ''military.'' Under Kennedy they ordinarily did not. Far from curbing the potential of the military-industrial complex, the Kennedy administration left it well equipped to fight on land, at sea, or in the air— anywhere, it seemed, in the world.

That ''anywhere'' was Vietnam. Since the Geneva accord of 1954, which had promised elections on the question of unifying the country in 1956, conditions there had steadily deteriorated. The Eisenhower administration, recognizing that Ho Chi Minh would win such elections, conspired with South Vietnam to see to it that they were never held. Instead, America spent some $2 billion by 1960 to support South Vietnam's Ngo Dinh Diem, a vehemently anticommunist Catholic nationalist. Diem, however, lacked Ho Chi Minh's popular acceptance, and by 1957 his opponents in the south, derisively labeled the Vietcong (Vietnamese Communists), were starting to rebel. When Kennedy took office, civil war was raging, and the Diem regime, though dictatorial and repressive, could not control roads more than 100 yards from urban centers—and these only at night.

Kennedy was perceptive enough to recognize the excesses of Diem's regime, especially its repressive treatment of Buddhists. In September 1963 he stated, ''I don't think that unless a greater effort is made to win popular support that the war can be won out there. In the final analysis it is their war. They are the ones who have to win it or lose it.'' When Diem balked at instituting reforms, Kennedy cut back economic aid. A month later, in

November, a military coup overthrew and killed Diem. Though Kennedy had not foreseen Diem's assassination, he knew in advance of the plot and made no attempt to prevent it. By letting the coup take place, the President showed that he did not want to associate America with ineffectively repressive regimes.

But Kennedy's growing disillusion with Diem never meant support for Ho Chi Minh. On the contrary, JFK regularly opposed the rebels in the south. "The Free World," he said, "must increasingly protect against and oppose communist subversive aggression as practiced today most acutely in Southeast Asia." His vice president, Lyndon Johnson, underscored America's commitment by going to Vietnam and publicly hailing Diem as the Winston Churchill of Southeast Asia. General Maxwell Taylor, a forceful advocate of larger American ground forces, and Walt W. Rostow, a top presidential adviser, insisted that Kennedy must step up aid to the Diem regime. By early 1963 McNamara and others were reporting confidently about favorable "kill ratios" and "actual body counts." By November America had some 17,000 military "advisers" in Vietnam, some of whom were engaging in combat and getting killed. This was more than eight times the number that had been stationed there at the end of Eisenhower's administration.

This escalation was not a prelude to an inevitable American involvement under President Johnson. Kennedy did not want to engage in a ground war in Southeast Asia. Had he lived, he might have acted with restraint. But the fact remains that Kennedy's stand on Vietnam, like his defense policy, was disingenuous. As president, it was his responsibility to educate the electorate about international complexities. His failure to do so, indeed his repetition of the dualistic clichés of the Cold War, revealed that he shared many of the assumptions of the Truman and Eisenhower years: communism was a united, world-wide conspiracy; America was the savior of the "free world"; technological superiority would overwhelm Asian opposition. Far from crossing "new frontiers" in foreign policy, he traveled over much old terrain.

The Johnson years, 1963–1968

Few presidents have received as much abuse as Lyndon Johnson, Kennedy's successor. By the late 1960s stories circulated about his towering ego, his crudity, his cruelty to members of his staff. Once he publicly addressed his press secretary, George Reedy, as a "stupid sonofabitch." He raged at another aide, Jack Valenti, "I thought I told you, Jack, to fix this fucking doorknob. . . . Where the goddam hell have you been?" The historian Eric Goldman, who served briefly as a consultant to the White House, repeated an alleged exchange between Johnson and a friend. Upset by criticism, the President supposedly asked, "why don't people like me?" The friend replied: "because, Mr. President, you are not a very likeable man."

Liberals especially distrusted Johnson. From 1948, when he squeaked into the Senate by eighty-seven votes, through the 1950s, when he worked with conservatives of the Eisenhower administration, they had found him uncooperative. They also observed his assiduous protection of southwestern oil and gas interests, his coolness to civil rights, and his close relations with hustlers like Bobby Baker, a top aide during his Senate years. In his fondness for wheeling and dealing, for long pointed collars and shiny suits, and for backroom stories, he seemed like a riverboat gambler, albeit with the drawl and the swagger of a Texas tycoon.

These unflattering portrayals overlooked other sides of Johnson. Though he alienated liberals, it was not because he was instinctively conservative but because he had to satisfy his Texas constituency. Indeed, he had begun his political career in the 1930s as an ardent New Deal congressman. Roosevelt himself had regarded him as future presidential material. Thereafter Johnson became an extraordinarily effective Senate majority leader from 1954 to 1960. As he grew more secure in his political base, he tentatively accepted many liberal programs, including the civil rights bill of 1957—which could not have become law without his patient negotiations on Capitol Hill.

I dreamed about 1960 myself the other night, and I told Stuart Symington [Democratic Senator from Missouri] and Lyndon Johnson about it in the cloakroom yesterday. I told them about how the Lord came into my bedroom, anointed my head and said, "John Kennedy, I hereby appoint you President of the U.S." Stuart Symington said, "That's strange, Jack, because I too had a similar dream last night in which the Lord anointed me and declared me, Stuart Symington, President of the United States and of Outer Space." Lyndon Johnson then said, "That's very interesting, gentlemen, because I too had a similar dream last night and I don't remember anointing either one of you."

Kennedy jokes about Johnson's egotism prior to the 1960 campaign.

Johnson's detractors also tended to ignore traits that made him one of the most dynamic chief executives in American history. One of these was his unflagging energy in working with Congress. Unlike Kennedy and Eisenhower, who disliked the hard negotiating involved in securing legislation, he undertook it himself. By 1968 this passion to be at the center of the action had worn him out. It deprived him of the assistance of men of ideas, who found him increasingly domineering. But it enabled him to know exactly how congressmen stood on issues and to move quickly in rewarding his friends and punishing his foes. No one since Roosevelt, his idol, had shown such careful attention to the details of legislation.

The President often resorted to what was known as the "Johnson Treatment," described by one senator as a "great overpowering thunderstorm that consumed you as it closed in on you." Johnson, the columnists Rowland Evans and Robert Novak explained, bore in on people he wished to convince, "his face a scant millimeter from his target, his eyes widening and narrowing, his eyebrows rising and falling. From his pockets poured clippings, memos, statistics, mimicry, humor, and the genius of analogy [which] made the Treatment an almost hypnotic experience and rendered the target stunned and helpless."

If the Treatment failed to work, Johnson was ready with other forms of pressure: seemingly endless phone calls, promises (or threats) concerning patronage, even simple appeals for justice. "You get the impression from reading all these [newspaper] stories that he's always twisting arms," one congressman noted, "but what he really twists is your heart. He says he's got to have your help, and tears are practically coming out of the telephone receiver."

In applying such methods Johnson had advantages denied Kennedy. Among these were friendships with many powerful figures on the Hill. Senators like Richard Russell of Georgia and Harry Byrd of Virginia had had little reason to help Kennedy; with Johnson, a crony of many years' standing, it was harder to be obstructive. Another advantage was his southern background, which made his support of civil rights all the more impressive. His Protestantism gave him an edge that Kennedy had lacked in handling the explosive question of aid to parochial schools. Above all, Johnson came to office at a time when Americans were shocked by Kennedy's assassination. As in 1933, they were yearning for purposeful leadership.

Johnson used these advantages brilliantly in late 1963 and 1964. On November 27, five days after the assassination, he made Kennedy's program his own by appearing before Congress and reminding it of the unfinished New Frontier, especially in the realm of civil rights. "No memorial oration or eulogy," he said, "could more eloquently honor President Kennedy's memory than the earliest possible passage of the civil rights bill for which he fought so long. . . . I urge you again, as I did in 1957 and again in 1960, to enact a civil rights law so that we can move forward to eliminate from this nation every trace of discrimination and oppression that is based upon race or color."

In 1964, Johnson persisted in similar appeals to carry out Kennedy's program—with breathtaking results. Congress approved the $13.5 billion tax cut Kennedy had called for in June 1963. It passed a controversial bill authorizing federal funds for mass transit. It quickly enacted an $800 million "war against poverty" program. And it passed the first effective civil rights bill since Reconstruction. The Civil Rights Act of 1964 created a Fair Employment Practices Committee, banned discrimination in public accommodations, gave the Attorney General injunctive powers in cases involving school segregation as well as voting rights, and authorized the government to withhold funds from public authorities practicing racial discrimination.

Given the national mood, these measures might have passed in any event. Still, Johnson made a difference. The poverty program, though originally conceived in the closing weeks of the Kennedy administration, owed its shape and scope to LBJ's efforts. The tax cut escaped the Senate Finance Committee only after he promised Senator Byrd, the committee chairman, that he would cut federal spending. The bill then passed the Senate, seventy-seven to twenty-one, with the consensus that he demanded. Johnson was most effective of all in shepherding the civil rights bill. Instead of settling for half a loaf, he encouraged House liberals to tack on tougher amendments to Kennedy's original bill. As moderates had warned, his action provoked a Senate filibuster. But Johnson held firm, and fence-sitting senators soon began to feel the pressure from home. After fifty-seven days the Senate invoked cloture for the first time in the history of civil rights legislation.

As if to ensure Johnson's continued success, the Republicans then nominated Senator Barry Goldwater of Arizona to oppose him in November. Right-wingers hailed the choice, for Goldwater was an avowed reactionary who opposed civil rights legislation and progressive federal taxation, and who called for bombing in Vietnam. At the GOP convention he antagonized moderates in his own party by courting support from the right-wing John Birch Society. "Extremism in defense of liberty is no vice," he proclaimed. His partisans proclaimed, "In Your Heart You Know He's Right," but opponents countered with "In Your Guts You Know He's Nuts."

In fact, Goldwater's nomination suggested a major trend of the future: the rise of ideology (especially of conservatism) in American politics. The successes of other right-wing politicians of the late 1960s and 1970s—Governor George Wallace of Alabama, Governor Ronald Reagan of California—revealed that many Americans were dissatisfied not only with liberalism but with the center as well. In 1964, however, Goldwater's ideology seemed particularly extreme. No major party candidate for the presidency had ever seemed farther from the mainstream of American political thought.

Johnson took full advantage of Goldwater's exposed position on the issues. The GOP stance on Vietnam, LBJ implied, was irresponsible. "We are not going South and we are not going North," he said on September 28. "We are going to continue to try to save their own freedom with their own men, with our leadership and our officer direction." On October 21 he added (in the same vein as FDR in 1940), "we are not going to send American boys nine or ten thousand miles away from home to do what Asian boys ought to be doing for themselves." On domestic questions he emphasized his liberal sympathies by naming Hubert Humphrey as his running mate, and he appealed to the center by reminding people of Goldwater's extremism. "Right here is the reason I'm going to win this thing so big," he told a friend. "You ask a voter who classifies himself as a liberal what he thinks I am and he says 'a liberal.' You ask a voter who calls himself a conservative what I am and he says 'a conservative.' You ask a voter who calls himself a middle-roader, and that is what he calls me. They all think I'm on their side."

To no one's surprise Johnson won overwhelmingly, by 43.1 million to 27.1 million. Goldwater carried only Arizona and five southern states. The GOP, once moribund in Dixie, now seemed wrecked everywhere else. Democrats also secured huge majorities of 68 to 32 in the Senate and 295 to 140 in the House. The enormous shifts in voting since 1960 showed that the electorate was becoming unpredictable and unstable in presidential elections.

Exhilarated, LBJ interpreted the election as a mandate for further domestic reform. "Hurry, boys, hurry," he told his aides. "Get that legislation up to the Hill and out. Eighteen months from now ol' Landslide Lyndon will be Lame-Duck Lyndon." Driven at a furious pace, the Democratic Congress responded with the most far-reaching legislation since 1935. Chief among its accomplishments were medicare and aid to elementary and secondary education. Medicare, funded by an increase in social security taxes, provided for health care to the aged. A corollary program, medicaid, offered free care to poor people of all ages who qualified for public assistance. The education act set aside an initial appropriation of $1 billion. Much supplemented in succeeding years, it gave the federal government an unprecedented role in educational policy.

Hardly pausing for breath, Congress approved many other reforms in 1965. It appropriated generously for manpower training, authorized $900 million to improve conditions in Appalachia, passed a housing act that

A supreme congressional politician, President Johnson was an incompetent and ineffective national politician. This should not have been too surprising. After all, he had had experience in only two national campaigns: one when he was the vice-presidential candidate, the other when he was running for President against a man Noam Chomsky [a radical antiwar intellectual] could have beaten. In his political instincts he was more a South American caudillo than a North American leader. . . . The President as a man impressed increasing numbers of Americans as high-handed, devious and disingenuous, the embodiment of a political system that wilfully deceived the people and denied them a voice in vital decisions.

Arthur Schlesinger, Jr., a liberal historian and Kennedy partisan, offers a widely held view of Johnson, 1969.

Selma, Alabama, 1965.
The Civil Rights Act of that year
prompted an intense
and often imaginative effort
to get blacks to register to vote.

included provisions for rent supplements, set aside $1.6 billion more for the war against poverty, and established the Economic Development Act for depressed areas with the potential for growth. It created the Department of Housing and Urban Development and the National Endowment for the Arts and the Humanities, authorized an additional $2.4 billion for education, including colleges and universities, and approved a new immigration law ending quotas based on pseudoscientific theories. When police in Selma, Alabama, roughed up blacks seeking to register to vote, new outrage exploded among civil rights advocates. Prodded by Johnson, Congress then approved the Civil Rights Act of 1965. This far-reaching piece of legislation authorized federal examiners to register voters, and it banned literacy tests. Along with passage of the twenty-fourth amendment (1964), which outlawed the poll tax in federal elections, it enabled thousands of formerly disfranchised people to register, to vote, and later to elect black officials in record numbers throughout the South. It was a fitting capstone to a congressional session of unparalleled productivity, and it made Johnson—once the whipping boy of liberals—the greatest champion of progressivism since FDR.

DISILLUSIONMENT WITH LIBERALISM

That very year, however, the euphoria began to disappear. Altruism turned to frustration, then to disenchantment. By 1966 Americans were tiring of listening to the "best and brightest"—the journalist David Halberstam's apt phrase describing the liberals, intellectuals, and "experts" who had ruled since 1961. Explaining this rapid change in mood tells much about the strengths and limitations of modern liberalism, about the stubbornness of the nation's problems, about the relative weakness of governmental institutions, and—in the last analysis—about the role of traditional attitudes.

This change of mood gradually affected Capitol Hill. Between 1966 and 1968 the lawmakers increased the minimum wage, created a Department of Transportation, and established a Model Cities program. In 1968 they approved another civil rights act—against discrimination in housing. But by then Congress was already cautious in authorizing funds for rent supplements, housing, and the war against poverty. For the next decade congressional advocates of reform remained as stymied as they had been from 1937 to 1963.

Johnson's programs, by falling far short of expectations, were partly to blame for these developments. Funds for Appalachia, many people observed, went primarily for short-run projects and to road-building, which gave out-of-state profiteers access to valuable raw materials. Aid to education failed to provide money for teachers' salaries or for renovation of urban schools, which continued to deteriorate. Medicare, too, left reformers dissatisfied, for it assisted only the elderly, was financed by regressive social security taxes, and failed to bring about reforms in the medical establishment.

The urban reforms of the Great Society (and of previous liberal administrations) caused particular disenchantment. Some programs, such as aid to mass transit and rent supplements, never received adequate appropriations. Public housing, started in 1937, suffered from many handicaps: insufficient funding, bureaucratic red tape, hostility from real estate interests, and fears by surrounding residents of "black invasions." By 1969 only 700,000 public housing units had been built, leaving some 4 million Americans in substandard dwellings. Urban renewal and rehabilitation (begun under Truman) was perhaps most controversial of all. In some cities these programs worked fairly well—much better, in fact, than critics were prepared to admit. Elsewhere, however, urban renewal resulted in "projects"—sterile, high-rise developments that deteriorated into zones of social pathology—or it destroyed viable communities (usually of blacks or other groups without political power) and replaced them with middle-income housing or commercial developments. "At a cost of more than three billion dollars," a liberal critic observed in 1965, "the Urban Renewal Agency has succeeded in materially reducing the supply of low-cost housing in American cities."

The urban poor complained especially loudly about federal welfare policies. Many government programs, such as aid to the blind, to the disabled, and to dependent children, continued to require state contributions—stipulations that resulted in wide variations and (especially in the poorer southern states) in wholly inadequate standards. Welfare recipients had to meet strict residency requirements (declared unconstitutional in 1969) and unnecessarily demeaning tests. Mothers who sought aid for dependent children had to prove that there was no man at home to provide support. This "absent father" rule may have helped to disrupt marriages. (It, too, was declared unconstitutional, in 1968.) All these provisions required an ever increasing bureaucracy of social workers. Though dedicated and humane, these workers offended militants who demanded an end to "snooping" and to governmental "paternalism" in general. Social workers, one young slum dweller protested, "are rat fink types. They act like they think we're not human. They think they've got all there is, and all they do is convert us to think and do what they think and do." Gilbert Steiner, a liberal expert on welfare programs, concluded in 1971 that the Kennedy–Johnson public assistance policies left a legacy of a "services approach that had failed, a work and training approach that could not get off the ground, an asserted interest in day care but no viable day care program, . . . and a steadily increasing number of AFDA [aid to families of dependent children] recipients."

Easily the most controversial of the Great Society programs was the much ballyhooed "war on poverty," which Johnson hailed as a "milestone in our 180-year search for a better life for our people." This broad-ranging program operated under a newly created Office of Economic Opportunity (OEO), which received close to $10 billion in federal money between 1965 and 1970. Among its programs were loans for farmers and rural coops, aid to migrant workers, work experience programs, and adult education. More significant were VISTA (volunteers in service to America), which was a "domestic peace corps" of young people who lived with and provided services to the poor; the Job Corps, residential centers offering counseling and job training for unskilled young people; and the Neighborhood Youth Corps, a program providing work and on-the-job training for students and dropouts. Most important of all were the community action agencies under the Community Action Program (CAP). These agencies, of which there were 1000 by the end of the decade, sought to develop neighborhood solutions to the problems of poverty. Some focused on educational programs such as Head Start for preschool children and Follow-Through for elementary school students. Others concentrated on legal services. Still others worked hard to develop family planning services or to provide day care centers for children. All the community action agencies were supposed to avoid "paternalism" by giving poor people "maximum feasible participation" in planning.

By the late 1960s, it appeared that the war on poverty was getting nowhere. Of all its efforts, only the Neighborhood Youth Corps and work experience programs were actually providing jobs to help the employable poor. Indeed, the war in Vietnam, by heating up the economy, did much more than did the OEO to create jobs. The unemployable poor—the aged, crippled, and, above all, nonsupported mothers and their dependent children—had to turn to the nation's creaking welfare "system." By 1969 the plight of such people (the number of mothers and dependent children on relief had risen from 3.5 million to 8 million since 1961) was so desperate that the Nixon administration proposed a program of family assistance payments setting a floor below which income would not be permitted to fall.

Many of the limitations of the war on poverty (and other programs) stemmed from lack of funds. Average expenditures per year by the OEO were approximately $1.7 billion. Even when added to the $5 billion per year for medicare and the $1 billion per year for poor school districts under the education act of 1965, this was a piddling sum (approximately $250 per poor person), which could not begin to take care of the 25 to 35 million Americans who were classified as poor in the mid- and late 1960s.

Even with proper funding, the war on poverty would have been burdened with its own dubious assumptions. Head Start, though praiseworthy in purpose, could not compensate for deprivations rooted in cultural and familial forces. Advocates of day-care centers wrongly assumed that there were large numbers of qualified people to run them, or that mothers would willingly deposit their children in them to accept menial employment. The Job Corps, it developed, was a very costly program that falsely assumed that the hard-core

An antipoverty worker tutors a child in Alabama.

poor could be trained to think and work like other people. By the late 1960s Job Corps centers were already beginning to be closed down.

The community action agencies were the most controversial of all the OEO programs. Though most of them were well run, a few fell into the hands of the wrong kinds of entrepreneurial leaders: in Syracuse, an extreme example, $7 million of the $8 million expended by mid-1967 went for salaries and administration—and only $1 million to the poor. Leaders in some communities soon adopted the fashionable revolutionary rhetoric and the racial separatism of the late-1960s (see chapter 14). Such leaders alarmed local politicans, who moved quickly to prevent federal money from flowing toward those rivals for power. In 1967 these politicians succeeded in getting Congress to require state approval of community action initiatives. Thus expired—in two years—the much-acclaimed stress on local administration and on "maximum feasible participation."

CAP suffered from other fundamental misconceptions. One of these was the assumption that poverty could be fought on a neighborhood basis. This view, useful in promoting participation by the poor, underestimated the mobility in and out of slums. The warriors against poverty also assumed— again with little evidence to guide them—that poor people could organize themselves. This was not always the case, for the "culture of poverty" in some (not all) areas tended to fragment, demoralize, and disorganize the poor. Elsewhere, racial and ethnic groups confronted one another. Contrary to the expectations of those who thought that community action could mobilize the poor against "power elites," the experience in many areas suggested that hard-core poverty was all but immune to attack by approaches such as CAP. In retrospect, it is reasonably clear that the poor would have benefited more from WPA-like public employment programs or from legislation guaranteeing a minimum annual income for all. Such programs would have done more to give poor people pride, economic security, and the ability to think of the future.

Some of these misconceptions stemmed from Johnson's passion for rapid accomplishment. He simply did not give Congress time to contemplate its actions. As the sociologist Nathan Glazer observed later, the war on poverty was enacted with "nothing like the powerful political pressure and long-sustained intellectual support that produced the great welfare measures of the New Deal." Donald Rumsfeld, head of the antipoverty effort under the Nixon administration, added that "few programs were ever so unformed at birth, and few were so completely and broadly defined, for good or ill, by the times in which they were implemented. Perhaps the story of Community Action must be told by a poet or a mystic rather than a politician or a historian."

Other critics complained that Johnson, like most New Deal liberals, relied too heavily on the presumed benefits of federal spending. Throw money at problems, he seemed to say, and they will go away. The journalist David Broder observed, "His primary purpose was to provide all the tangible benefits that Federal initiative could devise and Federal money could buy. There was no pause to consider how each of the new Federal programs meshed with all the others, or whether the function was one the national government could most appropriately undertake.'' To Broder and others Johnson's programs merely encouraged pressure groups (including welfare mothers) to demand ever greater sums from Uncle Sam. Johnson, critics concluded, was too much the bread-and-butter liberal who spent money as if there were no tomorrow.

To the extent that these critics perceived Johnson as a lavish spender they were unfair. As the war on poverty revealed, the money expended on domestic programs between 1965 and 1968 was modest. Much more was needed to attack social problems. Critics were closer to the mark, however, in suggesting that spending on welfare services—as opposed to providing public employment or a guaranteed minimum income—was no panacea. In this sense Johnson was indeed something of a paternalist—a politician trying to develop middle-class behavior and values in poor people whose primary needs were jobs and money.

Johnson's greatest error—and Kennedy's before him—was to promise so much. Kennedy had talked about getting the country moving again, about crossing new frontiers. Johnson went still further: there was to be a "war" on poverty, an end to racial injustice, a "Great Society." Such high-sounding rhetoric was inspiring, at least for a while. But it aroused unrealistic expectations, radical protest, middle-class backlash, the acrimony that settled over the nation by 1966 and the political conservatism that came about thereafter. It led others, including many young radicals, to blame Johnson for "running out of ideas" and to attack liberals in general. "Liberalism," one militant said, "drifts in smug self-satisfaction, preening itself with its pragmatic and value-free cleverness in social problem solving. . . . The time for radicalism has struck." As in the years after the New Deal reforms of 1933–35, much of the energy and idealism that might have been invested in improving the programs already passed was poured instead into alienated protests against the "establishment" reformers who had produced them.

It was unperceptive of such people to dismiss Johnson's programs or to denounce the liberal orthodoxies on which they drew. LBJ was much more than a simple opportunist, and his policies, especially in the realms of health and education, offered much to ordinary people. The civil rights acts of 1964 and 1965 were among the most far-reaching pieces of legislation passed in American history. In criticizing such reforms many radicals could do little more than demand more of the same, while Marxists called for changes that were simply unrealizeable within the framework of American values and institutions.

Still, by the late 1960s the disillusion with Johnsonism was not wholly groundless. LBJ's Vietnam policy (see chapter 14) was an unmitigated disaster that drained support—and funds—from domestic programs and divided the country. Moreover, like his idol FDR, Johnson stopped short of fundamental social change. He made no effort to reform the tax laws, to redistribute income, or to attack monopoly. He was slow to perceive the flaws in welfare and urban programs. Like other liberals, he tended to ignore evidence that the Welfare State did more, as the economist Kenneth Boulding put it, to redistrib-

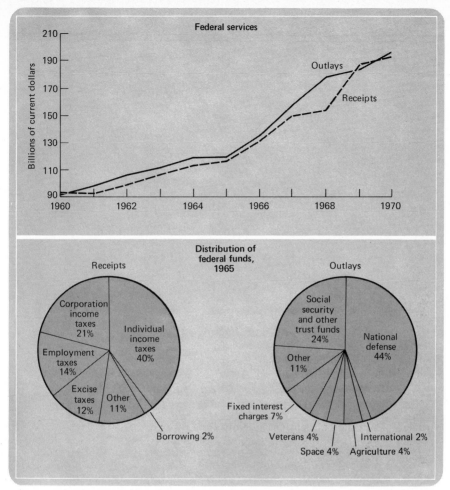

Federal services

SOURCE: U.S. Bureau of the Census, *Statistical Abstract of the United States: 1974,* 95th ed. (Washington, D.C., 1974), p. 220; distribution of funds projected by *Statistical Abstract of the United States: 1964,* p. 387

Growth of federal services, 1960–1970, and percent distribution of federal funds by function, 1965

ute income "toward the deserving middle class and the people who know how to get on the gravy train than it had for the poor."

Accordingly, many thoughtful observers began to question the state's ability to solve social problems. "There is mounting evidence," the writer Peter Drucker said, "that government is big rather than strong; that it is fat and flabby rather than powerful; that it costs a great deal and does not achieve much. . . . The citizen less and less believes in government and is increasingly disenchanted with it." James Sundquist, a liberal political scientist, added in 1968: "There are many signs that the capacity of the United States to make policies and establish programs in the domestic field has outrun its capacity, or its determination, to finance and administer them." With people such as these in doubt about welfare statism, it is not surprising that reformers were forced to the defensive after 1965.

PRACTICALLY INSUPERABLE PROBLEMS

Poverty in the Cities Johnson's critics also underestimated the size of the problems to be confronted. These, by the mid-1960s, revealed a socially divided nation. Racial tensions in the United States dwarfed those in any other advanced western society. Poverty, as books like Michael Harrington's *The Other America* (1962) revealed, affected as much as one-fifth of America's population, or nearly 40 million people, in 1960. The United States was a highly mobile society—perhaps the most mobile in the western world. The northward migration of blacks since World War II was particularly rapid. Between 1950 and 1970 the black population in metropolitan areas rose by seven million. Moreover, these cities offered fewer blue-collar opportunities than had been available to immigrants at the turn of the century. Thus it was that central cities stagnated or became dumping grounds for unemployed (or unemployable) rural migrants. In New York City, where the migrations were particularly large, the welfare load increased from 530,000 in 1965 to 1.2 million in 1972. This meant that one person in every six was on welfare and that the cost to the city was $1 billion per year. (CAP, by contrast, contributed only $50 million.) Many of LBJ's critics, radical as well as conservative, were too impatient to recognize the magnitude of these social problems and the reluctance of middle-class Americans to support the redistribution of income necessary to fight them.

America's urban problems reinforced romanticism concerning the frontier and the small town and in so doing impeded thoughtful discussion of remedies. Eric Sevareid, the liberal television broadcaster, told how warmly he (and others) remembered his small-town childhood. "I . . . loved . . . its memory always," he said of the town in which he had grown up. "It was, simply, *home*—and all of it home, not just the house but all the town. That is why childhood in the small towns is different from childhood in the city. Everything is home." Cities, by contrast, were "evil." Reflecting this antiurban bias, TV programs like *Ben Casey, Naked City,* and *East Side West Side* and movies such as *On the Waterfront* and *Pawnbroker* focused on the seamy side of city life.

Cities were not only seamy, Americans thought, but enclaves for minorities—Puerto Ricans, Orientals, Mexican-Americans, and above all, blacks, 80 percent of whom lived in urban areas by 1970. The "core" areas where these minorities lived were generally dirty, overcrowded, and—whites assumed—nests of drug addiction and violent crime. Like all stereotypes, this one was exaggerated in some respects: statistics on crime and drug addiction, never uniformly kept, were unreliable. The statistics on crime were misleading, for the baby boom of previous decades vastly increased the number of teenagers, the age group most likely to get arrested. Whites also failed to recognize the positive side of the cities, which offered wider economic opportunities than did farming regions or small towns, which languished in the postwar era. Compared to the black rural areas in the South, poverty-stricken Puerto Rico, or rural Mexico, America's cities seemed heaven-sent. But whites were correct in perceiving the "blackness" of core areas in the larger cities of the East and Midwest, in recoiling in fear from the spread of hard drugs on the streets, and in recognizing that ghetto areas were dangerous, especially after dark. Hence, whites continued to flee to the suburbs, which had 76 million people by 1970 (cities had 64 million). Confronted with such widespread hostility to cities—and to the blacks with which they were intimately identified—Johnson and urban reformers had difficulty finding support.

Those who continued to press for urban programs in the late 1960s were divided about what to do. Some, like Lewis Mumford, complained of the density of cities; others, such as Jane Jacobs, author of *The Death and Life of Great American Cities* (1963), thought that heterogeneous, closely settled neighborhoods such as Greenwich Village in New York were the ultimate in civilized living. Some reformers continued to press for public housing, but others complained that slums were a reflection, not a cause, of social disorganization. "Once upon a time," one reformer mused sadly, "we thought that if we could only get our problem families out of those dreadful slums, then papa would stop taking dope, mama would stop chasing around, and junior would stop carrying a knife. Well, we've got them in a nice new apartment with modern kitchens and a recreation center. And they're the same bunch of bastards they always were."

Advocates of racial justice were equally divided by the end of the decade. Most white reformers continued to favor federal initiatives to promote desegregation in housing, schools, and employment. Destroy the legal basis for discrimination, they said, and tensions would abate. Some liberals, however, developed doubts about cherished beliefs. In 1965, Daniel Moynihan authored a study for the government, *The Negro Family*. It stressed the social disorganization of black families. Despite increases in black income, he argued, illegitimacy and female-headed households characterized a larger number of nonwhite families than in the 1950s. A year later James Coleman and others published a massive statistical study, *Equality of Opportunity*, concerning American schools. They found that neither the level of spending for education nor desegregation made as much difference in explaining educational achievement as did socioeconomic class. Many activists challenged these findings, especially the Moynihan report, which appeared to resurrect old stereotypes about fun-lovin', indolent "darkies" who drifted from woman to woman. Find economic opportunities for black men, they argued, and families would stabilize. To others, however, reports such as these were unhappy reminders that class and cultural forces as well as "white racism" would continue to plague attempts to promote racial harmony.

The Great Society reformers also had the formidable task of trying to maintain harmony within the West's most polyglot society. According to the 1960 census, America had more than 19 million nonwhites (a term that included Orientals and American Indians as well as blacks), 9.3 million foreign-born whites, and 23.8 million people of mixed or foreign-born parents. The white ethnics alone comprised nearly 20 percent of the nation's population in 1960 of 183 million. Most of them lived unobtrusively, hoping to become accepted. But many jealously guarded their cultural identities, marrying within their own groups, and viewing outsiders with suspicion. The ethnic machines, which some people thought had been eclipsed by Roosevelt's welfare programs, continued to thrive in cities like Chicago, where Mayor Richard Daley ruled over a coalition of ethnic and professional groups. Quite obviously, the melting pot had failed to boil away America's religious, cultural, and ethnic divisions. So long as these existed, it remained difficult to mobilize a reform coalition based on class or occupational lines.

Economic interest groups further divided the potential progressive coalition. In small and relatively homogeneous nations, such as England or Sweden, it was possible (though very difficult even there) to plan ahead. Not so in the United States, where unions, businessmen, farmers, and professional groups joined self-conscious blacks and ethnics in competing for governmental favor. Almost all had pipelines to Congress or to the bewilderingly large federal bureaucracy that had "modernized" the American political system since the 1930s. Neither Johnson nor other postwar American presidents really had the power to control these groups or the bureaucrats who assisted them. Indeed, it was to fight back against these forces that Kennedy and Johnson dramatically increased the White House staff and that Nixon, even more anxious for control, resorted to a range of illegal intelligence-gathering activities.

Large corporations were by far the most powerful of these groups. By mid-decade one-half of the productive assets of American manufacturing was controlled by 150 corporations; two-thirds was held by 500. General Motors, America's largest corporation, made $2 billion in profits after taxes in 1965, a sum greater than the revenue for forty-eight of the fifty states. Its sales exceeded the Gross National Product of all but nine nations in the world. Other big companies spread into far corners of the world during the 1960s. By 1970 American firms sold some $200 billion worth of goods abroad, three-fourths of which was made in American-owned overseas plants. United States private investment abroad (including portfolio investment in overseas securities) grew from $19 billion in 1950 to $49 billion in 1960, and to $101 billion in 1968. International Telephone and Telegraph, among the largest of these "multinational" corporations, had operations in ninety countries, 400,000 employees, and a president who earned $812,000 a year in salary. Like other such corporations, it possessed enormous potential influence over American foreign policies.

Corporate influence at home was still more obvious. The large firms not only employed millions of Americans, but served as important social and

> *By all but the pathologically romantic, it is now recognized that this is not the age of the small man. But there is still a lingering presumption among economists that his retreat is not before the efficiency of the great corporation, or even its technological proficiency, but before its monopoly power. . . . This, by the uncouth, would be called drivel. Size is the general servant of technology, not the special servant of profits. The small firm cannot be restored by breaking the power of the larger ones. It would require, rather, the rejection of the technology which since earliest consciousness we are taught to applaud. It would require that we have simple products made from readily available materials by unspecialized labor. . . . If the market thus reigned, there would be, and could be, no planning. No elaborate organization would be required. The small firm would then, at last, do very well. All that is necessary is to undo nearly everything that, at whatever violence to meaning, has been called progress in the last half century. There must be no thought of supersonic travel, or exploring the moon, and there will not be many automobiles. . . .*
>
> J. K. Galbraith analyzes the "technostructure," 1968.

welfare institutions. Their investments in pension funds, which increased from $4 billion in 1940 to $100 billion in 1965, deeply affected the stock market and the level of general economic activity. The large corporations also continued to depend on, and to influence, government defense spending. Frequently unrestrained by competition, they remained free to increase prices, thus promoting inflation even in times of recession. As John Kenneth Galbraith argued in 1968, large corporations formed a potent "technostructure" that undermined the free market and made many of the nation's most fundamental decisions concerning production, wages, and technological change. J. P. Morgan would have been gratified.

If Johnson had been disposed to challenge the corporations—which he was not—he would have been unable to rely on their historic adversaries, the labor unions. Though union membership increased slightly in absolute numbers during the postwar years, the labor movement was hurt by the migration of many industries to the South, which was traditionally antiunion, and by the rapid expansion of the middle class, which limited the growth in blue-collar employment. Between 1955 and 1968 the percentage of unionized people in nonagricultural employment declined from 33 to 28 percent. Some of the stronger unions, such as the Teamsters (which had almost 2 million members by 1970), were plagued by corruption. The writer Norman Mailer concluded that such unions "sat closer to the Mafia than to Marx." Though Mailer exaggerated (as usual), he—and other critics—were right in noting the decline in labor militancy, which had been a cutting edge for reform in the 1930s. For every Walter Reuther, the socially conscious head of the United Automobile Workers, there were ten George Meanys, heirs to the Gompers tradition of placing the needs of union members before those of blacks or other poor people. Indeed, Meany, the durable head of the AFL, was often content to make deals with the large corporations: workers would get wage increases, and management an excuse to raise prices for consumers.

Such wage increases did not mean that industrial workers enjoyed lives of comfort, or even that they felt secure. On the contrary, they were among the first to be laid off during hard times, as in 1974–75. Their work on the assembly line seemed ever more tedious and alienating as definitions of the "good life" focused on the desirability of creative labor. Still, regularly employed industrial workers, like skilled craftsmen at the turn of the century, comprised the privileged elite of blue-collar labor. They enjoyed economic "clout" undreamed of in the 1930s. They used it to advance their own interests, not to promote the social welfare of others.

The Weakness of Government As reformers recognized only too well, governmental institutions reflected the power of these interest groups. Among these institutions was Congress, which regularly listened to influential constituents, not to reformers. "I have watched the Congress from either the inside or the outside, man and boy, for more than forty years," Johnson noted, "and I've never seen a Congress that didn't eventually take the measure of the president it was dealing with."

Other political institutions were almost as discouraging to reformers. The parties, for instance, depended upon an increasingly unstable and largely nonideological electorate. Instead of developing into forces for social change, they remained coalitions of quarrelsome interest groups. Similarly, state and local governments, while much expanded since the 1930s, lacked the financial resources (or the will) to enact significant reforms on their own, or even to contribute generously to federal-state welfare programs. America's federal system and decentralized parties made it essential that Johnson use every available presidential resource to enact *national* programs.

Federal bureaucracy, in some ways a modernizing influence, posed further hurdles to efficient social change. From 1947 to 1967 federal civilian employment increased some 30 percent—from 2 to 2.6 million. Most of this expansion occurred within the executive branch. Yet the growth was so uncoordinated that many liberals longed for the fresh, relatively simple days of Roosevelt's "alphabet soup," while others relied on approaches such as CAP, a deliberate attempt to set local pressures *against* the "dead hand" of bureaucracy. Still others, including Walter Heller, Johnson's liberal chairman of the Council of Economic Advisers, favored decentralization of administration through revenue-sharing with the states. (A Democratic Congress approved, and Nixon signed, revenue-sharing in the 1970s.) But Johnson, like his predecessors, often had to rely on the standard means of combatting bureaucracies: creating new ones as coordinators or rivals. The contrast between popular expectations and governmental performance, to say nothing of the cost of increased federal activity, prompted widespread doubts about the capacity of America's public institutions.

> *Legislators represent people, not trees or acres. Legislators are elected by voters, not farms or cities or economic interests. As long as ours is a representative form of government, and our legislatures are those instruments of government elected directly by and directly representative of the people, the right to elect legislators in a free and unimpaired fashion is a bedrock of our political system.*
>
> *Reynolds* v. *Sims* (1964), the Court's decision requiring reapportionment of state legislatures.

THE WARREN COURT: A CENTER OF CONTROVERSY

Johnson could not take much comfort from the most activist Supreme Court in American history. Liberal justices like Earl Warren, Hugo Black, William O. Douglas, and William J. Brennan, Jr., validated the sit-ins of the early 1960s and the civil rights acts of 1964 and 1965. In *Engel* v. *Vitale* (1962) and subsequent decisions they ruled against required prayers and Bible reading in public schools. In a series of cases starting with *Baker* v. *Carr* (1962) the Court struck at legislative malapportionment on both the state and national levels. Only population, it declared, could be the basis for representation. The Court then acted to broaden the rights of accused criminals. In *Gideon* v. *Wainwright* (1963) it declared that indigents charged with felonies in state courts had the right to free counsel; in *Escobedo* v. *Illinois* (1964) it stated that police must permit alleged offenders to consult with lawyers during interrogation; and in *Miranda* v. *Arizona* (1966) it required police to warn suspects that any statements they made could be used against them, and that they had the right to remain silent and to get free legal counsel. As if to antagonize traditionalists still further, the Court ruled against state laws banning the use of contraceptive devices, and it delivered a number of decisions against laws censoring allegedly pornographic material. All these cases marked significant departures from past judicial decisions.

These decisions infuriated conservatives. Southerners reacted as angrily as they had to *Brown* v. *Board of Education* in the 1950s. Traditionalists predicted (with some truth) that the apportionment decisions would involve the Court in what Justice Felix Frankfurter, a dissenter, called the "political thicket" of legislative districting. Catholics, fundamentalists, and others heatedly denounced the decisions concerning Bible reading in the schools, censorship, and contraception. Advocates of "law and order" complained that the Court was "coddling" criminals and hampering effective police work. In 1968 they pushed through the Crime Control and Safe Streets Act, which sanctioned so-called voluntary confessions in federal courts even if suspects were not informed of their rights. The act also authorized police to hold suspects for up to six hours before arraigning them, and to utilize wiretapping for a variety of purposes.

Most of these conservative complaints were considerably exaggerated.

Far from opposing religion, the Court did not prevent children or teachers from praying or from reading the Bible, and it permitted states to supply textbooks to parochial schools. It continued to hold that church property was exempt from taxation. Its decisions concerning criminals merely gave indigents in state courts the rights that they already possessed in federal courts and that wealthier law-breakers such as the Mafiosi had long enjoyed. Subsequent studies suggested that these decisions had little impact on police behavior—only on morale. The apportionment decisions were unprecedented— Warren himself regarded them as the most significant judgments of his tenure. But by the 1960s they seemed long overdue. By then only the Court could have broken the political logjams that had permitted gross overrepresentation for rural areas. Warren also exaggerated the impact of these decisions, for while they gave more political power to the growing suburban areas, they did relatively little to strengthen minority groups. The nation's most deliberately malapportioned institution, the United States Senate, remained constitutionally sacrosanct.

What mattered, however, was what people thought the Court was doing. With crime disturbing America's cities it was convenient to blame the Court's decisions concerning police behavior. As blacks became more "uppity," segregationists considered it equally fair to chastise the judges for abetting civil rights, and especially for decisions striking down laws against intermarriage and against sexual relations between blacks and whites. By 1966 a Harris poll discovered that 65 percent of Americans opposed the tribunal's actions concerning criminals. Millions of people, it seemed, saw in the liberalism of men like Warren the same misguided mollycoddling that they suspected in the Great Society.

These criticisms were the more forceful because the Court was an appointive institution whose jurisdiction in sociopolitical issues was unclear. Indeed, it was hard to ignore Justice Frankfurter's complaint that the Court was concerning itself with nonjudicial matters. Problems such as malapportionment, he insisted, were for popularly elected presidents and legislators to cure. To such critics, the reluctance of democratic institutions—Congress, the presidency, the states—to settle these problems was proof of the relative weakness of representative goverment.

Affluence—bane of social change?

Affluence also helped explain the movement from altruism to disenchantment in the late 1960s. For a time the unprecedented economic growth of the period assisted the activists. The New Economic Policy, reformers were able to maintain, proved that purposeful government did make a difference. Moreover, prosperity freed thousands of Americans, especially college students, from preoccupation with earning their daily bread. The altruism of the early 1960s, like that of the progressive era (but unlike that of the New Deal) coincided with a decided upswing in the business cycle and with the movement of thousands of people into the middle classes.

But affluence was a mixed blessing. In affecting so many people it prompted exaggerated expectations. Poor people, blacks, ethnics, though

Economic growth, 1961–1970, compared to select years before and after this period

	NATIONAL PRODUCT AND INCOME (In billions of current dollars)				PER CAPITA DISPOSABLE INCOME (In current dollars)
	GNP	PERCENT CHANGE FROM GNP OF PRECEDING YEAR (+ OR −)	NATIONAL INCOME	DISPOSABLE PERSONAL INCOME	
1940	99.7	+10.2	18.1	75.7	573
1945	211.9	+ 0.9	181.5	150.2	1,074
1949	256.5	− 0.4	217.5	188.6	1,264
1961	520.1	+ 3.2	427.3	364.4	1,984
1962	560.3	+ 7.7	457.7	385.3	2,065
1963	590.5	+ 5.4	481.9	404.6	2,138
1964	632.4	+ 7.1	518.1	438.1	2,283
1965	684.9	+ 8.3	564.3	473.2	2,436
1966	749.9	+ 9.5	620.6	511.9	2,604
1967	793.9	+ 5.9	653.6	546.3	2,749
1968	864.2	+ 8.9	711.1	591.0	2,945
1969	930.3	+ 7.6	766.0	634.4	3,130
1970	977.1	+ 5.0	800.5	691.7	3,376
1971	1,054.9	+ 8.0	857.7	746.4	3,605
1972	1,158.0	+ 9.8	946.5	802.5	3,843

SOURCE: Adapted from *Economic Report of the President*, 1975, p. 249, 267, 269 better off then ever before, knew from TV and other modern communications how much they were missing. Indeed, the gap between black income (rising) and white income (rising faster) was widening, not narrowing. If people had given Johnson's programs a chance to percolate, this gap might have closed a little. But like the sit-down strikers in 1937, the disaffected refused to wait. Like Roosevelt, Johnson ultimately found himself caught in a wave of social protest that he could do little to channel in constructive directions.

Prosperity also dulled reformism of many adults in the middle and upper middle classes. Though some of these people remained energetic supporters of social change, many others focused on taking care of themselves. For such people, gains in real income meant the chance to buy big cars and stereo sets, to travel, or simply to buy a home and settle down. This privatism helps to explain why support for social change did not run deep. Simultaneously, egocentric materialism unleashed revulsion in a minority of young people, whose strident protests gradually produced backlash among their elders.

This is another way of saying that American attitudes toward the needy had really changed rather little since the 1930s. Although people continued to believe that the state ought to help those who could not help themselves, they also retained much of their historic distrust of Big Government. Thus, when militants attempted to secure social as well as legal equality, this "silent majority" balked. It was this instinctive retreat from social reform that complicated the problems Johnson faced in trying to reduce racism, poverty, and injustice.

For all these reasons Johnson had to strike quickly. If he had waited for lengthy studies or debate, he would have missed the first chance in thirty years to get significant domestic legislation on the statute books. His dilemma suggests the plausibility of the cyclical theory of American reform, which holds that bursts of legislation, long blocked by Congress, by unstable parties, by state and local governments, by the affluence of the politically influential middle classes, by historic fears of Big Government, suddenly cascade over the barriers, only to be followed by troughs of complacency. This theory is not helpful in predicting when or why such bursts occur. But it helps explain why they dissipate so quickly. It suggests that Johnson, for all his limitations, deserves credit for appealing to the mood of altruism while he could.

Suggestions for reading

William Leuchtenburg's *A Troubled Feast** (1973) is the best account of domestic developments in the United States during the 1960s and early 1970s. Other helpful books are William O'Neill's idiosyncratic *Coming Apart* (1971); and Ronald Berman, *America in the Sixties** (1968), an intellectual history. James Sundquist's *Politics and Policy** (1968) is the most thorough account of policy-making; and Seyom Brown's *Faces of Power** (1968) is the most useful survey of developments in foreign affairs.

Other books on politics include Arthur Schlesinger, Jr., *A Thousand Days** (1965), and Theodore Sorenson, *Kennedy* (1965). Both are pro-Kennedy accounts written by insiders. James M. Burns, *John Kennedy** (1960), is a remarkably objective campaign biography. The same author's *Deadlock of Democracy** (1963) is an engaging interpretation of executive-congressional relations and presidential leadership from the late eighteenth century on. Books on electoral trends include Theodore White, *Making of a President, 1960** (1961), and *Making of a President, 1964* (1965); and Milton Cummings, ed., *The National Election of 1964** (1966). Studies using polling data and quantitative methods are V. O. Key, Jr., and Milton Cummings, *The Responsible Electorate . . . 1936–1960* (1968); and Angus Campbell et al., *The American Voter: An Abridgement** (1964). Other books dealing with aspects of the Kennedy administration are Lawrence Fuchs, *John Kennedy and American Catholicism* (1967); Grant McConnell, *Steel and the Presidency—1962** (1963); and Seymour Harris, *Economics of the Kennedy Years** (1964). Henry Fairlie, *The Kennedy Promise** (1973), is highly critical.

Lyndon Johnson's memoirs, *Vantage Point** (1971), are a self-serving account of his presidency. More critical is Robert Novak and Rowland Evans, *Lyndon B. Johnson: The Exercise of Power** (1966). So are two works by men who served in the Johnson administration: George Reedy, *The Twilight of the Presidency** (1970); and Eric Goldman, *Tragedy of Lyndon Johnson** (1965). The subject of welfare and antipoverty policy is well covered in Peter Marris and Martin Rein, *Dilemmas of Social Reform** (2nd ed., 1973); Sar Levitan, *The Great Society's Poor Law* (1969); and Gilbert Steiner, *State of Welfare* (1971). See also Richard Elman, *The Poorhouse State** (1966); Frances F. Piven and Richard A. Cloward, *Regulating the Poor: The Functions of Public Relief** (1972); and Ben Seligman, *Permanent Poverty** (1968). Jane Jacobs, *Death and Life of Great American Cities** (1961), is a provocative discussion of cities and urban policy, while Daniel Moynihan and Nathan Glazer, *Beyond the Melting Pot** (1963), reveals the ethnic dimensions of life in New York City. Joseph Goulden, *Meany* (1972), is helpful on the leader of the AFL. For civil rights in the early 1960s see Benjamin Muse, *The American Negro Revolution: From Nonviolence to Black Power, 1963–1967** (1968); Charles Silberman, *Crisis in Black and White** (1964), a very well written and provocative analysis; and Howard Zinn, *SNCC: New Abolitionists, 1964–65* (1964).

Books on foreign policy in the 1960s include Richard Walton, *Cold War and Counterrevolution** (1972), which is critical of Kennedy. Roger Hilsman, *To Move a Nation* (1967), is an interpretive account by a former member of the Kennedy administration. David Halberstam, *The Best and the Brightest* (1972), is a sustained critique of liberal foreign policy under Kennedy and Johnson. H. B. Johnson, *The Bay of Pigs* (1964), is helpful. For the missile crisis see Robert Kennedy, *13 Days* (1969); Elie Abel, *Missile Crisis** (1966); and especially Graham Allison, *Essence of Decision** (1971). Juan de Onis, *The Alliance that Lost its Way** (1970), laments the fate of the Alliance for Progress.

For Vietnam in the 1950s and early 1960s consult George M. Kahin and J. W. Lewis, *The United States and Vietnam** (1967); and Bernard Fall, *The Two Vietnams** (2nd rev. ed. 1967). Also helpful are Marvin Gettleman, ed., *Vietnam: History, Documents, and Opinions** (1970); and Neil Sheehan et. al., *The Pentagon Papers** (1971). Two books on military policies are William B. Bader, *The United States and the Spread of Nuclear Weapons* (1968); and A. C. Enthoven and K. W. Smith, *How Much is Enough? Shaping the Defense Program, 1961–1969* (1971). See also Richard Barnet and Ronald Müller, *Global Reach: The Power of the Multinational Corporations* (1974).

14

Turmoil

1965-1968

On March 31, 1968, a deeply lined, worn looking Lyndon Johnson appeared on television to announce his retirement from the presidency at the close of his tenure in January 1969. He said, "I shall not seek, and I will not accept, the nomination of my party for another term as president."

Though his announcement came as a surprise, it was greeted with relief by millions of Americans. By that time Gallup polls were reporting that only 36 percent of the people approved of his conduct of the presidency. Militants were so angry and threatening that Johnson hardly dared appear in public. Like Hoover before him, he had fallen victim to his own stubbornness and to unusually chaotic and turbulent times.

Among the many manifestations of this discord, which rent the country after 1965, three were outstanding. The first, the breakdown of the interracial civil rights movement, culminated in explosive social unrest, including race riots in the cities. The second, escalation of the fighting in Vietnam, led to massive antiwar activity. The third, the rise of radical protest movements and of the "counter culture," was in part the consequence of the other two and in part the cause of further divisions in society. Together these three forces produced domestic turmoil unprecedented in twentieth-century American history.

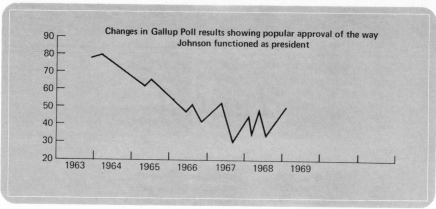

SOURCE: Adapted from Irish and Frank, *U.S. Foreign Policy*, p. 104

Johnson reached the peak of his popularity shortly after he assumed the presidency in 1964 when 80 percent of respondents approved of the way he conducted his office and reached a low in mid-1967 when only 32 percent approved of his presidency.

From interracialism to black power

Since 1960, when the sit-ins first attracted national attention, the civil rights movement had been the vanguard of domestic reform. In providing a cause worthy of sacrifice it sustained the idealism that assists broader movements for change. As early as 1963, however, internal divisions were beginning to split the interracial coalition. By 1966 this disintegration produced widespread disruption and disillusion.

One source of discord was the militants' awareness of the limits of legal action in combating racial discrimination in the South. More black children attended segregated schools in the Deep South in 1964 than in 1954, the year of the supposedly epochal *Brown* decision. Jim Crow laws flourished throughout the region. Despite legal guarantees, blacks (and many poor whites) still were denied the vote. Though the civil rights acts of 1964 and 1965 eventually rectified some of these abuses, they came too late to pacify activists.

Militants in the North grew equally angry by 1965. Whites, they complained, discriminated against all blacks in the crucially important areas of education and housing, where de facto segregation was the rule. Urban renewal, activists added, usually meant "Negro removal." James Baldwin commented bitterly that housing projects "are hated almost as much as policemen, and that is saying a great deal. And they are hated for the same reason: both reveal, unbearably, the real attitude of the white world, no matter how many liberal speeches are made." Like many others, Baldwin recognized that the civil rights acts did nothing to assist social welfare or racial justice in the North, where almost 50 percent of America's blacks lived by 1960.

Even before 1965 growing discontent among Negro slum dwellers led to an increase in the strength of the Black Muslims. Led by their Messenger, Elijah

Muhammed, the Muslims combined faith in Islam with vehement separatism, anti-Semitism, and black racism. Like Marcus Garvey (and Booker T. Washington), they called for black self-help. Whites, they said, were agents of the devil; blacks must consider them enemies and refuse to mingle with or intermarry with them. Integrationists such as Martin Luther King, Elijah Muhammed argued, were tools of white society.

This black racism did not become a mass movement: perhaps no more than 20,000 people belonged to the Muslims during the mid-1960s. But it appealed to outcasts whom the interracial organizations failed to attract. It enlisted Cassius Clay (later Muhammed Ali), the heavyweight boxing champion of the world. It promoted the rise of Malcolm X, a charismatic leader who broke with Elijah Muhammed in 1963 to form the Organization for Afro-American Unity before he was assassinated by black gunmen in February 1965. At the time Malcolm had accomplished almost nothing. But his death made him a martyr. His appeal, like that of the Muslims, exposed the bitterness that was affecting many blacks even at the peak of interracial cooperation in the early 1960s.

By 1964 racial and sexual tensions began to divide civil rights workers in the South. The idealistic white activists endured great discomfort and real danger in trying to register blacks to vote. Two of them, Andrew Goodman and Michael Schwerner, were killed along with James Chaney, a black, in Mississippi in 1964. But many northern white girls were shocked by what they perceived as the sexual aggressiveness of their black co-workers. Others—relatively affluent, upward-mobile college students—were staggered by what they thought to be the ignorance and laziness of blacks in the rural South. "I really don't understand how they [blacks] can sit on the porch from six in the morning until nine in the evening without crossing their legs," one white wrote. Another added, "[Negroes] speak our same language but they look at things differently. Religion, Sex. It's sort of a different culture." Still other whites, accustomed to assuming positions of leadership in biracial movements, grew resentful as blacks sought to direct their own revolution.

Blacks detected these white attitudes. The white activists, they observed, returned to exclusive northern suburbs when the registration drives were over, leaving blacks to face the angry segregationists in the South. Blacks complained also about the mass media, which exalted the idealism of the whites while taking the blacks for granted. And many black militants developed misconceptions of their own. Some of these misconceptions concerned sex. "I think all those white girls down here sat up North dreaming about being raped by some big black Negro," a southern black said, "and came down here to see what it was like." The problem of leadership was more divisive. Only black people, the militants argued, could understand the black experience. Whites, accordingly, had no business trying to direct the movement. Attitudes such as these proved that ethnocentrism was not the exclusive preserve of the white race. They helped prevent successful interracial drives for civil rights in the South after 1965.

Newark, N.J., site of a major race riot in 1967. Above, damaged area of the riot.
Below, armed police cars patrol the city.

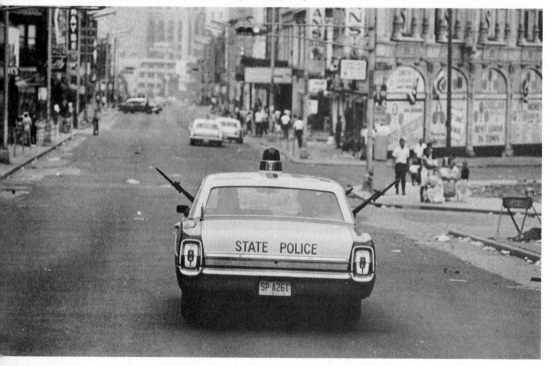

> *Certain fundamental matters are clear. Of these, the most fundamental is the racial attitude and behavior of white Americans toward black Americans. Race prejudice has shaped our history decisively in the past; it now threatens to do so again. White racism is essentially responsible for the explosive mixture which has been accumulating in our cities since the end of World War II.*
>
> President Johnson's commission on the urban riots concludes its account of the causes of urban disorder in the 1960s.

Militant young blacks came vehemently to distrust "paternalistic" white liberals as much as segregationists. President Kennedy, they believed, coopted the movement by preventing militants from taking a prominent role in the march on Washington in 1963. SNCC leaders from Mississippi complained—with only partial justice—that liberals had blocked their Freedom Democratic party delegation to the 1964 Democratic Convention. Integration and nonviolence, these blacks believed, were goals for "Uncle Toms." "Do I really want to be integrated into a burning house?" Baldwin asked. Whites, he added, would give in only under the threat of force—"the fire next time."

Baldwin was prophetic. One consequence of this bitterness was racial violence in northern cities. This began on a relatively small scale in Harlem and in Rochester in 1964. In August 1965, five days after Johnson signed the civil rights law, black rioting broke out anew in the Watts district of Los Angeles. It caused the death of thirty-five people and property damage estimated at more than $30 million. In 1966 minor disturbances occurred in Chicago and other places, and in 1967 the greatest explosions of all took place in Newark, where 26 died and more than 1000 were injured, and in Detroit, the worst conflagration since the Chicago race riot of 1919. At Detroit 43 died, and 2000 were hurt. Much of the city's black belt was burned or destroyed. In 1967 alone 83 people were killed in 164 disorders (8 of them major), causing more than $100 million in property damage.

To many observers, envy of white prosperity and consumer culture seemed to motivate the rioters. "The rebellion," one rioter conceded, " . . . was all caused by the commercials. I mean you saw all those things you'd never be able to get. . . . Men's clothing, furniture, appliances, color TV. All that crummy TV glamor just hanging out there." Other people blamed the disturbances on destitute migrants—"riffraff" cast adrift in strange cities. Others wishfully thought the rioters were engaged in fun and games, rather like students tearing up Ft. Lauderdale during spring vacation. Firm police action, it was believed, would restore order. Still others suggested that class conflict lay at the root of the trouble. Most of the troublemakers, they argued, were poor blacks, sometimes joined by poor whites. The violence, they added, was not directed against people, but at ghetto property.

Many of these explanations contained some truth, for motives varied. But

White and non-white family income, 1950–1970
(Percent distribution of families, by race of head of family)

	(In current dollars)			
WHITE FAMILIES	**UNDER $2,000**	**$2,000–$5,999**	**$6,000–$9,999**	**OVER $10,000**
1950	22.2	62.6	11.6	3.5
1955	15.3	54.1	23.8	6.8
1960	11.0	41.3	32.5	15.3
1965	7.7	30.1	35.3	27.1
1970	3.8	18.7	25.9	51.6
NON-WHITE FAMILIES				
1950	53.4	43.2	3.2	0.3
1955	39.7	51.7	7.9	0.6
1960	31.7	47.9	15.4	4.9
1965	20.7	49.7	20.5	9.0
1970	11.1	35.0	25.6	28.2

SOURCE: Adapted from *Statistical Abstract of the United States*, 1974, p. 382

if the reports of study commissions were accurate, the rioters included few "riffraff"—these were too disorganized and marginal to play much of a part. Rather, the majority of rioters were upward-mobile blacks who felt most deeply what President Johnson's commission called "white racism." Though these blacks had gained economically, they sensed that they had far to go to close the widening gap that separated them from the white middle classes, and that whites would never let them move out of the ghetto. Thus it was that some of the worst riots, as in Watts and Detroit, occurred where blacks were relatively well-off and relatively well treated—where expectations had been whetted the most. By 1965 these blacks were impatient, and they did not know where to turn. If violence be rational, theirs was.

Another cause—and consequence—of the riots was the developing cry for "black power." This phrase, which frightened whites throughout the late

> The media claims that I teach hate. Hate, like love, is a feeling. How can you teach a feeling? If Black people hate white people it's not because of me, it's because of what white people do to Black people. If hate can be taught, ain't no better teacher than white people themselves. I hate oppression. I am anti anybody who is anti-Black. Now if that includes most white people in America, it ain't my fault. That's just the way the bones break. I don't care whether or not white people hate me. It's not essential that a man love you to live. But "the man" has to respect you.
>
> H. Rap Brown of SNCC offers his view of race relations.

1960s, first gained currency in June 1966, when James Meredith was shot and wounded while making a demonstration walk from Memphis, Tennessee, to Jackson, Mississippi. King and others then moved in to complete the march. But Stokely Carmichael, the head of SNCC, rejected King's faith in white liberals and in nonviolence. "We have got to get us some black power," he said. "We have to organize ourselves to speak for each other. That's black power. We have to move to control the economics and politics of our community."

Other black militants made Carmichael sound like a moderate. H. Rap Brown, who took over as head of SNCC in 1967, explained that "John Brown was the only white man I could respect and he is dead. The Black Movement has no use for white liberals. We need revolutionaries. Revolutions need revolutionaries." Julius Lester, a SNCC field secretary, published a book entitled *Look Out Whitey! Black Power's Gon' Get Your Mama!* "Now it is over," he said, "the days of singing freedom songs and the days of combatting bullets and billy clubs with love. We Shall Overcome (and we have overcome our blindness) sounds old, outdated, and can enter the pantheon of the greats along with the IWW songs and the union songs. As one SNCC veteran put it after the Mississippi march, 'Man, the people are too busy getting ready to fight to bother with singing any more.'" Huey Newton, a leader of the Black Panthers, founded in 1966, added that blacks must arm themselves in defense against the police and the military. "We make the statement," he said, "quoting from Chairman Mao, that Political Power comes through the Barrel of a Gun."

In the cultural realm "black power" did much to develop pride among black people. Carmichael said, "The only thing we own in this country is the

James Meredith, shot during his one-man walk through Mississippi. Outrages such as this accelerated the movement toward black power.

color of our skins. . . . We have to stop being ashamed of being black. A broad nose, a thick lip, and nappy hair is us, and we are going to call that beautiful whether they like it or not.'' This ''Black Is Beautiful'' theme (which Langston Hughes and others had promoted in vain forty years earlier) cut down the sale of bleaches, hair straighteners, and other cosmetics that blacks had bought for decades in attempts to hide their racial characteristics. It affected advertising, films, art, and poetry. It led to courses in black history, to renewed appreciation for African culture, and to growing confidence among black people generally. As James Brown's popular song proclaimed, ''Say It Loud—I'm Black and I'm Proud.''

By using the rhetoric of violence, however, extremists like H. Rap Brown cut deep divisions into the civil rights movement. Roy Wilkins of the NAACP, whose legal defense fund had been indispensable to civil rights activists—and who was far from being an ''Uncle Tom''—said that such rhetoric was the ''father of hatred and the mother of violence.'' A. Philip Randolph, who had led the all-black march on Washington in 1941, considered the new version of black power a ''menace to peace and prosperity.'' King complained that ''returning violence for violence multiplies violence, adding deeper darkness to a night already devoid of stars. Darkness cannot drive out darkness; only light can do that.''

Hoping to prevent white ''backlash,'' these nonviolent leaders stressed that blacks could attain power through economic organization and voter solidarity. They insisted also that Carmichael, Brown, and other extremists represented only a very small minority of blacks. The moderates in the movement made other telling points against the separatist argument. First, it was ideologically puerile—romantic paramilitarism carried away by its own rhetoric. Second, it was unrealistic. Blacks, comprising only 11 percent of the population, would be destroyed if they relied on violence. Hatred and violence, King said, ''intensify the fears of the white majority, and leave them less ashamed of their prejudices toward Negroes.''

King, however, could not wish away either the urban riots or the extremist rhetoric of the militant minority, both of which antagonized whites. As early as June 1966, 85 percent of whites thought blacks were too demanding, compared to only 34 percent in 1964. House Republican leader Gerald Ford asked, ''how long are we going to abdicate law and order—the backbone of our civilization—in favor of a soft social theory that the man who heaves a brick through your window or tosses a fire bomb into your car is simply the misunderstood and underprivileged product of a broken home?'' Johnson himself grew peevish, especially when Rap Brown branded him a ''white honky cracker.'' After appointing a commission to study the riots, he rejected its call in 1968 for far-reaching federal reforms. ''They always print that we don't do enough,'' he snapped. ''They don't print what we do.''

Reactions like these did not mean that a ''white backlash'' was overrunning the country or that the civil rights movement had failed. Polls in the more peaceful years after the riots revealed that most Americans approved of the gains that had been made. The civil rights laws remained on the books, blacks registered and voted in unprecedented numbers, schools and universities were desegregated, even in the Deep South. By 1970 southern blacks enjoyed as much legal protection as blacks in the North, where de facto segregation had long prevailed. But black spokesmen began pressing for more social and economic equality, including the end of discrimination in housing, and busing to achieve racial balance in the schools. At this point many whites balked, and the struggle for racial justice entered a period of stalemate. The altruism that had characterized the civil rights movement in the early 1960s seemed eons past by 1968.

Vietnam, 1964–1968

Three days after Kennedy's assassination President Johnson conferred with Henry Cabot Lodge, Jr., America's ambassador to South Vietnam. Lodge confirmed what people already sensed: the assassination of Diem earlier in the month had increased political instability in South Vietnam, while doing nothing to facilitate the military struggle against the National Liberation Front, the predominantly communist political arm of the Vietcong rebels in the south. Another president, recognizing that South Vietnam was engaged in a civil war, might have refrained from increasing America's commitment of 17,000 men. But not Johnson, who persisted in blaming North Vietnam and China for the fighting in the south. As if echoing Winston Churchill, who had told FDR in World War II, "I did not become the King's first minister in order to preside over the liquidation of the Empire," Johnson told Lodge, "I am not going to be the president who saw Vietnam go the way China went."

In 1964 Johnson did his best to conceal this determined attitude from the electorate. Troop levels were increased, but only to 21,000. During the election campaign he ridiculed the notion that he would escalate the number of American soldiers in Vietnam. After the Vietcong attacked American facilities at Bien Hoa in October, he declared, "We are not going to drop bombs."

Even before the 1964 election, however, signs appeared of the Johnson deceptions that lay ahead. Early in August he announced that North Vietnamese torpedo boats had attacked American destroyers in the Tonkin Gulf thirty miles off North Vietnam. He suppressed the truth: that the American warships had been assisting South Vietnamese commando raids; that the destroyers had been in combat zones close to shore; and that the alleged assaults, on dark nights in rough seas, may have been imagined by nervous American officers. The supposed attacks, in any event, caused no damage. Feigning outrage, Johnson ordered American planes to smash North Vietnamese torpedo bases and oil installations—targets picked carefully two months earlier. He also asked Congress to authorize him to take " all necessary measures to repel any armed attack against the forces of the United States and to prevent

C H I N A

Red River

BURMA

U.S. bombing resumed,
spring 1972

N O R T H
V I E T N A M

DIENBIENPHU

Gulf of Tonkin

L A O S

HANOI

HAIPHONG

Haiphong harbor mined, May 1972

LUANG
PRABANG

U.S. bombing resumed in Hanoi—
Haiphong area, Dec. 1972

PLAINE DES
JARRES

U.S. bombing missions
Feb. 1965—March 1968

Demilitarized zone
U.S. bombing halted, Oct. 1968

VIENTIANE

Demarcation line, 1954

17°

QUANG TRI

T H A I L A N D

HUE

KHE SANH

DANANG

MY LAI

BANGKOK

C A M B O D I A

KONTUM

S O U T H
V I E T N A M

Mekong
River

PHNOMPENH

DUC LAP

Camrahn Bay

Gulf of Siam

AN LOC

TAY
NINH

XUAN
LOC

SAIGON

South China Sea

Mekong
Delta

→ Tet offensive, 1968

◁ U.S. invasion of Cambodia,
April—May, 1970

← South Vietnam invasion of
Laos, Feb. 1971

➤ Communist offensives in 1975

--- Communist states as of 1954

— Allies of the U.S. as of 1960

Unaligned states troubled by
insurgent forces as of 1960

Areas under communist control, 1973

Territories conquered by communist
forces as of April 16, 1975

Paris peace accords signed, Jan. 1973 (North and South Vietnam)

Vietnam war and fall of Indochina, 1954–1975

further aggression.'' An alarmed Congress acceded, unanimously in the House and eight-eight to two in the Senate. Like Truman after the North Korean invasion, Johnson never troubled to ask for a declaration of war. The Tonkin Gulf resolution gave him enough latitude to increase the American presence there over the next four years.

The escalation itself occurred early in 1965 after the Vietcong rebels killed 7 Americans and wounded 109 at Pleiku. Within twelve hours of getting the news, American planes retaliated by dropping bombs in the north. Three days later Johnson authorized regular bombing, again on targets chosen in 1964. In April, after Vietcong attacks had almost succeeded in blowing up the American embassy in Saigon, he stepped up the dispatch of ground troops. By early 1966 the United States had nearly 200,000 soldiers in South Vietnam.

When critics complained of American escalation, Johnson reminded them of his efforts for peace. In April 1965 he promised both sides long-term economic aid. On December 24, 1965, he called a bombing halt, which lasted until January 31, 1966. He made Averell Harriman an ambassador-at-large and sent him on well-publicized missions in search of peace. In October 1966 Johnson went to Manila to pledge that the United States would pull out of Vietnam within six months of the end of the shooting. Later in the year secret negotiations to end the war started in Poland.

It is unlikely that Johnson really expected these overtures to succeed. Instead, he remained fixed in his central goal: to keep South Vietnam within the noncommunist orbit. Because its pro-American puppet governments had little popular support, this policy required further escalation, which destroyed chances for accommodation. By mid-1966 America had 265,000 troops in South Vietnam; by the end of 1967 it had more than 500,000. The war cost an estimated $100 billion per year by 1968—the amount spent yearly on *all* federal expenditures as recently as 1964. Bernard Fall, the best-informed writer on Vietnam at the time, estimated that it cost the United States between $300,000 and $500,000 per enemy death as of early 1966.

Johnson relied heavily on massive bombing of North Vietnam. The attacks sought to destroy military installations, oil reserves, and railway lines and to slow down the flow of supplies from the north to the Vietcong. However, the raids were counterproductive. North Vietnam, which had given little aid to the Vietcong before 1965, responded to the attacks by stepping up its delivery of goods. The raids also smashed urban areas and killed countless North Vietnamese civilians. Frequently American bombers used napalm, an incendiary substance that set human flesh aflame.

In the south, American military action was equally barbaric and destructive. "Pacification" programs to secure the countryside entailed burning of villages, forcible uprooting of civilians, and desecration of ancestral burial grounds. "Search and destroy" missions—again using napalm—killed thousands of villagers. Overwhelming American firepower defoliated forests, destroyed rice crops, and shattered the economy. Some American troops perpetrated atrocities, such as the one in the village of My Lai in 1968, which resulted in the killing of 347 civilian men, women, and children. During Johnson's presidency the war caused the deaths of some 28,000 Americans, perhaps 100,000 South Vietnamese, and untold numbers of young Vietcong rebels. Civilian deaths approached a million.

A scene from Vietnam.

Long before Johnson left office opponents of the war inveighed against these policies. Like the more progressive isolationists in 1917 and 1940, they complained that the war was undermining support for reform at home. They protested the immorality of bombing civilians, the abuse of presidential power, and the impact of the war on America's relations with the rest of the world. Other critics, such as Walter Lippmann and the political scientist Hans Morganthau, pointed out that the United States had no economic or strategic interests in Vietnam worth such a commitment.

Johnson remained deaf to such arguments. Indeed, he brusquely dismissed dissidents within his administration. "Kennedy," one observer explained, "didn't mind disagreement. It didn't bother him. But disagreement really bothers this president. He is going to do what you dislike anyway; so let's not upset him by having an argument in front of him." Discussions with Johnson, his press secretary George Reedy recalled, were "really monologues in which one man is getting reflections of what he sends out." In such an atmosphere it was not surprising that few top-ranking officials dared dispute with him, or that those who did, like McNamara in 1967–68, left office. As late as March 16, 1968, six weeks after the devastating "Tet" offensive by the Vietcong, which brought pleas for deescalation from Deputy Secretary of Defense Paul Nitze, the new secretary of defense, Clark Clifford, and even from former Secretary of State Dean Acheson, a staunch anticommunist, Johnson held to his position. "Let's get one thing clear," he said. "I am not going to stop the bombing. I have heard every argument on the subject, and I am not interested in further discussion." Though he finally softened his stance two weeks later—announcing the end of bombing in the north (save near the demarcation line) and reporting that America was beginning peace talks in Paris— these were not concessions to his advisers but changes in tactics. The NLF demanded that America withdraw, and the talks in Paris went nowhere.

Johnson's stubbornness derived from many misconceptions. Among them was his characteristically American view of communism as a united, worldwide conspiracy. This attitude led him to ignore opportunities for Soviet-American détente, which had appeared real after Leonid Brezhnev and Aleksai Kosygin replaced the more erratic Khrushchev in October 1964. In Latin America it caused him to neglect the Alliance for Progress and, in 1965, to send marines to challenge left-wing forces in the Dominican Republic. In Southeast Asia it prompted him to ignore the simple fact that the conflict in South Vietnam was a civil war. Communist China, he said, was responsible for the "aggression" of Ho Chi Minh from the north. Resurrecting the SEATO pact of 1954 (which neither required nor authorized American military intervention), he insisted that the United States was doing in Vietnam what Truman had done in Korea.

By focusing on China, Johnson vastly underestimated the tenacity of the South Vietnamese rebels. Theirs was a war of revolution, not only against puppets like Diem but against decades of western imperialism. This revolutionary nationalism helped to explain why superior American fire power, to say nothing of 500,000 men, failed utterly to control the countryside. Short of dropping nuclear bombs on the entire Indo-Chinese peninsula, there was no military "solution" to the ideological conflict in Vietnam.

Johnson also placed exaggerated faith in money and technology. When the North Vietnamese ignored his offer of economic aid in 1965, he was uncomprehending. "I don't understand it," he said. "George Meany [head of the AFL] would've grabbed at a deal like that." Encouraged by the statistics of Secretary of Defense McNamara, he persisted in believing that American air superiority would eventually destroy the enemy. But the bombing failed to stem the flow of supplies from the north. Vietnam, an agricultural country where supply routes wound through dense cover, was one of the last places in the world where strategic bombing could have been effective.

Ironically, the appalling cost of these misconceptions prompted doubts in America about long-held liberal dogmas. Among these was the view that progressive government required a strong presidency. In domestic policy, this remained an article of liberal faith. In foreign affairs, however, it seemed that isolationists like Charles Beard and Robert Taft had been wise in demanding an important role for Congress. This distrust of the presidency did not prevent Johnson's successor from exceeding his constitutional authority. But suspicion of the White House did add immeasurably to the discord that tore the nation apart after 1965.

Another partial casualty of the war was globalism—the view that the United States must preserve "freedom" everywhere. The war in Vietnam ultimately proved that this was not possible. America was not omnipotent; it had to think about priorities. Most of those who turned against globalism were not isolationists—they supported the United Nations, NATO, and aid to Israel. But they called successfully for cuts in foreign aid, they demanded a reduced presence in Asia, and they looked for ways to defuse the Cold War. They pointed especially to the split between the Soviet Union and China. This break, already deep in the 1960s, led both communist nations to look for détente with the United States. Thanks in part to the rethinking of foreign policy engendered by Vietnam, even hard-liners like Richard Nixon were later induced to respond.

THE ANTIWAR MOVEMENT

Second thoughts such as these were but small consolation to Americans who by 1968 were suffering under the travails of the longest war in the nation's history. Besides devastating Vietnam, it shattered the reform coalition in the United States and ultimately promoted the most alarming inflation since 1946. As much as any other development of the decade, the war eclipsed the idealism and hopefulness of the Kennedy era and precipitated the unrest that gripped the country between 1965 and 1968.

America's mood:
the public's view of the most important
problem facing the country,
according to Gallup Poll results,
1964–1968

1964	Integration
1965	Vietnam
1966	Vietnam
1967	Vietnam
1968	Vietnam

SOURCE: Irish and Frank, *U. S. Foreign Policy*, p. 107

Leading this unrest was the most militant antiwar movement in American history. This crusade began slowly, primarily because Johnson delayed major escalation until 1965. The United States, most people agreed, could easily clean up the "mess" in Asia. But by late 1965 students were already starting to stage mass demonstrations, to conduct "bleed-ins" seeking blood for the Vietcong, to burn their draft cards, and to chant, "hey hey, LBJ, how many kids did you kill today?" A stop-the-bombing march in Washington in November 1965 attracted 20,000 protestors, including Norman Thomas, the veteran socialist leader, James Farmer, the head of CORE, Dr. Benjamin Spock,

*I have to speak
to some college students
about Vietnam—
could you rig up a tank
with a loudspeaker?*

By 1968 Johnson hardly dared appear in public.

author of the best-selling *Common Sense Book of Baby and Child Care,* the cartoonist Jules Feiffer, and the novelist Saul Bellow.

Many developments helped to swell the antiwar movement after 1965. One, of course, was the terrific American escalation, which became too obvious to hide by 1966. Another was the shocking coverage—in news photographs and on television—of American patrols burning Vietnamese villages, of refugees fleeing the smoke of battle, of horribly burned and wounded women and children, of mutilated American soldiers. These scenes of bloodletting, plus the mounting casualty figures, made it increasingly difficult for Americans to believe the White House and the Pentagon. The "credibility gap" added desperation and fury to the protests.

Young people, especially college students, provided much of the energy behind the antiwar movement. Many of these activists were veterans of the civil rights struggle, where they had learned the tactics of nonviolent mass protest. White civil rights workers, cut off from their cause after 1965 by advocates of black power, channeled their idealism to the cause of peace. Most agreed with Martin Luther King, Jr., who proclaimed that the United States was "the greatest purveyor of violence in the world."

Other young people had more personal reasons for joining the struggle against war: they did not want to fight in Vietnam. As draft calls mounted (from 5000 per month in 1965 to 50,000 per month in 1967), graduate students—who had previously secured exemptions—began to be inducted. Alarmed, they moved from quiet disagreement with the war to participation in "teach-ins" on campus to mass protests. Their frightened parents often supported them. By 1967 the antiwar crusade had become a broad-based movement including pacifists, leftists, civil rights activists, draft-age students, and substantial numbers of otherwise apolitical middle-class parents. By 1968, after the Tet offensive, these poeple were angry enough to demonstrate against the Pentagon, to challenge LBJ himself in the political arena, and to turn college campuses into cockpits of turmoil.

The youth rebellion

The growth of education in the postwar period was staggering. In 1940 the average level achieved by Americans was grade eight. At that time one out of six people of college age attended colleges or universities; one in twelve graduated. By the late 1960s the average grade level was twelve; 50 percent of college age youth went on to college; and more than 20 percent graduated. The nation's colleges and universities reflected the major themes of twentieth-century American history: affluence, professionalization, and the rise of the middle class.

Until the early 1960s most people welcomed these advances. The campuses were peaceful, and students appeared to worry more about fraternities and football than about social issues. In the Kennedy years, however, students became a little more politicized. Some joined New Leftist groups like the Students for a Democratic Society. Others led civil rights demonstrations, served in the Peace Corps, or labored in the war against poverty. These altruists were not a majority of students, let alone of young people generally. Indeed, only 12 percent of students identified themselves as part of the "New Left" even at the peak of activity in 1970. But the protestors attended some of the nation's largest and most prestigious universities. They were articulate. Their role in civil rights demonstrations at Birmingham and Selma suggested that they could make a difference in the world.

By the end of the decade, many of these campuses displayed the same turmoil that affected society at large. Beginning with a demonstration for free speech at Berkeley in 1964, youthful protest became steadily more radical. In 1968, agitators at Columbia seized the president's office and forced the university to shut down. Elsewhere, militants littered campus offices, stormed buildings, shouted down visiting speakers, staged strikes, and battled police ("pigs") called in to restore order. In all, 221 major demonstrations took place on the campuses between January and June 1968. Until 1971, when the campuses quieted down, America's universities seemed to be centers of revolution.

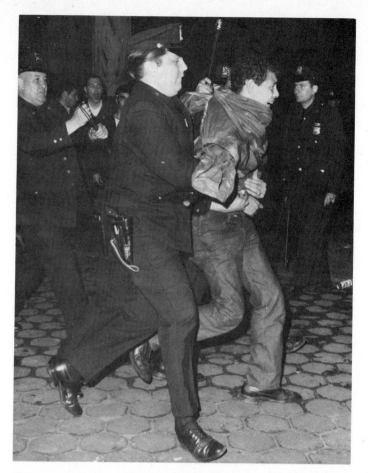

Police remove a demonstrator from the campus at Columbia University, May 1968. A total of 81 men and 50 women were arrested.

Among the forces prompting such unrest were the social divisions outside the university. Like the radicals in the 1930s, activists protested against racism, concentration of wealth, and the "power elite." Like many old conservatives, they complained about bureaucratic government, "snooping" by federal agencies, the draft, and "globalism." Like radical students elsewhere—for unrest gripped universities throughout the world at the time—they tended to question all authority. Their enemies were not the universities but racism, social inequality, and the military-industrial complex promoting war in Vietnam.

Other students concentrated their assaults on the universities. In this way they differed from the youthful radicals of the 1930s, who had tried to protect the campus from external pressures. Places like Berkeley, the new rebels complained, had become enormous bureaucratic institutions—"multiuniversities" that treated students like IBM cards. Urban universities like Harvard and Columbia, students protested, gobbled up surrounding areas once occupied by poor people. As the Vietnam war escalated, militants also protested against venerable campus institutions such as ROTC. Others busied themselves with exposing the connections between multiuniversities, scientific research, and the CIA. For all these students, universities were the most visible and most vulnerable manifestations of the repressive Establishment.

Idealistic students complained especially that universities were degree mills where young people had to do what they were told so that they could enter the Establishment at the age of twenty-two. Meanwhile, universities succeeded in keeping their captives out of the job market, which was to say out of the "real world." Using the arguments of anthropologists and psychiatrists, the protestors claimed that higher education prolonged adolescence and made students restless and impatient. Other critics, like Paul Goodman, went further and opposed compulsory education in general. "We have been swept on a flood-tide of public policy and popular sentiment," he argued, "into an expansion of schooling and an aggrandizement of school-people that is grossly wasteful of youth and effort and does positive damage to the young."

The restlessness that Goodman perceived helped explain why so many otherwise nonradical students lent their support to (or at least acquiesced in) the demands of antiestablishment minorities. It also helped to account for the lack of consistent ideology among the youthful militants. Unlike the radicals of the 1930s, many of whom were moved by Marx, the New Left of the 1960s (except for a handful of romantics who adored China's Mao or Cuba's Ché Guevara) eschewed programmatic approaches to revolution. Rather, they focused on tactics. Inspired by the civil rights demonstrations, and then by the attention given to advocates of black power, they moved quickly into confrontation strategies against the Vietnam war and the "power elite."

It later became almost fashionable to deride these militants. The campus unrest of the late 1960s, people began to argue, was orchestrated by a small minority, most of whom were sons and daughters of radicals in the 1930s. The militants, critics added, were affluent, self-indulgent hypocrites who were quick to join the Establishment after graduation; antiwar protestors wanted to escape the draft. Conservatives also reassured themselves with the notion that demographic imperatives prompted the campus unrest. High birth rates in the 1940s and early 1950s, they contended, created a uniquely large percentage of college age people by the late 1960s. No such revolt of youth, these analysts concluded, was likely to recur.

Though there was some truth in these observations, conservatives had to admit that the young people scored a few victories. Students forced temporary administrative and curricular reforms in many universities. Off campus they were the backbone of the civil rights and antiwar movements. Many of the protestors made permanent commitments to social change by fighting against environmental pollution, by enlisting in Common Cause, or by backing Ralph

Nader and other foes of commercial and governmental exploitation. Many worked for antiwar political candidates in 1968 and 1972. The student movement, like the struggle for black power, was neither wholly negative nor wholly wasted.

It was a fact, however, that many student victories were pyrrhic by 1968. Indeed, youthful excesses appalled many reformers as well as conservatives. Slogans such as "Don't Trust Anyone Over Thirty," to say nothing of well-publicized campaigns like the "Filthy Speech" movement at Berkeley, were hardly calculated to appeal to the majority of Americans. Neither were insults to "pigs" and other symbols of authority. Excesses such as these created backlash, divided the movement, and sapped its effectiveness.

The counter culture

If young people had contented themselves with unsettling the universities, they might have seemed relatively harmless. But many embraced what became known in the late 1960s as the counter culture. The overlapping of the two movements, radical protest and rebellion against the life styles and values of the 1950s, gave unprecedented visibility to the youth movement of the 1960s.

The surface manifestations of the counter culture in themselves alienated traditionalists. Increasing numbers of young men (and some adults) let their hair grow long, donned love beads, and dressed in faded jeans, work shirts, and sandals. Young women, slouching about without bras or shoes, talked of sexual freedom. Many of these people took marijuana or other more dangerous drugs, and they lived as "hippies" in rural communes or in seedy urban areas like San Francisco's Haight-Ashbury district. The very sight of such apparently unkempt people was offensive to many more staid Americans.

Traditionalists also grew alarmed at the taste in popular music that appeared to addict many young people by the late 1960s. Earlier in the decade idealistic youth had flocked to hear folk musicians like Bob Dylan, Malvina Reynolds, and Joan Baez sing gentle lyrics of social protest. Reynolds asked (in complaining about radioactivity), "What Have They Done to the Rain?" Pete Seeger chimed in, "Where have all the Flowers Gone?" Though lyrics such as these were socially-conscious, they were otherwise harmless enough. One radical complained that Baez talked only about "clouds, flowers, butterflies . . . and the like." Arlo Guthrie, a leading folk singer, conceded that "you don't accomplish very much singing protest songs to people who agree with you. Everybody just has a good time thinking they're right."

By the mid-1960s, many folk singers were turning away from themes of social protest. Why this was so remains somewhat unclear, but the immense popularity of rock groups like the Beatles, who carried only a vague and tardy social message, undoubtedly led many ambitious singers to concentrate on

The joys of communal living.

achieving a louder sound and more insistent beat. Moreover, the war in Vietnam induced growing anger and despair. As early as 1964 Dylan wrote, "i know no answer and no truth for absolutely no soul alive i will listen to no one who tells me morals there are no morals an' i dream a lot."

Within the next three years folk music of social protest gave way to rock, and then to still louder "acid rock." John Lennon, one of the Beatles, scored a hit with "Lucy in the Sky with Diamonds," and Dylan himself wrote "Mr. Tambourine Man." Both frankly embraced the use of drugs. Another singer explained, "You take the drugs, you turn up the music real loud, you dance around, you build up a fantasy." By the late 1960s the most popular entertainers included groups like the Doors and the Rolling Stones. Jim Morrison of the Doors relied primarily on sexuality for his effect. Twice arrested for indecent exposure, he was supposed to be able to hold an erection throughout a two-hour performance. Mick Jagger, leader of the Rolling Stones, unleashed not only sexual instincts but violence. In 1969 at Altamont in California he called on the Hell's Angels, a gang of motorcyclists, to keep order at one of the Stones' concerts. When the crowd grew unruly, the Angels stomped a black man to death on the stage.

Advocates of the counter culture neither sought nor welcomed such violence. By the end of the decade, however, they flocked happily to extravaganzas such as the "Woodstock" concert at Bethel, New York, in 1969. This attracted some 400,000 people. Some of them came to hear Baez, Jimi Hendrix, and others. But for three days the majority seemed content to lie about in the mud, to share marijuana, and even to fornicate in the open. "Everyone swam nude in the lake," a journalist wrote. "Balling was easier than getting breakfast, and the 'pigs' just smiled and passed out the oats."

There was much more to the counter culture than love-beads and rock concerts. True believers posed sharp challenges to existing values. For them there was a "generation gap." Like Dustin Hoffman, "hero" of the hit movie, *The Graduate* (1969), they rejected what they considered the hypocrisy of people over thirty. Their idols, to the extent to which they had any, were sensitive types like Salinger's Holden Caulfield, rough diamonds like Humphrey Bogart (whose movies enjoyed popular revivals in the 1960s), or even outlaws like Bonnie and Clyde, whose rejection of the "straight" world was romanticized in a movie in 1969. Paul Simon's song *Sound of Silence* symbolized the gigantic gap that prevented understanding between young people and their parents.

The "revolution," these youths believed, was cultural and generational. Young people must transcend the old culture and advance to new thresholds of freedom. To Charles Reich, whose *Greening of America* (1969) celebrated the new culture, this meant rejecting the materialism and competitiveness of previous epochs and embracing "Consciousness III." There people would live in a world of love, beauty, and peace. The counter culture, another writer suggested, meant a "vision of a new American identity—a collective identity that will be blacker, more feminine, more oriental, more emotional, more intuitive, more exuberant—and, just possibly, better than the old one."

Central to the ideas of these true believers was the conviction that older people were repressed. Adults, caught in what Paul Goodman called the "rat-race," were afraid to let themselves go. Herbert Marcuse, whose books appeared to support the counter culture, argued that affluence was abolishing poverty in society. Eros, the symbol of affluence and the end of scarcity, would ultimately conquer aggression. The avant garde must transcend repression to live by an "aesthetic ethos." As the historian John P. Diggins pointed out, beliefs such as these aligned the counter culturalists more closely with the "lyrical left" that had challenged middle-class values prior to World War I than with the "old" Marxist left of the 1930s. Like Randolph Bourne, the New Leftists believed that "imagination is revolution." They added that drugs helped to explode repressions. The key was "not politics but psychedelics."

Surmounting repression meant rejecting taboos about sex. If Eros was to conquer, people must feel free to indulge in premarital sex, to challenge nuclear families, even to practice homosexuality or lesbianism. Such attitudes were complemented by the widespread use of the Pill by the end of the decade. By 1970 traditionalists were appalled at the spread of "X-rated" movies, of "gay liberation," and even of "swingers" magazines featuring photos of naked people advertising their wares. One such magazine had a circulation of 50,000 by 1972. As never before, sexuality was becoming a virtue, and pornography a consumer durable.

If sex was one avenue to transcendence, rejection of science was another. Theodore Roszak, a leading proponent of the counter culture, argued that American society resembled a "world's fair in its final days, when things start to sag and disintegrate behind the futuristic façade." To overcome this technological debauch people needed to reject scientism, computerism, reason generally. Roszak's prose (like Marcuse's) left many things unclear. Was emotion, not intellect, to rule the world? But he was clear in yearning for a more decentralized, less industrialized, less competitive cosmos. It was to discover such an Eden that the true believers moved to rural communes and scratched at the soil with hand-made tools.

In this way the foes of the old culture joined others in the 1960s who swelled the age-old chorus against materialism. "American civilization," Norman Mailer cried, "had moved from the existential sanction of the frontier to the abstract ubiquitous sanction of the dollar bill." Another writer added "people no longer have opinions: they have refrigerators. . . . The only way to catch a spirit of the times is to write a handbook on home appliances." Like Andy Warhol, a "pop" artist who lavished his talents on painting such commercial symbols as Campbell's soup cans and Marilyn Monroe, these critics thought that consumerism was the essence of American culture.

To replace material values Roszak and others called for a return to spiritualism. By this they did not mean orthodox religious faiths. Rather, like Henry Thoreau and the transcendentalists, they wanted human beings to achieve enlightenment through communion with nature. People, Roszak said, must develop a "new culture in which the nonintellective capacities of personality" will predominate. This faith in intuition underlay the growing popularity in the 1960s of mysticism, astrology, and Oriental philosophy. Human beings, these people believed, must seek harmony with, not victory over, the natural world.

Such faith in nature led to a movement for ecology, which gripped thousands of Americans who otherwise had little use for the counter culture. Among these were scientists who raised frightening visions. Barry Commoner, a Washington University biologist, argued that nuclear explosions, automobiles, detergents, and pesticides polluted the environment and increased the percentage of carbon dioxide in the atmosphere. Soon, he warned, temperatures would increase, the polar ice caps would melt, and water would inundate the world's great seaports. Paul Ehrlich, author of *Population Bomb,* crusaded for birth control, the ultimate guarantee of environmental protection. Mothers' milk contained so much DDT, he said, that it would be banned if sold on the market. He added, "we must realize that unless we are extremely lucky everybody will disappear in a cloud of blue steam in twenty years."

Many scientists challenged such forecasts of doom. While conceding the misery caused by population growth in underdeveloped nations, they observed that the American birth rate was declining in the 1960s to the lowest level, except for the 1930s, in American history. Others insisted that pesticides such as DDT were necessary to grow food for the world's hungry masses. Alarmists like Commoner, they thought, failed to grasp Theodore Roosevelt's central point—that resources must be used wisely for orderly growth.

Still, there was no denying the central thrust of many of the ecologists: that modern American society was incredibly wasteful and destructive. Even the much-reduced birth rate resulted in the addition of 24 million people to America's population in the 1960s. This was the second largest increase (next to the 1950s) in the nation's history. Awareness of demands on resources led many people to recycle glass and paper, to join consumer movements, and to push the Pill. Others challenged the desirability of growth itself, thereby rejecting Kennedy's "new economics." The counter culturists could hardly take full credit for awakening these activists to the nation's wastefulness—conservation, after all, was not new to the 1960s. But their passion for the harmonious life helped the movement for ecology to spread. It was their most lasting legacy.

By the end of the decade it became increasingly clear that sharp differences divided the youth movement. While many members of the counter culture held vaguely New Left views on social issues, they were essentially nonpolitical. Their primary grievance was with adult culture, not with capitalism. New Leftists and black power advocates, accordingly, accused the "flower children" of trying to cop out of society, instead of fighting it. The crusade for sexual liberation, C. Wright Mills grumbled, was a "gonad theory of revolution." These differences, resembling nineteenth-century divisions between transcendentalists and abolitionists, split the young radicals in manifold ways and left them considerably less potent than alarmists perceived.

Extremists further undercut the appeal of the youthful counter culturists—just as they hurt the New Left. Among these were Jerry Rubin and Abbie Hoffman, self-styled leaders of the Yippies. They were long haired, unkempt looking, savagely expressive. "When in doubt, BURN," Rubin counseled in 1967. "Fire is the revolutionary's god. . . . Burn the flag. Burn churches. Burn. Burn. Burn." People should "farm in the morning, make music in the afternoon, and fuck wherever and whenever they want to." Rubin and Hoffman were essentially antipolitical. Like two callous Holden Caulfields, they were indulging themselves, not organizing a revolution. Yet their rhetoric—overcovered by the media—disgusted men and women of peace. It was easy for the public to lump together the hippies and the New Leftists and to perceive a united movement against the established ways of life.

People like Rubin especially appalled some of America's older leftists, who complained that the counter culture was anti-intellectual, self-indulgent, and elitist. One critic observed that Rubin and others mistook "vividness, intensity, and urgency for cultural sensitivity and responsible morality." Paul Goodman, commenting on his experiences with members of the counter culture, said, "they did not believe there was such a thing as the simple truth. To be required to learn something was a trap by which the young were put down and coopted. Then I knew that I could not get through to them. I had imagined that the worldwide student protest had to do with changing political and moral institutions, to which I was sympathetic, but I now saw that we had to do with a religious crisis of the magnitude of the Reformation in the fifteen hundreds, when not only all institutions but all learning had been corrupted by the whore of Babylon."

Calm observers of the counter culture later perceived these excesses. They also recognized that the huge majority of Americans still cherished the work ethic, nuclear families, and censorship of pornography. John Wayne and Vince Lombardi, the Spartan coach of the Green Bay Packers, remained more appealing than Dustin Hoffman. Indeed, it became steadily more obvious that there was a larger gap between blue-collar young people and the college elitists than there was between the generations.

In 1968, however, few people could be sure that the youth movements would lose momentum by the early 1970s. And many who sympathized with the goals of the militants—such as the end of the Vietnam war—shuddered at some of their methods. With the media playing up extremists like Rubin and Hoffman, with long-haired demonstrators battling police outside the Pentagon, with campuses in turmoil, with hippies advocating free and open sex, with blacks tearing up the ghettos, it seemed that traditional values and institutions were endangered. By 1968 "backlash" among "middle Americans," a vague term embracing blue-collar workers, conservatives, and others who were angry and frightened by domestic turmoil, was growing throughout the country.

Black Power, Red Power, Women's Power

The rise of protest movements and of the counter culture alerted other aggrieved Americans to the potential of group solidarity. By the end of the decade these too had become highly vocal and increasingly demanding. Their outbursts added to the turmoil of the times.

Among these were many ethnic leaders. Though the more acculturated groups—Irish-Americans, Italian-Americans—tended to work within the existing "system," others shared the rage that animated blacks. Leaders of the Puerto Ricans, who were treated as badly as blacks, staged strikes and demonstrations. American Indians, hidden away on arid reservations, conducted sit-ins to demand revision of old "treaties" with the government. Cesar Chavez, the charismatic leader of the National Farm Workers, championed the cause of "Chicanos" in California. With the aid of eastern sympathizers, who helped boycott nonunion produce, he secured modest concessions from the landowners.

Chavez, an organizer in the old CIO tradition, did not endorse separatism. Other disgruntled leaders did. Some Indians raised the flag of "red power." Radical Chicanos called for "brown power," or *La Raza,* a culture divorced from white American society. Like the advocates of black power, they represented minorities within their movements. But their militance forced the moderates to take tougher stands, and their tactics of direct action created confrontations with civil authorities. Their abrasiveness was an unpleasant reminder of the ethnocultural divisions in American society and of the obstacles that had prevented proscribed groups from developing more than the rudiments of a middle class.

"Power" ideologies also helped to promote a revival of feminism, which had been quiescent since the 1920s. As Betty Friedan pointed out in *The Feminine Mystique* (1963), an influential demand for equal rights, the intervening decades had actually witnessed setbacks for the feminist cause. Smaller percentages of women were in colleges in 1960 than in the 1920s. Women formed steadily lower percentages of the professionally employed (which included teachers) and of holders of M.A. and Ph.D. degrees. As late as the mid-1960s, 90 percent of school board members were men, although the school board was considered a woman's "place." Studies revealed that poverty and unemployment among women, especially among black women, were widespread in the 1960s and that the gap separating men's and women's wages was widening. Friedan and others protested particularly against the plethora of state laws discriminating against women. These prohibited women from serving on juries, from making contracts, and even from holding property. And women who wanted to enter politics were regularly rebuffed. Shirley Chisholm, a black congresswoman from New York, recalled that her sex was a larger obstacle than her color. "I was constantly bombarded by both men and women," she said, "that I should return to teaching, a woman's vocation, and leave politics up to men."

Long-developing demographic and economic trends helped feminists like Friedan to be heard. Thanks in part to the Pill, which permitted women to plan their lives with some assurance, and in part to the huge expansion of clerical opportunities, the growth in female employment accelerated. By 1965 more than 25 million women were regularly employed. Of married women with young children almost 40 percent held jobs by 1968—a startling increase of nearly 15 percent since the mid-1950s. The majority of these women worked because they needed the money, not because they wished to liberate themselves from the home. But the existence of such an army of female wage-earners virtually assured a decent reception to arguments for equal justice in work.

This healthy, normal baby has a handicap. She was born female.

When she grows up, her job opportunities will be limited, and her pay low. As a sales clerk, for instance, she'll earn half of what a man does. If she goes to college, she'll still earn less than many men with a 9th grade education. Maybe you don't care—but it's a fact—job discrimination based on sex is against the law. And it's a waste. Think about your own daughter—she's handicapped too.

Womanpower. It's much too good to waste.

The National Organization for Women makes a case.

At this point the civil rights and peace movements offered models for "women's power." They helped train women in direct action tactics. They revealed also that many male activists were chauvinists who expected women to wash dishes and cook the meals while others "manned" the barricades. The position of women in the struggle for racial justice, Carmichael had sneered, should be prone. Friedan explained, "the absolute necessity for a civil rights movement for women had reached such a point of subterranean explosive urgency by 1966, that it took only a few of us to get together to ignite the spark—and it spread like a chain reaction." With others she helped form the National Organization for Women in 1966. Soon NOW and other more militant groups were employing the same aggressive tactics—sit-ins, demonstrations, protest meetings—that had inspired activists for other causes.

These feminists battled for a variety of goals: exposing "sexism" in families, repealing antiabortion statutes, starting "consciousness-raising" courses, seeking sexual freedom. The majority of the feminists focused on the need for equal treatment. These women worked hard for an equal rights amendment to the Constitution, a dream of militant feminists since 1920. Like

Median annual earnings, by sex and occupation: 1962 to 1972

(In current dollars. Covers persons 14 years old and over as of March of following year. Earnings are for year-round full-time workers)

OCCUPATION GROUP	1962		1966		1970 [a]		1972 [a]	
	MALE	FEMALE	MALE	FEMALE	MALE	FEMALE	MALE	FEMALE
Total earnings	5,754	3,412	6,856	3,946	8,966	5,323	10,202	5,903
Professional, technical, kindred workers	7,621	4,840	9,203	5,779	12,255	7,850	13,542	8,744
Teachers, primary and secondary	6,584	5,183	7,629	5,910	9,883	7,856	11,310	8,706
Managers, officials, proprietors	6,907	3,744	8,826	4,472	11,665	6,369	13,486	7,024
Clerical and kindred workers	5,613	3,826	6,542	4,315	8,652	5,539	9,716	6,054
Salesworkers	6,225	2,607	7,553	3,066	9,765	4,174	11,610	4,445
In retail trade	4,956	2,573	6,150	3,002	7,633	3,874	8,254	4,137
Other Salesworkers	7,137	(B)	8,294	4,153	10,853	5,967	12,838	5,775
Craftsmen, foremen, and kindred workers	6,249	(B)	7,161	4,213	9,253	4,955	10,413	5,545
Foremen	7,350	(B)	8,104	4,250	10,531	5,223	11,497	5,972
Craftsmen	6,056	(B)	6,981	4,161	9,051	4,772	10,196	5,317
Operatives and kindred workers	5,335	3,156	6,135	3,387	7,644	4,465	8,747	5,004
Manufacturing	5,422	3,260	6,219	3,467	7,580	4,559	8,754	5,114

[a] Data may not be strictly comparable with those of previous years. (B) Not computed; base less than minimum required for reliability.
SOURCE: Adapted from *Statistical Abstract of the United States,* 1974, p. 361

blacks and ethnics, the activists crusaded for recognition of their past accomplishments, for courses in women's history, and for coeducation in sex-defined courses, such as woodworking for boys and home economics for girls. They made especially effective use of the prohibition of discrimination on grounds of sex in Title VII of the 1964 Civil Rights Act. This title had been added by segregationists who had hoped to weaken support for the entire bill. Once passed, it enabled women to employ the full force of the government in the struggle against discrimination in federally assisted employment and education.

For a variety of reasons, "women's liberation" did not prove so frightening in the 1960s as the related movement for black power. Women, after all, were already working in large numbers: to give them equal rights was only reasonable. The growth in female white-collar employment may also have altered traditional concepts of masculinity and blurred sex roles. If men were not ready for Unisex, they were prepared at least to admit that not all women must languish at home. Most important, the movement for women's liberation was nonviolent, and it was led by middle-class people. For all its vehemence, it was not likely to overturn society.

By 1968 traditionalists could take further comfort in the fissures that divided the movement. From the beginning most black women devoted their energies to the cause of civil rights for black men. Women's liberation, they insisted, was a diversion. Working-class women objected that the Equal Rights Amendment, which proposed to wipe out sex-oriented laws, would deprive them of protective labor legislation. Such splits were hardly surprising, for women comprised 51 percent of the population. Nor were they entirely new—similar divisions had weakened the feminist cause since the nineteenth century. Still, they permitted opponents of "women's lib" to anticipate further disagreements in the 1970s.

But these cracks in the movement could not hide the fact that the new feminism was more widespread than campaigns earlier in the century. Even women who called themselves moderates were free in criticizing the glorification of marriage and domesticity. For militant women, as for blacks and other minorities, agitation and turmoil were to be welcomed if they accelerated social change. For traditionalists, therefore, the "new" women seemed threatening. To such conservatives, the future of the nation seemed to hinge on the forthcoming electoral campaign of 1968.

The incredible campaign of 1968

On January 3, 1968, Senator Eugene McCarthy of Minnesota surprised the pundits by announcing he would challenge President Johnson on an antiwar platform. In many ways he seemed ill-suited to such a formidable task. A devout Catholic who had seriously considered becoming a monk and an intellectual who numbered the poet Robert Lowell among his advisers, he was hardly a typical representative of American politics. But for many people his stand on the war and his courage in challenging an incumbent president were qualifications enough. And when the Vietcong blasted American installations (including the embassy at Saigon) during the daring Tet offensive beginning January 31, the bankruptcy of Johnson's policies became painfully obvious. With thousands of student volunteers making campaign arrangements, McCarthy came close to beating Johnson in the New Hampshire primary on March 12. He seemed likely to win the next important confrontation, in Wisconsin on April 2. Johnson's awareness of McCarthy's popularity helped to precipitate his startling announcement on March 31 that he would not run for renomination.

Though McCarthy won with ease in Wisconsin, he immediately faced challenges within the Democratic party. Centrists in the Democratic coalition, including many labor leaders, leaned toward Vice-President Hubert H. Hum-

Above, Senator Eugene McCarthy and youthful supporters, 1968. Below, fervent Wallace supporters, 1968.

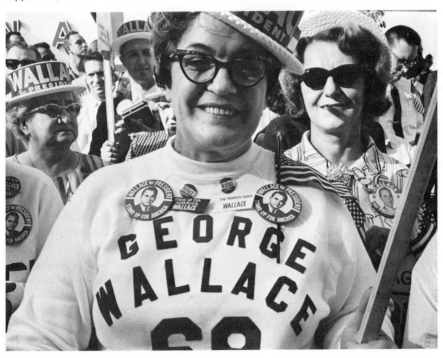

phrey. Right-wingers flocked to Governor George Wallace of Alabama, who was antiintellectual, openly racist, and hawkish on the war. No one doubted that Wallace commanded widespread support among segregationists in the South and among advocates of escalation. But he displayed much more than a sectional appeal. By denouncing the counter culture, the New Left, and the eastern Establishment, he appealed to many "middle Americans," ethnics, and blue-collar workers. His impressive showings in northern primaries—34 percent in Wisconsin, 30 percent in Indiana, 43 percent in Maryland—suggested that backlash was widespread indeed.

As the campaign progressed McCarthy also demonstrated his lack of appeal to blacks. In the best of times this weakness would have been a liability for a prospective Democratic candidate. But after April 4 it became doubly serious. On that day James Earl Ray, a white exconvict, shot and killed Martin Luther King on the balcony of a Memphis motel. Outraged blacks responded immediately by rampaging through ghettos in Chicago, Washington, and other American cities. McCarthy was naturally appalled by the assassination. But most blacks continued to regard him as the candidate of the white student elite—which in large part he was. Someone else would have to be found who could unite the black masses and antiwar activists and appeal to the center as well.

That someone was Robert Kennedy, who announced his candidacy after the New Hampshire primary. His belated entry earned him few plaudits for courage, and McCarthy supporters abused him for his opportunism. But Kennedy possessed useful assets. He was rich, intelligent, highly organized, and charismatic. More than all other candidates in 1968, he aroused passionate support among blacks, Chicanos, and many Catholics and blue-collar workers. By calling for deescalation of the war he gradually cut into McCarthy's support among the white student Left. Though he lost to McCarthy in a primary in Oregon, he won impressively everywhere else. He peaked on June 4 when he won the biggest test of all in California.

Whether he could have gone on to win the nomination is hard to judge. Perhaps not, for the Johnson loyalists hated him. But, in any case, he never got the chance. On the night of the California primary, as he walked down a kitchen corridor in a Los Angeles hotel, he was shot and killed by Sirhan Sirhan, a crazed Jordanian immigrant. To millions of blacks and poor people his assassination, following so closely on the murder of King, was the ultimate tragedy. It was also "proof" of the violence and divisions that rent American society.

Kennedy's death eliminated the last chance for the triumph of the antiwar forces at the Democratic convention in Chicago. McCarthy stayed in to the end, but his defeat in California exposed his limitations as a vote getter. Kennedy partisans tried to make a candidate of Senator George McGovern, an antiwar liberal from South Dakota. At that late date, however, McGovern excited little enthusiasm. After bitter struggles over the seating of delegates, the party regulars excluded most of the insurgents. They then chose Hum-

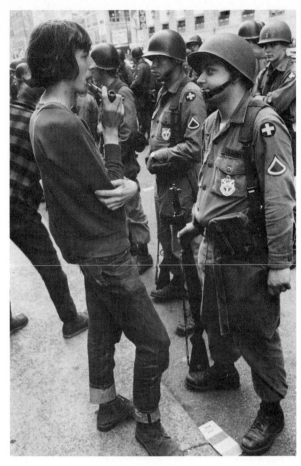

A demonstrator confronts a National Guardsman at the 1968 Democratic national convention in Chicago.

phrey by a margin of more than two to one over McCarthy and McGovern and balanced the ticket by naming liberal-leaning George Muskie, a senator from Maine, as the vice-presidential nominee. As in most Democratic conventions since the 1920s, the slightly left-of-center coalition within the party had triumphed.

These nominations seemed almost worthless as a result of the tumult that convulsed Chicago. As the convention opened, left-wing protesters moved into the city. Most of them were nonviolent whites working for McCarthy. Others, however, were determined to provoke confrontations with Mayor Richard Daley, who had earned notoriety after King's assassination by ordering his police to "shoot to kill" arsonists and to "shoot to maim" looters. Daley erected chain-link fences and barbed wire to protect the convention site and surrounded it with police. Some of the activists responded by taunting and insulting the "pigs," who then charged wildly into crowds, clubbing and gassing passersby as well as demonstrators. The "police riot," as the Walker Report later described it, shattered what hope had remained for rapprochement between the Democratic center and the youthful Left. For Humphrey, "beneficiary" of this police activity, the convention was a disaster.

Richard Nixon, the Republican nominee, seemed certain to profit from this Democratic disarray. His victory at the GOP convention was a triumph of ambition, persistence, and party loyalty. After losing to Kennedy in 1960, he had failed in a race for the governorship of California in 1962. Tired and petulant in defeat, he had told reporters, "You won't have Nixon to kick around any more, because, gentlemen, this is my last press conference." Thereafter, he had been a conscientious party worker, supporting Goldwater in 1964 and traveling widely for GOP congressional candidates in 1966. His smooth performance during the preconvention campaign outflanked right-wingers who had supported California governor Ronald Reagan and liberals who had favored governors Nelson Rockefeller of New York and George Romney of Michigan. It also misled many who had disliked him in the past. "The Nixon of 1968," said Theodore White, chronicler of presidential elections, "was so different from the Nixon of 1960 that the whole personality required reexplanation. . . . There was . . . a total absence of bitterness, of the rancor and venom that had once colored his remarks."

As the campaign developed, Nixon failed to generate enthusiasm. Despite his appeals for "law and order," a rightist slogan, it was clear that George Wallace, running as the presidential candidate of the American Independence party, would capture much of the right-wing vote. Nixon also waffled on Vietnam. In 1966 he had proclaimed, "we believe this is a war that has to be fought to prevent World War III." By early 1968 he was saying that America must "end the war," but refusing to say how or when he would do it. And many people, remembering his partisan, Red-baiting past, refused to believe there was a "new Nixon." As if these were not handicaps enough, he yoked himself to Governor Spiro Agnew of Maryland, his choice for vice-president. Inexperienced and maladroit, Agnew repeatedly insulted ethnic groups. He was one of the most ill qualified vice-presidential candidates in modern times.

Humphrey, meanwhile, labored earnestly to salvage what he could from the discord of the convention. Many union leaders, distrusting the GOP, gave him their support. So did some black spokesmen, who recalled his enthusiasm for civil rights as far back as the 1948 convention. Humphrey built bridges with the antiwar supporters by edging away, though much too slowly for McCarthy, from Johnson's policies. And he benefited from the energetic campaigning of Muskie, a Catholic who appealed to many ethnic voters. On October 31, when Johnson announced that he was stopping all bombing in North Vietnam, it seemed that Humphrey might have a chance.

Johnson's move came too late. Moreover, the South Vietnamese rejected his course of action, and the chances for peace quickly disappeared. On election day Nixon and Agnew triumphed over the Democrats. Considering the woeful state of the GOP in 1964, their victory was impressive. It suggested that voters were becoming much less partisan, indeed, more independent,

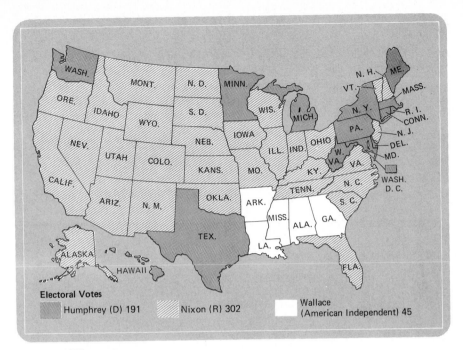

Electoral Votes

| Humphrey (D) 191 | Nixon (R) 302 | Wallace (American Independent) 45 |

Election, 1968

than they had been in the heyday of the Democratic coalition under Roosevelt.

The results, however, hardly gave Nixon much cause for rejoicing. In winning he got 31,770,222 votes, less than 1 percent more than Humphrey's 31,267,744. He took only 43 percent of the total vote, the smallest share for a victor since Wilson's in 1912. Like Eisenhower before him, he failed to dent the large Democratic majorities in Congress. Analysts concluded that a higher turnout among blacks would have given Humphrey the margin for victory, and that the Democratic coalition, though slipping, had not disappeared. Voters, they added, had not been attracted to Nixon. As in so many presidential elections since World War II, they had rejected the loser, not accepted the winner.

This negativism showed most clearly in the votes for Wallace and his warlike running mate, General Curtis LeMay. Although Wallace carried only five states (all in the Deep South), he won 9.9 million votes. This was 13.5 percent of the turnout, the highest for any third party candidate since Robert La Follette in 1924, and the highest ever for a candidate on the Right. Wallace's supporters included large numbers of northerners as well as southerners, young people as well as old, blue-collar workers (who defied union spokesmen) as well as wealthy conservatives. His appeal proved that a significant cross section was disgusted with the major parties, with radical youth, with liberalism generally. It showed also that millions still wanted to win the war, even if it meant adopting Le May's suggestion of bombing North Vietnam into the Stone Age. For people such as these Nixon's victory over Humphrey was small consolation.

The Left was even more discouraged than was the Right by the campaign of 1968. Nixon had campaigned on the slogan of "Bring Us Together Again." But he had shown little discernible longing to include in his happy circle the antiwar activists, the blacks, or young people generally. He had denounced the liberal Supreme Court, talked threateningly (though vaguely) about restoring "law and order," and hinted (again vaguely) about cutting back Great Society programs. Given the frustration, indeed the fury, felt by many activists, his victory did not augur well for social peace in the years ahead.

The dissatisfaction of both Right and Left should presumably have comforted the center. To a degree it did. Moderates considered it cause for congratulation that the American people had gone peaceably to the polls and had authorized without protest a transfer of great political power from one party to the other. As so often in the American past, the two-party system had helped to undermine extremes and to preserve the legitimacy of elected officials. This stability was impressive amid such turbulent events.

But thoughtful analysts also asked: stability for what? In being forced to choose between two middle-of-the-road candidates (Wallace was never a plausible winner) the voters had been given no real opportunity to express themselves. And in remaining so vague, Nixon had done little to enlighten them. Millions probably voted for him because of the violence they associated with the radicals in the Democratic party. But did they want Nixon to dismantle the Great Society? Polls suggested not. Millions also supported him because they were tired of "Johnson's war." But did that mean they expected Nixon to stop the fighting or to escalate it? Here the polls were disturbing, for they showed that Americans were frustrated and confused by the war. McCarthy's supporters, for instance, included many who wanted to end the conflict by moving in with the full force of American military power.

This confusion and ambiguity was the most unsettling feature of the campaign of 1968. Far from toning down the discord of the previous three years, it frustrated reactionaries as well as radicals and reduced even the center to apprehensiveness and uncertainty. As Americans were shortly to discover, the stability they had bought by letting Nixon "Bring Us Together Again" was to be short-lived indeed.

Suggestions for reading

Useful starting points for understanding Johnson's foreign policy are Philip L. Geyelin, *Lyndon B. Johnson and the World* (1966); and Richard J. Barnet, *Intervention and Revolution: U. S. and the Third World** (1969), a far-ranging analysis. For the intervention in the Dominican Republic see Theodore Draper, *Dominican Revolt** (1968); and Jerome Slater, *Intervention and Negotiation* (1970). Vietnam policy is covered in Townsend Hoopes, *Limits of Intervention** (1973); Chester Cooper, *Lost Crusade*

(1971); and Seymour Hersh, *My Lai* (1970). See especially Frances Fitzgerald, *Fire in the Lake** (1972), which exposes the impact of war on Vietnamese culture.

Books on domestic unrest include the Report of the National Advisory Commission on Civil Disorders* (1968); and the report of the Scranton Commission on Campus Violence* (1970). Hugh Davis Graham and Ted Gurr, *Violence in America** (1969), provides some historical background. See also Robert Fogelson, *Violence as Protest* (1971); and Robert Conot, *Rivers of Blood, Years of Darkness** (1968), which deals with the riot in Watts. Two eye-witness books by Norman Mailer are *Armies of the Night** (1968) on the demonstration at the Pentagon in 1968; and *Miami and the Siege of Chicago** (1968) on protest at the national conventions.

Among the many books on young people in the 1960s are Kenneth Keniston, *Young Radicals** (1968); Lewis Yablonsky, *Hippie Trip* (1968); Lewis Feuer, *The Conflict of Generations* (1969); and Seymour Lipset, *Rebellion in the University* (1972). Books read widely at the time are Theodore Roszak, *Making of a Counter Culture** (1969); and Charles Reich, *Greening of America** (1970). Paul Goodman, *Growing Up Absurd** (1960), is a lucid account of what alienated young people. Charles Silberman, *Crisis in the Classroom** (1970); and David Riesman and Christopher Jencks, *The Academic Revolution* (1969), cover their subjects thoroughly. Paul Jacobs and Saul Landau, eds., *New Radicals** (1966), is a useful anthology. Books dealing with left-wing ideology include Peter Clecak, *Radical Paradoxes: Dilemmas of the American Left, 1945–1970* (1973); Edward Baccioco, *The New Left: Reform to Revolution* (1974); and Irwin Unger, *The Movement: A History of the American New Left, 1959–1972** (1974). See also John Diggins, *The American Left in the Twentieth Century** (1973).

For the attitudes of militant blacks in the 1960s see James Baldwin, *The Fire Next Time** (1963); Malcolm X, *Autobiography** (1965); Stokeley Carmichael and Charles Hamilton, *Black Power** (1967); and Julius Lester, *Look Out Whitey* (1968). Peter Coleman, *The Death and Life of Malcolm X* (1973), is excellent. E. U. Essien-Udom, *Black Nationalism** (1962), describes the Black Muslims. Surveys of other minorities include Matt Meier and Feliciano Rivera, *The Chicanos** (1972); Stan Steiner, *La Raza** (1970); and Oscar Lewis, *La Vida** (1966), on Puerto Ricans. Michael Novak, *Rise of the Unmeltable Ethnics* (1970), describes the failure of the melting pot.

Books that help in understanding the rise of feminism are Robert Lifton, ed., *The Woman in America** (1965); Lois Banner, *Women in Modern America** (1974); and the book by William Chafe cited in chapter 6. Important feminist statements are Betty Friedan, *The Feminine Mystique** (1963); and Germaine Greer, *The Female Eunuch** (1972).

For politics, especially in 1968, consult the thorough account by Lewis Chester, et. al., *An American Melodrama** (1970). Theodore White, *Making of a President, 1968** (1969), is useful. Marshall Frady, *Wallace** (1970), is entertaining and provocative. David Halberstam, *The Unfinished Odyssey of Robert Kennedy* (1968); and Jeremy Larner, *Nobody Knows: Reflections on the McCarthy Campaign of 1968* (1970), add insights. Richard Scammon and Ben Wattenberg, *The Real Majority* (1970), is a well-written, balanced account of recent electoral trends.

15

The unsettled 1970s

In his first inaugural President Nixon repeated the "bring us together" note he had sounded during his campaign. "We are torn by division," he said. "To a crisis of the spirit, we need an answer of the spirit. And to find that answer, we need only look within ourselves. . . . We cannot learn from one another until we stop shouting at one another—until we speak quietly enough so that our words can be heard as well as our voices. For its part, government will listen."

No leader relishes the thought of presiding over a fractured society, and Nixon was no exception. He took extreme measures in his effort to impose "unity" on the nation. But except for an interlude in 1972, when he triumphed spectacularly in his quest for reelection, the goal of consensus eluded him. Indeed, his own failings did much to divide the country. So it was that Gerald Ford of Michigan, who replaced Nixon in 1974, assumed leadership of a worried country. It remains to be seen whether subsequent presidents can resolve or reduce the conflicts inherited from Nixon and whether the nation can harness the modernizing forces that have transformed American life in the twentieth century. Can the United States extend economic and social progress, curb the military-industrial complex, and find the sense of purpose and idealism appropriate to the future?

Limited advances, 1969–1973

There were some slight grounds for optimism even during the first few years of Nixon's tumultuous presidency. Racial unrest seemed to subside. Contrary to expectations, the ghettos had quieted in the summer of 1968, and they stayed relatively peaceful throughout the early 1970s. Some people attributed the calm to prosecutions that had driven militants like Carmichael and Rap Brown into jail or exile. Others concluded that blacks had come to doubt the wisdom of destroying their own property. As one Watts leader put it, "the rioting phase, where we burn down businesses in our own areas, is over. The whole movement is in another direction—toward implementing black power and finding our own dignity as a people."

To a limited extent blacks achieved these aims. Thanks to the Supreme Court, which ruled in 1969 *(Alexander* v. *Holmes)* that school desegregation must proceed "at once," the percentage of blacks in formerly all-black schools fell from 68 percent to 18 percent between 1968 and 1970. Statistics revealed that blacks, though still failing to capture a larger share of the national income, were developing a sizeable middle class: the proportion of employed blacks who earned $10,000 or more increased from 5 percent to 28 percent during the 1960s. The number who attended college rose between 1966 and 1970 by 85 percent—to 434,000. And blacks began to make use of the vote. By 1971 there were 13 black congressmen, 81 mayors, 198 state legislators, and 1,567 black local office-holders. These advances were significant. Few people in 1960 could have predicted them. Nevertheless, discrimination still plagued the nation. The controversy over busing in the schools, perhaps the most acrimonious domestic issue of the early 1970s, showed that many white Americans still refused to accept residential integration or to go much beyond tokenism in the schools.

Feminists, too, made modest gains in the 1970s. Writers like Robin Morgan, author of *Sisterhood Is Powerful* (1970), and Germaine Greer, author of the *Female Eunuch* (1971), advanced the economic, psychological, and physiological justifications for women's liberation. Others, including self-proclaimed lesbians like Kate Millett, led a growing campaign for sexual freedom. In 1972 activists founded *Ms,* the first militant feminist magazine to attract a sizeable circulation. In the same year Congress approved legislation banning sex discrimination in colleges and universities receiving federal aid. In 1973 the Supreme Court (*Doe* v. *Bolton, Roe* v. *Wade)* ruled against state laws prohibiting abortions, and both houses of Congress approved the Equal Rights Amendment, which feminists had been seeking for fifty years. A total of twenty-two states—of thirty-eight needed—ratified the amendment the same year.

Thereafter, feminism suffered reverses. Many black women continued to oppose the movement. So did large numbers of married working women—who were too intent on keeping their jobs (or on earning enough money to

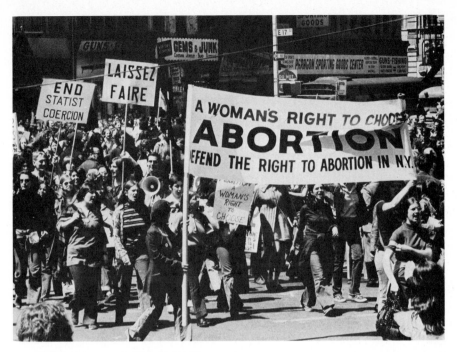

Feminists on the march, New York City.

return to the home) to spend time on campaigns for women's rights. NOW moderates complained that lesbians and sexual radicals exposed the movement to distortion and ridicule. Other articulate women led a countermovement. One of their most forceful leaders, Phyllis Schlafly, was a conservative whose idols were Thomas Edison, Elias Howe (inventor of the sewing machine), and Clarence Birdseye, all of whom had promoted comforts of domesticity. "A man's first significant purchase," she said, "is a diamond for his bride, and the largest financial investment of his life is a home for her to

> The women's movement promises to affect radically the life of virtually everyone in America. Only a small part of the population suffers because it is black, and most people have little contact with minorities. Women are 51 percent of the population, and chances are that every adult American either is one, is married to one, or has close social or business relations with many.
>
> The feminist revolution will overturn the basic premises upon which these relations are built—stereotyped notions about the family and the roles of men and women, fallacies concerning masculinity and femininity, and the economic division of labor into paid work and homemaking.
>
> If the 1960s belonged to the blacks, the next ten years are ours.
>
> Lucy Komisar, an activist for women's liberation, explains her goals (1970).

live in." Reflecting this attitude, Nixon vetoed a bill in 1973 that would have provided funds for day-care centers. Meanwhile, antifeminists campaigned against ratification of the ERA, which they said would destroy the "special place" of women in the home.

Yet feminists, like blacks, could take some comfort in the progress they had made since the early 1960s. Though NOW still had fewer than 40,000 members in 1975, it had grown steadily since its formation in 1966. A majority of women told pollsters that they approved the general goals of the movement. Of all the protest movements that started in the 1960s—for peace, for black power, for brown power—women's liberation seemed most durable.

Other reformers took limited pleasure in accomplishments of the Democratic Congresses between 1969 and 1972. The legislators voted increases in social security benefits and extended the life of the 1965 Voting Rights Law. They approved an act regulating campaign spending and authorized eighteen-year-olds to vote in federal elections. The Twenty-sixth Amendment to the Constitution, ratified in 1971, extended the voting rights of eighteen-year-olds to state and local elections. Though Congress fell far short of attacking the nation's festering urban and racial problems, it did increase funding for some domestic purposes. In part because of a recession that descended on the economy in 1969, spending for food stamps—to go to 11 million poor people—rose from $250 million in 1969 to $2.2 billion in 1971. Nonmilitary federal expenditures as a percentage of the GNP almost doubled between 1969 and 1972.

The lawmakers occasionally proved responsive to the pressures for environmental conservation applied constantly by Ralph Nader and others in the early 1970s. Among the important measures approved were the Water Quality Improvement Act, which attempted to control pollution caused by industry and power companies; the Clean Air Act, which called for changes in the manufacture of automobiles; and the Resource Recovery Act, which promoted recycling of solid wastes. Congress also refused funds for the Super Sonic Transport (SST), a huge, noisy airplane that the administration had strongly favored. In 1971 Congress created the Environmental Protection Agency and empowered it to bring suits against corporate or municipal leaders who violated federal standards. Despite these laws, many corporations (especially in the automobile industry) found ways to evade or to postpone stringent regulation. Careless oil drilling and pumping, which had ruined beaches and marine life off Santa Barbara in 1969, continued to cause damage. Most alarming, Americans continued to squander resources at an alarming rate. But as the birth rate approached the point of zero population growth, the hope remained that the nation could learn to exist without destroying its environment.

Nixon could claim little credit for these developments. Indeed, he was cool to legislation for social welfare or environmental protection. But many observers welcomed his apparent expertise in the realm of foreign affairs. Here he, like Kennedy, paid little attention to the State Department. Its secretary until late 1973, William Rogers, played an insignificant role in policy making. Nixon relied instead on Dr. Henry Kissinger, his national security adviser. Kissinger, a German emigré who had become a professor of government at Harvard, was a highly skilled negotiator and a persuasive exponent of power politics. The way to avoid nuclear catastrophe, he believed, was to seek détente with the Soviet Union and China. These powers, with Japan and western Europe, could cooperate with the United States to prevent brush fires from escalating into World War III.

Kissinger's policies did not work wonders in 1969–71. In the Middle East they failed to end tensions heightened by Israel's stunning victory over Arab countries in the Six-Day War of 1967. Nixon and Kissinger also did not deserve much credit for the limited détente that did develop with Russia and China by 1972. Rather, these communist powers, at odds with each other, assumed considerable initiative for developing better relations with the West. Still, the administration helped to defuse the Cold War and to reverse the tide of postwar American foreign policy. Nixon, once the cold warrior extraordinaire, had revealed his capacity for change.

The President even seemed to make progress toward deescalating the war in Vietnam. In 1969 he announced the Nixon Doctrine, which proclaimed that allies could expect American aid, but not troops, when confronted with internal revolt. He added that he would end the draft within two years. Encouraged by Secretary of Defense Melvin Laird, he propounded Vietnamization, as it became called. The United States, Nixon said, would build up the Vietnamese military so that it could stand on its own. To back up this policy the President began withdrawing American troops. In 1968 there had been 543,000; by September 1972 there were only 39,000. Though later developments revealed the serious limitations of Vietnamization, the troop withdrawals were a popular step toward disengagement.

The persistence of discord

From the beginning of Nixon's presidency, however, the discord of the Johnson years persisted. For the universities, in fact, the spring of 1969 was the most disruptive to date. Police moved in to restore order at Howard, Massachusetts, Pennsylvania State, and San Fernando State. Conflicts between black and white students erupted in violence at the University of Wisconsin and City College of New York. Harvard students invaded University Hall, rifled files, and were thrown out by state police. And at Cornell armed blacks seized the student union, leading the university president to capitulate to their demands. The backlash that followed such demonstrations—perpetrated by a small minority of students—was one of many forces that culminated in scanty funding for colleges and universities in the early 1970s.

Militant black students at Cornell University, 1969.

Economic divisions plagued society at large. The 1970s were for public service employees what the 1930s had been for industrial workers. Teachers, nurses, policemen, garbage collectors, firemen, and transit employees formed militant unions, picketed city hall, and staged walkouts that would have seemed revolutionary in Calvin Coolidge's day. A strike of postal workers tied up the nation's mails for a week and forced the national guard to take charge in New York City. Despairingly, Congress established an independent postal service that was expected to soften discontent. Inflation stemming from a war-heated economy accounted for much of this conflict. So did new visions of the "good life" and meaningful work. White-collar and service workers in the 1970s, like so many Americans in the prosperous postwar years, were joining the revolution of rising expectations.

Continuing violence was particularly frightening. In early 1970 bombs tore up the Manhattan offices of IBM, General Telephone and Electronics Corporation, and Mobil Oil. Antiwar revolutionaries claimed credit for the explosions. Shortly thereafter two black militants, followers of Rap Brown, were killed when one of their homemade bombs went off prematurely. And in March 1970 three young radicals, one of them a socially prominent young woman who had recently graduated from Swarthmore, were blown to pieces in their "bomb factory" in Greenwich Village. Two other revolutionaries, cut and bleeding, fled from the scene.

These were but the most striking manifestations of apparent social upheaval in the years after 1968. In New York City bomb threats averaged 1000 a month in 1969–70. Within fifteen months 368 bombs actually exploded. In 1970 the FBI reported 35,202 assaults on policemen, four times the number in 1960. People were not even safe in the air: skyjacking diverted seventy-one planes in 1969 alone. The drug traffic seemed particularly frightening. When rock stars Jimi Hendrix and Janis Joplin died from overdoses, some of the worst fears seemed confirmed.

The most shocking violence of the early 1970s took place in prisons, many of which were breeding grounds for racial confrontations between convicts and authorities. One such outbreak occurred in August 1971 at San Quentin prison, where George Jackson, one of the three black "Soledad brothers" (actually not related), was caged for allegedly having killed a white guard at Soledad prison a year earlier. Using a smuggled pistol, Jackson broke out of his cell and demanded the release of twenty-seven prisoners. He then murdered three white guards and two trusties before falling in a rain of shots himself. Militants, outraged by his death, dressed him in a black panther uniform and gave him a martyr's funeral.

Jackson's death helped to trigger the most bloody prison riot in American history. This occurred at Attica, New York State, home of 2,254 convicts, 75 percent of whom were black or Puerto Rican. All the 383 guards were white, and racial incidents were common. In September 1971 angry blacks staged a rebellion that was quickly joined by more than 1200 inmates. They grabbed 39 hostages, seriously hurt a guard, barricaded themselves in a cell block, and issued demands on the warden. When the prisoners threatened to cut the throats of their hostages, the authorities waited no longer. In the assault which followed, police gunfire killed 30 prisoners and 10 guards. To some observers, like *The New York Times*'s Tom Wicker, the Attica riot displayed the urgent need for prison reform. To many others it was "proof" of the savagery of the criminal population—especially of blacks—and of the need for "law and order."

NIXON AT BAY, 1969–1971

Nixon, of course, was not to blame for such violence. But to many Americans—progressives, college activists, blacks—he was an unsympathetic figure. Between 1969 and mid-1971 they grew increasingly hostile to the President. They focused on four themes: his personal style, his domestic policies, his "southern strategy," and Vietnam.

Objections to Nixon's style ranged from the frivolous to the profound. Americans who had looked to the White House for cultural leadership disliked his patronage of pro football, middlebrow music, and Norman Vincent Peale. Others considered him banal, hypocritical, and sanctimonious. People wondered about his close friendships with C. G. ("Bebe") Rebozo, a wealthy real estate operator, and with Robert H. Abplanalp, a businessman, who helped

Nixon finance the purchase of property worth $600,000 at Key Biscayne, Florida, and San Clemente, California. Nixon's taste for regal living, it was revealed later, cost the government $10 million in improvements and security measures. To his critics, "Tricky Dick" was becoming "King Richard."

Nixon's style was above all secretive and suspicious. Extremely sensitive to criticism, he avoided contacts with the press. Faced with important decisions, he frequently slipped off to the presidential retreat at Camp David, Maryland, or to one of his tightly guarded compounds in Florida and California. There he would summon up the courage to act. Even his cabinet found him remote and nonsupporting. Two of the more popular among his appointees, Secretary of the Interior Walter Hickel and HEW Secretary Robert Finch, left or were fired by the end of 1970. Like reporters, they complained that Nixon surrounded himself with a much-expanded White House staff of ambitious, unscrupulous young lawyers, public relations men, and advertising executives. Among them were attorneys John Dean and Charles Colson, and Jeb Stuart Magruder, a young businessman. Nixon's closest domestic advisers, H. R. Haldeman and John R. Erlichman, had no experience in government. Tough, cold, and utterly devoted to their boss, they excluded visitors, insulted important politicians, and narrowed the circle of decision-making. Not even Lyndon Johnson at his most highhanded had seemed so inaccessible as Nixon.

The President's economic policies aroused special concern. Some of his angriest critics, susprisingly enough, were conservatives. When Nixon proclaimed, in January 1971, "I am now a Keynesian," they were appalled. They were equally shocked to discover that the budget deficit for the 1970–71 fiscal year amounted to more than $23 billion, only $2 billion less than the record set during Johnson's last year in office. Nixon's endorsement of unbalanced budgets provided added evidence of his flexibility (critics said of his lack of principle), and of the political clout enjoyed by pressure groups.

Conservatives had other complaints about Nixon's domestic policies. They resented Hickel's rigorous enforcement of the laws protecting the environment. They grumbled especially about the influence of Daniel Patrick Moynihan, a Harvard professor whom Nixon named to head the newly created Urban Affairs Council. Under Moynihan's persistent coaching Nixon endorsed the controversial Family Assistance Plan, which would have guaranteed an income of $1600 a year (plus food stamps valued at $800 or more) to a family of four. The plan promised cash payments to the hitherto neglected working poor. Michael Harrington, a socialist, termed FAP "the most radical idea since the New Deal." But Democrats in Congress ultimately sidetracked the measure—in part because they demanded more generous benefits, in part because they disliked Nixon, in part because the President (to gain conservative support) appeared to threaten able-bodied heads of households with loss of benefits if they failed to register for job training or to accept work. Congress's rejection of the measure meant that America's creaking welfare "system" staggered on.

Most criticism of the President's domestic policies came from liberals. They recognized that Nixon, like Kennedy, was primarily interested in foreign affairs. Indeed, Nixon once commented, "I've always thought this country could run itself domestically without a President." He added, "all you need is a competent cabinet to run the country at home." This attitude antagonized reformers, most of whom could not get past the "Berlin Wall" erected by Haldeman and Erlichman. Congress objected also to presidential pressure in 1969 for the funding of antimissile (ABM) development. Though Nixon won that fight, by one vote, it cost him what little chance he had had of working harmoniously with the Democratic Congresses of his administration. Long before Congress counterattacked in 1973–74, many of its most influential members were barely on speaking terms with the White House.

The liberals were particularly critical of Nixon's handling of the economy, which grew ragged and unstable between 1969 and 1972. The administration's tight money policy, they claimed, harmed investment and impeded construction. The failure to set forth price and wage guidelines encouraged round after round of inflationary settlements between management and labor. A $2.5 billion tax cut, which Nixon signed in December 1969, further fed inflation. By 1971 the country was experiencing the worst of all possible worlds: inflation (5.3 percent in 1970) and recession (6 percent unemployment) at the same time. At fault, said Democratic party chieftain Lawrence O'Brien, were "Nixonomics." O'Brien explained, "All the things that should go up—the stock market, corporate profits, real spendable income, productivity—go down, and all the things that should go down—unemployment, prices, interest rates—go up."

NIXON'S SOUTHERN STRATEGY

Most objectionable of all to progressives was the administration's "southern strategy." In its broad outlines this reflected the argument of Kevin Phillips, a Justice Department aide who wrote *The Emerging Republican Majority* in 1969. To Phillips the preeminent need of the GOP was to outflank men like Governor Wallace by 1972. This meant securing the votes of "middle Americans"—southern whites, blue-collar workers, Catholic ethnics, suburbanites, conservatives. It meant stressing the theme of "law and order," discrediting activist students, and paying relatively little attention to the wishes of blacks, Hispanic-Americans, and others who were predominantly Democratic anyway.

This southern strategy helps to explain Nixon's civil rights policies. These were a mixture of forward and backward movements. To assist blacks Nixon instituted the so-called Philadelphia Plan, which required unions working on federal projects to accept quotas of blacks as apprentices and to admit them when training was completed. To secure black support he named James Farmer, a leading activist, as an assistant secretary of HEW. He told Farmer that he wanted to do "what's right" for blacks. "I care," he added. "I just hope people will believe that I DO care."

During the two years that Farmer stayed with HEW, however, he was unable to penetrate the Berlin Wall. Like other advocates of civil rights, he confronted the influence of Attorney General John Mitchell, a Nixon law partner who emerged as the strongest figure in the new cabinet. Under Mitchell the Department of Justice attempted (unsuccessfully) to prevent extension of the voting rights act of 1965. He also brought suit to delay school desegregation guidelines in Mississippi. Outraged attorneys in the civil rights divisions of the Justice Department and HEW protested vigorously. Though the Supreme Court's ruling for desegregation "at once" foiled Mitchell's effort, he had shown the white South that the administration cared.

Mitchell's passion for "law and order" led him into several other blunders between 1969 and 1971. One was his attempt to prosecute antiwar demonstrators. Among the many activists he had arrested were the "Harrisburg Seven," the "Gainesville Eight," and others who were tried in groups. The trial of the "Chicago Seven," including the Yippies Jerry Rubin and Abbie Hoffman, degenerated into a shouting match between the unruly defendants and a judge so biased that his decision against them was later overruled. Capping efforts to stifle dissent, Mitchell brought suit in 1971 to stop publication of the so-called Pentagon papers, a forty-seven-volume, 2.5-million-word summary that documented the escalation of the war in Vietnam prior to 1969. The Supreme Court, however, ruled against prior restraint of publication in the press, and lesser courts sustained the antiwar demonstrators. The court decisions revealed the continuing independence of the judiciary from executive activity. They suggested also Mitchell's disregard for civil liberties. For a guardian of "law and order" it was an unedifying performance.

The southern strategy came gradually to dictate the administration's choice of justices to fill vacancies in the Supreme Court between 1969 and 1972. The first nominee, Warren Earl Burger of Minnesota, was a well-qualified moderate named to replace Chief Justice Warren, who retired after sixteen years on the bench. The Senate confirmed him quickly. Mitchell's next choice was Judge Clement F. Haynsworth, Jr., a South Carolinian. Union leaders, civil rights advocates, and progressives opposed him. Early supporters wavered when they learned of conflict-of-interest charges marring Haynsworth's judicial record. In November 1969 the Senate, including seventeen Republicans, rejected him.

The Senate's action infuriated Nixon, who called the attacks on Haynsworth "brutal, vicious . . . and unfair." His temper high, he carelessly nominated Mitchell's next choice, G. Harrold Carswell, a Floridian who served on the court of appeals. Suspecting Nixon's political motives, opponents produced evidence to show Carswell's racial bias. Law professors throughout the country exposed his mediocrity as a judge. Accordingly, the Senate, including thirteen Republicans, rejected him in April 1970. Adhering to the southern strategy, Nixon burst out, "I understand the bitter feelings of millions of Americans who live in the South. They have my assurance that the day will come when judges like Carswell and Haynsworth can and will sit on the High Court.''

After circulating the names of other mediocre candidates, Nixon finally searched for qualified nominees who could command congressional support. By 1972 he had named three. The first, Judge Harry Blackmun of Minnesota, held views that resembled Burger's. The second, Lewis F. Powell, Jr., had been a president of the American Bar Association. The third, Assistant Attorney General William H. Rehnquist, was a young Goldwater Republican who was developing a reputation as a thoughtful exponent of conservative jurisprudence. The Senate confirmed all three.

Nixon's actions enhanced his standing in the South. But they antagonized Congress. And they failed to produce a tractable Court. Though the four new appointees often voted together, they showed little disposition to reverse the decisions of the Warren Court, and they did not comprise a majority. In addition to the abortion and Pentagon papers cases—both of which annoyed the administration—the Burger Court voted unanimously in 1971 that busing was necessary and proper if other means failed to achieve school desegregation. Though later decisions concerning busing left the issue in doubt, it was clear that Burger and his associates would not block the movement for racial justice.

In the next few years the Court continued to antagonize conservatives. In 1972 it held, five to four, that state laws that authorized the death sentence were unconstitutional because they gave too much discretion to judges and juries. The decision did not outlaw the death sentence per se—thirty-two states passed new laws authorizing it by 1975—but it stopped executions for the time being, and it prompted renewed litigation that branded the death penalty unconstitutional "cruel and unusual punishment." The court also ruled that the government had to get a court order before employing wiretapping against suspected subversives. And in 1974 it ruled, eight to nothing, that Nixon must turn over damning tape recordings to a district court. The President, like many of his predecessors in the White House, experienced the rugged independence of the judicial branch.

Vietnam, Cambodia, and Laos

Nixon's most divisive policies before 1973 were in the realm where he had seemed so assured: foreign policy. His problem was simple: Vietnamization was not working. As American troops were withdrawn, the North Vietnamese and the Viet Cong proved more than a match for the forces of South Vietnam's Dictator Nguyen Van Thieu. To compensate, Nixon authorized unpublicized bombing raids on neighboring Cambodia, which the enemy was using as a sanctuary. These raids, some 3,600 beginning early in 1969, failed to stop the communists. Encouraged by the Joint Chiefs, Nixon then toyed with the idea of sending American troops into Cambodia. But such an attack could not be concealed, and Prince Norodim Sihanouk, Cambodia's ruler, would have objected. The President's hands were tied.

In March 1970 the situation changed suddenly. Lon Nol, a rightist, staged a successful coup against Sihanouk. With the way now open for invasion, Nixon wasted little time. On April 30 he appeared on television to announce that an attack was underway to destroy the North Vietnamese sanctuaries. He did not mention the failure of Vietnamization, and he said nothing about the secret bombing raids of the previous fourteen months. The fact that American soldiers were invading a neutral nation did not seem to trouble him. On the contrary, he spoke fiercely. "We will not be humiliated," he explained. "We will not be defeated. If when the chips are down the United States acts like a pitiful helpless giant, the forces of totalitarianism and anarchy will threaten free nations and free institutions throughout the world. It is not our power but our will that is being tested. . . ." He added that the invasion might make him a "one-term President . . . but I have rejected all political considerations in making this decision . . . I would rather be a one-term President than be a two-term President at the cost of seeing America become a second-rate power and see this nation accept the first defeat in its proud 190-year history."

Nixon miscalculated badly. In Cambodia the attack was of dubious merit. According to American estimates, the invasion succeeded in killing more than 11,000 soldiers and in capturing stores of food and ammunition. By

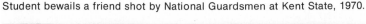

Student bewails a friend shot by National Guardsmen at Kent State, 1970.

reducing some of the military pressure on Thieu's forces, it may have given Vietnamization a little more time. But allied casualties were 1,138 dead and 4,911 wounded. The invasion failed to drive the enemy out of Cambodia. Worst of all, the assault dragged Cambodia itself into full-scale civil war. Within five years Lon Nol's increasingly unpopular regime was to fall to a nationalistic form of communism.

INTENSIFICATION OF ANTIWAR SENTIMENT

At home Nixon's action prompted stirrings—at last—of independence in Congress, which repealed the 1964 Gulf of Tonkin resolution. The invasion also led to tragedy in Ohio. Two nights after Nixon announced his move students at Kent State University firebombed the ROTC building, causing Ohio Governor James Rhodes to call in the national guard. For a time it seemed that calm would return. But on May 4 students threw rocks and bottles at the guardsmen, who responded with tear gas. When the soldiers ran out of gas, they retreated nervously up a hillside. They were out of range of rocks, and in no danger. Some of the guardsmen then stopped, turned, and began to shoot. A girl screamed, "my God, they're killing us." When the firing stopped, four students lay dead, and eleven were wounded. The Justice Department, acting under Mitchell's orders, failed to call a federal grand jury to review the tragedy, and it was not until 1974 that eight guardsmen were

Kent State University, 1970.

indicted (and acquitted) on criminal charges of violating the students' civil rights.

The deaths at Kent State unleashed a torrent of protest, especially on the campuses, which erupted for the third consecutive spring. Within the month demonstrations disrupted more than 400 universities; more than 250 had to be closed down before the end of the semester. By May 9 weekend, some 100,000 students descended on Washington in protest. A week later at Jackson State College in Mississippi two black students were killed and eleven wounded when police fired indiscriminately into a dormitory. President William J. McGill of Columbia University commented accurately that it was the "most disastrous month of May in the history of American higher education."

Nixon's first reaction was to discredit the students. "These bums . . . blowing up the campuses," he said, " . . . burning up the books, storming about." After the bloodshed at Kent State he commented that the shootings should "remind us once again that when dissent turns to violence it invites tragedy." But the protests worried him, and before dawn on May 9 he got out of bed and stole off to talk to demonstrators camped near the Lincoln Memorial. He intended to be responsive, conciliatory, understanding. But the ensuing dialogue exposed the gulf that separated him from the demonstrators. To California students he talked about surfing; to those from Syracuse he posed questions about the college football team. When he left to eat breakfast in a Washington hotel, he had done nothing to placate his opposition.

The campus disorders also heightened the President's desire to curb dissent. Already he had arranged to tap the phones of thirteen top government officials whom he suspected of leaking stories about the bombings in Cambodia, and of four journalists who had published them. Now, in June 1970, he tried to form a special national security committee composed of top people from the CIA, FBI, and Defense Intelligence Agency, and headed by FBI chief J. Edgar Hoover. The committee would have the power to engage in electronic surveillance, stage break-ins, open mail, and infiltrate college campuses. Hoover, however, spiked the plan by refusing to serve. Though a staunch anticommunist, he wanted no part of illegal operations that would damage the reputation of the FBI. Disappointed, Nixon had to put the plan aside for a while.

Instead, he relied on the vitriolic rhetoric of his vice-president, Spiro Agnew, who outdid himself during the congressional campaigning of 1970. Dissidents, Agnew said, were "parasites of passion," "ideological eunuchs," an "effete corps of impudent snobs who characterize themselves as intellectuals." The press was an "unelected elite," a "tiny and closed fraternity of privileged men . . . enjoying a monopoly sanctioned and licensed by the government." Agnew's assaults dovetailed neatly with the southern strategy and appealed to "middle Americans" who disliked the radical students and the "metromedia" of the eastern seaboard. But Agnew was practically threatening the media with censorship. Not since the days of the sedition and espionage acts during World War I had an administration acted so menacingly toward its opponents.

Perhaps for this reason, the Nixon-Agnew strategy backfired politically. In the election of 1970 the GOP gained two seats in the Senate but lost twelve in the House. They dropped eleven governorships, to trail twenty-nine to twenty-one nationwide. That winter a Gallup poll showed that only 49 percent of Americans, a new low, approved of the administration. Maine's Democratic Senator Edmund Muskie, who had made an extraordinarily effective election-eve broadcast, moved ahead of the President, 47 percent to 39 percent. It seemed possible that Nixon would be a one-term president.

During the first six months of 1971 Nixon did little to better his fortunes. The economy continued to skid. Inflation mounted. The nation faced an unfavorable balance of trade for the first time since the depression year of 1893. The press carried alarming stories of drug addiction, desertion, and mutiny among the troops in Vietnam. Courting further confrontations with antiwar spokesmen, Nixon intervened on behalf of Lieutenant William Calley, Jr., whom the army had convicted of murdering twenty-two civilians at My Lai in 1968. The President had him removed from the stockade pending appeal and promised personally to review the case. He also had charges of stealing government property brought against Daniel Ellsberg, a McNamara protégé and Rand Corporation employee who had released the Pentagon papers to the press. Some of Nixon's aides even drew up an "enemies list." It included such threats to the state as James Reston, Jane Fonda, Barbra Streisand, Paul Newman, and many others.

Nixon compounded his difficulties with yet another adventure in Southeast Asia. This was an invasion of Laos by South Vietnamese troops in February. Its aim, like the assault on Cambodia in 1970, was to cut off sanctuaries and supply routes winding into Vietnam. The incursion was also to display the fighting capacity of the South Vietnamese, who were to go it alone this time. When the attack was over in April, Nixon announced proudly, "tonight I can report that Vietnamization has succeeded." Press accounts showed otherwise. The enemy inflicted 50 percent casualties—3800 South Vietnamese killed and 4500 wounded—in six weeks. Only heavy bombing by the United States—again in a neutral country—prevented still more shocking losses.

Predictably, the invasion of Laos provoked demonstrations. This time the universities were relatively quiet—perhaps because students remembered Kent State, perhaps because protest on the campuses had seemed ineffective in the past. Instead, students and antiwar veterans—by then a growing lobby—headed for Washington. Their protests were orderly, and Washington police made no attempt to harass them. But the arrival in late April of the so-called Mayday tribe changed the situation. Though these activists, perhaps 15,000 strong, were nonviolent, they vowed to "stop the government." They threw trash into streets, abandoned cars at intersections, and milled about. This was too much for Mitchell, who sent in police, national guardsmen, and army troops. Using truncheons and tear gas, they arrested 12,614 people in four days and penned them in open spaces like Robert F. Kennedy Memorial Stadium. Mitchell said that the government had "stopped a repressive mob from robbing the rights of others." The courts, appalled, threw out the arrests as violations of civil rights. Once again the Nixon administration, which had promised to bring the nation together, had helped to drive it apart.

The great turnabout, 1971–1972

In mid-1971 the administration began a turnabout that dramatically improved its fortunes. Nixon began it in July by announcing that he would visit the People's Republic of China early in 1972. Critics grumbled that the proposed trip was a public relations stunt. Others complained that Chiang Kai-shek was being abandoned—indeed, the General Assembly of the United Nations voted three months later to seat Mao Tse-tung's regime. Still others pointed out that Red China, which felt threatened by the Soviet Union, was simply using the United States, and that the visit would poison American relations with Japan, the most highly industrialized nation in Asia. But most Americans were as pleased as they were surprised by Nixon's announcement. Kissinger's efforts for détente with the great powers were apparently paying off. The Cold War was thawing at last.

A month later Nixon made an equally dramatic announcement: the New Economic Policy. To improve the nation's balance of payments, he said, the United States would permit the dollar to find its own level—to "float" in the international exchange markets. He also called for a 10 percent tax on many imports, the repeal of important excise taxes, and tax breaks for industries that undertook new investment. To bring inflation to a halt, wages, prices, and dividends would be frozen for ninety days, and controlled (in so-called Phase II) thereafter.

Many of Nixon's critics refused to credit him with these policies. His new Secretary of the Treasury John Connally, a Democrat, seemed the more likely initiator. Still, the changes were startling. Permitting the dollar to float in its weakened condition was largely the same as devaluing it. To many Americans this was a rude shock. Establishing controls seemed even more incredible, for Nixon, who had served unhappily as a young lawyer with the Office of Price Administration in World War II, had adamantly rejected such a policy earlier in the year. But if Americans were surprised, they were pleased by the administration's show of resolve—and by the gains that appeared to follow. As the dollar declined in value (eventually by about 9 percent), American exports became cheaper, and the balance of trade seemed to improve. Controls temporarily slowed down the rate of inflation. Stock prices jumped encouragingly, until the Dow Jones industrial average broke 1000 for the first time in history, in November. The President's amazing turnabout was literally paying off.

In the next few months Nixon's economic policy seemed less assured. Even before the introduction of Phase II in November, the government's wage and price commissions began to give way before the pressure of unions and of business interests. Inflation, which controls had checked, began to accelerate again. Disgruntled, the AFL-CIO refused to cooperate any longer in March 1972. For the rest of the year—indeed for the next few years—the rising cost of living became an increasingly vital concern.

But Nixon's pyrotechnic diplomacy in early 1972 helped conceal the faults of his economic policies. His visit to China in February 1972, though accomplishing little that was concrete, was elaborately staged for the American television audience. It greatly enhanced his stature. Kissinger's handling of Moscow was even more dazzling. When North Vietnam mounted an offensive on March 30, Nixon responded by bombing the north for the first time in three years, and by dropping mines in the harbor of Haiphong, a provocative step that not even Johnson had dared to take. Yet the Soviet Union, anxious not to drive the United States and China closer together, posed no objections. On the contrary, it welcomed Nixon with open arms when he visited Moscow in May. In an amiable series of meetings the President and Brezhnev agreed to collaborate on space exploration, to limit deployment of antiballistic missiles, and to freeze offensive missiles for the next five years. The trips to Moscow and Peking marked the high points of the Nixon-Kissinger foreign policy.

By this time the President's campaign for reelection was well underway. Here he took no chances. In 1971 he had already formed the Special Investigations Unit, which placed on its payroll such security "experts" as G. Gordon Liddy, a former Treasury employee, and ex-CIA operatives E. Howard Hunt, Jr., and James McCord, Jr. These "plumbers," outfitted illegally by the CIA, burglarized the office of Daniel Ellsberg's psychiatrist in an unsuccessful attempt to find compromising evidence. In 1971 Nixon had also formed the Committee to Re-elect the President. CREEP disbursed funds for "dirty tricks" aimed at embarrassing potential opponents like Wallace and Muskie. It arranged to tap the phone of the secretary of Lawrence O'Brien, chairman of the Democratic National Committee. And it collected a record $60 million, much of it in violation of existing laws against corporate contributions to political campaigns.

In mapping out his campaign the President had more than the usual amount of luck. Senator Edward Kennedy of Massachusetts, once the most popular Democratic challenger, had seriously harmed his chances in 1969 when he had driven his car off a bridge on the island of Chappaquiddick near Martha's Vineyard. The crash caused the death by drowning of a passenger, Mary Jo Kopechne. Senator Edward Muskie, the front-runner early in 1972, was damaged politically by his tearful response to a letter contrived by a "dirty trickster" in the employ of CREEP and published during the New Hampshire primary. George Wallace, who scored well in Democratic primaries in the North as well as in the South and seriously threatened Nixon's chances in November, was shot on May 15 by a deranged white youth, Arthur H. Bremer. Though Wallace survived, the shots paralyzed him for life and removed him from the presidential race. As it turned out, Wallace's withdrawal practically guaranteed Nixon the election.

As if charmed, the President benefited from disarray within the Democratic party. With Muskie and Wallace out of the race, the two remaining contenders, Senators Hubert Humphrey of Minnesota and George McGovern of South Dakota, traded damaging accusations in the crucial California primary in early June. Though McGovern won, thereby assuring himself the nomination, Humphrey argued persistently that McGovern's economic program—which included giving $1000 to every American—was both costly and tough on the middle class. The charges proved useful to the GOP in the election campaign.

The Democratic convention added to McGovern's problems. Based on a quota system that favored blacks, women, and young people while discriminating against labor unions, urban political machines, congressional leaders, and ethnic groups, the convention alienated the traditional support of the Democratic party and exposed McGovern to the charge that he (like Goldwater in 1964) was the candidate of a lunatic fringe. As if to ensure McGovern's defeat, the delegates nominated as his running mate Senator Thomas Eagleton of Missouri. Eagleton, young, liberal, articulate, then disclosed that he had twice been hospitalized for psychiatric care. Under enormous pressure to reject Eagleton, McGovern at first proclaimed his support of the vice-presidential candidate, only to reverse himself and secure Eagleton's withdrawal. R. Sargent Shriver, a Kennedy brother-in-law who had headed the Peace Corps and the war on poverty, took Eagleton's place. McGovern, whose integrity had been a major asset, now struck many people as indecisive and self-righteous.

In an effort to redeem himself, McGovern moved to the attack. He criticized Nixon's handling of the war, which had caused 15,000 deaths since January 1969. He rapped the administration's economic policies. He charged the President with dropping an antitrust suit against ITT in return for a campaign contribution of $400,000. And he tried to implicate Nixon in a burglary on June 17 of the Democratic National Committee headquarters in Washington's Watergate Hotel.

The Watergate affair, as it became known, deeply worried Nixon, who knew of CREEP's involvement in it. Citing national security reasons, he got Haldeman to stop the FBI from investigating the incident. Later in the campaign he authorized payments of more than $460,000 in hush money to keep Hunt and some of his collaborators from implicating higher-ups in the administration. Publicly, he and other ranking Republicans disclaimed any involvement in the affair. Nixon said inaccurately in late August that his counsel, John Dean, had conducted a "complete investigation" that showed that "no one in the White House staff, no one in this administration, presently

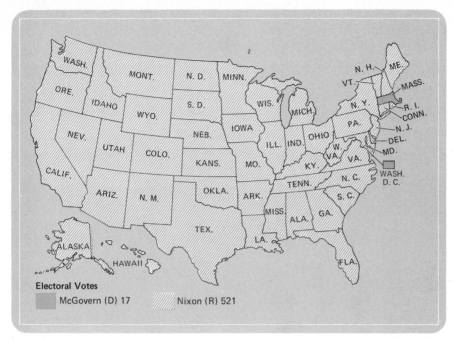

Electoral Votes

McGovern (D) 17   Nixon (R) 521

Election, 1972

employed, was involved in this very bizarre incident." He concluded: "what really hurts in matters of this sort is not the fact that they occur, because over-zealous people in campaigns do things that are wrong. What hurts is if you try to cover them up."

Americans apparently believed such protestations of innocence. Indeed, they had little choice, for the Democrats lacked evidence at the time to implicate the White House. The voters were also impressed with Nixon's conduct of foreign policy. Despite the failures of Vietnamization, troop with-drawals were continuing, and casualty lists, which had shown around 300 American deaths per week in late 1968, totaled near zero by September 1972. A month later, on October 26, Kissinger held a televised press conference to announce a breakthrough in the negotiations he had been conducting with the enemy in Paris. "Peace," he declared grandiloquently, "is at hand."

Kissinger's misleading announcement clinched victory for the team of Nixon and Agnew, which took 47 million votes to 29 million for McGovern and Shriver. This was 60.7 percent of the vote, the highest percentage in modern American history except for that won by Johnson in 1964. Nixon carried every state except Massachusetts and the District of Columbia, for a margin in the electoral college of 521 to 17. Representative John G. Schmitz of California, who headed the American party after Wallace was shot, got only 1.1 million—one-ninth of the total Wallace had received four years earlier. Dr. Spock, who ran on the People's party ticket, won but 74,000. Nixon's critics bravely explained that turnout had been low and pointed out that Democrats still held wide margins in Congress. But it was impossible to deny that the voters had endorsed the President. At least for the time being Nixon was a resounding political success.

Acrimony again, 1973–1975

INTERNATIONAL PROBLEMS

Those who hoped for harmony after the election were immediately disillusioned. Kissinger's forecast of peace, it developed, was inaccurate, primarily because General Thieu refused to agree to the deals the United States and North Vietnam were making without his knowledge. By mid-December the prospects for peace seemed as remote as ever.

Nixon, safely reelected, reacted sharply by authorizing the most savage bombing of North Vietnam in the twelve-year history of American involvement in the war. General Alexander Haig, Kissinger's deputy, described it aptly as the "brutalizing" of the north. Some of the bombs hit a hospital in Hanoi; others damaged a camp holding American prisoners of war. The enemy, better defended than in the past, shot down fifteen B-52 planes (each costing $8 million) and captured ninety-eight American airmen in two weeks.

The resumption of bombing may have achieved its aim: two weeks after starting it Nixon announced peace negotiations would soon resume. At the same time, he stopped the raids. More important in North Vietnam's attitude may have been pressure to settle from Russia and China, both of whom were tired of the war. In any event, the negotiations succeeded in establishing a cease-fire beginning January 28. An agreement signed by the United States, North Vietnam, South Vietnam, and the Vietcong's Provisional Revolutionary Government (PRG) decreed that in the next sixty days America would remove its 23,700 remaining troops, and the enemy would return 509 prisoners of war. The future of Vietnam—left vague—was to be determined by negotiations, not by force.

The agreement brought to an end, after twelve years, the presence of western combat troops in Vietnam. In that time the dead included 56,000 Americans, 5200 allied soldiers, 184,000 South Vietnamese, and an estimated 925,000 North Vietnamese. Approximately five times these numbers were wounded. The total of refugees, and of civilian deaths, in Vietnam, Laos, and Cambodia could only be guessed at—undoubtedly in the millions. In the face of such statistics it is not surprising that many Americans, relieved at the prospect of withdrawal, accepted Nixon's statement that he had bought "peace with honor."

Thoughtful observers knew better. In part because Nixon had secretly assured Thieu of military support in the event of communist gains, South

Desperate Vietnamese refugees try to board an American evacuation plane at Da Nang, April 1975.

Vietnam refused from the start to recognize the PRG, to consider communist participation in a coalition government, or to work earnestly to restrain its combat forces. Faced with this all-or-nothing attitude, the PRG and North Vietnam pressed on for a military solution, and fighting ravaged the country again. In response America dispatched bombing raids over Laos, propped up the deteriorating regime of Lon Nol in Cambodia, and sent billions more in military equipment to sustain Vietnamization. For a time in early 1973 Nixon even considered resuming saturation bombing of North Vietnam, refraining only for fear of domestic turmoil. Russia and China, meanwhile, aided Hanoi and the Vietcong. Knowledgeable onlookers suspected Nixon's secret under-standing with Thieu and knew that the unpopular, repressive regime in Saigon would collapse without American support.

Whether America learned the correct "lessons" from the war also remains to be seen. World War I, after all, had taught the "virtues" of noninvolve-ment; World War II had encouraged globalism. By 1973 Americans seemed fairly sure about two things: first, that they could not protect the whole world; and second, that Southeast Asia should fight its own civil wars. Holding to such views, Congress forbade the President to undertake any military action whatever in Indo-China after August 15, 1973. It also approved, over Nixon's veto, the War Powers Act of 1973. Henceforth the White House would have to give Congress a full explanation within forty-eight hours for the dispatch of

America's mood:
the public's view of the most important
problem facing the country,
according to Gallup Poll results,
1969–1974

1969	Vietnam
1970	Reducing crime
1971	Inflation
1972	Vietnam
1973	High cost of living
1974	Energy crisis

SOURCE: Irish and Frank, *U. S. Foreign Policy*, p. 107

American troops abroad. Presidents must withdraw such troops within sixty days unless Congress specifically authorized them to stay. In 1975, when the administration wanted to intervene again in Cambodia and Vietnam, the War Powers Act stood in its way. As in 1919, the presidential excesses prompted a resurgence of congressional will.

It was too much to expect, however, that the withdrawal of American troops would bring an end to the nation's problems. On the contrary, continuing deficits in the balance of payments resulted in further devaluation of the dollar—this time of 10 percent—by February 1973. Rising inflation forced Nixon to reintroduce price controls, first on petroleum products and meat, and then (in June) on all retail prices. The controls lasted sixty days. On the moral plane, militant Indians on the Oglala Sioux reservation in South Dakota reminded Americans of injustice at home. Rising in anger at Wounded Knee, site of a massacre of Indians eighty-three years before, they seized eleven hostages and demanded redress of their grievances. Federal authorities responded by surrounding the Indians and blocking the flow of food. Before the siege ended eleven weeks later, outbreaks of shooting had killed one Indian and wounded one FBI man. The protracted confrontation settled nothing of consequence.

Withdrawal from Vietnam also failed to deliver the nation from overseas involvements. These became obvious in October 1973, when Israel and the Arab states went to war again. As in 1948, 1956, and 1967, the Israelis showed their military superiority. But this time the Arabs inflicted costly losses on their enemies, and it became clearer than ever that the future of Israel depended on continuing American support. In the next two years Kissinger, who became secretary of state in October 1973, shuttled back and forth to the Middle East in an effort to promote some understanding between the antagonists. Though he made progress with Egypt, he found Israel reluctant at first to return territory gained in the 1967 war. He also could not placate the Palestine Liberation Organization, which represented the million-plus Arabs displaced from their lands in Israel. Meanwhile the Soviet Union continued to provide arms to the Arabs and to persecute Jews at home. Soviet-American détente was quite obviously limited.

The Middle East war had the further effect of drawing the often quarrelsome Arab states closer together. Using oil as a weapon, they cut back on shipments of oil to their enemies, including the United States. Thereafter, they hiked their prices. These actions dramatically exposed the dependence of the industrialized nations on oil—the great powers, one observer cracked, were now the United States, Russia, Saudi Arabia, Kuwait, and Abu Dhabi. The increase in oil prices also caused the most frightening wave of inflation to date throughout the industrialized noncommunist world. Nixon called for voluntary restraint in the use of gasoline and heating oil. But he refused to impose rationing, to investigate high oil company profits, or to develop a long-range policy for the conservation of energy resources. Inflation continued to mount, the stock market to plummet, and the economy to stagnate.

A popular president might have been able to act resourcefully against these problems. But a host of revelations in 1973–74 combined to undermine Nixon's standing. One showed that the CIA had been involved in a military coup in September 1973 that overthrew Chile's Salvador Allende, the Western Hemisphere's first popularly elected Marxist leader. Though the CIA denied

A militant Indian at Wounded Knee, South Dakota, heads through bitter cold to church, March 1973.

Middle East, 1947–1975

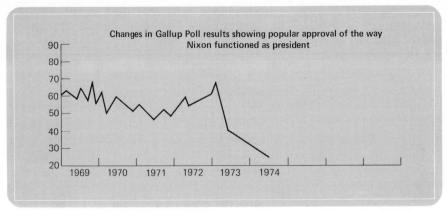

Changes in Gallup Poll results showing popular approval of the way Nixon functioned as president

SOURCE: Adapted from Irish and Frank, *U.S. Foreign Policy*, p. 104, and *Gallup Opinion Index*, no. 111, Sept. 1974, p. 11

Nixon's popularity peaked in late 1969 and early 1973 when 68 percent of respondents approved of his handling the presidency and reached a low of 24 percent shortly before he resigned in 1974.

the charges, other rumors about the agency's excesses placed it also on the defensive. (One such rumor, that the CIA had hired Mafiosi to kill Fidel Castro in 1961, was later confirmed.) Nixon and Kissinger, like most of America's postwar leaders, wanted satellites in the Western Hemisphere.

WATERGATE

Charges of corruption further harmed the administration in 1973–74. In October 1973 Vice-President Agnew, champion of law and order, had to resign when it was revealed that he had cheated on his income taxes and had taken more than $100,000 in payoffs from contractors between 1966 and 1972. The IRS then disclosed that Nixon himself owed more than $400,000 in back taxes and penalties. Other critics showed that CREEP had solicited huge corporate campaign contributions, illegal under the 1972 campaign financing law, that the government had spent millions on improvements to the presidential properties in Florida and California, and that the administration had raised subsidies to milk producers, who thereupon contributed $527,500 to the Republican campaign chest. The trail of corruption surrounding the election was winding dangerously close to the Oval Office.

The President's major problem was the Watergate burglary. Though he did his best to cover up his involvement in the affair, hard-working reporters from the *Washington Post* and other papers gave him no rest. Neither did the Senate Select Committee on Campaign Practices headed by folksy Sam Ervin of North Carolina. Judge John Sirica of the United States district court of the

District of Columbia, which heard the cases of the burglars in early 1973, was perhaps the most persistent of all. Imposing stiff sentences on Hunt, Liddy, McCord, and four others in March, he read a letter from McCord that stated that higher-ups in the administration were involved.

A series of disclosures between April and July of 1973 sustained Sirica's point of view. On April 27 Patrick Gray, who had been acting chief of the FBI since Hoover's death a year earlier, resigned after admitting that he had burned incriminating documents concerning Watergate and related matters. Three days later evidence linking the White House to the cover-up forced the resignations of Haldeman and Erlichman. In May the revelation that the FBI had tapped Daniel Ellsberg's phone conversations in 1969–70 caused the dismissal of the government's case against him involving the Pentagon papers. In June, John Dean, who had turned against his White House associates, testified that the President himself had been involved in the cover-up. And a month later a White House aide revealed that Nixon had taped many of the conversations concerning the affair. This disclosure set off a year-long war in which the Senate, Judge Sirica, and federal prosecutors fought the President for access to the tapes.

Nixon claimed to be appalled by these revelations. On April 30 he appeared on prime time TV to announce the resignations of Haldeman and Erlichman and to emphasize his diligent quest for the facts. Next to him as he spoke were a picture of his family and a bust of Abraham Lincoln. "The easiest course," he explained, "would be for me to blame those to whom I delegated the responsibility to run the campaign. But that would be a cowardly thing to do. . . . In any organization the man at the top must bear the responsibility. . . . I accept it. . . . There can be no whitewash at the White House. . . . I love America. . . . God bless America and God bless each and every one of you."

In an attempt to promote public confidence in his conduct the President brightened the image of his administration. To head the FBI he picked William Ruckelshaus, an Indianan who then headed the Environmental Protection Agency. To run the Justice Department, the prosecuting arm of the government, he named Elliot Richardson, his secretary of defense. Both men had reputations for courage and integrity. The President even accepted Richardson's choice for a special Watergate prosecutor. This was Archibald Cox, a Harvard law professor. Cox, Nixon said, would have full cooperation from the White House.

When Cox insisted on going to court for the tapes, however, Nixon demanded that Richardson fire him. Claiming executive privilege, the President added that he would personally edit a summary of the transcripts. Richardson, refusing to do Nixon's bidding, resigned in late October. Ruckelshaus, who had become Richardson's deputy, agreed with Richardson, and was fired. The solicitor general, next in command at the Justice Department, then discharged Cox. In the ensuing uproar, Nixon felt compelled to yield some of the tapes, to name a new special prosecutor, Leon Jaworski of Texas, and to tell the public over TV, "I am not a crook." But he refused to give up all the tapes, and Jaworski, as tenacious as Cox, kept up the legal struggle in late 1973 and early 1974.

During this time the President continued to profess his innocence. On April 29, 1974 he appeared on TV again to announce that he was releasing transcripts of the tapes. These, he said, "will at last, once and for all, show that what I knew and what I did with regard to the Watergate cover-up were just as I described them to you from the very beginning." On other occasions he angrily blamed the press for his dilemma and insisted that impeachment, which the House Judiciary Committee began considering seriously in May 1974, would "jeopardize" world peace and endanger the American political system. As if to prove his indispensability, he toured the Middle East and Moscow in June and July. Though he attracted sizeable crowds, he accomplished little, in part because the Watergate affair was undermining his effectiveness abroad as well as at home. "Every negotiation," Kissinger said later, "was getting more and more difficult because it involved the question of whether we could, in fact, carry out what we were negotiating."

By this time the pressure on Nixon to release all the tapes was overwhelming. But Nixon had good reason to refuse such requests, because between

The cartoonist Herblock comments on Watergate, 1973.

May 5 and 7, 1974, he had listened carefully to them himself. He knew then, if not long before, that they proved his obstruction of justice. Accordingly, he cited "executive privilege" and national security as his reasons for keeping the recordings. His lawyers, none of whom were told the facts, were instructed to resist Jaworski's requests for the tapes and to appeal the matter to the Supreme Court.

On July 24 a unanimous Court gave its answer. It agreed that a president could withhold "military, diplomatic, or sensitive national security material." To this extent executive privilege gained explicit judicial sanction for the first time. But the judges went on to insist that the Court, not the president, had the right to "say what the law is," and that the Watergate affair, a criminal proceeding, did not involve "national security." The claim for executive privilege, therefore, had to "yield to the demonstrated, specific need for

I have discovered that according to a secret tape of June 23, 1972, I AM a crook.

evidence in a pending criminal trial," and the President must turn over "forthwith" the sixty-four recordings demanded by his foes. Judge Sirica could listen to the tapes and release relevant portions to Jaworski, who would be free to give them to Congress.

A few days later the House Judiciary Committee acted against the President by voting to impeach him on three counts. The first, passed twenty-seven to eleven, charged him with obstruction of justice. Nixon, the committee said, had made or caused to be made false statements, withheld relevant and material evidence, interfered with investigations by the FBI, the Justice Department, special prosecutors, and Congress, approved the payment of hush money to witnesses, and lied to the American people. The second charge, approved twenty-eight to ten, accused Nixon of abusing his presidential authority by resorting to illegal wiretapping and by using the FBI, CIA, and Internal Revenue Service against American citizens. A third charge hit him for refusing to turn over the tapes, after receiving a congressional subpoena, to the committee.

Some of the President's friends were consoled by the failure of the committee to approve two other articles of impeachment. One concerned his secret bombing of Cambodia in 1969–70; the other accused him of enriching himself with public funds while president. But most observers recognized that the three other charges were damaging enough to Nixon's standing. The committee, indeed, had deliberated long and responsibly, and its concluding debates, carried on radio and TV, did much to restore faith in Congress as an institution. There was little doubt that the House would endorse the committee's conclusions by wide margins. If the Senate could corral a two-thirds majority for conviction—and that seemed entirely possible—Nixon would have to leave office.

After these developments, some of Nixon's supporters called on him to resign immediately. His opponents feared that he would try to destroy the tapes rather than turn them over to Sirica. Nixon followed neither course. Instead, he procrastinated until August 5, when he finally released the tapes that proved his involvement in the cover-up. He admitted that he had concealed them, even from his own lawyers, but insisted that he had done nothing to warrant conviction by the Senate.

The Senate clearly disagreed. So did the American people, who felt betrayed by the President's lies over the previous twenty-six months. In the next few days Republicans as well as Democrats indicated they would vote for conviction. Deprived of support, the President resigned on August 9, 1974. Vice-president Gerald Ford of Michigan, whom Nixon had appointed to succeed Agnew earlier in the year, was immediately sworn in as the next president.

Nixon's resignation, while welcomed by many people at home and abroad, enabled him to avoid the Senate trial that might have established clearly the extent of his involvement in the Watergate affair. Worse, it left many questions unanswered. What self-incriminating documents had the administration hoped to steal at Watergate? Also, suppose Nixon had never taped the conversations? Having done so, suppose he had destroyed the tapes, along with logs that showed what they contained? What if some future president, having committed some egregious act, concealed such misconduct by claiming executive privilege based on the existence of "military, diplomatic, or sensitive national security material?" Such questions suggested that future presidents might still find ways of acting above the law. The imperial presidency, which the founding fathers had feared—and which twentieth-century chief executives from TR on had done so much to create—might again endanger constitutional processes and lead to paralysis of the state.

Subsequent disclosures did little to dispel such fears. These disclosures revealed a new kind of corruption. The men around Grant, Harding, and other scandal-stained presidents had acted primarily for financial gain. Many of Nixon's criminal subordinates, however, truly believed that their ends—defined as everything from reelection of the President to the maintenance of world peace—justified the means. They had no qualms about subverting democratic institutions and civil liberties. Colson, Nixon's counsel, had exclaimed, "for the President I would walk over my grandmother if necessary." Liddy added that Watergate was "an intelligence-gathering operation of one group of persons who were seeking to retain power against another group of persons who were seeking to acquire power. That's all it was. It's like brushing your teeth. It's basic." Defending the cover-up, CREEP director Magruder added that "after the Democrats nominated Senator McGovern, we felt that we were protecting the honorable peace that the President was bringing to Vietnam. . . . We were not covering up a burglary, we were safeguarding world peace." He concluded, "we wanted to win the election and we wanted to win it big. Just as a corporation wants to dominate its market, our reelection committee wanted to dominate that year's election. . . . We were past the point of halfway measures or gentlemanly tactics."

In the aftermath of Watergate

The resignation of Nixon brought to the fore problems that excitement over Watergate had helped to obscure. Most of the afflictions that had troubled the nation in the twentieth century—racial injustice, urban blight, economic inequality, sex discrimination, oppression of Indians and Hispanic-Americans—remained serious. Still more pressing at the time were inflation, which was increasing at the rate of 14 percent per year in late 1974, recession, which caused the GNP to fall 9 percent in the last quarter of 1974, instability in the Middle East, and the collapse—which became complete in April 1975—of the regimes of Lon Nol and General Thieu. The fall of Phnom Penh, Cambodia's capital, took place as President Ford and 100,000 others commemorated the

President Gerald Ford delivers his first state of the union address to Congress, January 1975. Vice-President Nelson Rockefeller sits behind him.

battles of Lexington and Concord 200 years earlier. The shots that had been heard 'round the world were losing their force.

Americans worried about the capacity of their new leaders to deal with these problems. In his lengthy political career Ford had shown little interest in fighting urban or racial problems. He was largely uninformed concerning fiscal policy. Confronted with recession, he insisted at first on tax increases and other deflationary measures that would have worsened the situation. He was handicapped also by his lack of a popular mandate. Both he and his new vice-president, former Governor Nelson Rockefeller of New York, were Republicans facing the most aroused and self-assertive Democratic Congresses in recent memory. Thanks to the Twenty-fifth Amendment (1967), which authorized presidents to nominate (and Congress to confirm) vice-presidents, both men were nonelective officials. The United States, which had done so much to advance the cause of political democracy 200 years earlier, would have to wait more than 2 years before being governed by a president chosen by popular vote.

President Ford then compounded doubts about his ability by pardoning his predecessor. He did so, he said, because he wanted people to forget the recent past and because Nixon had suffered enough. A few weeks later, when Nixon almost died after an operation on his leg for phlebitis, Ford's compassion seemed appropriate. Whether the pardon was proper was another matter. Men like Erlichman, Haldeman, Mitchell, Dean, and Magruder—and many lesser officials—were either in jail or appealing convictions for crimes ranging from perjury to obstruction of justice. These people, like many Americans, wondered about the fairness of a system that punished the little fish while the shark escaped scot-free. Americans found it equally impossible to forget the deceit and hypocrisy that had contaminated governmental institutions since the mid-1960s. As one magazine phrased it earlier, the United States seemed to have swung half circle in the 200 years of its existence: "from George Washington, who could not tell a lie, to Richard Nixon, who could not tell the truth."

As if to register their alienation, the voters showed little interest in the off-year elections of 1974. Democrats gained throughout the nation. But only 45 percent of eligible voters cast their ballots. In a nation supposedly governed by popular majorities, this was hardly encouraging. The turnout of youth was especially poor: only 21 percent of people aged eighteen to twenty bothered to vote. Students, indeed, seemed amazingly quiescent in contrast to a few years earlier. With the economy deteriorating they worried about finding jobs or getting into graduate schools, and seldom engaged in sustained protest. The historian C. Vann Woodward commented, "Rarely in history has publicized activism been replaced so rapidly by apparent apathy, student dissent by silence."

Many Americans in the mid-1970s shared the students' worries about the future. Though the nation was calmer than it had been in the turbulent years of the late 1960s, no one could be confident that domestic tranquility would last. Some observers feared that the approach of zero population growth, for the first time in American history, signaled not only the end of economic expansion but also a more general loss of confidence. The last frontiers, it appeared, had been conquered; it was time to consolidate and pull back. Others, lamenting the continuing coexistence of inflation and recession, foresaw increasing government control over a stagnant economy. Robert Lekachman, a respected economist, wrote, "I think we are entering a long period of slower growth. I take seriously the resource scarcities. We've reached the end of cheap energy. . . . The prospects for improvement in the American standard of life thus are much less than they've been."

Reflecting these doubts, many observers concluded that the nation was becoming a "business civilization" like that of the 1920s: materialistic, hollow, lacking in securely held values or sense of purpose beyond individual self-aggrandizement. The rise of such a society, critics said, exposed the mixed blessings of modernization, which had unleashed a revolution in expectations along with economic growth and technological progress. Restless, cranky, divided, Americans seemed psychologically unfulfilled and impossible to satisfy.

American foreign policy gave special cause for concern. In 1975 the United States operated a defense budget of $104 billion—an increase of $15 billion over the amount needed during the years of involvement in Vietnam in 1972–74. America also sold arms to more than 130 countries and maintained military commitments with forty nations. Most of these forty were NATO or Latin American countries. Other commitments included South Korea, a repressive dictatorship, Japan, Taiwan, the Philippines, Australia, and New Zealand. Two danger zones, West Berlin and Israel, were not covered by treaty, but appeared to be integral parts of America's worldwide defense perimeter. With naval vessels circling the globe, planes ever in the air, 8500 strategic nuclear weapons in full deployment, and more than 400,000 troops stationed overseas in the cause of Pax Americana, the once uncommitted United States ran the risk of constant military involvement.

The Ford administration quickly showed its readiness to use part of this formidable arsenal. In May 1975 Cambodia captured the *Mayaguez,* an American merchant vessel sailing near its shores. When the anti-American government of Cambodia was slow to answer United States protests, Ford authorized an attack by 350 marines on Koh Tang, a nearby island where the crew was wrongly believed to be held. The assault, accompanied by bombing in Cambodia, marked a heavy overreaction to a minor incident. It cost the United States fifteen dead, three missing, and fifty wounded. It was probably unnecessary, for Cambodia was in the process of returning both ship and crew at the time. But many Americans exulted in Ford's show of steel. The incident suggested that they cared little for consultation, that they had learned almost nothing from ten years of trauma over Vietnam, and that deep down they were a little like schoolyard bullies—afraid, uncertain, and insecure.

It was nonetheless possible in the mid-1970s to contemplate the future with guarded optimism. Whatever the President's faults, he appeared honest and open. Some people hailed him as a Republican Harry Truman. Ford also proved willing to compromise. When Congress rebuffed his conservative economic policies in late 1974, he reversed himself to favor a multibillion-dollar tax cut, an increase in unemployment benefits, and a thoroughly Keynesian budget that envisaged a deficit of $52 billion. His turnabout did little to arrest inflation—it may in fact have made it a little worse—and it failed to end the worst recession since the 1930s. Unemployment, hovering at around 9 per cent in 1975 (affecting more than eight million people) had not been so high since 1940. Still, Ford's flexibility relieved observers who had feared a return to Hooverism. Congress acted quickly to expand on his proposals.

Americans with a sense of history also recognized that the strife of the immediate past had brought progress as well as pain. Indeed, it may be that conflict necessarily accompanies progressive social change. The forces of technology, industrialization, and economic growth had made the nation incomparably richer than it had been in 1776, or—more to the point—than in 1940 or 1960. The civil rights revolution had brought the most impressive gains

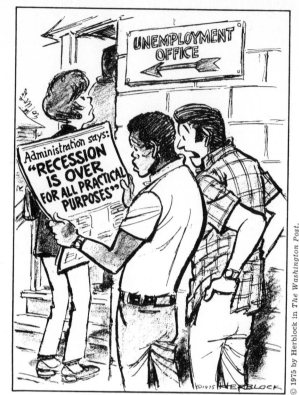

It's just that they don't consider us a practical purpose.

© 1975 by Herblock in *The Washington Post.*

for blacks since emancipation. Supreme Court decisions had broadened the civil rights and civil liberties of the people. The Cold War, with its attendant threat of nuclear catastrophe, had softened. The country's political institutions, apparently so flawed, had remained stable under pressure of war, assassinations, and incomparable presidential abuse. The virtues of a free press, an independent judiciary, and an alert Congress had rarely been so clearly revealed. For all the nation's problems, it had withstood a public airing of its deficiencies that would have disrupted many other countries in the world. For these and some other blessings the United States could take cautious pride.

Suggestions for reading

Books on Richard Nixon include Earl Mazo and Stephen Hess, *Nixon: A Political Portrait** (1968); Jules Witcover, *The Resurrection of Richard Nixon* (1970), which covers the years of 1960–68; Gary Wills, *Nixon Agonistes** (1970); Bruce Mazlish, *In Search of Nixon** (1971), a psychological inquiry; and Rowland Evans and Robert Novak, *Nixon in the White House** (1971), the best account of the first two years of his presidency. Other books that deal with politics and policies of the 1970s are Leonard Silk, *Nixonomics** (1972); Jules Witcover, *White Knight: The Rise of Spiro Agnew* (1972); Robert S. Ansom, *McGovern* (1972); Richard Harris, *Decision* (1971), on the Carswell nomination; and Daniel Moynihan, *Politics of a Guaranteed National Income** (1973).

Important books on political trends include Walter Dean Burnham, *Critical Elections and the Mainstream of American Politics** (1972), a stimulating analysis of twentieth-century developments; Walter De Vries and V. L. Torrance, *The Ticket Splitters* (1972); Samuel Lubell, *The Hidden Crisis in American Politics** (1970); Frederick G. Dutton, *The Changing Sources of Power* (1971); and David S. Broder, *The Party's Over** (1972). See also Theodore White, *Making of a President, 1972** (1973); Kevin Phillips, *The Emerging Republican Majority** (1969); and Richard Scammon and Ben Wattenberg, *The Real Majority** (1970). Among the books on Watergate are Carl Bernstein and Bob Woodward, *All the President's Men** (1974), a devastating account by two *Washington Post* reporters; and Raoul Berger, *Impeachment: The Constitutional Problems* (1974).

Sources for foreign policy include Henry Brandon, *The Retreat of American Power* (1973); David Landau, *Kissinger* (1972); R. W. Tucker, *The Radical Left and American Foreign Policy** (1971); and Arthur Schlesinger, Jr., *The Imperial Presidency* (1973), which narrates the impact of foreign policy on the executive branch. See also V. Brodine and Mark Seldon, eds., *Open Secret: The Nixon-Kissinger Doctrine in Asia* (1972); Lloyd Gardner, ed., *The Great Nixon Turnaround* (1973); Morton Halperin, *Defense Strategies for the Seventies* (1971); Leonard Mosley, *Power Play* (1973), on oil companies in the Middle East; and Adam Yarmolinsky, *The Military Establishment: Its Impact on American Society* (1971).

Domestic unrest in the 1970s is the subject of many books, including J. A. Michener, *Kent State: What Happened and Why* (1973); I. F. Stone, *Killings at Kent State* (1971); George Jackson, *Soledad Brother: The Prison Letters of George Jackson* (1970); Tom Wicker, *A Time to Die* (1975), on the Attica riot; Ramsey Clark, *Crime in America* (1970); and Robert C. Wood, *The Necessary Majority: Middle America and the Urban Crisis* (1972). An important book dealing with the growth of corporate power is J. K. Galbraith, *The New Industrial State** (1971).

Among the books that focus on environmental issues are Paul Erlich, *Population Bomb** (1968); Barry Commoner, *The Closing Circle** (1971); Garrett De Bell, ed., *The Environmental Handbook* (1970); and R. F. Buckhorn, *Nader: The People's Lawyer* (1972). See also Emma Rothschild, *Paradise Lost: The Decline of the Auto-Industrial Age* (1973).

Unrest among American Indians is the subject of: A. M. Josephy, ed., *Red Power** (1971); Stan Steiner, *The New Indians** (1968); and Sar Levitan and Barbara Hetrick, *Big Brother's Indian Programs** (1971).

The Constitution
of the
United States
of America

We the people of the United States, in Order to form a more perfect Union, establish Justice, insure domestic Tranquility, provide for the common defence, promote the general Welfare, and secure the Blessings of Liberty to ourselves and our Posterity, do ordain and establish this Constitution for the United States of America.

ARTICLE I

Section 1. All legislative Powers herein granted shall be vested in a Congress of the United States, which shall consist of a Senate and House of Representatives.

Section 2. The House of Representatives shall be composed of Members chosen every second Year by the People of the several States, and the Electors in each State shall have the Qualifications requisite for Electors of the most numerous Branch of the State Legislature.

No Person shall be a Representative who shall not have attained to the Age of twenty-five Years, and been seven Years a Citizen of the United States, and who shall not, when elected, be an Inhabitant of that state in which he shall be chosen.

[Representatives and direct Taxes shall be apportioned among the several States which may be included within this Union, according to their respective Numbers, which shall be determined by adding to the whole Number of free Persons, including those bound to Service for a Term of Years, and excluding Indians not taxed, three fifths of all other Persons.][1] The actual Enumeration shall be made within three Years after the first Meeting of the Congress of the United States, and within every subsequent Term of ten Years, in such Manner as they shall by Law direct. The Number of Representatives shall not exceed one for every thirty Thousand, but each State shall have at Least one Representative; and until such enumeration shall be made, the State of New Hampshire shall be entitled to chuse three, Massachusetts eight, Rhode Island and Providence Plantations one, Connecticut five, New-York six, New Jersey four, Pennsylvania eight, Delaware one, Maryland six, Virginia ten, North

The Constitution and all amendments are shown in their original form. Parts that have been amended or superseded are bracketed and explained in the footnotes.

[1]Modified by the Fourteenth and Sixteenth amendments.

Carolina five, South Carolina five, and Georgia three.

When vacancies happen in the Representation from any State, the Executive Authority thereof shall issue Writs of Election to fill such Vacancies.

The House of Representatives shall chuse their Speaker and other Officers; and shall have the sole Power of Impeachment.

Section 3. The Senate of the United States shall be composed of two Senators from each State, [chosen by the Legislature thereof,][2] for six Years; and each Senator shall have one Vote.

Immediately after they shall be assembled in Consequence of the first Election, they shall be divided as equally as may be into three Classes. The Seats of the Senators of the first Class shall be vacated at the Expiration of the second Year, of the Second Class at the Expiration of the fourth Year, and of the third Class at the Expiration of the sixth Year, so that one-third may be chosen every second Year; [and if Vacancies happen by Resignation, or otherwise, during the Recess of the Legislature of any State, the Executive thereof may make temporary Appointments until the next Meeting of the Legislature, which shall then fill such Vacancies].[3]

No Person shall be a Senator who shall not have attained to the Age of thirty Years, and been nine Years a Citizen of the United States, and who shall not, when elected, be an Inhabitant of that State in which he shall be chosen.

The Vice-President of the United States shall be President of the Senate, but shall have no vote, unless they be equally divided.

The Senate shall chuse their other Officers, and also a President pro tempore, in the absence of the Vice-President, or when he shall exercise the Office of the President of the United States.

The Senate shall have the sole Power to try all Impeachments. When sitting for that purpose, they shall be on Oath or Affirmation. When the President of the United States is tried, the Chief Justice shall preside. And no person shall be convicted without the Concurrence of two thirds of the Members present.

Judgment in Cases of Impeachment shall not extend further than to removal from Office, and disqualification to hold and enjoy any Office of honor, Trust, or Profit under the United States: but the Party convicted shall nevertheless be liable and subject to Indictment, Trial, Judgment, and Punishment, according to Law.

Section 4. The Times, Places and Manner of holding Elections for Senators and Representatives, shall be prescribed in each state by the Legislature thereof; but the Congress may at any time by Law make or alter such Regulations, except as to the Places of Chusing Senators.

The Congress shall assemble at least once in every Year, and such Meeting shall [be on the first Monday in December,][4] unless they shall by Law appoint a different Day.

Section 5. Each House shall be the Judge of the Elections, Returns and Qualifications of its own Members, and a Majority of each shall constitute a Quorum to do Business; but a smaller number may adjourn from day to day, and may be authorized to compel the Attendance of absent Members, in such Manner, and under such Penalties, as each House may provide.

Each House may determine the Rules of its Proceedings, punish its Members for disorderly Behavior, and, with the Concurrence of two thirds, expel a Member.

Each House shall keep a Journal of its Proceedings, and from time to time publish the same, excepting such Parts as may in their Judgment require Secrecy; and the Yeas and Nays of the Members of either House on any question shall, at the Desire of one fifth of those Present, be entered on the Journal.

Neither House, during the Session of Congress, shall, without the Consent of the other, adjourn for more than three days, nor to any other Place than that in which the two Houses shall be sitting.

[2]Superseded by the Seventeenth Amendment.
[3]Modified by the Seventeenth Amendment.

[4]Superseded by the Twentieth Amendment.

Section 6. The Senators and Representatives shall receive a Compensation for their Services, to be ascertained by Law, and paid out of the Treasury of the United States. They shall in all Cases, except Treason, Felony, and Breach of the Peace, be privileged from Arrest during their Attendance at the Session of their respective Houses, and in going to and returning from the same; and for any Speech or Debate in either House, they shall not be questioned in any other Place.

No Senator or Representative shall, during the Time for which he was elected, be appointed to any civil Office under the Authority of the United States, which shall have been created, or the Emoluments whereof shall have been increased, during such time; and no Person holding any Office under the United States shall be a Member of either House during his continuance in Office.

Section 7. All Bills for raising Revenue shall originate in the House of Representatives; but the Senate may propose or concur with Amendments as on other bills.

Every Bill which shall have passed the House of Representatives and the Senate, shall, before it become a Law, be presented to the President of the United States; If he approve he shall sign it, but if not he shall return it, with his Objections, to that House in which it shall have originated, who shall enter the Objections at large on their Journal, and proceed to reconsider it. If after such Reconsideration two thirds of that House shall agree to pass the bill, it shall be sent, together with the objections, to the other House, by which it shall likewise be reconsidered, and if approved by two thirds of that House, it shall become a Law. But in all such Cases the Votes of both Houses shall be determined by Yeas and Nays, and the names of the Persons voting for and against the Bill shall be entered on the Journal of each House respectively. If any Bill shall not be returned by the President within ten Days (Sundays excepted) after it shall have been presented to him, the Same shall be a Law, in like Manner as if he had signed it, unless the Congress by their Adjournment prevent its Return, in which Case it shall not be a Law.

Every Order, Resolution, or Vote to which the Concurrence of the Senate and House of Representatives may be necessary (except on a question of Adjournment) shall be presented to the President of the United States; and before the Same shall take Effect, shall be approved by him, or being disapproved by him, shall be repassed by two thirds of the Senate and House of Representatives, according to the Rules and Limitations prescribed in the Case of a Bill.

Section 8. The Congress shall have Power To Lay and collect Taxes, Duties, Imposts and Excises, to pay the Debts and provide for the common Defence and general Welfare of the United States; but all Duties, Imposts and Excises shall be uniform throughout the United States;

To borrow money on the credit of the United States;

To regulate Commerce with foreign Nations, and among the several States, and with the Indian Tribes;

To establish an uniform Rule of Naturalization, and uniform Laws on the subject of Bankruptcies throughout the United States;

To coin Money, regulate the Value thereof, and of foreign Coin, and fix the Standard of Weights and Measures;

To Provide for the Punishment of counterfeiting the Securities and current Coin of the United States;

To establish Post Offices and post Roads;

To promote the Progress of Science and useful Arts, by securing for limited Times to Authors and Inventors the exclusive Right to their respective Writings and Discoveries;

To constitute Tribunals inferior to the Supreme Court;

To define and punish Piracies and Felonies committed on the high Seas, and Offenses against the Law of Nations;

To declare War, grant Letters of Marque and Reprisal, and make Rules concerning Captures on Land and Water;

To raise and support Armies, but no Appropriation of Money to that Use shall be for a longer Term than two Years;

To provide and maintain a Navy;

To make Rules for the Government and Regulation of the land and naval forces;

To provide for calling forth the Militia to execute the Laws of the Union, suppress Insurrections and repel Invasions;

To provide for organizing, arming, and disciplining the Militia, and for governing such Part of them as may be employed in the Service of the United States, reserving to the States respectively, the Appointment of the Officers, and the Authority of training the Militia according to the discipline prescribed by Congress;

To exercise exclusive Legislation in all Cases whatsoever, over such District (not exceeding ten Miles square) as may, by Cession of particular States, and the acceptance of Congress, become the Seat of the Government of the United States, and to exercise like Authority over all Places purchased by the Consent of the Legislature of the State in which the Same shall be, for the Erection of Forts, Magazines, Arsenals, dock-Yards, and other needful Buildings;—And

To make all Laws which shall be necessary and proper for carrying into Execution the foregoing Powers, and all other Powers vested by this Constitution in the Government of the United States, or in any Department or Officer thereof.

Section 9. The Migration or Importation of such Persons as any of the States now existing shall think proper to admit shall not be prohibited by the Congress prior to the Year one thousand eight hundred and eight, but a tax or duty may be imposed on such Importation, not exceeding ten dollars for each Person.

The privilege of the Writ of Habeas Corpus shall not be suspended, unless when in Cases of Rebellion or Invasion the public Safety may require it.

No Bill of Attainder or ex post facto Law shall be passed.

[No capitation, or other direct, Tax shall be laid unless in Proportion to the Census or Enumeration herein before directed to be taken.][5]

[5]Modified by the Sixteenth Amendment.

No Tax or Duty shall be laid on Articles exported from any State.

No Preference shall be given by any Regulation of Revenue to the Ports of one State over those of another: nor shall Vessels bound to, or from, one State, be obliged to enter, clear, or pay Duties in another.

No Money shall be drawn from the Treasury, but in Consequence of Appropriations made by Law; and a regular Statement and Account of the Receipts and Expenditures of all public Money shall be published from time to time.

No Title of Nobility shall be granted by the United States: And no Person holding any Office of Profit or Trust under them, shall, without the Consent of the Congress, accept of any present, Emolument, Office, or Title, of any kind whatever, from any King, Prince, or foreign State.

Section 10. No State shall enter into any Treaty, Alliance, or Confederation; grant Letters of Marque and Reprisal; coin Money; emit Bills of Credit; make any Thing but gold and silver Coin a Tender in Payment of Debts; pass any Bill of Attainder, ex post facto Law, or Law impairing the Obligation of Contracts, or grant any title of Nobility.

No State shall, without the Consent of the Congress, lay any Imposts or Duties on Imports or Exports, except what may be absolutely necessary for executing its inspection Laws: and the net Produce of all Duties and Imposts, laid by any State on Imports or Exports, shall be for the Use of the Treasury of the United States; and all such Laws shall be subject to the Revision and Control of the Congress.

No State shall, without the Consent of Congress, lay any duty of Tonnage, keep Troops, or Ships of War in time of Peace, enter into any Agreement or Compact with another State, or with a foreign Power, or engage in War, unless actually invaded, or in such imminent Danger as will not admit of delay.

ARTICLE II

Section 1. The executive Power shall be vested in a President of the United States of

America. He shall hold his Office during the Term of four years, and, together with the Vice-President, chosen for the same Term, be elected, as follows:

Each State shall appoint, in such Manner as the Legislature thereof may direct, a Number of Electors, equal to the whole Number of Senators and Representatives to which the State may be entitled in the Congress: but no Senator or Representative, or Person holding an Office of Trust or Profit under the United States, shall be appointed an Elector.

[The Electors shall meet in their respective States, and vote by Ballot for two persons, of whom one at least shall not be an Inhabitant of the same State with themselves. And they shall make a List of all the Persons voted for, and of the Number of Votes for each; which List they shall sign and certify, and transmit sealed to the Seat of the Government of the United States, directed to the President of the Senate. The President of the Senate shall, in the Presence of the Senate and House of Representatives, open all the Certificates, and the Votes shall then be counted. The Person having the greatest Number of Votes shall be the President, if such Number be a Majority of the whole Number of Electors appointed; and if there be more than one who have such Majority, and have an equal Number of Votes, then the House of Representatives shall immediately chuse by Ballot one of them for President; and if no Person have a Majority, then from the five highest on the List the said House shall in like Manner chuse the President. But in chusing the President, the Votes shall be taken by States, the Representation from each State having one Vote; a quorum for this Purpose shall consist of a Member or Members from two-thirds of the States, and a Majority of all the States shall be necessary to a Choice. In every Case, after the Choice of the President, the Person having the greatest Number of Votes of the Electors shall be the Vice-President. But if there should remain two or more who have equal votes, the Senate shall chuse from them by Ballot the Vice-President.][6]

The Congress may determine the Time of chusing the Electors, and the Day on which they shall give their Votes; which Day shall be the same throughout the United States.

No person except a natural-born Citizen, or a Citizen of the United States, at the time of the Adoption of this Constitution, shall be eligible to the Office of President; neither shall any Person be eligible to that Office who shall not have attained to the Age of thirty-five years, and been fourteen Years a Resident within the United States.

[In Case of the Removal of the President from Office, or of his Death, Resignation, or Inability to discharge the Powers and Duties of the said Office, the same shall devolve on the Vice-President, and the Congress may by Law provide for the Case of Removal, Death, Resignation, or Inability, both of the President and Vice-President, declaring what Officer shall then act as President, and such Officer shall act accordingly, until the disability be removed, or a President shall be elected.][7]

The President shall, at stated Times, receive for his Services a Compensation, which shall neither be increased nor diminished during the Period for which he shall have been elected, and he shall not receive within that Period any other Emolument from the United States, or any of them.

Before he enter on the execution of his Office, he shall take the following Oath or Affirmation:—"I do solemnly swear (or affirm) that I will faithfully execute the Office of President of the United States, and will, to the best of my Ability, preserve, protect, and defend the Constitution of the United States."

Section 2. The President shall be Commander in Chief of the Army and Navy of the United States, and of the Militia of the several States, when called into the actual Service of the United States; he may require the Opinion, in writing, of the principal Officer in each of the executive Departments, upon any subject relating to the Duties of their respective Offices, and he shall have Power to Grant Reprieves and

[6]Superseded by the Twelfth Amendment.

[7]Modified by the Twenty-fifth Amendment.

Pardons for Offenses against the United States, except in Cases of Impeachment.

He shall have Power, by and with the Advice and Consent of the Senate, to make Treaties, provided two thirds of the Senators present concur; and he shall nominate, and by and with the Advice and Consent of the Senate, shall appoint Ambassadors, other public Ministers and Consuls, Judges of the supreme Court, and all other Officers of the United States, whose Appointments are not herein otherwise provided for, and which shall be established by Law: but the Congress may by Law vest the Appointment of such inferior Officers, as they think proper, in the President alone, in the Courts of Law, or in the Heads of Departments.

The President shall have Power to fill up all Vacancies that may happen during the Recess of the Senate, by granting Commissions which shall expire at the End of their next Session.

Section 3. He shall from time to time give to the Congress Information of the State of the Union, and recommend to their Consideration such Measures as he shall judge necessary and expedient; he may, on extraordinary occasions, convene both Houses, or either of them, and in Case of Disagreement between them, with respect to the Time of Adjournment, he may adjourn them to such Time as he shall think proper; he shall receive Ambassadors and other public Ministers; he shall take Care that the Laws be faithfully executed, and shall Commission all the Officers of the United States.

Section 4. The President, Vice-President and all civil Officers of the United States, shall be removed from Office on Impeachment for, and Conviction of, Treason, Bribery, or other high Crimes and Misdemeanors.

ARTICLE III

Section 1. The judicial Power of the United States, shall be vested in one supreme Court, and in such inferior Courts as the Congress may from time to time ordain and establish. The Judges, both of the supreme and inferior Courts, shall hold their Offices during good Behaviour, and shall, at stated Times, receive for their Services, a Compensation, which shall not be diminished during their Continuance in Office.

Section 2. The judicial Power shall extend to all Cases, in Law and Equity, arising under this Constitution, the Laws of the United States, and treaties made, or which shall be made, under their Authority;—to all Cases affecting ambassadors, other public ministers and consuls;—to all cases of admiralty and maritime Jurisdiction;—to Controversies to which the United States shall be a Party;—to Controversies between two or more States;— [between a State and Citizens of another State;]—between Citizens of different States, —between Citizens of the same State claiming Lands under Grants of different States, and between a State, or the Citizens thereof, and foreign States, Citizens or Subjects.

In all Cases affecting Ambassadors, other public Ministers and Consuls, and those in which a State shall be Party, the supreme Court shall have original Jurisdiction. In all the other Cases before mentioned, the supreme Court shall have appellate Jurisdiction, both as to Law and Fact, with such Exceptions, and under such Regulations as the Congress shall make.

The trial of all Crimes, except in Cases of Impeachment, shall be by Jury; and such Trial shall be held in the State where the said Crimes shall have been committed; but when not committed within any State, the Trial shall be at such Place or Places as the Congress may by Law have directed.

Section 3. Treason against the United States, shall consist only in levying War against them, or in adhering to their Enemies, giving them Aid and Comfort. No Person shall be convicted of Treason unless on the Testimony of two Witnesses to the same overt Act, or on Confession in open Court.

The Congress shall have power to declare the Punishment of Treason but no Attainder of Treason shall work Corruption of Blood, or Forfeiture except during the Life of the Person attainted.

[8]Modified by the Eleventh Amendment.

ARTICLE IV

Section 1. Full Faith and Credit shall be given in each State to the public Acts, Records, and judicial Proceedings of every other State. And the Congress may by general Laws prescribe the Manner in which such Acts, Records and Proceedings shall be proved, and the Effect thereof.

Section 2. The Citizens of each State shall be entitled to all Privileges and Immunities of Citizens in the several States.

A Person charged in any State with Treason, Felony, or other Crime, who shall flee from Justice, and be found in another State, shall on demand of the executive Authority of the State from which he fled, be delivered up, to be removed to the State having Jurisdiction of the crime.

[No Person held to service or Labour in one State, under the Laws thereof, escaping into another, shall, in Consequence of any Law or Regulation therein, be discharged from such Service or Labour, but shall be delivered up on Claim of the Party to whom such Service or Labour may be due.][9]

Section 3. New States may be admitted by the Congress into this Union; but no new State shall be formed or erected within the Jurisdiction of any other State; nor any State be formed by the Junction of two or more States, or parts of States, without the Consent of the Legislatures of the States concerned as well as of the Congress.

The Congress shall have Power to dispose of and make all needful Rules and Regulations respecting the Territory or other Property belonging to the United States; and nothing in this Constitution shall be so construed as to Prejudice any Claims of the United States, or of any particular State.

Section 4. The United States shall guarantee to every State in this Union a Republican Form of Government and shall protect each of them against Invasion; and on Application of the Legislature, or of the Executive (when the Legislature cannot be convened) against domestic Violence.

[9]Superseded by the Thirteenth Amendment.

ARTICLE V

The Congress, whenever two-thirds of both Houses shall deem it necessary, shall propose Amendments to this Constitution, or, on the Application of the Legislatures of two-thirds of the several States, shall call a Convention for proposing Amendments, which, in either Case, shall be valid to all Intents and Purposes, as part of this Constitution, when ratified by the Legislatures of three-fourths of the several States, or by Conventions in three-fourths thereof, as the one or the other Mode of Ratification may be proposed by the Congress; Provided that no Amendment which may be made prior to the Year One thousand eight hundred and eight shall in any Manner affect the first and fourth Clauses in the Ninth Section of the first Article; and that no State, without its Consent, shall be deprived of its equal Suffrage in the Senate.

ARTICLE VI

All Debts contracted and Engagements entered into, before the Adoption of this Constitution, shall be as valid against the United States under this Constitution as under the Confederation.

This Constitution, and the Laws of the United States which shall be made in Pursuance thereof; and all Treaties made, or which shall be made, under the Authority of the United States, shall be the supreme Law of the Land; and the Judges in every State shall be bound thereby, any Thing in the Constitution or Laws of any State to the Contrary notwithstanding.

The Senators and Representatives before mentioned, and the Members of the several State Legislatures, and all executive and judicial Officers, both of the United States and of the several States, shall be bound by Oath or Affirmation to support this Constitution; but no religious Test shall ever be required as a qualification to any Office or public Trust under the United States.

ARTICLE VII

The Ratification of the Conventions of nine States shall be sufficient for the Establishment of this Constitution between the States so ratifying the same.

Done in Convention by the Unanimous Consent of the States present the Seventeenth Day of September in the Year of our Lord one thousand seven hundred and Eighty seven, and of the Independence of the United States of America the Twelfth. In Witness whereof We have hereunto subscribed our Names.

Articles in Addition to, and Amendment of, the Constitution of the United States of America, Proposed by Congress, and Ratified by the Legislatures of the Several States, Pursuant to the Fifth Article of the Original Constitution.

AMENDMENT I[10]

Congress shall make no law respecting an establishment of religion, or prohibiting the free exercise thereof; or abridging the freedom of speech, or of the press; or the right of the people peaceably to assemble, and to petition the Government for a redress of grievances.

AMENDMENT II

A well regulated Militia, being necessary to the security of a free State, the right of the people to keep and bear Arms shall not be infringed.

AMENDMENT III

No Soldier shall, in time of peace, be quartered in any house, without the consent of the Owner, nor in time of war, but in a manner to be prescribed by law.

AMENDMENT IV

The right of the people to be secure in their persons, houses, papers, and effects, against unreasonable searches and seizures, shall not be violated, and no Warrants shall issue, but upon probable cause, supported by Oath or affirmation, and particularly describing the place to be searched, and the persons or things to be seized.

[10]The first ten amendments were passed by Congress September 25, 1789. They were ratified by three-fourths of the states December 15, 1791.

AMENDMENT V

No person shall be held to answer for a capital or otherwise infamous crime, unless on a presentment or indictment of a Grand Jury, except in cases arising in the land or naval forces, or in the Militia, when in actual service in time of War or public danger; nor shall any person be subject for the same offence to be twice put in jeopardy of life or limb; nor shall be compelled in any criminal case to be a witness against himself, nor be deprived of life, liberty, or property, without due process of law; nor shall private property be taken for public use, without just compensation.

AMENDMENT VI

In all criminal prosecutions, the accused shall enjoy the right to a speedy and public trial, by an impartial jury of the State and district wherein the crime shall have been committed, which district shall have been previously ascertained by law, and to be informed of the nature and cause of the accusation; to be confronted with the witnesses against him; to have compulsory process for obtaining witnesses in his favor, and to have the Assistance of Counsel for his defence.

AMENDMENT VII

In suits at common law, where the value in controversy shall exceed twenty dollars, the right of trial by jury shall be preserved, and no fact tried by a jury, shall be otherwise reexamined in any Court of the United States, than according to the rules of the common law.

AMENDMENT VIII

Excessive bail shall not be required, nor excessive fines imposed, nor cruel and unusual punishments inflicted.

AMENDMENT IX

The enumeration in the Constitution, of certain rights, shall not be construed to deny or disparage others retained by the people.

AMENDMENT X

The powers not delegated to the United States by the Constitution, nor prohibited by it to the States, are reserved to the States respectively, or to the people.

AMENDMENT XI (1798)[11]

The Judicial power of the United States shall not be construed to extend to any suit in law or equity, commenced or prosecuted against one of the United States by Citizens of another State, or by Citizens or Subjects of any Foreign State.

AMENDMENT XII (1804)

The Electors shall meet in their respective States and vote by ballot for President and Vice-President, one of whom, at least, shall not be an inhabitant of the same State with themselves; they shall name in their ballots the person voted for as President, and in distinct ballots the person voted for as Vice-President, and they shall make distinct lists of all persons voted for as President, and of all persons voted for as Vice-President, and of the number of votes for each, which lists they shall sign and certify, and transmit sealed to the seat of the government of the United States, directed to the President of Senate;—The President of the Senate shall, in the presence of the Senate and House of Representatives, open all the certificates and the votes shall then be counted;— The person having the greatest number of votes for President, shall be the President, if such number be a majority of the whole number of Electors appointed; and if no person have such majority, then from the persons having the highest numbers not exceeding three on the list of those voted for as President, the House of Representatives shall choose immediately, by ballot, the President. But in choosing the President, the votes shall be taken by states, the representation from each state having one vote; a quorum for this purpose shall consist of a member or members from two-thirds of the states, and a majority of all the states shall be necessary to a choice. [And if the House of Representatives shall not choose a President whenever the right of choice shall devolve upon them, before the fourth day of March next following, then the Vice-President shall act as President, as in the case of the death or other constitutional disability of the President.][12]—The person having the greatest number of votes as Vice-President, shall be the Vice-President, if such number be a majority of the whole number of Electors appointed, and if no person have a majority, then from the two highest numbers on the list, the Senate shall choose the Vice-President; a quorum for the purpose shall consist of two-thirds of the whole number of Senators, and a majority of the whole number shall be necessary to a choice. But no person constitutionally ineligible to the office of President shall be eligible to that of Vice-President of the United States.

AMENDMENT XIII (1865)

Section 1. Neither slavery nor involuntary servitude, except as a punishment for crime whereof the party shall have been duly convicted, shall exist within the United States, or any place subject to their jurisdiction.

Section 2. Congress shall have power to enforce this article by appropriate legislation.

AMENDMENT XIV (1868)

Section 1. All persons born or naturalized in the United States, and subject to the jurisdiction thereof, are citizens of the United States and of the State wherein they reside. No State shall make or enforce any law which shall abridge the privileges or immunities of citizens of the United States; nor shall any State deprive any person of life, liberty, or property, without due process of law; nor deny to any person within its jurisdiction the equal protection of the laws.

Section 2. Representatives shall be apportioned among the several States according to their respective numbers, counting the whole number of persons in each State, excluding Indians not taxed. But when the right to vote at any election for the choice of electors for President and Vice-President of the United States, Representatives in Congress, the Executive and Judicial officers of a State, or the members

---

[11]Date of ratification.

[12]Superseded by the Twentieth Amendment.

of the Legislature thereof, is denied to any of the male inhabitants of such State, being twenty-one years of age, and citizens of the United States, or in any way abridged, except for participation in rebellion, or other crime, the basis of representation therein shall be reduced in the proportion which the number of such male citizens shall bear to the whole number of male citizens twenty-one years of age in such State.

Section 3. No person shall be a Senator or Representative in Congress, or elector of President and Vice-President, or hold any office, civil or military, under the United States, or under any State, who, having previously taken an oath, as a member of Congress, or as an officer of the United States, or as a member of any State legislature, or as an executive or judicial officer of any State, to support the Constitution of the United States, shall have engaged in insurrection or rebellion against the same, or given aid or comfort to the enemies thereof. But Congress may by a vote of two-thirds of each House, remove such disability.

Section 4. The validity of the public debt of the United States, authorized by law, including debts incurred for payment of pensions and bounties for services in suppressing insurrection or rebellion, shall not be questioned. But neither the United States nor any State shall assume or pay any debt or obligation incurred in aid of insurrection or rebellion against the United States, or any claim for the loss or emancipation of any slave; but all such debts, obligations, and claims shall be held illegal and void.

Section 5. The Congress shall have the power to enforce, by appropriate legislation, the provisions of this article.

AMENDMENT XV (1870)

Section 1. The right of citizens of the United States to vote shall not be denied or abridged by the United States or by any State on account of race, color, or previous condition of servitude—

Section 2. The Congress shall have power to enforce this article by appropriate legislation.

AMENDMENT XVI (1913)

The Congress shall have power to lay and collect taxes on incomes, from whatever source derived, without apportionment among the several States, and without regard to any census or enumeration.

AMENDMENT XVII (1913)

The Senate of the United States shall be composed of two Senators from each State, elected by the people thereof, for six years; and each Senator shall have one vote. The electors in each State shall have the qualifications requisite for electors of the most numerous branch of the State legislatures.

When vacancies happen in the representation of any State in the Senate, the executive authority of such State shall issue writs of election to fill such vacancies: *Provided,* That the legislature of any State may empower the executive thereof to make temporary appointments until the people fill the vacancies by election as the legislature may direct.

This amendment shall not be so construed as to affect the election or term of any Senator chosen before it becomes valid as part of the Constitution.

AMENDMENT XVIII (1919)[13]

Section 1. After one year from the ratification of this article the manufacture, sale, or transportation of intoxicating liquors within, the importation thereof into, or the exportation thereof from the United States and all territory subject to the jurisdiction thereof for beverage purposes is hereby prohibited.

Section 2. The Congress and the several States shall have concurrent power to enforce this article by appropriate legislation.

Section 3. This article shall be inoperative unless it shall have been ratified as an amendment to the Constitution by the legislatures of the several States, as provided in the Constitution, within seven years from the date of the submission hereof to the States by the Congress.

---

[13]Repealed by the Twenty-first Amendment.

AMENDMENT XIX (1920)

The right of citizens of the United States to vote shall not be denied or abridged by the United States or by any State on account of sex.

Congress shall have power to enforce this article by appropriate legislation.

AMENDMENT XX (1933)

Section 1. The terms of the President and Vice-President shall end at noon on the 20th day of January, and the terms of Senators and Representatives at noon on the 3d day of January, of the years in which such terms would have ended if this article had not been ratified; and the terms of their successors shall then begin.

Section 2. The Congress shall assemble at least once in every year, and such meeting shall begin at noon on the 3d day of January, unless they shall by law appoint a different day.

Section 3. If, at the time fixed for the beginning of the term of the President, the President elect shall have died, the Vice-President elect shall become President. If a President shall not have been chosen before the time fixed for the beginning of his term, or if the President elect shall have failed to qualify, then the Vice-President elect shall act as President until a President shall have qualified; and the Congress may by law provide for the case wherein neither a President elect nor a Vice-President elect shall have qualified, declaring who shall then act as President, or the manner in which one who is to act shall be selected, and such person shall act accordingly until a President or Vice-President shall have qualified.

Section 4. The Congress may by law provide for the case of the death of any of the persons from whom the House of Representatives may choose a President whenever the right of choice shall have devolved upon them, and for the case of the death of any of the persons from whom the Senate may choose a Vice-President whenever the right of choice shall have devolved upon them.

Section 5. Sections 1 and 2 shall take effect on the 15th day of October following the ratification of this article.

Section 6. This article shall be inoperative unless it shall have been ratified as an amendment to the Constitution by the legislatures of three-fourths of the several States within seven years from the date of its submission.

AMENDMENT XXI (1933)

Section 1. The eighteenth article of amendment to the Constitution of the United States is hereby repealed.

Section 2. The transportation or importation into any State, Territory, or possession of the United States for delivery or use therein of intoxicating liquors, in violation of the laws thereof, is, hereby prohibited.

Section 3. This article shall be inoperative unless it shall have been ratified as an amendment to the Constitution by conventions in the several States, as provided in the Constitution, within seven years from the date of the submission hereof to the States by the Congress.

AMENDMENT XXII (1951)

No person shall be elected to the office of the President more than twice, and no person who has held the office of President, or acted as President, for more than two years of a term to which some other person was elected President shall be elected to the office of the President more than once.

But this Article shall not apply to any person holding the office of President when this Article was proposed by the Congress, and shall not prevent any person who may be holding the office of President, or acting as President, during the term within which this Article becomes operative from holding the office of President or acting as President during the remainder of such term.

AMENDMENT XXIII (1961)

Section 1. The District constituting the seat of Government of the United States shall appoint in such manner as the Congress may direct:

A number of electors of President and Vice-President equal to the whole number of Senators and Representatives in Congress to which the District would be entitled if it were a

State, but in no event more than the least populous State; they shall be in addition to those appointed by the States, but they shall be considered for the purposes of the election of President and Vice-President, to be electors appointed by the State; and they shall meet in the District and perform such duties as provided by the twelfth article of amendment.

Section 2. The Congress shall have power to enforce this article by appropriate legislation.

AMENDMENT XXIV (1964)

Section 1. The right of citizens of the United States to vote in any primary or other election for President or Vice-President, for electors for President or Vice-President, or for Senator or Representative in Congress, shall not be denied or abridged by the United States or any State by reason of failure to pay any poll tax or other tax.

Section 2. The Congress shall have power to enforce this article by appropriate legislation.

AMENDMENT XXV (1967)

Section 1. In case of the removal of the President from office or of his death or resignation, the Vice-President shall become President.

Section 2. Whenever there is a vacancy in the office of the Vice-President, the President shall nominate a Vice-President who shall take office upon confirmation by a majority vote of both Houses of Congress.

Section 3. Whenever the President transmits to the President pro tempore of the Senate and the Speaker of the House of Representatives his written declaration that he is unable to discharge the powers and duties of his office, and until he transmits to them a written declaration to the contrary, such powers and duties shall be discharged by the Vice-President as Acting President.

Section 4. Whenever the Vice-President and a majority of either the principal officers of the executive department or of such other body as Congress may by law provide, transmit to the President pro tempore of the Senate and the Speaker of the House of Representatives their written declaration that the President is unable to discharge the powers and duties of his office, the Vice-President shall immediately assume the powers and duties of the office as Acting President.

Thereafter, when the President transmits to the President pro tempore of the Senate and the Speaker of the House of Representatives his written declaration that no inability exists, he shall resume the powers and duties of his office unless the Vice-President and a majority of either the principal officers of the executive department or of such other body as Congress may by law provide, transmit within four days to the President pro tempore of the Senate and the Speaker of the House of Representatives their written declaration that the President is unable to discharge the powers and duties of his office. Thereupon Congress shall decide the issue, assembling within forty-eight hours for that purpose if not in session. If the Congress, within twenty-one days after receipt of the latter written declaration, or, if Congress is not in session, within twenty-one days after Congress is required to assemble, determines by two-thirds vote of both Houses that the President is unable to discharge the powers and duties of his office, the Vice-President shall continue to Discharge the same as Acting President; otherwise, the President shall resume the powers and duties of his office.

AMENDMENT XXVI (1971)

Section 1. The right of citizens of the United States, who are eighteen years of age or older, to vote shall not be denied or abridged by the United States or by any State on account of age.

Section 2. The Congress shall have power to enforce this article by appropriate legislation.

Presidential elections, 1900-1972

YEAR	NUMBER OF STATES	CANDIDATES	PARTIES	POPULAR VOTE (In thousands)	ELECTORAL VOTE	PERCENTAGE OF POPULAR VOTE"
1900	45	WILLIAM McKINLEY	Republican	7,218	292	51.7
		William J. Bryan	Democratic; Populist	6,356	155	45.5
		John C. Wooley	Prohibition	208		1.5
1904	45	THEODORE ROOSEVELT	Republican	7,628	336	57.4
		Alton B. Parker	Democratic	5,084	140	37.6
		Eugene V. Debs	Socialist	402		3.0
		Silas C. Swallow	Prohibition	258		1.9
1908	46	WILLIAM H. TAFT	Republican	7,675	321	51.6
		William J. Bryan	Democratic	6,412	162	43.1
		Eugene V. Debs	Socialist	420		2.8
		Eugene W. Chafin	Prohibition	253		1.7
1912	48	WOODROW WILSON	Democratic	6,296	435	41.9
		Theodore Roosevelt	Progressive	4,118	88	27.4
		William H. Taft	Republican	3,486	8	23.2
		Eugene V. Debs	Socialist	900		6.0
		Eugene W. Chafin	Prohibition	206		1.4
1916	48	WOODROW WILSON	Democratic	9,127	277	49.4
		Charles E. Hughes	Republican	8,533	254	46.2
		A. L. Benson	Socialist	585		3.2
		J. Frank Hanly	Prohibition	220		1.2
1920	48	WARREN G. HARDING	Republican	16,143	404	60.4
		James N. Cox	Democratic	9,130	127	34.2
		Eugene V. Debs	Socialist	919		3.4
		P. P. Christensen	Farmer-Labor	265		1.0
1924	48	CALVIN COOLIDGE	Republican	15,718	382	54.0
		John W. Davis	Democratic	8,385	136	28.8
		Robert M. La Follette	Progressive	4,831	13	16.6
1928	48	HERBERT C. HOOVER	Republican	21,391	444	58.2
		Alfred E. Smith	Democratic	15,016	87	40.9

SOURCE: Adapted from *Historical Statistics of the United States*, p. 682; *Statistical Abstract of the United States: 1974*, p. 422
"Candidates receiving less than 1 percent of the popular vote have been omitted. For that reason the percentage of popular vote given for any election year may not total 100 percent.

YEAR	NUMBER OF STATES	CANDIDATES	PARTIES	POPULAR VOTE (In thousands)	ELECTORAL VOTE	PERCENTAGE OF POPULAR VOTE"
1932	48	FRANKLIN D. ROOSEVELT	Democratic	22,809	472	57.4
		Herbert C. Hoover	Republican	15,758	59	39.7
		Norman Thomas	Socialist	881		2.2
1936	48	FRANKLIN D. ROOSEVELT	Democratic	27,752	523	60.8
		Alfred M. Landon	Republican	16,674	8	36.5
		William Lemke	Union	882		1.9
1940	48	FRANKLIN D. ROOSEVELT	Democratic	27,307	449	54.8
		Wendell L. Willkie	Republican	22,321	82	44.8
1944	48	FRANKLIN D. ROOSEVELT	Democratic	25,606	432	53.5
		Thomas E. Dewey	Republican	22,014	99	46.0
1948	48	HARRY S. TRUMAN	Democratic	24,105	303	49.5
		Thomas E. Dewey	Republican	21,970	189	45.1
		J. Strom Thurmond	States' Rights	1,169	39	2.4
		Henry A. Wallace	Progressive	1,157		2.4
1952	48	DWIGHT D. EISENHOWER	Republican	33,936	442	55.1
		Adlai E. Stevenson	Democratic	27,314	89	44.4
1956	48	DWIGHT D. EISENHOWER	Republican	35,590	457	57.6
		Adlai E. Stevenson	Democratic	26,022	73	42.1
1960	50	JOHN F. KENNEDY	Democratic	34,227	303	49.9
		Richard M. Nixon	Republican	34,108	219	49.6
1964	50	LYNDON B. JOHNSON	Democratic	43,126	486	61.1
		Barry M. Goldwater	Republican	27,176	52	38.5
1968	50	RICHARD M. NIXON	Republican	31,785	301	43.4
		Hubert H. Humphrey	Democratic	31,275	191	42.7
		George C. Wallace	American Independent	9,906	46	13.5
1972	50	RICHARD M. NIXON	Republican	47,170	520	60.7
		George S. McGovern	Democratic	29,170	17	37.7

Illustration Credits

Page 2, The Byron Collection, Museum of the City of New York; 11, Chicago Historical Society; 12, Amalgamated Clothing Workers of America; 13, Library of Congress; 14, Lewis Hine, George Eastman House; 27, (top left) Culver; (top right) Jacob Riis, Museum of the City of New York; (bottom) Culver; 29, Hazleton Area Public Library, Hazleton, Pa.; 34, Library of Congress; 50, Wallace Kirkland; 53, Library of Congress; 54, New York Public Library Picture Collection; 55, Lewis Hine, George Eastman House; 56, Tamiment Library, New York University; 58, Brown Brothers; 61, Missouri Historical Society; 65, Culver; 66, Brown Brothers; 76, Culver; 83, New York Public Library Picture Collection; 87, Brown Brothers; 92, Culver; 94, Chicago Historical Society; 100, *L'Illustration;* 108, Culver; 109, Library of Congress; 113, *Punch,* August 27, 1913; 114, Brown Brothers; 116, Courtesy of Mrs. Lydia G. Minor; 117, Historical Pictures Service; 121, Historical Pictures Service; 122, Historical Pictures Service; 125, National Archives; 130, National Archives; 134, National Archives; 135, Historical Pictures Service; 138, (all) National Archives; 139, (top left) National Archives; (top right) Culver; (bottom) United Press International; 144, Culver; 146, Culver; 151, Historical Pictures Service; 156, Courtesy, Ford Archives; 159, Amistad Research Center Collection; 161, (top) Michigan Historical Commission; (bottom) Brown Brothers; 167, United Press International; 176, (both) Stanley King Collection; 178, Culver; 184, Smithers Collection; 186, Brown Brothers; 189, Brown Brothers; 196, Culver; 199, (top) © 1929 by The New York Times Company, reprinted by permission; 199, (bottom) Culver; 201, Brown Brothers; 202, Library of Congress; 206, (top left) Ewing Galloway; (top right) Freelance Photographers Guild; (bottom) Wide World; 211, United Press International; 216, The Ben and Beatrice Goldstein Foundation; 224, United Press International; 227, J. Doyle Dewitt Collection; 230, National Archives; 231, The Franklin D. Roosevelt Library; 232, United Press International; 237, The Franklin D. Roosevelt Library; 240, United Press International; 243, Library of Congress; 244, National Archives; 250, Wide World; 251, United Auto Workers; 253, Freelance Photographers Guild; 257, J. Doyle Dewitt Collection; 266, Imperial War Museum; 278, Bishop, *St. Louis Star-Times;* 279, The Franklin D. Roosevelt Library; 281, *Punch,* January 1941; 288, U.S. Navy Photo; 294, Library of Congress; 295, Library of Congress; 300, United Press International; 302, The Franklin D. Roosevelt Library; 311, Culver; 314, Kaiser Industries Corporation; 317, (top right) Culver; (bottom) Library of Congress; 320, U.S. Department of Labor; 324, Wide World; 325, Wide World; 327, Wide World; 328, U.S. Army Photo; 339, United Press International; 352, Eve Arnold, Magnum; 361, John Dominis, Time-Life Picture Agency; 362, Carl Mydans, Time-Life Picture Agency; 365, Cornell Capa, Magnum; 366, United Press International; 370, Bill Owens, Magnum; 373, Arthur Tress, Magnum; 374, Drawing by Claude, © 1956 The New Yorker Magazine, Inc.; 391, © 1956, Cartoon from *Herblock's Special for Today,* Simon & Schuster, 1958; 398, © 1956, Cartoon from *Herblock's Special for Today,* Simon & Schuster, 1958; 404, Elliott Erwitt, Magnum; 410, Flip Schulke, Black Star; 412, Hank Walker, Time-Life Picture Agency; 418, Charles Moore, Black Star; 419, *Ebony Magazine;* 423, Wright, *Miami News;* 431, Bruce Davidson, Magnum; 434, Richard Bellak, Black Star; 448, Wide World; 452, (both) Bob Adelman, Magnum; 455, Wide World; 460, Philip Jones Griffiths, Magnum; 463, Brooks, *Birmingham News;* 465, Wide World; 468, Bonnie M. Freer, Photo Trends; 474, NOW Legal Defense/Education Fund; 477, (top) Charles Harbutt, Magnum, and (bottom) Roger Malloch, Magnum, both from *Crisis in America,* published by Ridge Press and Holt Rinehart & Winston; 479, Roger Malloch, Magnum; 484, Wide World; 487, Bettye Lane; 490, B. Curtis, Black Star; 496, *Valley Daily News,* Tarentum, Pa.; 497, John A. Darnell, Time-Life Picture Agency; 505, United Press International; 507, United Press International; 511, © 1973 by Herblock in the *Washington Post;* 512, Editorial Cartoon by Bill Sanders, courtesy of Field Newspaper Syndicate; 515, Wide World; 518, © 1975 by Herblock in the *Washington Post.*

Index

nental missiles; Nuclear weaponry

Armstrong, Neil, 414

Army Department and McCarthyism, 352, 355, 386

Arnold, Henry, 299

Arnold, Matthew, 9–10

Arnold, Thurman, 214, 215; *Folklore of Capitalism* by, 214; *Symbols of Government* by, 214

Art, 38, 378, 456; abstract, 40; Pop, 470; Regionalist, 219; and social criticism, 217. *See also* Painting

Arthur, Chester A., 102

Asia, TR policy, 106–7; U.S. economic interests in, 284. *See also* Open Door policy

Aswan Dam, 402

AT&T, 162, 204

Atom bomb, 274, 292, 326, 327, 345, 386; Russia's, 351, 355. *See also* Nuclear weaponry

Attica, N.Y., 491

Australia, 364, 401

Austria, 209, 273

Austria-Hungary, 118

Automobile industry, 132–33, 209, 488; and the economy, 160, 162; planned obsolescence, 163; sit-down strikes, 249

Automation, 384. *See also* Computers; Electronics

Automobiles, 22, 23, 159, 160, 161, 164–65, 375

Aviation, 22

Azerbaijan oil rights, 338

Babbitt (Lewis), 67, 179, 180

Baby boom, 318, 380

Back-to-Africa movement, 188, 190, 191

Back-to-the-land movement, 218

Baez, Joan, 467, 469

Bailey, Josiah, 261

Bailey, Thomas, 309

Baker, Bobby, 427

Baker, Newton, 37, 137, 140

Baker, Ray Stannard, 62, 131; *Following the Color Line* by, 62; on TR, 85

Baker v. *Carr*, 443

Baldwin, James, 450, 453

Baldwin, Roger, 140

Ballinger, Richard, 89–91

Banking, 24–25, 85, 96, 162, 254; bank holiday, 234–35; in

depression, 200–1, 207–8, 209; farm credits, 95, 96, 97; FDIC, 235; Federal Reserve banks, 95–96; RFC, 227, 262, 264; WW I loans, 117–18, 126

Bara, Theda, 166

Barnes, Harry Elmer, 288

Barnett, Ross, 417, 418

Baruch, Bernard, 132, 133, 231, 341

Bataan defeat, 291

Batista, Fulgencio, overthrown by Castro, 403

Baum, Lyman Frank, General Jinjur by, 61; *The Wonderful Wizard of Oz* by, 9, 61

Bay of Pigs invasion, 421–22, 424

Beard, Charles, 171, 269, 277, 278–79, 461; *Open Door at Home* by, 270

Beatles, 467, 468

Bedroom communities, 373

Beecher, Henry Ward, 29

Beer, sale of legalized, 235

Belgium, 116

Bell, Daniel, 383; *The End of Ideology* by, 383

Bellamy, Edward, 36, 37, 38, 48, 54; *Looking Backward* by, 37

Bellow, Saul, 463; *Adventures of Augie March* by, 378; *Dangling Man* by, 378; *Herzog* by, 378

Benchley, Robert, 212

Benedict, Ruth, 170

Bennett, Constance, 204

Benson, Ezra Taft, 392–93, 394

Benton, Thomas Hart, 219

Berger, Victor, 140

Berkeley free speech demonstration, 464, 465–66

Berle, Adolph, Jr., 162, 170, 379, 383

Berlin, Irving, 316

Berlin wall, 422, 423

Bernays, Edward, 164

Beven, Ernest, 360

Beveridge, Albert, 79, 105

Biddle, Francis, 330

Big business, 30, 80, 85, 175; and FDR, 133, 239, 254, 255, 256, 260, 262, 264; and Hoover, 226; and Kennedy, 415–16; and the military, 314–15; and NRA, 236–37; partnership with Federal government, 132, 133

Big government, 309, 391, 416; and far Right, 387; distrust of, 446

Big Three, 339

Bigotry, 407

Bill of Rights, 141, 388, 411; and Red scare, 144

Birmingham Ala., 464; and use of police dogs, 417, 418, 420

Birth control, 14, 57–58, 470

Birth of a Nation, 65, 160, 185

Birth rate, 211, 318, 471, 488

Bissell, Richard, Jr., 421

Black, Hugo, 4, 5, 186, 259, 443

Black Is Beautiful theme, 456

Black Muslims, 191, 321, 450–51

Black Panthers, 455

Black power, 450, 454–57, 466, 467, 471, 472, 473

Black Star shipping line, 190

Blacklist, 118

Blackmun, Harry, 495

Blacks, 47, 61, 62, 74, 98, 159, 171, 191, 438, 439, 440, 444, 450, 478, 480; accommodationists, 63, 64, 65, 66; back-to-Africa movement, 188, 190, 191; expectations, 319, 396, 418, 454; gains, 258, 319, 418, 486, 489; income, 446, 486; migration, South to North, 66, 134, 187, 246, 311, 438; militant, 63, 64, 65, 66, 135, 136, 188–91, 193, 256, 257, 319–21, 450, 455; nationalists, 64; in 1920s, 187–92; separatists, 451; separate but equal doctrine, 80, 387; and unions, 134, 517. *See also* Discrimination; Segregation; Voting rights

Blough, Roger, 416

Boas, Franz, 43

Bogart, Humphrey, 469

Bohemians, 178, 181, 183, 217

Bolshevik revolution, 142, 146, 147, 216, 343

Bolsheviks, 164, 344

Bonus army, 229

Boorstin, Daniel, 383; *The Genius of American Politics* by, 383

Bootleggers, 183

Borah, William, 150, 268

Borglum, Gutson, 229

Boston, 6; machine politics, 10; police strike, 142, 143, 175

Boulder Dam, 174, 226

Boulding, Kenneth, 437

Bourne, Randolph, 41, 180, 469

Bow, Clara, 166

Bowles, Chester, 312, 331, 334

Brace, Charles Loring, *The Dangerous Classes of New York* by, 12

nedy, 471; Korean War boom, 357; mass purchasing power, 209–10; and New Deal, 236–42, 255, 262, 264; Nixon policies, 493, 500–1, 506; and Vietnam War, 434; WW I, 117, 118, 132, 134; WW II, 295, 308, 309, 333. *See also* Fiscal policy; Inflation

Economy Act, 235, 245

Eden, Anthony, 304

Edison, Thomas, 182, 183, 487

Education, 26, 62, 329, 439, 464; adult, 433; agricultural extension, 170; antipoverty programs, 433, 434; compulsory, 36, 49, 466; discrimination in, 450, 475; elementary, 430, 433; federal aid to, 262, 308, 333, 336, 337, 349, 350, 394, 414, 415, 432, 475; progressive, 44–46, 214, 382; secondary, 430; and social science, 214–15; vocational, 170, 382

Egypt, 402, 403, 507

Ehrlich, Paul, 470–71; *Population Bomb* by, 470

Eight-hour day, 7, 84, 91

Eighteenth Amendment, 67

Eightieth Congress, 347

Einstein, Albert, 170, 298

Eisenhower, Milton, 403

Eisenhower, Dwight D., 346, 389–96, 412, 481; and big business, 391; and Cold War, 396–405; and Congress, 392, 401, 428; and Cuba, 406–7; and Dulles, 399–403; Doctrine, 403; economic policies, 389, 393–94; foreign policy, 398, 403; and Khrushchev, 403–4; and McCarthy, 390–91; 1952 election, 365, 366, 367, 388, 408; 1956 election, 388, 391, 408; and Vietnam, 400, 425, 426; and U-2 incident, 403–5; in WW I, 298, 300, 301, 303, 306

Elections: direct (popular, of senators), 49, 71–72; direct primary, 69, 71, 72, 73; electoral reform, 71–73; initiative, 49, 69, 70, 71, 72, 91; midterm (off-year). *See* Midterm elections; presidential. *See* Presidential elections; recall, 49, 71, 72, 91–92; referendum, 49, 69, 70, 71, 72

Electronics, 384

Elijah Muhammed, 450–51

Eliot, Charles, 116

Elkins Act, 83, 85

Ellsberg, Daniel, 499, 501, 510

Ely, Richard T., 32, 69

Employment. *See* Federal civilian employees; Workers

Employment Act, 333

Encyclopedia Britannica, 191

Engels, Friedrich, 31; *The Condition of the Working Class* by, 50

Engel v. *Vitale,* 443

Emerson, Ralph Waldo, 38

England. *See* Great Britain

Englebrecht, Helmuth, (coauthor) *Merchants of Death* by, 271

Environment: and behavior, 163, 170; Environmental Protection Agency, 488, 510; pollution, 466, 470, 488, 492

Equal Rights Amendment, 476, 486, 488

Erlichman, John R., 492, 493, 510, 516

Ervin, Sam, 509

Espionage Act, 54, 137, 140, 141

Escobedo v. *Illinois,* 443

Establishment, 416, 466, 478; antiestablishment minorities, 466

Ethiopia, 269, 272

Ethnic groups, 18–19, 174, 184, 252, 355, 383, 478; anticommunism of, 344; anti-interventionism of, 277; anti-Versailles peace treaty, 152, 153; ethnocentrism, 15, 20, 451; ethnocultural divisions, 5, 78, 178, 473; and politics, 10, 69, 72, 472; rise of consciousness of, 187–93, 472

Europe, 341–42

Evans, Hiram Wesley, 186, 187

Evans, Rowland, 428

Evans, Walker, 219, 220

Evolution, 29, 184–85

Executive agencies, 174

Executive Office of the President, 261

Expatriates, 179, 181, 183

Export-Import Bank, 270

Exports, 104, 132, 171, 344; cash and carry (WW II), 273; decline (1930–32), 227; growth (1934–39), 270

Fair Deal, 329, 333, 337, 347

Fair Employment Practices Commission, 320–21, 333, 429

Fall, Albert, 175

Family, 40, 81–82, 380; in the depression, 197, 211–13, 221; nuclear, 470, 472; WW II, 318

Family Assistance Plan, 434, 492

Farley, James A., 232

Farmer, James, 463, 493–94

Farming, 7, 23, 176, 200, 206, 209, 252, 308; and AAA, 239–42; acreage reduction, 239, 241; agribusiness, 174, 349, 350; allotment plan, 239; Brannan plan, 349, 350; Commodity Credit Corporation, 239; cooperatives, 174, 226, 227; and credit, 95, 96, 97, 174; farm bloc, 393; Farm Credit Administration, 239; Farm Security Administration, 203, 241; government assistance, 329, 393; large-scale, 48, 262; loans, 226, 227, 433; lobbying, 440; price supports, 239, 241; protective legislation, 174, 308; Rural Electrification Administration, 239; share cropping, 62; Soil Conservation Service, 239; tenant, 62, 204, 218, 220, 241, 261

Farrell, James T., *Studs Lonigan* by, 218, 220

Fascism, 215, 216, 218, 275, 277, 343, 346; in Spain, 273

Faubus, Orval, 395, 396

Faulkner, William, 220

Fay, Charles N., *Business in Politics* by, 182

Federal Bureau of Investigation, 388, 416, 465, 491, 498, 509; and Watergate, 502, 510

Federal civilian employees, 78, 173, 235, 309, 442; security risk checks, 386, 387; subversive activities boards (loyalty boards), 337, 353, 354

Federal Communications Commission, 77

Federal Deposit Insurance Corporation, 235

Federal Emergency Relief Administration, 235, 245

Federal government: centralization, 165; employees. *See* Federal civilian employees; executive branch, 77, 110; executive budget, 173–74; expansion, 225, 307–15; and industrialization, 86; labor controls, 96; partnerships with business, 132–33; restored faith in, 235; revenue sharing with states, 442; spending. *See* Federal spending; weak-

Heflin, Thomas, 193
Heller, Walter, 442
Hell's Angels motorcycle gang, 469
Hemingway, Ernest, 181; *For Whom the Bell Tolls* by, 218, 220; *Old Man and the Sea* by, 220, 375; *To Have and Have Not* by, 218
Hendrix, Jimi, 491
Hepburn Act, 83, 84, 85–86
Herberg, Will, 382
Herskovitz, Melville, 170
Hewitt, Alexander, 68, 69
Hickel, Walter, 492
Hicks, Granville, 216
High Schools, 26, 169; enrollment during depression, 203–4
Highways, 160, 206; construction of, 22, 96, 97, 132, 395; federal act for, 394, 395
Hill, Napoleon, *Think and Grow Rich* by, 221
Hillman, Sidney, 52
Himmler, Heinrich, 296
Hirohito, 287
Hiroshima bombing, 292, 297, 300, 326, 327
Hippies, 467, 472
Hiss, Alger, 354
Hitler, Adolf, 149, 216, 269, 272, 276, 283, 292, 296, 303, 344; America and, 275–82, 342; European aggression in WW II, 273–75, 285; persecution of Jews, 269, 277, 283; Roosevelt and, 282–83; and Russia, 275, 281, 282
Hobby, Oveta Culp, 392
Ho Chi Minh, 400, 425, 426, 461
Hoffman, Abbie, 471, 472, 494
Hoffman, Dustin, 469, 472
Hofstader, Richard, 382
Holding companies, 162, 207, 208; control bill, 254, 255
Holland, German invasion of, 285
Holli, Melville, 68
Holmes, Oliver Wendell, Jr., 44, 46; *The Common Law* by, 44; on Espionage Act, 141
Home Owners Loan Corporation, 235
Homosexuality, 470
Hoover, Herbert, 165, 166, 171, 174, 182, 183, 226–30, 231, 232, 233, 234, 254, 267, 269, 368, 389, 408, 409; anti-interventionism of, 277; election of, 177; FDR on, 226; Food Administration, 133; and foreign affairs, 268–69; and gov-ernment reorganization, 329; public works spending by, 263; as Secretary of Commerce, 175, 187
Hoover, J. Edgar, 143, 498, 509
Hoovervilles, 201
Hopkins, Harry, 235, 238, 242, 243, 244, 291, 304, 306
Horney, Karen, *The Neurotic Personality of Our Time* by, 215
House, Edward, 118, 120, 121, 145, 152
House Judiciary Committee, Nixon impeachment charges, 511, 513
House of Representatives, 79, 420; *Panay* incident, 274; un-American Activities Committee, 261; and WW I, 124, 126
House-Grey memorandum, 120
Housing: post WW II, 373, 380; public. *See* Public housing; suburban, 373
Houston, 6; race riot (1917), 134; suburban growth, 372
Howard University student demonstrations, 489
Howe, Frederic, 144–45
Howells, William Dean, 39
HUD. *See* Department of Housing and Urban Development
Huerta, Victoriano, 112, 113, 115
Hughes, Charles Evans, 96, 123, 172, 174, 175, 259
Hughes, Langston, 188, 190, 456
Hull, Cordell, 270, 272, 274, 286, 287, 291, 306
Hull House, 50, 51
Humphrey, George, 392, 393
Humphrey, Hubert H., 346, 348, 388, 389, 406, 430, 480; presidential candidate, 1968, 476, 478–79, 480, 481, 502
Hungarian revolution (1956), 397, 398, 401, 405
Hunt, E. Howard, 501, 502, 509
Hunter, Robert, *Poverty* by, 26, 28
Hutchins, Robert, 214–15
Hydrogen bomb, 386, 398

IBM. *See* International Business Machines
ICC. *See* Interstate Commerce Commission
Iceland, 282; U. S. occupation, 280
Ickes, Harold, 238, 258, 274, 312, 330

Immigration, 6, 15–20, 32, 37, 107; act (1924), 192; anti-immigrationists, 15–16, 19, 186; Chinese exclusion, 15; ethnic conflicts, 192–93; Japanese exclusion, 172; literacy tests, 15; and out-migration, 18; quotas, 15, 172, 337, 431; restrictions, 15–16, 20, 47, 49, 172, 178, 192; West Indian, 190, 191; and Wilson, 93, 97
Immigration Restriction League, 20, 47
Immigrants, 4, 5, 15–20, 74; in city machine politics, 10–11, 68, 69
Imperialism, 103–15; interventionist policy, 111, 112, 113, 172, 173, 268. *See also* Realpolitik; Roosevelt Corollary; Third World
Imports, 104, 500
Income, 383, 384; of blacks, 486; distribution, 209, 262, 316, 331, 338, 385, 414, 436, 437, 438; national, 158, 200, 262, 316; personal, 158; tax on, 26, 80, 83, 88, 95, 96, 97, 134, 309; and wealth tax, 254, 255, 262; widening gap between black and white, 446
Independents, 1936 election, 258
Indians. *See* American Indians
Indo-China: Geneva accord, 400; and Japan, 285, 286, 287, 292; U.S. aid to French in, 364, 400. *See also* Cambodia; Laos; Vietnam
Individualism, 9, 182, 210, 218, 332
Industrial Workers of the World, 53–55, 57; suppression of (WW I), 140, 142
Industrialization, 2, 21–32, 37, 74, 86, 517; impact on labor, 28, 31; and monopolies, 24, 25; and progressivism, 47; and urban growth, 6, 24
Infant mortality, 26
Inflation, 48, 462, 499, 506, 514, 517; labor–management settlements, 493; and oil prices, 507; and Phase II, 500, 501; post–WW II, 334, 337; price and wage controls, 500, 501; with recession, 493, 516; WW I, 133, 142, 154
Initiative, 49, 69, 70, 71, 72, 92
Installment buying, 160, 163, 198, 207
Insull, Samuel, 162, 207

Intellectuals, 41, 214, 220; and McCarthyism, 355; 1920s, 179–81, 183; 1950s, 383; and progressivism, 179–81, 183

Intelligence services, 336. *See also* Central Intelligence Agency; Defense Department; Federal Bureau of Investigation; Military

Intercontinental ballistic missiles, 398, 501; antimissile (ABM) development, 493; Soviet, in Cuba, 423; U.S., in Turkey, 424

Interest groups, 5, 32, 38, 50, 73, 78, 225, 241–42, 262, 264, 308, 332, 337, 350, 368, 440, 441; and McCarthyism, 354–55. *See also* Pressure groups

Internal Security Act, 353

International Business Machines, 204, 250, 380, 490

International Ladies Garment Workers Union, 52

International peace movement, 111, 115

International Telephone and Telegraph, 440, 502

Internationalism, 150, 153

Interracialism, 449, 450

Interstate commerce, 254

Interstate Commerce Commission, 85–86, 88, 195

Interventionism, 112, 113, 172, 173, 268, 269–70, 272, 403, 461

Intolerance, 15, 136, 141, 144, 356; patterns of, 192–93; of whites to blacks, 191–92

Inventions, 21–23. *See also* Technology

Investment, 230, 260, 262, 263, 384; foreign, in U.S., 104, 132; and recovery, 248; U.S., abroad, 104, 132, 171–72, 440

Investment Trusts, 207, 208

IQ tests, 192

Iran: CIA in, 403; and Stalin, 338, 339, 343

Irish immigrants, 5, 16, 68

Irish-Americans, 116, 152, 258, 472

Islam, 451

Isolationism, 127, 342, 344; in 1920s and 1930s, 153; and Japan, 285, 292; and League of Nations, 149, 150, 153; pre–WW II, 267, 270, 272, 277, 279, 282, 283, 342, 344, 461; and Versailles treaty, 149, 150, 153; and WW I, 116

Israel, 462. *See also* Arab-Israeli conflict

Italian immigrants, 18–19

Italian-Americans, 152, 311, 472

Italy, 109, 148, 152, 273; Communist party in, 307, 341, 342; invasion of Ethiopia, 269, 272; Tripartite Pact, 283, 286; Versailles peace conference, 145, 146; WW I, 123; WW II, 297, 301

ITT. *See* International Telephone and Telegraph

Iwo Jima, 326

IWW. *See* Industrial Workers of the World

Jackson, George, 491

Jackson State College, 498

Jacobs, Jane, 433; *The Death and Life of Great American Cities* by, 439

Jagger, Mick, 468–69

James, Henry, 10

James, William, 9, 35, 46, 47, 170

Japan, 148, 149, 172, 173, 268, 286, 292, 325, 489; Anti-Comintern Pact with Germany, 283, 286; atomic bombing of, 326–28; and China, 111–12: invasion of (1937), 273, 285, 286, 290; and East Indies, 285, 286, 287, 290; fourteen-part note, 287, 289; and Indo-China, 285, 286, 287, 292; and Korea, 283; and Manchuria, 112, 147, 268, 269, 283; *Panay,* sinking, 274; Pearl Harbor attack, 172, 287, 288–90; and Russia, 286, 326, 363; Tripartite Pact, 283, 286; and U.S., 283–92; U.S. declaration of war against, 288; Versailles peace conference, 146, 148; V-J Day, 328, 329; WW II surrender, 328, 329

Japanese in California, 20

Japanese-Americans, 311, 312

Jawboning, 226

Jaworski, Leon, 510–11, 513

Jazz, 40, 159, 188

Jencks v. *U.S.,* 387, 388

Jenner, William, 337, 353, 387

Jewish immigrants, 16, 17

Jews, 18, 192; anti-Semitism, 185, 186, 192, 193; FDR support by, 258; Hitler persecution of, 269, 277, 283; Zionism, 193

Jim Crow practices, 258, 395, 418,

450; Justice Department suits, 349

Jingoism, 102, 103, 111

Job Corps, 433, 434–35

John Birch Society, 386, 387, 429

John Reed clubs, 216

Johnson, Hiram, 69, 70, 149; on FDR, 258; on Wilson, 145

Johnson, Hugh, 237, 238

Johnson, James Weldon, 65, 188

Johnson, Lyndon B., 348, 368, 406, 407, 427–44, 449, 460, 461, 463, 476, 492; commission on urban disorders, 453, 454, 456; and congress, 428, 441; election of, 430, 503; Great Society of, 388, 414; problems confronting, 438–42; reforms, 411; as Senator, 377, 388, 389, 427; Tonkin Gulf resolution, 282, 401, 457; and Vietnam War, 426, 429–30, 457, 463; and war on poverty, 429, 431, 432, 433–38

Johnson, Tom, 37, 67, 68, 69

Joint Chiefs of Staff, 336, 421, 496

Jones, Bobby, 182

Jones, Jesse, 312

Jones, Samuel, 37, 68, 69

Joplin, Janis, 491

Jordan, 403

Jordan, David Starr, 20

Judiciary, 44, 91–92, 518

Jurisprudence, 170, 171, 214

Justice Department, 143, 260, 310, 352, 392, 493, 494, 497, 510; civil rights suits, 418, 420; NRA code violation prosecution, 236; suit ends segregation in southern airports, 418; voting rights suits, 418

Juvenile courts, 51

Juvenile delinquency, 318

Kansas City, 6; Pendergast Machine, 325, 330

Kearny, 282

Keats, John, 373–74; *The Crack in the Picture Window* by, 373

Kefauver, Estes, 348, 387, 388, 416

Kelley, Florence, 20, 50, 57

Kellog-Briand Pact, 268

Kempton, Murray, 390

Keniston, Kenneth, 382

Kennan, George, 270, 307, 338, 342, 344, 353, 361, 375, 396, 399, 405, 424–25

Kennedy, Edward, 501

Kennedy, John F., 355, 427, 436,

Metropolitan life style, 160
Mexican revolution, 112–15
Mexican-Americans in city enclaves, 438
Mexico, 111; and Germany, WW I, 123
Middle class, 4, 48, 209, 408; and college attendance, 464; growing backlash, 472; growth of, 157, 159, 371–79, 464; move into, 445; sexual permissiveness, 169
Middle East, 514; nationalism in, 403; October War (1973), 506–7; Six-Day War (1967), 489; Soviet pressure on, 397, 398; Suez crisis, 402–3. *See also* Arab-Israeli conflict
Midterm elections: 1914, 97; 1918, 134, 145; 1930, 228–29; 1934, 242; 1938, 260; 1954, 388, 393; 1958, 407; 1962, 419; 1970, 498–99; 1974, 516
Midway battle, 296
Migration: blacks, South to North, 66, 134, 187, 246, 319, 438; city to suburbs, 439; in depression, 202, 211; 1950s, 372; rural to city, 4, 212
Militarism, 140, 269
Military, 357; aid, 336, 341; and big business, 314–15; and Cold War, 398; and intelligence community, 405; and NATO, 350
Military-industrial complex, 133, 312, 315, 326, 405, 425, 465, 485
Milk subsidies and campaign contributions, 509
Millett, Kate, 486
Millis, Walter, *Road to War* by, 271
Mills, C. Wright, 379, 380, 471; *Power Elite* by, 379
Minimum wages, 52, 308, 336, 349, 394, 413, 432; NRA guarantees, 236; and Supreme Court, 81, 259–60
Mining, 23, 209; and IWW, 53, 54; safety legislation, 88; and strikes, 29, 53, 83, 84, 142, 335; and unions, 52, 335. *See also* Coal mining
Minor, Robert, 116
Minority groups: in city enclaves, 438; in population, 440; and "power" ideologies, 472–73. *See also* Black power; Red power; Women's power
Miranda v. *Arizona,* 443

Mississippi, 134; disfranchisement of blacks, 64; killings during black voting registration efforts, 451; school desegregation, 494
Mississippi River valley flood control, 174
Missouri Pacific Railroad, 203
Mitchell, Billy, 172
Mitchell, John, 494, 497, 499–500, 516
Mitchell, Margaret, *Gone with the Wind* by, 219
Mitchell, Wesley, 170
Mobil Oil bombing, 490
Mobility, 438; geographical, 4, 31, 212, 246, 316; social, 4, 19, 31, 188; and slums, 435; and tension, 4–15
Model Cities program, 432
Modernity in 1920s, 157, 161, 166
Modernization, 46, 73, 294, 516, 225–64
Mohawk Valley Formula, 251
Moley, Raymond, 232, 236, 237, 256–57
Molotov, Vyacheslav Mikhailovich, 345
Monetary policy, 208, 263; Federal Reserve banks, 95–96
Monopolies, 24, 25–26, 44, 252, 436; and antimonopolists, 237; and FDR, 261, 262, 264; protection of small business from, 329; and TR, 84, 85, 89. *See also* Corporations; Trusts
Monroe, Marilyn, 166, 381, 470
Monroe Doctrine, 110, 149
Moody, Dwight,. 36
Morgan, J. P., 25, 26, 30, 44, 82–83, 89, 96, 117, 162, 175, 227, 441
Morgan, Robin, *Sisterhood is Powerful* by, 486
Morgenthau, Hans, 460
Morgenthau, Henry, 274
Morgenthau Plan, 297
Morrison, Jim, 468
Movies, 22, 65, 141, 165, 166, 168, 211–19, 381; antiurban bias, 438; and censorship, 212; X-rated, 470. *See also* Film industry
Moynihan, Daniel, 439, 492; *The Negro Family* by, 439
Muckrakers, 43, 67
Muhammed Ali, 451
Muir, John, 90
Muller v. *Oregon,* 45, 81
Multiuniversities, 466
Mumford, Lewis, 145, 216, 439

Muncie, Indiana, Lynds' sociological studies of, 166, 168, 197, 221
Munich conference, 273, 274, 292, 306, 344, 360, 363
Municipal government and public services, 78
Municipal ownership of public utilities, 67, 68
Municipal reform, 37, 69, 73
Munitions industry, 271; Senate investigation, 271; in WW I, 139, 271. *See also* Arms and munitions
Murphy, Frank, 311
Music: acid rock, 468; "coon songs," 65; folk, 467, 468; jazz, 40, 159, 188; of 1920s, 166; rock, 467–68; social protest, 467, 468; WW I songs, 122
Muskie, George, 479, 480, 499, 501, 502
Mussolini, Benito, 180, 192; invasion of Ethiopia, 269, 272
My Lai, civilian murders in, 499
Myrdal, Gunnar, 321
Mysticism, 470

NAACP. *See* National Association for the Advancement of Colored People
Nader, Ralph, 467, 488
Nagasaki bombing, 292, 297, 326
Nasser, Gamal Abdel, 402, 403
Nathan, George Jean, 41
National American Women's Suffrage Association, 58, 59, 60
National Association for the Advancement of Colored People, 47, 49, 50, 63, 73, 256, 320, 417, 456
National Association of Manufacturers, 30
National Broadcasting Company, 160, 162
National Consumers' League, 50, 169
National Defense Education Act, 394
National Defense Research Committee, 298
National Endowment for the Arts and the Humanities, 431
National Farm Workers (union), 473
National forests, 90
National Guard, 122
National Labor Relations Act,

80, 83, 85; safety regulation, 88; securities regulation, 83–84

Randolph, A. Philip, 189, 190, 193, 320, 321, 456

Rankin, Jeanette, 288

Rationing, 314

Rauschenbusch, Walter, 36; *Christianity and the Social Crisis* by, 37

Ray, James Earl, 478

Rayburn, Sam, 389, 417

Reagan, Ronald, 429, 480

Real estate, 160, 192

Realpolitik, 106–10, 111

Rebozo, C. G. ("Bebe"), 491

Recall, 49, 71, 72, 91–92

Recession, 514, 515, 517, 518; 1913, 117; 1937–38, 260, 262; 1950s, 393–94; 1969, 488; with inflation, 493, 516

Reconstruction, 396, 429

Reconstruction Finance Corporation, 226, 227, 312

Red Cross, 59, 187

Red decade, 213

Red scare, 142–45, 154, 178, 356

Reed, James, 149

Reed, John, 41, 216

Referendum, 49, 69, 70, 71, 72, 91

Reform movements, 7, 35–74; assault on genteel values, 40–43; genteel tradition, 38–40; 19th century, 35–47; social Darwinism under siege, 43–47. *See also* Social reform

Regulatory commissions, 73; federal, 77, 91, 95, 96; state, 70–71, 80

Rehnquist, William H., 495

Reich, Charles, *Greening of America* by, 469

Religion, 171, 381; fundamentalist, 183, 184–85; and political issues, 72

Republican party, 69, 82, 86, 174, 348; Congressional majority, 134, 145, 367; liberation plank, 399, 401; National Committee, 363; nonvoting in presidential elections, 347; partisan politics and League of Nations, 150; and Taft, 89; 1912 election, 88, 91–92, 94; 1932 election, 233; 1936 election, 257, 258; 1952 election, 367; 1960 election, 394

Resettlement Administration, 241

Resource Recovery Act, 488

Reston, James, 392, 393, 416, 420, 499

Reuben James, 282

Reuther, Walter, 251, 346, 383, 441

Revenue Act, 96

Revenue sharing, 442

Revisionism: Eisenhower administration, 405; Korean War, 358–59; and Pearl Harbor, 288–90; and WW I, 271

Revolution, 142, 144; Bolshevik, 142; of counter culture, 469; proletarian worldwide, 215–16, 343; socioeconomic, 112. *See also* Radicalism

Reynolds, Malvina, 467

Reynolds v. *Sims,* 443

Rhineland, 148; Hitler invasion, 269

Rhodes, James, 497

Rice, Elmer, *Adding Machine* by, 162

Richardson, Eliot, 510

Ridgway, Matthew, 357

Riesman, David, 374–75; *The Lonely Crowd* by, 374

Right, 419, 429; ascendancy of, 385–89; disaffected groups in, 252; FDR's wartime diplomacy criticized by, 303–5; New Deal criticized by, 254, 255, 256; 1930s, 225, 234; 1968 campaign, 382; post–WW II, 185; Radical, 386–87, 429–30; WPA criticized by, 243–44

Riis, Jacob, 6, 11; *How the Other Half Lives* by, 36

Ripley, William Z., 20; *Races of Man* by, 19

River development, 83, 174

Rivers, Mendell, 444

Roberts, Owen, 259

Robinson, Edwin Arlington, 42

Robot, 162

Rochester race riot (1964), 453

Rockefeller: John D., 25, 142; John D., Jr., 79; Nelson, 480, 515

Rockwell, Norman, 375

Roe v. *Wade,* 486

Roethke, Theodore, "The Reckoning" by, 222

Rogers, Will, 206, 211, 227, 234

Rogers, William, 489

Rolling Stones, 468, 469

Roman Catholic Church: and Al Smith, 178, 192, 406; and Kennedy, 406, 407, 415

Romney, George, 480

Roosevelt, Eleanor, 41, 218, 231, 258, 365, 406

Roosevelt, Franklin D., 177, 206, 226, 231–61, 267, 274, 279, 308, 328, 329, 332, 333, 344, 345, 348, 350, 367, 427, 428, 430, 436, 440, 442, 446, 457; Asian policy, 290–93, 303–7; bank closing, 200–1; and big business, 133, 239, 254, 255, 256, 260, 262, 264; Casablanca conference, 297, 301; and Chiang Kai-shek, 303, 305; and Churchill, 296, 297, 301, 302, 303, 304, 305; concentration on Europe, 296–97; and Congress, 260, 261, 264, 308; death of, 325; destroyer deal with Great Britain, 275–76; domestic policies, 270, 277, 308; elections of: 1932, 233, 234; 1936, 252, 256, 258, 308; 1940, 280, 308, 348; 1944, 308; European invasion, 300–2; foreign affairs, 269–70, 283; and Hitler, 282–83; lend lease, 280, 281, 282, 307; New Deal. *See* New Deal; Pearl Harbor attack, 287–88; quarantine speech, 273–74; and Stalin, 301–7; Supreme Court reform plan, 258–60, 264; unconditional surrender policy, 297–98; wartime diplomacy, 303–7; Yalta conference, 305, 306

Roosevelt, Franklin D., Jr., 346

Roosevelt, Theodore, 23, 30, 38, 39, 40–43, 44, 51, 59, 81–86, 111, 124, 128, 231, 406, 471; and antitrust suits, 82, 83, 84; Asian policy, 106–7; Caribbean policy, 109–10; and Congress, 82, 83, 95; and conservation, 83, 85, 90, 471; Corollary, 109, 110, 268; election of, 83; expansionist foreign policy, 104, 105; legacy of, 85–86; New Nationalism of, 84; and Panama Canal, 107–8, 109; and the Philippines, 103; Portsmouth peace conference, 106–7; as Progressive party candidate, 82–84, 85; *Realpolitik* of, 106–10; and Rough Riders, 81; San Juan Hill, 81; and Spanish American War, 81, 102; Square Deal of, 84; and Taft, 87–88, 106; and Wilson, 94, 96, 97; WW I, 122

Root, Elihu, 82

Root-Takahira Agreement, 107

Rosenberg, Julius and Ethel, 354

Vietnam, 103, 115, 293, 300, 329, 405; election for unification, 401, 425; Geneva accord, 400–1, 425; temporary division, 400–1. *See also* North Vietnam; South Vietnam

Vietnam War, 422, 425–26, 429, 434, 449, 457–64, 465, 466, 467, 476; antiwar sentiment, 460, 462–64; and Cambodia, 495–97, 498; casualties, 459, 502, 503, 504; cost of, 459, 517; and Johnson, 426, 429–30, 457, 463; and Laos, 499; and Nixon, 480, 489, 491, 495–97, 501, 502, 503, 504–5; peace talks, 459, 503, 504; Pentagon papers, 494, 495; Tet offensive, 460, 464, 476; Tonkin Gulf resolution, 282, 401, 457, 458, 497; troop withdrawal, 489, 495, 503, 504; U.S. bombing, 457, 459, 460, 495–97, 501, 504; U.S. economic aid offer, 459, 461

Vietnamization, 489, 495, 496, 497, 499, 503, 505

Vinson, Fred, 329–30

VISTA, 433

V-J Day, 328, 329

Vladivostok, 147

Vocational training, 170

Volstead Act, 67

Voting, 177–78, 348, 516; blacks in elective offices, 486; by blacks, 60, 64, 179; decline in, 72–73, 347; by ethnics, 60, 178; literacy tests for, 60; and poll tax, 333; qualifications for, 69; religions and ethnic issues, 72; by women, 59, 176, 177, 178. *See also* Presidential elections

Voting registration, 69, 72; of blacks in South, 431, 451

Voting rights, 429, 431; denial of, 450; extension to eighteen-year-olds, 488; Justice Department suits in support of, 418; Law, 488, 494; in South, 396. *See also* Disfranchisement

Wages, 23, 31, 48, 210, 441; controls, 500, 501; dollar, 30; minimum, 30, 91, 158–59, 175, 209; WW I, 132; widening gap between men's and women's, 473

Wagner, Robert, 177, 248, 261

Wagner Act. *See* National Labor Relations Act

Walker, Francis, 19

Walker, Jimmy, 10

Wall Street, bombing, 143

Wallace, George, 418, 429, 477, 478, 480, 481, 493, 501–2, 503; 1968 election, 55

Wallace, Henry A., 239, 241, 308, 330, 339, 341, 342, 343; forms new Progressive party, 346, 383; 1948 election, 348

War, 102, 115; economic motive for, 271; fear of, 271; outlaw of aggressive, 268

War Industries Board, 132, 133

War Labor Board: WW I, 132; WW II, 309

War Powers Act, 505–6

War Production Board, 309, 312, 313

War Resources Board, 312

Warhol, Andy, 470

Warren, Earl, 346, 394; Supreme Court under, 387, 388, 411, 443–44

Washington, Booker T., 63, 64 189, 451

Washington, D.C.: all-black march, 320, 456; antiwar demonstrations, 498, 499; bonus army in, 229; civil rights march, 419, 453; segregation in, 395; stop the ˎbombing march, 462–63

Washington Conference, 172

Washington State, 59

Water Quality Improvement Act, 448

Watergate, 175, 502–3, 509–14; and CREEP, 502; and impeachment proceedings, 511, 513; Nixon's taped conversations, 495, 510–13; resignation of the president, 513–14; and Supreme Court, 512–13

Watson, John B., 163

Watts riot, 453, 454, 486

Wayne, John, 378, 472

Wealth, 35, 84, 255; corporate, 162; distribution of, 26, 209; Gospel of, 29; national, 26; tax on, 254, 255, 262

Weaver, Robert, 418

Webb-Pomerene Act, 132

Wechsler, James, 214

Wedemeyer, Albert, 350, 351

Welch, Robert, 386–87

Welfare, 247, 307, 394, 488; categorical assistance, 245, 246;

Family Assistance Plan, 492; federal level, 235, 242–45, 259, 492; federal-state funding, 245–47, 429, 432–33, 442; food stamps, 492; political machine services, 10

Welfare capitalism, 30, 32, 175, 182, 210, 215, 248, 348

Welfare state, 38, 49, 52, 264, 329, 332, 337, 368, 437

West, Mae, 212

West Berlin: airlift, 342; and East German access, 422; Russian blockade, 342, 354

West Germany, in NATO, 364

West Indian migrants, 191

Western Federation of Miners, 52, 85

Wheeler, Burton, 3–4, 5, 252, 254, 259, 280, 292

White, William Allen, 63, 275; on politics, 228; on Roosevelt, 82

White, Theodore, 480

White House staff, 261, 440, 492, 502, 503, 510

Whyte, William H., Jr., *Organization Man* by, 374, 376

Wicker, Tom, 491

Wilder, Thornton, 217; *Our Town* by, 375

Wilkins, Roy, 456

Willard, Frances, 66–67

Willkie, Wendell, 255, 275, 280

Willow Run, Mich., 313

Wilson, Charles E., 392, 393, 400

Wilson, Edmund, 216, 218, 219, 220

Wilson, Woodrow, 56, 79, 88, 91, 92–98, 101, 136, 137, 140, 142, 177, 226, 269, 304, 310, 399, 481; Asian policy, 111–12; and big business, 132; and civil liberties, 174; Clemenceau on, 146, 149; and Congress, 95–96, 123–24, 133, 134, 174; and Democratic party, 96, 97, 98; domestic program of, 95, 96, 133, 134; elections: 1912, 92, 94; 1916, 123; evaluation of, 96–98; Federal Reserve banks established by, 95, 96; foreign policy of, 111–15, 145–53; Fourteen Points of, 146, 147; and Haiti, 112; Hiram Johnson on, 145; and immigration, 15, 16, 93, 98; Jim Crow practices developed by, 98, 258; and League of Nations, 145–53; and Mexico, 112–15; neutrality efforts of, 115–28; New Freedom of, 93, 96, 132; and

A
B 6
C 7
D 8
E 9
F 0
G 1
H 2
I 3
J 4